Recent Developments in Monetary Policy
Volume II

The International Library of Critical Writings in Economics

Series Editor: Mark Blaug

Professor Emeritus, University of London, UK
Professor Emeritus, University of Buckingham, UK

This series is an essential reference source for students, researchers and lecturers in economics. It presents by theme a selection of the most important articles across the entire spectrum of economics. Each volume has been prepared by a leading specialist who has written an authoritative introduction to the literature included.

A full list of published and future titles in this series is printed at the end of this volume.

Wherever possible, the articles in these volumes have been reproduced as originally published using facsimile reproduction, inclusive of footnotes and pagination to facilitate ease of reference.

For a list of all Edward Elgar published titles visit our site on the World Wide Web at
www.e-elgar.com

Recent Developments in Monetary Policy Volume II

Edited by

Alec Chrystal

Professor of Money and Banking
Sir John Cass Business School, City University London, UK

and

Paul Mizen

Professor of Monetary Economics
School of Economics
University of Nottingham, UK

THE INTERNATIONAL LIBRARY OF CRITICAL WRITINGS IN ECONOMICS

An Elgar Reference Collection
Cheltenham, UK • Northampton, MA, USA

Published by
Edward Elgar Publishing Limited
The Lypiatts
15 Lansdown Road
Cheltenham
Glos GL50 2JA
UK

Edward Elgar Publishing, Inc.
William Pratt House
9 Dewey Court
Northampton
Massachusetts 01060
USA

A catalogue record for this book is available from the British Library

Library of Congress Control Number: 2009922749

Mixed Sources
Product group from well-managed
forests and other controlled sources
www.fsc.org Cert no. SA-COC-1565
© 1996 Forest Stewardship Council
FSC

ISBN 978 1 84542 449 7 (2 volume set)

Printed and bound in Great Britain by MPG Books Ltd, Bodmin, Cornwall

Contents

Acknowledgements

The editors and publishers wish to thank the authors and the following publishers who have kindly given permission for the use of copyright material.

American Economic Association for article: Ben S. Bernanke and Mark Gertler (2001), 'Should Central Banks Respond to Movements in Asset Prices?', *American Economic Review, Papers and Proceedings*, **91** (2), May, 253–7.

Banco de Espana for article: Alan S. Blinder (2006), 'Monetary Policy Today: Sixteen Questions and about Twelve Answers', in S. Fernandez de Liz and F. Restoy (eds), *Central banks in the 21st Century*, Banco de Espana, July, 1–65.

Bank of England for articles: Charles Goodhart (1999), 'Central Bankers and Uncertainty', *Bank of England Quarterly Bulletin*, February, **39** (1) 102–14; Mervyn King (1999), 'Challenges for Monetary Policy: New and Old', *Bank of England Quarterly Bulletin*, November, 397–415.

Bank for International Settlements for article: Charles Bean (2003), 'Asset Prices, Financial Imbalances and Monetary Policy: Are Inflation Targets Enough?', *BIS Working Papers*, No. 140, September, 1–29.

Blackwell Publishing Ltd for articles: Michael Woodford (2000), 'Monetary Policy in a World Without Money', *International Finance*, **3** (2), July, 229–60; Bennett T. McCallum (2000), 'Theoretical Analysis Regarding a Zero Lower Bound on Nominal Interest Rates', *Journal of Money, Credit and Banking*, **32** (4), November, 870–904; Marvin Goodfriend (2000), 'Overcoming the Zero Bound on Interest Rate Policy', *Journal of Money, Credit and Banking*, **32** (4), November, 1007–35; Charles Goodhart (2001), 'What Weight Should Be Given to Asset Prices in the Measurement of Inflation?', *Economic Journal*, **111** (472), June, F335–F356; John B. Taylor (2007), 'Thirty-Five Years of Model Building for Monetary Policy Evaluation: Breakthroughs, Dark Ages, and a Renaissance', *Journal of Money, Credit, and Banking*, **39** (1), February, 193–201; Michael Woodford (2008), 'How Important Is Money in the Conduct of Monetary Policy?', *Journal of Money, Credit and Banking*, **40** (8), December, 1561–598.

Brookings Institution Press for article: Paul Krugman (1998), 'It's Baaack: Japan's Slump and the Return of the Liquidity Trap', *Brookings Papers on Economic Activity*, **2**, 137–87, refs.

Elsevier for article: Athanasios Orphanides (2003), 'Monetary Policy Evaluation with Noisy Information', *Journal of Monetary Economics*, **50** (3), April, 605–31.

Federal Reserve Bank of St Louis for articles: Bennett T. McCallum (2001), 'Monetary Policy Analysis in Models Without Money', *Federal Reserve Bank of St. Louis Review*, **83** (4), July/August, 145–60; Marvin Goodfriend (2005), 'The Monetary Policy Debate Since October 1979: Lessons for Theory and Practice', *Federal Reserve Bank of St. Louis Review*, **87** (2, Part 2), March/April, 243–62; Ben S. Bernanke, Alan S. Blinder and Bennett T. McCallum (2005), 'Panel Discussion I: What Have We Learned Since October 1979', *Federal Reserve Bank of St. Louis Review*, **87** (2, Part 2), March/April, 277–91.

Every effort has been made to trace all the copyright holders but if any have been inadvertently overlooked the publishers will be pleased to make the necessary arrangement at the first opportunity.

In addition the publishers wish to thank the Library of Indiana University at Bloomington, USA, for their assistance in obtaining these articles.

Part I
Monetary Policy and Asset Prices

[1]

QUANTITATIVE POLICY IMPLICATIONS OF NEW NORMATIVE MACROECONOMIC RESEARCH[†]

Should Central Banks Respond to Movements in Asset Prices?

By BEN S. BERNANKE AND MARK GERTLER*

In recent decades, asset booms and busts have been important factors in macroeconomic fluctuations in both industrial and developing countries. In light of this experience, how, if at all, should central bankers respond to asset price volatility?

We have addressed this issue in previous work (Bernanke and Gertler, 1999). The context of our earlier study was the relatively new, but increasingly popular, monetary-policy framework known as *inflation-targeting* (see e.g., Bernanke and Frederic Mishkin, 1997). In an inflation-targeting framework, publicly announced medium-term inflation targets provide a nominal anchor for monetary policy, while allowing the central bank some flexibility to help stabilize the real economy in the short run. The inflation-targeting approach gives a specific answer to the question of how central bankers should respond to asset prices: Changes in asset prices should affect monetary policy *only* to the extent that they affect the central bank's forecast of inflation. To a first approximation, once the predictive content of asset prices for inflation has been accounted for, there should be no additional response of monetary policy to asset-price fluctuations.[1]

In use now for about a decade, inflation-targeting has generally performed well in practice. However, so far this approach has not often been stress-tested by large swings in asset prices. Our earlier research employed simulations of a small, calibrated macroeconomic model to examine how an inflation-targeting policy (defined as one in which the central bank's instrument interest rate responds primarily to changes in expected inflation) might fare in the face of a boom-and-bust cycle in asset prices. We found that an aggressive inflation-targeting policy rule (in our simulations, one in which the coefficient relating the instrument interest rate to expected inflation is 2.0) substantially stabilizes both output and inflation in scenarios in which a bubble in stock prices develops and then collapses, as well as in scenarios in which technology shocks drive stock prices. Intuitively, inflation-targeting central banks automatically accommodate productivity gains that lift stock prices, while offsetting purely speculative increases or decreases in stock values whose primary effects are through aggregate demand.

Conditional on a strong policy response to expected inflation, we found little if any additional gains from allowing an independent response of central-bank policy to the level of asset prices. In our view, there are good reasons, outside of our formal model, to worry about attempts by central banks to influence asset prices, including the fact that (as history has shown) the effects of such attempts on market psychology are dangerously unpredictable. Hence, we concluded that inflation-targeting central banks need not respond to asset prices, except insofar as they affect the inflation forecast.

In the spirit of recent work on robust control, the exercises in our earlier paper analyzed the performance of policy rules in worst-case

[†] *Discussants:* Robert Shiller, Yale University; Glenn Rudebusch, Federal Reserve Bank of San Francisco; Kenneth Rogoff, Harvard University.

* Woodrow Wilson School, Princeton University, Princeton, NJ 08544 (e-mail: bernanke@princeton.edu), and Department of Economics, New York University, 267 Mercer St., 7th floor, New York, NY 10003 (e-mail: mark.gertler@econ.nyu.edu), respectively. We thank Fabio Natalucci and Michele Cavallo for excellent research assistance, and Simon Gilchrist for helpful comments.

[1] As discussed in what follows, an additional response is warranted in theory if changes in asset prices affect the natural real rate of interest, though we find this effect to be quantitatively small in our simulations. Also, this prescription is not intended to rule out short-term interventions to protect financial stability.

scenarios, rather than on average. However, the more conventional approach to policy evaluation is to assess the expected loss for alternative policy rules with respect to the entire probability distribution of economic shocks, not just the most unfavorable outcomes. That is the approach taken in the present article. We conduct stochastic simulations of the same model we used earlier to evaluate the expected performance of alternative policy rules. We consider stock-price "bubble" shocks, technology shocks, and the two in combination. Although the policy-evaluation approach is different from our previous work, the results of these simulations are complementary to what we found earlier. We find again that an aggressive inflation-targeting rule stabilizes output and inflation when asset prices are volatile, whether the volatility is due to bubbles or to technological shocks; and that, given an aggressive response to inflation, there is no significant additional benefit to responding to asset prices.

I. The Model and the Simulation Method

The model we use is essentially the same as in Bernanke and Gertler (1999), which in turn was an extension of the framework developed in Bernanke et al. (2000). Broadly, the model is a standard dynamic new-Keynesian model, augmented in two ways. First, it incorporates an informational friction in credit markets, by means of the assumption that monitoring of borrowers by lenders is costly. This credit-market friction gives the model a "financial accelerator," a mechanism by which endogenous changes in borrowers' balance sheets enhance the effects of exogenous shocks. For example, in our model a boom in stock prices raises output not only via conventional wealth and Tobin's q effects, but also by increasing the net worth of potential borrowers. As borrowers become wealthier and thus more able to self-finance, the expected deadweight losses of external finance decline, further increasing investment and output.

The second modification, introduced in Bernanke and Gertler (1999), is to allow an additive, non-fundamental component in stock prices. We model this non-fundamental component as an exogenous stochastic process. Innovations to this process are drawn randomly each period from a normal distribution. The effect of

a given innovation on stock prices persists into the subsequent period with fixed probability, set equal to one-half in our simulations. If an innovation persists, it grows at a rate equal to a fixed parameter a times the fundamental rate of return on capital, divided by the probability of continuation. If the parameter a were to equal 1.0, the non-fundamental component would be a rational bubble, in the sense of Olivier Blanchard and Mark Watson (1982). To preserve long-run stationarity, we choose instead $a = 0.99$, so that the non-fundamental component has a weak mean-reverting tendency. Agents are assumed to know the statistical process that drives bubbles, though they do not know in advance their ultimate magnitude or duration. The primary effect of a bubble is to increase aggregate demand, by increasing consumers' wealth and by improving the balance sheets of borrowers.

The model is calibrated as in Bernanke and Gertler (1999), except that here we have increased the elasticity of Tobin's q with respect to investment from 0.5 to 2.0, as is consistent with the evidence. In addition, to introduce more realistic persistence in the response of Tobin's q to productivity shocks, we introduce diminishing returns into the production of new capital goods, though this modification does not materially affect the results.

We considered simulations of the model, under alternative monetary-policy rules, for (i) random draws of the bubble process, (ii) random draws of the technology shock, and (iii) combinations of shocks to the bubble and to technology. As described earlier, the duration and hence the maximum size of each bubble are stochastic. Because our linear approximation becomes less accurate as the bubble becomes very large, we assume that bubbles that have lasted five periods collapse with certainty in the sixth period. Depending on the monetary-policy rule, a positive one-standard-deviation initial bubble shock that lasts the full five periods can cause stock prices to rise 25–30 percent above their steady-state values. Experiments confirmed that our qualitative results are not affected by allowing the bubble to run for a maximum of seven periods (the unconditional probability of a bubble lasting more than seven periods is less than 1 percent). Technology shocks are modeled as permanent shifts in total factor productivity (TFP). The standard devia-

TABLE 1—BUBBLE SHOCKS ONLY

Policy rule (π, s, y)	σ_y	σ_π
1.01, 0, 0	0.83	2.85
1.01, 0.05, 0	0.45	9.44
1.01, 0.1, 0	0.76	14.77
1.01, 0, 0.5	0.37	4.11
2, 0, 0	0.34	0.10
2, 0.05, 0	0.33	0.17
2, 0.1, 0	0.32	0.42
2, 0, 0.5	0.32	0.09
3, 0, 1	0.29	0.07

TABLE 2—TECHNOLOGY SHOCKS ONLY

Policy rule (π, s, y)	σ_y	σ_π
1.01, 0, 0	0.73	6.23
1.01, 0.05, 0	0.18	25.06
1.01, 0.1, 0	0.48	42.24
1.01, 0, 0.5	0.28	2.79
2, 0, 0	0.24	0.14
2, 0.05, 0	0.22	0.28
2, 0.1, 0	0.19	0.62
2, 0, 0.5	0.22	0.05
3, 0, 1	0.21	0.05

TABLE 3—BUBBLE AND TECHNOLOGY SHOCKS

Policy rule (π, s, y)	σ_y	σ_π
1.01, 0, 0	3.47	40.84
1.01, 0.05, 0	1.92	94.13
1.01, 0.1, 0	3.91	180.77
1.01, 0, 0.5	1.08	19.49
2, 0, 0	0.80	0.64
2, 0.05, 0	0.68	1.26
2, 0.1, 0	0.58	2.89
2, 0, 0.5	0.70	0.44
3, 0, 1	0.68	0.23

tion of innovations to TFP is assumed to be 1 percent of its initial level.

As for policy rules, we considered simple rules relating the central bank's nominal interest rate to next period's expected inflation, the current level of the stock market, and the output gap (defined as actual output less output under flexible prices and with no credit frictions). The response of the interest rate to expected inflation was varied between 1.01 and 3, the response to log stock prices between 0 and 0.2, and the response to the output gap between 0 and 2. For each choice of rule parameters, we calculated the unconditional variances of the output gap and inflation, as well as the overall loss, as measured by various quadratic loss functions in the output gap and inflation.

II. Simulation Results

Representative simulation results are shown in the tables. For each table, in the first cell of each row, the triple of numbers indicates the policy rule being evaluated. The first number of the triple is the response of the nominal interest rate to expected inflation (π), the second number is the response of the interest rate to the log of the price of capital, or Tobin's q (s), and the third number is the response of the interest rate to the output gap (y). The second and third columns show the unconditional variances of the output gap, σ_y, and inflation, σ_π, both in percentage points. With no discounting, quadratic losses for each policy can be calculated directly as linear combinations of these variances. Table 1 shows results for the case of bubble shocks only, Table 2 covers the case of technology shocks only, and Table 3 reports

results for simulations in which both bubble shocks and technology shocks are drawn in each period. For the last case, we assumed that the correlation of bubble shocks and technology shocks is 0.9, to capture the idea that bubbles may be more likely to develop when fundamentals are also strong. However, the results were similar when this correlation was set to other values, including zero.

The clearest conclusion to be drawn from Tables 1–3 is that "aggressive" inflation-targeting rules, in which the response of the nominal interest rate to expected inflation is 2 or 3, strongly dominate "accommodative" rules, in which the response to expected inflation is 1.01 (a value that barely satisfies the stability condition that real interest rates rise when expected inflation rises). The superiority of aggressive inflation-targeting holds for both types of shocks and their combination. The reduction in inflation variability from aggressive inflation-targeting is particularly striking, as might be expected, but in nearly all cases variability of the output gap is also reduced.

256   AEA PAPERS AND PROCEEDINGS   MAY 2001

Our simulations suggest that good policy rules will react sensitively to expected inflation, but consistent with the widely held view that inflation-targeting should be applied "flexibly," they show that policy should respond to the output gap as well. Indeed, with equal weighting of the output gap and inflation in the loss function, we find that the policy (3, 0, 1) performs best across the different scenarios (conditional on a relatively coarse grid search). Notice that this policy involves zero weight on stock prices.

Although the optimal policy (for equal weighting of output and inflation) never involves a response to stock prices, we can see from Tables 1–3 that adding a stock-price response to a rule that targets only inflation typically leads to a small reduction in variability of the output gap. Compare, for example, the policies (2, 0, 0), (2, 0.05, 0), and (2, 0.1, 0) in each of Tables 1–3. Our interpretation of this effect is as follows: A shock to stock prices (either from a bubble or from technology) may temporarily change the natural real rate of interest, a change that in principle should be accommodated by a fully optimal policy rule. Putting a small weight on stock prices therefore may help a bit, at least in some circumstances and on some dimensions.

However, shocks to stock prices are not unique in this regard; by the same logic, monetary policy should respond to *any* shock that changes the natural real rate of interest; there is no theoretical justification for singling out the stock market. Indeed, as noted, the simulations show that allowing the policy rule to respond to the output gap eliminates any benefits of responding to stock prices. Admittedly, the output gap is difficult to measure, but we are more confident in economists' ability to measure the output gap than to measure the fundamental component of stock prices; the percentage standard deviation of estimates of stock-price fundamentals surely far exceeds that of potential output. In addition, the behavior of inflation provides a real-time indicator of the magnitude of the output gap, whereas there is no analogous indicator to provide confirmation of estimates of stock fundamentals.

In any case, our simulations show that the small benefits in terms of reduced output-gap variability of responding to stock prices are likely to be outweighed by the associated increase in inflation variability. For example, in the case of technology shocks (Table 2), the policy (2, 0.1, 0) is to be preferred to (2, 0, 0) only if the loss-function weight on output-gap variability exceeds 0.9, and to the policy (3, 0, 1) only if the weight on output-gap variability exceeds 0.96. Similar results obtain for the other scenarios. We conclude that for plausible parameter values the central bank should not respond to asset prices.

III. Relation to the Literature

There has been considerable debate on the appropriate role of asset prices in the formulation of monetary policy. Recent contributions include Charles Goodhart (2000), Nicoletta Batini and Edward Nelson (2000), and Andrew J. Filardo (2000). The paper most closely related to our work, however, is by Stephen Cecchetti et al. (2000). Indeed, a portion of their paper employs simulations of the model of Bernanke and Gertler (1999), the same model used in this paper. Contrary to our findings, however, Cecchetti et al. claim to find strong support for including stock prices in the central bank's policy rule. What accounts for this striking difference in conclusions?

In computing their preferred policy rules, Cecchetti et al. do not take into account either the probabilistic nature of the bubble or the possibility that shocks other than a bubble may be driving asset prices. Specifically, Cecchetti et al. "optimize" the policy rule with respect to a single scenario, a bubble shock lasting precisely five periods, rather than with respect to the entire probability distribution of shocks, including shocks other than bubble shocks. Effectively, their procedure yields a truly optimal policy only if the central bank (i) knows with certainty that the stock-market boom is driven by non-fundamentals and (ii) knows exactly when the bubble will burst, both highly unlikely conditions.[2] In contrast, we find (Table 1) that,

---

[2] Even so, under reasonable parametrizations, our aggressive inflation-targeting rule performs nearly as well as the optimal policy based on these extraordinary information assumptions. It appears otherwise in Cecchetti et al. (2000) because they report the loss under our rule divided by the loss under their optimal rule, where the latter is a number close to zero. However, by any reasonable metric, the *absolute* difference in losses is very small.

VOL. 91 NO. 2   *POLICY IMPLICATIONS OF MACROECONOMIC RESEARCH*   257

even if the central bank is certain that a bubble is driving the market, once policy performance is averaged over all possible realizations of the bubble process, by any reasonable metric there is no consequential advantage of responding to stock prices. Moreover, a too-aggressive response to stock prices can create significant harm in that scenario.[3] Batini and Nelson (2000) find an analogous result for bubbles in the real exchange rate.

A deficiency of the literature to date is that the nonfundamental component of stock prices has generally been treated as exogenous. Our own view is that the macroeconomic stability associated with inflation-targeting is likely to reduce the incidence of panic-driven financial distress that could destabilize the economy, but this question is clearly deserving of further research.

REFERENCES

Batini, Nicoletta and Nelson, Edward. "When the Bubble Bursts: Monetary Policy Rules and Foreign Exchange Market Behavior." Working paper, Bank of England, 2000.

Bernanke, Ben and Gertler, Mark. "Monetary Policy and Asset Volatility." *Federal Reserve Bank of Kansas City Economic Review*, Fourth Quarter 1999, *84*(4), pp. 17–52.

Bernanke, Ben; Gertler, Mark and Gilchrist, Simon. "The Financial Accelerator in a Quantitative Business Cycle Framework," in J. Taylor and M. Woodford, eds., *Handbook of macroeconomics*. Amsterdam: North-Holland, 2000, pp. 1341–93.

Bernanke, Ben and Mishkin, Frederic. "Inflation Targeting: A New Framework for Monetary Policy?" *Journal of Economic Perspectives*, Spring 1997, *11*(2), pp. 97–116.

Blanchard, Oliver and Watson, Mark. "Bubbles, Rational Expectations, and Financial Markets," in P. Wachtel, ed., *Crisis in the economic and financial structure*. Lexington, MA: Lexington Books, 1982, pp. 295–316.

Cecchetti, Stephen; Genberg, Hans; Lipsky, John and Wadhwani, Sushil. *Asset prices and central bank policy*. London: International Center for Monetary and Banking Studies, 2000.

Filardo, Andrew J. "Monetary Policy and Asset Prices." *Federal Reserve Bank of Kansas City Economic Review*, Third Quarter 2000, *85*(3), pp. 11–37.

Goodhart, Charles. "Asset Prices and the Conduct of Monetary Policy." Working paper, London School of Economics, 2000.

---

[3] In results not reported here, we find that the harm from targeting stock prices can rise significantly if the nonfundamental component of stock prices affects spending less than does the fundamental component, as seems consistent with the evidence.

[2]

The Economic Journal, 111 (*June*), F335–F356. © Royal Economic Society 2001. Published by Blackwell Publishers, 108 Cowley Road, Oxford OX4 1JF, UK and 350 Main Street, Malden, MA 02148, USA.

WHAT WEIGHT SHOULD BE GIVEN TO ASSET PRICES IN THE MEASUREMENT OF INFLATION?*

Charles Goodhart

Besides the theoretical (Alchian/Klein, 1973) case for including asset prices in measures of inflation, there is also a practical case, that some asset prices, notably housing, are closely associated with the main trends in inflation, and via 'bubbles and busts' with output disturbances. Attempts to use the pure Alchian/Klein methodology in practice give excessive weight to unstable asset prices, but there are more appropriate weighting schemes, derived either from econometrically measured relationships or from final expenditures. Either way, the statistical treatment of housing is crucial, and is being discussed in Eurostat.

My dictionary (Longman) defines inflation as a fall in the value of money, *not* as a rise in the consumer price index. If I spend my money now on obtaining a claim on future housing services by buying a house, or on future dividends by buying an equity, and the price of that claim on housing services or on dividends goes up, why is that not just as much inflation as when the price of current goods and services rises? We spend much of our money on such purchases; the value of gross purchases of houses, in those cases where a mortgage was taken out, was 18.5% of post tax income of the household sector in 1999. In the same year the net value of other financial savings of the household sector was 5.5% of post tax income.

The argument that an analytically correct measure of inflation should take account of asset price changes was made most forcefully by Alchian and Klein in 1973, and has never, in my view, been successfully refuted on a *theoretical* plane, though, as we shall see, in Section 2.1 their *particular* proposals have severe, perhaps incapacitating, *practical* deficiencies. It was, therefore, a surprise that, at the Conference on 'The Measurement of Inflation', (Silver and Fenwick, 2000), at which an earlier version of this paper, (then entitled 'Time, Inflation and Asset Prices'), was given, there was no other paper concerning asset prices, and how such asset prices, of houses, land, and various other investments, real or financial, might, or might not, fit into a measure of inflation. At the moment most such asset price changes are, in principle, given zero weight, with the index supposedly reflecting only the price of purchases of current consumption of goods and services.

In practice the distinction between the purchase of a durable asset and current consumption is not easy to make. When I buy an overcoat or a golf

*My thanks are primarily due to Philip Laochamroonvorapongse, Raoul Minetti and Paul Robinson for research assistance and advice. I am also most grateful for comments and suggestions from Bill Allen, Don Brash, David Clementi, Nick Davey, Paul Fisher, Neal Hatch, Steve Machin, Jim O'Donoghue, Shigenori Shiratsuka, Mick Silver, Ralph Turvey, John Vickers and Sushil Wadhwani. I remain, however, personally responsible for all the contents of this paper, whether sensible or otherwise.

club, I expect to benefit from, and consume, their services over many years; yet official data attribute all such consumption, and the pricing thereof to the year of purchase. This problem is particularly acute with so-called consumer durables, (though the average useful life of these may well be often less than that of clothes and shoes); this results in some arcane distinctions in practice; thus the purchase price of new cars has been excluded from the RPI in the United Kingdom (because of the difficulty of observing individually bargained discounts), whereas the price of second-hand cars is included, though partly as a proxy for the former, (see the Office for National Statistics (ONS), Technical Manual for the RPI, 1998). We shall deal with the even more complex case of how to treat house prices in Section 3. The point here is that the current RPI and CPI statistics are *not* pure measures of the price of current consumption, but a practically convenient, (though fuzzy at the edges), mix of prices of short-lived consumer quasi-durable and durable assets alongside the prices of current consumables and services.

Some argue that the question of the appropriate treatment of asset prices in the measurement of inflation has been effectively settled by custom and usage. Thus an anonymous referee of the previous version of this paper, (who advised rejection), wrote as follows:-

'The problem is that the fall in the value of money should be measured by the reciprocal of the increasing [sic] in the general level of prices, which is a concept impossible to be measured. What we can do is to measure the increases in some basket which can reproduce the general movements of prices. It is commonly agreed that this basket is the consumers' one. As we need to measure the inflation, the best way to do it seems to be using the CPI. Of course, we may question whether to extend the basket in order to take asset price changes into account, but the practical implications appear so severe to advise against any attempt in this direction (as pointed out by Alchian and Klein).'

This involves a number of sweeping assertions.

As Ralph Turvey, one of our leading experts in this field, has often stated, for example in Turvey *et al.* (1989), Chapter 2 and in (2000*b*), especially the Chapter on 'Purpose determines concepts and coverage', what kind of index you should want depends on the use that you intend to make of it. Let me rephrase that question. When you want the monetary authorities to control inflation, exactly what do you want to mean by inflation? Current goods and services inflation can sometimes be far from being the same as changes in the value of money, especially when there is a combination of stable consumption prices and wildly fluctuating asset prices, as in Japan over the last two decades. What should we mean by the word 'inflation'?

Of course, there are many uses to which a CPI or an RPI is put for which the focus on the costs of current consumption of goods and services is entirely appropriate. But is that same concentration on the costs of current consumption alone also appropriate when one wishes to concentrate on a general measure of inflation? Put alternatively what measure of inflation should be, in principle at least, the main focus for monetary policy?

How can one answer that last question? We shall try to divide the question into two parts. First, in Section 1, we shall discuss arguments for including asset prices *in principle* in the measurement of inflation, for the purposes of monetary policy. Here we shall discuss the general theoretical case for so doing (1.1), basing this on the analysis of Alchian and Klein (1973); then we shall turn to practical, empirical policy considerations (1.2), arguing that paying attention to asset prices, in a more formalised manner, could help to protect against the worst errors of policy; finally we shall review why inflation is supposed to harm welfare (1.3), and suggest that welfare losses would be reduced if the inflation measure to be stabilised at a low level also incorporated asset prices.

Even if the arguments *in principle* for including asset prices in measures of inflation, for monetary policy purposes, were to be accepted, the question would still remain how to do so in practice.

Such practical questions revolve around the issue of what *weightings* to give asset prices in the construction of a price index. This is the topic of Section 2. As is well known, but we shall repeat (2.1), the theoretical arguments of Alchian and Klein (1973) imply such high weights on volatile asset prices, that the resulting price indices become unstable, unreliable and unusable. But that does *not* eliminate the case for any inclusion of asset prices in price indices. Other, more moderate, weighting schemes which are both analytically defensible and practicable, can be found. We shall discuss two such approaches. The first involves the weighting of asset prices according to their empirical relationships with goods and services prices (2.2). One such exercise was undertaken in Cecchetti *et al.* (2000); another was carried out by Goodhart and Hofmann (2000). The second weighting system is based, even more simply, on the proportion either of total personal incomes, or of total final expenditures, actually spent on assets (2.3).

Arguments, such as are made here, do not command mainstream support amongst economists (see Gertler *et al.*, 1998; and Bernanke and Gertler, 2000), largely perhaps because they are concerned whether excessive weight might be given to volatile financial assets (eg equities), thereby making the price index more unstable and less useful. The purpose of Sections 2.2 and 2.3 is to demonstrate that such an outcome need not occur. Nevertheless, the result of such disagreements amongst economists has been to halt moves towards any generalised incorporation of asset prices into price indices and associated measures of inflation.

But the one area, in this respect, where the immediate practical policy issues are too intense to be bundled away, concerns housing. Housing costs are such a large element in personal spending that the issue cannot be ignored. National statisticians *have* to decide how to deal with housing costs, even if they then – as they do in some countries – find the problems so severe that they decide to exclude (some, or all, aspects of) housing altogether from their statistical measures. We touch, rather briefly on some of the alternative treatments of housing in consumer price indices in Section 3.

Even if, analytically, the case for some more formalised inclusion of asset prices in the appropriate price index (and measurement of inflation) is strong, we are not starting from a blank chart, with a new beginning. This country, and others, have used the RPI (and CPI in some cases) in its existing, or amended, form – as in the case of RPIX as a target for the Monetary Policy Committee – for policy purposes and as a component element in contracts, eg indexed contracts for many years. Continuity, certainty and simplicity all argue against chopping and changing existing procedures. So in the Conclusions, we do not argue for replacing the present measures, but of paying rather more attention to accompanying, alternative measures which *do* give a more appropriate weighting to asset prices.

1. Why Asset Prices Should Have a Role in the Measurement of Inflation

1.1. *The Theoretical Case*

This case was brilliantly expressed by the economists, Alchian and Klein, in their paper 'On the Correct Measure of Inflation' as long ago now as 1973. They state that the CPI and the GNP deflator, p. 173,

> 'are frequently considered to be the operational counterparts of what economists call "the price level". They, therefore, often are used as measures of inflation and often are targets or indicators of monetary and fiscal policy. Nevertheless, these price indices, which represent measures of current consumption service prices and current output prices, are theoretically inappropriate for the purpose to which they are generally put. The analysis in this paper bases a price index on the Fisherian tradition of a proper definition of intertemporal consumption and leads to the conclusion that a price index used to measure inflation must include asset prices.'

Alchian and Klein, following the lead of Irving Fisher (1906) and Samuelson (1961), argue that the utility of any situation is 'a function of a vector of claims to present and future consumption', and hence one should try to assess whether prices have risen, or fallen, by looking at whether the prices of an iso-utility vector of current and future goods and services has risen, or fallen, (p. 175). But futures prices for future consumption goods and services are not generally available, and hence one should proxy these by a full set of asset prices, pp 176–7.

Alchian and Klein are aware of the difficulties of the course they propose.

> Thus, p. 187, '[W]ithout future contracts in all commodities, the explicit futures prices and quantities needed for construction of a wealth price index are unavailable. Current prices of assets of different life lengths provide a theoretical substitute since they embody present prices of

expected future service flows. But both the asset prices and asset quantities necessary for this index are extremely expensive to determine. We must have prices of a very broad spectrum of assets on which we presently have very little information. Our data must include prices of generally nonmarketable assets, such as human capital, and of assets of varying durability, so that we are able to produce the exact optimum current and future consumption service flows by adjusting the asset mix. We may not be able to determine all these prices with any reasonable expenditure of resources, ...'

Moreover, as noted on p. 188,

'[E]ven if asset prices and quantities were available, we would have significant problems in the interpretation of asset price changes. A change in the market value of an asset may reflect (i) a change in the price of an unchanged future service flow from the asset, (ii) a shift in preferences for this asset's service relative to other assets, (iii) a shift in preferences for present consumption relative to future consumption, or (iv) a change in the anticipated magnitude of service flow from the asset. Any or all of these changes are likely to be occurring simultaneously and therefore the cause of a change in a particular asset price is difficult to determine. Changes (ii) and (iii) represent a shift in tastes while (iv) represents a change in asset quality; however, they are not conceptually different from the problems encountered in constructing the presently used indices.'

They conclude, p. 189, that,

'The empirical problems involved are enormous. But whatever efforts may be made in this direction and whatever the results, we believe it is an error to assign all of the change in common stock and other asset prices to changes in anticipated future service flows with no change in present prices of such future flows... which is what is implicitly done now in commonly used price indices that ignore asset prices.'

1.2. *The Practical Case*

Many of the most serious and intractable problems of monetary policy relate to the question of whether, and how if at all, the authorities should respond to asset price fluctuations. How we define inflation is quite likely to influence the conduct of monetary policy in practice, whatever should happen in principle.

The most obvious recent case is Japan. If you look at the paths for the level of Consumer Prices, Fig. 1, or for the rate of inflation of consumer prices, defined as the percentage increase in the CPI in each quarter over the same quarter in the preceding year, Fig. 2, then the outcome for Japan appears superior to that of Australia, United States or United Kingdom. The generally accepted desideratum is for low and stable inflation; some, eg Goodfriend and King (2000) even advocate aiming for complete price stability. Fig 1 demon-

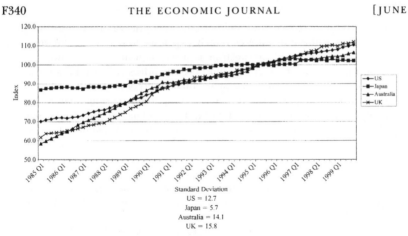

Source: OECD, *Main Economic Indicators*, various volumes.

Fig. 1. *Consumer Prices*
1995 = 100

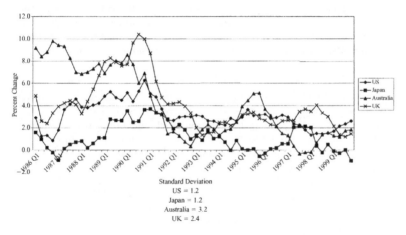

Fig. 2. *Consumer Prices*
(% Change Over Same Quarter of Previous Year)

strates that Japan has approximated more closely to this desideratum with patently lower inflation than its comparators, and Fig 2 shows, though less clearly, that it has also had more stable inflation than its comparators.

Yet most of us do not regard Japan's monetary policy as having been exemplary. Why not? The main reason for a more adverse judgment is that the policy makers in Japan were not able to prevent an asset price bubble and bust over this same period. This bubble and bust occurred in both the equity and real estate markets. I have argued elsewhere, (Goodhart and Hofmann, 2000, and 2001), that the real estate market has the more important linkages with financial intermediation, real output and the CPI/RPI, but movements in equity prices have been more eye-catching, and both are shown below.

Fig. 3 shows the relative movements in equity prices for these same four countries. In the United States, United Kingdom and Australia, there are temporary peaks, in 1987 Q3 and 1994 Q1, with subsequent downturns, but otherwise the series trend strongly upwards over the whole period. In Japan, in contrast, a massive rise until 1989 Q4 is followed by a collapse until 1992 and subsequent stagnation. Moreover the volatility of Japanese share prices, as measured by the standard deviation of year on year percentage changes (each quarter relative to the same quarter a year ago), shows that this (at 24) is double that in the United States and United Kingdom (at 12), (Australia is 19).

Nevertheless, as reported in Cecchetti *et al.* (2000) and Goodhart and Hofmann (2000), (also OECD, 2000), the linkages between housing prices and both output and CPI/RPI inflation measures are much stronger, than those between equity prices and output/inflation. In Fig. 4 we show the time path of housing prices in these same four countries. The same bubble and bust is evident in Japan. In the United Kingdom there is a much stronger cyclical pattern, with a very sharp rise until 1989, a sharp decline until 1993, and a fairly steady rise thereafter. In Australia much the same pattern occurs. In contrast in the United States there has been much less cyclical volatility in housing prices, at least over the whole country. The relationship between local cycles in real estate prices and activity remains to be fully explored.

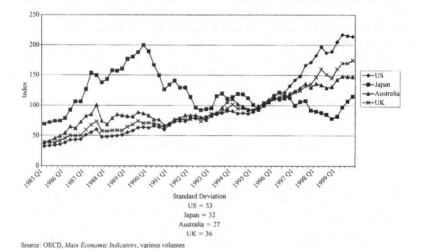

Standard Deviation
US = 53
Japan = 32
Australia = 27
UK = 36

Source: OECD, *Main Economic Indicators*, various volumes

Fig. 3. *Share Prices*
1995 = 100

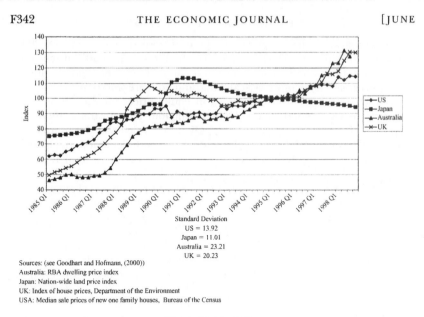

Standard Deviation
US = 13.92
Japan = 11.01
Australia = 23.21
UK = 20.23

Sources: (see Goodhart and Hofmann, (2000))
Australia: RBA dwelling price index
Japan: Nation-wide land price index
UK: Index of house prices, Department of the Environment
USA: Median sale prices of new one family houses, Bureau of the Census

Fig. 4. *Housing Prices*
1995 = 100

These discrepant patterns in asset prices, especially in housing prices, appear to have had some influence on the path of real output, the levels of which are shown in Fig. 5 and the percentage change over the same quarter in the previous year in Fig. 6. The rapid rate of growth in real output in Japan until the end of 1991 is then replaced by a period of halting growth. In the United Kingdom and Australia, there is a cyclical peak in 1990, following the end of the housing boom, with a subsequent recession until 1992. The United States has the steadiest time path for output growth, just as it has also had the steadiest time path for housing price inflation.

The interaction between asset prices, especially real estate, and output, has been recently examined in several studies (Cecchetti *et al.*, 2000; Goodhart and Hofmann, 2000, 2001; Filardo, 2000; and OECD, 2000), and found to be significant.

How, if at all, should the monetary authorities then react to such asset price changes, and how, if at all, should such asset price changes be incorporated into our measures of inflation?

These two questions, of action and measurement, are intimately linked. So long as asset price changes are *not* incorporated in the measure of inflation which the authorities are required to stablilise, the authorities are likely to express audible worries about 'exuberance' and 'sustainability', but in practice find themselves largely incapable of any (preemptive) action in response to asset price changes themselves in advance of any (consequential) effects coming through onto current goods and services prices, paralysed in practice

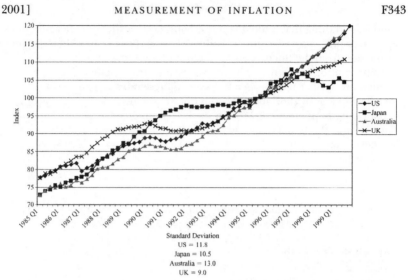

Standard Deviation
US = 11.8
Japan = 10.5
Australia = 13.0
UK = 9.0

Source: OECD Statistics, Quarterly National Accounts, 1998 and 1999.

Fig. 5. *Gross Domestic Product*
1995 = 100

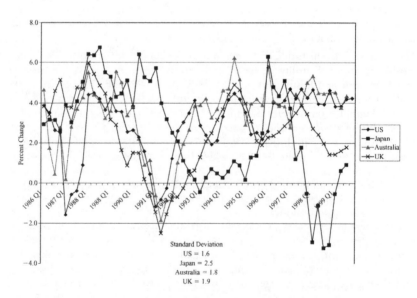

Standard Deviation
US = 1.6
Japan = 2.5
Australia = 1.8
UK = 1.9

Fig. 6. *Gross Domestic Product*
(% Change Over Same Quarter of Previous Year)

– and a good thing that is too, many, perhaps most, academic colleagues would reply stressing, *inter alia*, the volatility of asset prices, and their frequent dysjunction from the fluctuations of the rest of the economy.

There is also, perhaps, a hint of an asymmetric approach to asset price fluctuations, ie that it is proper to lower interest rates to counter steep asset price declines, as in 1987 and 1988, but not to raise them to counter asset price increases. Perhaps some perception of this asymmetry has been a supporting factor behind the remarkable 'bull-run' of equity prices which these diagrams illustrate. This was noted in the *Financial Times* on Monday, August 30th 1999, (the day before the Conference on the Measurement of Inflation), when reporting on the monetary conference at Jackson Hole, Gerard Baker reported that,

> 'Mr Greenspan devoted his entire contribution to the enlarged role asset prices play in the formulation of policy. But, though he has warned repeatedly in the past that equity prices have become overvalued, he focussed more on trying to understand the forces that have driven prices higher. And, for all the attention he and his colleagues are paying to Wall Street, it is still highly unclear how it will impact policy.
>
> Indeed, the only certainty, he confirmed, was that the Fed would be forced to cut rates if the market fell sharply. This has given rise recently to concerns that the central bank is unwittingly contributing to a form of moral hazard – that it stands by ready to prop up the market if it fails, but will do nothing to stop it going up too high.'

1.3. *The Welfare Case*

Economists have historically struggled to understand why inflation is so widely disliked. After all, utility is, (one might think), provided by real things, eg consumption and leisure; money is mostly just a veil; and a *fully* anticipated rate of inflation should have no costs, unless currency is restricted to have a zero nominal interest rate, in which case second-order costs are involved in replenishing a reduced stock of currency more often from ATMs.

But we owe to Leijonhufvud (1981) the realisation that any fully anticipated, and hence *fully* controlled, inflation can be transformed into a zero inflation rate with an appropriate monetary reform, (with some consequential benefit in reducing computational costs). So any non-zero inflation rate is by definition at least partially unanticipated, and therefore leads to losses and benefits on contracts and prices/wages based on incorrect expectations. The greater the deviation of actual from expected inflation, the more extreme will be the losses (and gains).

With most ordinary people being risk averse, such added uncertainty lowers utility. In order to avoid losses, when inflation rises to high levels, double digit and above, much more effort has to be made not only to estimate likely inflationary pressures, but also to withdraw from market positions that might leave one unduly exposed to risk. Some markets cease to function at all, eg long term corporate bond markets, and prices in others become less informative of relative scarcities. Be that as it may, empirical research suggests that when inflation rises over around 10% it has a significant adverse effect on output. While one can argue that bringing inflation down from, say, 7% to 2% per annum has no clear benefit in terms of raising *trend output*, and a transitional output cost on the way down, there are two counter-arguments. First, there is a continuing loss from the higher inflation itself, to offset against the transitional loss. Second, and perhaps more important, a monetary authority which is not prepared to try to offset stochastic shocks around an *optimal* inflation target is not likely to be able to prevent political, and other, pressures to allow inflation first to creep, and then to gallop, upwards to a point at which trend output growth is worsened. So an inflation target, *au fond*, is there in order to prevent monetary disturbances from affecting output, to provide the basis of financial stability in which growth can prosper.

If one then asks what *measurement* of inflation will do this job best, the answer, I would suggest, depends on the relationship between fluctuations in the inflation series and in the output series. If fluctuations in one measured inflation series have a more significant positive effect on fluctuations in the output series than those of a second measured inflation series, then the first series is to be preferred.

The practical policy concerns outlined already in Section 1.2 suggest that extreme cycles in asset prices, bubbles and busts, are liable to cause problems. In the Appendix we try to quantify this relationship by examining how far fluctuations of output around their trend are associated with volatile movements in prices, where we take as our price series, CPI, housing prices, equity prices and the exchange rate. We examine this relationship for 14 countries, mostly over the period from the early 1970s to 1998, using quarterly data.

The basic series are themselves extremely noisy, and few of the fits are close. Nevertheless for several countries the strongest relationship, after that between consumer price volatility and instability in output, is between fluctuations in housing prices and fluctuations in output around its trend. Movements in share prices and in exchange rates have less relationship with fluctuations in output.

In so far as the welfare effect of inflation relates ultimately to its impact on output and on consumption per head, the implication of this preliminary study is that the most relevant measure of inflation *should* give considerable weight to housing prices, though less, perhaps none, to equity prices. The econometric instability of the relationship between exchange rates and output implies that no weight should be given to them beyond their indirect effect already picked up in the CPI. This provides yet another reason for doubting the use of Monetary Conditions Indices (MCI) combining interest and exchange rates via some weighting function as a measure of the (overall?) stance of monetary policy (eg Batini and Turnbull, 2000).

Clearly, however, the relative weights to be given to the various assets (in some cases, perhaps, zero), is the crucial issue, and it is to this issue that we turn in Section 2.

2. What Weights Should be Given to Asset Prices in the Construction of a Price/Inflation Index?

2.1. *The Alchian/Klein Theoretical Position*

As one might have expected, greater efforts have been made to follow up Alchian and Klein's conceptual proposals with concrete empirical and numerical estimates in Japan, than anywhere else. Shiratsuka (1996, 1998 and 1999) and Shibuya (1992) have taken the lead on this, though also see Shimizu (1992), and Goodhart in a paper presented at a Conference at the Bank of Japan (1995). The conclusions are, however, largely negative about the value and usefulness of such a constructed index. Asset price changes are caused by too many factors, and many of such assets, such as land prices and human capital, are too badly measured. Moreover, unless the rate of subjective time discount, or time preference, is taken to be very high, an empirical application of the Alchian/Klein approach will give a huge weighting on asset prices relative to current goods prices (in Shibuya's exercise 0.97 and 0.03 respectively). And this relatively large weight on asset prices, of course, then exaggerates all the idiosyncratic causes of variance in asset prices as a measure of, or guide to, inflation more generally. Shiratsuka concludes, p. 19, that

> 'Although the concept of a dynamic equilibrium price index is highly evaluated from the viewpoints of theoretical consistency, it is difficult for monetary policy makers to expect the DEPI to be more than supplementary indicators for inflation pressures. This is because such modification of the conventional price indices is hardly operational.'

2.2. *An Empirically Based Measure*

The main recent work on this is by Cecchetti, *et al.* (2000), particularly Section 3, and also Section 4.

Thus they write:-

> 'There is a notion pervading much of the discussion of the inclusion of asset prices in measures of inflation, and it concerns that idea that asset-price movements somehow give information about *future* inflation.....
>
> However, note that if the underlying justification for inclusion of asset prices in the measure of inflation is that they help to predict future inflation, then it is far from obvious that they should attract a weight based on the discount rate. Instead, the weight should be more closely related to their relative contribution to an inflation forecast.
>
> But once we formulate the problem in this way, we can see that the issue of including or excluding any given nominal price is an empirical one, having to do with their informativeness about the common trend. If, for example, we knew that the price of a particular variety of shoes never

experienced any relative price changes, then we could save government statistical agencies quite a bit of money. Alternatively, if there were only two goods in the economy, and they experienced substantial relative price shocks, then focussing attention on one price alone, rather than a properly constructed average, would be very misleading.

The computation of a DFI [Dynamic Factor Index] involves the calculation of the relative weights to put on the different prices that we observe. Starting with a set that includes asset prices, we can ask whether their inclusion adds any information to our estimate of the common trend?

We study the properties of two sets of price data. First, we examine a same set of quarterly data for 12 countries used by Goodhart and Hofmann (2000). The data are described in the appendix to their paper. Table 3.1 [not shown here] reports the implied weights for consumer prices, housing prices and stock prices, using the full sample that they have available. The results are what we would expect. Since stock prices are so much more volatile than consumer prices, their implied weight is very low, never exceeding 2.5%, and usually below 2%. Housing is quite a different story, however, because in this case prices can have a substantial effect.

To examine this a bit further, we have collected a more comprehensive monthly data set for the United States, with a sample from the beginning of 1967 through 1999. Here we are able to assemble data for energy prices, food prices, housing purchase prices, housing rental and operating costs (labeled 'CPI Shelter'), stock prices, and a residual category of the consumer price index that excludes food, energy and shelter. Here we look at the inflation rate over 12-month period, and examine the consequences of computing variances of rolling ten-year periods. The results are reported in Table 3.2 [not shown here], and suggest that stock prices are much too volatile to be useful in computing a price index, but that the treatment of housing is crucial. . .

The conclusion from this expository exercise is that straightforward attempts to include asset prices in measures of inflation need to proceed with care. While there may be justification for including equity prices, their inclusion is likely to create more problems than they solve. Specifically, the extremely high variance of stock returns (hundred of times that of conventional inflation measures) will simply add noise. Housing, though, needs to be considered very carefully. Here, we believe that there is clear room for improvement of price indices.'

In a similar vein Goodhart and Hofmann (2000) have examined the relationship between CPI inflation and previous values of sets of explanatory variables, examining whether the inclusion of certain asset prices, notably housing, equities and the yield spread improves the fit.

Our conclusion was that:-

> 'If there is a message in these results, it is that monetary variables in general, and house price movements in particular, need to be given more weight in the assessment of inflation, particularly at a two-year horizon, than is done in some current models, which primarily incorporate the monetary transmission mechanism via the effects of real interest rates on real expenditures (and of nominal interest rates on exchange rates)...
>
> At the beginning of this paper we noted that most economists would agree that movements in asset prices *should* be taken into account by the monetary authorities in so far as they signal changes in expected inflation. What we have done here is to run a horse-race between a benchmark forecasting equation with and without a set of non-standard asset prices. We claim that such asset prices, especially house prices, do help in the majority of cases in the context of our data set to assess (predict) future CPI inflation.'

Thus one method of weighting asset prices in a reformed price index is to use weights derived from empirical studies of the econometric relationships between the various series.

2.3. *A Statistically Based Measure*

Another alternative is to relate the weights to the share of expenditures on each item. The CPI and RPI concentrate on personal expenditures, but omit almost entirely expenditures on real and financial assets. Thus direct (net) expenditures on buying houses (from other sectors, ie houses built by the company sector or sold to it from the government sector, when public sector dwellings are sold to their occupants) amounted to slightly over $3\frac{1}{2}\%$ of the usage of personal incomes in the United Kingdom in 1999. So the weight on the price of new housing could be that same percentage.

Besides being (net) purchasers of houses, households save by buying, mostly financial, assets. Changes in such asset prices affect the value of money, as much as changes in current goods and services prices. A net acquisitions approach is, perhaps, the best.

What one is buying with a financial asset is a claim to a flow of interest or dividend payments. Dividend payments change over time, and there will be expectations of these which may turn out to be correct, or not. But the present level of dividends is measurable, and a rise in the price of a claim on such a dividend, or more simply in the case of a rise in the price of a claim on an interest payment, (though there is default risk here), seems (to me) a perfectly reasonable measure of inflation.

The argument may be made that the household sector, even after taking into account indirect purchases via financial intermediaries such as pension funds, may be net sellers of financial assets, as for example currently in the United States. In that case, the higher the price/dividend ratio the lower would be measured inflation. But that also seems reasonable. The more that I am a net seller of something high valued, the higher is my utility, and the better-off I am for a given cash income.

Why should one be concerned only with the level of inflation affecting individuals (persons), taking no notice of the inflationary pressures on other domestic sectors, companies and government? Perhaps particularly if one is concerned about the conceptual and practical difficulties of taking account of (volatile) financial assets in a measure of inflation, a much broader index, covering all domestic sectors, (so that financial assets net out, ignoring net claims on the rest of the world for this purpose), would seem suitable.

The GDP deflator at least has a broader coverage than the RPI or CPI, and includes estimates of prices of newly produced investment goods and houses. In that sense it partly avoids one of the main deficiencies of the narrow focus of the RPI/CPI measure of inflation.

It has, however, other drawbacks. It does not, for example, resolve the theoretical problems identified by Alchian and Klein. Thus they state, p. 181, that the GNP deflator

> 'includes the prices of newly produced assets but does not include the prices of previously existing items of wealth and therefore is conceptually distinct from our iso-utility wealth price index. Therefore, although it is useful for other purposes, a current output price index also provides a biased estimate of changes in the money cost of consumer utility... Prices of already produced assets will, we conjecture, generally be more flexible than prices of currently produced goods, which are based on current costs that are often made less flexible by long-term contracts.'

Moreover, this deflator is a somewhat arbitrary and abstract concept partly obtained as a derived residual which coordinates estimates of nominal and real output, themselves measured with considerable error. As a consequence it is only available quarterly, and is subject to large revisions as often as the output measures are changed. It is a somewhat noisy series. Few understand its conceptual basis, and even fewer pay it much attention as a preferred measure of inflation.

A better index that has been developed in response to user requests for such a broader measure of inflation is the Final Expenditure Price Index, or FEPI, see Wall (1997; 2000); and Wall and O'Donoghue (2000); also note a similar exercise being undertaken in Australia, see Woolford (2000). While these indices have been constructed to overcome several of the deficiencies of the GDP deflator as a broader measure of inflation, they are still somewhat experimental and, in some fields, problematical. Wall's (2000) paper is concerned with one such difficult area, concerning the public sector, and Woolford's paper touches on others. A few years' experience will be required before it will be possible to discern exactly how valuable these additional and broader measures of inflation will be to our assessments of such trends. In these, as in other, measures of inflation the treatment of owner-occupied housing tends to remain a stumbling block, though FEPI does contain an index for new dwellings as a component of its investment index.

3. Housing

Perhaps, these arguments on the appropriate treatment of asset prices in an inflation index reach their most practical and operational nub in the treatment of housing. For a large proportion of the population, our house is our most important and valuable asset. Personal expenditures on housing services, in one form or another, downpayment, mortgage payments, rent and repairs represent a considerable chunk of personal expenditures. So, statisticians, and others, can hardly avoid trying to decide how to deal with this major question for the construction of price indices.

The International Labour Organisation (ILO) manual (Turvey *et al.*, 1989), also see Turvey (2000 *a*), and ONS (1998), lists three general approaches to the treatment of housing. The first is the net acquisition approach, which is the change in the price of newly purchased owner-occupied dwellings, weighted by the net purchases of the reference population. This is an asset-based measure, and therefore comes close to my preferred measure of inflation as a change in the value of money, though the change in the price of the stock of existing houses rather than just of net purchases would in some respects be even better. It is, moreover, consistent with the treatment of other durables. A few countries, eg Australia and New Zealand, have used it, and it is, I understand, the main contender for use in the Euro-area Harmonised Index of Consumer Prices (HICP), which currently excludes any measure of the purchase price of (new) housing, though it does include minor repairs and maintenance by home owners, as well as all expenditures by tenants.

The second main approach is the payments approach, measuring actual cash-outflows, on down-payments, mortgage repayments and mortgage interest, or some subset of the above. This approach always, however, includes mortgage interest payments. This, though common, is analytically unsound. First, the procedure is not carried out consistently across purchases. Other goods bought on the basis of credit, eg credit card credit, are usually not treated as more expensive on that account (though they have been in New Zealand). Second, the treatment of interest flows is not consistent across persons. If a borrower is worse off in some sense when interest rates rise, then equivalently a lender owning an interest bearing asset is better off; why measure one and not the other? If I sell an interest-earning asset, say a money market mutual fund holding, to buy a house, why am I treated differently to someone who borrows on a (variable rate) mortgage? Third, should not the question of the price of any purchase be assessed separately from the issue of how that might be financed? Imports, inventories and all business purchases tend to be purchased in part on credit. Should we regard imports as more expensive, when the cost of trade credit rises? Money, moreover, is fungible. As we know from calculations of mortgage equity withdrawal, the loan may be secured on the house but used to pay for furniture. When interest rates rise, is the furniture thereby more expensive? Moreover, the actual cash out-payments totally ignore changes in the on-going value of the house whether by depreciation, or capital loss/gain, which will often dwarf the cash flow. Despite its problems, such a cash payment approach was used in the United Kingdom until 1994 and still is in Ireland.

As the RBNZ (1997) put it,

> 'The rate of interest paid in order to advance consumption in time is not a "price" any more than the rate of interest on saving is a "negative price". Consumers do not "consume" debt. They consume the goods and services purchased with borrowed funds in the same way as they consume out of current income or past savings. The CPI should measure current consumption prices, not the way in which that consumption is financed. It is for these reasons that interest rates are excluded from the national accounts and GST frameworks and from the CPIs of most OECD countries.'

The third approach is some variation of a user-cost approach. The most straight-forward, and perhaps the best of these, is to pretend that all housing is rented, and ask what is the change in the cost of renting current housing services. There is a practical difficulty with this in many countries, in that the rented sector in reality is too dissimilar and often too small to provide a good basis for calculation, though the United States, Germany, Denmark and the Netherlands try to use this approach. Meanwhile, of course, I have a difficulty in principle, which is that people buy houses; they mostly do not rent them. This means that this kind of rental approach consciously aims to ignore the cost of buying access now to such future rental services.

In the absence of a sufficiently large rental market, there is a plethora of approximations to a user cost approach. The method used now in the United Kingdom, following the advice of the RPI Advisory Committee (1994), and also in Canada, Sweden and Finland, is a combination of mortgage payments plus depreciation at replacement cost. Analytically this really is a dog's breakfast. I have already stated why I believe that the use of mortgage payments is wrong. As for depreciation, it is neither a cash payment, nor the true change in the price of an asset over any period, since depreciation over any period is likely to be dwarfed by shifts in the current value of the asset.

An even more theoretical user-cost approach is to measure the cost foregone by living in an owner-occupied property as compared with selling it at the beginning of the period and repurchasing it at the end (see Blinder, 1980). But this gives the absurd result that as house prices rise, so the opportunity cost falls; indeed the more virulent the inflation of housing asset prices, the more negative would this measure become. Although it has some academic aficionados, this flies in the face of common sense; I am glad to say that no country has adopted this method.

In view of all these difficulties it is, perhaps, not surprising that another popular option is to exclude owner-occupied housing from the index altogether: none of France, Belgium, Italy, Spain, Greece, Austria, Luxembourg or Portugal here included it in their index, at least when a survey of such practices was taken in 1998. And currently, neither does the HICP. A working-party at Eurostat is considering owner-occupied housing costs in the HICP. At present it is bound by law from including prices that are non-observable or do not involve an actual monetary transaction. Partly for this reason, the method, I understand, that is most likely to be implemented, if one is at all, is the purchase price of new houses bought by the household sector from another sector (eg the corporate or government sectors).[1]

4. Conclusions

In the earlier sections of this paper I have set out some general arguments for incorporating asset prices into measures of price indices and inflation. Yet there is also a very strong case for leaving our present measures unchanged. The status quo has the inestimable advantage that it has the power of inertia on its side. Change is disruptive, perhaps even more so in the statistical world than elsewhere, and the case for change has to be demonstrable to have a chance. It is of crucial importance to have a nominal inflation target in the first place which is understood and reliable. Monkeying about with it on minor points of academic nicety could provoke confusion and cynicism. So long as all such measures are cointegrated the choice between measures is less important than having and sticking with the measure with which we have already become accustomed.

Moreover, there are strong arguments for keeping the status quo. On the negative side it can be correctly claimed that the valuation of asset prices depends on expectations about the future. Such expectations are hard to measure, ephemeral, not facts as price tags are facts, and often falsified; ex ante is not the same as ex post. If I should expect the price of London housing services to rise in future at a steady 10% per annum, a two-room flat in, shall we say, Notting Hill priced at £$\frac{1}{2}$ million is not expensive, but cheap!

The more positive argument is that there is no *necessity* for the authorities to remain paralysed into inaction in the face of asset price changes, even with the present definition of inflation. In so far as those, like me, concerned about asset price changes can demonstrate econometrically that asset price changes *now* feed through significantly into *future* goods and services inflation, then the authorities should react *now*. And if they cannot find such a robust link, then it is right to ignore such asset price movements.

What does, I believe, emerge from the empirical studies which have been done is that the links between equity prices (and exchange rates) and subsequent movements in output and (goods and services) inflation is weak. In

---

[1] However, there are several technical issues which need to be resolved before the incorporation of such indices into the HICP. As a first step, Member States agreed in September 2000 to develop pilot indices. This work will involve a consideration of the measurement problems and an analysis of the behaviour of the results. Member States will then consider in due course whether the new series should be integrated in the HICP. I am grateful to Mr. Jim O'Donoghue of the ONS for this information.

contrast, the relationship between housing price movements and subsequent output and inflation is much stronger. So, the appropriate methodology for incorporating measures of housing price inflation into our overall statistics for inflation remains an urgent and important issue. It cannot be dismissed or ignored. It has to be addressed.

London School of Economics

Appendix

If utility is derived from real variables, then our concern about inflation must relate primarily with respect to its effect in distorting such real variables from their equilibrium path. Hence the definition of inflation that is most relevant would seem to be that most closely related to such deviations. We attempt to measure this by examining the relationship between the variability of output around its trend and the variability of consumer prices and of a set of asset prices (exchange rate, share prices and house prices).

The countries in the sample are: Australia, Belgium, Canada, Denmark, Finland, France, Germany, Ireland, Japan, Netherlands, Norway, Sweden, United Kingdom and United States. The data period is quarterly (annually for Germany) from early 1970s to 1998 (see Table 1 for details).

There were difficulties in selecting an appropriate indicator for the variability of the series, eg simple standard deviations led to overlapping observations. After some experimentation, we decided to measure the variability of each variable as the *absolute difference of its growth rate from its trend value*. In particular for each variable the growth rate at quarter t was calculated as the growth rate of the variable from the corresponding quarter of the previous year. So for each variable we ended up with four series, one for the growth rate of the variable between the first quarters of consecutive years, the second for the growth rate between the second quarters and so on (for Germany we ended up with one series for each variable because house prices were only available with annual frequency). Both for simplicity and to avoid overfitting we used a linear trend for all the series.

Having calculated this indicator for all the variables, we specified two alternative models, running therefore eight regressions for each country (2 for Germany):

$$\left| Dev\,GDP \right|_t = C + \left| Dev\,GDP \right|_{t-1} + \left| Dev\,CPI \right|_t + \left| Dev\,EXCH \right|_t + \left| Dev\,SP \right|_t + \left| Dev\,HP \right|_t \quad (1)$$

$$\left| Dev\,GDP \right|_t = C + \left| Dev\,GDP \right|_{t-1} + \left| Dev\,CPI \right|_{t-1} + \left| Dev\,EXCH \right|_{t-1} + \left| Dev\,SP \right|_{t-1}$$

$$+ \left| Dev\,HP \right|_{t-1} \quad (2)$$

where $DevX = \Delta \ln X - TREND\Delta \ln X$. The two models differ only in their lag structure. In the first model fluctuations of asset and consumer prices are expected to affect the volatility of GDP (as measured by our proxy) instantaneously, while in the second model they are expected to affect the volatility of output with a lag of one year. Both models included an autoregressive term because of the strong autocorrelation in the growth rate of output.

Table 1
Variables, Data Sources and Periods of Estimation

Country	Variable (and definition) Unless alternatively specified Consumer price inflation: change in CPI Output: Real GDP Exchange rate: Effective nominal exchange rate Share prices: share price index	Data sources Unless alternatively specified CPI: IMF Exchange rate, Share prices: IMF and OECD	Period of estimation
Australia	Exchange rate: US Exchange rate House prices: RBA dwelling price index	House prices: Central Bank	1972–98
Belgium	House prices: average housing prices	House prices: Central Bank	1973–98
Canada	House prices: average resale housing price index	House prices: Canadian real estate association	1973–98
Denmark	House prices: house price index for single family houses	House prices: Central Bank	1973–98
Finland	House prices: national house price index	House prices: Central Bank	1973–98
France	House prices: price of old apartments in Paris	House prices: Chambres des Notaires	1973–98
Germany	House prices: residential house price index	House prices: Aufina/Era	1973–98
Ireland	Output: industrial production House prices: average prices of new houses	House prices: Department of the Environment	1978–98
Japan	House prices: nation-wide land price index	House prices: Japan Real Estate Institute	1973–98
Netherlands	House prices: average housing prices	House prices: Central Bank	1973–98
Norway	House prices: national house price index	House prices: Central Bank	1973–98
Sweden	House prices: single family house price index	House prices: Central Bank	1978–98
UK	House prices: index of house prices	House prices: Department of the Environment	1972–98
US	House prices: median sales prices of new one-family houses	House prices: Bureau of the Census	1972–98

The exact definition of the variables, the data sources and the periods of estimation are reported in Table 1. In Table 2 we summarise the results of our exercise recording the number and name of the countries for which the specified explanatory variable was significant and with the expected sign in i regressions (the full results are available on request).

All the series were extremely noisy, and the included explanatory variables appear to have power in explaining the volatility of GDP only in *some* of the regressions (concentrated in *a few* countries). However, despite the necessary caution, this simple exercise suggests that the variable that appears best in explaining the volatility of GDP is the volatility of consumer prices, as might have been expected. Perhaps more interesting is that the volatility of house prices appears the second most important explanatory variable with at least three countries (Germany, Netherlands, and UK) for which we found reasonable evidence of its importance. By comparison we only found reasonable evidence (ie significance in at least three equations) for share prices in one

Table 2
Summary of the Results

Number of equations	Share prices	House prices	Exchange rate	CPI	GDP
4	1 (Japan)	1 (Germany: 1 out of 2)*	0	1 (Netherlands)	0
3	0	2 (Netherlands, UK)	0 (Belgium, Japan)	2	0
2	3 (Finland, UK, US)	1 (Finland)	1 (Denmark)	3 (Denmark, France, US)	3 (Australia, Belgium, Japan)
1	3 (Australia, Canada, Netherlands)	2 (Canada, US)	2 (France, UK)	4 (Canada, Finland, Ireland, Sweden)	3 (Denmark, Netherlands, US)

Note: Cell (i, j) reports the number and the name of the countries for which variable j resulted significant (at least at the 10% level) and with the expected (positive) sign in i of the eight regressions run for the country.
* For Germany, since house prices were available with annual frequency, we ran one regression for each model.

country (Japan). The least important regressors appeared to be the autoregressive term (GDP(-1)) and the exchange rate.

Therefore, and with due caution, if we were to infer policy implications from this simple exercise, we would be tempted to propose a role for house prices in the measurement of inflation (besides consumer prices), but no role for share prices or for the exchange rate.

References

Alchian, A. A. and Klein, B. (1973). 'On a correct measure of inflation', *Journal of Money, Credit and Banking*, vol. 5 (1), pt.1 (February), pp. 173–91.
Batini, N. and Turnbull, K. (2000). 'Monetary conditions indices for the UK: a survey', Bank of England, unpublished mimeograph, September.
Bernanke, B. and Gertler, M. (2000). 'Monetary policy and asset price volatility', in *New Challenges for Monetary Policy*, proceedings of the 1999 Jackson Hole Conference, Kansas City: Federal Reserve Bank of Kansas City.
Blinder, A. (1980). 'The consumer price index and the measurement of recent inflation', *Brookings Papers on Economic Activity*, vol. 2, pp. 539–73.
Cecchetti, S., Genburg, H., Lipsky, J. and Wadhwani, S. (2000). *Asset Prices and Central Bank Policy*, Report prepared for the Conference 'Central Banks and Asset Prices', organised by the International Center for Monetary and Banking Studies and CEPR in Geneva on May 5.
Filardo, A. (2000). 'Monetary policy and asset prices', *Federal Reserve Bank of Kansas City Economic Review*, Third Quarter, pp. 11–37.
Financial Times, (1999). Gerard Baker on 'Wall St asks Fed questions – and may hold the answers', Monday, August 30th, p. 3.
Fisher, I. (1906). *Nature of Capital and Income*, New York: Macmillan.
Gertler, M., Goodfriend, M., Issing, O. and Spaventa, L. (1998). 'Asset prices and monetary policy, four views', Pamphlet, Bank for International Settlements and Centre for Economic Policy Research.
Goodfriend, M. and King, R. (2000). 'The case for price stability', Paper presented for the First ECB

Central Banking Conference, 'Why Price Stability', Frankfurt, (November), forthcoming in Conference Proceedings (2001).

Goodhart, C.A.E. (1995). 'Price stability and financial fragility', in (K. Sawamoto, Z. Nakajima and H. Taguchi. eds.) *Financial Stability in a Changing Environment*, London: Macmillan, Chapter 10, pp. 439–510.

Goodhart, C. and Hofmann, B. (2000). 'Do asset prices help to predict consumer price inflation?', *The Manchester School Supplement*, vol. 68, pp. 122–40.

Goodhart, C. and Hofmann, B. (2001). 'Asset prices and the conduct of monetary policy', paper presented at the Swedish Riksbank Conference on Monetary Policy, June 2000, forthcoming in Proceedings.

Leijonhufvud, A. (1981). 'Inflation and economic performance', published as a 'Kieler Vortag' pamphlet, Kiel: Institute fur Weltwirtschaft.

OECD, Secretariat, Economics Department, (2000). 'House prices and economic activity', note, ECO/CPE (2000) 16 (October).

Office for National Statistics, (1998). *The Retail Prices Index: technical manual*, London: H.M. Stationery Office.

Reserve Bank of New Zealand, (1997). 'Recommendation to the 1997 CPI Revision Advisory Committee', (May), web pages http://www.rbnz.govt.nz/cpi.htm.

RPI Advisory Committee, (1994). 'Treatment of owner occupiers' housing costs in the retail prices index', Central Statistical Office, Cmnd 2717.

Samuelson, P. (1961). 'The evaluation of "social income": capital formation and wealth', in (F. Lutz and D. Hague, eds.), *The Theory of Capital*, London: Macmillan.

Shibuya, H. (1992). 'Dynamic equilibrium price index: asset prices and inflation', *Bank of Japan Monetary and Economic Studies*, Institute for Monetary and Economic Studies, Bank of Japan, vol. 10 (1), pp. 95–109.

Shimizu, Y. (1992). 'Problems in the Japanese financial system in the early 1990s', *Hitotsubashi Journal of Commerce and Management*, vol. 27 (November), pp. 29–49.

Shiratsuka, S. (1996). 'Shisan kakaku hendo to bukka shisu (Asset price fluctuations and price index)', *Kin'yu Kenkyu*, Institute for Monetary and Economic Studies, Bank of Japan, vol. 14 (4), pp. 45–72 (in Japanese).

Shiratsuka, S. (1997). 'Inflation measures for monetary policy: measuring the underlying inflation trend and its implication for monetary policy implementation', *Bank of Japan Monetary and Economic Studies*, vol. 15 (2), pp. 1–26.

Shiratsuka, S. (1998). *'Bukka no keizai bunseki'*, (Economic analysis of inflation measures), University of Tokyo Press, (in Japanese).

Shiratsuka, S. (1999). 'Asset price fluctuation and price indices', Institute for Monetary and Economic Studies, Bank of Japan, Discussion Paper No. 99-E-21.

Silver, M. and Fenwick, D. (2000). *Proceedings of the Measurement of Inflation Conference* (in 1999), Eurostat, Office for National Statistics and Cardiff University, Cardiff Business School.

Turvey, R. (2000a). 'Owner-occupiers and the price index', *World Economics*, vol. 1 (3), (July–September), pp. 153–9.

Turvey, R. (2000b). *Consumer Price Index Methodology, a manual*, www.turvey.demon.co.uk, (November format).

Turvey, R, Sellwood, D. J., Szuke, B. J., Donkers, H. W. J. *et al.*, Marret, M. A., Clements, L. C. *et al.*, Woodhouse, T. J. and Hanson, K. M. (1989). *Consumer Price Indices*, Geneva: International Labour Organisation.

Wall, D. (1997). 'Developments of a final expenditure prices index', *Economic Trends*, No. 526, September, pp. 30–50.

Wall, D. (2000). 'The final expenditure prices index (FEPI): improving the index of government prices and other issues', in (M. Silver and D. Fenwick eds.), *Proceedings of the Measurement of Inflation Conference*, Eurostat, Office for National Statistics and Cardiff University: Cardiff Business School, pp. 511–6.

Wall, D. and O'Donoghue, J. (2000). 'Development plans for the final expenditure price index', *Economic Trends*, No. 555, (February), pp. 51–4.

Woolford, K. (2000). 'Measuring inflation: a framework based on domestic final purchases', in (M. Silver and D. Fenwick eds.), *Proceedings of the Measurement of Inflation Conference*, Eurostat, Office for National Statistics and Cardiff University: Cardiff Business School, pp. 518–34.

[3]

Asset prices, financial imbalances and monetary policy: are inflation targets enough?

Introduction[1]

On the face of it, the last decade and a half has been a successful period for most developed country central banks. Compared to the previous 15 years inflation has been low and relatively stable. Moreover, price stability has not been achieved at the expense of the real economy, as growth has also been relatively stable and unemployment has been falling in a number of countries.

Notwithstanding the good macroeconomic outturns there has, however, been a growing concern that the achievement of price stability may be associated with heightened risks of financial instability, particularly so in the aftermath of the collapse of the dotcom bubble and the more recent wider correction to share values. Appreciating asset values and debt accumulation have, in some countries, led to stretched household and corporate balance sheets that are vulnerable to the sort of equity price corrections witnessed recently. That has led some commentators to question the quasi-consensus that monetary policy should be directed exclusively at maintaining price stability and its role in combating financial instability should be restricted to minimising any adverse consequences when overvaluations are corrected or as financial imbalances unwind.

The heterodox view is neatly summarised by Crockett (2003; italics in original):

> "(I)n a monetary regime in which the central bank's operational objective is expressed *exclusively* in terms of short-term inflation, there may be insufficient protection against the build up of financial imbalances that lies at the root of much of the financial instability we observe. This could be so if the focus on short-term inflation control meant that the authorities did not tighten monetary policy sufficiently pre-emptively to lean against excessive credit expansion and asset price increases. In jargon, if the monetary policy reaction function does not incorporate financial imbalances, the monetary anchor may fail to deliver financial stability."

In this paper I examine the view that inflation targeting alone, whether explicit or implicit, is not enough and that there is a case for an additional monetary response to asset price movements and/or developing financial imbalances in order to reduce the risks of future financial instability. My view, in a nutshell, is that (flexible) inflation targeting is best thought of as a description of the objective function of the policymaker rather than entailing an explicit monetary policy reaction function. The abrupt unwinding of asset price misalignments and/or financial imbalances that may lead to financial instability will also invariably be associated with significant macroeconomic instability. A forward-looking flexible inflation targeting central bank should bear in mind those longer-run consequences of asset price bubbles and financial imbalances in the setting of current interest rates. There is thus no need for an additional response of monetary policy to be specified, though inflation targeting central banks may need to look out further into the future than is usual in order to take on board these considerations.

The remainder of the paper is organised as follows. In the next section, I review some of the recent literature on the extent to which monetary policy should respond to asset prices, and in particular to asset price bubbles. While it may well be appropriate for interest rates to respond to asset prices, among many other economic indicators, I conclude that such a response is consistent with inflation targeting. In the subsequent section I characterise the optimal monetary policy in a simple New Keynesian macroeconomic model in which financial imbalances play a role and where their subsequent unwinding may lead to a credit crunch or similar financial distress. The possibility of credit crunches turns out to affect the design of the optimal policy in a subtle, and perhaps surprising, way. I also consider a variety of other ways that incipient financial imbalances could impinge on the conduct of an optimal monetary policy. Finally I illustrate some of the difficulties in deciding whether an asset price is misaligned, or an imbalance poses a potential threat to macroeconomic stability, by considering the recent evolution of house prices and consumer debt in the United Kingdom.

---

[1] Prepared for the conference on "Monetary stability, financial stability and the business cycle" at the Bank for International Settlements, Basel, 28-29 March 2003. I am grateful to the discussants, Ignazio Visco and Sushil Wadhwani, to participants at the conference, and to Peter Andrews, Francesco Giavazzi and Ed Nelson for useful comments. The views expressed are those of the author and do not reflect those of either the Bank of England, the Monetary Policy Committee or the BIS.

Asset prices and monetary policy: some recent views

The conventional view that monetary policy can do little more than deal with the fallout from the unwinding of asset price bubbles has been clearly ennunciated by Chairman Greenspan (2002):

> "Such data suggest that nothing short of a sharp increase in short-term rates that engenders a significant economic retrenchment is sufficient to check a nascent bubble. The notion that a well-timed incremental tightening could have been calibrated to prevent the late 1990s bubble is almost surely an illusion. Instead, we ... need to focus on policies to mitigate the fallout when it occurs and, hopefully, ease the transition to the next expansion."

But not everyone subscribes to this view, and there has recently been a lively literature debating the extent to which monetary policy should respond to asset price movements (see eg Batini and Nelson (2000), Bernanke and Gertler (1999, 2001), Cecchetti et al (2000), Cecchetti et al (2002), Taylor (2001)). Thus on the one hand Bernanke and Gertler (1999) conclude that:

> "The inflation targeting approach dictates that central banks should adjust monetary policy actively and pre-emptively to offset incipient inflationary and deflationary pressures. Importantly for present purposes, it also implies that policy should not respond to changes in asset prices, except insofar as they signal changes in expected inflation."

Against this, Cecchetti et al (2000) argue:

> "A central bank concerned with both hitting an inflation target at a given time horizon, and achieving as smooth a path as possible for inflation, is likely to achieve superior performance by adjusting its policy instruments not only to inflation (or its inflation forecast) and the output gap, but to asset prices as well. Typically modifying the policy framework in this way could also reduce output volatility. We emphasize that this conclusion is based on our view that reacting to asset prices in the normal course of policymaking will reduce the likelihood of asset price bubbles forming, thus reducing the risk of boom-bust investment cycles."

Each of these contributions evaluates the appropriateness of a policy response to asset prices by exploring the efficacy of a variety of interest rate reaction functions in simple calibrated stochastic model economies in which asset prices play some explicit role. Thus both Bernanke and Gertler (1999, 2001) and Cecchetti et al (2000) employ a dynamic New Keynesian model, modified to allow for credit market frictions and exogenous asset price bubbles. The credit market frictions arise from agency problems in the credit market, so that internal finance is cheaper than external finance and the external finance premium depends on the firm's financial position. In particular, a rise in the firm's share price increases the available collateral and leads to a reduction in the marginal cost of external funds, and a consequent increase in borrowing and investment. Furthermore, the equity price may differ from fundamentals by an exogenous and stochastic bubble component, which grows exponentially but may collapse. During the build-up of such a bubble the external finance premium falls, and investment, aggregate demand and future potential output rise, whereas when the bubble collapses the process reverses.

But despite the apparent similarity of the models employed, the two sets of authors come to strikingly different conclusions about whether it is wise for the monetary authorities to condition their short-term interest rate on the equity price. Cecchetti et al (2002) argue that a key difference lies in different assumptions about what shocks are present and exactly what the monetary authorities are allowed to observe.

Similarly, Batini and Nelson explore whether feedback to the interest rate from the exchange rate (which may or may not contain a bubble) is advisable in a New Keynesian model of a small open economy in which the real exchange rate influences both demand and supply and the exchange rate is determined via uncovered interest parity. They find that for an optimised rule, there is apparently no gain to reacting separately to the exchange rate. Yet Cecchetti et al (2002), using essentially the same model, find that under some circumstances feedback from the exchange rate leads to higher welfare than not responding. Again, the key difference appears to lie in the assumptions about what shocks are present and exactly what the monetary authorities know.

Now, at one level it may not seem surprising that different assumptions about the stochastic structure of the economy and what the authorities can observe/infer may lead to different conclusions about the appropriateness of adjusting interest rates in the light of asset price movements. And few people would disagree that the authorities should take account of asset price movements insofar as they affect the outlook for output and inflation. But the question is whether some additional response is called for, as the above quotes should make clear. In addressing this issue, I think it is fruitful to look at exactly how the above authors go about trying to answer that question.

Essentially, all these contributions evaluate whether the addition of asset prices - or an estimate of the bubble component therein - to a simple feedback rule for the policy rate instrument leads to a lower value of a suitable loss function. Two general classes of simple rule are employed.

Either an augmented Taylor rule:

(1) $i_t = i^*_t + \phi_\pi \pi_t + \phi_y x_t + \phi_q q_t,$

where i_t is the nominal interest rate, i^*_t is the "natural" level of the nominal interest rate, π_t is inflation (strictly, the deviation from target), x_t is the deviation of output from its flexible-price level, ie the output gap, and q_t is an asset price (relative to some suitably defined normal or equilibrium value).

Or else an augmented inflation forecast targeting rule:

(2) $i_t = i^*_t + \mu_\pi E_t \pi_{t+k} + \mu_q q_t,$

where E_t denotes the mathematical expectation conditional on information available to the policymaker at time t and k is some suitably chosen time horizon.

The authorities are assumed to have a period loss function that is quadratic in the deviation of inflation from target and in the output gap:

(3) $L_t = \pi_t^2 + \lambda x_t^2,$

where for simplicity the inflation target is set to zero. The associated expected objective function, Λ_t, is

(4) $\Lambda_t = E_t[(1-\beta)L_t + \beta\Lambda_{t+1}],$

where β is a discount factor. As β tends to unity, so this loss function tends to a simple weighted average of the conditional variances of inflation about the target and of the output gap. One can then think of searching over the parameters in the Taylor-type rule (1) and the inflation forecast targeting rule (2) to find the values of the feedback coefficients that minimise the loss function (3 and 4), and this is what the papers in this literature in essence do.

However, it is worth recalling that, despite their appeal, Taylor-type rules imply feedback from a relatively restricted state vector and the optimal feedback rule can only be written as a Taylor rule in very simple settings. The same is true of inflation forecast targeting rules, which furthermore are dynamically inconsistent (see Svensson (2001)). A relevant question is why we should be interested in whether an asset price, or indeed any other variable for that matter, appears in some ad hoc class of feedback rule, even though the coefficients of that rule may have been optimised? It seems more instructive to ask first what an optimal rule looks like, and then consider how asset prices ought to figure in it. One might then go on to consider whether particular simple rules represent sufficiently close approximations to the optimal rule to be useful guideposts for policy.

In order to say more we need first to assume something about the structure of the economy. Suppose, for illustrative purposes, the demand side is given by a forward-looking IS schedule, including the asset price:

(5) $x_t = E_t x_{t+1} - (i_t - E_t \pi_{t+1} - r^o_t)/\sigma + \chi q_t + v_t,$

where r^o_t is the flexible-price real interest rate (ie the natural real interest rate) and v_t is an aggregate demand shock. The IS schedule is augmented by a suitable intertemporal arbitrage condition determining the asset price (including, perhaps, a bubble component or a stochastic risk premium). And the supply side is given by a New Keynesian Phillips curve

(6) $\pi_t = \beta E_t \pi_{t+1} + \kappa x_t + u_t,$

where u_t is a supply (cost) shock. Both shocks are observed by the monetary authorities and for simplicity are assumed to be serially uncorrelated.

Then, as shown by Svensson and Woodford (1999), Svensson (2002) and Giannoni and Woodford (2002), the optimal policy under commitment, from the "timeless perspective", satisfies the first-order condition, for all $k \geq 0$:

$$(7) \qquad E_t\pi_{t+k} = -(\lambda/\kappa)(E_tx_{t+k} - E_tx_{t+k-1}).$$

This optimal targeting rule describes a plan that the conditional expectations of the two target variables should satisfy.[2] This optimal plan equates the marginal rate of transformation between output and inflation that is embodied in the supply schedule with the marginal rate of substitution that is embodied in the loss function. It ensures that inflation will be brought back to target, but at a rate that recognises the consequences for activity. Svensson has characterised an optimality condition of this type as describing "flexible inflation forecast targeting".

Combining the first-order conditions for periods t and $t+1$ with the supply schedule (6), one can also characterise the optimal choice of the output gap in terms of lagged activity and the supply shock as:

$$(8) \qquad x_t = \gamma_x x_{t-1} + \gamma_u u_t,$$

where $\gamma_x = \{[(1+\beta+\kappa^2/\lambda) - [(1+\beta+\kappa^2/\lambda)^2 - 4\beta]^{1/2}\}/2\beta$ and $\gamma_u = -\kappa\gamma_x/\lambda$.

A key feature of condition (7) is that it contains neither the policy instrument,[3] nor indeed anything to do with the structure of the demand side of the economy. In particular, there is no role for asset prices.[4] So in that sense the analysis supports the conventional wisdom as summarised in the quote above from Bernanke and Gertler - with the modification that policy responds to changes in asset prices only insofar as they signal changes in expected inflation or *growth*.

Is this a reasonable interpretation of what inflation targeting central banks are about, as opposed to an inflation forecast targeting rule like (2)? Take for instance the statutory objective of the Bank of England since it was given operational independence in 1997. The *Bank of England Act* (1998) charges the Bank "to maintain price stability, and subject to that to support the economic policy of (the) government, including the objectives for growth and employment". An annual *Remit* from the Chancellor of the Exchequer then defines price stability - currently as an annual rate of inflation of 2.5% for RPIX at all times - and also fleshes out the "economic policy of the government", namely the maintenance of a high and stable rate of growth. This can be thought of as defining the bliss point for inflation, but instructing the Monetary Policy Committee to seek to achieve it in a way that avoids undue volatility in economic activity. However, the remit is non-specific about the relative weight that we should put on deviations of output from potential and deviations of inflation from target. Both King (1997) and Bean (1998) discuss the UK inflation targeting regime in these terms; the latter also explores the consequences of the incompleteness of the remit.

Similarly, the objectives of the Reserve Bank of Australia (RBA), another inflation targeting central bank, as laid out in the *Reserve Bank Act* (1959) are "to ensure that ... monetary and banking policy ... is directed ... (so as to) contribute to: the stability of the currency ...; the maintenance of full employment ...; and the economic prosperity and welfare of the people". The counterpart of the UK *Remit* from the Chancellor in Australia is the joint *Statement on the Conduct of Monetary Policy* between the Governor and the Treasurer. The target is for an inflation rate for the underlying CPI of 2-3% "over the cycle". Again the "first-level" target for inflation is specified explicitly, together with a general injunction that the central bank should care about the level of activity. I think this view of what monetary policymakers are seeking to achieve is also a fair description of central banks like the Federal Reserve or the European Central Bank that do not describe themselves explicitly as inflation targeters.

---

[2] Suppose instead that supply were given by an accelerationist Phillips curve: $\pi_t - \pi_{t-1} = \kappa x_t + u_t$. The optimality condition would then be: $E_t[\sum_{k=0}^{\infty} \beta^k\pi_{t+k}] = -(\lambda/\kappa)E_tx_{t+k}$. Consequently, the argument that asset prices only matter insofar as they affect expected inflation or growth still holds.

[3] If the objective function contains a term in the interest rate, as in Woodford (1999), then the policy instrument appears in the optimality condition. It is then, however, a rather different animal from the instrument rules (1) and (2).

[4] In an open economy subtle issues arise as to whether the real exchange rate should also appear in the optimality condition (7) as a result of the impact of the terms of trade on consumer prices. Under some assumptions the closed economy model of the text can be translated directly into an open economy setting (see eg Clarida et al (2001)), but under other formulations that is not necessarily the case. However, it is clear that the presence of the real exchange rate in the optimality condition under such circumstances has little to do with arguments about the appropriate response to asset price bubbles.

But that does leave open the extent to which asset prices should affect the setting of the instrument, because they will affect the outlook for growth and inflation. Given the optimality condition (7), or its counterpart for the output gap written in terms of observables (8), the IS schedule (5) can be used to back out the associated value of the instrument, i_t. Clearly this reaction function in general will contain the asset price, q_t. That is consistent with the views of Cecchetti et al (2002), though the finding that the inclusion of asset prices in an augmented Taylor or inflation forecast targeting rule reduces the expected loss does not imply an independent role for asset prices *beyond* their impact on the outlook for inflation and growth. And in fairness to Cecchetti et al (2002), they never really claim that it does.

In my view, the substantive issue that divides those who advocate a more activist response to asset prices from those who do not is really the extent to which asset price movements are informative about the prospects for inflation and growth, and whether pre-emptive action against a bubble is either possible or effective. Here, it is worth recalling the difficulty of establishing significant and stable econometric relationships between asset prices and subsequent movements in output or inflation; see eg Stock and Watson (2001) for a recent survey. But there are good reasons why such links should be unstable as asset prices can move for a variety of reasons, each of which may have different implications for growth and inflation.

For instance, even if valued according to their fundamentals, equity prices could fall because of a reduction in expected future earnings, an increase in the expected risk-free discount rate, or a change in the equity risk premium. And that reduction in earnings might come about because of, for example, a fall in the expected rate of growth of productivity, an increase in corporate taxes, or an increase in product market competition. And finally, equity prices may include a non-fundamental or bubble component. But these various shocks all have rather different implications for growth and inflation, either qualitatively or quantitatively.

That suggests that an automatic response to any single asset price is likely to be in general inappropriate, as stressed by Goodfriend (2002). As an aside we might note that this applies not only to equity prices, but also to exchange rates. Monetary conditions indices (MCIs) that weight together nominal interest rates and the exchange rate are often used to indicate whether monetary conditions have changed, on the argument that a fall in the exchange rate - seen as a monetary variable - boosts demand in the same way as does a reduction in nominal interest rates. But this ignores the fact that the exchange rate can change for a variety of reasons, including shifts in preferences or productive potential at home or abroad, changes in current or expected interest rates, changes in portfolio preferences and risk premia, and bubbles and fads. The nature of the shock, as well as the initial degree of over- or undervaluation of the exchange rate, will affect the pass-through into activity and inflation and thus also the appropriate monetary response.

The danger in following MCIs slavishly in setting policy is well illustrated by the experience of New Zealand during the Asia crisis. An MCI was at that time used as the operating target for implementing monetary policy, so the depreciation of the New Zealand dollar during 1997-98 led more or less automatically to an increase in domestic interest rates. But the depreciation of the Kiwi dollar was part of a more general depreciation of currencies in the region, and was associated with a contraction in the markets for New Zealand exports. A more appropriate monetary response would have been to reduce interest rates rather than raise them, as in fact the Reserve Bank of Australia did. That Australian economic performance was noticeably better than that of New Zealand over this period was no accident, and prompted the abandonment of the MCI as the operating target of monetary policy the following year.

But the fact that asset prices may move for a variety of reasons is not a justification for ignoring them completely. Rather, as stressed by Cecchetti at al (2002), it is an argument for using the full array of asset prices and other information in order to try to extract an estimate of the underlying shocks driving them. Drawing such inferences from the co-movements of a set of variables is something that empirical economists and policymakers frequently do already and even an imperfect estimate of the underlying shocks is better than ignoring the information altogether. The case in principle for exploiting the information contained in asset prices thus seems irrefutable, though the difficulties involved in doing so may be considerable and due recognition needs to be paid to the imprecision of the resulting estimates.

As to the possibility of preventing asset price bubbles and misalignments through pre-emptive action, I am rather more sceptical. As with the more general problem of imbalances discussed below, early diagnosis of such problems is fraught with difficulties. Once one can be fairly confident that a bubble has emerged, it is probably too late to take significant action against it without causing just the disruption to the real economy that one wants to avoid. If one is confident that an asset price bubble will continue, then one might want to raise interest rates in order to try to moderate it. But the presence of lags between an interest rate change and its effect on the real economy means that if one expects the bubble to burst imminently, then policy relaxation is appropriate now in order to prepare for the fallout. Tightening policy to deal with an asset price bubble may thus end up being counterproductive if the bubble then bursts, so that the economy is subject to the twin deflationary impulses of an asset price collapse and the lagged policy tightening. Gruen and Plumb (2003) explore this issue and show that the informational requirements necessary to make such activist policy effective are extreme. At best there seems likely to be only a very narrow window of opportunity during which action is likely to be effective.

Financial imbalances and monetary policy

Borio and Lowe (2002) argue persuasively that the issue is not really whether monetary policy should respond to asset price bubbles per se. Rather, booms and busts in asset prices - which may reflect the presence of bubbles, but may also reflect shifts in assessments of the underlying fundamentals - should be seen as part of a broader set of symptoms that typically also include a build-up of debt and frequently a high rate of capital accumulation. Thus during a period of exuberance - irrational or otherwise - optimism about future returns drives up asset values, prompting private agents to borrow in order to finance capital accumulation. Moreover, appreciating asset values raise the value of collateral, hence facilitating the accumulation of debt. During the upswing, balance sheets may look healthy as the appreciation in asset values offsets the build-up of debt. But if that optimism turns to pessimism, leading to a correction in asset valuations and a sharp deterioration in net worth, then financial distress may be the result as the financial imbalances are exposed. That is particularly likely to be the case if financial intermediaries respond to the deterioration in their own and their creditors' balance sheets by tightening credit conditions. This process may apply to the corporate sector and productive capital, but may equally well apply to the household sector and housing capital.

Borio and Lowe also argue that while low and stable inflation may promote financial stability overall, such financial imbalances can nevertheless build up in a low inflation environment. Indeed, beneficial supply shocks - resulting either from faster productivity growth or from structural or institutional reform - are likely both to lower inflationary pressure and to foster the build-up of such imbalances. And that may be aggravated when monetary policy has a high degree of counterinflationary credibility as excessive expansion in aggregate demand beyond the natural rate of output may have only limited impact on inflationary pressures.

In order to explore some of the implications of debt-financed asset accumulation for the conduct of monetary policy, I shall employ a simple New Keynesian macroeconomic model of the sort considered above, though modified to allow for debt-financed capital accumulation and the possibility of credit crunches.

There are two types of agents in the economy: households and firms. Households, who are infinitely lived, supply labour, consume and can borrow and lend freely. All debt lasts a single period and is denominated in real terms. Households also own a non-tradable diversified portfolio of shares in firms, so that all profits are returned to households in lump sum form. Firms are monopolistic competitors, and nominal prices are fixed with a fraction of prices being reset each period as in the standard New Keynesian Phillips curve. Capital lasts a single period, has to be installed a period in advance, and is financed entirely by borrowing from households.

Credit crunches occur with a fixed probability,[5] ρ. When they do occur their effect is to lower the level of supply in the economy. One rationalisation for this could be that a credit crunch leads to bankruptcies and the necessary administration or reorganisation of the firm's assets absorbs resources. Another could be that firms need access to working capital within the period in order to pay their workers, buy inputs, etc. If firms cannot get access to the required working capital then their supply will necessarily be curtailed. So in effect a credit crunch is treated as a negative shock to total

---

[5] Though the impact of the crunch if it occurs is endogenous. It might seem natural to also make the probability of a crunch depend on policy, but this complicates the analysis significantly.

factor productivity, though it reflects events in financial markets rather than a change in the technical capabilities of the economy. Moreover, if a credit crunch does occur, it is assumed to be more severe the higher the level of overall debt outstanding. An individual firm's borrowing decision has a negligible impact on *overall* debt. Consequently, firms ignore the impact of their borrowing on the severity of any future credit crunch, ie there is a negative externality present.[6]

The production function is Cobb-Douglas in capital and labour:

(9) $y_t = a_t + \alpha k_t + (1-\alpha) n_t$,

where y_t is (the logarithm of) output in period t, a_t is (the logarithm of) total factor productivity in period t, k_t is (the logarithm of) the capital stock at the start of period t, inherited from the previous period and n_t is (the logarithm of) employment in period t. Total factor productivity is given by the process:

(10) $a_t = e_t - \varepsilon_t [\varpi + \omega (d_t - E_{t-1} y_t)]$,

where e_t is a shock to the technology, d_t is the (logarithm of) debt outstanding and ε_t is an indicator variable that takes the value unity if a credit crunch occurs and zero otherwise. The severity of the credit crunch is assumed to depend on the debt-output ratio. We write (10) in terms of expected output at the start of the period rather than realised output because the latter depends on whether a credit crunch occurs or not. Making the extent of the credit crunch depend on ex post output complicates the analysis considerably.

Equation (9) may be inverted to give labour demand conditional on the level of output

(11) $n_t = (y_t - a_t - \alpha k_t)/(1-\alpha)$,

The demand for capital is then obtained by minimising expected costs, conditional on the expected future level of output and recognising that employment will subsequently be determined through the labour requirement equation (11):

(12) $k_{t+1} = E_t y_{t+1} - E_t a_{t+1} + (1-\alpha)(E_t w_{t+1} - E_t p_{t+1} - r_t + v_t)$

            $= E_t n_{t+1} + E_t w_{t+1} - E_t p_{t+1} - r_t + v_t$,

where w_t is (the logarithm of) the nominal wage in period t, p_t is (the logarithm of) the price level in period t, r_t is the real rate of return on debt and v_t can be thought of as representing a shock to "animal spirits", ie irrationally over- or underoptimistic expectations. For simplicity, v_t is assumed to be serially uncorrelated, and here and elsewhere inessential constants are normalised to zero through appropriate choice of units.

Following Calvo (1983), prices are set on a staggered basis, with those firms that are able to change their price choosing an optimal one based on expected marginal cost.

(13) $\pi_t = \beta E_t \pi_{t+1} + \delta m_t + u_t$,

where $m_t (= w_t - p_t + n_t - y_t)$ is (the logarithm of) marginal cost and u_t is a shock to the markup, assumed uncorrelated for simplicity.

Turning to the household sector, we assume that savings are a constant fraction of income, and labour supply is an increasing function of the real wage alone:

(14) $w_t - p_t = \phi n_t$.

It is, of course, possible to develop the model along standard lines with an intertemporal optimality equation for consumption of the usual form and a corresponding intratemporal optimality condition for labour supply. However, that leads to a rather more complex dynamic structure without changing the nature of the basic insights. For that reason I prefer a simpler, albeit more ad hoc, approach.

Given the constant savings rate assumption, an IS schedule can then be obtained from (12) and using the fact that marginal cost is equal to the labour share:

(15) $y_t = E_t y_{t+1} + E_t m_{t+1} - r_t + v_t$.

---

[6]   Of course, the first-best policy may well be to look for other instruments that tackle the market failures more directly, such as prudential capital requirements, etc. But it is nevertheless fruitful for central bankers to ask what monetary policy should look like in a second-best world where those market failures are still present.

This is similar to the standard expression, except for the appearance of expected marginal cost.

Using equations (11) and (14), marginal cost is

(16) $m_t = (\alpha+\phi)y_t/(1-\alpha) - (1+\phi)(a_t + \alpha k_t)/(1-\alpha)$.

The flexible price level of output, $y^p{}_t$, is then obtained by setting $m_t = 0$:

(17) $y^p{}_t = v(a_t + \alpha k_t)$,

where $v = (1+\phi)/(\alpha+\phi)$. The model may then be condensed into the two equations:

(18) $\pi_t = \beta E_t \pi_{t+1} + \kappa x_t + u_t$,

where $x_t (= y_t - y^p{}_t)$ is the output gap and $\kappa = \delta(\alpha+\phi)/(1-\alpha)$, and:

(19) $x_t = \eta E_t x_{t+1} + r^p{}_t - r_t + v_t$,

where $r^p{}_t = E_t y^p{}_{t+1} - y^p{}_t$ is the natural real rate of interest and $\eta = (1+\phi)/(1-\alpha)$ ($= \kappa v/\delta$). Aside from the coefficient on the expected output gap in (19), this is isomorphic to the standard New Keynesian model considered in Section 2, though the impact of interest rates on demand is via their effect on investment rather than consumption.

We now consider the policymaker's control problem. Crucially, we assume that the policymaker would like to stabilise output around its *technically* feasible level:

(20) $y^*_t = v(e_t + \alpha k_t)$.

When there is no credit crunch, this is just the same as the flexible price equilibrium, $y^p{}_t$. But when a credit crunch occurs, there will be a gap between the two, which is larger the greater is the current debt-output ratio. The relevant gap, x^*_t is:

(21) $x^*_t = (y_t - y^p{}_t) + (y^p{}_t - y^*_t)$

          $= x_t - v\varepsilon_t[\varpi + \omega(k_t + r_{t-1} - E_{t-1}y_t)]$

          $= x_t - v\varepsilon_t[\varpi + \omega\kappa E_{t-1}x_t/\delta + v_{t-1})]$.

where we have used the fact that $d_t = k_t + r_{t-1}$. Note that the impact of the credit crunch is not affected directly by the rate of interest in the preceding period. A higher rate of interest reduces capital formation and debt accumulation during period $t-1$, but that is nullified by the higher interest payments on the debt. Consequently, the total amount that has to be repaid is left unchanged. Clearly, whether an increase in the rate of interest in period $t-1$ raises or lowers the debt stock in period t depends on the semi-elasticity of borrowing with respect to the interest rate. In the present case that is unity, so the two effects exactly offset.

Equation (21) implies that:

(22) $E_{t-1}x^*_t = (1-\rho\omega\eta)E_{t-1}x_t - v\rho\varpi + \omega v_{t-1})$.

Using this, the Lagrangian for the optimisation problem at date τ may be written:

(23) $\Omega_\tau = E_\tau[\sum_{t=\tau}^{t=\infty} \beta^{t-\tau}\{(\pi_t^2 + \lambda x^{*2}_t)/2 + \varphi_t(\pi_t - \beta\pi_{t+1} - \kappa x^*_t - z_t)\}]$

where $z_t = \kappa\varepsilon_t[v\varpi+\omega v_{t-1}) + \omega\eta E_{t-1}x^*_t]/(1-\rho\omega\eta) + u_t$. The first-order conditions are:

(24) $0 = E_\tau\pi_t + \varphi_t - \varphi_{t-1}$ for all $t \geq \tau$, with $\varphi_{\tau-1} = 0$

(25) $0 = \lambda x^*_\tau - \kappa\varphi_\tau$

(26) $0 = \lambda E_\tau x^*_t - \kappa\varphi_t/(1-\rho\omega\eta)$ for all $t > \tau$

Integrated first-order conditions analagous to equation (7) may then be obtained by eliminating the multipliers:

(27) $E_\tau\pi_t = -[\lambda(1-\rho\omega\eta)/\kappa](E_\tau x^*_t - E_\tau x^*_{t-1})$

The structural similarity to the standard model of Section 2 - obtained by setting ρ to zero - makes it easy to see the impact of the possibility of a credit crunch on the design of the optimal policy. Assuming that $\omega\rho\eta < 1$, introducing the possibility of a credit crunch is similar in effect to reducing the weight on output in the policymaker's objective function.

That there is apparently less incentive to stabilise current output when the economy is overheating and building up larger imbalances today[7] may appear counterintuitive. However, recall that this simple model is forward-looking in nature, and that an increase in interest rates today will not affect the severity of any credit crunch tomorrow because of the assumption that the interest semi-elasticity of borrowing is unity. But policy *does* affect debt levels through another channel, namely expectations of the future output gap. If the output gap is expected to be large and positive in the future, then that will boost capital accumulation today, so raising the future debt stock and the costs associated with a credit crunch.

In the standard model, without the possibility of a credit crunch, the optimal policy in the face of a temporary positive supply shock, such as a reduction in wage push or a fall in the markup, exploits the fact that a credible commitment to hold output above potential in the future raises inflation today via the expectations term in the New Keynesian Phillips curve. Given the desirability of avoiding large deviations in output from potential, the optimal response therefore involves a small, but persistent, deviation of output from potential in response to the temporary supply disturbance, rather than returning inflation to target through a larger, but more short-lived, output gap. When there is a possibility of a credit crunch, however, the gradualist response to the beneficial supply shock generates additional expected future costs. Consequently, the optimal policy involves more variation in the output gap today and less persistence than the standard setup.

This somewhat paradoxical result is unlikely to be robust, and the model no doubt omits many of the more important channels whereby imbalances can accumulate and unwind. Nevertheless, it illustrates the fact that allowing for the accumulation and unwinding of imbalances may affect the design of policy in subtle ways, as well as the more obvious ones.

Other considerations

Though the model illustrates one way financial imbalances might affect the design of an optimal monetary policy, it misses a number of other considerations. Importantly, it does not incorporate an explicit role for asset prices and misses the inherent non-linearities that may be present. Falling asset prices reduce collateral and may induce a sharp change in the behaviour of potential borrowers as collateral constraints start to bind. That can act as an important amplification and propagation mechanism, as in the work of Kiyotaki and Moore (1997). Bordo and Jeanne (2002) construct a model in which firms can only borrow against collateral, and a credit crunch occurs if asset prices fall sufficiently. As in the model above, the credit crunch then leads to a loss of output. The resulting model is highly non-linear, and Bordo and Jeanne show that an appropriately forward-looking policy that responds to the initial asset price inflation and build-up of debt by pre-emptively raising interest rates[8] dominates a purely reactive policy that responds to current inflation and activity.

Bordo and Jeanne go on to conclude that this demonstrates that a monetary policy that reacts only to output and inflation is insufficient, and that a (non-linear) response to asset prices, etc is also desirable. They suggest this is inconsistent with inflation targeting. However, Bordo and Jeanne assume a standard loss function that is quadratic in the output gap and inflation. If one accepts the argument that an inflation target is really a statement about the objective function rather than the reaction function, a flexible inflation targeter would also choose their recommended policy. But their analysis does suggest that a richer interest rate reaction function may be required in the pursuance of that inflation target.

Financial instability and credit crunches are probably of the greatest significance when they adversely affect the supply potential of the economy, as in the model of this section and Bordo and Jeanne. But even without such adverse supply effects, the unwinding of financial imbalances may cause problems for the design and conduct of monetary policy. In most settings the appropriate response to the fall in aggregate demand occasioned by the unwinding of cumulative imbalances, triggered say by a fall in asset prices or a downward revision in expectations about future income or earnings, is simply to offset the shock to demand by lowering interest rates. But this may not be possible if the zero lower

---

[7]   Recall that the constant savings rate assumption implies that higher output must be associated with higher capital formation and therefore more debt accumulation.

[8]   This channel is absent in the model described in this paper because of the assumption that the semi-elasticity of debt with respect to the interest rate is unity.

bound on nominal interest rates starts to bind. Although other monetary policy options may be available, including purchases of a broader range of assets than the central bank usually undertakes, as well as more exotic approaches such as taxing money balances à la Gesell, their effectiveness is less certain than conventional interest rate policy. Consequently, it will make sense to conduct a policy during the period of accumulating imbalances that reduces the likelihood of encountering the zero lower bound as the imbalances unwind.

Stochastic simulations with macroeconometric models suggest that, at an average inflation rate of 2%, the fraction of time spent at the zero lower bound is likely to be around 2%. And even for an average inflation rate of 1%, the corresponding figure is only up to around 5% (see the studies surveyed in Yates (2003)). That might appear to suggest this is not likely to be a very serious issue. But those stochastic simulations assume shocks similar to those experienced in the past. The unwinding of imbalances is likely to be sharp, particularly in the context of a credit crunch or similar financial instability, and so corresponds to shock realisations in the bottom tail of the distribution. That suggests the presence of the zero lower bound on interest rates provides a more compelling argument for pre-emptive action to prevent the build-up of imbalances in the first place.[9]

A second consideration in relation to the impact on demand arises from the fact that a sharp unwinding of imbalances is likely to make aggregate demand somewhat less predictable than normal. Knowledge of the current state of the economy is highly imperfect - unlike in the models above - and increased uncertainty about demand will inevitably be transmitted into greater variability in activity. Moreover, the impact of interest rate changes on aggregate demand is also likely to become more uncertain in such an environment, especially if credit channel effects assume greater importance or if there is a credit crunch. Greater uncertainty about policy multipliers will then impact on the optimal policy setting, eg as in the seminal analysis of Brainard (1967).

In this case one would expect there to be something of a trade-off facing the policymaker. Action taken today to reduce the build-up of imbalances might pay off in the longer term by reducing the future uncertainty that the policymaker will face as the imbalances unwind. But, as before, this seems entirely consistent with the approach of flexible inflation targets, taken as a description of the objectives of policy rather than the route whereby they are achieved.

Identifying imbalances: a case study

These considerations suggest that even inflation targeters - indeed especially inflation targeters - should take cognisance of the risks to future macroeconomic stability posed by cumulating financial imbalances and/or asset price misalignments. No additional consideration of asset prices or financial imbalances need be introduced into the description of the objectives of policy beyond inflation and activity. But as it may be some while before imbalances unwind or misalignments correct, the policymaker does need to look sufficiently far ahead in assessing the risks to the outlook posed by the build-up of imbalances and misalignments.

A key issue is, of course, the identification of threatening imbalances before they grow too large. But without the wisdom of hindsight, it is often hard to identify those that pose a real threat, as rapid debt accumulation or large asset price movements may be a rational and justified response to changes in the economic environment. The empirical results of Borio and Lowe (2002), building on Kaminsky and Reinhart (1999), seek to develop indicators of imminent financial crises based on the joint behaviour of asset prices, credit and investment and using only information available to the policymaker at the time. Such indicators will no doubt be a useful addition to the armoury of central banks, but early diagnosis of incipient imbalances is always likely to be difficult. By the time it is obvious that there is a problem, it may be too late to do much about it - at least with conventional macroeconomic tools - without causing the macroeconomic instability that the policymaker wishes to avoid.

Moreover, as noted by a number of authors, the greater counterinflationary credibility of monetary policy in the last decade or so itself complicates the identification of imbalances (see eg Borio and Lowe or Goodfriend (2002)). Debt accumulation is likely to prove excessive if it is associated with

---

[9] Note that this argument suggests that greater uncertainty may lead to greater policy activism, in contrast to the classic Brainard (1967) result.

unsustainably high levels of activity. When credibility was low, levels of activity above the natural rate tended to show up relatively quickly in accelerating inflation. But a feature of the last decade has been the apparent flattening of the short-run output-inflation trade-off (see Graph 1). There are at least three possible reasons for this. First, New Keynesian models of nominal price inertia relying on the presence of menu costs suggest that the slope of the output-inflation trade-off should be flatter at low average inflation rates (Ball et al (1988)). Second, models of the Phillips curve in which expectations of inflation play a role - whether of the Friedman-Phelps-Lucas or New Keynesian varieties - suggest that an increase in activity above the natural rate will raise inflation less if those expectations are well anchored. Consequently, the enhanced belief that monetary policy will be used to stabilise inflation will itself help to keep inflation low. Moreover, that credibility will also help to stabilise long-term interest rates. Third, increased competitive pressures in product markets, associated in particular with increased international trade, may also act to restrain inflationary pressures.

Graph 1

UK Phillips curve 1967-2001

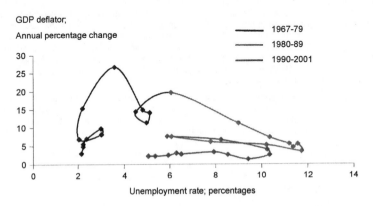

US Phillips curve 1967-2001

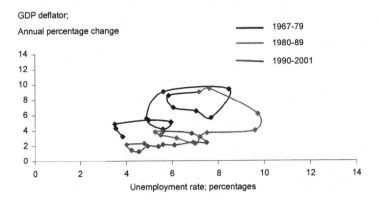

Sources: IMF; OECD.

11

In such a world, excess debt accumulation and levels of demand above the natural rate will not immediately show up in higher inflation rates. Moreover, that in itself may encourage market participants and policymakers to believe that the natural rate of output is higher than it really is. That in turn is likely to boost asset prices, further raising demand. Instead of showing up in inflation, the excess demand will show up in other indicators, such as profit rates, measures of labour shortage and the like. That suggests focusing attention on other indicators, as well as inflation, in identifying when demand is excessive and imbalances are unsustainable.

Rather than add to the body of work that seeks to develop early-warning indicators of potentially dangerous imbalances, I conclude with a review of current developments in the United Kingdom that illustrates the difficulties in assessing whether or not asset price movements and credit growth constitute a potential problem. A key feature of the UK economy in the past six years has been the buoyancy of household spending, which has consistently grown faster than output, in both real and nominal terms (see Graph 2). And associated with that has been a build-up of household debt and rapid house price inflation (see Graphs 3 and 4). Moreover, the Bank's Monetary Policy Committee has over the past two years sought to offset the impact of the global slowdown by relaxing policy in order to further boost domestic spending, and in particular private consumption. That has added to the accumulation of household debt and raised house prices further. Is there any evidence that the financial imbalances in the UK household sector have reached the point where they might pose a threat to the economic outlook?

Graph 2

Consumption to GDP ratio

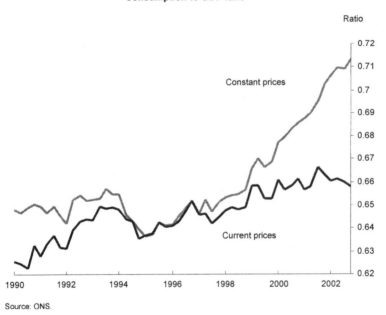

Source: ONS.

In addressing this question, it is helpful first to ask why consumer demand might have been so buoyant. Standard theory suggests that it should be "permanent" income rather than current income that drives consumer spending, though the extent to which households will intertemporally shift expenditures will also depend on the cost of borrowing and the return to saving. The recent strong growth in consumption has coincided with robust growth in real disposable household incomes and falling unemployment, and for a while also with rising equity prices. So one explanation for the strength of consumer spending is that households have been revising up their assessment of their permanent income. To the extent that there has indeed been an increase in households' permanent income, then we would expect consumption growth in due course to fall back in line - or strictly speaking a little below - the rate of growth of their income, with the extra accumulated debt being gradually repaid. But if expectations prove to be overoptimistic then a sharper future correction to consumer spending is likely.

Furthermore, a significant fraction of the increase in real household incomes has been associated with the substantial improvement in the terms of trade - up 13% since 1996 (see Graph 5). An important issue is whether the improvement from this source is permanent, reflecting the exploitation of comparative advantage, or whether it is associated instead with a temporarily high level of the exchange rate, in which case real incomes and consumption will eventually both drop back. The answer to this question is not obvious.

A second explanation for the rapid growth in consumer spending and debt is easier access to, or cheaper, borrowing. This is where house prices enter the picture. The most important channel through which house prices affect consumer spending is probably not via a conventional wealth effect. Rather it is through increasing the value of the collateral against which owners - who would otherwise be credit-constrained - can borrow, or else by allowing them to borrow at lower rates. The higher house prices of recent years have allowed owner-occupiers to increase their borrowing, using the proceeds in part to boost spending. That is reflected in high rates of mortgage equity withdrawal, currently estimated to be equivalent to about 7% of personal disposable income (see Graph 3).

Graph 3

Household debt and mortgage equity withdrawal

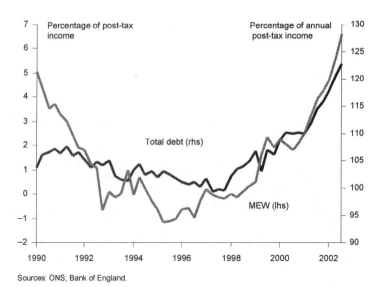

Sources: ONS; Bank of England.

But why has the price of houses risen? The demand for housing services should be driven by the same factors that drive the demand for consumer goods and services, ie permanent income. Graph 4 also shows the evolution of house prices relative to the nominal value of consumer spending per household (a proxy for consumers' estimates of their permanent income). That ratio has risen sharply in recent years, although the picture is not quite as dramatic as when house prices are compared to earnings.

Graph 4

**House price to nominal consumption per household
ratio and house price to earnings ratio**

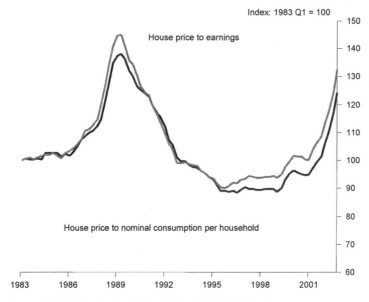

Index: 1983 Q1 = 100

Sources: Halifax; Office of the Deputy Prime Minister; ONS; Bank of England.

So something else has also been driving house prices, and with them the value of the collateral against which owner-occupiers can borrow. At first glance Graph 4 might seem to indicate an incipient house price bubble, but there are at least three reasons why the demand for housing might have risen more than might be suggested simply by looking at permanent income. First, the transition to a low inflation environment implies that nominal interest rates should also be lower on average. As standard mortgages entail an even flow of nominal payments over the life of the mortgage, the initial real payments on a given nominal debt are smaller than they would be if inflation and interest rates were high, with the real burden of payments towards the end of the loan period being correspondingly greater. Shifting the pattern of real payments into the future in this way makes households that are constrained by their cash flow more willing or able to borrow, thus driving up the demand for housing. But a legitimate concern is that borrowers may not have fully factored in the corresponding increase in future real payments. Second, increased competition amongst lenders and the application of better credit scoring techniques may have increased the supply of loans. And third, population growth and demographic developments - more people wanting to live alone and an increased desire for second homes - will also have boosted demand.

In addition, on the supply side of the market, the rate of construction of new dwellings in the United Kingdom has lagged behind the expansion in the number of households, in part because of a shortage of land and the impact of planning restrictions. Graph 6 shows that the ratio of dwellings to households - a measure of spare capacity in the housing market - has been steadily falling over the last two decades. One might reasonably expect that this might also be reflected in higher house prices relative to nominal consumption per household.

Graph 5

Terms of trade

1995 = 100

Source: ONS.

Graph 6

Ratio of dwellings to household[1]

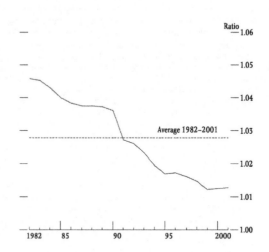

[1] Figures for the stock of dwellings are for 31 December each year prior to 1991 and 31 March from 1991 onwards. This may account for most of the fall in the ratio in 1991.

Source: Office of the Deputy Prime Minister.

15

In sum, there are good reasons why a higher house-prices-to-consumption ratio (or house-prices-to-earnings ratio) might be warranted by underlying economic developments. But there is inevitably very considerable uncertainty about the underlying equilibrium value of house prices. An optimal monetary policy almost certainly would dictate a differential response to a movement in house prices associated with a misalignment to one that is associated with movements in the fundamentals. Yet diagnosing whether there is a misalignment is far from straightforward.

Whether the movement in house prices is justified by fundamentals or not is clearly also central to assessing whether there is any danger posed by the build-up of household debt that is the counterpart to the increase in the value of housing wealth. But even if a sharp correction were to occur to house prices, it would not necessarily imply a correspondingly sharp fall in household spending. Net household wealth would fall, but rational consumers would spread the required adjustment over the rest of their lives. Even consumers who were credit-constrained and had previously exploited the higher collateral to increase their borrowing would not need to cut back their spending sharply unless the lender were to foreclose on them for some reason.[10]

The high outstanding debt levels could, however, increase the impact on consumer spending of other adverse shocks to activity, especially those leading to higher unemployment. Households with adequate liquid assets or who can still access the credit market would not need to cut back their consumption much if they experience a spell of unemployment, assuming it does not harm their future earning potential. Instead they would simply run down their savings or borrow more. On the other hand, households with no assets, and who cannot borrow, would be forced to cut back spending in line with their reduced income. So the impact of this adverse shock on aggregate consumption will be greater, the higher the fraction of constrained households. Furthermore, that fraction will tend to be higher, the greater the amount of debt already extended.

So a key question is whether those who hold the debt are particularly likely to be exposed to adverse shocks, such as job loss, and whether they have other assets that they could run down. The good news is that it is those households who hold the most debt who also tend to have higher income and more assets (see Graph 7). But this is not very surprising as most of the debt is in the form of mortgages and bigger mortgages are typically associated with more expensive houses!

Perhaps more relevant in assessing the potential vulnerability of the household sector to shocks is the matching of debts to liquid assets. Here the news is not quite so good. Graph 8 illustrates the distribution of total liabilities and liquid assets across individual households, drawn from a 10% random sample of the 5,000 households in the 2000 British Household Panel Survey. It is notable that a large fraction of households are positioned on one or other axis. In particular, roughly a third had no liquid assets to speak of. This suggests that the financial position of the household sector might be rather less resilient than is suggested merely by looking at aggregate balance sheet data.

This contemporary example illustrates the problem that policymakers have in assessing whether potentially dangerous financial imbalances are developing or whether credit growth and asset price appreciation is simply the consequence of sustainable movements in the economic fundamentals. Moreover, even if imbalances are developing, information at the microeconomic level may well be required to evaluate the potential problems that may be caused by their unwinding - looking at aggregate data may not be sufficient to reveal whether there is a problem or not.

---

[10] Note that the mere fact that the value of the collateral is less than the value of the loan does not necessarily imply the borrower will choose to walk away from the debt and forfeit the asset. Some borrowers may, for reputational reasons, prefer to repay their debts even though are worth more than the value of the collateralised asset. Hence lenders, having extended the loan on the basis of what turns out to be a temporarily inflated collateral value, may prefer not to foreclose.

Graph 7

**Average financial assets, housing wealth and debt
at different levels of household indebtedness (2000)**

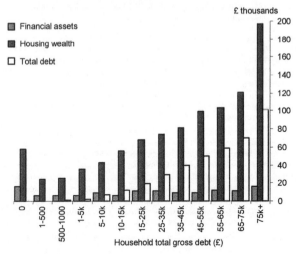

Sources: BHPS; Bank calculations.

Graph 8

**Distribution of total liabilities and liquid assets
across individual households**

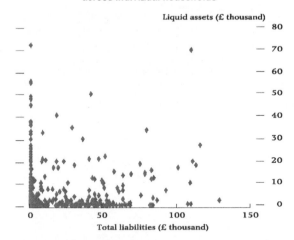

Note: The full BHPS survey for 2000 contains information on the total liabilities and the liquid assets of more than 5,000 households. Households in the upper percentile of either the liquid assets or the total liabilities distribution were removed. This graph is based on a random 10% sample of the remaining households, with each dot representing one of those households.

Source: British Household Panel Survey, 2000.

17

Concluding remarks

Financial imbalances, asset price misalignments and the instability that may result as they unwind and correct may pose significant problems for monetary policymakers. Achieving price stability is no guarantee that financial instability can be avoided. But taking account of financial imbalances in the design of monetary policy does not require a change in the formal structure of inflation targets. Significant financial instability invariably will also have a significant impact on activity and inflation. The attraction of inflation targets is that they focus on the goals of policy - not the means by which they are achieved, as is the case under regimes such as money supply targets and fixed exchange rates. An inflation targeting regime that specifies a "first-level" target for the inflation rate, but requires the policymaker to take on board the implications for activity in seeking to achieve it, is a practical solution to the problem of describing the principal's objective function. A flexible inflation targeter - in the specific sense of Svensson - therefore does not require the explicit addition of financial imbalances or asset prices to be added to their remit. Rather the implications of possible imbalances and misalignments for the macroeconomic goal variables must necessarily be factored into the assessment of expectations of future growth and inflation in order to execute the optimal plan. So the answer to the question posed in the title of this paper is: Yes, (flexible) inflation targets are enough. But taking on board the possible risks posed by cumulating financial imbalances may require a shift in the rhetoric of inflation targeters towards the longer term.

But more investigation is needed into understanding the way in which financial imbalances and asset price misalignments in practice affect economic prospects. There are at least two distinct sets of issues where further work would be useful. First, it would be helpful to advance our ability to detect when rapid credit expansion and asset price increases are symptomatic of the development of underlying imbalances that are susceptible to future correction, rather than simply reflecting sustainable movements in the underlying economic fundamentals. Second, improving our understanding of how imbalances unwind and their associated costs would facilitate the design of appropriate policies, on both the monetary and regulatory front. It is safe to assume that these two issues will remain on the agenda for both monetary economists and central bankers for many years to come.

References

Ball, L, N G Mankiw and D Romer (1988): "The new Keynesian economics and the output-inflation tradeoff", *Brookings Papers on Economic Activity*, 1.

Batini, N and E Nelson (2000): *When the bubble bursts: monetary policy rules and foreign exchange market behaviour*, mimeo, Bank of England.

Bean, C R (1998): "The new UK monetary arrangements: a view from the literature", *Economic Journal*, 108, pp 1795-809.

Bernanke, B S and M Gertler (1999): "Monetary policy and asset volatility", *Federal Reserve Bank of Kansas City Economic Review*, 84(4), pp 17-52.

—— (2001): "Should central banks respond to movements in asset prices?", *American Economic Review*, 91(2), pp 253-7.

Bordo, M and O Jeanne (2002): "Boom-busts in asset prices, economic instability and monetary policy", *Centre for Economic Policy Research Discussion Paper 3398*.

Borio, C and P Lowe (2002): *Asset prices, financial and monetary stability: exploring the nexus*, mimeo, BIS, Basel.

Brainard, W (1967): "Uncertainty and the effectiveness of monetary policy", *American Economic Review, Papers and Proceedings*, 57, pp 411-25.

Calvo, G (1983): "Staggered prices in a utility maximizing framework", *Journal of Monetary Economics*, pp 383-98.

Cecchetti, S G, H Genberg, J Lipsky and S Wadhwani (2000): "Asset prices and central bank policy", *Geneva Reports on the World Economy*, 2, International Centre for Monetary and Banking Studies and Centre for Economic Policy Research.

Cecchetti, S G, H Genberg and S Wadhwani (2002): "Asset prices in a flexible inflation targeting framework", in *Asset price bubbles: the implications for monetary, regulatory and international policies*, (eds W C Hunter, G G Kaufman and M Pomerleano), MIT Press, pp 427-44.

Clarida, R, J Gali, and M Gertler (1999): "The science of monetary policy: a new Keynesian perspective", *Journal of Economic Literature*, 37, pp 1661-707.

—— (2001): "Optimal monetary policy in open versus closed economies: an integrated approach", *American Economic Review*, 91(2), pp 248-52.

Crockett, A (2003): *International standard setting in financial supervision*, Institute of Economic Affairs Lecture, Cass Business School, London, 5 February.

Giannoni, M P and M Woodford (2002): *Optimal interest rate rules: II. Applications*, mimeo, Princeton University.

Goodfriend, M (2002): "Interest rate policy should not react directly to asset prices", in *Asset price bubbles: the implications for monetary, regulatory and international policies*, (eds W C Hunter, G G Kaufman and M Pomerleano), MIT Press, pp 427-44.

Greenspan, A (2002): *Economic volatility*, speech at a symposium sponsored by the Federal Reserve Bank of Kansas City, Jackson Hole, Wyoming.

Gruen, D and M Plumb (2003): *Is it clear how monetary policy should respond to asset-price bubbles?*, mimeo, Australian Treasury and Reserve Bank of Australia.

Kaminsky, G and C Reinhart (1999): "The twin crises: the causes of banking and balance-of-payments problems", *American Economic Review*, 89(3), pp 473-500.

King, M A (1997): "The inflation target five years on", *Bank of England Quarterly Bulletin*.

Kiyotaki, N and J H Moore (1997): "Credit cycles", *Journal of Political Economy*, 105(2), pp 211-48.

Rotemberg, J and M Woodford (1997): "An optimization-based econometric framework for the evaluation of monetary policy", *NBER Macroeconomics Annual*, pp 297-345.

Stock, J H and M W Watson (2001): "Forecasting output and inflation: the role of asset prices", *NBER Working Paper*, 8180.

Svensson, L (2001): *Requiem for forecast-based instrument rules*, mimeo, IIES, Stockholm University.

—— (2002): "What is wrong with Taylor rules?", *Journal of Economic Literature*.

Svensson, L and M Woodford (1999): *Implementing optimal policy through inflation-forecast targeting*, mimeo.

Taylor, J B (2001): "The role of the exchange rate in monetary-policy rules", *American Economic Review*, 91(2), pp 263-7.

Woodford, M (1999): "Optimal monetary policy inertia", *NBER Working Paper*, 7261.

Yates, A (2003): "Monetary policy and the zero bound to nominal interest rates", *Bank of England Quarterly Bulletin*, 43(1), pp 27-37.

Discussion of "Asset prices, financial imbalances and monetary policy: are inflation targets enough?", by Charles Bean

Ignazio Visco[1]

Introduction

Whether and how monetary policy should react to asset price misalignments and financial imbalances is a time-honoured question for both the central banking and the academic professions. This question has gained even more relevance as we have been through the New Economy bubble and, following the recent Japanese experience, risks of deflation are no longer confined to the footnotes of macroeconomic textbooks. Charlie Bean's paper is therefore very much welcome, not least as he is a distinguished member of both professions. The paper is a rich blend of theory, empirical analysis and policy considerations. The question whether monetary policy should explicitly react to asset prices is rephrased as "Is inflation targeting enough?", and the answer is unequivocal: "Yes, it is enough", provided it is "flexible".

In what follows I shall address three issues: (i) Is this answer too general?; (ii) Is "flexible inflation targeting", as advocated by Bean, operational?; (iii) Given real world non-linearities, could there be a case, even within an inflation targeting framework, for monetary policy explicitly reacting to asset price misalignments?

Too general a framework?

Following Svensson,[2] Bean makes clear that flexible inflation targeting (FIT) is not a policy reaction function but a monetary policy framework that depends on an explicit intertemporal *loss* function, a *model* of the economy and the nature of *shocks* affecting the economy. Typically, the loss function is quadratic in the deviation of actual inflation from an inflation target, π, and a measure of the output gap, x. In this framework, forecasts of policy objectives and implied policy instruments that satisfy "optimal" trade-offs are generated. These trade-offs are obtained by equating the marginal rate of transformation (MRT) between π and x (from the model's supply function) to the marginal rate of substitution (MRS) between these two objectives (from the policymaker's loss function). In a linear model of the economy, with a forward-looking rational expectations supply function such as the one considered by Bean, the trade-off is completely characterised by the ratio $-\lambda/\kappa$.

In this case there is no explicit role for other variables or demand shocks. They enter the implicit policy rules through their effects on the forecasts of π and x.[3] As exemplified in the model examined in Section 3 of the paper, (linear) supply shocks also affect the trade-off. In particular, Bean assumes that total factor productivity depends linearly on firms' outstanding debt that is, in turn, dependent on the capital stock, as firms borrow against collateral. The higher the debt-output ratio, the sharper the credit crunch. This takes place, however, with a given and constant probability. Reflecting the model changes (that is the new MRT) the trade-off in this case is $-\lambda\psi/\kappa$ (with ψ likely to be less than one). Thus, the fact that, as Bean puts it, "there is apparently less incentive to stabilise current output" is a consequence of the particular forward-looking supply function adopted in the model, not of the

---

[1]   Bank of Italy. The views expressed are those of the author and do not reflect those of the Bank of Italy or those of the BIS.

[2]   See, for example, Svensson (2002).

[3]   Implicit policy rules may be derived by combining the trade-off and the model equations and solving for the policy instruments.

preferences of the policymaker. A different result would be obtained with a backward-looking supply function and/or adaptive expectations.[4]

Within a FIT framework, then, if it is possible to identify asset price misalignments that would eventually affect the economy (ie the paths of inflation and output), they should be countered proactively, as suggested by Cecchetti et al (2000).[5] In particular, forecasts of future inflation and output gaps should extend over longer horizons than is typically the case (ie longer than one or two years). In fact, as suggested by Bernanke and Gertler (2001), the relevant asset price effects are those on expected inflation and growth and they possibly take place with considerable lags. In agreement with Bernanke and Gertler, and differently than Cecchetti et al,[6] Bean concludes that specific instrument rules (such as Taylor or inflation forecast targeting rules), possibly augmented to include asset prices or financial imbalances as separate arguments, are *inefficient* compared to the optimal "time-consistent" targeting of the FIT type. In other words, in the latter framework, reaction to asset prices should not be "over and above" their effects on π and x.

At this level of generality, a FIT framework accommodates various sources of information besides the variables and the parameters contained in a particular model of the economy. It allows for the use of judgement in the evaluation of the effects of asset prices and financial imbalances on the economy, as well as the feedback to changes in the policy instruments. And the specification of a loss function in terms of both inflation deviations and output gaps allows for the inflation targeting to be conducted as "flexibly" as desired. It would be difficult then to disagree with Bean's conclusions, but one may ask whether this might be too general a framework to provide an actual guide for monetary policymaking. It is indeed striking that, as Charlie Bean writes, "this view of what monetary policymakers are seeking to achieve is also a fair description of central banks like the Federal Reserve or the European Central Bank".

Also the main conclusion of the paper, that monetary policy should counter asset price misalignments and/or financial imbalances so long as they affect the arguments of the authorities' loss function, may not match what prominent central bankers say and do. Consider, for instance, the following statement: "... central banks do not respond to gradually declining asset prices. We do not respond to gradually rising asset prices. We do respond to sharply reduced asset prices ... But you almost never have the type of 180-degree version of the seizing up on the up side. If indeed such an event occurred, I think we would respond to it".[7]

How operational is FIT?

It is evident that the more flexible a framework is, the more likely its ability to encompass a large number of cases. In practice, however, it would be interesting to understand whether FIT is something more than just specifying a loss function with current and future inflation as a specific monetary policy target, together with the output gap (with a substitution coefficient of λ). The computation of the trade-off is model-dependent, as it is crucially affected by the shape of the supply function. As mentioned, it is especially important to establish whether past inflation has a significant effect on output decisions and whether the assumption of rational expectations can be maintained. That the framework asks for a serious discussion on the shape of the supply function taking place among monetary policymakers should not be considered a weakness. Even if central banking is as much art as science, the exercise of judgment is also dependent on an interpretation of the real world, and forcing monetary policymakers to come out not only with their preferences on the final objectives, but also with their views on the supply function, should be seen as a constructive challenge.

Besides the specification of the loss function and a view of how the economy operates, two elements seem however to be essential ingredients of FIT. The first is some sort of commitment not to change

---

[4]   On the puzzling dynamic effects of monetary policy in forward-looking models of inflation-unemployment dynamics, see Mankiw (2001).

[5]   See also Cecchetti et al (2003).

[6]   See also Blanchard (2000).

[7]   Greenspan (1999), p 143.

policy without "new" information having become available. This is technically achieved in Bean's paper by following Svensson and Woodford[8] in deriving the trade-off equations under commitment from "the timeless perspective". As this is an important condition, it would have been interesting if Bean had discussed how it could be achieved in practice. Even more importantly, transparency is a key element of the framework. However, not only it is doubtful whether this is part of the framework within which all the central banks characterised by Bean as (explicitly or implicitly) engaged in flexible inflation targeting operate, but also it is by no means clear how they should communicate the perception of risks associated with an asset price misalignment or a bubble.

To account for the effects of asset prices, Bean suggests that "... central banks may need to look out further into the future than is usual ...". A number of issues come immediately to mind with regard to this recommendation. They refer respectively to the identification of asset price misalignments, the evaluation of their effects on the real economy and the proper communication strategy that should be followed.

First of all, it is essential to understand how asset price misalignments develop and how they may produce financial imbalances. Identification of misalignments and imbalances is not an easy task, but it should not be considered impossible. One might start by considering whether asset prices appear to be sharply deviating from some sort of historical averages.[9] Then, it would be natural to ask whether these deviations are justified by observed changes in fundamentals, referring for instance, in the case of stock prices, to complex entities, such as price-earnings ratios, that are often used by practitioners and policymakers. Consider, for example, the New Economy bubble. It is certainly possible that productivity increases linked to the New Economy have not been negligible. However, on the basis of calculations founded on the discounted dividend model or Gordon formulae, already in early 1998 a consensus was being established that stock prices (especially but not only in the Nasdaq) were rising without correspondence to fundamental variables such as changes in discount factors, opportunity costs and risk premiums.[10]

For another example, consider the case study conducted by Bean in Section 4 of his paper. From a preliminary, though thorough, analysis of the risk that recent property prices in the United Kingdom might be substantially misaligned, Bean concludes that while this risk cannot be easily dismissed, it might be too early to conclude that relevant imbalances have already built up. While this is a relatively optimistic assessment, I am more inclined to conclude from Bean's evidence that the odds that a sharp correction in house prices might take place are not negligible. Given the related build-up of household debt, this could lead to severe consequences for the economy. In any case, this example shows how subjective the assessment may be and how important it is to evaluate the possible impact of asset price changes on the final variables of interest.[11]

In fact, a crucial question to be answered is what do we know about the effects of asset price misalignments, and related imbalances in equity, real estate and currency markets, as well as in bank credit and government debt. My reading of the empirical literature is that these effects are in general considered to be small and financial asset price movements are generally found to play a relatively minor role in the transmission of monetary policy. But this conclusion may be seriously biased, as these are often likely to be *rare* and *extreme* events. Even if, when they materialise, the effects of asset price changes are usually strong, in macroeconometric estimates they are likely to be dominated over the sample by "normal time" observations and, being relatively rare, they frequently end up being dummied out. In other words, their effects on the real economy are *rarely* and partly captured by our

---

[8]   See Svensson and Woodford (2003) and Svensson (2002).

[9]   As is done, for example, in Bordo and Jeanne (2002b).

[10] For the use of the discounted dividend models and derivations, see Gordon (1962). The use of Gordon formulae is similar to the more sophisticated econometric tests conducted by Shiller, Campbell and others, for which I refer to the discussion in Herrera and Perry (2003). See, for a mid-1998 examination of stock market prices associated with the New Economy developments, OECD (1998), where warnings of risk of substantial deviation of US stock prices from some historical norms (as well as the implicit anticipation of a return to those norms) were advanced.

[11] Even if there is a misalignment in the UK market for real estate, it is not obvious that it would be for monetary policy to respond to it. On one side, there might be effects on aggregate demand that could lead to inflationary pressures and monetary policy should obviously take them into account. On the other side, in this case the use of prudential instruments, which would lead to pricing differently the value of the collateral against which borrowing takes place, might be a better solution.

empirical models, and are often treated as exogenous shocks. Also, if captured, the econometric estimates might be *extremely* imprecise.

Much more empirical work is therefore needed (on wealth effects, asset prices, expectations and credit channels), and microeconomic information should be extensively used. But substantial uncertainty will undoubtedly remain, not least because the effects of (monetary policy) changes on asset prices and quantities depend on rather hazy channels such as consumer and business confidence, expectations and "animal spirits". This would add to the uncertainty due to the fact that, as observed by Bean, these effects are likely to materialise over long time horizons. Even if, as suggested by Bean and Svensson, FIT might be a general framework for the conduct of monetary policy in "normal" times, since the precision of forecasts can only decline over time it is debatable whether trade-offs that depend on forecasts that extend far in the future and are by their very nature rather uncertain turn out to be stable enough to provide reliable guidance for current policy decisions.

Finally, if asset price changes and financial imbalances must be taken into account in the formulation of monetary policy, as Bean readily acknowledges (even if not "in addition" to forecasts), as I have mentioned above a substantial problem must necessarily arise concerning the transparency of policy decisions, and especially the way they are communicated to markets and the public at large. In fact, if central banks do respond to asset price misalignments, monetary authorities should explain, within a general FIT framework of the kind advocated in Bean's paper, how they affect the forecasts, and therefore interest rate decisions. But this may be difficult to assess and in the end much judgment needs to be exercised. While in principle this could be accommodated within a FIT framework, that judgment, and the inevitable uncertainty attached to it, would in turn affect the market response in a direction and a magnitude difficult to predict. This would make the assessment of the odds of a sharp asset price correction even more difficult.

A complex, non-linear real world

So far, I have considered the case, examined explicitly by Bean, where asset price misalignments affect the economy through linear demand or supply shocks. In Section 3.1, Bean also briefly discusses the possibility that supply shocks are non-linear or that demand shocks are "unconventional". Also in these cases, Bean concludes that FIT is the proper framework to follow in designing a policy response to financial imbalances and asset price shocks.

Also in the model recently studied by Bordo and Jeanne (2002a, 2002b), financial imbalances affect total supply. Differently than in the model considered in Section 3 of Bean's paper, the probability of a credit crunch (ρ in Bean's notation) is not constant but rises with the debt burden (ie the stock of debt and the rate of interest). The conclusion is straightforward: monetary policy should respond to asset prices, and this response would be rather complex. In particular, not only are the trade-offs between output and inflation affected by the shock, but also the policy response should *explicitly*, no longer implicitly through forecasts of inflation and output, and *non-linearly* react to asset price misalignments and related financial imbalances.

I find both the analysis and the conclusions of Bordo and Jeanne's papers suggestive and thorough. And so, it seems to me, does Bean. Bordo and Jeanne, however, also conclude that inflation targeting is insufficient as a policy framework, while Bean disagrees with such a conclusion. To an extent this appears to be just a semantic issue, as is clear from Bean's observation that a "flexible inflation targeter" would follow Bordo and Jeanne's suggested policy. In fact, they also "assume a standard loss function that is quadratic in the output gap and inflation", and "an inflation target is really a statement about the objective function rather than the reaction function".

Again, the level of generality of FIT, as exposed by Bean, is very high. I do not see how one can today disagree with the view that a good central bank should conduct monetary policy by looking at the forecasts of the variables of interest (affected by demand and supply shocks, including those on asset prices) and taking into account the relevant trade-offs in order to reach the targets that are more appropriate. Indeed, FIT seems also to accommodate the case of unconventional shocks that may cause a severe fall in aggregate demand through the unwinding of cumulative imbalances. The standard response would be "simply to offset the shock ... by lowering interest rates". As these may encounter a zero lower bound, Bean also appears to support the recommendation of leaving some room to manoeuvre in good times. Indeed, Bean recognises that the unwinding of imbalances would result in higher uncertainty in demand and greater output variability. And he readily acknowledges, following the suggestion from Brainard's (1967) seminal paper, that being more prudent today (to reduce the build-up of imbalances) pays off by reducing future uncertainty. As in the other cases, this is also found to be entirely consistent with the definition of FIT as "a description of the objectives of policy rather than the route whereby they are achieved".

Given the objectives of policy, however, policy decisions have to follow. Bean suggests that monetary policy should not neglect asset price misalignments and possibly bubbles, and the financial imbalances that are related to them. In this he agrees with Borio and Lowe (2002) and others, that while the issue is not "whether monetary policy should respond to asset price bubbles per se", excessive build-up of debt should not be left unanswered. He seems also to agree with what he defines as the "heterodox" view summarised by Crockett (2003), that "authorities [should] tighten monetary policy sufficiently pre-emptively to lean against excessive credit expansion and asset price increases". Where Bean seems to disagree is with Crockett's following statement that "if the monetary policy reaction function does not incorporate financial imbalances, the monetary anchor fails to deliver financial stability", with possibly serious consequences for the real economy. In his FIT framework, in fact, Bean shows that there is no need to explicitly design a monetary policy reaction function directly incorporating asset prices, as it is sufficient to derive the trade-offs between inflation and output gaps consistent with the policy objectives and the supply function of the economy.

Bean's analysis is clear and well presented. As he illustrates, FIT is a framework that can be defined generally enough to accommodate judgment and information extraneous from the necessarily simple representations of the economy provided by even the more sophisticated econometric models typically available to central banks. However, it should be recognised that Bean's formal analysis only covers the case of relatively simple imbalances and shocks that affect *linearly* the demand and supply decisions of households and firms. As also discussed in Bean's paper, the real world is generally complex and non-linear. Even within a well-specified FIT framework, the *implicit* monetary policy reaction function would then also be non-linear (and possibly very complex, as it would not be possible to rely on certainty equivalence). As in the example considered by Bordo and Jeanne (2002a), it is rather likely that this reaction function, even if not in the simple form of an augmented Taylor rule, would depend on asset prices and financial imbalances.[12]

As Bean recognises, such a world is characterised by a high degree of uncertainty. This follows from the fact that asset prices may affect the real economy with long lags, and over time the precision of forecasts necessarily falls. It also follows from the fact that statements on the timing and the effects of credit crunches or the sharp unwinding of imbalances can only be expressed in terms of subjective probabilities. Even the communication strategy that accompanies transparent policy decisions such as those taken by a central bank committed to a FIT framework might add to the overall uncertainty. In general, with uncertainty of this sort it pays to be more prudent. Indeed, if shocks turn out to positively and permanently affect the real economy, some additional monetary restriction would probably not make a big difference; if they were going to result in a bubble, some extra restriction would probably prove valuable. The question, as always in the difficult art of central banking, is how much restriction would be needed, and this calls for more study and experimentation. But it hardly calls in general, as Bordo and Jeanne (2002b) aptly put it, for "benign neglect".

---

[12] As a Taylor rule is often used as a *description* of how monetary policy is *normally* conducted, it might turn out that for some purposes a linear rule that expresses interest rates as functions not only of deviations of inflation from the target and output from potential but also of asset price misalignments could be a simple and linear approximation of how central banks would behave in a non-linear and complex environment. Rather than a "Taylor rule" as we have come to know it, after John Taylor the economist, we may think of it as a "Taylor approximation", after Brook Taylor the mathematician ...

References

Bernanke, B and Gertler, M (2001): "Should central banks respond to movements in asset prices?", *American Economic Review*, May, pp 253-7.

Blanchard, O J (2000): "Bubbles, liquidity traps, and monetary policy", in R Mikitani and A S Posen, *Japan's financial crisis and its parallels to the US experience*, Institute for International Economics, Washington DC, pp 185-93.

Bordo, M D and O Jeanne (2002a): "Boom-busts in asset prices, economic instability and monetary policy", *NBER Working Paper*, no. 8966.

——— (2002b): "Monetary policy and asset prices: does 'benign neglect' make sense?", *International Finance*, 5(2), pp 139-64.

Borio, C and P Lowe (2002): "Asset prices, financial and monetary stability: exploring the nexus", *BIS Working Papers*.

Brainard, W (1967): "Uncertainty and the effectiveness of monetary policy", *American Economic Review*, May, pp 411-25.

Cecchetti, S, H Genberg, J Lipsky and S Wadhwani (2000): "Asset prices and central bank policy", *Geneva report on the world economy 2*, CEPR and ICMB.

Cecchetti, S, H Genberg and S Whadwani (2003): "Asset prices in a flexible inflation targeting framework", in W C Hunter, G G Kaufman and M Pomerleano, *Asset price bubbles*, MIT Press, Cambridge, Mass, pp 427-44.

Crockett, A (2003): *International standard setting in financial supervision*, Institute for Economic Affairs Lecture, Cass Business School, London, 5 February.

Gordon, M (1962): *Investment, financing and valuation of the corporation*, Irwin, Homewood, Illinois.

Greenspan, A (1999): "Comment in the general discussion of 'Monetary policy and asset price variability', by B Bernanke and M Gertler", in *New challenges for monetary policy*, Federal Reserve Bank of Kansas City, Jackson Hole Symposium, p 143.

Herrera, S and G E Perry (2003): "Tropical bubbles: asset prices in Latin America, 1980-2001", in W C Hunter, G G Kaufman and M Pomerleano (eds), *Asset price bubbles*, MIT Press, Cambridge, Mass, pp 127-62.

Mankiw, N G (2001): "The inexorable and mysterious trade-off between inflation and unemployment", *Economic Journal*, May, pp C45-C61.

OECD (1998): "Recent equity market developments and implications", Chapter V in *OECD Economic Outlook*, no 64, Paris.

Svensson, L (2002): "What is wrong with Taylor rules? Using judgment in monetary policy through targeting rules", *NBER Working Paper 9421*.

Svensson, L and M Woodford (2002): "Implementing optimal policy through inflation-forecast targeting", in B S Bernanke and M Woodford (eds), *Inflation targeting*, University of Chicago Press, Chicago, forthcoming.

Discussion of "Asset prices, financial imbalances and monetary policy: are inflation targets enough?", by Charles Bean

Sushil Wadhwani[1]

I would like to thank the organisers for inviting me. I have known Charlie for a long time, and it is a great privilege to be given the opportunity to comment on this paper.

Before moving on to substantive issues, it is important that I clarify a possible misunderstanding first. Essentially Charlie sets up a "straw man", which he then sets about knocking down. Since Stephen Cecchetti, Hans Genberg and myself are associated with the "straw man" view - you might call us the "straw men" - it is obviously important that I set the record straight.

Charlie repeatedly emphasises that, in a flexible inflation targeting framework, if you look at the entire future path of expected inflation and growth, there is no independent role for asset prices. He asserts that we argue otherwise.

To quote our paper:

> "It is also important to emphasise that our proposal is wholly consistent with the remit of inflation-targeting central banks, as we are recommending that while they might **react** to asset price misalignments, they must **not** target them". (Cecchetti et al (2002), abstract)

> "This paper is **not** about what the central bank objective should be. Instead, we are concerned with how an inflation-targeting central bank can most effectively fulfil its objectives." (Cecchetti et al (2002), p 2)

So what then is the controversy about?

The key issue in the debate, in my opinion, is that in practice much of interest rate setting is not driven by looking at inflation and growth forecasts at all horizons, but is based on rules of thumb. In particular, inflation targeting is usually based on inflation forecasts one to three years out, often with a focus on a fixed horizon such as two years. This can have the effect that asset price misalignments get an insufficient weight in policymaking.

At the Geneva conference when we first presented our work three years ago, Ueda-san argued that a Japanese central banker who was looking 10 years out would have been raising rates in 1987-88. But, given that the central bank was focused on inflation only one or two years out, it was more difficult to justify raising rates (see Cecchetti et al (2000), pp 111-12).

We are simply proposing that, where the reaction function includes fixed-horizon inflation forecasts, it should also incorporate asset price misalignments.

As we said in 2000:

> "A purist might argue that the central bank should really look at inflation forecasts at several (all) future time periods ... such a policy might not be easy to implement ... The proposal for incorporating asset price misalignments can be interpreted as an alternative way of allowing for considerations relating to longer time-horizons" (Cecchetti et al (2000) p 51).

Hence, our view was simply that including asset price misalignments would help us to do better than existing rules of thumb.

---

[1]   Wadhwani Asset Management LLP. The views expressed are those of the author and not those of the BIS.

But why focus on rules of thumb?

There are those like Charlie, who argue that improving on existing rules of thumb is not interesting or relevant. Instead, one should just use the theoretically "optimal" policy rule. Recall that, in this case, that might involve reacting to a 10-year-ahead inflation profile. My heart sinks at the thought of having to attempt to implement such a rule.

(1) Practical considerations. It is very time-consuming to agree on a two-year profile for inflation, let alone going out many years into the future. Also many of the econometric models that underlie such forecasts perform particularly badly at longer horizons.

(2) It is what most central banks do in practice. Therefore, unsurprisingly, for most of the period I was on the Bank of England Monetary Policy Committee (MPC), the emphasis was on the two-year-ahead horizon. This was reflected in the substantial time spent on deciding whether the inflation forecast was 2.4, 2.5 or 2.6% at the two-year-ahead horizon. Of course, towards the end of my term on the MPC, the relationship may have become a little less tight. But, even then, for the majority of members of the committee, the two-year-ahead point forecasts remained central.

In many other inflation targeting countries, the central bank also relies on a fixed-horizon element in the target set for the central bank (for example, Sweden and New Zealand).

(3) Ease of communication. Both internally and in terms of how policy is communicated to the public, simple rules are much easier to work with. In particular, if the inflation target is more easily understood, inflation expectations will be better anchored, providing crucial support to the success of monetary policy.

(4) Accountability. If the framework is vague, it is difficult to make the central bank accountable.

Avoiding bubbles

Charlie asserts that:

> "... the design of monetary policy does not require a change in the formal structure of inflation targets" (p 18).

I disagree.

A clear and explicitly enunciated role for asset prices in the inflation targeting framework has the advantage that bubbles will be discouraged. Having a transparent reaction function consisting of the two-year-ahead inflation forecast plus an asset price misalignment adjustment could potentially make bubbles less likely to occur.

One key point is that the simulation work in the literature significantly understates the benefits of including asset price misalignments in the reaction function. It doesn't allow for the Kent-Lowe (1997)/Allen-Gale (2000) effect - ie the impact that the central bank can have on the probability of the bubble growing, by signalling that it will respond.

For example, in the United Kingdom in the last two years, the Bank of England has provided no clear steer on the housing market, with different members expressing different views. A transparent rule of thumb would have made it easier to affect expectations, and might have reduced the degree of the house price misalignment.

Charlie seems sympathetic to the "conventional view" that monetary policy can do little more than deal with the fallout from the unwinding of asset price bubbles and explicitly quotes Chairman Greenspan on this issue. But, this is potentially dangerous as it is asymmetric, and, more importantly, no attempt is made to affect expectations during the period that the bubble is inflating.

27

Other work

Of course, many people have done interesting work on why the reaction function should be modified - not just to include asset price misalignments but to make it richer more generally. Andrew's address at the beginning of this conference summarised much of this work (eg Borio and Lowe (2002) and Bordo and Jeanne (2002)).

I believe that it is important that central banks use richer reaction functions than the existing ones that seem to feed off fixed-horizon inflation forecasts, and Charlie's paper does not do enough justice to the need for such modifications.

Lack of clarity of current UK framework

While the current UK framework has many advantages, there is a lack of clarity on asset prices and imbalances. The "flexibility" of the framework in this area has meant that MPC members have, in the last two to three years, had a whole host of views on how they should react to the imbalances. This has therefore been confusing to the public.

In particular, some members have reacted differently to the exchange rate "misalignment" and the house price/consumption "misalignment". According to our suggested rule of thumb:

(1)   Since unsustainable house price growth could lead to a crash and very low inflation three to four years out, interest rates should initially have been higher than warranted by the two-year-ahead forecast to prevent a build-up of debt and house prices.

(2)   But, acting in the opposite direction, since the exchange rate was higher than warranted, interest rates should have initially been set lower than otherwise. This would have helped keep the exchange rate lower, thereby reducing the size of its eventual crash.

However, some members did not apply this same logic to both misalignments. The same members argued for higher interest rates because of the housing market, in line with our proposed rule of thumb. But, at the same time, these members argued that the strength of sterling also argued for higher interest rates. The reasoning was that this meant there was a risk of future exchange rate falls, stimulating inflation at some uncertain point.

So the so-called flexible inflation targeting allows people to be inconsistent in their treatment of misalignments in different asset markets. It would be much better to have a transparent and consistent rule of thumb in that case.

Conclusion

I enjoyed reading Charlie's paper, and am grateful for the opportunity of being here today. However, I do hope that the Bank of England and other central banks decide to adopt superior rules of thumb (which include asset price misalignments) when setting policy.

References

Allen, F and D Gale (2000): "Bubbles and crises", *The Economic Journal*, 110, January, pp 236-55.

Bordo, M and O Jeanne (2002): "Monetary policy and asset prices: does 'benign neglect' make sense?", *International Finance*, 5(2), pp 139-64.

—— (2002): "Boom-busts in asset prices, economic instability and monetary policy", *Centre for Economic Policy Research Discussion Paper 3398*.

Borio, C and P Lowe (2002): "Asset prices, financial and monetary stability: exploring the nexus", *BIS Working Papers*, no 114.

Cecchetti, S, H Genberg, J Lipsky and S Wadhwani (2000): "Asset prices and central bank policy", *ICMB/CEPR Report*, no 2.

Cecchetti, S, H Genberg, and S Wadhwani (2002): "Asset prices in a flexible inflation targeting framework", *National Bureau of Economic Research Working Paper 8970*.

Kent, C and P Lowe (1997): "Asset-price bubbles and monetary policy", *Research discussion paper*, Reserve Bank of Australia, RDP 9709.

Part II
Low Inflation, Zero Bounds

[4]

PAUL R. KRUGMAN
Massachusetts Institute of Technology

It's Baaack: Japan's Slump and the Return of the Liquidity Trap

THE LIQUIDITY TRAP—that awkward condition in which monetary policy loses its grip because the nominal interest rate is essentially zero, in which the quantity of money becomes irrelevant because money and bonds are essentially perfect substitutes—played a central role in the early years of macroeconomics as a discipline. John Hicks, in introducing both the IS-LM model and the liquidity trap, identified the assumption that monetary policy is ineffective, rather than the assumed downward inflexibility of prices, as the central difference between Mr. Keynes and the classics.[1] It has often been pointed out that the Alice in Wonderland character of early Keynesianism—with its paradoxes of thrift, widows' cruses, and so on—depended on the explicit or implicit assumption of an accommodative monetary policy; it has less often been pointed out that in the late 1930s and early 1940s it seemed quite natural to assume that money was irrelevant at the margin. After all, at the end of the 1930s interest rates were hard up against the zero constraint; the average rate on U.S. Treasury bills during 1940 was 0.014 percent.

Since then, however, the liquidity trap has steadily receded both as a memory and as a subject of economic research. In part, this is because in the generally inflationary decades after World War II nominal interest rates have stayed comfortably above zero, and therefore central banks have no longer found themselves "pushing on a string." Also, the experience of the 1930s itself has been reinterpreted, most notably by

---

1. Hicks (1937).

138   *Brookings Papers on Economic Activity, 2:1998*

Milton Friedman and Anna Schwartz.[2] Emphasizing broad aggregates rather than interest rates or the monetary base, Friedman and Schwartz argue, in effect, that the Depression was caused by monetary contraction; that the Federal Reserve could have prevented it; and implicitly, that even the great slump could have been reversed by sufficiently aggressive monetary expansion. To the extent that modern macroeconomists think about liquidity traps at all (the on-line database EconLit lists only twenty-one papers with that phrase in title, subject, or abstract since 1975), their view is basically that a liquidity trap cannot happen, did not happen, and will not happen again.

But it has happened, and to the world's second-largest economy. Over the past several years, Japanese money market rates have been consistently below 1 percent, and the Bank of Japan plausibly claims that it can do no more; yet the Japanese economy, which has been stagnant since 1991, is sliding deeper into recession. Since Japan is such an important economy, and its slump threatens to shatter the already fragile prospects for economic recovery in the rest of Asia, understanding what is going wrong there has become quite urgent. And there is also a deeper reason for concern: if this can happen to Japan, perhaps it can happen elsewhere. In short, it is time to reexamine the theory of liquidity traps, which has turned out not to be irrelevant after all.

But surely economists already understand liquidity traps well enough to formulate policy. Can we not just pull the old models out of the basement, dust them off, and put them to work? In effect, that is what policymakers at the U.S. Treasury and elsewhere have done: drawing on the simple liquidity trap framework that appeared in macroeconomics textbooks a generation or so ago, they have urged Japan to follow the classic recovery strategy of pump-priming fiscal expansion. (Since hardly anybody in the thoroughly urbanized societies of modern America and Japan has any idea what it means to prime a pump, I hereby suggest that we rename this the jump-start strategy.) Macroeconomics has, however, moved on in several ways that require a rethinking of the issue.

In particular, one might identify three strands of modern thought that are missing from the classic IS-LM analysis. First is the intertemporal

2. Friedman and Schwartz (1963).

Paul R. Krugman 139

nature of decisions. Economists now understand, perhaps better than fifty years ago, that how one formulates expectations is a crucial matter in macroeconomic analysis, and that a good first pass assumption is that these expectations are rational. Second is the openness of the economy. Although the Britain of Keynes and Hicks was actually a quite open economy, with a share of trade in GDP more than twice that of modern Japan, their analysis, and almost all subsequent analysis of the liquidity trap, ignores foreign trade and capital mobility. It is a justifiable strategic simplification; but since many of the disputes surrounding Japan's direction involve the future of the country's current account and exchange rate, one needs to know what happens when this assumption is relaxed. Finally, traditional IS-LM analysis neglects the role of financial intermediaries. But how one interprets the experience of the 1930s hinges crucially on how broad a monetary aggregate one chooses; and the same has turned out to be true in recent arguments over Japan. Furthermore, one school of thought about the Depression argues that a troubled banking system lay at the heart of the problem; a similar view has become near orthodoxy about contemporary Japan. So one needs at least a basic sense of how financial intermediation fits into the picture of the liquidity trap.

There are two major parts to this paper. The first is an extended generic discussion of the causes and consequences of liquidity traps. I use a succession of small, highly stylized models to address both the traditional questions regarding liquidity traps and a number of novel issues. The central new conclusion of this analysis is that a liquidity trap fundamentally involves a credibility problem—but it is the inverse of the usual one, in which central bankers have difficulty convincing private agents of their commitment to price stability. In a liquidity trap, the problem is that the markets believe that the central bank *will* target price stability, given the chance, and hence that any current monetary expansion is merely transitory. The traditional view that monetary policy is ineffective in a liquidity trap, and that fiscal expansion is the only way out, must therefore be qualified: monetary policy will in fact be effective if the central bank can credibly promise to be irresponsible, to seek a higher future price level.

My theoretical analysis also appears to refute two widely held beliefs. First, international capital flows, which allow a country to export savings to the rest of the world, are not a surefire guarantee against a

liquidity trap; because goods markets remain far from perfectly integrated, the required real interest rate in terms of domestic consumption
can be negative even if capital is perfectly mobile and there are positive-
return investments abroad. A corollary is that a successful monetary
expansion, in which the central bank does create expectations of inflation, will probably be less of a beggar thy neighbor policy, expanding
demand at the rest of the world's expense, than is widely imagined.

Second, putting financial intermediation into a liquidity trap framework suggests, *pace* Friedman and Schwartz, that it is quite misleading
to look at monetary aggregates under these circumstances: in a liquidity
trap, the central bank may well find that it cannot increase broader
monetary aggregates, that increments to the monetary base are simply
added to reserves and currency holdings, and thus both that such aggregates are no longer valid indicators of the stance of monetary policy
and that their failure to rise does not indicate that the essential problem
lies in the banking sector.

In the second part of the paper, I turn to some specific questions
surrounding Japan. I survey other analysts' estimates to consider four
main issues. First is the size of Japan's output gap. I argue that this is
probably considerably larger than the standard estimates, and hence
that the need for expansionary policy is even greater than is commonly
supposed. Second is the reason for the apparent large gap between
saving and willing investment at full employment. Third is the relevance of Japan's banking woes to its macroeconomic malaise. Although
the conventional wisdom is that Japanese banks are at the center of the
problem, I argue that they have played less of a causal role than is
widely assumed. Finally, I make a first attempt at quantifying the size,
duration, and side effects of the inflation that would be needed to lift
Japan out of its trap.

The Theory of Liquidity Traps

It is useful, in considering Japan's liquidity trap, to begin at a high
level of generality, to adopt what one might almost call a philosophical
stance. Popular discussion of the current situation has a strong tendency
to plunge too quickly into the specifics, to cite one or another structural
issue as *the* problem, missing the central point that whatever the details

of its history, Japan is now in a liquidity trap, so that the generic issues surrounding such traps apply.

A liquidity trap may be defined as a situation in which conventional monetary policies have become impotent, because nominal interest rates are at or near zero: injecting monetary base into the economy has no effect, because base and bonds are viewed by the private sector as perfect substitutes. By this definition, a liquidity trap could occur in a flexible price, full-employment economy; and although any reasonable model of the United States in the 1930s or Japan in the 1990s must invoke some form of price stickiness, one can think of the unemployment and output slump that occurs under such circumstances as what happens when an economy is trying to have deflation—a deflationary tendency that monetary expansion is powerless to prevent.

This may seem a peculiar way of putting the issue, but it does highlight the central mystery of a liquidity trap, and the reason why structural explanations, in a fundamental sense, cannot by themselves resolve that mystery. For if there is one proposition with which everyone in macroeconomics agrees it is that, aside from the possibility that price stickiness will cause monetary expansion to be reflected in output rather than prices, increases in the money supply raise the equilibrium price level. Indeed, the normal view is that money is roughly neutral: that an increase in the money supply produces a roughly equiproportional increase in the general price level.[3] Or to be more specific, an increase in outside money—the monetary base—must raise prices.

Putting the issue this way immediately reveals that many of the common explanations of why Japanese monetary policy is ineffectual are wrong, or at least inadequate. One often hears, for example, that

3. Strictly speaking, in traditional models money is not quite neutral when the private sector holds nominal claims on outside agents, such as government debt, because changes in the price level then have wealth effects on these assets, a point emphasized by Metzler (1951). Even leaving aside empirical doubts about the importance of the Metzler effect and theoretical questions about its relevance (with Ricardian equivalence the effect goes away), this complication can at most dampen the effect of money on the price level, but cannot eliminate it.

That said, many macroeconomists bristle at the mention of monetary neutrality. The reason for their disdain is the widespread belief (which I share) that because prices are not perfectly flexible, increases in the money supply often get reflected mainly in output rather than in prices. However, this has nothing to do with the puzzle of a situation in which increases in outside money can raise neither output nor prices, and indeed seem powerless to prevent deflationary pressures.

the real problem is that Japan's banks are troubled, and hence that the Bank of Japan cannot increase monetary aggregates; but outside money is supposed to raise prices regardless of the details of the transmission mechanism. Aside from the bad loans, one also often hears that corporations have too much debt, that the service sector is overregulated and inefficient, and so on. All of this may be true and may depress the economy for any given monetary base, but it does not explain why *increases* in the monetary base should fail to raise prices, or output, or both. Recall that the neutrality of money is not a conditional proposition; it does not depend on banks being in good financial shape, or the service sector being competitive, or corporations not taking on too much debt. Money (which is to say, outside money) is supposed to be just plain neutral.[4]

So how is a liquidity trap possible? The answer lies in a little-noticed escape clause in the standard argument for monetary neutrality: an increase in the money supply in the current *and all future* periods will raise prices in the same proportion. There is no corresponding argument that a rise in the money supply that is not expected to be sustained will raise prices equiproportionally—or indeed at all.

In short, approaching the question from this high level of abstraction suggests that a liquidity trap involves a kind of credibility problem. A monetary expansion that the market expects to be sustained (that is, matched by equiproportional expansions in all future periods) will always work, whatever structural problems the economy might have; if monetary expansion does not work—if there is a liquidity trap—it must be because the public does not expect it to be sustained. To firm up this insight, one needs a specific model.

Money, Interest, and Prices: A Minimalist Model

Although the idea of a liquidity trap is normally bound up with the IS-LM model, there are several compelling reasons not to start with that model here. Many macroeconomists believe that IS-LM is too ad

4. This summary of the standard remarks about Japan does not contradict my earlier assertion that almost everyone believes that money is approximately neutral. My point here is that to my knowledge nobody has made this connection; that is, nobody has noticed that to say that monetary expansion is ineffective at raising output is equivalent to saying that it is ineffective at fighting deflation, and that this conflicts with the almost universally held belief in the near neutrality of money.

hoc to be worthy of serious consideration. Some of us do not share that view and continue to regard Hicks's construction as a very useful heuristic device. Still, it is important to stress that the possibility of a liquidity trap does not depend on the ad hoc nature of the IS-LM model, that it can occur in a model that dots its microeconomic *i*'s and crosses its intertemporal *t*'s. Also, as shown above, a liquidity trap fundamentally involves expectations and credibility; using models that explicitly recognize the intertemporal aspects of the problem helps to clarify this point. Let me therefore move immediately to an explicit intertemporal model that establishes relationships among output, money, prices, and interest rates. I then use this model as a base for a series of thought experiments and extensions.

Consider a one-good, representative agent economy (in which, however, agents must purchase their consumption from others). Suppose, initially, that the good is inelastically supplied, so that one can simply think of each agent as receiving a given endowment y_t in each period. For concreteness, the utility function is assumed to take the form

$$(1) \qquad U = \frac{1}{1 - \rho} \sum c_t^{1-\rho} D^t,$$

where c is consumption within a period, ρ is relative risk aversion, and D is the discount factor.

The simplest way to introduce money into this model, one that has the added advantage of avoiding the suspicion that the conclusions are dictated by arbitrary assumptions about the way money enters utility, is to assume a cash in advance constraint. Specifically, within each period agents are assumed to go through a two-stage process. At the beginning of each period there is a capital market, in which individuals can trade cash for one-period bonds, with nominal interest rate i_t. Their consumption during the period is constrained by the cash with which they emerge from this trading: the nominal value of consumption, $P_t c_t$, cannot exceed money holdings, M_t. After the capital market is held, each individual purchases his desired consumption, while receiving cash from the sale of his own endowment.

Government policy can take two forms. First, it is assumed that the central bank is able to engage in open market operations during the beginning of period capital market, by buying or selling bonds. Second, at the end of the period the government can collect or distribute lump sum taxes and transfers. The government must obey its own intertemporal budget constraint, which takes into account the seignorage that results from money creation.

Analyzing this model in general requires careful specification of the budget constraints of both individuals and the government, and of intertemporal choices. However, if one makes some simplifying assumptions, the model's implications can be derived with almost no algebra. Assume that from the second period onward, output (and therefore also consumption) will remain constant at a level y^*, and that the government will also hold the money supply constant at a level M^*. Then one can immediately guess at the solution from period two on: the price level will remain constant at $P^* = M^*/y^*$, and the interest rate will also be constant at a rate $i^* = (1 - D)/D$. It is straightforward to confirm that this is indeed an equilibrium: one plus the real interest rate equals the ratio of marginal utility in any two successive periods; because the nominal interest rate is positive, individuals have an incentive to acquire only as much cash as they need, so all money will indeed be spent on consumption.

All of the action, then, goes into determining the price level and interest rate in the first period (I use letters without subscripts to represent first period output, consumption, interest rate, and so forth). The first relationship comes from the monetary side. Under normal circumstances—that is, when the nominal interest rate is positive—individuals will hold no more cash than they need to make their consumption purchases. Thus the cash in advance constraint will be binding: $Pc = Py = M$, so that

$$(2) \qquad\qquad P = M/y.$$

Under normal circumstances there is a simple proportional relationship between the money supply and the price level.

The second relationship comes from intertemporal choice. By holding one less yen in period one, an individual gives up $1/P$ units of first period consumption but allows himself to consume $(1 + i)/P^*$ additional units in period two. At an optimum, this change must leave him indifferent. But the marginal utility of consumption in period one, given the assumed utility function, is $c^{-\rho}$; the marginal utility in period two is $D(c^*)^{-\rho}$. It follows that one must have

Paul R. Krugman   145

Figure 1. Relationships between Prices and the Interest Rate

Interest rate

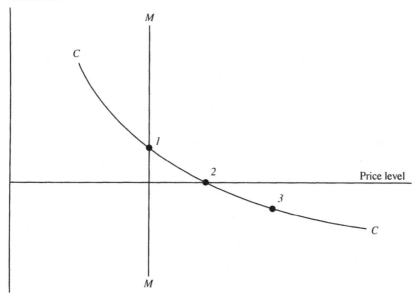

Source Author's model as described in text

(3) $(c/c^*)^{-\rho} = DP(1 + i)/P^*,$

or, since consumption must equal output in each period,

(4) $1 + i = \dfrac{P^*}{DP} (y^*/y)^{\rho}.$

This says that the higher is the current price level, the lower is the nominal interest rate. The easiest way to think about this is to say that there is an equilibrium real interest rate, which the economy will deliver whatever the behavior of nominal prices. Meanwhile, since the future price level P^* is assumed held fixed, any rise in the current level creates expected deflation; hence higher P means lower i.

The two relationships are shown in figure 1 as *MM* and *CC*, respectively; as drawn, they intersect at point 1, simultaneously determining the interest rate and the price level. It is also immediately apparent that an increase in the first period money supply will shift *MM* to the right, leading to a higher price level and a lower nominal (but not real) interest rate. While this is surely the normal case, however, there is also another possibility.

The Liquidity Trap in a Flexible Price Economy

Suppose that one starts with an economy in the equilibrium described by point 1 in figure 1 and imagines an initial open market operation that increases the first period money supply. (Throughout, one imagines that the money supply remains unchanged from period two onward—or equivalently, that the central bank will do whatever is necessary to keep the price level stable from period two onward.) Initially, as I have shown above, this operation will increase the price level and reduce the interest rate. And such a monetary expansion can clearly drive the economy down the *CC* curve as far as point 2. But what happens if the money supply is increased still further, so that the intersection of *MM* and *CC* is at point 3, with a negative nominal interest rate?

The answer clearly is that the interest rate cannot go negative, because money would then dominate bonds as an asset. Therefore it must be that any increase in the money supply beyond the level that would push the interest rate to zero is simply substituted for zero interest bonds in individual portfolios (the bonds being purchased by the central bank in its open market operation!), with no further effect on either the price level or the interest rate. Because spending is no longer constrained by money, the *MM* curve becomes irrelevant; the economy stays at point 2, no matter how large the money supply.

Note that the interest rate at point 2 is zero only on one-period bonds; it would not be zero on longer term bonds, such as consols. This is important if one is trying to map the model onto the current situation in Japan, or for that matter in the United States during the 1930s: long rates in Japan are still positive, but short-term rates are indeed very close to zero.

A good way to think about what happens when money becomes irrelevant under such circumstances is to bear in mind that one is holding the long-run money supply fixed at M^*, and therefore also the long-run price level at P^*. So when the central bank increases the current money supply, it lowers the expected rate of money growth, M^*/M, and also (if it does succeed in raising the price level) the expected rate of inflation, P^*/P. One knows that in this full-employment model the economy will have the same *real* interest rate whatever the central bank does. Since the nominal interest rate cannot become negative, however, the economy has a minimum rate of inflation, or a maximum rate of deflation.

Now suppose that the central bank in effect tries to impose a rate of deflation that exceeds this maximum, by making the current money supply, *M*, large relative to the future supply, *M**. In this case the economy will simply cease to be cash-constrained, and any excess money will have no effect: the rate of deflation will be the maximum consistent with a zero nominal rate, and no more.

This may seem a silly thought experiment. Why would a central bank try to impose massive deflation? But the maximum rate of deflation need not be large, or even positive. Suppose that the required real rate of interest is negative; then the economy ''needs'' inflation, and an attempt by the central bank to achieve price stability will lead to a zero nominal interest rate and excess cash holdings.

The condition under which the required real interest rate is negative is straightforward in this simple endowment economy. Market clearing will require a negative real interest rate if the marginal utility of consumption in period two is greater than that in period one, which will be the case if the economy's future output is expected to be sufficiently less than its current output. Specifically, given the assumed utility function, the required real interest rate is negative if

(5) $$(y/y^*)^\rho < D.$$

This condition might seem peculiar. After all, one normally thinks of economies as growing rather than shrinking. One possible answer involves an equity premium, another involves demography; but I reserve this issue for discussion below.

In a flexible price economy, the necessity of a negative real interest rate does not cause unemployment. This conclusion may surprise economists who recall the tortured historical debate about the liquidity trap, much of which focused on whether wage and price flexibility were effective means of restoring full employment. In this model the problem does not arise, but for a reason that is a bit unusual: the economy deflates now in order to provide inflation later. That is, if the current money supply is so large compared with the future supply that the nominal rate is zero, but the real rate needs to be negative, *P* falls below *P**; the public then expects the price level to rise, which provides the necessary negative real interest rate. And to repeat, this fall in the price level occurs regardless of the current money supply, because any excess money will simply be hoarded, rather than added to spending.

At this point one has a version of the liquidity trap: money becomes irrelevant at the margin.[5] But aside from frustrating the central bank—which finds itself presiding over inflation no matter what it does—this trap has no adverse real consequences. To turn the analysis into a real problem, in both senses, one must introduce some kind of nominal rigidity.

The Hicksian Liquidity Trap

Suppose that the consumption good is produced, rather than simply appearing, with a maximum productive capacity y^f in period one. And suppose, also, that this productive capacity need not be fully employed. In particular, this paper assumes simply that the price level in period one is predetermined, so that the economy now acquires a Keynesian feel, and monetary policy can affect output. In period two and subsequently, output will still be assumed to take on the value y^*.

In this sticky price world, the levels of period one consumption and output must still be equal, but output adjusts to consumption rather than the other way around. Given the utility function, and the assumption that consumption will be y^* in period two, one can immediately write an expression for current real consumption, which becomes the IS curve determining real output:

$$(6) \qquad c = y = y^*(P^*/DP)^{1/\rho}(1 + i)^{-1/\rho}.$$

5. Some commentators on an earlier draft of this paper seemed to believe that this possibility of monetary irrelevance depends on the assumption that the central bank is expected to defend a future price-level target, as opposed to an inflation rate target—that money becomes irrelevant only because the central bank creates expectations of future deflation. But when the equilibrium real interest rate is negative, the liquidity trap emerges even if all the central bank wants is to keep prices stable. And the assumption that the central bank has an inflation target leads to even more paradoxical results. Since the economy needs inflation, attempting to keep the rate of change of prices constant means that there is no equilibrium price level: prices simply fall without limit.

If one makes the more realistic assumption that prices are downward sticky in the short to medium run, this paradox disappears. In this case, a committment to price stability, measured either by a predetermined target level or by inflation from the current level, will still imply a liquidity trap when the full-employment real rate is negative.

Figure 2. Relationships between Output and the Interest Rate

Interest rate

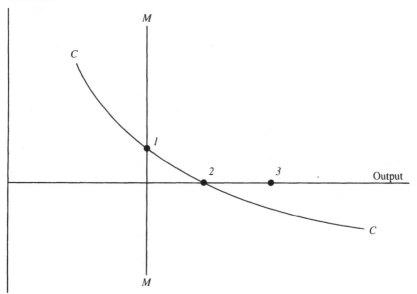

Source Author's model as described in text

Figure 2 illustrates the joint determination of the interest rate and output in this case. The IS curve, as just indicated, shows how output will be determined by consumption demand, which is decreasing in the interest rate. Meanwhile, as long as the nominal interest rate is positive, the cash in advance constraint will be binding, giving the *MM* curve

(7) $$y = M/p.$$

Increasing the money supply can now increase output, up to a point; specifically, up to point 2. But what if productive capacity is at point 3? The same argument as in the previous section applies: since the nominal interest rate cannot become negative, any increase in money beyond the level that drives the rate to zero will simply be substituted for bonds, with no effect on spending. And therefore no open market operation, however large, can get the economy to full employment. In short, the economy is in a classic Hicksian liquidity trap.

Under what conditions will such a liquidity trap occur? One possi-

bility is that P is high compared with P^*; that is, people expect deflation, so that even a zero nominal rate is a high real rate. The other
possibility, however, is that even if prices are expected to be stable, y^f
is high compared with the future—or equivalently, people's expected
future real income is low compared with the amount of consumption
needed to use today's capacity. In that case, it may take a negative real
interest rate to persuade people to spend enough now, and with downwardly inflexible prices that may not be possible.

To put it yet another way, closer to the language of applied macroeconomics, if people have low expectations about their future incomes,
even with a zero interest rate they may want to save more than the
economy can absorb. (In this case, the economy cannot absorb *any*
savings; I address that point below.) And therefore, no matter what the
central bank does with the current money supply, it cannot reflate the
economy sufficiently to restore full employment.

So I have now shown that a fully specified model, fudging neither
the role of money nor the necessity of making intertemporal choices,
can indeed generate a liquidity trap. The model does, however, omit
some important aspects of standard macroeconomic models. Perhaps
most notable, it has no investment, no foreign trade or capital mobility,
and no financial intermediation, so that all money is outside. Can the
same story be told if these elements are introduced?

Investment, Productive Capital, and Tobin's q

One way of stating the liquidity trap problem is to say that it occurs
when the equilibrium real interest rate—the rate at which saving and
investment would be equal at potential output—is negative. An immediate question is how this can happen in an economy in which, in
contrast with the simple endowment economy described above, productive investment can take place and the marginal product of capital,
while it can be low, can hardly be negative.

One answer that may be extremely important in practice is the existence of an equity premium. If the equity premium is as high as the
historic U.S. average, the economy could find itself in a liquidity trap
even if the rate of return on physical capital is as high as 5 or 6 percent.

A further answer is that the rate of return on investment depends not
only on the ratio of capital's marginal product to its price, but also on

the expected rate of change of that price. An economy in which Tobin's q is expected to decline could offer investors a negative real rate of return despite having a positive marginal product of capital.

This point is easiest to make if one considers an economy with not capital but land (which can serve as a sort of metaphor for durable capital); and also if one temporarily departs from the basic framework to consider an overlapping generations model, in which each generation works only in its first period of life but consumes only in its second. Let A be the stock of land, and L_t be the labor force in period t, defined as the number of individuals born in that period. Given the special assumption that the young do not consume during their working years but use all their income to buy land from the old, one has a very simple determination of q_t, the price of land in terms of output: it must be true that

$$(8) \qquad\qquad q_t A_t = w_t L_t,$$

where w_t is the marginal product of labor. So in this special setup, q is not a forward-looking variable; it depends only on the size of the current labor force.

The expected rate of return on purchases of land, however, is forward looking. Let R_t be the marginal product of land, and r_t the rate of return for the current younger generation. Then

$$(9) \qquad\qquad 1 + r_t = \frac{R_{t+1} + q_{t+1}}{q_t}.$$

Now suppose that demographers project that the next generation will be smaller than the current one, so that the labor force, and hence (given elastic demand for labor) the real price of land, will decline. Then even though land has a positive marginal product, the expected return from investing in land can, in principle, be negative.

This is a highly stylized example, which begs many questions. Nevertheless, it at least establishes that a liquidity trap can occur despite the existence of productive investment projects.

International Mobility of Goods and Capital

Many writers on Japan have assumed that one solution to the apparent excess of saving over investment, even at a zero interest rate, is simply to invest the excess savings abroad. In a recent influential study, Andrew Smithers suggests that over the long term, Japan should run capital account deficits (and hence current account surpluses) of no less than 10 percent of GDP.[6] The general view seems to be that an open economy can always extricate itself from a liquidity trap as long as there are profitable investment opportunities overseas. The main problem is the political one of persuading the rest of the world to accept the corresponding trade surpluses.

Unfortunately, the economics of capital export are not as favorable as this analysis suggests. The limited integration of markets for goods and services turns out to prevent capital flows from equalizing real interest rates in terms of domestic consumption, even when the mobility of capital itself is perfect. The fact is that in large economies like Japan or the United States, the bulk of employment and value added is in goods and services that remain nontradable despite modern communications and transportation technology. And this large nontradable share may well mean that capital export, even at a zero interest rate, is not enough to escape a liquidity trap.

This argument can be made in the language of conventional open economy IS-LM models. In such models it is usual to tie down the exchange rate by assuming that the market expects the real exchange rate to return to some normal value in the long run. The current real exchange rate is then determined off this long-run rate via the real interest differential between domestic and foreign bonds. So a monetary expansion that lowers nominal, and hence real, interest rates at home will produce a real depreciation, and this real depreciation will increase net exports at any given level of output. However, there is a limit to the size of the stimulus that this depreciation can generate: because the real exchange rate is expected to revert to its normal level, even a zero interest rate will produce only a finite real depreciation. If trade is a small share of GDP and if the price elasticities of imports and exports are also fairly small—both of which conditions are true in econometric models of large economies, if not in reality—even near perfect capital mobility may provide only limited extra scope for monetary expansion.

But should one believe this story? While the open economy IS-LM model may be a highly useful heuristic device for thinking about short-

6. Smithers (1998).

Paul R. Krugman   153

and medium-run macroeconomic issues, many economists doubt that it is really trustworthy, especially in considering such fundamental questions as the scope for international capital flows. And in any case, the thrust of this paper is to remove the stigma of the ad hoc nature of the liquidity trap concept. It may therefore be helpful to supplement this conventional view with a restatement in terms of a variant of my basic intertemporal model.

Consider a somewhat modified version of the basic model, in which the economy produces and consumes two goods, one tradable (T) and the other nontradable (N). Utility takes the form

$$(10) \qquad U = \frac{1}{1 - \rho} \sum_t D^t \left[c_{Tt}^\tau \, c_{Nt}^{1-\tau} \right]^{1-\rho} .$$

In general, one would want to give the economy a transformation curve between N and T at any point in time. For simplicity, I assume that the transformation curve is right-angled; that is, the economy receives exogenous endowments of the two goods in each period. It can, however, borrow and lend on world markets at a given real interest rate r_T in terms of the tradable good, so consumption of that good need not be the same as production.

Does this assumed perfect capital mobility therefore imply that the domestic real interest rate must equal the world rate? Not if inflation is measured in terms of either the nontraded good or a consumption basket that includes both traded and nontraded goods. This is most easily seen by considering the special case in which ρ is equal to one; that is, in which equation 10 takes the special form

$$(11) \qquad U = \sum_t D^t [\tau \ln(c_{Tt}) + (1 - \tau)\ln(c_{Nt})].$$

In equation 11, utility becomes separable between tradables and nontradables. For each good, the relationship between consumption growth and the real interest rate must obey the rule $1 + r = D^{-1}(c_{t+1}/c_t)$. Whereas in the tradable sector relative consumption is determined by the exogenous real interest rate, however, in the nontraded sector (assuming full employment) it will be the other way around: because consumption of nontradables must equal production, the real interest rate in terms of nontraded goods will have to adjust to the path of production. As a result, it is entirely possible that the market-clearing real interest rate in terms of nontraded goods will be negative, even with perfect capital mobility; and if the traded share in the consumption basket is small enough, the overall domestic real rate may be negative even if the world real rate is positive.

Now introduce the possibility of unemployment, by making the nominal price of nontradables downwardly rigid, and consider the effects of a temporary monetary expansion—that is, one that increases the money supply in the first period but does not change expectations about money supplies in later periods. Such a monetary expansion will lower the nominal interest rate, with different effects on the two sectors. In tradables, the real interest rate is tied down by world capital markets, so there must now be expected deflation in traded goods prices. But the future price is also tied down by the assumption that the monetary expansion is only temporary. So the current price of tradables must rise, in order to allow for the subsequent fall. There must therefore be a nominal depreciation of the exchange rate.

The situation in nontradables will be exactly as in the economy as a whole in the closed economy model: the lower nominal rate will also be a lower real rate, and both consumption and production will increase.

The important point is that both for the exchange rate and for non-tradable production, the zero constraint on the nominal interest rate can be binding. That is, even at a zero interest rate, the output increase and the nominal depreciation will have finite magnitudes—and the economy may not be able to go all the way to full employment.

Incidentally, in this log utility case, monetary expansion has no effect on the current account. This is so because the separability of the utility function means that consumers in effect must make completely separate decisions on tradable and nontradable consumption over time; and since the real interest rate on tradables does not change, there is no reallocation between present and future consumption of those goods. This is obviously an artifact of the assumption that ρ is equal to one; I discuss the consequences of larger ρ below.

Financial Intermediation and Monetary Aggregates

Attempts to make sense of the origins and persistence of the Great Depression in the United States hinge crucially on how one interprets the radical divergence between the growth of monetary base and that

Paul R. Krugman 155

Figure 3. U.S. Monetary Trends, 1929–39

Index, 1929 = 100

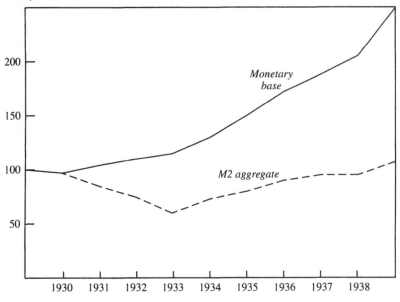

Source Temin (1976, p. 5)

of broader aggregates during the period. Figure 3 shows the familiar picture presented slightly differently from the standard representation (with both monetary base and M2 presented as indexes constructed so that 1929 equals 100). It shows that monetary base actually rose during the early years of slump and continued to rise steeply throughout the 1930s. By contrast, M2 fell by more than a third and did not surpass its 1929 level until 1939. These basic facts underlie two influential views of the Depression. One, suggested by Friedman and Schwartz, is that a broad aggregate like M2 is the proper measure of the money supply, that the Depression occurred because the Fed allowed broad money to fall so much, and that recovery was so long delayed because the needed increase in broad money was equally long delayed.[7] The other view, associated with Ben Bernanke and Russell Cooper and Dean Corbae, among others, is that the dramatic decline in the money mul-

7. See Friedman and Schwartz (1963).

tiplier was the signature of a major episode of financial disintermediation; and that this disintermediation, which may be thought of more
nearly as a supply-side than a demand-side phenomenon, was the cause
of the sustained slump.[8] However, monetary explanations of the Great
Depression have been criticized, most notably by Peter Temin, who
suggests that the decline in monetary aggregates was a result rather than
a cause of the slump, and perhaps could not have been prevented by
the Federal Reserve.[9]

Since the Depression is the main historical example for liquidity trap
economics, and since one quite often hears similar arguments made
about contemporary Japan, it is important to ask how financial intermediaries and monetary aggregates fit into the liquidity trap story.
Fortunately, it is quite easy to sketch out how this could be done, using
a framework that might be described as "cash in advance meets
Diamond-Dybvig" (a formal exposition of this framework is given in
appendix A). In their classic paper, Douglas Diamond and Philip Dybvig introduce a demand for liquidity by making individuals uncertain
about their own consumption needs; only after they have made commitments to illiquid investments do they discover whether they are
"type one" consumers, who derive utility from consumption in period
one but not period two, or "type two" consumers, who do the reverse.[10]
This dilemma can be resolved by a class of financial intermediaries that
allow individuals to withdraw funds on demand, but are able to make
illiquid investments because the number of early withdrawals is predictable. Although Diamond and Dybvig are mainly concerned with
showing how such a system could be vulnerable to self-fulfilling bank
runs, one can also use their approach as a device for putting inter-
mediates and monetary aggregates into the basic model of this paper.

To do this, return to a one-good endowment economy, but now
suppose that at the beginning of each period a three-step process takes
place, as follows: (1) individuals trade currency for bonds in a capital
market and are also able to make deposits at a class of banks,
(2) individuals discover whether they derive utility from consuming in
the current period, (3) those who do want to consume withdraw the
necessary cash from their bank accounts.

8. See Bernanke (1994); Cooper and Corbae (1997).
9. See Temin (1976).
10. Diamond and Dybvig (1983).

Paul R. Krugman 157

The determination of the real interest rate is somewhat more complex in this setup, because while the representative agent assumption may hold ex ante, it does not hold ex post. However, given the equilibrium real rate, it is straightforward to see what must happen in the financial sector. As long as the nominal interest rate is positive, individuals will have no incentive to hold on to cash; instead, they will deposit enough money in their bank accounts to cover their cash needs if they do turn out to be type one consumers. Banks, in turn, will have to hold enough of the deposits they receive in cash to cover such withdrawals; again, given a positive nominal interest rate, they will hold no more than the minimum required, putting the rest in bonds. So at the beginning of the period, a monetary aggregate defined as currency plus deposits will actually consist of no currency, but a volume of deposits that is a multiple of the base money held as reserves. And any increase in that base will, under conditions of full employment, lead to an equal proportional increase in both deposits and the price level.

But if the nominal interest rate is driven to zero, consumers and banks will become indifferent between holding monetary base and bonds—and consumers will also be indifferent between both of these and bank deposits. Exactly what happens to an increase in the monetary base under these conditions is indeterminate: it could be absorbed by consumers, who might substitute cash for either bonds or bank deposits in their portfolios; or the extra base could be absorbed by banks, which will simply hold excess reserves. Of these three possibilities, only the one in which consumers substitute cash for bonds (rather than deposits) will have any effect on a currency-plus-deposits measure of the money supply. Either a substitution of cash for deposits or an addition of base money to reserves will reduce bank credit but leave the monetary aggregate unchanged. And in any case, there will be no effects on the price level, nor on output if prices are sticky.

Applying what one of my colleagues calls the principle of insignificant reason, one may surmise that an increase in monetary base will lead to substitution in all three directions. This means that under liquidity trap conditions, such a base expansion will (1) expand a broad aggregate slightly, but only because the public holds more currency; (2) actually reduce deposits, because some of that currency substitutes for deposits; and (3) reduce bank credit even more, because banks will add to reserves.

The implications of this thought experiment should be obvious. If an economy is truly in a liquidity trap, failure of broad monetary aggregates to expand is not a sign of insufficiently expansionary monetary policy: the central bank may simply be unable to achieve such an expansion because additional base is either added to bank reserves or held by the public in place of bank deposits. However, this inability to expand broad money does not mean that the essential problem lies in the banking system; it is to be expected even if the banks are in perfectly fine shape.

The point is important and bears repeating: under liquidity trap conditions, the normal expectation is that an increase in high-powered money will have little effect on broad aggregates, and may even lead to a decline in bank deposits and a larger decline in bank credit. This seemingly perverse result is part of the looking-glass logic of the situation, irrespective of the problems of the banks, per se.

Fiscal Policy

One can now consider possible policy responses to an economy in a liquidity trap. The classic Keynesian answer is fiscal expansion, which clearly does work in an IS-LM framework. How does it look in a modernized version of liquidity trap theory?

The framework developed above is strongly biased against finding any useful role for fiscal policy, because the representative agent, intertemporal optimization approach implies Ricardian equivalence. This bias does not represent an empirical judgment: it is an accidental by-product of modeling decisions made for the sake of simplicity on other fronts. True, a number of commentators have suggested (mainly because of the apparent ineffectiveness of Japanese efforts at fiscal stimulus to date) that Japan may come closer to Ricardian equivalence than most countries, and it is interesting, at least as an exercise, to think through the implications of such equivalence.[11] But in reality, fiscal

11. Suppose that one really believed that Japan was Ricardian equivalent, or nearly so. The first and most obvious implication is that changes in taxes and transfers should have no effect. In the practical discussion of Japanese policy, there has been much concern over whether tax cuts should be temporary or "permanent." If one really believes in Ricardian equivalence, this discussion is irrelevant, unless one believes that a permanent tax cut will constrain future government purchases of goods and services.

A second, less obvious, point is that under liquidity trap conditions the multiplier on

policy would surely have some impact. Two questions about that impact follow, one qualitative and one quantitative.

The qualitative question is whether a temporary fiscal stimulus can have permanent effects. If current income has very strong impacts on spending, so that the marginal propensity to spend (consumption plus investment) is actually greater than one over some range, there can be multiple equilibria. A liquidity trap may therefore represent a low-level equilibrium, and a sufficiently large temporary fiscal expansion could jolt the economy out of that equilibrium into a region where conventional monetary policy worked again.

It seems to be part of the folk wisdom in macroeconomics that this is in fact how the Great Depression came to an end: the massive one-time fiscal jolt from the war pushed the economy into a more favorable equilibrium. However, Christina Romer contends that most of the output gap created during 1929–33 had been eliminated before there was any significant fiscal stimulus.[12] She argues that the main explanation

---

government expenditures—for example, public works projects—should be exactly one: that is, such projects will generate exactly as much additional income as the government spends. This may be seen directly, by the fact that in the basic model current consumption is tied down by the Euler condition; if current policy cannot either raise expected future consumption or change the real interest rate, it cannot change current consumption. Alternatively, note that the extra income generated by government spending will be matched by an exactly equal present-discounted value of future tax liabilities. Either way, government spending will not generate any second-round increase in private spending.

A third point, which has not been appreciated in some recent discussion, is that if temporary tax cuts will not raise consumption, any other policy that can be reinterpreted as a temporary tax cut or transfer will be equally ineffectual. For example, several foreign commentators have suggested that the Japanese government promote consumption by issuing vouchers that must be spent within some short period. But individuals could presumably use the vouchers for purchases that they would otherwise have made with cash; and if they take the future tax liability implied by the vouchers into account, they will do so, with no increase in spending.

A surprising corollary is that what is normally regarded as the most extreme inflationary monetary policy possible, a helicopter drop of cash, is just as ineffective in a liquidity trap as an open market operation. Since in a liquidity trap money and bonds are perfect substitutes, it is no different from a lump sum transfer of bonds to the public, which, by Ricardian equivalence, has no effect.

These extreme results are, of course, implications of the strong assumption of completely rational, forward-looking consumption behavior.

12. Romer (1992). Significant fiscal stimulus began in 1941 (before Pearl Harbor—a massive military buildup was already under way). One's assessment of whether the economy had largely recovered from the Great Depression prior to the onset of massive wartime spending partly depends on the choice of denominators. By 1940, real GDP

of that expansion was a sharp decline in real interest rates, which she attributes to monetary policy (although most of the decline in her estimate of the real interest rate is actually due to changes in the inflation rate rather than the nominal interest rate). Indeed, Romer estimates that for most of the recovery period ex ante real rates were sharply negative, ranging between − 5 and − 10 percent.[13]

My point is that the end of the Depression, which is the usual, indeed perhaps the sole, motivating example for the view that a one-time fiscal stimulus can produce sustained recovery, does not actually appear to fit the story line too well. Much, though by no means all, of the recovery from that particular liquidity trap seems to have depended on inflation expectations that made real interest rates substantially negative.

If temporary fiscal stimulus does not jolt the economy out of the doldrums, however, a recovery strategy based on fiscal expansion would have to continue the stimulus over an extended period. Which raises the quantitative question of how much stimulus is needed, for how long—and whether the consequences in terms of government debt are acceptable.

Credibility and Monetary Policy

It may seem strange to have a subsection mentioning monetary policy, given that up to this point the paper has stressed the ineffectuality of such policy in a liquidity trap. However, as I noted at the beginning,

---

had risen 70 percent from its 1933 level, but it was only 11 percent above its 1929 level, so that a significant output gap surely remained. The "half full or half empty" issue is apparent in the contrast between Romer's discussion and that of Gordon (1988). While Gordon views the U.S. economy in 1939 as stuck, Romer emphasizes growth rates of more than 8 percent in 1939 and 1940.

13. For this calculation, Romer uses commercial paper rates, which did decline somewhat even in nominal terms. However, the spread between commercial paper and Treasury bills is presumably to some extent endogenous. T-bill rates averaged 0.515 percent in 1933—roughly the same as Japanese rates today. While they did fall to virtually zero by the end of the decade, any fall in real rates using this measure of nominal interest would be almost entirely dominated by changes in inflation expectations.

Indeed, seen through the lens of the analysis in the present paper, Romer's evidence seems to suggest a somewhat different interpretation of events. One might think of her findings as showing that the real expansion of the economy—and the associated rise in prices—was the result of a rise in inflation expectations, which reduced real interest rates when nominal rates were already at the floor. Without this expected inflation, the expansion of monetary base that Romer emphasizes would have been ineffectual.

only temporary monetary expansions are ineffectual. If a monetary expansion is perceived to be permanent, it will raise prices (in a full-employment model) or output (if current prices are predetermined). The mechanism may be seen immediately from equation 6: a rise in the expected future price level P^* will shift out the IS curve in the current period.

The ineffectuality of monetary policy in a liquidity trap is really the result of a looking-glass version of the standard credibility problem: monetary policy does not work because the public expects that whatever the central bank may do now, given the chance, it will revert to type and stabilize prices near their current level. If the central bank can credibly promise to be irresponsible—that is, convince the market that it will in fact allow prices to rise sufficiently—it can bootstrap the economy out of the trap. Again, although she does not put it this way, Romer's analysis of the U.S. recovery over 1933–41 suggests that just such a bootstrap process was the main cause of the growth in output.

Proposals for "managed inflation," first widely aired a few months ago, have since drawn a number of questions.[14] One may as well go through those most frequently asked, and their answers.

Why inflation—isn't an end to deflation good enough? In terms of the analysis given above, price stability is not an option for an economy in a liquidity trap. The economy needs inflation, because it needs a negative real interest rate; the deflationary pressures actually being manifested represent the economy trying to generate that needed inflation by reducing current prices compared with the future price level. The only way to avoid lowering the current level is to raise the expected future level.

Isn't inflation a bad thing? Again, in terms of my analysis, a liquidity trap economy is "naturally" an economy with inflation; if prices were completely flexible, it would get that inflation regardless of monetary policy, so a deliberately inflationary policy is remedying a distortion rather than creating one. One might also arrive at the recommendation of inflation by a quite different route: Friedman's famous theory of the optimum quantity of money.[15] Although he says that the economy should deflate at the rate of time preference, the proper interpretation

14. Managed inflation gained widespread attention following a posting on the author's worldwide web site, "Japan's Trap," in May 1998.

15. Friedman (1969).

of this logic is that the economy should deflate at the market-clearing real rate of interest. For a liquidity trap economy, where that market-clearing rate is negative, this means a negative rate of deflation—that is, inflation.

Won't expected inflation produce perverse incentives? In terms of the models, at least, a fall in the real interest rate achieved through expected inflation is identical in its effects to one produced through a fall in nominal interest rates, when that is possible. There is no reason in principle to expect the increase in spending generated by a commitment to inflation to be any different in character from that generated by a conventional monetary expansion in an economy that starts with positive nominal rates.

Won't an inflationary policy lead to a plunge in the exchange rate and become a beggar thy neighbor policy at the rest of the world's expense? Because expected inflation plays the same role in a liquidity trap economy as do interest rate reductions under more normal circumstances, inflating one's way out of a trap is no more (and no less) a beggar thy neighbor policy than any monetary expansion under flexible exchange rates. But what is the beggar thy neighbor aspect of monetary policy, anyway?

In the traditional open economy IS-LM model developed by Robert Mundell and Marcus Fleming, and also in large-scale econometric models, monetary expansion unambiguously leads to currency depreciation.[16] But there are two offsetting effects on the current account balance. On one side, the currency depreciation tends to increase net exports; on the other side, the expansion of the domestic economy tends to increase imports. For what it is worth, policy experiments on such models seem to suggest that these effects very nearly cancel each other out. Table 1 presents estimates from the comprehensive, if somewhat elderly, comparison of eleven models by Jeffrey Frankel.[17] For each model, it shows the second year effects on the exchange rate and the current account of a monetary expansion sufficient to raise real United States GNP by 1 percent. The exchange rate impacts are substantial, the current account impacts negligible. To the extent that these estimates are correct, they suggest that in a large economy with fairly small

16. Mundell (1963); Fleming (1962).
17. Frankel (1988).

Paul R. Krugman 163

Table 1. Second Year Effects on the U.S. Exchange Rate and Current Account after a Monetary Expansion to Raise Real GNP by 1 Percent

Percent

Model[a]	Exchange rate	Current account[b]
DRI	−8.1	−0.02
EEC	−4.0	−0.07
EPA	−5.3	−0.03
LINK	−2.3	−0.01
LIVERPOOL	−39.0	−3.1
MCM	−4.0	−0.05
MINIMOD	−5.7	−0.07
MSG	−6.7	−0.21
OECD	−1.6	−0.13
VAR	−7.6	−0.04
WHARTON	−1.4	−0.17
Summary statistic		
Median	−5.3	−0.03

Source: Frankel (1988).
a. Models are fully identified by Frankel.
b. As a percentage of GNP.

trade shares, expected inflation will produce a significant currency depreciation but have small impact on the current account.[18]

I have been trying to get beyond the IS-LM model, however. How does the result look in an intertemporal open economy model? Assume the utility function given in equation 10, exogenous output of traded goods, and sticky prices or excess capacity in the nontraded sector. If the nominal interest rate is positive, ordinary monetary policy can raise output of the nontraded good; if the economy is in a liquidity trap, expectations of future monetary expansion can achieve the same result.

18. In the case of Japan, many people want the economy to act as a "locomotive"—to run much smaller current account surpluses, thereby aiding the recovery of neighboring economies. Perhaps the important point to make here is that even a large recovery in Japanese output would have only a small locomotive effect, unless accompanied by a substantial strengthening of the yen. Typical estimates of the short-run income elasticity of import demand are around 2; given Japan's import share in GDP of approximately 0.1, this means that a 5 percentage point recovery would, at an unchanged real exchange rate, reduce Japan's surplus by roughly 1 percent of GDP (some $35 billion). And only a fraction of this swing would come vis-à-vis the troubled emerging economies of Asia. The only way to get a much larger locomotive effect would be for Japan to pursue a Reagan-style expansion, in which the exchange rate appreciates substantially. However, given that Japan is having great difficulty achieving any type of recovery, advocating a currency appreciation seems rather strange.

Table 2. Beggar Thy Neighbor Coefficients

	τ		
ρ	*0.2*	*0.3*	*0.4*
2	0.167	0.231	0.286
3	0.286	0.375	0.444
4	0.375	0.474	0.545

Source: Author's calculations as described in text.

The question is what impact this expansion has on the current account, which in this framework amounts to asking what happens to consumption of the traded good.

One can take a shortcut here, if one imagines that the expansion is "brief," in the sense that one can ignore the effect of the current account on the future investment income of the country. Removing this assumption would only reinforce the results. In the case of a brief expansion, it is possible to calculate analytically a "beggar thy neighbor coefficient," defined as the ratio of the increase in the expanding country's current account surplus (measured as a share of GDP) to the percentage increase in its GDP. Appendix B shows that

$$(12) \qquad\qquad B = -\frac{1 - \rho}{1 - \rho - (1/\tau)},$$

where ρ is relative risk aversion and τ is the traded share of consumption (and hence value added in the economy). One sees immediately that in the special case of ρ equal to 1, a monetary expansion has no effect on the expanding country's current account, which is roughly what the econometric exercises in table 1 indicate. If relative risk aversion is higher than 1, there will to some extent be expansion by means of inflation, as a result of a widened current account surplus, but the extent will depend inversely on how open the economy is, as measured by τ. Table 2 shows beggar thy neighbor coefficients for a range of values of ρ and τ. If one believes the folk wisdom that relative risk aversion is something like 2, and judgmentally assumes that the tradable share in the Japanese economy is not much more than 0.2, the implication is that an inflationary policy that raised Japanese output by as much as 5 percent relative to baseline would require an expansion of the current

Paul R. Krugman   165

Table 3. Depreciation Coefficients

	τ		
ρ	0.2	0.3	0.4
2	1.67	1.54	1.43
3	2.14	1.88	1.67
4	2.5	2.11	1.82

Source: Author's calculations as described in text.

account surplus of something like 1 percent of GDP. This is far short of the huge surpluses envisaged by Smithers and others.[19]

One can also calculate the real depreciation—as measured by the change in a domestic price index with weights τ and $1 - \tau$ relative to the price of traded goods—associated with a 1 percent increase in real GDP achieved through inflationary expectations. It can be shown that this depreciation is

(13)
$$1 + \frac{1-\tau}{\tau} \cdot \frac{1-\rho}{1-\rho-\dfrac{1}{\tau}} .$$

Table 3 shows depreciation coefficients for a range of values of ρ and τ. These numbers look generally small, compared with the model simulations in table 1. I discuss why this might be so in the second part of the paper.

Summary

I have offered a quick tour of a rather extensive and unfamiliar territory, the land of the liquidity trap. Perhaps the most important lesson to be learned from this tour is the strangeness of the territory: once an economy really is in a liquidity trap, much of the conventional wisdom of macroeconomics ceases to apply—indeed, applying conventional models to the liquidity trap universe implies some quite unconventional conclusions. Aside from the observation that international capital mobility makes less difference than most economists probably suppose (an observation that actually applies to open economy macroeconomics in general), I would highlight two conclusions in particular.

19. Smithers (1998).

First, one must be careful about making inferences from divergences between the growth of monetary base and of broad monetary aggregates. The failure of aggregates to grow need not indicate dereliction on the part of the central bank; in a liquidity trap economy the central bank in principle cannot move broad monetary aggregates. Likewise, the observation that although the central bank has slashed interest rates and pumped up monetary base, the broader money supply has not grown, does not necessarily imply that the fault lies in the banking system; it is just what one would expect in a liquidity trap economy.

Second, whatever the specifics of the situation, a liquidity trap is always the product of a credibility problem: the public believes that current monetary expansion will not be sustained. Structural factors can explain why an economy needs expected inflation; they can never imply that *credibly sustained* monetary expansion is ineffective.

Japan's Trap

Table 4 presents some standard summary statistics on Japan's economic performance since 1981. It makes the familiar point that following rapid growth to 1991, the economy has gone through an extended period of very slow growth. The breakpoint shown in the table, however, is actually 1992 rather than 1991. The reason is that the Japanese economy appeared to be overheated in 1991, so that part of the slowdown in growth as measured from that date can be simply viewed as the correction of an unsustainable boom. Inflationary pressures had clearly eased by 1992, though, and the low growth rate thereafter is a better indicator of the economy's true shortfall. It is clear that Japan will have a significant decline in real GDP for 1998; and the unemployment rate has already risen above 4 percent.

There are two striking features of these dreary numbers. The first is the extent of the slowdown. In the period 1981–92 Japan grew at an average rate of 3.7 percent. It ended the period with the same unemployment rate as it had started with, and with a lower inflation rate; in short, potential as well as actual output would seem to have risen at about 3.7 percent annually over the period. If one had projected that growth rate forward, one would have overpredicted 1998 output by about 14 percent.

Paul R. Krugman   167

Table 4. Economic Performance in Japan, 1981–97
Percent

Year	Real GDP growth	Inflation	Unemployment rate	Money market interest rate
1981	3.2	4.1	2.2	. . .
1982	3.1	1.8	2.4	. . .
1983	2.3	1.8	2.7	. . .
1984	3.9	2.6	2.7	6.5
1985	4.4	2.1	2.6	6.6
1986	2.9	1.8	2.8	5.1
1987	4.2	0.1	2.8	4.2
1988	6.2	0.7	2.5	4.5
1989	4.8	2.0	2.3	5.4
1990	5.1	2.3	2.1	7.7
1991	3.8	2.7	2.1	7.2
1992	1.0	1.7	2.2	4.3
1981–92 average	3.7	2.0	2.5	5.7
1993	0.3	0.6	2.5	2.9
1994	0.6	0.2	2.9	2.3
1995	1.5	−0.6	3.1	1.2
1996	3.9	−0.5	3.4	0.6
1997	0.9	0.6	3.4	0.6
1993–97 average	1.4	0.1	2.4	1.5

Source: *International Financial Statistics*, 1998.

The second feature is the low interest rates of recent years; Japanese money market rates have been below 1 percent since 1995. It is true that Japan has not pushed money market rates down to their absolute minimum—at the time of writing, there are still 43 basis points to go— but the economy is clearly in a very good approximation to liquidity trap conditions.

How important a role does this liquidity trap play in the growth slowdown and current slump? In principle, the great bulk of the slow-down might represent a reduction in the rate of potential output growth; in that case, even a successful stimulative policy would have only a small payoff, so that freeing the economy from its liquidity trap is not a particularly urgent issue. It is therefore important to estimate the gap between actual and potential output.

For the United States, the output gap is usually estimated by com-bining an estimate of the natural rate of unemployment with an estimate of the Okun's Law coefficient between changes in unemployment and

168   *Brookings Papers on Economic Activity, 2:1998*

Figure 4. Okun's Law for Japan, 1982–91

Change in unemployment

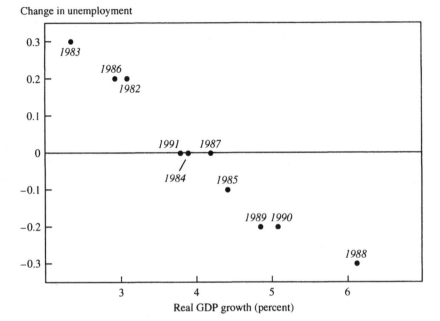

Real GDP growth (percent)

Source: *International Financial Statistics,* 1998.

in real GDP. Although Japan's measured unemployment rate has traditionally moved much less than that of the United States, there is actually a surprisingly close Okun's Law relationship in the 1982–91 period, as shown in figure 4. The slope of the apparent relationship is about three times as steep as for the United States: it apparently took about 6 percentage points of excess growth to reduce the unemployment rate by 1 percentage point. If one were to take the average 2.5 percent unemployment rate in the period before the slump as an estimate of the natural rate, the 3.4 percent unemployment rate in 1997 would therefore seem to imply an output gap of more than 5 percent in that year—and with potential output presumably still growing while output slumps, by the end of 1998 the gap could be as great as 10 percent.

Most published estimates of Japan's output gap are far smaller. Many of these estimates, notably those of the International Monetary Fund, are based on the Hodrick-Prescott filter, which minimizes a weighted sum of squared deviations of actual from potential output and squared

Paul R. Krugman 169

Figure 5. U.S. Gross Domestic Product, 1919–39

ln GDP

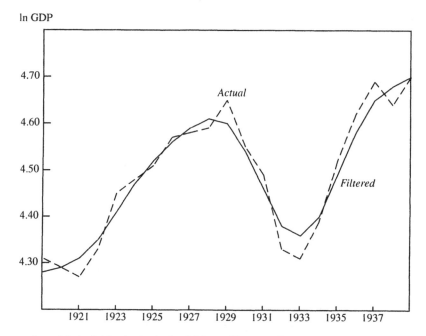

Source: Author's calculations based on data from U S Bureau of Economic Analysis (1973).

changes in the growth rate of potential output.[20] The main practical advantage of this method is that it can be used even when there are secular changes in both potential growth rates and the natural rate of unemployment. However, Hodrick-Prescott has severe disadvantages when applied to an economy that undergoes a sustained slump. First, it imposes the assumption that average deviations from potential are zero over the whole period, so that when the economy slumps, the filter automatically reevaluates earlier periods as times of above-potential output, reducing the estimated shortfall. Second, any sustained drop in output gets built into the estimated potential growth rate. As a result, it systematically understates the actual shortfall from potential. A stark, if somewhat unfair, way to make this point is to apply the Hodrick-Prescott filter to the United States in the interwar period, as shown in figure 5. For this figure, the smoothing parameter λ is set at 25; but a

20. See Giorno and others (1995) for a description.

Figure 6. Output Gap for Japan, 1982–97

Percent

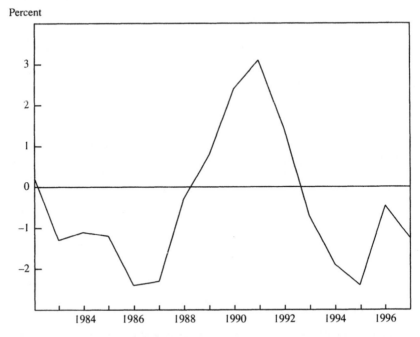

Source. *OECD Economic Outlook*, June 1998

wide range of values of λ yields the conclusion that output was in excess of potential by 1935.

The Organisation for Economic Co-operation and Development (OECD) has adopted a more complex technique to assess Japan's output gap; its most recent estimates are shown in figure 6.[21] Nonetheless, the estimated output gap in 1997 is remarkably small: − 1.2 percent. This seems to be due to the fact that although the OECD does not engage in simple Hodrick-Prescott filtering, it updates estimates of normal worker hours and worker productivity in such a way that possibly cyclical components get reinterpreted as structural trends. Figure 7 provides a nice illustration of this process at work, by contrasting the estimates of potential growth in the 1995 study by Giorno and others that introduced the OECD's current method with the potential growth estimates that appear in the most recent *OECD Economic Outlook*. As recently as

21. The OECD methodology is described in Giorno and others (1995).

Paul R. Krugman 171

Figure 7. OECD Estimates of Japanese Potential Growth, 1987–97

Percent

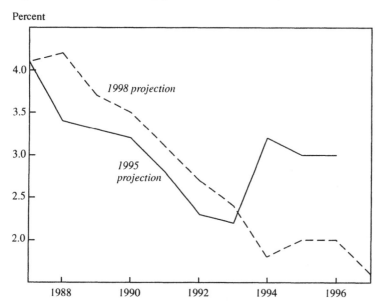

Source: Giorno and others (1995); *OECD Economic Outlook*, June 1998

three years ago, the OECD estimated Japan's potential growth at 3 percent; now it has marked it down to 1.6 percent. Applying the earlier 3 percent potential growth to the period since 1994, the 1997 output shortfall rises to 4.6 percent; not too far short of the estimate suggested by the Okun's Law calculation for Japan.

If the Japanese output gap was 3 to 4 percent in 1997, if potential output growth is 2 to 3 percent, and if, as now seems certain, output falls throughout 1998, the output gap at the end of 1998 will quite probably exceed 7 percent. Obviously there is no precision in this estimate; my guess is that in retrospect it will seem clear that Japan's 1998 output gap was 8 percent or more. But one can make a very strong case that it will exceed 5 percent, so that demand-side policies to close that gap are of very real importance.

Saving and Investment

A liquidity trap occurs when desired saving exceeds desired investment at full employment, even at a zero short-term interest rate. As

Table 5. Private Consumption as a Share of GDP, Japan and the United States, 1991–97

Percent

Year	Japan	United States
1991	57.1	67.1
1992	57.8	67.6
1993	58.6	68.0
1994	59.7	67.8
1995	60.1	68.2
1996	59.9	68.2
1997	60.6	67.9

Source: *International Financial Statistics,* 1998.

argued in the first part of this paper, for some purposes it does not matter why this is the case, as long as it is. Still, the intepretation of Japan's problem, and to some extent the policy implications, do depend on how one views the apparent excess saving.

Table 5 shows ratios of consumption to GDP for Japan and the United States since 1991. Two familiar observations stand out. One is that Japan's consumption ratio remains very low by comparison with the United States. A vast literature has attempted to explain this disparity; this paper has nothing to add to it. The other observation is that Japan's consumption ratio has not declined in the 1990s; if anything, it has risen slightly. This suggests that the shift into liquidity trap territory might reflect declining investment demand rather than rising saving supply.

How significant is the difference between U.S. and Japanese consumption ratios? Consider the 1997 difference of approximately 7 percentage points of GDP. If U.S. consumers were suddenly to start behaving like their Japanese counterparts, this would be the equivalent of a 7 percent of GDP negative fiscal impulse. Suppose that the Fed then tried to offset that contraction with looser monetary policy. Would it be able to do so, or would the U.S. find itself in liquidity trap territory? Recall that the emergence of budget deficits of approximately 3 percent of GDP in the 1980s was widely held to have raised real short-term interest rates by 3 or 4 percentage points; the difference between Japanese and U.S. consumption shares is more than twice as large a shock. Another approach is to ask what the impact of such a monetary-fiscal switch would be in a variety of standard econometric models, such as those considered in table 1. Table 6 reports estimates of the impact of

Paul R. Krugman 173

Table 6. Effect on U.S. Short-Term Interest Rates of a Fiscal-Monetary Switch Equivalent to a 1 Percent Decline in the Consumption Ratio
Percent

Model[a]	
DRI	−4.3
EEC	−4.4
EPA	−5.3
LINK	−1.9
LIVERPOOL	−2.2
MCM	−4.3
MINIMOD	−2.9
MSG	−3.3
OECD	−2.3
TAYLOR	−0.7
VAR	−0.4
WHARTON	−5.3
Summary statistic	
Median	−3.1

Source· Frankel (1988, pp. 21, 23)
a Models are those used in table 1

a monetary-fiscal switch equivalent to a 1 percent decline in the consumption ratio; both the mean and the median effects are a 3 percentage point decline in the short-term interest rate.

It is easy to find reasons why such exercises might overstate the case; structural models probably tend to understate the spending impact of a sustained reduction in the interest rate. But even this crude comparison makes it substantially less surprising than one might have supposed that Japan, with its low consumption, has indeed found itself in a liquidity trap. In fact, this exercise suggests that the real puzzle is not why Japan is now in a liquidity trap, but why the trap did not materialize sooner. How was Japan able to invest so much, at relatively high real interest rates, before the 1990s? The most obvious answer is some version of the accelerator: investment demand was high because of Japan's sustained high growth rate, and therefore ultimately because of the high rate of potential output growth. In that case, the slump in investment demand in the 1990s may be explained in part by a slowdown in the underlying sources of Japanese potential growth, and especially in prospective potential growth.

As noted above, there is considerable uncertainty about the actual rate of Japanese potential growth in the 1990s. Nonetheless, it is likely that there has been a slowdown in the rate of increase in total factor productivity, even cyclically adjusted. It is certain, however, that Japan's long-run growth must slow, even at full employment, because of demographics. Through the 1980s, Japanese employment expanded at 1.2 percent annually.[22] However, the working-age population has now peaked: it will decline at 0.7 percent annually over the next thirty years, and—if demographers' projections about fertility are correct—at a remarkable 1.0 percent for the twenty-five years thereafter.[23] As suggested by the discussion of investment and Tobin's q in the first part of this paper, such prospective demographic decline should, other things equal, depress expectations of future q, and hence also depress current investment.

The looming shortage of working-age Japanese people has been visible for a long time; indeed, the budgetary consequences of an aging population have been a preoccupation of the Ministry of Finance and an important factor inhibiting expansionary fiscal policy. One reason why this prospect did not start to affect long-term investment projects earlier is the "bubble economy" of the late 1980s. Businesses may have believed that total factor productivity would grow rapidly enough to make up for a declining work force. However, the bubble economy may also have masked the underlying decline in investment opportunities, and hence delayed the day of reckoning. Moreover, that bubble economy left a legacy of large debts and troubled bank balance sheets, which are widely regarded as the main culprits of Japan's current plight.

Banking Problems

Japan clearly faces a huge problem of bad bank loans; the current conventional wisdom places their value at a trillion dollars. These bad loans are in part a legacy of the burst of the asset bubble of the 1980s, reinforced by the consequences of the subsequent slow growth. Clearly Japan will need to engage in a cleanup operation dwarfing that of the U.S. thrift crisis, especially as measured against Japan's smaller economy. Inevitably, also, the form and funding of that cleanup will be central political preoccupations. But how central are the problems of banks to the country's macroeconomic difficulties?

This may seem an odd question to ask. Disruption of financial inter-

22. *OECD Economic Outlook*, December 1997, p. A23.
23. Organisation for Economic Co-operation and Development (1997, p. 113).

Paul R. Krugman   175

Table 7. Japanese Financial Data, 1994–97

Index, 1994 = 100

Year	Monetary base	M2 plus certificates of deposit	Bank credit
1994	100.0	100.0	100.0
1995	107.8	103.3	100.8
1996	117.0	106.5	100.6
1997	125.6	110.6	100.9

Source: *International Financial Statistics,* 1998

mediation has clearly played a crucial role in many if not most historical financial crises, including the current crisis in the emerging economies of Asia. Also, to many economists it seems a priori obvious that if conventional monetary policy has become ineffective, the reason must be that the troubles of the banks have blocked the usual channels of central bank influence.

A casual look at the data does seem to support the view that the Japanese problem with monetary policy lies in the banks. Table 7 shows developments in high-powered money, broad money, and bank credit since the end of 1994. It is evident that a fairly rapid growth in monetary base has failed to produce an equivalent growth in broad monetary aggregates, and has actually been accompanied by stagnation in bank credit. However, recall the discussion of financial intermediation under liquidity trap conditions in the first part of this paper: given an economy in a liquidity trap, this sort of disconnect between monetary base, aggregates, and bank credit is to be expected even if the banks are financially healthy. It is not evidence that the banks' troubles aggravated the problem.

It is important to realize that Japan has not (yet?) suffered from any widespread run by depositors—in this sense, Japanese banks are like the U.S. thrifts, whose financial woes were widely recognized well before the cleanup began, but whose depositors remained calm because of an underlying government guarantee. As a result, Japanese banks have not been forced into the kinds of fire-sale liquidations of loans, abrupt removal of credit lines, and so forth, that produce a classic bank-centered financial crisis: the kind of crisis that has afflicted its emerging-economy neighbors.

In the absence of a bank run, however, how would one expect a bank of questionable solvency to behave? Would it restrict credit? The text-book answer is just the opposite: as long as an insolvent or near insol-vent bank is able to hold on to deposits thanks to government guarantee, it has an incentive to overlend to risky projects.[24] In effect, the game is "heads I win, tails the taxpayer loses." Indeed, one could argue that since the bubble burst, Japan's financial institutions have actually been in the situation of U.S. thrifts before the crackdown, with the moral hazard of their position creating a bias toward too much rather than too little lending.

This is not merely abstract speculation. Japan has already, in regard to the *jūsen* (nonbank subsidiaries of financial institutions, specializing in housing loans), gone through a miniature version of the systemwide bank cleanup that it must now undertake. According to Thomas Cargill, Michael Hutchinson, and Takatoshi Ito, *jūsen* lending actually grew rapidly in 1990–91, even as asset deflation was underway, "as a result of funds provided by agricultural cooperatives and their prefectural associations."[25] Because these agricultural cooperatives had strong po-litical influence, they were able to take large risks while counting on implicit government guarantees. The result was behavior strongly rem-iniscent of that of the U.S. thrifts. Indeed, Cargill, Hutchinson, and Ito offer a striking example of lending driven by moral hazard in the case of two credit cooperatives that failed in November 1994. The relevant authorities apparently knew that these cooperatives were insolvent more than a year before their actual closure; presumably the management knew considerably earlier. Nonetheless, in the two years before the institutions were closed, both their deposits and their loans expanded rapidly.

How can the logic of excessive lending by banks be reconciled with tales of credit crunch? The immediate answer is that such tales are a very recent phenomenon. An informal search of news archives finds few alle-gations of credit rationing in Japan before the second half of 1997; even well into the fall of that year, a number of observers questioned whether there was really any credit crunch, or at least, whether it was serious. Only by early 1998 did the credit squeeze become widely accepted.

24. This line of argument now plays a major role in discussions of the troubles in the emerging economies of Asia; see McKinnon and Pill (1997); Krugman (1998); Corsetti, Pesenti, and Roubini (1998).

25. Cargill, Hutchinson, and Ito (1997, p. 121).

Paul R. Krugman   177

A review of press reports also makes the reasons for the emergence of credit constraints in late 1997 quite clear. The immediate forcing event was the announcement, in October 1997, of new capital adequacy standards, to be effective from April 1998. To meet this standard, banks began cutting back on loans that would have required larger capital backing. In other words, the financial problems of the banks only became a drag on aggregate demand when the government began half-hearted efforts to come to grips with those problems.

More generally, one can argue that since late 1997, the prospect that the government would eventually seize some but not all banks has created a new incentive for banks near the edge to dress up their balance sheets, in order to make the cut. The payoff to those successful in this endeavor is, loosely speaking, that they will live to make bad loans again; or to say it somewhat differently, they want to stay out of government hands at least for a while, in order to capture the value of the put option implied by government deposit guarantees.

This should all sound familiar to economists in the United States. A mild form of the same ailment appeared in 1990–92, when the size of the savings and loans bailout had become apparent, and it was widely said that commercial banks might be next. As in the Japanese case, the credit crunch appeared not during the years when banks were getting into financial trouble, but when it began to look likely that the government would do something about the situation.

But if the threat of bank closures or seizures is causing a credit crunch that has deepened Japan's slump, why engage in bank reform at all? The answer is that cleaning up bad banks is a *microeconomic* policy, undertaken to remove the distortion in the direction of investment that results from moral hazard—and also to limit the eventual liability of the government, since (as both the U.S. savings and loans case and Japanese experience with credit cooperatives so graphically demonstrate) delay only multiplies the losses. That it might reduce aggregate demand as a side effect is of little relevance. Under normal circumstances, the macroeconomic effects of this or any other move toward microeconomic efficiency that happens to discourage spending can simply be offset with a looser monetary policy. Japan's problem is that because it is in a liquidity trap, the normal disconnect between microeconomic and macroeconomic policy no longer applies.

Policy Options and Their Consequences

Given all that I have said, it is useful to review Japan's policy options and ask how well they would work. Current discussion focuses on three basic alternatives, which are not mutually exclusive.

FISCAL EXPANSION. This is the classic remedy for a liquidity trap and has been pursued by Japan in a sort of stop-go fashion for much of the period since 1992. At the time of writing, the traditional emphasis on public works seems to have given way to a new emphasis on "permanent" tax cuts.

There are two major questions about fiscal expansion as a remedy for Japan, one strictly economic, one political. The economic issue is whether an adequate expansion is possible without creating an unacceptable impact on the government's long-term fiscal position. Much discussion of fiscal stimulus in Japan seems to be predicated on some form of pump-priming (or jump-starting): the idea that a brief period of stimulus will jolt the economy back into a favorable equilibrium. However, there is no good evidence for such a multiple-equilibria view; indeed, Romer has argued that even the historical episode usually invoked in support of that view, the U.S. recovery from the Great Depression, has been misinterpreted.[26] An alternative view is that Japan has a long-term deficiency of demand due to low rates of time preference combined with negative population growth—and also an output gap of 7 percent or more—so that the size and duration of the deficits implied would be very large.[27] If one expects interest rates to stay near zero indefinitely, the level of government debt hardly matters. But if one expects that at a sufficiently distant date real rates will become strongly positive again, the eventual size of that debt becomes an important concern.

The political point is that Japan—like the United States during the New Deal—appears to have great difficulty in working up political nerve for a fiscal package anywhere close to that required to close the output gap. Exactly why this is so is an interesting question, but beyond this paper's scope.

---

26. Romer (1992).

27. A useful indication of the seriousness of the situation in Japan is that ten-year government bond rates are now less than 0.7 percent, suggesting that investors expect the country to be in or near a liquidity trap for at least a decade.

Paul R. Krugman 179

This surely does not, however, mean that fiscal policy should be ignored as part of the policy mix. On the general Brainard principle—when uncertain about the right model, throw a bit of everything at the problem—one would want to apply fiscal stimulus. (Not even I would trust myself enough to go for a purely Krugman solution.) But it seems unlikely that a mainly fiscal solution will be enough.

BANKING REFORM. Japan clearly needs to clean up its financial system. Many commentators seem to believe that this urgent microeconomic step will also make a major contribution to solving the macroeconomic problem. However, as shown above, the financial problems of the banks have until recently biased them toward lending too much rather than too little.

Ironically, indications that the Japanese government is finally getting its nerve up to do something about the banks have probably been a significant factor in the economy's slide over the past year. From a macroeconomic as opposed to microeconomic view, a situation in which the government is expected to start seizing banks but has not yet done so is the worst of all possible worlds. The most important thing is to get on with the job and get it over with. If Japanese authorities behave true to form and carry out bank seizures and closures slowly, initially adopting excessively lenient criteria and only gradually tightening them, credit constraints could be a depressing factor on the economy for years to come.

Moreover, a radical, forceful bank cleanup—which basically settles the issue and leaves the remaining banks reasonably sure that they will not be taken over—would in principle leave the banking system no more willing to lend, and in fact somewhat less so, than it was a year ago. The reason is that until the second half of 1997, at least some banks were driven by moral hazard to take excessive risks in their lending; once the system has been cleaned up, that extra boost to aggregate demand will be gone.

In short, a financial cleanup is vital on microeconomic grounds; and given that it must be done, on macroeconomic grounds it is best done quickly. But it is unlikely to bootstrap Japan out of its liquidity trap.

MANAGED INFLATION. Thanks to the Internet (Nouriel Roubini has become the Matt Drudge of the Asian crisis), proposals that Japan adopt an inflation target as an answer to its liquidity trap have become the subject of widespread, if not always well-informed, discussion. The logic of such an approach is laid out in the first part of this paper. In Japan's case, there would be three main issues: implementation, the appropriate target, and the likely effects.

How can a country in a liquidity trap—that is, where increases in the money supply seem to have no effect—engineer inflation? As I have shown, the problem is essentially one of credibility. If the central bank can credibly commit to pursue inflation where possible, and ratify inflation when it comes, it should be able to increase inflationary expectations despite the absence of any direct traction on the economy by means of current monetary policy. Indeed, if one views monetary policy in terms of nominal interest rates, a credible commitment to inflation can seem to be a pure bootstrap policy: interest rates need never fall; all that is required is a promise not to raise them when the economy expands and prices begin to rise.

How in fact to create these expectations is, in a sense, outside the usual boundaries of economics. However, one obvious suggestion is that Japan deal with its inverted credibility problem through legislation giving the Bank of Japan an inverted version of the price stability targets now in force in a number of countries: it would be enjoined to achieve an inflation rate of not less than x percent over y years. (If this does not work, appendix C discusses several ways in which the necessary inflation expectations might nonetheless be generated.)

And this raises the question of the appropriate inflation target. A key insight is that the objective of the inflation target is not particularly exotic: it is simply to reduce the real interest rate sufficiently to bring the economy back to potential output. Although this real interest reduction must be achieved via inflation, because the nominal interest rate is up against the zero constraint, in other respects it should act just like a conventional monetary expansion. So one can estimate the size of the necessary inflation simply by asking how large a real interest rate reduction would normally be needed to eliminate an output gap as large as Japan's.

One might also note that while the theoretical models of the first part of this paper were cast in terms of a one-period liquidity trap, economists have no real idea of how long a ''period'' is. However, Japan's liquidity trap looks like a fairly long-term problem; also, investment and exchange rates are generally believed to be driven by long-term interest rates. Therefore Japan probably requires a sustained period—

Paul R. Krugman　　　　　　　　　　　　　　181

Table 8. Reduction in U.S. Long-Term Interest Rates That Would Expand Real GNP by 1 Percent
Percent

Model[a]	
DRI	−0.82
EEC	−1.80
LINK	−0.64
MCM	−0.68
MINIMOD	−0.30
OECD	−0.94
TAYLOR	−0.30
WHARTON	−2.70
Summary statistic	
Median	−0.75

Source: Bryant and others (1988).
a. Models are those used in table 1.

at least a decade—of inflation, to reduce the real long-term rate sufficiently to close the output gap.

At this point, matters become difficult. The size of Japan's output gap is highly uncertain, although it is probably well over 5 percent. Worse yet, there is no consensus on the stimulative effect of a given interest rate reduction. As in earlier discussions, it may be useful to look not at the small number of estimates for Japan, but at the larger range of estimates for that other large, relatively closed advanced economy, the United States. Table 8 shows estimates of the reduction in long-term interest rates needed to expand real U.S. GDP by 1 percent, using the various standard econometric models introduced in table 1.

Given the uncertainties, any number is a matter of multiplicative guesswork. I would suggest the following series of leaps of faith: although Japan's current output gap is probably well over 5 percent, the combination of fiscal stimulus and—if all goes well—clarification of which banks will be taken over and which will not, should reduce that gap by several percentage points. Therefore managed inflation would need to close a remaining gap of, say, 4 to 5 percentage points. Looking at the median estimate in table 8, this would require an inflation target of 3 to 3.75 percent. So, to give a bit of extra room (one can always raise nominal interest rates if the economy seems to be overheating—as long as the inflation target is met), how about 4 percent inflation for fifteen years?

This target should not really be taken seriously. Rather, it should serve mainly to stimulate serious research. And there is probably time for such research, since it will take some time before the idea of managed inflation overcomes the instinctive negative reactions of many policymakers.

What side consequences might one expect from such a solution to Japan's slump? In particular, what would happen to the current account and the value of the yen? Recall that a policy of managed inflation is, in principle, simply a monetary expansion by other means. Typical estimates suggest that a monetary policy that expands output by 1 percent leads to a depreciation on the order of 5 percent. So the implied yen depreciation from such a policy would be on the order of 20 to 25 percent—a number that is probably less uncertain than the required inflation rate discussed above, although still more of a stimulus to debate than a serious estimate.

Concluding Remarks

Japan's economic difficulties are widely viewed as essentially political: if only the politicians would bite the bullet, they would get their country moving again. But in fact it has been far from clear what exactly Japan should be doing—which is to say that the problems are not so much political as conceptual.

In this paper I have argued that to understand Japan's problems one needs to revive and modernize the theory of the liquidity trap, a concept that once played a major role in macroeconomics, but has virtually disappeared from economic discourse in the past twenty years. Taking liquidity traps seriously does not, it turns out, require a rethinking of the fundamentals of macroeconomics; liquidity traps can quite easily be generated in basically conventional models that meet the modern criteria of rational behavior and intertemporal consistency. It is even possible to have full-employment, flexible price analyses of the liquidity trap. However, applying conventional modeling to liquidity trap conditions produces unconventional conclusions and policy recommendations. My claim is that strange as they may seem, these conclusions are the best guide available for dealing with Japan's malaise.

Nor is Japan, important as it is, the sole issue. Nobody thought that a liquidity trap could happen in Japan; now that it has, one should wonder whether it could happen elsewhere. Germany and France currently have short-term interest rates of only 3.5 percent, and Europe faces Japanese-style demographics; could a liquidity trap happen to the European Monetary Union? Economists now know that the liquidity trap is not a historical myth: it can and does really happen sometimes, and we had better try to understand it.

APPENDIX A

Financial Intermediation and Monetary Aggregates in a Liquidity Trap

IN THE TEXT, I sketch out how one might think about the role of financial intermediaries and the behavior of monetary aggregates in a liquidity trap. This appendix describes that "cash in advance meets Diamond-Dybvig" approach more fully.

Consider, for simplicity, a full-employment endowment economy that lasts for only two periods, with each individual receiving an endowment y_1 in period one, y_2 in period two. In the aggregate there is no uncertainty; however, each individual is uncertain ex ante about when he will want to consume. The assumed utility function takes the form

$$(14) \qquad U = HU_1(c_1) + (1 - H)U_2(c_2),$$

where H takes on the value 1 with probability π, value 0 with probability $1 - \pi$. So in the population there will be fractions π of first period consumers, $1 - \pi$ of second period consumers.

One wants to make this a cash in advance economy. But finite horizons pose problems for a fiat-money economy, while trying to have an infinite horizon would complicate the simple Diamond-Dybvig-type logic considerably. As a device for sidestepping these problems, assume that each individual is issued with a quantity of money M^* at the beginning, which must be repaid at the end. The government may, however, inject additional money into the economy via open market operations, as described below.

Within each period, consumers must pay in cash before they receive income from selling their own endowments. As in the basic model in the text, they are able to trade cash for bonds at the beginning of the first period (including bonds issued or purchased by the government in open market operations). However, in order to motivate financial intermediaries, assume that a consumer does not know his own type until after the capital market; so he can no longer simply acquire just enough cash for planned purchases within the period.

This is where financial intermediaries come in. Assume that there exist banks which accept deposits during the initial capital market, then allow customers to withdraw their deposits if they turn out to have H equal to 1. (Bank runs are left on one side for this paper!) Deposits earn competitive interest if not withdrawn.

Thus the sequence of events looks like this:

—Consumers come into existence and receive the money supply $M*$.

—A capital market is held; consumers deposit money in banks, and open market operations may increase or decrease the monetary base.

—Consumers learn their type.

—They withdraw their funds if necessary.

—Consumers receive income from sale of their endowment, receive bonds and deposits, and pay or receive whatever tax or transfer is needed.

—Consumers purchase second period consumption.

—They receive income from sales of endowment, and repay their money to the government.

In this setting, the real interest rate is determined independent of the money supply. Each individual gets to spend the present value of his endowment in the appropriate period. Thus a period one consumer will get to purchase units of the good in period one; but since a fraction π of consumers is type one,

$$(15) \qquad \pi[y_1 + y_2/(1 + r)] = y_1,$$

implying that the real interest rate is

$$(16) \qquad 1 + r = \frac{\pi y_2}{1 - \pi y_1}.$$

Assume, provisionally, that the nominal interest rate is positive. Then the behavior of consumers and banks is straightforward. Consumers will borrow, establishing bank accounts equal to Pc_1, the amount they will spend if they are type one; they will hold no cash. Banks, however, need hold only a fraction π of their deposits in reserves and will hold no more than necessary; they lend the rest out (which is how consumers get the money for the deposits). So bank deposits will be a multiple $1/\pi$ of the monetary base; the velocity of base will be 1, that of deposits π. And from here on, the model will work in pretty much the same way as the pure outside money model in the text.

But what happens if the government increases M relative to M^* to such an extent that the nominal interest rate goes to zero—which can clearly happen here, just as in the simple endowment model with no uncertainty. First, consumers become indifferent between holding cash and holding deposits; second, they become indifferent between cash and bonds; finally, banks also become indifferent between cash and bonds. At this point any further open market bond purchase by the government could be absorbed in any combination of three ways: (1) consumers could create new bonds to sell to the government and simply hold extra currency; (2) banks could sell bonds to the government and add the cash to their reserves; (3) consumers could sell bonds to the government instead of borrowing from banks.

It is indeterminate which would happen, since none of these actions has any effect on either real variables or the price level. Action 1 would lead to some increase in common definitions of the money supply; the others would not. Action 3 would lead to an actual decline in bank credit. So as stated in the text, it is actually normal for increases in the monetary base to have little effect on broader aggregates, and even to reduce bank credit, when the economy is in a liquidity trap.

APPENDIX B

Current Account and Real Exchange Rate Consequences of Monetary Expansion

IN THE TEXT, I introduce a simple traded-nontraded good model to discuss the possibility of a liquidity trap despite the possibility of capital movement. In that model a monetary expansion—current money in a positive interest environment or expected future money in a liquidity trap—can raise output of the nontraded good. But what is the impact on the current account? In this model, that question reduces to the question of what happens to traded-good consumption.

One can simplify this issue by starting with an economy in which trade is balanced, and normalizing initial prices of both traded and nontraded goods to one. In that case, one initially has that

$$(17) \qquad \frac{c_T}{c_N} = \frac{\tau}{1 - \tau}.$$

One can further simplify the issue by supposing that the monetary expansion, which leads to an increase in the production and consumption of nontraded goods, is "brief," in the sense that it does not have a significant effect on the country's net investment income from abroad. In that case, one knows that the levels of consumption of both traded and nontraded goods in later periods will be unchanged, and hence also that the marginal utility of each good in later periods will be unchanged. However, the real interest rate on traded goods is given by the world capital market. Hence even in the current period the marginal utility of traded goods will remain unchanged, as

$$(18) \qquad \frac{\partial U}{\partial c_T} = \tau c_T^{\tau(1-\rho)-1} c_N^{(1-\tau)(1-\rho)}.$$

Now suppose that there is a monetary expansion. This will lead to an increase in c_N, which is also the increase in GDP at initial prices. It may also lead to either a fall or a rise in c_T, which corresponds to a move toward current account surplus or deficit. The change in c_T associated with a small rise in GDP can be evaluated as follows. First, note that

$$(19) \qquad \frac{\partial^2 U}{\partial c_T^2} = \tau(\tau(1-\rho)-1)c_T^{\tau(1-\rho)-2} c_N^{(1-\tau)(1-\rho)}$$

and that

$$(20) \qquad \frac{\partial^2 U}{\partial c_T \partial c_N} = \tau(1-\tau)(1-\rho)c_T^{\tau(1-\rho)-1} c_N^{(1-\tau)(1-\rho)-1}.$$

Finally,

$$(21) \quad \frac{\partial c_T}{\partial c_N} = -\frac{\dfrac{\partial^2 U}{\partial c_T \partial c_N}}{\dfrac{\partial^2 U}{\partial c_T^2}} = -\frac{(1-\tau)(1-\rho)}{\tau(1-\rho)-1}\frac{c_T}{c_N} = -\frac{1-\rho}{1-\rho-\dfrac{1}{\tau}},$$

which is the "beggar thy neighbor coefficient" described in the text.

APPENDIX C

Creating Inflation Expectations

SUPPOSE THAT one believes that Japan needs a negative real interest rate on a sustained basis, but also that a pure bootstrapping policy—in which the announcement of an inflation target generates the expansion that eventually creates the inflation—is infeasible. Then Japan should apply some temporary policy that moves the economy to a position where monetary policy does have traction and use that traction to generate sustained inflation.

In this case, the temporary fiscal jolt comes into its own. The strategy would work along the following lines: a large fiscal expansion would be applied, with interest rates kept at zero, and sustained even as the economy began to develop inflation. Ideally, the fiscal stimulus would then be phased out gradually, just slowly enough for rising expectations of inflation to take up the slack. The important point is that monetary policy would have to remain accommodating, not only up to the point of full employment, but as inflation rose to the necessary level.

What kind of fiscal policy would be appropriate? One answer might be an explicitly temporary investment tax credit, which would encourage more or less the same kind of spending as the immediate creation of inflation expectations.

204   *Brookings Papers on Economic Activity, 2:1998*

References

Bernanke, Ben S. 1994. ''The Macroeconomics of the Great Depression: A Comparative Approach.'' Working Paper 4814. Cambridge, Mass.: National Bureau of Economic Research (August).

Bryant, Ralph C., and others, eds. 1988. *Empirical Macroeconomics for Interdependent Economies*, supplemental volume. Brookings.

Cargill, Thomas, Michael M. Hutchinson, and Takatoshi Ito. 1997. *The Political Economy of Japanese Monetary Policy*. MIT Press.

Cooper, Russell, and Dean Corbae. 1997. ''Financial Fragility and the Great Depression.'' Working Paper 6094. Cambridge, Mass.: National Bureau of Economic Research (July).

Corsetti, G., Paolo Pesenti, and Nouriel Roubini. 1998. ''Paper Tigers? A Preliminary Assessment of the Asian Crisis.'' Unpublished paper. New York University.

Diamond, Douglas W., and Philip H. Dybvig. 1983. ''Bank Runs, Deposit Insurance, and Liquidity.'' *Journal of Political Economy* 91(3): 401–19.

Eichengreen, Barry, and Jeffrey D. Sachs. 1985. ''Exchange Rates and Economic Recovery in the 1930s.'' *Journal of Economic History* 45(4): 925–46.

Fleming, J. Marcus. 1962. ''Domestic Financial Policies Under Fixed and Under Floating Exchange Rates.'' *IMF Staff Papers* 9: 369–79.

Frankel, Jeffrey A. 1988. ''Ambiguous Policy Multipliers in Theory and in Empirical Models.'' In *Empirical Macroeconomics for Interdependent Economies*, edited by Ralph C. Bryant and others. Brookings.

Friedman, Milton. 1969. *The Optimum Quantity of Money and Other Essays*. Chicago: Aldine.

Friedman, Milton, and Anna Jacobson Schwartz. 1963. *A Monetary History of the United States*. Princeton University Press.

Fuhrer, Jeffrey C., and Brian F. Madigan. 1997. ''Monetary Policy when Interest Rates Are Bounded at Zero.'' *Review of Economics and Statistics* 79(4): 573–85.

Giorno, Claude, and others. 1995. ''Potential Output, Output Gaps and Structural Budget Balances.'' *OECD Economic Studies* 24: 167–209.

Gordon, Robert J. 1988. ''Back to the Future: European Unemployment Today Viewed from America in 1939.'' *BPEA, 1:1988*, 271–304.

Hicks, John Richard. 1937. ''Mr. Keynes and the 'Classics.' '' *Econometrica* 5(2): 147–59.

Krugman, Paul R. 1998. ''What Happened to Asia?'' Unpublished paper. Massachusetts Institute of Technology.

McKinnon, Ronald I., and Huw Pill. 1997. ''Credible Economic Liberaliza-

Paul R. Krugman 205

tions and Overborrowing.'' *American Economic Review, Papers and Proceedings* 87(2): 189–93.

Metzler, Lloyd A. 1951. ''Wealth, Saving, and the Rate of Interest.'' *Journal of Political Economy* 59(2): 93–116.

Mundell, Robert A. 1963. ''Capital Mobility and Stabilization Policy under Fixed and Flexible Exchange Rates.'' *Canadian Journal of Economics and Political Science* 29(4): 475–85.

Obstfeld, Maurice, and Kenneth Rogoff. 1995. ''Exchange Rate Dynamics Redux.'' *Journal of Political Economy* 103(3): 624–60.

———. 1996. *Foundations of International Macroeconomics*. MIT Press.

Orphanides, Athanios, and Volker Wieland. 1998. ''Monetary Policy Effectiveness when Nominal Interest Rates Are Bounded at Zero.'' Unpublished paper. Board of Governors of the Federal Reserve System (June).

Organisation for Economic Co-operation and Development. 1997. *Economic Surveys: Japan*. Paris.

Romer, Christina D. 1992. ''What Ended the Great Depression?'' *Journal of Economic History* 52(4): 757–84.

Smithers, Andrew. 1998. *Japan's Problems of Debt and Demography*. London: Smithers and Co.

Summers, Lawrence. 1991. ''How Should Long-Term Monetary Policy Be Determined?'' *Journal of Money, Credit, and Banking* 23(3, pt. 2): 625–31.

Temin, Peter. 1976. *Did Monetary Forces Cause the Great Depression?* W.W. Norton.

U.S. Bureau of Economic Analysis. 1973. *Long-Term Economic Growth, 1860–1970*. Department of Commerce.

Wolman, Alexander. Forthcoming. ''Staggered Price Setting and the Zero Bound on Nominal Interest Rates.'' Federal Reserve Bank of Richmond *Economic Quarterly*.

Woodford, Michael. 1998. ''Public Debt and the Price Level.'' Unpublished paper. Princeton University (May).

[5]

BENNETT T. MCCALLUM

Theoretical Analysis Regarding a Zero Lower Bound on Nominal Interest Rates

This paper explores several issues concerning a possible zero lower bound (ZLB) including its theoretical rationale; the magnitude of effects of low sustained inflation on real interest rates; the validity of analyzing monetary policy in models with no monetary variables; and the dynamic stabilizing properties of Taylor rules in a ZLB context. The most important argument, however, is that if the short nominal rate is immobilized at zero, there nevertheless exists a route for monetary stabilization policy to be effective—via the foreign exchange market. Its quantitative importance is examined in a calibrated, optimizing, open-economy model.

THE OBJECT OF THIS PAPER is to explore theoretical issues relating to the idea that there exists a zero lower bound on nominal interest rates and to the possibility that such a bound might interfere with the conduct of monetary policy in an environment of low inflation. The possibility of such an impediment has been mentioned over the years by Vickrey (1954), Phelps (1972), Okun (1981), and Summers (1991); recently it has been analyzed quantitatively by Fuhrer and Madigan (1997), Rotemberg and Woodford (1997), Orphanides and Wieland (1998), Wolman (1998), Reifschneider and Williams (1999), and possibly others. There has been little explicit theoretical analysis, however, the main exception that I am aware of being some work in progress by Woodford (1999).

Interest in the subject of a zero lower bound—which will be abbreviated below as ZLB—has been greatly enhanced in recent years by the success that central banks have had in reducing average inflation rates to the range of 1–3 percent (per annum), and by the failure of Japanese stabilization policy to prevent a prolonged macroeconomic slump in which short-term nominal interest rates[1] have fallen to figures approximating zero. Many writers have suggested, especially in the journalistic literature, that such a situation leaves a central bank helpless to provide macroeco-

The author is indebted to Miguel Casares, Larry Christiano, Marvin Goodfriend, Dale Henderson, Allan Meltzer, Edward Nelson, Athanasios Orphanides, Neil Wallace, Alex Wolman, and Michael Woodford for helpful comments and suggestions.

1. Henceforth, the term "interest rate" should be understood to mean nominal interest, unless the modifier "real" is included or very obviously implied.

BENNETT T. MCCALLUM *is the H. J. Heinz Professor of Economics in the Graduate School of Industrial Administration, Carnegie Mellon University. E-mail:* bm05@andrew.cmu.edu

Journal of Money, Credit, and Banking, Vol. 32, No. 4 (November 2000, Part 2)

nomic stimulus. This point of view has been contested by Goodfriend (1997), Krugman (1999), Meltzer (1999), and others.

The discussion below takes up a number of distinct issues and utilizes a variety of analytical models. It begins in section 1 with a simple but explicit analysis of the source of a possible ZLB on interest rates. Next, section 2 introduces an argument to the effect that most formal analysis has overstated the restrictiveness of the ZLB by failing to recognize forces that tend to raise steady-state real rates of interest when maintained (that is, policy target) inflation rates are lowered. Section 3 returns to models with inflation-invariant steady-state real rates and reconsiders the popular practice of analyzing monetary policy in models with no monetary variables. It is argued that neglect of monetary variables is theoretically inappropriate, but probably not quantitatively important. The main analysis, concerning the effectiveness of monetary policy in a ZLB situation, is put forth in sections 4 and 5. The first of these argues that if the one-period nominal interest rate is for some reason fixed at zero (or some other value), there is nevertheless a route for monetary stabilization policy operating via the foreign exchange market. Then in section 5 the quantitative importance of this stabilization approach is investigated by means of a structural macroeconomic model developed and utilized previously. Section 6 takes up a somewhat esoteric topic concerning dynamic stability analysis and expresses disagreement with some alarming views recently put forth. Finally, section 7 provides a concluding overview. Because of the variety of topics considered, different models are used from section to section. Unfortunately, some accompanying changes in notation are needed, to which the reader should be alert.

1. THE SOURCE OF A ZERO LOWER BOUND

Let us begin with an elementary but explicit analysis of the theoretical basis for the common-sense belief that nominal interest rates cannot be negative. For this purpose it will be useful to consider an extremely simple general equilibrium model that abstracts from uncertainty and sticky prices, both of which will be introduced later in the paper. Thus we imagine an economy populated by a large number of identical (but independently acting) households, a typical one of which seeks at time 1 to maximize the objective function

$$u(c_1) + \beta u(c_2) + \beta^2 u(c_3) + \dots$$

subject to a sequence of constraints for $t = 1,2,\dots.$

$$f(n_t,k_t) - tx_t = c_t + k_{t+1} - (1-\delta)\,k_t + (1+\pi_t)m_{t+1}$$

$$- m_t + (1+\pi_t)\,(1+R_t)^{-1}\,b_{t+1} - b_t + w_t\,(n_t-1)$$

$$+ \psi(c_t,m_t)\,. \tag{1}$$

Here c_t denotes consumption[2] during period t while $y_t = f(n_t, k_t)$ is the output produced by the household from inputs of labor (n_t) and the services of capital (k_t), in
accordance with the well-behaved production function $f(n_t, k_t)$. The economy should
be thought of as one in which there are many distinct goods; households specialize in
production but choose consumption bundles c_t that include many differentiated
goods. As has become well known, the formulation shown can then be justified by
assuming that c_t is a CES index of the various goods while P_t indexes the money
price of one consumption bundle and is appropriately related to the prices of the distinct goods.[3] In (1), tx_t reflects lump-sum taxes net of transfers from the government,
$\pi_t = (P_{t+1} - P_t)/P_t$; m_t is real money balances held by the household at the start of t;
and b_{t+1} is the number of bonds purchased in t, each for the price $(1 + R_t)^{-1}$, and re-
deemed in $t + 1$ for one unit of money.

The final term in (1), $\psi(c_t, m_t)$, reflects the transaction-facilitating properties of
money, that is, the economy's medium of exchange (MOE). Over a range corresponding to normal conditions the function ψ has partial derivatives satisfying
$\psi_1(c_t, m_t) > 0$ and $\psi_2(c_t, m_t) < 0$, but at very low inflation rates the latter inequality
may not hold, as will be discussed shortly. Thus the assumption is that the act of acquiring the many-good bundles consumed during t requires an expenditure of resources on transaction services, in addition to the purchase price of the goods. The
magnitude of this expenditure increases with c_t, but is decreased—at least up to a
point—by larger holdings of real money balances, which make it less likely that their
holder will have to resort to barter or hastily negotiated credit arrangements to effect
desired purchases.[4] There are, of course, other analytical devices for representing
this transaction-facilitating property of the MOE. Quite common are cash-in-advance and money-in-utility-function specifications, and I have often promoted the
"shopping time" approach that expresses transaction requirements in terms of time
rather than tangible resources. By and large, the messages conveyed by most of these
devices are the same.[5] But the resource transaction-cost variant represented in (1) is
somewhat cleaner analytically and so will be utilized throughout most of the present
paper.

Assuming that $f(\ )$, $u(\ )$, and $\psi(\ )$ are such that interior solutions are obtained, the
household's first-order conditions for optimality in the problem stated above include,
for $t = 1,2...$:

---

2. More specifically, c_t is the number of many-commodity bundles consumed during t, as discussed
below.

3. See, for example, the treatments in Rotemberg and Woodford (1997, pp. 308–10), Blanchard and
Fischer (1989, pp. 376–81), or Obstfeld and Rogoff (1996, pp. 236–38, 661–65).

4. There has been a sizeable volume of theoretical work in recent years that seeks to provide a firm mi-
crotheoretic basis for the MOE role of money; leading examples are Kiyotaki and Wright (1989), Lacker
and Schreft (1996), and Wallace (1997). The specification of $\psi(\ )$ used here is intended to serve as a reduced-form shorthand for these analyses, one that is suitable for macroeconomic (but not microeconomic)
issues. The model does not explain which asset society has somehow selected as the MOE, but the discussion presumes that it is paper money issued by a governmentally sponsored central bank.

5. An exception is that the cash-in-advance setup implies an interest-inelastic money demand function.

$$u'(c_t) - \lambda_t[1+\psi_1(c_t,m_t)] = 0 ; \tag{2}$$

$$f_1(n_t,k_t) - w_t = 0 ; \tag{3}$$

$$-\lambda_t + \beta\lambda_{t+1} [f_2(n_{t+1}, k_{t+1}) + 1-\delta] = 0 ; \tag{4}$$

$$-\lambda_t(1+\pi_t) + \beta\lambda_{t+1}[1 - \psi_2(c_{t+1},m_{t+1})] = 0 ; \tag{5}$$

$$-\lambda_t(1+\pi_t)(1+R_t)^{-1} + \lambda_{t+1} \beta = 0 . \tag{6}$$

Here λ_t is the Lagrange multiplier attached to constraint (1). There are also transversality conditions (TCs) pertaining to the household's choice problem. Presuming them to hold, equations (1)–(6) determine optimal time paths for c_t, m_{t+1}, k_{t+1}, n_t, b_{t+1}, and λ_t in response to market- or policy-determined values of w_t, π_t, tx_t, and R_t.

For general equilibrium, we have, in addition to relations (1)–(6), the following:

$$n_t = 1 ; \tag{7}$$

$$m_t = M/P_t ; \tag{8}$$

$$g_t - tx_t = (1+\pi_t) m_{t+1} - m_t + (1+\pi_t) (1+R_t)^{-1}b_{t+1} - b_t ; \tag{9}$$

$$\pi_t = (P_{t+1}-P_t)/P_t . \tag{10}$$

Here (7) and (8) are market-clearing conditions, (9) is the identity that reflects the government's budget constraint, and (10) is the inflation definition mentioned above—all expressed in per-household terms where relevant. We assume that the government—a combination of a central bank that issues high-powered money M_t and a fiscal authority—exogenously determines time paths for the variables g_t, b_t, and M_t. Then the model's ten equations (plus TCs) determine time paths for c_t, m_t, k_t, n_t, λ_t, tx_t, w_t, R_t, P_t, and π_t.

If we were to append the Fisher identity

$$1 + r_t \equiv (1+R_t) (1+\pi_t)^{-1} , \tag{11}$$

then equations (4) and (6) would imply

$$1 + r_t = f_2(n_{t+1},k_{t+1}) - \delta + 1 , \tag{12}$$

that is, that the real rates of return on bonds and capital are equalized. If the model featured uncertainty regarding tastes or technology, then the differing risk characteristics of bonds and capital would introduce a stochastic differential in these returns. We now ask, is there anything in the equations governing market equilibrium in the system at hand that is suggestive of a ZLB on the value of R_t? For an answer, we combine (5) and (6) to obtain

$$1 + R_t = 1 - \psi_2(c_{t+1}, m_{t+1}),\qquad(13)$$

which says that the interest rate R_t equals -1 times the partial derivative of transaction costs with respect to real money balances. The latter may be described as the marginal service yield from holding money balances; thus our condition (13) can also be written as

$$R_t = -P_{t+1}\frac{\partial\psi(c_{t+1}, m_{t+1})}{\partial M_{t+1}}.\qquad(14)$$

This equality is similar to (24) on p. 32 of Friedman (1969), under the assumption that bonds provide no nonpecuniary services to their holders.

From the foregoing it is apparent that any bounds pertaining to R_t are going to be decisively influenced by limits on $\psi_2(c_t, m_t)$. If $\psi_2 < 0$ strictly, then we would have the implication $R_t > 0$. But it seems rather implausible that such would be the case. One would expect to have $\psi_{22} > 0$ over an extended range, so that the marginal service yield on m_t decreases as the quantity of money held grows larger. But at some point, say $m^*(c_t)$, real money holdings would be so large in relation to spending—for example, ten times as large as annual spending flows!—that additional money holdings would not provide any extra services. Then $-\psi_2$ would fall to zero at $m = m^*(c)$. Suppose then, that $\psi(c_t, m_t)$ is such that the relationship between $-\psi_2$ and m_t is (for given c_t) as depicted in Figure 1, top panel. Then with $\psi_2(c_t, m_t) \leq 0$, condition (13) implies $R_t \geq 0$. In this way we obtain, via formal analysis, a ZLB on the one-period interest rate.

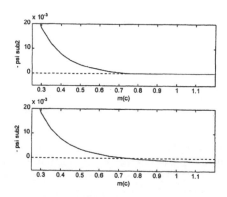

FIG. 1. Alternative Specifications of Transaction Cost Function

Continuing this line of thought, however, it seems apparent that $\psi(c_t,m_t)$ in (1) should be regarded as reflecting transaction services together with any storage costs associated with money. If the economy's MOE were metallic coins or uncoined bullion, then storage costs would clearly be relevant. But even with paper money, which we are presuming to be relevant for the analysis at hand, one can imagine that stocks of money balances could be so large that storage costs at the margin would become non-negligible.[6] In that case Figure 1, bottom panel, would be relevant, and a ZLB on R_t would not be implied. To the author, this case seems most relevant.[7] It is, nevertheless, rather difficult to imagine that such storage costs could permit R_t to be negative by more than a few basis points in any currently conceivable circumstances.

The main point of the foregoing discussion is that the presence or absence of a ZLB on (short-term) nominal interest rates depends upon the properties of the function or constraint of the model that represents the transaction-facilitating properties of the economy's MOE, together with any storage costs necessitated by stocks of the MOE. Strictly speaking, then, it seems to be logically unsatisfactory to discuss the topic of a ZLB in the context of a model that takes no explicit position concerning the properties of $\psi(c_t, m_t)$ or some analogous function that depicts the transaction and storage cost properties of the MOE.

Before proceeding, it will be useful to prepare some background for the next topic by noting one of the steady-state properties of the system at hand. With no population growth and no technical progress, a steady-state equilibrium must have constant values of c_t, y_t, k_t, r_t, and m_t so the rates of growth of P_t and M_t must be equal: the inflation rate must equal the rate of growth of the money stock. But furthermore (4) implies that

$$\lambda = \beta\lambda[f_2(n,k) + 1-\delta] \tag{15}$$

holds in a steady state, so that

$$1/\beta = 1 + \rho = 1 + f_2(n,k) - \delta, \tag{16}$$

that is, that $r = f_2(n,k) - \delta = \rho$. Of course the latter implies via (11) that

$$1 + R = (1+\rho)(1+\pi). \tag{17}$$

If then the rate of money growth μ and inflation were negative and greater in absolute value than ρ, a negative value of R would be implied. Suppose, then, that the central bank were to destroy money at a constant rate $-\mu$ larger than ρ and that the nature of

---

6. With paper money, pure storage costs would depend upon nominal rather than real money balances. But one can construct a relationship such as that of Figure 1 (bottom panel) nevertheless, contingent upon some assumption regarding the composition of bills by denomination. For "storage" costs that reflect insurance or guard services, the relationship would pertain to real balances in any case.

7. For some supportive argumentation, see Thornton (1999).

$\psi(\ )$ is such that $\psi_2(\ ) \leq 0$ so that there is a ZLB on R. It would then appear to be the case that no steady-state equilibrium is possible, when $-\mu > \rho$.

The property just derived should be regarded, in my judgment, as a weakness of the model at hand—a defect due to the model's assumption that the steady-state equilibrium value of r is totally independent of the ongoing inflation rate. This superneutrality property is a useful approximation for thinking about macro-monetary issues, but is a rather special property of models with time-separable, infinite-horizon utility functions for the household agents. Not all well-known models possess this property, however, as we shall review in the next section.

2. REAL-RATE EFFECTS OF INFLATION

The present section considers the possibility that a permanent reduction in the central bank's inflation target—a fall in the long-run average inflation rate—may not sharply reduce the "policy buffer" between the average level of R_t and the ZLB because of an increase in the steady-state real rate, r.[8] The reason is that a decreased pecuniary yield differential between capital and money may induce wealth-holders to allocate a larger fraction of their wealth to money and less to capital. As this occurs, the marginal product of capital will tend to rise, carrying the real yield on paper assets along with it. We need to consider whether such effects can be of quantitative importance.

Effects of this type cannot obtain in the Sidrauski-Brock model of section 1, of course, but can in models in which individuals have finite lifetimes. For our formal analysis, let us for simplicity adopt an overlapping-generations (OG) setup in which agents live for only two periods, keeping in mind that such periods must be thought of as (say) twenty-five years in duration.

Notation for our model is similar, but not identical, to that of McCallum (1987). Thus c_t denotes consumption when young, and x_{t+1} consumption when old, of an individual born in period t. Such an individual's utility function when young is $u(c_t, x_{t+1})$, which we specialize to the separable form

$$u(c_t, x_{t+1}) = v(c_t) + \beta v(x_{t+1}) . \tag{18}$$

Here the discount factor must be recognized to pertain to a period of twenty-five years. Thus for an annual rate of time preference of 0.025, we would have $\beta = (1.025)^{-25} = 0.5394$.

When young, individuals supply one unit of labor inelastically and earn a real wage of w_t. Old individuals cannot work, but can and do operate production processes using capital goods (obtained from their savings when young) and hired labor of youths. Let $y_t = f(n_t, k_t)$ denote output in t of an old producer who has k_t units of capital to use and hires n_t young workers.

8. The policy buffer term is taken from Clouse et al. (1999).

Young individuals can hold their savings $w_t - c_t$ in the form of capital, bonds, or money. Let k_{t+1}, b_{t+1}, and ξ_t denote capital, bond, and real-money holdings at the end of t. Then the young person's budget constraint is

$$w_t = c_t + k_{t+1} + b_{t+1}(1+r_t)^{-1} + \xi_t , \tag{19}$$

and when old in $t+1$ this person will be constrained by

$$x_{t+1} = f(n_{t+1}, k_{t+1}) + (1-\delta)k_{t+1} - w_{t+1} n_{t+1} + b_{t+1} + \xi_t P_t/P_{t+1}$$

$$+ tr_{t+1} - \psi(x_{t+1}, m_{t+1}) . \tag{20}$$

Here $tr_{t+1} = -tx_{t+1}$ denotes lump-sum transfers to an old person in $t + 1$, while money holdings are

$$m_{t+1} = \xi_t P_t/P_{t+1} + tr_{t+1} \tag{21}$$

and $\psi(x_{t+1}, m_{t+1})$ represents transaction costs of consuming in old age. The function ψ has the same general interpretation as in section 1, although it is more strained by the extreme length of a period in the present setting.[9]

Maximization of (18) subject to (19), (20), and (21) yields the following first-order optimality conditions for a young individual:

$$v'(c_t) = \beta v'(x_{t+1}) [f_2(n_{t+1}, k_{t+1}) + 1-\delta]/[1+\psi_1(x_{t+1}, m_{t+1})] ; \tag{22}$$

$$f_1(n_{t+1}, k_{t+1}) = w_{t+1} ; \tag{23}$$

$$v'(c_t) = \beta v'(x_{t+1}) (P_t/P_{t+1})[1 - \psi_2(x_{t+1}, m_{t+1})]/[1+\psi_1(x_{t+1}, m_{t+1})] ; \tag{24}$$

$$r_t = f_2(n_{t+1}, k_{t+1}) - \delta . \tag{25}$$

These plus (19), (20), and (21) determine the individual's choices of c_t, x_{t+1}, k_{t+1}, n_{t+1}, b_{t+1}, m_{t+1}, and ξ_t given exogenous (to the individual) values of w_t, w_{t+1}, tr_t, P_t/P_{t+1}, and r_t.

We assume that population growth proceeds at the rate v, so that $1 + v$ is the number of young persons per old person in each period. Then for general equilibrium, we must have for each $t = 1,2,...$

$$n_t = 1 + v , \tag{26}$$

---

9. It is natural to ask why no such shopping considerations apply to young consumers. For simplicity we assume that they must obtain their goods by barter since they have no assets when born. The cost of conducting barter exchanges should then be included also, but has been omitted for simplicity. It would appear that this omission should not have major misleading effects on the analysis that follows.

$$M_t/P_t = (1+v)\,\xi_t\,,\tag{27}$$

where M_t = money supply per old person in t, after transfers, and the government budget identity

$$P_t(g_t + tr_t) = (1+v)M_t - M_{t-1} + (1+v)P_t b_{t+1}(1+r_t)^{-1} - P_t b_t\,.\tag{28}$$

Assuming that the government sets time paths for g_t (government purchases), M_t, and b_t, the ten listed equations determine equilibrium paths for the variables c_t, x_t, k_{t+1}, n_t, m_t, ξ_t, P_t, tr_t, w_t, and r_t ($t = 1,2,\dots$).[10]
   In a steady-state equilibrium, we have constant values for c, x, m, ξ, k, w, r, b, $\pi = (P_{t+1}/P_t)-1$, tr, and $n = 1+v$. In this context, $r = f_2(1+v, k)-\delta$ and $w = f_1(1+v,k)$. But determination of the value of k is not independent of m and P_t/P_{t+1}. For simplicity, let us eliminate g and b from the model. Then the relevant set of conditions determining k, c, x, and m is

$$v'(c) = \beta v'(x)[f_2(1+v,k) + 1-\delta] \,/\, [1+\psi_1(x,m)]\,;\tag{29}$$

$$v'(c) = \beta v'(x)[1-\psi_2(x,m)] \,/\, [1+\psi_1(x,m)](1+\pi)\,;\tag{30}$$

$$f(1+v,k) + (1-\delta)k = x + (1+v)c + (1+v)k + \psi(x,m)\,;\tag{31}$$

$$f_1(1+v,k) = c + k + m/(1+v)\,.\tag{32}$$

Here equations (29), (31), and (32) include the four endogenous variables c, x, k, and m. Therefore their values cannot be determined without use of (30), where the inflation rate π appears. If we treat π as exogenous—determined by the average growth rate of M—then the monetary authority's choice of π will typically affect the steady-state value of k and therefore r.
   Our objective now is to see whether the effect of π on r is quantitatively large enough to be of policy significance. Thus we need to calibrate the model at hand. For the production function we take $y = A\,n^{.64}\,k^{.36}$ and choose A to yield a realistic value of k/y. In annual terms the latter would be about 3 so, in our setup with twenty-five-year periods, we need k/y in the range of about 0.1–0.2. In equilibrium, $n = 1+v$ so if we take population growth to be 1 percent per year we obtain $n = (1.01)^{25} = 1.2824$. We also want the real rate of interest to be around 2.0–4.0 percent per year. It turns out that together these requirements suggest a value of $A = 20$. For the twenty-five-year depreciation rate, we use $\delta = 0.90$, which implies that about 10 percent of gross output goes to depreciation. For our utility function, an intertemporal

---

   10. In this setup, $m_t = M_t/P_t$ is not assumed but can be shown to be implied by the equilibrium conditions. Also implied is the overall resource constraint $f(n_t, k_t) + (1-\delta)k_t = x_{t+1} + (1+v)c_t + (1+v)k_{t+1} + g_t + \psi(x_t,m_t)$.

elasticity of substitution of 0.25 seems appropriate,[11] so we specify $u(c) = (1-\theta)^{-1}c^{1-\theta}$ with $\theta = 4$, which implies $u'(c) = c^{-4}$.

Turning now to the transaction cost function $\psi(x,m)$, let us suppose that the cost per unit of purchases declines with m/x, according to

$$\psi(x,m)/x = a_1(x/m)^{a2} \qquad a_1, a_2 > 0 . \tag{33}$$

From a relation analogous to (13) we have that the elasticity of money demand with respect to the nominal interest rate equals $-1/(1+a_2)$. To yield a conservatively small value of 0.2, we then set $a_2 = 4$. Finally, to keep the ratio of m to k (or m to y) realistically small, we specify $a_1 = 0.1 \times 10^{-8}$. With these values, we consider annualized inflation rates of 10, 5, 2, 1, 0, -2, -5, and -10 percent. In terms of our twenty-five-year periods, these imply values of π as shown in Table 1. Steady-state values of c, x, k, and m are also reported in Table 1 for these alternative inflation rates. It will be observed that real money balances rise and the capital stock falls as inflation rates are reduced toward zero, and then on into the negative range. The real rate of interest—the marginal product of capital net of depreciation—is shown in the final column in annualized percentage terms. It rises quite slowly with reduced inflation, but climbs more significantly as deflation ranges are encountered. Indeed, in the model at hand, it seems to rise enough to keep the nominal interest rate positive in all cases, even with substantial deflation. That finding accords with the type of effect that this section was designed to investigate.

In quantitative terms, however, Table 1 results are unlikely to provide much reassurance to policymakers concerned with the issue raised by Summers, Okun, and others, which has to do with cyclical stabilization, not the potential infeasibility of sizeable steady-state deflation rates. In that regard, our quantitative results suggest that the increase in the steady-state real interest rate associated with a reduction in inflation from 2 percent to 0 percent (per year) would be negligible. Accordingly, we henceforth ignore the effects of inflation on the average real rate of interest, and re-

TABLE 1
EFFECTS OF INFLATION ON STEADY-STATE REAL INTEREST RATE

Infl.,% pa	π	c	x	k	m	r, % pa
10	9.835	16.39	16.47	6.781	0.178	3.86
5	2.386	16.33	17.21	6.719	0.239	3.89
2	0.641	16.28	17.44	6.672	0.288	3.90
1	0.283	16.26	17.49	6.648	0.308	3.91
0	0.000	16.23	17.53	6.617	0.333	3.93
-2	-0.397	16.14	17.57	6.510	0.408	3.97
-5	- .723	13.72	16.19	3.947	1.958	5.26
-10	- .928	5.86	9.70	0.462	3.261	11.11

11. Virtually identical results were obtained with an elasticity of 0.4, that is, $\theta = 2.5$.

turn to models of the Sidrauski-Brock type in which the steady-state real rate r is invariant to alternative maintained inflation rates.

3. THE ROLE OF MONETARY VARIABLES IN POLICY ANALYSIS

At this point we resume the main line of argument. Much practical monetary policy analysis during recent years has been conducted, as is well known, in models that include no monetary variables whatsoever. Instead, they consist of the three following components: (i) an IS-type relation (or set of relations) that specifies how interest rate movements affect aggregate demand and output; (ii) a price-adjustment equation (or set of equations) that specifies how inflation behaves in response to the output gap and to expectations regarding future inflation; and (iii) a monetary policy rule that specifies each period's settings of an interest rate instrument. These settings are typically made in response to recent or predicted values of the economy's inflation rate and its output gap—as, for example, in the case of a Taylor rule. Examples of such analytical work, stemming from conferences held by NBER and the Sveriges Riksbank (in collaboration with IIES of Stockholm University), are presented in Taylor (1999) and in the June 1999 issue of the *Journal of Monetary Economics* (vol. 43, no. 3). This practice of conducting monetary policy analysis in models with no monetary variables is of particular interest in situations in which interest rates are close to a ZLB. But before turning to that case, it will be useful to consider the absence of monetary variables from a more general perspective.

As a point of reference, let us write out a simple specification of the IS-AS-MP type under discussion.[12] Symbols are basically the same as in section 1, but in addition we let $\bar{y}_t$ be the natural-rate value of y_t, that is, the value that would prevail in the absence of any price stickiness in the economy, and define $\bar{p}_t$ as the associated price level. Also, let v_t and e_t represent shocks to spending and monetary policy behavior. We suppose that $\bar{y}_t$ is generated exogenously, influenced perhaps by the shock v_t. Then the schematic model is given by the following three equations:

$$\log y_t = b_0 + b_1(R_t - E_t\Delta\log p_{t+1}) + b_2(\log g_t - E_t\log g_{t+1})$$

$$+ E_t y_{t+1} + v_t \; ; \tag{34}$$

$$\log p_t - \log p_{t-1} = (1-\alpha)(\log \bar{p}_{t-1} - \log p_{t-1})$$

$$+ E_{t-1}(\log \bar{p}_t - \log \bar{p}_{t-1}) \; ; \tag{35}$$

$$R_t = E_{t-1}\Delta\log p_{t+1} + \mu_0 + \mu_1(E_{t-1}\Delta\log p_{t+1} - \pi^*)$$

$$+ \mu_2(\log y_t - \log \bar{y}_t) + e_t \; . \tag{36}$$

12. Here AS and MP stand for aggregate supply and monetary policy, respectively.

Here (36) is a Taylor-style (1993a) policy rule, with a forward-looking flavor, and (35) is a particular price-adjustment specification that will be discussed below in section 4. For present purposes, our concern is with the IS-type relationship (34) about which we ask: can it be given an adequate theoretical foundation?

In fact, a reasonably satisfactory justification has become quite well known from a number of papers, including Kerr and King (1996), Rotemberg and Woodford (1997), McCallum and Nelson (1999c), and Clarida, Gali, and Gertler (1999), among others. It can be outlined briefly as follows. Consider the optimizing model presented in section 1 and note that equations (4) and (12) can be combined to yield

$$\lambda_t = \beta \lambda_{t+1}(1+r_t) , \tag{37}$$

where λ_t is the shadow value (in utility units) of a unit of output in t while r_t is the real rate of interest. Suppose then that the transaction-cost function $\psi(c_t, m_t)$ is separable, so that its first partial derivative with respect to c_t can be written as $\psi_1(c_t)$. Then using (2) for λ_t we can substitute into (37) and obtain

$$u'(c_t)/[1+\psi_1(c_t)] = \beta u'(c_{t+1})(1+r_t)/[1+\psi_1(c_{t+1})] . \tag{38}$$

Now the latter is a relationship that determines a household's choice of c_t in response to r_t and its expectations regarding c_{t+1}. Taking a log-linear approximation, then, we can obtain[13]

$$\log c_t = b_0' + E_t \log c_{t+1} + b_1' r_t \tag{39}$$

where $b_1' < 0$. In the literature, derivations such as the foregoing have usually been presented in models in which the transaction-facilitating property of money is expressed by including m_t as an argument of the utility function, rather than in the manner involving our transaction-cost approach. But the basic idea is the same. And in either case, a disturbance term will appear on the right-hand side of (39) if there is a serially correlated preference shock appearing appropriately in the utility function.

Next, armed with (39) we make use of the economy's overall resource constraint. A log-linear approximation is written as

$$\log y_t = \omega_1 \log c_t + \omega_2 \log i_t + \omega_3 \log g_t \tag{40}$$

where i_t denotes investment in period t. The weights ω_j sum to 1.0 and reflect average shares of the three components. We substitute (39) into (40) for c_t and solve out $E_t c_{t+1}$ using (40), thereby obtaining

$$\log y_t = b_0 + b_1 r_t + b_2(i_t - E_t i_{t+1}) + b_3(g_t - E_t g_{t+1}) + E_t y_{t+1} + v_t . \tag{41}$$

---

13. For a summary of useful approximation formulae, see Uhlig (1997).

882 : MONEY, CREDIT, AND BANKING

The latter is the "expectational IS function" that we set out to justify. It might be mentioned that applications have often ignored the investment and government spending terms. In the case of investment, that practice is rationalized by treating capital as a fixed constant (for example, Rotemberg and Woodford (1997)) or by treating log investment as an exogenous random walk [McCallum and Nelson (1999c)].[14] If assumed exogenous, government spending can be included easily. Thus we end up with a relation basically equivalent to (34).

At this point let us return our attention to the system (34), (35), (36). If g_t is excluded, or assumed exogenous, then the system is complete in the sense that y_t, p_t, and R_t are the only endogenous variables. To append a money demand function, which could be derived in the model of section 1 by solving (13) for m_{t+1}, would be redundant. The only role of such a function would be to describe the path of the nominal money stock M_t that would be necessary to support the R_t policy rule (36). Including this relation in the model would therefore have no effect on time paths of the variables y_t, p_t, and R_t.

But, of course, it should be clear that this conclusion depends upon the absence of any term involving real money balances in the expectational IS function (34). And that absence depends upon the assumption, inserted provisionally three paragraphs ago, that the transaction-cost function $\psi(c_t, m_t)$ is *separable* in c_t and m_t. An obvious task, then, is to reconsider that crucial assumption. But my own position has already been introduced in section 2, where it is suggested that a plausible specification for $\psi(\ )$ would be of the form

$$\psi(c_t, m_t) = c_t a_1 (c_t/m_t)^{a_2} \tag{42}$$

with $a_1, a_2 > 0$. This function is clearly not separable so the issue becomes one involving quantitative magnitudes. Is the role of real money balances in the IS function likely to be quantitatively important?[15]

To approach that question, let us see how the IS function would be specified under the assumption that (42) is the relevant specification for transaction costs. Then equation (2) can be written (assuming that $u'(c_t) = c_t^{-\theta}$) as

$$\lambda_t = c_t^{-\theta} /[1 + (1+a_2)a_1(c_t/m_t)^{a_2}] \tag{43}$$

and a log-linear approximation would be

$$\log \lambda_t = -\theta \log c_t - \phi(\log c_t - \log m_t), \tag{44}$$

provided that ϕ/a_2 is small relative to 1.0, where $\phi = a_1(1+a_2)a_2(c/m)^{a_2}$.[16] Substitution of (44) into the log of (37) followed by rearrangement yields

14. A formulation with endogenous investment, together with an analysis of the constant-capital assumption, is developed by Casares and McCallum (1999).

15. This is apparently the way that Woodford (1999) views the issue.

16. Here (c/m) is interpreted as a steady-state value. Similar usages appear below, for example, in (46).

$$\log c_t = E_t \log c_{t+1} + (\theta+\phi)^{-1}[\phi(\log m_t - E_t \log m_{t+1}) - r_t - \log \beta]$$

$$+ \textit{disturbance} . \tag{45}$$

Clearly, then, combination of the latter with (40) would result in an IS function like (41) but including an additional term, equal to

$$[(c/y)\phi/(\phi+\theta)](\log m_t - E_t \log m_{t+1}) . \tag{46}$$

In sum, we have found that nonseparability of $\psi(c,m)$ implies that a term involving real money balances appears in the expectational IS function based on optimizing analysis, and if the form of $\psi(c,m)$ is as given in (42) then the additional term can be approximated by expression (46). It is clearly of interest, then, to obtain an idea of the magnitude of the attached coefficient, that is, the term in brackets in (46).

To do so we again draw on the implication that the money demand equation in the model under discussion would be of the form (13), which we now write as

$$R = a_1 a_2 (c_t/m_t)^{1+a_2} . \tag{47}$$

Then an assumed money demand elasticity with respect to R_t of -0.2 would again suggest a value of $a_2 = 4$. To calibrate a_1, let us express R and c/m in units pertaining to annual time periods. Then for R a value of 0.05 would be reasonably appropriate and for c/m a value of 5.[17] These choices yield $a_1 = 0.05/4(5)^5 = 4 \times 10^{-6}$. Also let $\theta = 2.5$. Thus we have $\phi = 20(4 \times 10^{-6})(5)^4 = 0.05$ and $\phi/(\phi+\theta) = 0.05/(0.05 + 2.5) = 0.0199$. Consequently, the coefficient attached to $\log m_t - E_t \log m_{t+1}$ in the IS function is estimated by our calibration exercise to be smaller than 0.02. Of course, there are numerous uncertainties and approximations involved, but the figure obtained seems to be too small to justify any confidence that the effect of real money terms in the IS function would be economically sizeable, contingent upon our basic model specification.

Woodford (1999, Sect. 3.1) suggests a considerably larger number (approximately 0.1) for the comparable slope coefficient, primarily because he assumes a much larger value for the intertemporal elasticity of substitution in consumption.[18] Nevertheless, he concludes that there is no prospect from this source for escape from a liquidity trap situation—one with R_t at a ZLB—because approximations such as those used above break down in the vicinity of satiation with monetary transaction services. Woodford's reasoning seems to be correct, but we will consider the liquidity trap issue more generally in the next section.

First, however, it should be noted that some analysts—most notably Meltzer (1999)—argue that monetary variables cannot legitimately be ignored in policy

---

17. For the latter, we use recent U.S. ratios of consumption to M1.

18. That Woodford uses a money-in-the-utility-function formulation, rather than (42), seems an inessential difference.

analysis because they are related to market outcomes in a manner that does not work through a real-money-balance term in an IS function. Instead, Meltzer argues that the relevant transmission process involves adjustment in the relative prices of assets that are not recognized in simple models such as the ones used here [and by Woodford (1999)]. Of course, Meltzer is correct to say that it is a gross simplification of reality to pretend that economies include only two assets.[19] Whether monetary policy can be used to systematically influence the relevant relative asset prices is, however, an open question.[20] Also, modeling of the relevant transmission process is both necessary and difficult. For one such relative price it does seem clear, however, that there are systematic effects of monetary policy that are both relevant and comprehensible. That argument will be spelled out in the following section.

4. STABILIZING MONETARY POLICY IN A LIQUIDITY TRAP

Probably the most contentious and important topic under consideration is the idea that the potential stabilizing powers of monetary policy can be nullified by the occurrence of a "liquidity trap," that is, a situation in which the central bank's usual policy instrument R_t cannot be lowered past a prevailing ZLB (or possibly some negative lower bound as suggested in Figure 1B). The purpose of the present section is to argue, by means of an expository model, that even in a liquidity trap there is scope for monetary stabilization policy provided that the economy is internationally open—as all actual economies are.[21] Then the argument will be evaluated quantitatively in an optimizing model in section 5.

We begin by specifying a schematic model designed for illustrative purposes. The macroeconomic structure will consist of an open-economy IS sector, with no real-money terms included, a price-adjustment relation, and a monetary policy rule. For the IS sector we have

$$y_t = E_t y_{t+1} + b_0 + b_1(R_t - E_t \Delta p_{t+1}) + b_2(x_t - E_t x_{t+1}) + v_t ; \tag{48}$$

$$x_t = c_1(s_{t-1} - p_{t-1}) + c_2 y_{t-1} . \tag{49}$$

Here (48) is an expectational IS function of the type described above, in which now y_t denotes the log of output, p_t the log of the price level, and x_t the log of net exports.[22] (Please note the *change in notation* relative to sections 1 and 3!) The disturbance term v_t, taken for simplicity to be white noise, reflects taste shocks. As

19. That is the case for the model of this section because (abstracting from uncertainty) capital and bonds are perfect substitutes.

20. In Casares and McCallum (1999) the model includes bonds and capital goods that are not perfect substitutes, because of capital adjustment costs. But their relative prices are not influenced by the systematic component of monetary policy.

21. I am indebted to Edward Nelson for encouraging me to pursue the approach developed in this section and the one to follow.

22. More precisely, x_t is the log of exports minus the log of imports.

suggested by optimizing analysis, $b_1 < 0$ and $b_2 > 0$. In the real interest rate term, R has been written without a subscript so as to reflect the hypothesized liquidity trap situation, that is, that the one-period nominal interest rate R_t is held fixed over time by some force not explicitly modeled but presumed to reflect a ZLB or some such constraint. Relation (49) represents effects of relative prices and incomes on net exports. We treat foreign prices and income as constant, so $s_t - p_t$ represents the modeled economy's (log) real exchange rate, s_t being the log of the domestic price of foreign exchange. We presume, as is quite standard, that $c_1 > 0$ and $c_2 < 0$.[23] A one-period lag is assumed for simplicity, but distributed-lag effects would not fundamentally alter the model. It is necessary, in the present simplified setup, that the effect of $s_t - p_t$ on x_t not be entirely contemporaneous, for reasons discussed below in footnote 25. (No such assumption will be used, however, in the more complete model of section 5.)

Next, regarding price-adjustment behavior we posit that

$$p_t - p_{t-1} = (1-\alpha)(\bar{p}_{t-1} - p_{t-1}) + E_{t-1}(\bar{p}_t - \bar{p}_{t-1}), \tag{50}$$

where $\bar{p}_t$ represents the price that would be market-clearing in the absence of nominal stickiness. With $0 < \alpha < 1$ price level stickiness is implied, however. McCallum and Nelson (1999a) show that (50) is equivalent to the Barro-Grossman-Mussa-McCallum "P-bar" model, which is one of the few sticky-price formulations that implies satisfaction of the natural-rate hypothesis of Lucas (1972). They also show that (50) is equivalent (assuming demand function log-linearity) to the condition

$$E_{t-1}\tilde{y}_t = \alpha \tilde{y}_{t-1}, \tag{50'}$$

where $\tilde{y}_t = y_t - \bar{y}_t$, with $\bar{y}_t$ representing the (log) natural-rate value of output, that is, the value that would prevail with fully flexible prices. Relation (50') can be used instead of (50) in a model, analytical or numerical, to significantly facilitate the analysis.

For simplicity suppose that $\bar{y}_t = \bar{y}$. Then equations (48)–(50) contain the endogenous variables y_t, x_t, s_t, and p_t. We close the system with the following monetary policy rule:

$$s_t - s_{t-1} = \mu_0 - \mu_1(\Delta p_t - \pi^*) - \mu_2 E_{t-1}\tilde{y}_t + e_t \tag{51}$$

where $\mu_1, \mu_2 > 0$. Thus when inflation is low and/or expected output is below its natural-rate value, the rate of depreciation of the exchange rate Δs_t is increased. This is accomplished via central bank purchases of foreign exchange at a pace more rapid than is normal. Such an action reflects expansionary monetary policy, conducted in accordance with the rule (51), designed to stabilize Δp_t toward its target value π^* and

---

23. In the next section, a model is presented in which the import component of (49) is modeled in an optimizing fashion.

$\bar{y}_t$ toward zero (y_t toward $\bar{y}_t$). In (51), e_t represents the unsystematic "shock" component of monetary policy, which we take to be white noise. The constant term μ_0 is set equal to the average real rate of interest, which is $-b_0/b_1$.

The MSV rational expectations solution to the system (48)–(51) can be obtained as follows.[24] Write (49) in first difference form $\Delta x_t = c_1(\Delta s_{t-1} - \Delta p_{t-1}) + c_2(y_{t-1} - y_{t-2})$, and substitute into (48) in place of $E_t \Delta x_{t+1}$. That step yields[25]

$$y_t = E_t y_{t+1} + b_1(R - E_t \Delta p_{t+1}) - b_2 E_t[c_1(\Delta s_t - \Delta p_t) + c_2(y_t - y_{t-1})] + v_t . \quad (52)$$

Then (50), (51), and (52) comprise a system for which the MSV solution is of the form

$$y_t = \phi_{10} + \phi_{11}y_{t-1} + \phi_{12}v_t + \phi_{13}e_t ; \quad (53)$$

$$\Delta p_t = \phi_{20} + \phi_{21}y_{t-1} + \phi_{22}v_t + \phi_{23}e_t ; \quad (54)$$

$$\Delta s_t = \phi_{30} + \phi_{31}y_{t-1} + \phi_{32}v_t + \phi_{33}e_t . \quad (55)$$

Thus we have $Ey_{t+1} = \phi_{10} + \phi_{11}y_t$, $E_t \Delta p_{t+1} = \phi_{20} + \phi_{21}y_t$, and $E_t \Delta s_{t+1} = \phi_{30} + \phi_{31}y_t$ with y_t given by (53). Substitution into (50)–(52) and application of the undetermined coefficients procedure indicates that the solution values (ignoring constants) are as follows, where $\Phi \equiv 1 - \alpha + b_1\phi_{21} + b_2 c_2$:

$$\phi_{11} = \alpha \qquad\qquad\qquad \phi_{12} = 1/\Phi \qquad \phi_{13} = -b_2 c_1 / \Phi$$

$$\phi_{21} = \frac{b_2 c_2(1-\alpha) - b_2 c_1 \alpha \mu_2 - \alpha(1-\alpha)}{b_1 - c_1 b_2(1-\mu_1)} \qquad \phi_{22} = 0 \qquad \phi_{23} = 0$$

$$\phi_{31} = \alpha\mu_2 + \mu_1\phi_{21} \qquad\qquad\qquad \phi_{32} = 0 \qquad \phi_{33} = 1 \qquad (56)$$

Unfortunately, it is not possible to determine the sign of ϕ_{21} or therefore Φ on the basis of the qualitative specification given above. Nevertheless, it can be seen from (56) that as $\mu_1 \to \infty$, that is, as the strength of policy response to $\Delta p_t - \pi^*$ increases without bound, $\phi_{21} \to 0$ and therefore the variance of $\Delta p_t - \pi^*$ goes to zero. Also, as $\mu_2 \to \infty$, $\phi_{21} \to \pm\infty$, so $1/\Phi \to 0$ causing the variability of y_t relative to $E_{t-1}y_t = \alpha y_{t-1}$ to approach zero. So the exchange-rate-based stabilization rule (51) possesses policy effectiveness. The extent to which this is quantitatively significant will be explored, in a somewhat larger model that is realistically calibrated, in the following section.

---

24. Here MSV stands for "minimum state variable." For a recent discussion that characterizes the MSV solution as the solution that excludes "bubble" components, together with the exposition of an algorithm that yields the unique MSV solution in a very broad class of linear models, see McCallum (1999b).

25. Here it can be seen why a purely contemporaneous version of (49) is unsatisfactory in the present setup: it would introduce $E_t \Delta p_{t+1}$ rather than Δp_t into (52), and then Δp_t would appear nowhere in the system.

Before turning to that exploration it will be appropriate to provide some additional discussion concerning the nature of policy rule (51). First, is such a rule feasible? Is it possible, that is, for a central bank to control an economy's nominal exchange rate under liquidity trap conditions, with (domestic) agents satiated with the transaction-facilitating services of money and a short-term nominal interest rate equal to zero? In that regard it must be noted that, in a model of the type under discussion, the left-hand-side variable in the policy rule is not literally an instrument but rather an indicator variable. Assuming that the model applies to quarterly or monthly time periods, that is, the value of Δs_t on the left-hand side of (51) can be viewed as an intermediate "operating target" to be obtained by day-to-day or hour-by-hour manipulation of other tools (for example, open-market purchases) serving literally as the central bank's instrument. The issue, then, is whether a central bank can, based on virtually continuous observation of its exchange rate s_t, push it in the desired direction? There are limits to how far a central bank can reduce s_t, that is, appreciate its currency, since it will always hold at most a finite stock of foreign exchange reserves. But depreciation, that is, upward movement of s_t, is the crucial requirement in the situation under discussion. And it seems clear that there would be no economic limit to the upward movement of s_t that could be engineered by central bank purchases (with high-powered money) of foreign exchange.[26]

The idea that s_t can be used as an instrument variable (in the relevant sense) is not a new one. For a number of years, for example, economists associated with the Reserve Bank of New Zealand (RBNZ) used s_t as the instrument variable in analytical descriptions of RBNZ policy; see, for example, Grimes and Wong (1994) or Hansen and Margaritis (1993). Alternatively, Ball (1999), Gerlach and Smets (1999), and others have described the use by several countries of a "monetary conditions index" as an instrument variable. There are various definitions of a monetary conditions index (MCI), but those that I have seen all feature measures that in some fashion combine a short-term interest rate and an exchange rate. One plausible, dimensionally coherent definition would be

$$mci_t = \omega R_t - (1-\omega)\Delta s_t .\tag{57}$$

Clearly, in a ZLB situation this mci_t measure would reduce to use of a Δs_t instrument, as specified in (51). Thus there seems to be significant practical evidence of two types, as well as a priori reasoning, to support the hypothesis that use of a Δs_t instrument is feasible. Nevertheless, more discussion will be provided, immediately.

In the model presented above, there are two nonstandard features. The first is that R_t is held fixed at $R_t = 0$; that feature is imposed so as to address the issues concerned with monetary policy in a ZLB situation. The second feature is that the model apparently does not include a relationship reflecting uncovered interest parity (UIP). In that regard, most analysts (including myself) would normally include UIP as one

---

26. Of course, there might be political limits, but that is a different matter altogether, outside the scope of the present paper.

component of an open-economy macroeconomic model—despite the existence of mountains of empirical evidence that are, at least on the surface, strongly inconsistent with UIP on a quarter-to-quarter basis.[27] So how is UIP avoided here? The answer is as follows.

It is well known that, to be consistent with the data, UIP relations must include a discrepancy term, typically referred to as a risk premium. Thus UIP in empirical models is typically expressed as

$$R_t - R_t^* = E_t \Delta s_{t+1} + \xi_t, \tag{58}$$

where the risk premium ξ_t has a large variance relative to shock terms and furthermore is serially correlated.[28] Recently it has been common practice to treat ξ_t as generated exogenously, but there are theoretical reasons for believing that it would be related to the relative amounts of outside domestic and foreign nominal liabilities outstanding. For example, a hypothesis widely entertained during the 1970s might be expressed as

$$\xi_t = \lambda[B_t - (B_t^* - s_t)] + \zeta_t \tag{59}$$

where B_t and B_t^* are logs of domestic and foreign government debt (including base money) and ζ_t is an exogenous stochastic shock term. Substituting and recognizing that lags could be involved, we then write

$$R_t - R_t^* = (E_t s_{t+1} - s_t) + \lambda (L)[B_t - B_t^* + s_t] + \zeta_t, \tag{60}$$

which is similar to equations prominent in several older writings of Dornbusch (for example, 1980, p. 169, and 1987, p. 7). This "portfolio balance" hypothesis has receded from its earlier prominence because empirical studies by Frankel (1982, 1984), Dooley and Isard (1983), and others failed to find empirical support. But it seems implausible to believe that no such relation obtains in fact, that is, that ξ_t is totally unaffected by the $B_t - B_t^*$ variable. And if such a relation does obtain, then our procedure above is fully justified. For (60) indicates that even with $R_t = R$, s_t can be affected by purchases of foreign exchange since they alter the value of $B_t - B_t^*$. Yet the precise specification of relation (60) need not be known, and the relation need not be included in the model, for exactly the same reason that money demand functions are not needed in analyses that presume use of an interest rate instrument. Thus appending (60) to the model (48)–(51) would have no effect on the implied behavior of Δp_t, x_t, y_t, or Δs_t; it would merely specify the magnitude of open-market purchases of foreign exchange needed to implement the Δs_t policy rule (51).

27. A standard reference is Lewis (1995). For data averaged over long time periods, see Flood and Taylor (1997).

28. In McCallum and Nelson (1999b), the variance is by far the largest of any exogenous disturbance and the process is an AR(1) with coefficient 0.5. These values were taken from evidence in Taylor (1993b).

BENNETT T. McCALLUM : 889

Still another way of expressing the argument is as follows. Suppose that policy rule (51) is relevant but the economy is not in a liquidity trap. Then let strict UIP be included as part of the model and note that R_t is determined endogenously. In that determination of R_t, the UIP relation plays a major role—one might say that UIP is the "proximate determinant" of R_t. Next suppose that the economy in question has a fixed nominal exchange rate. Then $E_t \Delta s_{t+1} = 0$ in all periods so the UIP condition implies that the home-foreign interest rate differential is constant over time; in that case the home country's central bank has no influence on R_t, not even temporarily. Most practical analysts would not, however, accept that conclusion. Instead they would view this lack of influence over R_t as a medium-term tendency, and would contend that on a month-to-month or quarter-to-quarter basis the central bank can influence R_t, keeping it temporarily high or low relative to the relevant foreign rate. But that contention implies that strict UIP does not hold on a period-to-period basis. Instead the home-foreign interest differential can be temporarily influenced by policy actions of the central bank as suggested by formulation (60).[29] Some evidence supportive of this position has been provided by Stockman (1992).

5. QUANTITATIVE APPLICATION

Our objective now is to provide quantitative support for the position developed in the previous section, viz., that a policy feedback rule with an exchange rate instrument can provide macroeconomic stabilization in a situation in which interest rate manipulation is infeasible because of a ZLB. The basic research strategy is to adopt a quantitative open-economy macroeconomic model, alter the policy rule so as to use Δs_t rather than R_t as the left-hand-side instrument or indicator variable, and impose the constraint that $R_t \equiv 0$. The latter step requires that some relationship in the model be ignored to avoid over-determination of the endogenous variables; the relationship that we ignore is UIP.

The model to be used here as a starting point is the small-scale, open-economy, quarterly model based on explicit optimizing analysis that is developed by McCallum and Nelson (1999b). It has been utilized subsequently—together with an additional variant—by McCallum (1999a); the next three paragraphs constitute an adaptation of descriptive material taken from the last-mentioned paper.

Basing one's analysis on the assumption of explicit optimizing behavior by the modeled individuals in a general equilibrium setting is obviously not sufficient—and perhaps not necessary—for the creation of a structural model that is specified with reasonable accuracy relative to economic reality. The optimizing general equilibrium approach can be very helpful in this respect, however, since it eliminates potential internal logical inconsistencies that are possible when this source of intellectual discipline is absent. The model at hand, henceforth termed the M-N model, has a simple basic structure since it depicts an economy in which all individuals are infinite-lived and alike. As with many recent models designed for policy analysis, it assumes that goods prices are "sticky," that is, adjust only slowly in response to changes in conditions. It differs from many previous efforts in this genre, however, in three ways. First, the gradual price-adjustment specification satisfies the strict version of the natural-rate hypothesis. Second, the modeled economy is open to international trade of goods and securities. And, third, individuals' utility functions do not feature time separability, but instead depart in a manner that reflects habit formation.

This last feature is specified as follows. A typical agent desires at t to maximize $E_t(U_t + \beta U_{t+1} + \ldots)$, where the within-period measure U_t is specified as

$$U_t = \exp(v_t)(\sigma /(\sigma -1))[C_t/C_{t-1}{}^h]^{(\sigma-1)/\sigma} + (1-\gamma)^{-1}[M_t/P_t]^{1-\gamma}. \tag{61}$$

Here C_t is a CES consumption index, M_t/P_t is real domestic money balances, v_t is a stochastic preference shock, and h is a parameter satisfying $0 \leq h < 1$. With $h = 0$, preferences feature intertemporal separability, but with $h > 0$ there exists "habit formation" that makes consumption demand less volatile.

The open-economy aspect of the model is one in which produced goods may be consumed in the home economy or sold abroad. Imports are exclusively raw materials, used as inputs in a production process that combines these materials and labor according to a CES production function. Capital accumulation is not modeled endogenously, but securities are traded internationally. The relative price of imports in terms of domestic goods, that is, the real exchange rate, affects the demand for exports and imports, the latter in a explicit maximizing fashion. Nominal exchange rates and the home country one-period nominal interest rate are related in the M-N model by a version of uncovered interest parity that realistically includes a stochastic and highly variable "risk premium" term [as in Taylor (1993b) and many multi-country econometric models]. That relationship is not included, however, in the present application.

Price adjustments conform to the P-bar model, mentioned above, but with capacity output $\bar{y}_t$ now treated as a variable that depends upon raw material inputs and the state of technology, the latter driven by an exogenous stochastic shock that enters production in a labor-augmenting fashion.[30] As mentioned above, price-adjustment behavior implies $E_{t-1}\tilde{y}_t = \alpha \tilde{y}_{t-1}$, so application of the unconditional expectation operator yields $E\tilde{y}_t = \alpha E\tilde{y}_t$, and with $\alpha \neq 0$ this implies $E\tilde{y}_t = 0$ regardless of the monetary policy rule employed. This strict natural-rate property is not a feature of the Calvo-Rotemberg or Fuhrer-Moore models of price adjustment. Indeed, there are very few sticky-price models that have the natural-rate property, the only other one that I know of being Gray-Fischer style nominal contracts that imply limited persistence of $\tilde{y}_t$ magnitudes.

The foregoing paragraphs should provide the reader with a broad qualitative overview of the basic M-N model. Quantitatively, the model is calibrated by refer-

---

30. As mentioned above, we treat capital as exogenously determined.

ence to empirical relationships estimated in various studies with U.S. data.[31] In terms of openness, a crucial consideration in the present context, the U.S. economy is of course quite similar to Japan or to Euroland (that is, the members of the European monetary union). For a complete description of the model, the reader may consult McCallum and Nelson (1999b), with an additional price-adjustment variant described in McCallum (1999a).[32]

Our objective now is to combine the M-N model with policy rule (51),[33] generate rational expectations solutions, and then characterize the effects of monetary policy on the behavior of inflation and the output gap $\tilde{y}_t$. In considering policy effects, we shall devote some attention to the unsystematic (shock) component e_t, but will place more emphasis on the systematic part of policy behavior since in practice it accounts for most of the variability of policy instruments.[34] In this analysis use will be made of impulse response functions and also stochastic simulations. In these simulations, all constant terms are set to equal zero—a standard practice in work of this type—so the standard deviation of Δp_t can be interpreted as the root-mean-square-error (RMSE) value of $\Delta p_t - \pi^*$ and the standard deviation of $\tilde{y}_t$ as the RMSE value of $y_t - \bar{y}_t$. In all cases, the reported magnitudes are mean values (of standard deviations) averaged over one hundred replications, with each run pertaining to a sample period of two hundred quarters (after fifty-three start-up periods are discarded). Calculation of the RE solutions are conducted using the algorithm of Paul Klein (1997).

A first set of results is presented in Table 2. There for each μ_1, μ_2 combination, the three reported values are standard deviations of Δp_t, $\tilde{y}_t$, and Δs_t, respectively. Going down each column we see that increases in the feedback policy coefficient μ_1 serve to decrease the variability of inflation around its (implicit) target value. Similarly, in each row we see that increases in μ_2 typically decrease the variability of $\tilde{y}_t$, although not strongly in the region $0 < \mu_2 < 1$. Simultaneously, increases in μ_2 serve to increase the variability of inflation over most of the range considered. Thus it is clear that the systematic component of monetary policy is relevant for inflation and output gap stabilization in the ZLB situation under analysis, much as is the case with more familiar policy rule studies.

A more graphic way to represent the stabilizing effects of the policy rule is by means of impulse response functions. Several figures presented below plot responses of y_t (not $\tilde{y}_t$), p_t, Δp_t, q_t, s_t, and R_t to a unit realization of various shocks appearing in the system.[35] In Figure 2A, responses to a unit realization of the v_t taste shock [see equation (61)] are reported for policy rule parameter values of $\mu_1 = 1$ and $\mu_2 = 1$. In Figure 2B the experiment is the same except that μ_1 is increased to ten, reflecting a

---

31. Notably, the value of 0.8 for h in (61) was estimated by Fuhrer (1998).

32. One small change effected in the latter reference and utilized here is to use 0.95 rather than 1.00 for the autoregressive coefficient in AR(1) processes generating technology and foreign income shocks.

33. For the standard deviation of the policy shock term e_t, I have used 0.01. This is much larger than is estimated for actual policy rules with an R_t instrument, but is only one-fourth as large as standard deviations of Δs_t for major economies under current policy regimes.

34. For an argument to this effect—but presuming an interest rate instrument—see McCallum (1999a).

892 : MONEY, CREDIT, AND BANKING

TABLE 2

SIMULATION RESULTS WITH BASIC MODEL
Standard Deviations of Δp_t, $\bar{y}_t$, and Δs_t

Value of μ_2	0.0	0.5	1.0	5.0	10.0
Value of μ_1					
0.0	2.19	2.00	2.55	8.36	12.25
	1.53	1.48	1.42	0.97	0.68
	3.98	4.05	4.16	5.91	7.31
0.5	1.46	1.26	1.53	5.57	8.64
	1.59	1.52	1.44	1.09	0.81
	4.06	4.14	4.17	5.15	6.20
1.0	1.12	0.93	1.04	4.00	6.63
	1.53	1.53	1.45	1.14	0.92
	4.18	4.17	4.25	5.07	6.21
5.0	0.47	0.38	0.33	1.09	2.16
	1.59	1.53	1.53	1.36	1.24
	4.67	4.61	4.61	4.85	5.81
10.0	0.29	0.24	0.21	0.53	1.14
	1.54	1.53	1.54	1.43	1.37
	4.92	4.91	4.86	4.84	5.30

much stronger monetary policy reaction to departures of inflation from its target level. A comparison of the lower left-hand panels of these two figures shows that the response of inflation to the shock is greatly muted by the stronger policy reaction represented in the second case. Also, the middle right-hand panels reveal clearly the stronger reaction of the Δs_t instrument in this case.

Some readers may be surprised by the negative response of p_t to a positive realization of v_t. There is no clear-cut reason to believe that anything is logically amiss in the model, for the behavior of p_t to a real shock in any dynamic optimizing framework depends in subtle ways on details of the specification.[36] There are, however, some aspects of the model at hand that are not fully consistent with the time series properties of important macroeconomic variables. Most prominent of the failures, perhaps, is the rather small amount of inflation persistence in the basic M-N model.[37] In McCallum (1999a), this problem is attacked by replacing the P-bar price-adjustment relation (53) with the following:

$$\Delta p_t = 0.5 \, E_t \, \Delta p_{t+1} + 0.5 \, \Delta p_{t-1} + \alpha_1 \bar{y}_t + u_t \,. \tag{62}$$

35. Here and below q_t denotes the log of the real exchange rate.

36. In the present model, the response of Δp_t to $v_t > 0$ would be positive if v_t were an AR(1) process with autocorrelation coefficient of 0.5.

37. There is some persistence of Δp_t shown in Figure 2, which is not the case for several prominent models with sticky price levels (see Nelson 1998), but not much.

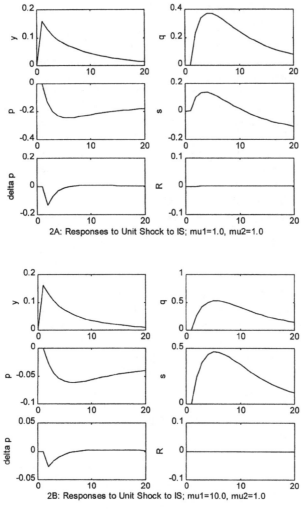

FIG. 2. Impulse Responses to IS Shock, Basic Model

The latter, which is similar but not identical to the specification of Fuhrer and Moore (1995),[38] imparts a good bit of persistence to the inflation process as can be seen readily from the lower left-hand panels in parts A and B of Figure 3.

Table 3 and Figures 3A and 3B report results analogous to those presented previously for the M-N model with the P-bar price-adjustment relation. In the version with (62) replacing (53) the qualitative conclusions are much the same: the variability of π_t and $\tilde{y}_t$ is smaller with larger values of μ_1 and μ_2, respectively. The figures in Table 3 suggest that inflation variability is quite weakly responsive to μ_1, but the main reason for this finding is that a sizeable fraction of the inflation variability is directly due to the presence of the u_t shock term in the price-adjustment rule (62). That component of the variance of Δp_t is only slightly affected by policy. The standard deviation of the output gap, by contrast, appears slightly more responsive to μ_2 in Table 3 than in Table 2.

Figures 3A and 3B present impulse response functions for cases analogous to those in Figures 2A and 2B, that is, cases with $\mu_1 = 1$ and $\mu_1 = 10$, respectively ($\mu_2 = 1.0$ in both cases). The lower left-hand panels show that the muting of Δp_t responses to this particular taste shock is quite slight, although definitely perceptible. The exchange rate (instrument) reactions are, of course, much larger in the part B panels Of most interest in these figures, probably, are the inflation responses—for two reasons. First, inflation now rises in response to a positive v_t realization, in contrast with Figure 2. Second, the shape of the impulse response function suggests that there is considerable persistence of inflation in the model at hand—which in fact there is.

TABLE 3

SIMULATION RESULTS IN MODEL WITH EQUATION (62)
Standard Deviations of Δp_t, $\tilde{y}_t$, and Δs_t

Value of μ_2	0.0	0.5	1.0	5.0	10.0
Value of μ_1					
0.0	3.56	3.68	3.78	4.55	5.16
	2.83	2.32	1.96	1.48	1.58
	4.00	4.16	4.42	8.13	15.26
0.5	3.52	3.48	3.66	4.37	4.83
	2.90	2.37	2.13	1.46	1.44
	4.29	4.38	4.66	8.35	14.59
1.0	3.42	3.45	3.39	4.20	4.60
	2.88	2.51	2.14	1.49	1.39
	4.99	5.09	5.27	8.88	14.57
5.0	3.13	3.10	3.10	3.39	3.78
	3.37	3.24	3.04	2.14	1.64
	13.72	13.56	13.42	14.34	16.81
10.0	2.82	2.92	2.85	3.02	3.30
	3.80	3.87	3.60	2.85	2.24
	23.41	23.87	23.15	21.93	22.19

38. The present implementation follows McCallum (1999a) in setting $\alpha_1 = 0.0032$ and $\sigma_u = 0.002$.

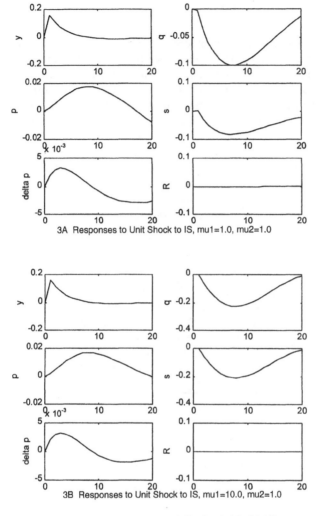

FIG. 3. Impulse Responses to IS Shock, Model with (62)

896 : MONEY, CREDIT, AND BANKING

To conclude this section, let us turn to the unsystematic component of monetary policy—that is, e_t shocks. The results are shown in Figures 4 and 5, the former pertaining to the basic M-N model and the latter to the variant with price-adjustment equation (62). Part A of each figure has $\mu_1 = 1.0$, $\mu_2 = 1.0$ and part B has $\mu_1 = 10.0$, $\mu_2 = 1.0$. In these figures we see that the strength of policy reaction to $\Delta p_t - \pi^*$ has

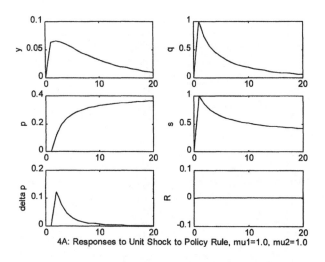

4A: Responses to Unit Shock to Policy Rule, mu1=1.0, mu2=1.0

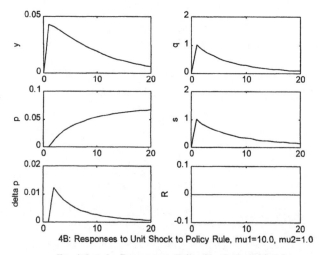

4B: Responses to Unit Shock to Policy Rule, mu1=10.0, mu2=1.0

FIG. 4. Impulse Responses to Policy Shock, Basic Model

a major effect on the responses of both inflation and also the output gap, with larger values of μ_1 reducing Δp_t responses sharply and y_t responses considerably. Again, incidentally, inflation persistence shows up as a property of the model with (62). All in all, our quantitative results support the proposition that monetary policy can be effectively stabilizing even with R_t frozen in a liquidity trap.

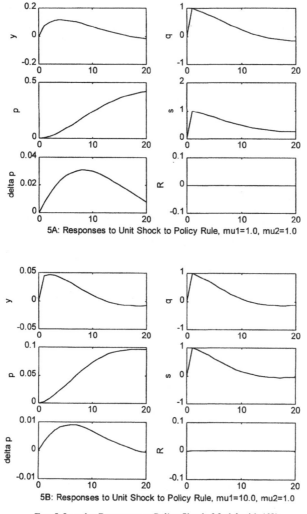

FIG. 5. Impulse Responses to Policy Shock, Model with (62)

898 : MONEY, CREDIT, AND BANKING

6. ISSUES REGARDING DYNAMIC ANALYSIS

In this section the object is to consider some slightly esoteric issues concerning dynamic analysis. This discussion is included because several writers—for example, Benhabib, Schmitt-Grohë, and Uribe (1998), Krugman (1999), and Reifschneider and Williams (1999)—have suggested that recognition of the existence of a ZLB has drastic effects on the dynamic properties of models that include interest rate policy rules such as the Taylor rule. It is my own belief that these particular effects represent theoretical curiosa that are not relevant for practical policy analysis, even granting the possibility of a ZLB-induced liquidity trap.[39]

The argument here will be conducted in the context of a simple example. To maintain some continuity in the face of the various topics considered in this paper, let us adopt the model of section 3, but simplified by elimination of government purchases and stochastic shocks.[40] Also, we now use notation such that y_t and p_t represent *logs* of output and the price level. Finally, and merely for simplicity, we let $\mu_2 = 0$ in the Taylor rule, making it one of the inflation-targeting variety. With those amendments, the model (34)–(36) can be written as

$$y_t = E_t y_{t+1} + b_0 + b_1 (R_t - E_t \Delta p_{t+1}) \tag{63}$$

$$\Delta p_t = (1-\alpha) (\bar{p}_{t-1} - p_{t-1}) + E_{t-1}(\bar{p}_t - \bar{p}_{t-1}) \tag{64}$$

$$R_t = -b_0/b_1 - \mu_1 \pi^* + (1+\mu_1)\Delta p_t . \tag{65}$$

Thus we have, as in section 3, an expectational IS function consistent with optimizing behavior, a price-adjustment relation that features some inflation persistence yet satisfies the natural-rate hypothesis, and a policy rule that is designed to stabilize inflation around the target value π^*.

Before seeking a rational expectations solution, we again express (64) as

$$E_{t-1}y_t = \alpha y_{t-1} \tag{53''}$$

and combine (63) with (65) as follows:

$$y_t = E_t y_{t+1} + b_1[(1+\mu_1)\Delta p_t - \mu_1 \pi^* - E_t \Delta p_{t+1}] . \tag{66}$$

In this system (53''),(66) there is only one relevant state variable, y_{t-1}, so the unique "bubble-free" or "fundamentals" MSV solution will be of the form

$$y_t = \phi_{10} + \phi_{11} y_{t-1} \tag{67}$$

---

39. It should be unnecessary to mention that many accomplished theorists are likely to disagree with my views on this particular issue.

40. This streamlining is irrelevant for the issues at hand.

BENNETT T. McCALLUM : 899

$$\Delta p_t = \phi_{20} + \phi_{21} y_{t-1} \tag{68}$$

and it is clear from (53″) that $\phi_{10} = 0$ with $\phi_{11} = \alpha$.[41] Substitution of $E_t y_{t+1} = \alpha(\alpha y_{t-1})$ and $E_t \Delta p_{t+1} = \phi_{20} + \phi_{21}(\alpha y_{t-1})$ into (66), followed by application of the undetermined coefficients (UC) logic, yields the following solution for inflation:

$$\Delta p_t = \pi^* + [\alpha(1-\alpha)/b_1(1+\mu_1-\alpha)]\, y_{t-1}\,. \tag{69}$$

Thus Δp_t equals π^* on average and would fluctuate around that value if stochastic shocks were included in the system.

Suppose, however, that in obtaining a solution the analyst specified that Δp_{t-1} is a relevant state variable, even though it appears nowhere in the system (63), (53″), (65). Then instead of (68) we would have

$$\Delta p_t = \phi_{20} + \phi_{21} y_{t-1} + \phi_{22} \Delta p_{t-1}\,. \tag{70}$$

Again (53″) would imply that $y_t = \alpha y_{t-1}$, but application of the UC procedure would now imply that the solution value for ϕ_{22} is either 0 or $1+\mu_1$. Thus for Δp_t we would obtain either the same solution as before, equation (69), or else

$$\Delta p_t = -\,\mu_1 \pi^* - [(1-\alpha)/b_1]\, y_{t-1} + (1+\mu_1)\Delta p_{t-1}\,. \tag{71}$$

The latter gives π^* as the steady-state value of inflation (when $y_t = 0$ and $\Delta p_t = \Delta p$), but with $\mu_1 > 0$ as suggested by Taylor the dynamic behavior of Δp_t would be explosive. If the system "begins" with $\Delta p_{t-1} > \pi^*$, inflation will increase explosively; if the initial value is less than π^*, then it will approach $-\infty$, according to (71).[42]

In the absence of a ZLB, $\Delta p_t \to -\infty$ would be ruled out as a solution path in a complete version of the model because it would violate a transversality condition necessary for optimizing behavior. But with recognition of a ZLB, it becomes apparent that inflation cannot behave as specified by (71) when the ZLB is encountered. Instead, the outcome is that Δp_t approaches the negative value $b_0/b_1 = -\bar{r}$, which corresponds to $R_t \to 0$. Thus the Taylor rule has, in this case, failed to stabilize inflation around its target value.[43] For a graphical representation, see Figure 6, which is—so as to permit a two-dimensional diagram—drawn for the special case with complete price flexibility (that is, $y_t = 0$). If the system begins with an initial inflation rate below π^*, it will approach $-\bar{r}$ in an oscillatory fashion. In the absence of the ZLB, by contrast, inflation would approach $-\infty$ according to (71) so a transversality condition that ruled out such a path would lead the analyst back to (69).

---

41. It should be emphasized that y_t would not be policy-invariant if the system included stochastic shocks.

42. Here the word "begins" is put in quote marks because the MSV approach suggests that any beginning or initial value is irrelevant.

43. Related problems are emphasized, in a limited-participated model, by Christiano and Gust (1999).

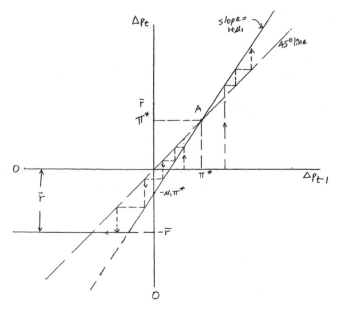

FIG. 6. Inflation Dynamics in Model (63)-(65)

My own conclusion is quite different. It is that the last ZLB solution is not economically relevant.[44] It is a bubble solution that results from designating Δp_{t-1} as a relevant state variable even though it does not appear in the system (that is, is in my terminology a redundant state variable). It is my belief that emphasis on such bubble or non-fundamental solutions constitutes a perversion of the original objectives of rational expectations analysis.[45] But in any event it can be noted that the MSV solution (69), which clearly is a RE solution to the model at hand, is entirely well behaved so long as $\pi^* > b_0/b = -\bar{r}$. In Figure 6 this solution implies that Δp_t is determined at point A in each period. With $y_t = 0$, there are no dynamic adjustments—which is natural since there are no shocks and no relevant state variables other than y_{t-1} (which equals zero in Figure 6, though not in the more general case considered algebraically).

Furthermore, it should also be noted that the non-MSV solution (71) implies that inflation explodes toward $+\infty$ if the system "begins" with a value above π^*, since fully developed models typically include no transversality condition that would preclude such behavior. (Again see Figure 6.) Thus if one is inclined to doubt the stabi-

---

44. Woodford (1999, sect. 3) also argues that the solution of the previous paragraph is unlikely to prevail in actual economies, but his reasoning is different and will often lead to conclusions that do not agree with mine.

45. The second objective, in addition to ruling out the possibility of persistently maintained expectational errors, was to provide an objective list—dictated by the model—of relevant determinants of expectations.

lizing property of Taylor rules, or interest-instrument rules for inflation targeting, then this doubt should logically exist without any regard to ZLB considerations!

The foregoing analysis is not specific to the model utilized, but applies rather generally (I believe) to models with optimizing IS functions and either flexible prices or forward-looking price-adjustment specifications.[46] In particular, it would apply to price-adjustment relations of the Calvo-Rotemberg type or the more general form (62). I have not used either of these in the foregoing example for expositional convenience: the former gives a MSV solution with no relevant state variables—a case that is expositionally confusing as well as dull—while the latter leads to a cubic expression for the counterpart of the coefficient ϕ_{22} in (70) and is therefore difficult to work with analytically (although the analysis is quite manageable in numerical systems such as those of section 5).

7. CONCLUSION

We conclude with a brief overview. The present paper has explored a number of distinct theoretical issues that are relevant to recent discussions regarding the possibility of a zero lower bound (ZLB) on nominal interest rates and the implications of such a bound for monetary policy in regimes with low inflation. First, the paper seeks to spell out an explicit theoretical rationale for the idea that a ZLB may exist and indicates that its validity depends upon the assumption that it is costless at the margin to store money (the economy's medium of exchange). It is argued that the foregoing assumption is probably not correct, strictly speaking, so that negative interest rates are possible. But the quantitative extent of the phenomenon is almost certainly very small. Second, an investigation is conducted of the extent to which the absence of superneutrality will lead to an increase in the steady-state real rate of interest as steady-state inflation is reduced (and turned negative) by sustained policy. The conclusion based on a quantitative overlapping-generations model is that this effect is unlikely to be of much importance in the context of stabilization issues, although it is of considerable theoretical relevance as it suggests that real rates would rise sufficiently to keep an economy's steady-state nominal rate positive even with sizeable rates of deflation. Next, the analysis returns to models with the property of real-interest invariance to maintained inflation and explores the suitability of the common practice of conducting monetary policy analysis in models with no monetary variables. It is argued that this practice is almost certainly unjustified in a strict sense, but again the quantitative magnitude of the omitted effects is estimated to be very small.

The most important analysis, from the perspective of current policy issues, is that of sections 4 and 5. In the former it is shown analytically that even if short-run nominal interest rates are fixed at zero, there nevertheless exists a route for monetary pol-

---

46. The specification used on pp. 7–10 of Reifschneider and Williams (1999) includes IS and price-adjustment relations that are entirely backward looking.

icy actions to exert stabilizing effects on inflation and output (relative to capacity). This route, available in any economy that is open to foreign trade of goods and securities, works by a policy rule that adjusts the rate of depreciation of the exchange rate, acting in the role of an instrument variable, so as to meet stabilization objectives. The analysis presumes that strict uncovered interest parity does not prevail on a period-by-period basis, a presumption for which there is much empirical justification. Then in section 5 the quantitative magnitude of this stabilization strategy is investigated by means of simulations with a small but complete macroeconomic model, one that is designed to be consistent with optimizing analysis and calibrated to U.S. quarterly data. The results suggest that the extent of stabilization that can be obtained by this exchange rate approach is substantial.

Finally, recent warnings concerning some alarming theoretical results, obtained with Taylor-style policy rules in optimizing models that recognize the existence of a ZLB, are reconsidered. It is argued that these anomalous and undesirable effects obtain only when nonfundamental "bubble" solutions are considered despite the existence of fundamental solutions. Consequently, it is suggested—but not established conclusively—that the empirical relevance of such effects is highly dubious. Furthermore, if bubble solutions are considered then undesirable outcomes occur even if there is no ZLB.

LITERATURE CITED

Ball, Laurence. "Policy Rules for Open Economics." In *Monetary Policy Rules*, edited by John B. Taylor. Chicago: University of Chicago Press, 1999.

Benhabib, Jess, Stephanie Schmitt-Grohë, and Martin Uribe. "The Perils of Taylor Rules." Working paper, 1998.

Blanchard, Oliver J., and Stanley Fischer. *Lectures on Macroeconomics*. Cambridge, Mass.: MIT Press, 1989.

Casares, Miguel. "Dynamic Analysis in an Optimizing Monetary Model with Transaction Costs and Endogenous Investment." Working paper, 1999.

Casares, Miguel, and Bennett T. McCallum. "An Optimizing IS-LM Framework with Endogenous Investment." Working paper, Carnegie Mellon University, 1999.

Christiano, Lawrence J., and Christopher J. Gust. "Comment." In *Monetary Policy Rules*, edited by John B. Taylor. Chicago: University of Chicago Press, 1999.

Clarida, Richard, Jordi Gali, and Mark Gertler. "The Science of Monetary Policy: A New Keynesian Perspective." *Journal of Economic Literature* 37 (December 1999), 1661–1707.

Clouse, James, Dale Henderson, Athanasios Orphanides, David Small, and Peter Tinsley. "Monetary Policy When the Nominal Short-Term Interest Rate Is Zero." Working paper, Board of Governors of the Federal Reserve System, 1999.

Dooley, Michael P., and Peter Isard. "The Portfolio-Balance Model of Exchange Rates and Some Structural Estimates of the Risk Premium." International Monetary Fund *Staff Papers* 30 (December 1983), 683–702.

Dornbusch, Rudiger. "Exchange Rate Economics: Where Do We Stand?" *Brookings Papers on Economic Activity* (3), 537–584, 1980.

_____. "Exchange Rate Economics: 1986." *Economic Journal* 97 (March 1987), 1–18.

Flood, Robert P., and Andrew K. Rose. "Fixes: Of the Forward Discount Puzzle." *Review of Economics and Statistics* 78 (November 1996), 748–52.

Flood, Robert P., and Mark P. Taylor. "Exchange Rate Economics: What's Wrong with the Conventional Macro Approach." In *The Microstructure of Foreign Exchange Markets,* edited by Jeffrey A. Frankel, Giampaolo Galli, and Alberto Giovannini, pp. 261–94. Chicago: University of Chicago Press, 1996.

Frankel, Jeffrey A. "A Test of Perfect Substitutability in the Foreign Exchange Market." *Southern Economic Journal* 49 (October 1982), 406–16.

_____. "Tests of Monetary and Portfolio Balance Models of Exchange Rate Determination." In *Exchange Rate Theory and Practice*, edited by John F.O.Bilson and Richard C. Marston, pp. 239–60. Chicago: University of Chicago Press, 1984.

Friedman, Milton. *The Optimum Quantity of Money and Other Essays*. Chicago: Aldine Publishing Co., 1969.

Fuhrer, Jeffrey. "An Optimization-Based Model for Monetary Policy Analysis: Can Habit Formation Help?" Working paper, Federal Reserve Bank of Boston, 1998.

Fuhrer, Jeffrey, and Brian Madigan. "Monetary Policy When Interest Rates Are Bounded at Zero." *Review of Economics and Statistics* 79 (November 1997), 573–85.

Fuhrer, Jeffrey, and George C. Moore. "Inflation Persistence." *Quarterly Journal of Economics* 109 (March 1995), 127–59.

Gerlach, Stephan, and Frank Smets. "MCIs and Monetary Policy." Working paper, BIS, 1999.

Goodfriend, Marvin. "Comments." In *Towards More Effective Monetary Policy*, edited by Iwao Kuroda, New York; St. Martin's Press, 1997.

Grimes, Arthur, and Jason Wong. "The Role of the Exchange Rate in New Zealand Monetary Policy." In *Exchange Rate Policy and Interdependence*, edited by Ruben Glick and Michael M. Hutchinson. New York: Cambridge University Press, 1994.

Hansen, Eric, and Dimitri Margaritis. "Financial Liberalization and Monetary Policy in New Zealand." *Australian Economic Review* (4th Quarter 1993), 28–36.

Kerr, William, and Robert G. King. "Limits on Interest Rate Rules in the IS Model." Federal Reserve Bank of Richmond *Economic Quarterly* 82 (Spring 1996), 47–75.

Kiyotaki, Nobuhiro, and Randall Wright. "On Money as a Medium of Exchange." *Journal of Political Economy* 97 (August 1989), 927–54.

Klein, Paul. "Using the Generalized Schur Form to Solve a System of Linear Expectational Difference Equations." Working paper, Stockholm University, 1997.

Krugman, Paul. "It's Baaack: Japan's Slump and the Return of the Liquidity Trap." *Brookings Papers on Economic Activity* (No. 2 1998), 137–87.

_____. "Deflationary Spirals." The Official Paul Krugman Web Page, 1999.

Lacker, Jeffrey M., and Stacey L. Schreft. "Money and Credit as Means of Payment." *Journal of Monetary Economics* 38 (August 1996), 3–23.

Lewis, Karen. "Puzzles in International Financial Markets." In *Handbook of International Economics*, vol. 3, edited by Gene M. Grossman and Kenneth Rogoff. Amsterdam: Elsevier Science, 1995.

Lucas, Robert E., Jr. "Econometric Testing of the Natural-rate Hypothesis." In *The Econometrics of Price Determination*, edited by Otto Eckstein. Washington, D.C.: Board of Governors of the Federal Reserve System, 1972.

McCallum, Bennett T. "The Optimal Inflation Rate in an Overlapping-Generations Economy with Land." In *New Approaches to Monetary Economics*, edited by William A. Barnett and Kenneth Singleton. New York: Cambridge University Press, 1987.

_____. "Analysis of the Monetary Transmission Mechanism: Methodological Issues." In *The Monetary Transmission Process: Recent Developments and Lessons for Europe*. London: Macmillan Publishers, forthcoming, 1999a.

904 : MONEY, CREDIT, AND BANKING

_____. "Role of the Minimal State Variable Criterion in Rational Expectations Models." *International Tax and Public Finance* 6 (November 1999b), 621–39.

McCallum, Bennett T., and Edward Nelson. "Performance of Operational Policy Rules in an Estimated Semiclassical Structural Model." In *Monetary Policy Rules*, edited by John B. Taylor. Chicago: University of Chicago Press, 1999a.

_____ "Nominal Income Targeting in an Open-Economy Optimizing Model." *Journal of Monetary Economics* 43 (June 1999), 553–78, b.

_____. "An Optimizing IS-LM Specification for Monetary Policy and Business Cycle Analysis." *Journal of Money, Credit, and Banking* 31 (August 1999, Part 1), 296–316, c.

Meltzer, Allan H. "The Transmission Process." In *The Monetary Transmission Process: Recent Developments and Lessons for Europe*. London: Macmillan Publishers, 1999.

Nelson, Edward. "Sluggish Inflation and Optimizing Models of the Business Cycle." *Journal of Monetary Economics* 42 (October 1998), 303–22.

Obstfeld, Maurice, and Kenneth Rogoff. *Foundations of International Macroeconomics*. Cambridge, Mass.: MIT Press, 1996.

Okun, Arthur M. *Prices and Quantities: A Macroeconomic Analysis*. Washington, D.C.: Brookings Institution, 1981.

Orphanides, Athanasios, and Volker Wieland. "Price Stability and Monetary Policy Effectiveness When Nominal Interest Rates Are Bounded at Zero." Working paper 1998–35, Finance and Economics Discussion Series, Federal Reserve Board, 1998.

Phelps, Edmund S. *Inflation Policy and Unemployment Theory*. London: Macmillan Press, 1972.

Reifschneider, David, and John C. Williams. "Three Lessons for Monetary Policy in a Low Inflation Era." Working paper, Federal Reserve Board, 1999.

Rotemberg, Julio J., and Michael Woodford "An Optimization-Based Econometric Framework for the Evaluation of Monetary Policy." In *NBER Macroeconomics Annual 1997*, edited by Ben S. Bernanke and Julio J. Rotemberg. Cambridge, Mass.: MIT Press, 1997.

Stockman, Alan C. "International Transmission under Bretton Woods." In *A Retrospective on the Bretton Woods System*, edited by Michael P. Bordo and Barry Eichengreen, pp. 317–48. Chicago: University of Chicago Press, 1992.

Summers, Lawrence. "How Should Long-Term Monetary Policy Be Determined?" *Journal of Money, Credit, and Banking* 23 (August 1991, Part 2), 625–31.

Taylor, John B. "Discretion versus Policy Rules in Practice." *Carnegie-Rochester Conference Series on Public Policy* 39 (December 1993), 195–214, a.

_____. *Macroeconomic Policy in a World Economy*. New York: W. W. Norton, 1993b.

_____. *Monetary Policy Rules*, editor. Chicago: University of Chicago Press, 1999.

Thornton, Daniel L. "Nominal Interest Rates: Less Than Zero?" Federal Reserve Bank of St. Louis *Monetary Trends* (January 1999), 1.

Uhlig, Harald. "A Toolkit for Analyzing Nonlinear Dynamic Stochastic Models Easily." Working paper, Tilburg University, 1997.

Vickrey, William S. "Stability through Inflation." In *Post-Keynesian Economics,* edited by Kenneth T. Kurihara. New Brunswick, N.J.: Rutgers University Press, 1954.

Wallace, Neil. "Absence-of-Double-Coincidence Models of Money: A Progress Report." Federal Reserve Bank of Minneapolis *Quarterly Review* 21 (Winter 1997), 2–20.

Wolman, Alexander S. "Staggered Price Setting and the Zero Bound on Nominal Interest Rates." Federal Reserve Bank of Richmond *Economic Quarterly* 84 (Fall 1998), 1–24.

Woodford, Michael. *Interest and Prices*, chapter 2. Manuscript, 1999.

[6]

MARVIN GOODFRIEND

Overcoming the Zero Bound on Interest Rate Policy

The paper proposes three options for overcoming the zero bound on interest rate policy: a carry tax on money, open market operations in long bonds, and monetary transfers. A variable carry tax on electronic bank reserves could enable a central bank to target negative nominal interest rates. A carry tax could be imposed on currency to create more leeway to make interest rates negative. Quantitative policy—monetary transfers and open market purchases of long bonds—could stimulate the economy by creating liquidity broadly defined. A central bank needs more fiscal support than usual from the Treasury to pursue quantitative policy at the interest rate floor.

PRICE STABILITY creates a problem for interest rate policy. In the decade following the Korean War, CPI inflation averaged about 1.5 percent per year in the United States and the three-month nominal Treasury bill rate ranged between 1.5 and 3.5 percent. With fully credible price stability, nominal short rates could average as low as 1 percent.[1] Fisher (1930) pointed out that if a commodity could be stored costlessly over time, then the rate of interest in units of that commodity could never fall below zero.[2] Fisher's reasoning is self-evident in the case of money. No one will lend money at negative nominal interest if cash is costless to carry over time. Therefore, the power of open market operations to lower short-term interest rates to fight deflation and recession is strictly limited when nominal rates are already low on average.[3]

This paper benefitted from conversations with A. Broaddus, M. Dotsey, B. Hetzel, T. Humphrey, R. King, J. Lacker, B. McCallum, J. Reese, A. Stockman, J. Weinberg, V. Wieland, and A. Wolman, and from the discussants at this conference, R. Bryant and C. Freedman. The paper also benefitted from a preliminary workshop at the European Central Bank and a presentation at the University of Toronto.

1. Ex post real Treasury bill rates from 1926 to 1997, excluding the wartime peg years, average about 1 percent per year. See Ibbotson (1998).

2. See pages 186–94.

3. Because the inconvenience and physical costs of storing currency are not literally zero at the margin, nominal interest rates can be slightly negative. In fact, the nominal yield on Japanese Treasury bills became slightly negative during the Asian financial crisis last autumn when nominal rates were already very low. Investors were willing to pay for the safety and convenience of government bonds rather than incur the cost of storing currency. Mogi and Zuckerman (1998).

Nominal yields on U.S. Treasury bonds and notes calculated in the standard way became negative in the 1930s. However, Cecchetti (1988) shows that nominal rates only appeared to be negative by correcting the apparent negative yields for an institutional "exchange privilege" on bonds.

The behavior of nominal rates near the zero bound is discussed in detail in sections 2.1 and 2.2 below.

MARVIN GOODFRIEND *is Senior Vice President and Policy Advisor at the Federal Reserve Bank of Richmond. E-mail:* Marvin.Goodfriend@rich.frb.org

Keynes (1936) was very much concerned with the consequences for macroeconomics and monetary policy of the zero bound on nominal interest rates.[4] That concern was revived by Summers (1991,1996) and Fischer (1996). Summers and Fischer argue that central banks should target inflation in a range as high as 3 percent per year so that the inflation premium would make room for nominal interest rates to fall an additional three percentage points before hitting the zero bound. In section 1 I review this and other suggestions for dealing with the zero bound that have appeared in the literature. None of the alternatives is entirely satisfactory.

In the main body of the paper I propose three options that could allow a central bank to overcome the zero bound on interest rate policy: a carry tax on money, open market purchases in long bonds, and monetary transfers. The first half of the paper considers the mechanics of lowering the floor on nominal interest rates by imposing a storage (carry) tax on money. The second half explores the power of open market purchases and monetary transfers to stimulate the economy when nominal interest rates are at the zero (or lower) bound given by the cost of carry on money.

Following Fisher's insight, I recommend that a central bank put in place systems to raise the cost of storing money by imposing a carry tax on its monetary liabilities. If a cost of carry were imposed on money, then expansionary open market operations could make nominal interest rates negative. Lenders could be made to accept negative nominal interest on loans rather than pay the carry tax on money. Although Keynes (1936) and others mentioned the possibility of taxing money for this purpose, the idea has never been taken seriously because of its administrative costliness, and because the zero bound was not an issue until the return to price stability.[5] In light of recent advances in payments technology and the less than satisfactory alternatives, imposing a carry tax on money seems to be a reasonable way of dealing with the zero bound. I present and develop a proposal for imposing a carry tax in section 2.

Under my proposal, the floor on short-term nominal interest rates would be determined by the carry tax imposed by a central bank on electronic reserve balances. When interest rates are pressed against that floor, a monetary policy committee could vary the carry tax in order to adjust its interest rate target. The carry tax would anchor the short end of the yield curve much as, say, the intended federal funds rate does today in the United States. To assure that the carry tax on electronic reserve balances sets the economy's nominal interest rate floor, a carry tax could also be imposed on currency and vault cash. I discuss how this might be done, too.

In section 3 I recommend that a central bank supplement its carry tax (interest rate) policy with quantitative monetary policy—open market operations and monetary transfers. When the short-term nominal interest rate is pressed against the cost-

4. See Chapter 17. Lerner (1952) clarifies some of the analysis in that chapter. See, in particular, Lerner's concluding section.

5. See Keynes (1936, chapter 17, p. 234 and chapter 23, pp. 353–58), Dahlberg (1938, chapters 7 and 8), Fisher (1933, chapter 3), and Hart (1948, chapter 20, pp. 443–47). Keynes (1936, chapter 23) credits Silvio Gesell with idea for imposing carrying costs on money in order to lower the floor on nominal interest rates. In a recent paper, Buiter and Panigirtzoglou (1999) revive Gesell's idea for imposing a periodic stamp tax on currency. They show in a dynamic macromodel, how Gesell's tax on money allows the model economy to escape a liquidity trap.

of-carry floor, a central bank can pursue independently a monetary aggregate target. The variable carry tax would be a powerful policy instrument. However, making interest rates increasingly negative would create stress for lenders and people heavily dependent on interest income. Open market purchases and monetary transfers could stimulate spending without lowering the interest rate floor. More importantly, a central bank could use quantitative policy to see to it that a contraction of monetary assets or an excess demand for liquid assets in the economy does not precipitate or exacerbate a downturn, or preclude a recovery.[6]

I begin the analysis in section 3 by distinguishing between narrow and broad notions of liquidity. Liquidity is provided in the narrow sense when the medium of exchange makes possible a saving of "shopping time" in transactions.[7] The economy is satiated with liquidity services in the narrow sense when the nominal interest rate is pressed against the cost-of-carry floor. I define liquidity broadly as a service yield provided by assets according to how easily they can be turned into cash, either by a sale or by serving as collateral for external finance. Liquidity services defined broadly are valued because they can be used to minimize one's exposure to the external finance premium in the sense of Bernanke and Gertler (1995). In my view, liquidity broadly defined is at the heart of the leverage that quantitative policy can exert when the nominal interest rate is at the cost-of-carry floor.

Building on the notion of broad liquidity services, I describe in detail the transmission mechanism by which open market purchases would help to offset an adverse aggregate demand shock when nominal and real interest rates are bounded at zero. The mechanism involves the portfolio rebalancing channel stressed by monetarists such as Friedman (1969) and Meltzer (1995) and the credit channel stressed by Bernanke and Gertler (1995) and follows from the attempt on the part of asset holders to rearrange their portfolios after an injection of liquidity. To be effective at the zero bound, open market purchases have to be undertaken in longer-term rather than short-term securities. This has potentially far-reaching fiscal consequences that I consider in detail.

I conclude section 3 by evaluating the feasibility and desirability of transferring money to the public in order to stimulate spending. For a central bank committed to price stability it turns out that money transfers could not exert an effect on spending by permanently relaxing budget constraints. However, money transfers could stimulate spending through the portfolio rebalancing and credit channels. Given a commitment to price stability, I recommend that monetary transfers be used in conjunction with open market purchases as a means of injecting money into a depressed economy. The need to drain money to stabilize inflation after the economy recovers (by reversing monetary transfers or by selling long bonds with unexpected capital losses) could greatly increase government debt in the hands of the public. I identify the perceived burden of the additional public debt as a potential cost of using quantitative policy to stimulate the economy.

6. Meltzer (1999) and Romer (1992) present interesting discussions of the role of money in various historical episodes of recession and recovery.
7. The "shopping time" model of money demand is discussed in McCallum and Goodfriend (1987).

1010 : MONEY, CREDIT, AND BANKING

In section 4 I consider a number of practical issues that arise in connection with the carry tax and quantitative policies. Clearly, the central bank and the Treasury would need legislation in order to impose a carry tax on money. The most serious objection to the carry tax is that the public might not hedge itself adequately against negative nominal interest rates. The public could do so by holding long bonds. But the public is shy of the inflation risk in bonds. To reassure the public, the legislature should mandate a price stability objective for the central bank. The Treasury should provide an adequate supply of long bonds. And the central bank should use its economic education programs to teach the public the benefits of holding long bonds.

One of the main points of the paper is that quantitative monetary policy needs more fiscal support from the Treasury than usual to be effective at the interest rate floor. To make large-scale open market operations in long bonds credible, the Treasury must indemnify the central bank against unexpected capital losses. Fortifying the central bank against capital losses would commit the Treasury to expand the public debt, perhaps substantially, in support of monetary policy. That fiscal commitment might require legislation. If so, then quantitative monetary policy might need new legislation, too, in order to be effective when the nominal interest rate is at its cost-of-carry floor.

The paper concludes with a brief summary.

1. A REVIEW OF PRIOR PROPOSALS

The zero bound problem arises because real interest rates must fluctuate to stabilize the economy over the business cycle. When a central bank has full credibility for maintaining price stability, inflation expectations are firmly anchored and a central bank produces the required real interest rate movements by managing its target for short-term nominal interest rates. With zero expected inflation, however, the zero bound on nominal interest rates implies that expected real interest rates cannot be negative.

The zero bound is a potential problem for two reasons. First, negative real interest rates may have helped the economy to recover from recessions in the past, particularly in periods of financial market stress. Second, deflation expectations in economic downturns can actually raise expected real interest rates when nominal rates are at the zero bound, with perverse effects on demand and employment.[8] The possibility of a deflation spiral worries economists and central bankers alike.[9] Nominal interest rates

---

8. Clouse et al. (1999) report that real short-term interest rates were negative in most of the twelve recessions in the United States since the early 1930s. The major exceptions occurred in the two recessions of the 1930s and in the post–World War 2 recession, when deflation actually pushed real rates up as the economy turned down.

Fisher (1930) points out on page 192 that "there is no absolutely necessary reason inherent in the nature of man or things why the rate of interest in terms of any commodity should be positive rather than negative." The interest rate is a relative price reflecting the cost of using a commodity today in terms of future units of that commodity. Barro (1987) explains the role of the real interest rate in macroeconomics as the central intertemporal relative price.

9. See Benhabib, Schmitt-Grohé, and Uribe (1999), Mints (1950, chapter 3), and Reifschneider and Williams (2000).

might only need to be negative occasionally and temporarily. If they are not free to do so, however, recessions could be much deeper and longer than otherwise.

The zero bound is more than an academic concern. Short-term nominal interest rates hit the zero bound in the Great Depression and are zero in Japan today.[10] Reports of deflation and unemployment in Japan and China, in particular, have sensitized the press and the public around the world to the problem of deflation and deficient aggregate demand.[11] The concern on the part of economists, central bankers, and the public about these issues has given rise to a series of suggestions for dealing with the zero bound.

As mentioned in the introduction, Summers and Fischer suggest that a central bank should target an average rate of inflation of up to 3 percent. Their recommendation gets support from macroeconometric studies that suggest that the risk in more frequent and longer-lasting recessions associated with zero inflation may be significant but that an inflation rate of 1 to 3 percent may be sufficient to alleviate most of that risk.[12]

The problem with this proposal is that it accepts some risk of a potentially disastrous outcome. Much higher inflation on average would be needed to rule out the disastrous outcome with confidence. Yet, the costs of substantially higher inflation are significant in themselves. Thus, higher inflation does not really afford a satisfactory solution to the problem.

Krugman (1998, 1999) proposes that if the zero bound is actually hit, a central bank should hold the nominal rate down and target a moderate rate of inflation for some period of time to make the real interest rate negative. The problem with this recommendation is that Krugman does not explain how a central bank could create inflation at the zero bound. One would think that a central bank with the power to create inflation would have the power to stimulate spending directly.

In practice it would be difficult for a central bank to steer an economic recovery after deliberately unleashing inflation.[13] Moreover, the resort to inflation whenever the zero bound was hit would create an environment in which inflation scares could become a problem. The central bank would not know when and how much inflation might be needed to respond to a given downturn in the economy. Hence, the public's expectations of inflation could become highly variable. Inflation scares could themselves become a significant destabilizing source of shocks to the economy.

Wolman (1998) shows that a fully credible policy rule might make the zero bound irrelevant for monetary policy. Wolman's point is that if prices are sticky but inflation is flexible, then a credible policy rule could overcome the zero bound by moving inflation and inflation expectations around a zero inflation average. But Wolman also

---

10. See Hayami (1999) and Okina (1999) for discussions of monetary policy from the Bank of Japan's perspective.

11. See Abelson (1998), "Could It Happen Again?" (1999), "Deflation and All That" (1997), Faison (1999), Uchitelle (1999). See also Krugman (1999).

12. See Fuhrer and Madigan (1997), Orphanides and Wieland (1998), Reifschneider and Williams (2000), Svensson (1999), and Tetlow and Williams (1998).

13. If for some reason the economy had already undergone a severe deflation, then reflation would be called for to reverse the decline in the price level in order to reverse debt deflation effects. See Bernanke and Gertler (1995).

points out that if inflation is sticky, then his argument loses much of its force. Moreover, in practice a central bank may not have enough credibility for such an activist rule to work well.[14]

McCallum (2000) suggests that a central bank confronting the zero bound should adopt the foreign exchange rate as its policy instrument. Specifically, he proposes following a monetary policy rule that varies an exchange rate policy instrument to stabilize inflation and output. This is not the place to discuss the operating characteristics of McCallum's exchange rate rule. To get an idea of how an exchange rate instrument might work, however, suppose that a country pegged its currency at a much depreciated foreign exchange rate. The exchange rate depreciation, then, would create an increase in net exports, the nominal short interest rate would immediately match the foreign currency interest rate, and prices would move up over time in proportion to the exchange rate depreciation. The expected inflation would imply a low or even negative real interest rate for a while.

The problem with an exchange rate oriented monetary policy is that it could be perceived as working at the expense of its trading partners, and it might not work very well at all for a very large country such as the United States. If the United States adopted such a policy to lift itself out of a deflationary, zero bound trap, it might export deflation and recession without helping itself much.

Finally, consider a collection of policy possibilities discussed by Clouse et al. (1999) more closely related to current central bank practices.[15] These authors doubt that open market purchases of long bonds could push long-term interest rates much closer to zero. According to the expectations theory of the term structure of interest rates, Clouse et al. note that to move long rates closer to zero a central bank must somehow credibly commit itself to maintain zero short-term rates even if higher short rates turn out to be desirable in the future. Clouse et al. suggest that a central bank could write options on future short rates at zero interest to give itself more incentive to keep rates down. Whether this could work is questionable given the overwhelming pressures to take interest rate policy actions that seem correct at a particular point in time. Moreover, the marginal gain to be had by moving long-term interest rates closer to zero might not be worth the loss of credibility for price stability after a recovery was underway.

Clouse et al. also consider purchases of private sector debt and more extensive discount window lending. The idea is that such policies could reduce private credit spreads and help finance credit-constrained firms. The credit channel plays an important role in the transmission mechanism. But it doesn't follow that credit allocation by a central bank is beneficial. Direct lending to individual firms at reduced credit spreads crowds out private lenders who require higher spreads. Deciding

---

14. The work of Rotemberg and Woodford (1999) and Woodford (1999b) emphasizes the idea that credibility can be exploited to minimize the chances that the short-term nominal rate will hit zero. However, their work does not focus on what a central bank could or should do if the zero bound is actually encountered.

15. See Lebow (1993) for an early analysis of practical options.

which firms deserve credit assistance puts a central bank in a difficult political situation. Credit allocation is incompatible with central bank independence.[16]

Subsidized lending involves the assumption of credit risk. The assumption of credit risk in the absence of increased monitoring and controls creates moral hazard. Therefore, central bank lending should be used sparingly only to stabilize financial markets. Lending should not be used as part of a package of policies to stimulate economic recovery more generally.[17]

2. IMPOSING A CARRY TAX ON MONEY

My goal in this section is to show how a variable carry tax on electronic bank reserves at a central bank could be made to function like an interest rate policy instrument when the zero bound on short-term nominal interest rates is a constraint on monetary policy. First, I describe the nature of the zero bound when there is currency but no banking system. Second, I add a banking system and describe the interaction of the various types of monetary instruments and interest rates that would coexist. Third, I explain how a carry tax imposed by a central bank on electronic bank reserves would affect the interbank rate, deposit rates, the loan rate, and bond rates. Fourth, I consider the technological feasibility of imposing a carry tax on money. Fifth, I compare the costs of the carry tax and the inflation tax alternatives for dealing with the zero bound on nominal interest rates.

2.1 The Zero Bound in a Currency Economy

McCallum (2000) points out that the behavior of the nominal interest rate near zero depends decisively on the behavior of the net marginal service yield on money with respect to increases in the quantity of real money balances. If the net marginal service yield asymptotes to zero, and money is costless to carry at the margin relative to nominal bonds, then the nominal interest rate also asymptotes to zero.[18] There is a zero bound in this case, but the nominal rate never reaches it. No matter how large real money balances become, people will hold more with a small reduction in the nominal interest rate. Lucas's (2000) "shopping time" model of money demand exhibits this behavior. Money demand is never satiated in Lucas's model.

On the other hand, if the marginal service yield becomes zero beyond some quantity of real money balances and there is no cost of carry, then the nominal interest rate could hit the zero bound, and people could become indifferent between holding money or bonds. This possibility arises in the "cash in advance" model studied in Cole and Kocherlakota (1998).

---

16. The statement in the text follows from a fundamental principle of independent central banking given in section 4.

17. See Goodfriend and Lacker (1999).

18. If there is a small marginal cost of storing bonds, then the nominal interest rate asymptotes to a small positive value so that the net nominal return to holding bonds is also zero.

A more realistic model might have a shopping time transactions technology and a small marginal physical cost of storing currency relative to bonds. The net marginal service yield on currency would then asymptote to a slightly negative value reflecting the small physical cost of storing currency.[19] The nominal interest rate could become negative in this case, but only slightly so.

2.2 Banking and the Zero Bound

A banking system gives the public the opportunity to obtain monetary services from deposits in addition to currency. Moreover, banks themselves get monetary services from vault cash and from electronic reserve balances at a central bank. Here I discuss how the various forms of money coexist and what determines their relative demands and interest rates near the zero bound.

As is common practice, suppose that a central bank does not charge a storage cost or a user fee for the transaction services it provides on electronic reserve balances. Further assume that banks' demand for reserves exhibits a declining marginal service yield as in Frost (1971). The absence of storage costs and user fees on electronic reserve balances at the central bank sets a zero interest rate floor on the interbank interest rate regardless of the physical cost of storing currency.

The interbank rate represents a cost of loanable funds for a particular bank. Hence, if a central bank pushed the interbank rate to zero, banks would respond by lowering the bid rates on other sources of loanable funds such as certificates of deposit and time deposits. Banks would try to purchase securities to earn higher yields. Competition among banks would pull short rates down to zero and move longer-term rates down with the average of expected future short rates over the relevant horizon. Loan rates and rates on risky securities would come down as far as their credit spreads would allow.

Banks would trim costs by eliminating interest on transactions deposits and imposing a fee to cover transactions services. Competitive pricing of transactions services would have two parts, a per period, per dollar fee to cover the overhead cost of providing the services (with average or minimum balance requirements), and a marginal fee per transaction.[20] The public would hold transactions deposits to the point where the marginal service yield was zero, net of the per period, per dollar service fee. Insured time deposits would pay zero interest and incur a smaller service charge than transactions deposits. Finally, currency would be held up to the point where its marginal service yield, net of storage costs, was also zero. If, for example, the marginal service yield behaved according to Lucas's version of the shopping time transactions technology, then the demand for currency would be satiated at the zero bound if there were a small marginal physical cost of storing currency.[21]

To repeat, in the presence of a banking system there is a zero bound on nominal

---

19. If bonds are also costly to store, then the nominal interest rate asymptotes to a value equal to the marginal cost of storing bonds minus the marginal cost of storing currency.

20. Stavins (1999, pp. 6–8) discusses the pricing of transactions services.

21. Wolman (1997) shows that the welfare consequences of low or negative rates of inflation turn importantly on whether currency is actually satiated or not at zero interest.

interest rates regardless of the physical cost of storing currency. The zero bound, however, results from the fact that a central bank typically charges no user fee for the transactions services on electronic reserve balances and stores bank reserves for free.

2.3 Imposing the Carry Tax

What would happen if a central bank were to impose a per period, per dollar carry tax on electronic bank reserves when the interbank interest rate was pressed to zero? Competition among banks to avoid the carry tax would push the interbank below zero by the cost of carry. The interbank rate would go no lower because banks would not lend reserves at a loss greater than the storage cost on electronic reserves. As long as open market purchases maintained the downward pressure on interest rates, the interbank rate would be governed by the carry tax.

Banks would continue to charge service fees on deposits, but they would match the negative cost of funds in the interbank market by offering equally negative interest on deposits. Banks would reach for higher (zero) yields on short-term securities. However, they would only succeed in pushing short-term interest rates below zero by the size of the cost of carry. Likewise, long-term interest rates would become negative if banks expected the central bank to sustain negative short-term interest rates sufficiently far into the future. Loan rates and rates on risky securities would be bid down and could also become negative if the carry tax were large enough.

Thus, it is feasible for a central bank to make nominal interest rates negative throughout the economy by imposing a cost of carry on electronic bank reserves. The only qualification is that nominal interest rates could not be made more negative than the dollar value of the physical cost of storing vault cash or currency. Otherwise, banks would store reserves as vault cash; and the public would not lend at negative interest greater than the marginal physical cost of storing currency.

The inconvenience and expense of storing large volumes of currency and vault cash would probably preclude large-scale hoarding if nominal rates were made only slightly negative for a relatively short period of time. If negative rates of perhaps 4 or 5 percent were expected to persist for a year or more, however, banks and the public would probably hoard currency rather than lend it, setting a floor closer to zero below which a central bank could not push nominal interest rates.

To deal with this problem a central bank could also impose a carry tax on vault cash and currency.[22] The carry tax on currency could be varied with the carry tax on electronic reserves. Or the carry tax on currency could temporarily be fixed high enough, say, at 5 percent per year, so that the central bank could move nominal interest rates in a range from zero to negative 5 percent by varying the carry tax on electronic bank reserves alone.[23]

---

22. Physical costs of storing coin are probably large enough at the margin that storing large values of cash as coin would not be a cost-effective means of avoiding negative nominal interest rates.

23. In principle, as an alternative to imposing a carry tax on currency, banks could agree to suspend the payment of currency for deposits whenever a carry tax was imposed on electronic reserves at the central bank. Currency and deposits each have a comparative advantage in making payments. Currency is more efficient for small transactions made in person, and checkable deposits are useful for making larger

2.4 Technological Feasibility

Modern payments system technology makes it possible to impose and vary a carry tax on electronic bank reserves at the central bank. With a system to do so in place, the zero bound would cease to be a technological constraint on interest rate policy. Whenever the intended target for the interbank interest rate reached zero, the policy committee could activate a daily tax on electronic reserve balances that would make the interbank rate negative. By calibrating the daily tax as a percent per annum, the policy committee could adjust the cost of carry so as to move the interbank rate in twenty-five basis point steps and continue to make interest rate policy exactly as it does today. [24]

To supplement the carry tax on electronic reserves, a carry tax could be imposed on currency by imbedding a magnetic strip in each bill. The magnetic strip could visibly record when a bill was last withdrawn from the banking system. A carry tax could be deducted from each bill upon deposit according to how long the bill was in circulation since last withdrawn and how much carry tax was "past due." Likewise, a carry tax could be assessed on currency held as vault cash in banks.

In the United States the average period between acquisitions of cash is about two weeks, so currency stays in circulation for about a week at a time. [25] Therefore, a carry tax on the order of 5 percent per year would require a tiny 0.1 cents tax per dollar on the average deposit. Banks would be assessed a carry tax for the period that currency was in their vaults. There is little reason to think that the use of the monetary base would change much in response to the occasional imposition of a carry tax. Jefferson (1997) reports that the velocity of the monetary base has remained near 3.3 since 1980, a period in which the inflation tax averaged around 4 percent per year, and was over 10 percent in the early 1980s.

Most currency received in payment is immediately deposited in the banking system. For the vast majority of bills in circulation that were "current" or nearly so, people might very well ignore the tiny tax due at the next deposit date when accepting cash. Since merchants would make most of the currency deposits, they might take the trouble to collect the carry tax on currency from customers. Otherwise, the carry

---

payments at a distance. The respective demands for the two monies would be well-defined. The imposition of a negative nominal interest rate coupled with a suspension would cause the deposit price of currency to jump to the point that the expected negative deposit return to holding currency matched the negative nominal rate on deposits.

This mechanism is reminiscent of the temporary suspensions that occurred in the United States prior to the establishment of the Federal Reserve. For instance, currency went to a few percent premium over deposits for a few months during the suspension that occurred in the aftermath of the banking panic of 1907.

Suspending the payment of currency for deposits would avoid the cost of imposing a carry tax on currency. After the initial capital gain, however, currency would bear the same expected negative return as deposits. Moreover, the proposal would involve the inconvenience of dealing with a fluctuating deposit price of currency. Furthermore, the possibility of making a capital gain on currency relative to deposits when a suspension occurs would create destabilizing speculative runs on the banking system. Such attacks would be annoying and costly for banks. Effort invested in attacking banks would be a waste of resources from society's point of view.

24. John Taylor's (1993) interest rate rule could be adapted to situations when the nominal rate was made negative.

25. See Porter and Judson (1996, Table 1, p. 887).

tax on currency would amount to a kind of sales tax paid by merchants. Either way, prices would adjust to determine the ultimate incidence of the carry tax.

The carry tax would serve as a powerful deterrent to hoarding currency. Currency that was hoarded and "past due" would only be accepted at a discount sufficient to cover the arrears. Since the carry tax on currency would equal or exceed the negative interest rate, the public would deposit or lend currency in excess of the transactions demand rather than hoard it.

2.5 The Carry Tax versus the Inflation Tax

Overcoming the zero bound on nominal interest rates is costly, whether accomplished by imposing a carry tax or an inflation tax. Ultimately one must compare the costs of imposing a carry tax with those of imposing an inflation tax to determine the most efficient means of dealing with the zero bound. This is not the place to assess quantitatively the respective costs.[26] It is useful, however, to compare the nature of the costs arising from the two alternatives. As is the case in public finance, we should consider both the distortionary and the administrative costs of the inflation tax and the carry tax alternatives.

The inflation tax would incur permanent distortionary costs to enable a central bank to create negative real interest rates on occasion. The carry tax would be imposed temporarily only on those occasions when a negative nominal interest rate was needed. Moreover, on those occasions no distortion would be introduced by the imposition of a carry tax. Imposing a carry tax temporarily to move the nominal interest rate below zero would have no effect on the opportunity cost of holding money. And imposing a carry tax at the zero bound to offset the effect of expected deflation on the real interest rate likewise would leave the opportunity cost of holding money unchanged.[27] Of course, if a carry tax on currency were fixed below the carry tax on electronic bank reserves, then currency demand would be distorted temporarily while the carry taxes were in effect.

The carry tax is costly mainly because systems have to be put in place to enable a central bank to impose it. There would be permanent administrative costs involved in operating and maintaining such systems. Currency would be more sophisticated and more costly to produce. Systems would have to be put in place at banks and automatic teller machines to read bills, assess the carry tax, and visibly record the bills "current." Substantial development and installation costs would have to be paid to put these systems into practice.

Such considerations notwithstanding, the case for the carry tax solution to the zero bound problem is a compelling one for a number of reasons. First, an occasional

26. The costs of inflation are well known and have been documented and measured extensively elsewhere. See, for instance, Feldstein (1997), Fischer (1996), Goodfriend (1997), Lucas (2000), Summers (1991, 1996), Wolman (1997), and references therein.

27. An exogenously imposed carry tax would be distortionary. Consider a permanent carry tax on money. In balanced growth, the real interest rate is governed by time preference, intertemporal substitutability, and the growth rate. A carry tax on money would not affect the real interest rate in balanced growth. It would, however, raise the consumption interest opportunity cost of holding money and cause people to economize on real money balances.

imposition of the carry tax could guarantee that the zero bound would never be a problem for monetary policy. The permanent inflation tax could not guarantee that, unless inflation was targeted at a relatively high and costly rate. Second, varying the carry tax would enable interest rate policy to be made exactly as it is today. Third, long bond rates could be made to move closer to or below zero. Fourth, the carry tax would allow a central bank to deal directly with deflation expectations by making nominal interest rates negative.[28] Fifth, ongoing progress in payments technology is reducing the cost of putting systems in place to impose a carry tax. Sixth, systems to impose a carry tax could be utilized to pay interest on bank reserves and currency when nominal interest rates exceed zero, reducing the distortions that arise in that case.

3. OPEN MARKET OPERATIONS AND MONETARY TRANSFERS

In section 2 I considered lowering the floor on nominal interest rates by imposing a carry tax on money. In this section I explore the power of open market purchases and monetary transfers to stimulate the economy when nominal interest rates are at the zero (or lower) bound given by the cost of carry on money. The quantitative and carry tax policies could complement each other. Temporarily negative real interest rates are a powerful stimulant to spending, but they are costly for people holding liquid assets and for those heavily dependent on interest income. Quantitative policy could stimulate spending even if the nominal interest rate were fixed at the cost-of-carry floor. A central bank should pursue quantitative policy at the zero bound to make sure that a contraction of monetary assets in the economy or an excess demand for money does not cause or contribute to an economic downturn, or prevent a recovery.

Ordinarily open market operations support a central bank's interest rate policy by accommodating the demand for money at the opportunity cost given by the spread between the interest rate instrument and the zero cost of carry on reserves and currency.[29] In effect, open market operations support the opportunity cost spread; they do not determine the level of interest rates. For a constant spread maintained by open market operations, we could just as well imagine that a carry tax (or carry interest) could be varied to manage the level of interest rates.[30]

When nominal rates are pressed against the cost-of-carry floor, whether that cost

---

28. The deflation trap in Benhabib et al. (1999) arises because of the assumed zero bound on nominal interest rates. Benhabib et al. show that as long as there is a zero bound, deflation expectations can put the economy on a trajectory to the deflationary equilibrium. Using the carry tax to overcome the lower bound on nominal rates eliminates the deflationary equilibrium in their model and the possibility of a deflationary spiral.

29. For the purpose of this discussion, one may take the price level and the real transactions variable in the money demand function as given. The general point holds in slightly different form in a fully dynamic, flexible price model.

30. Hall (1999) proposes that a central bank pay interest on reserves, and vary the spread between the market rate and the own rate on reserves as the policy instrument. If one interprets his interest on reserves as a negative cost of carry, then his analysis can be seen to be related to the discussion here.

MARVIN GOODFRIEND : 1019

is zero or not, open market purchases become an independent policy instrument free to pursue targets for the monetary base or broader monetary aggregates. When such is the case, a central bank can use the carry tax to manage interest rate policy and open market operations to manage quantitative monetary policy.[31]

In section 3.1 I begin to think about quantitative monetary policy at the interest rate floor by distinguishing between what I define as narrow and broad notions of liquidity services. In section 3.2 I evaluate two potential impediments to the effectiveness of open market operations: banks and restrictions that limit open market purchases to short-term bonds. In section 3.3 I set the stage for the analysis that follows by describing how the economy would adjust to an adverse aggregate demand shock without either a reduction in interest rates or an expansion of the monetary base.

In section 3.4 I describe the channels by which expansionary open market operations could counteract the effect of an adverse demand shock when interest rates are at the cost-of-carry floor. The mechanism by which increases in the monetary base are transmitted to spending involves the portfolio rebalancing channel emphasized by monetarists such as Friedman (1969) and Meltzer (1995) and the credit channel emphasized by macroeconomists such as Bernanke and Gertler (1995).[32]

In section 3.5 I evaluate the role that monetary transfers might play in supporting quantitative monetary policy. To the extent that a central bank reverses monetary injections to stabilize the price level after the economy recovers, quantitative policy may result in an increase in public debt. I identify the perceived burden of the public debt as a potential cost of using quantitative policy to stimulate the economy.

3.1 Narrow and Broadly Defined Liquidity Services

For the purpose of thinking about quantitative monetary policy when the interest rate is at the cost-of-carry floor, I distinguish between narrow and broad notions of liquidity services. Narrow liquidity services are those provided by the medium of exchange allowing the public to economize on "shopping time" in transactions. Once the short nominal interest rate has fallen to the cost of storing money, an expansionary open market operation cannot relax the transaction constraint any further to free shopping time for more productive uses.[33] At that point the economy may be said to be satiated in narrow liquidity services provided by the medium of exchange.[34]

I define liquidity broadly as a service yield provided by assets according to how easily they can be turned into cash, either by sale or by serving as collateral for external financing. Liquidity services defined broadly are valued because they can be used to minimize one's exposure to the external finance premium in the sense of Bernanke and Gertler (1995).

---

31. McCallum's (1988) monetary base policy rule could be adapted to this situation.

32. See Friedman (1969, pp. 229–34 and 255–56).

33. Woodford (1999a, p. 87) makes this point forcefully.

34. Note that the reduction of the opportunity cost of holding the medium of exchange to zero and the reduction of the purchasing power of money to zero are two different things. The real demand for the medium of exchange is satiated at the point that the marginal services yield net of the cost of carry becomes zero. At that point the average value, that is, purchasing power of the medium of exchange, is still positive. See Johnson (1969).

Bernanke and Gertler explain that imperfect information and costly enforcement of contracts create a wedge between the cost of funds raised externally (through the issuance of imperfectly collateralized debt) and internal funds.[35] They call the wedge the external finance premium. The premium reflects the deadweight costs associated with the principal-agent problem that typically exists between lenders and borrowers.[36] Among the factors reflected in the premium are the lender's expected costs of evaluation, monitoring, and collection. Bernanke and Gertler emphasize that the external finance premium fluctuates with conditions in the economy. The premium is negatively related to the net worth, that is, the balance sheet health of firms and household borrowers.[37] The cost of funds to bank dependent borrowers is inversely related to the capital cushion of banks themselves.

I regard liquidity services broadly defined as an attribute of an asset that allows its owner to minimize his exposure to the cost of external finance. From this perspective, all assets provide broadly defined liquidity services to one degree or another. Generally speaking, liquidity services contribute to an asset's value together with the asset's direct utility or productive services.[38] Monetary assets such as currency and bank deposits are valued primarily for their implicit liquidity services yield. The implicit liquidity services yield accounts for a smaller share of the total return to holding short-term bonds, and a smaller share still of the return to longer-term bonds and nonfinancial assets.[39]

Consider unimproved land. With a haircut off market value to shield a lender from price fluctuations, unimproved land makes good collateral for a loan because it is inexpensive to monitor. For large parcels, the price risk can be considerable because it takes time and effort to find a buyer. But since a large fraction of the market value of unimproved land can be borrowed against with a relatively small external finance premium, implicit liquidity services provided by unimproved land can be substantial.

In what follows, I assume that the implicit marginal broad liquidity services yield declines (given income, consumption, and wealth) as the aggregate stock of monetary assets increases. Generally speaking, this would be so because the greater abundance of liquidity reduces the exposure of households and firms to the external finance premium. Liquidity broadly defined is at the heart of the leverage that quantitative monetary policy can exert when the nominal interest rate is at the cost-of-carry floor.[40]

35. This paragraph is taken directly from Bernanke and Gertler (1995, pp. 34–35), with minor changes and omissions.

36. "Among the factors reflected in the premium are the lender's expected costs of evaluation, monitoring, and collection; the 'lemons' premium that results from the fact that the borrower inevitably has better information about its prospects than does the lender; and the costs of distortions in the borrower's behavior that stem from moral hazard or from restrictions in the contract intended to contain moral hazard (for example, restrictive covenants or collateral requirements)" Bernanke and Gertler (1995, p. 35).

37. See Mishkin (1978) for an analysis of the household balance sheet in the Great Depression.

38. Keynes (1936) argued this way in chapter 17.

39. Heaton and Lucas (1996) find that transactions costs in the stock market can produce an equity premium of about half of the observed value. Fifty percent of the equity premium in their model is accounted for by the marginal implicit liquidity services yield on short-term bonds.

40. Diamond (1997), Freeman (1985), and Holmström and Tirole (1998) may be interpreted as analyzing broad liquidity services provided by bank deposits, currency, and government bonds, respectively, in models with an external finance premium.

3.2 Banks, Long Bonds, and Open Market Purchases

Could banks short-circuit open market purchases by simply holding newly created reserves instead of lending them? Ordinarily, the answer would be no. Banks could be expected to maintain a minimum reserve to deposit ratio. At the interest rate floor, however, banks could be slower to rebalance their portfolios. Without an accompanying decline in interest rates it might be more difficult to attract new borrowers. If the economy were depressed, the external finance premium could be elevated and acceptable borrowers harder to find. Moreover, at the interest rate floor there is little advantage to buying securities. Thus, an open market acquisition of reserves by banks might not stimulate lending very much, at least initially. Large-scale open market purchases, however, could deplete banks of their securities and put cash in the hands of the nonbank public.

If the public were satiated with liquidity services narrowly defined at the interest rate floor, the public would simply replace short-term securities sold to the central bank with nontransactions bank deposits. Since the two assets are very close substitutes in terms of the broadly defined liquidity services that they provide, open market operations in short-term securities wouldn't matter much. To be effective at the interest rate floor, open market purchases must be undertaken in longer-term securities.[41]

Long bonds would provide relatively little liquidity services per dollar of market value if interest rates were temporarily zero or negative. Bondholders would be exposed to an elevated risk of capital loss due to uncertainty about the timing and magnitude of the rise in short-term interest rates that would accompany an economic recovery. Consequently, long bonds would get a more than usual haircut off market value when used as collateral for external finance. Moreover, the increased risk of

---

Heaton and Lucas (1996) show quantitatively that the equity premium is very sensitive to the stock of short-term government bonds available and is reduced when an outside supply of bonds is increased. Bond holdings provide liquidity services broadly defined by allowing borrowing constrained individuals to smooth consumption without paying transactions costs.

We can interpret the findings as follows. When the stock of outside bonds is small and the marginal implicit liquidity services yield is high, the explicit premium on equity relative to bonds is large because the implicit marginal liquidity yield on bonds is large. As the per capita inventory of bond holdings increases, individuals are better protected against having to smooth consumption by paying large transactions costs to sell other assets. The required explicit bond return rises as the marginal implicit liquidity services yield falls, that is, the explicit equity premium falls.

See Barro (1974) for an early discussion of liquidity services provided by government bonds.

41. In principle, a central bank could buy long-term assets besides bonds. Government bonds or highly-rated private bonds are preferable because they are the most convenient assets to monitor and manage. If the stock of bonds proved inadequate, then assets such as land or gold might be purchased as well. Purchases of foreign currency denominated bonds would also be an option.

Long bonds, land, gold, and foreign exchange all expose the central to unexpected capital losses due to rising interest rates. A central bank could purchase medium-term bonds to minimize its exposure to higher interest rates. However, to achieve the same increase in net broad liquidity, open market operations might have to be carried out on a correspondingly greater scale with little change in exposure to interest rate risk.

A central bank could buy relatively short-lived producer or consumer durables and lease these to the public. Such transactions would amount a substitution of central bank credit for private short-term financing of the durables. The net liquidity effect would reflect the injection of base money minus the loss of private short-term securities. And purchasing durables for the central bank portfolio would involve non-negligable administrative and management costs. This option looks like a more costly version of the previous one.

A central bank could also inject liquidity into the economy by overpaying for assets. Overpaying amounts to making monetary transfers. Transfers are considered in sections 3.5 and 4.2 below.

capital loss would raise the cost of making a market in long bonds and increase their cost of sale. Thus, open market purchases that "monetize" longer-term bonds when interest rates are low could increase substantially broadly defined monetary liquidity.

3.3 An Adverse Aggregate Demand Shock

This section sets the stage for the analysis in section 3.4 of quantitative monetary transmission at the zero bound. The preliminary analysis here assumes that the public expects no change in the real rate of interest, both because the price level is expected to remain constant and because the central bank is not expected to change its short-term interest rate instrument. Such a situation could arise in an economy characterized by credible price stability with the short-term nominal rate at the zero bound.[42] Assume that an adverse aggregate demand shock takes the form of an expected temporary decline in future income prospects.[43]

Since expected permanent income has fallen, households cut current consumption to a level that they expect to sustain through the hard times. Specifically, households wish to save a greater share of current income. Likewise, firms cut current investment, expecting less demand for output. Assuming that the macroeconomy is characterized by monopolistic competition and sticky money output prices, the cut in aggregate demand translates into a decline in firm demand for labor. In this Keynesian world, the perceived decline in income prospects causes real income to fall.

Households and firms react to the actual decline in income by cutting consumption and investment further. The contraction reaches bottom when the rate at which households wish to save out of current income just equals the investment that firms are willing to do. The bottom is reached because as current income looks worse relative to future income, households wish to save less out of current income. If gross investment demand holds up reasonably well, income stabilizes at not too low a level.[44]

Turning to the asset markets, consider first consumer durables, for example, cars and houses. The rise in the marginal utility of current consumption due to the cut in consumption spending makes the initial consumption price of durables too high. Hence, the price of durables falls to the point that the expected return makes owning durables worthwhile.[45] Firm profits and the marginal product of capital are adversely affected by the decline in demand and employment. And the prices of physical capital and claims to intellectual and organizational capital fall as well.

---

42. Assume that long-term interest rates are anchored by the expected path of future short rates up to a term premium and a liquidity spread according to the expectations theory of the term structure.

43. Since I am holding the real interest rate fixed, I am really focusing on what happens inside the disturbance term in the popular "forward-looking IS function" that plays an important role in modern models of monetary policy. See, for example, Kerr and King (1996). The aggregate demand shock, the quantitative monetary policy response, and the effect of quantitative policy on the economy all reside in the disturbance term.

44. By making real interest rates negative, a central bank could encourage investment and lower the saving rate at any level of income. Income would stabilize at a higher level than with no reduction in the real interest rate.

45. In principle, if the central bank made real interest rates sufficiently negative, the price of durables could rise enough to create an expected depreciation.

The fall in asset prices, in turn, negatively influences consumption and investment. The fall in the prices of consumer durables and physical capital relative to their cost of production induces a cutback in investment and a further contraction in aggregate demand, income, and production.[46] The collapse in asset values reduces net worth, the capital of banks, and the value of collateral available for loans. This raises the external finance premium and depresses current spending further. The rise in the external finance premium amplifies the asset price declines and deepens and prolongs the downturn.

To complete the picture, consider the potential that exists for deflation in this depressed economy. If the output gap were large and expected to persist, then firms would try to cut their relative product prices in an effort to increase market share and offset the decline in profits. In aggregate, of course, attempts to cut relative prices would only cause the general price level to fall. That said, an output gap expected to be temporary could result in relatively little price cutting and little deflation. The outcome for deflation would depend critically on the public's confidence in the central bank's power to bring the economy back to full employment reasonably quickly.[47]

Consider the depressed economy from a monetary perspective. On net, the contraction increases the demand for liquidity services broadly defined. Yet a decline in bank lending and an increase in the desired ratio of reserves to deposits probably reduces the stock of monetary assets. Ordinarily, an increase in the implicit marginal liquidity services yield would precipitate an equivalent reduction of explicit returns on liquid assets, for example, short-term securities, relative to expected explicit returns on illiquid assets. But with nominal short-term interest rates at the cost-of-carry floor, the required increase in the expected explicit yield spread between illiquid and liquid assets must show up as an increase in the expected explicit yield on relatively illiquid assets. Thus, the prices of illiquid assets fall relative to the prices of liquid assets to produce the required expected explicit return differential. Lower net worth elevates the external finance premium and raises the value of broad monetary liquidity further. At a minimum, a central bank should use quantitative monetary policy to offset any tendency for a contraction in monetary assets or a rise in the value of broad liquidity services to depress aggregate demand and employment.

3.4 Monetary Transmission at the Interest Rate Floor

Starting from the depressed state described above, consider what would happen if a central bank increased the monetary base by purchasing long bonds from the nonbank public. The object is to describe the transmission mechanism by which open

---

46. Adjustment costs may be involved in the production and installation of consumer and producer capital goods so that aggregate investment responds relatively smoothly to a change in asset prices relative to their costs of production. If the contraction is not too long, we can ignore the effect of investment on stocks, on the marginal service yield of consumer durables, and on the marginal product of capital.

47. See Goodfriend and King (1997) for a discussion of the relationship between the output gap, the markup, and inflation in the modern New Synthesis style macromodel. From the perspective of the New Synthesis, the stickiness of real interest rates and the price level in the face of the adverse demand shock causes the markup to rise as employment and nominal wages fall. Real business cycle reasoning in the New Synthesis context sees the decline in employment as resulting from the temporarily elevated markup tax.

market purchases help to offset the adverse aggregate demand shock independently of the nominal and real interest rate on bonds. The mechanism involves the portfolio rebalancing channel identified by monetarists and the credit channel by which a monetary expansion reduces the external finance premium. Even though I describe the two channels sequentially, it should be emphasized that I regard them as thoroughly intertwined, since broad liquidity services are closely related to the external finance premium.

Consider the portfolio rebalancing channel of monetary transmission. By expanding the monetary base in exchange for long bonds, open market purchases reduce somewhat the high implicit marginal liquidity services yield on monetary assets. As a result, holders of monetary assets seek to rebalance their portfolios by acquiring less liquid assets including consumer durables, physical capital, and claims to intellectual and organizational capital. The public cannot rid itself of the excess aggregate monetary liquidity. But the attempt to rebalance portfolios reverses somewhat the fall in asset prices that accompanied the adverse demand shock. Portfolio balance is achieved when the prices of less liquid assets have regained enough of their lost ground that their expected return has fallen in line with the reduced implicit liquidity yield on monetary assets.[48]

The higher price of assets induces households to consume more out of current income. At the same time the rise in asset prices relative to their cost of production revives investment. The reduced saving rate, and the increase in investment reverse somewhat the contraction in income, consumption, and employment. The rise in the marginal product of physical and organizational capital and in firm profits, and the fall in the marginal utility of consumption, raise asset prices still further.

Now consider the credit channel of monetary transmission. A reduction in the external finance premium is achieved both by the increase in monetary assets and by the rise in asset prices. Balance sheets of households and firms are repaired to a degree. Collateral values reflate, net worth increases, and banks see an increase in capital. Bank lending revives with a decline in the premium on external finance. Credit spreads narrow. Spending increases because the cost of borrowing against future income prospects falls. Greater spending, in turn, has multiplier effects on current income and accelerator effects on investment.[49] Thus, we see that determined open market operations have the power to stimulate spending independently of any effect operating through the real interest rate on bonds.

There are complications, however. One involves the role of expectations and the credibility of open market policy. Open market purchases raise asset prices today by creating expectations that asset prices will be higher tomorrow and so on until the

48. If the real interest rate on bonds is negative, then a decrease in expected future appreciation creates a partially offsetting benefit to holding the asset related to the negative real interest rate on bonds.

49. King (1993, p. 77), describes simulations of the effect of a persistent change in the money stock in a quantitative sticky-price macromodel with a rational expectations investment function. He reports that persistent changes in the demand for final output lead to quantitatively major shifts in the investment demand schedule at given real interest rates. The effects are generally sufficiently important that real interest rates actually rise with a persistent monetary expansion rather than fall. His findings support the idea advanced here that a determined, persistent monetary expansion would stimulate spending without a fall in the interest rate.

economy recovers fully. Open market operations must create a kind of bridge for asset prices. In order to value assets, the public works backward from the future expected recovery. Working backward from such a future period, the public will construct the path of sustainable asset prices based on its view of the way monetary assets influence nonmonetary asset prices, and its view of the central bank's future intentions for open market purchases.

Such reasoning suggests that open market operations are not likely to exert a simple contemporaneous influence on asset prices and spending. The effect of open market operations will depend on expectations for future operations, much as the effect of a current interest rate policy action depends on expectations for future short rates. Quantitative monetary policy is not inherently more difficult to pursue than interest rate policy; but central banks have much more experience pursuing the latter.[50]

There will have to be some experimentation. Ordinarily, relatively small changes in aggregate bank reserves are sufficient to support interest rate policy actions. At the interest rate floor, however, open market purchases must influence liquidity broadly defined in order to be effective. That may require large-scale injections of monetary base, perhaps orders of magnitude larger than usual. Economists will have to develop and estimate models of how the monetary base influences the economy independently of interest rate policy. Costly portfolio adjustment will have to be a feature of such models.[51] Divisia indexes designed to track the liquidity services yield of broad monetary aggregates could help guide quantitative policy.[52] A central bank will have to rely more heavily on information in asset price movements than it does today.

All this should not be seen as too discouraging for quantitative policy, however. With short-term interest rates already at the cost-of-carry floor, large-scale purchases of long bonds would present little risk to the economy. The main complications would involve relations between the central bank and the Treasury, and public debt policy more generally, as discussed in sections 3.5 and 4.2 below.

3.5 Monetary Transfers

Monetary transfers could supplement open market purchases as a means of injecting liquidity into a depressed economy. Transfers that raise permanent income have the potential to stimulate spending independently of an effect operating through either interest rates or asset prices. Hence, monetary transfers should be considered as part of a policy package to help offset an adverse shock to aggregate demand at the interest rate floor.

---

50. One can understand interest rate policies commonly pursued by central banks today without considering money supply or money demand. See, for example, Kerr and King (1996) and Woodford (1999, part 2.2). Models that ignore money presume that a central bank has full credibility for a future price level target or a path for the price level. It should not be forgotten, however, that the credibility for a price path objective devolves from a central bank's power to manage the monetary base to enforce it, if necessary. It was the collapse of credibility for low inflation that caused the Federal Reserve to move temporarily from interest rate to monetary targeting in 1979 to bring inflation down.

51. Christiano and Eichenbaum's (1992) work on the liquidity effect of open market operations highlights the important role played by portfolio adjustment costs.

52. See Barnett and Spindt (1982).

A central bank must be prepared to reverse monetary injections after the economy recovers in order to maintain price stability. Reversing transfers, or reversing open market purchases of long bonds with unexpected capital losses, would increase government debt in the hands of the public. I identify the perceived burden of public debt as a potential cost of using quantitative monetary policy to stimulate the economy at the interest rate floor.

3.5.1 Transfers and Spending. There are opportunities for a central bank to make transfers.[53] For example, monetary transfers would be delivered by financing with money creation a government budget deficit created by cutting taxes. Open market purchases are transfers to the extent that the public is Ricardian and government bonds are not net wealth.[54] And a central bank would transfer money to the public by buying long bonds at low or negative nominal interest and subsequently selling them back to the public with unexpected capital losses.

According to the permanent income hypothesis, money transfers would directly and substantially affect spending on nondurables and services only to the extent that they are expected to be repeated and permanent. Transfers expected to be nonrecurring or reversed in the future would tend to be saved. There are two possibilities. The first is that the economic recovery raises income and real wealth enough to absorb the monetary transfers as permanent additions to the public's desired stock of monetary assets. The public would save the monetary transfers to the extent that it expected this outcome.

The second possibility is that the public's demand for money does not rise to absorb the monetary transfers after the economy recovers. In this case, higher prices would dissipate the wealth effect of monetary transfers as the public attempted to spend its excess money balances. A central bank committed to price stability, however, would reverse any monetary transfers expected to create inflation. Thus, the public could expect any excess (inflationary) monetary transfers to be reversed by the central bank.

Monetary transfers could be reversed in one of two ways. The government could temporarily increase taxes relative to spending. In this case the public would pay the temporarily higher taxes with the transfers it had saved. Alternatively, the central bank could sell securities, in which case the public would receive a stream of interest payments matched by an offsetting stream of higher taxes.

The above argument suggests that monetary transfers should not be expected to exert an effect on spending by permanently relaxing budget constraints for the average household or firm. Nevertheless, transfers would exert the same portfolio rebalancing and credit channel effects on asset prices and spending as open market purchases.[55] Moreover, in severely depressed conditions it might be useful for a cen-

---

53. Mints (1946, 1950, pp. 205–12) considers and recommends various methods of delivering monetary transfers to the public.

54. The application of the Ricardian view of public debt to open market operations is discussed in Barro (1987, pp. 395-96) and Mundell (1971, chapter 1). See also Barro (1974).

55. Monetary injections may be said to exert a wealth effect in the sense that they reduce the external finance premium. This is analogous to a wealth effect exerted when the short-term nominal rate moves closer to zero. In both cases wealth is created by reducing a distortion. The interest rate and asset price

tral bank temporarily to finance a tax cut with money creation in order to distribute money widely throughout the economy. Such transfers might be particularly effective in getting credit-constrained households and firms to spend. The effect on spending might be strengthened if it were known that any need to drain money in the future would be accomplished with open market sales rather than by running in reverse the tax cut by which the monetary transfers were initially distributed. Given a commitment to price stability that disciplines a central bank to reverse monetary injections to prevent inflation, monetary transfers could be used in conjunction with open market purchases to stimulate a depressed economy.

3.5.2 Reversing Monetary Injections, Capital Losses, and the Public Debt. The need to reverse monetary transfers by selling short-term bonds or by reversing open market purchases of long bonds with unexpected capital losses has consequences for the credibility of quantitative policy. Quantitative policy would lack credibility if a central bank were unable to take capital losses. Moreover, either of the above operations results in a permanent increase of government debt in the hands of the public. Quantitative policy would also lack credibility if the country were unwilling to accept a resulting increase of government debt in the hands of the public, or unwilling to run a budget surplus in the future to retire the increased debt.

Consider open market operations. As pointed out above, monetary targeting is effective only if the public believes that sufficient monetary stimulus is forthcoming, and that the monetary stimulus will not be withdrawn before the economy recovers. Such a commitment exposes a central bank to considerable risk of capital loss on its long bonds due to uncertainty about the timing and magnitude of the rise in short-term interest rates that would accompany a recovery.[56] If the public thinks that the central bank is unwilling to take losses on its long bonds, then the central bank's monetary targeting policy will lack credibility.

To help assure the credibility of quantitative policy, the Treasury could agree to indemnify the central bank against capital losses. Recapitalization per se would be costless. It would just involve transferring Treasury securities to the central bank, which would return the interest to the Treasury. The problem is solved unless the central bank has to drain money initially injected by purchasing long bonds after those bonds have taken unexpected capital losses. In that case only a fraction of the money could be drained by selling the long bonds themselves. The rest would have to be drained by selling some of the additional public debt that was issued by the Treasury to recapitalize the central bank. In this case, there would be an increase in the stock of government dept in the hands of the public after the economy and interest rates return to normal.

Now consider monetary transfers. When a central bank transfers money to the public by monetizing a government tax cut, for example, the central bank acquires

---

substitution effects seem to be more important for the transmission of monetary policy than the wealth effect.

56. There would seem to be little scope for minimizing capital losses due to higher interest rates by buying assets other than long-term bonds. See note 41.

1028 : MONEY, CREDIT, AND BANKING

newly issued public debt as an asset. If the public debt is short term, then the monetary transfer can be reversed subsequently by selling that debt to the public with little risk of capital loss. There would be, nevertheless, an increase of government debt in the hands of the public.

Since a larger stock of public debt mainly increases transfer payments, it is costly in the aggregate only to the extent that it involves distorting taxes. Of course, a larger stock of outstanding public debt may be beneficial to the extent that it increases liquidity in the economy. Moreover, the additional debt would be forthcoming only if the economic recovery were secure. Yet the tax liabilities associated with interest payments on the debt could prove to be unpopular. In judging how much to encourage a central bank to use quantitative monetary policy at the interest rate floor, a society would have to evaluate any perceived burden of the public debt against the power of quantitative policy to act forcefully against economic downturns.

4. PRACTICAL CONSIDERATIONS

This section addresses practical issues that arise in connection with the proposed policies. The discussion is in two parts. I consider the carry tax first. Then I take up quantitative policy and issues connected with open market operations and monetary transfers.

4.1 The Carry Tax

Keynes (1936) endorsed a carry tax on money in principle.[57] But he objected that the tax would be impractical on the grounds that money was not unique in having liquidity services attached to it. He appears to have been thinking in terms of a permanent tax on currency, and he argued that substitutes for currency such as bank money, call debts, foreign money, and jewelry would take the place of currency if the latter were taxed.[58]

Keynes's objections would appear to have little force. Currency and non-interest-bearing deposits have been taxed by inflation and reserve requirements for decades. The financial services industry responded by paying interest on deposits, offering new monetary assets such as money market mutual funds, economizing on reserves, and finding ways to avoid reserve requirements. But there was no move away from the monetary base as the medium of exchange.[59] Moreover, a carry tax only would be imposed if the zero bound became a constraint on monetary policy. Impositions of the carry tax would be relatively infrequent and of relatively short duration, and less onerous than the inflation tax and the reserve requirement tax.

---

57. Keynes (1936, p. 234).

58. Keynes (1936, p. 357).

59. As mentioned in section 2.4 above, Jefferson (1997) shows that St. Louis home base velocity has remained near 3.3 since 1980, a period in which the inflation tax averaged around 4 percent and was over 10 percent in the early 1980s.

Hart (1948), too, endorsed a carry tax on money in principle but thought it impractical.[60] He reasoned that a negative nominal interest rate might be hard for the public to accept. Hart agreed, however, that imposing "melting money," as he called it, should be reconsidered if other methods for dealing with a deficiency of aggregate demand proved unworkable. The problem with Hart's position is that systems for imposing a carry tax would have to be put in place well ahead of time. The public might find such systems and the occasional imposition of a carry tax acceptable, however, if the government agreed to use the systems to pay interest on bank reserves and currency when short-term interest rates exceed zero.

Dahlberg (1938), a proponent of the carry tax idea, worried about its legality.[61] But he noted that even the conservative Supreme Court of 1933–36 supported Congress' constitutional power over the nation's money in abrogating contractual gold clauses.[62] Dahlberg pointed out that several states taxed bank deposits as personal property, and that in the last century the Federal government taxed state banks 10 percent on all bank notes outstanding.

The Federal Reserve and the Treasury would need legislation to impose a carry tax, but one would not expect that power to be unconstitutional. In fact, one could make a case that the power to impose a "user fee" on money from time to time should be granted to the central bank in support of the nation's commitment to maintain full employment with stable prices.

Buiter and Panigirtzoglou (1999) worry that "past due" bills might simply circulate like counterfeit currency. Given the nature of the public's use of currency discussed above, however, and the fact that most currency is deposited by merchants, this would not appear to be a problem. Merchants might object that the carry tax amounts to a sales tax. But merchants might be persuaded to go along by pointing out that the carry tax would encourage their customers to spend and make their own borrowing costs negative.

The regressivity of the carry tax is a concern. In response, a few hundred dollars of bank deposits per person could be exempt from the negative interest consequences of the tax, with a government rebate financed out of the carry tax proceeds.

The most serious impediment to imposing a carry tax on money involves the harm it could do if the public were not adequately positioned to withstand a period of negative interest rates. Individuals dependent on interest income such as the elderly would be hurt most. But anyone counting on interest income could be hurt.

An initiative to introduce systems to impose a carry tax should be accompanied by a program to encourage individuals to position their portfolios for the possibility of negative nominal interest rates. In particular, the public should be advised and strongly encouraged to arrange its financial affairs so as not to be excessively dependent on short-term interest income. The responsibility for educating the public could be assumed by the central bank as part of its economic education programs. The eco-

---

60. Hart (1948, pp. 443–47).
61. Dahlberg (1938, p. 97).
62. See Kroszner (1999).

1030 : MONEY, CREDIT, AND BANKING

nomic education part of the implementation of a carry tax would be as important as developing and installing systems to impose the tax itself.

Long bonds are a natural hedge against a period of low or negative interest rates. But the public is shy of the inflation risk in bonds. To reassure the public, and support the central bank's program to encourage the holding of long bonds, the legislature should mandate a price stability objective for the central bank. The Treasury might help to supply long bonds if need be.

4.2 Quantitative Policy

One of the main points of the paper is that quantitative monetary policy needs more fiscal support than usual in order to be effective at the interest rate floor. The relationship between the central bank and the Treasury must be more intimate. To help guide our sense of how that relationship should work, consider the following principle of independent central banking:

"Monetary policy should be used to stabilize the macroeconomy regardless of the fiscal concerns of the Treasury. A fully independent central bank contributes importantly to economic stability. Independence insulates a central bank from short-run inflationary pressures to stimulate employment. It also frees a central bank from having to get legislative approval for its policy actions so that a central bank can react quickly and decisively to macroeconomic and financial market shocks. The legislature bestows independence only because it is necessary for a central bank to do its job effectively. Hence, the presumption is that a central bank ought to perform only those functions absolutely necessary to stabilize the macroeconomy."[63]

Independence requires accountability. An independent central bank should have its goals mandated to it by the legislature. The analysis in this paper suggests that the central bank should be directed to give priority to price level stability and to employ monetary policy to facilitate employment and economic growth.

The principle of independent central banking says that a central bank should not assume unnecessary fiscal burdens. A central bank should not purchase long bonds if it does not need to. Thus, if the short-term nominal interest rate is comfortably above zero, a central bank should do open market operations in short-term bonds. However, when the price level is stable and nominal interest rates are near zero, a central bank must be prepared to purchase long bonds in order to make quantitative policy effective at the interest rate floor. The problem is that a central bank can't do so without the fiscal support of the Treasury.

A second part of the fundamental principle is that the Treasury should support monetary policy with fiscal policy.[64] Accordingly, the Treasury should do two things. First, the Treasury should maintain a sufficiently large stock of outstanding long bonds for the central bank to purchase, if it needs to, at the interest rate floor. In this regard the legislature might consider authorizing the central bank to purchase long-

---

63. With minor changes, this paragraph comes from Goodfriend (1994, p. 573).

64. Fiscal accommodation ordinarily occurs because the Treasury accepts whatever interest earnings transfers it gets from the central bank arising from changes in a central bank's portfolio as a result of its monetary policy actions.

term assets other than government bonds in case there is an insufficient supply of the latter.[65]

Second, the Treasury ought to indemnify the central bank against capital losses on long bonds so that the central bank could aggressively pursue quantitative policy to stimulate a depressed economy.[66] To facilitate the indemnification, the Treasury should allow the central bank to accumulate, in a capital account, coupons earned on long bonds purchased to stimulate the economy. Moreover, the central bank should be empowered to enlarge its surplus capital to provide additional protection for its financial independence. Completely fortifying the central bank against capital losses would commit the Treasury to expand the public debt, perhaps substantially, in support of monetary policy. Such enhanced fiscal support of monetary policy might require legislation.

To further protect its financial independence, the central bank should routinely hold a share of its portfolio in long bonds to hedge its interest income against the possibility that short rates may go to zero or become negative. In return for a legislative commitment to price stability and the fiscal support of the Treasury, the central bank should be willing to consider monetizing a tax cut with money creation as long as monetization is consistent with price stability. As mentioned above, in severely depressed conditions temporarily transferring money widely and in large quantity to the public might be a valuable policy option.

5. CONCLUSION

I proposed and developed three options for overcoming the zero bound on interest rate policy: a carry tax on money, open market operations in long bonds, and monetary transfers. In the first half of the paper I explained how a variable carry tax on electronic bank reserves could allow a central bank to target negative nominal interest rates. When short-term interest rates are pressed against the cost-of-carry floor, the carry tax would anchor the short end of the yield curve much as the intended federal funds rate does today in the United States. A carry tax on currency could supplement the carry tax on electronic reserves by creating more leeway to make interest rates negative.

In the second half of the paper I discussed how quantitative policy—open market purchases and monetary transfers—could stimulate spending at the interest rate floor

---

65. The Federal Reserve Act would have to be amended to allow the Fed to do so. See Small and Clouse (1999).

66. There is a well-known instance in which the U.S. Treasury protected its long bond holders from capital losses. The 1951 Treasury—Federal Reserve Accord freed the Federal Reserve from pegging long bond rates at 2.5 percent. As part of the processes of allowing long-term interest rates to move higher, the Treasury agreed to exchange at par some long bonds with a 2.5 percent coupon for long bonds with a 2.75 percent coupon. Long-term rates moved up to about 2.75 percent soon after the Accord. And bondholders that participated in the conversion managed to avoid capital losses. The Fed had been accumulating long bonds prior to the Accord as a result of its support of bond prices. The Treasury's exchange offer allowed the Fed to escape capital losses on its substantial holdings of long bonds. See Eichengreen and Garber (1990).

by creating liquidity broadly defined. I described in some detail how quantitative policy could act independently of interest rate policy through a portfolio rebalancing channel and a credit channel of monetary transmission. The need for a central bank to drain money (by reversing monetary transfers or by selling long bonds with unexpected capital losses) to stabilize the price level after an economy recovers could greatly increase government debt in the hands of the public. I identified the perceived burden of this additional public debt as a potential cost of using quantitative policy to stimulate spending. I also pointed out that a central bank would need more fiscal support than usual from the Treasury to effectively pursue quantitative monetary policy at the interest rate floor.

LITERATURE CITED

Abelson, Reed. "If Deflation Hits It's a Whole New Game." *New York Times*, November 22, 1998, 1, 9.

Barnett, William, and Paul Spindt. "Divisia Monetary Aggregates: Compilation, Data, and Historical Behavior." Staff Studies 116, Board of Governors of the Federal Reserve System, May 1982.

Barro, Robert. "Are Government Bonds Net Wealth?" *Journal of Political Economy* 82 (November/December 1974), 1095–1117.

———. *Macroeconomics*. New York: John Wiley, 1987.

Benhabib, Jess, Stephanie Schmitt-Grohë, and Martin Uribe. "The Perils of Taylor Rules." Manuscript, New York University, 1999.

Bernanke, Bernard, and Mark Gertler. "Inside the Black Box: The Credit Channel of Monetary Policy Transmission." *Journal of Economic Perspectives* 9 (Fall 1995), 27–48.

Buiter, Willem, and Nikolaos Panigirtzoglou. "Liquidity Traps: How to Avoid Them and How to Escape Them." Working Paper 7245. Cambridge, Mass.: National Bureau of Economic Research, July 1999.

Cecchetti, Stephen G. "The Case of the Negative Nominal Interest Rates: New Estimates of the Term Structure of Interest Rates during the Great Depression." *Journal of Political Economy* 96 (December 1988), 1111–41.

Christiano, Lawrence J., and Martin Eichenbaum. "Liquidity Effects and the Monetary Transmission Mechanism." *American Economic Review* 82 (May 1992), 346–53.

Clouse, James, Dale Henderson, Athanasios Orphanides, David Small, and Peter Tinsley. "Monetary Policy When the Norminal Short-Term Interest Rate Is Zero." Manuscript, Board of Governors of the Federal Reserve System, 1999.

Cole, Harold L., and Narayana Kocherlakota. "Zero Nominal Interest Rates: Why They're Good and How to Get Them." Federal Reserve Bank of Minneapolis *Quarterly Review* 22 (Spring 1998), 2–10.

"Could It Happen Again?" *The Economist* (February 20, 1999), 19–25.

Dahlberg, Arthur. *When Capital Goes On Strike*. New York: Harper, 1938.

"Deflation and All That." *The Economist* (November 15, 1997), 77–8.

Diamond, Douglas. "Liquidity, Banks, and Markets." *Journal of Political Economy* 105 (October 1997), 928–56.

Eichengreen, Barry, and Peter Garber. "Before the Accord: U.S. Monetary-Financial Policy 1945–51." Working paper 3380. Cambridge, Mass.: National Bureau of Economic Research, June 1990.

Faison, Seth. "Fearing Deflation, Chinese Set Limits on New Factories." *New York Times,* August 19, 1999, 1.

Feldstein, Martin. "The Costs of Going fom Low Inflation to Price Stability." In *Reducing Inflation: Motivation and Strategy,* edited by Christian D. Romer and David H. Romer, pp. 123–66. Chicago, University of Chicago Press, 1997.

Fischer, Stanley. "Why Are Central Banks Pursuing Long-Run Price Stability?" In *Achieving Price Stability,* pp. 7–34. Kansas City: Federal Reserve Bank of Kansas City, 1996.

Fisher, Irving. *The Theory of Interest.* Fairfield, N.J.: Augustus M. Kelley, 1986. (Reprint of 1930 edition)

_____. *Stamp Scrip.* New York: Adelphi Co., 1933.

Freeman, Scott. "Transactions Costs and the Optimal Quantity of Money." *Journal of Political Economy* 93 (February 1985), 146–57.

Friedman, Milton. *The Optimum Quantity of Money and Other Essays.* Chicago: Aldine Publishing Co., 1969.

Frost, Peter A. "Banks' Demand for Excess Reserves." *Journal of Political Economy* 79 (July/August 1971), 805–25.

Fuhrer, Jeff, and Brian Madigan. "Monetary Policy When Interest Rates Are Bounded at Zero." *Review of Economics and Statistics* 79 (November 1997), 573–85.

Goodfriend, Marvin, "Why We Need an Accord for Federal Reserve Credit Policy." *Journal of Money, Credit, and Banking* 26 (August 1994, Part 2), 572–80.

_____. "Monetary Policy Comes of Age: A 20th Century Odyssey." Federal Reserve Bank of Richmond *Economic Quarterly* (Winter 1997), 1–22.

Goodfriend, Marvin, and Robert King. "The New Neoclassical Synthesis and the Role of Monetary Policy." In NBER *Macroeconomics Annual,* edited by Ben Bernanke and Julio Rotemberg, pp. 231–82. Cambridge, Mass.: MIT Press, 1997.

Goodfriend, Marvin, and Jeffery M. Lacker. "Limited Commitment and Central Bank Lending." Federal Reserve Bank of Richmond *Economic Quarterly* (Fall 1999).

Hall, Robert. "Controlling the Price Level." Working paper 6914. Cambridge, Mass.: National Bureau of Economic Research, January 1999.

Hart, Albert G. *Money, Debt, and Economic Activity.* New York: Prentice-Hall, 1948.

Hayami, Masaru. "On Recent Monetary Policy." Bank of Japan, Tokyo, June 1999.

Heaton, John, and Deborah Lucas. "Evaluating the Effects of Incomplete Markets on Risk Sharing and Asset Pricing." *Journal of Political Economy* 104 (June 1996), 443–87.

Holmström, Bengt, and Jean Tirole. "Private and Public Supply of Liquidity." *Journal of Political Economy* 106 (February 1998), 1–40.

Ibbotson, R. *Stocks, Bonds, Bills, and Inflation.* Ibbotson Associates, 1998.

Jefferson, Philip N. "Home Base and Monetary Base Rules: Elementary Evidence from the 1980s and 1990s." Manuscript. Board of Governors of the Federal Reserve System, April 1997.

Johnson, Harry. "Pesek and Saving's Theory of Money and Wealth: A Comment." *Journal of Money, Credit, and Banking* 1 (August 1969), 535–37.

Kerr, William, and Robert G. King. "Limits on Interest Rate Rules in the IS Model." Federal Reserve Bank of Richmond *Economic Quarterly* 82 (Spring 1996), 47–75.

Keynes, John Maynard. *The General Theory of Employment, Interest, and Money.* London: McMillan and Company, 1957. (first edition 1936).

King, Robert G. "Will the New Keynesian Macroeconomics Resurrect the IS-LM Model." *Journal of Economic Perspectives* 7 (Winter 1993), 57–82.

Kroszner, Randall S. "Repudiaton of the Gold Index Clause in Long-Term Debt during the Great Depression." Graduate School of Business, University of Chicago, 1999.

1034 : MONEY, CREDIT, AND BANKING

Krugman, Paul. "It's Baaack: Japan's Slump and the Return of the Liquidity Trap." *Brookings Papers on Economic Activity* 2 (1998), 137–87.

_____. *The Return of Depression Economics*. New York: W.W. Norton and Company, 1999.

Kynge, James, and Peter Montagnon. "China Warns Over Its Ability to Halt Deflation." *Financial Times* (February 7, 1999), 1.

Lebow, David. "Monetary Policy at Near Zero Interest Rates." Manuscript. Board of Governors of the Federal Reserve System, July 1993.

Lerner, Abba P. "The Essential Properties of Interest and Money." *Quarterly Journal of Economics* 66 (May 1952), 172–93.

Lucas, Robert. "Inflation and Welfare." *Econometrica* 68 (March 2000), 247–74.

McCallum, Bennett. "Robustness Properties of a Rule for Monetary Policy." *Carnegie-Rochester Conference Series on Public Policy* 29 (Autumn 1988), 173–204.

_____. "Theoretical Analysis Regarding a Zero Lower Bound on Nominal Interest Rates." *Journal of Money, Credit, and Banking* 32 (November 2000, Part 2), 870–904.

McCallum, Bennett, and Marvin Goodfriend. "Demand for Money: Theoretical Studies." In *The New Palgrave: A Dictionary of Economics*, edited by John Eatwell, Murray Milgate, and Peter Newman, pp. 775–80. New York: The Stockton Press, 1987.

Meltzer, Allan H. "Monetary Credit and (Other) Transmission Processes: A Monetarist Perspective." *Journal of Economic Perspectives* 9 (Fall 1995), 49–72.

_____. "The Transmission Process." Prepared for the Bundesbank Conference on the Monetary Transmission Process, March 1999.

Mints, Lloyd. "Monetary Policy." *The Review of Economic Statistics* 28 (May 1946), 60–9.

_____. *Monetary Policy for a Competitive Society*. New York: McGraw-Hill, 1950.

Mishkin, Frederic. "The Household Balance Sheet in the Great Depression." *Journal of Economic History* 38 (December 1978), 918–37.

Mogi, Chikako, and Gregory Zuckerman. "T-Bills' Yield in Japan Shifts to the Negative." *Wall Street Journal,* November 6, 1998, C1, C19.

Mundell, Robert. "Money, Debt, and the Rate of Interest." In *Monetary Theory*, pp. 5–13. Pacific Palisades, Calif.: Goodyear Publishing Co., 1971.

_____. "The New Danger." *The Economist,* February 20, 1999, 15.

Okina, Kunio. "Monetary Policy under Zero Inflation — A Response to Criticisms and Questions Regarding Monetary Policy." *Monetary and Economic Studies*, Bank of Japan 17 (December 1999), 157–82.

Orphanides, Athanasios, and Volcker Wieland. "Price Stability and Monetary Policy Effectiveness When Nominal Interest Rates Are Bounded at Zero." Manuscript, Board of Governors of the Federal Reserve System, 1998.

Porter, Richard D., and Ruth A. Judson. "The Location of U.S. Currency: How Much Is Abroad?" *Federal Reserve Bulletin* (October 1996), 883–903.

Reifschneider, David, and John C. Williams. "Three Lessons for Monetary Policy in a Low Inflation Era." *Journal of Money, Credit, and Banking* 32 (November 2000, Part 2).

Romer, Christina D. "What Ended the Great Depression." *Journal of Economic History* 52 (December 1992), 757–84.

Rotemberg, Julio, and Michael Woodford. "Interest Rate Rules in an Estimated Sticky Price Model." In *Monetary Policy Rules* (A National Bureau of Economic Research Conference Report) edited by John B. Taylor, pp. 57–126. Chicago: University of Chicago Press, 1999.

Small, David, and James Clouse. "The Limits of the Federal Reserve Act: What Types of Policy Actions May the Federal Reserve Undertake?" Manuscript. Board of Governors of the Federal Reserve System, May 1999.

Stavins, Joanna. "Checking Accounts: What Do Banks Offer and What Do Consumers Value?" Federal Reserve Bank of Boston *New England Economic Review* (March/April 1999), 3–13.

Summers, Laurence. "How Should Long-Term Monetary Policy Be Determined." *Journal of Money, Credit, and Banking* 23 (August 1991, Part 2), 625–31.

_____. "Commentary: Why Are Central Banks Pursuing Long-Run Price Stability?" In *Achieving Price Stability*, pp. 35–43. Kansas City: Federal Reserve Bank of Kansas City, 1996.

Svensson, Lars E.O. "How Should Monetary Policy Be Conducted in an Era of Price Stability." Manuscript, Institute for International Economic Studies, August 1999.

Taylor, John B. "Discretion versus Policy Rules in Practice." *Carnegie-Rochester Conference Series on Public Policy* 39 (December 1993), 195–214.

Tetlow, Robert, and John C. Williams. "Implementing Price Stability: Banks, Boundaries and Inflation Targeting." Working paper, Board of Governors of the Federal Reserve System, Washington, March 1998.

Uchitelle, Louis. "Reviving the Economics of Fear." *New York Times,* July 2, 1999, C1.

Wolman, Alexander. "Staggered Price Setting and the Zero Bound on Nominal Interest Rates." Federal Reserve Bank of Richmond *Economic Quarterly* 84 (Fall 1998), 1–24.

_____. "Zero Inflation and the Friedman Rule: A Welfare Comparison." Federal Reserve Bank of Richmond *Economic Quarterly* 83 (Fall 1997), 1–21.

Woodford, Michael. "Interest and Prices." Manuscript, Princeton University, April 1999a.

_____. "Optimal Monetary Policy Inertia." Working paper 7261, National Bureau of Economic Research, July 1999b.

Part III
Role of Money in Monetary Policy

[7]
Monetary Policy in a World Without Money*

Michael Woodford
Princeton University.

Abstract

This paper considers whether the development of 'electronic money' poses any threat to the ability of central banks to control the value of their national currencies through conventional monetary policy. It argues that, even if the demand for base money for use in facilitating transactions is largely or even completely eliminated, monetary policy should continue to be effective. Macroeconomic stabilization depends only upon the ability of central banks to control a short-term nominal interest rate, and this would continue to be possible, in particular through the use of a 'channel' system for the implementation of policy, like those currently used in Canada, Australia and New Zealand.

*Prepared for a conference on 'The Future of Monetary Policy', held at the World Bank on July 11, 2000. The paper was written during my tenure as Professorial Fellow in Monetary Economics at the Reserve Bank of New Zealand and Victoria University of Wellington, and I thank both institutions for their hospitality and assistance. I would also like to thank David Archer, Barry Bosworth, Roger Bowden, Andy Brookes, Kevin Clinton, Ben Friedman, Arthur Grimes, Bruce White, and Julian Wright for helpful discussions, Tim Hampton for providing me with New Zealand data, and Gauti Eggertsson for research assistance. Opinions expressed here should not be construed as those of the Reserve Bank of New Zealand.

230 *Michael Woodford*

I. Introduction

The revolution in information technology (IT) all around us has led to eager speculation about the ways in which business practices may be fundamentally transformed. The promise of the 'New Economy' has excited the imaginations both of young people seeking careers with a bright future and investors hoping for dazzling capital gains. Many executives in the established firms of the 'old economy' must also ask themselves, with some trepidation, how precarious their present market situations may be. Among those institutions of the 'old economy' that ask if they may soon be rendered obsolete, we may now list central banks, who are beginning to ask themselves if their capacity to stabilize the value of their national currencies may not be eroded by the development of electronic means of payment.

The alarm has been raised in particular by a widely discussed recent essay by Benjamin Friedman (1999).[1] Friedman begins by proposing that it is something of a puzzle that central banks are able to control the pace of spending in large economies by controlling the supply of 'base money' when this monetary base is itself so small in value relative to the size of those economies. The scale of the transactions in securities markets through which central banks such as the US Federal Reserve adjust the supply of base money is even more minuscule when compared to the overall volume of trade in those markets. He then argues that this disparity of scale has grown more extreme in the past quarter century as a result of institutional changes that have eroded the role of base money in transactions, and that advances in IT are likely to carry those trends still farther in the next few decades.[2] In the absence of aggressive regulatory intervention to head off such developments, the central bank of the future will be 'an army with only a signal corps' – able to indicate to the private sector how it believes that monetary conditions should develop, but not able to do anything about it if the private sector has opinions of its own.

Mervyn King (1999) has recently offered an even more radical view of the (somewhat more distant) future, in a discussion of the prospects for central banking in the twenty-first century. King proposes that the twentieth century was the golden age of central banking – a time in which central banks rose to an unprecedented importance in economic affairs, notably as a result of the rise of managed fiat currencies as a substitute for the commodity money of the past – and one in which they achieved an influence that they may never

---

[1]For an example of the attention given to Friedman's analysis in the press, see 'Who Needs Money?', *The Economist*, January 22, 2000.

[2]Henckel et al. (1999) review similar developments, though they reach a very different conclusion about the threat posed to the efficacy of monetary policy.

again have, as the development of 'electronic money' eliminates their monopoly position as suppliers of means of payment. King's discussion is more elegiac than alarmist; he does not suggest that regulation could do much to hold off the progress of technology and, instead, proposes that central bankers display a degree of humility, lest they be hustled from the stage with undue indignity.

II. Will Money Disappear, and Does it Matter?

But do prospective advances in IT really threaten central banks' capacity to regulate the overall level of spending in the economy, and hence to stabilize the general level of prices? The claim that they do depends, first, on the premise that the effectiveness of monetary policy depends on the private sector's need to hold base money (directly or indirectly, through financial intermediaries) in order to execute purchases of goods and services, and second, on the premise that improved methods of information processing should substantially, or even completely, eliminate the need to hold base money. Let us first consider the nature of this second claim.

The monetary base – the liabilities of the central bank that are held by private parties so as to facilitate payments – can be broadly divided into two parts: the *currency* (notes and coins) that private parties hold for use as a means of payment, and the *reserves* that commercial banks hold in accounts at the central bank in connection with the transactions services that they supply their customers. These bank reserves, in the typical textbook account, are held in proportion to the size of the transactions balances (such as checking accounts) that the public maintains at the banks, owing to the existence of legal reserve requirements; and this still accounts for most of actual bank reserves in a country like the USA. In countries such as the UK, Sweden, Canada, Australia and New Zealand, among others, there are instead no longer any reserve requirements, but commercial banks still hold *settlement balances* with the central bank so as to allow them to clear the payments made by their clients.[3] Regardless of the component of the monetary base with which we are concerned, the private sector's demand for such assets is plausibly proportional to the money value of transactions in the economy, and it is in this way that it is often supposed that variations in the supply of base money directly determine the flow of spending in dollar terms.

How should advances in IT affect the demand for base money of these various types? The most obvious possibility is through the development of

---

[3]See Borio (1997), Sellon and Weiner (1996, 1997) and Henckel et al. (1999) for further discussion of the worldwide trend toward reduction or elimination of such requirements.

232   *Michael Woodford*

convenient ways of executing payments that might in the past have required the use of currency. Electronic funds transfer at point of sale (EFTPOS), already quite common in countries like New Zealand, is an obvious example. The widespread use of stored value cards, currently being experimented with in a number of countries might well erode the demand for currency even more significantly, by being practical for use in an even broader range of purchases, owing to the absence of a need for communication with the buyer's bank.

Charles Goodhart (2000) has argued that currency is unlikely ever to be completely replaced, owing to its uniquely convenient features as a means of payment and, as we shall see, this is in any event not the potential innovation that poses the greatest challenges to current methods of implementation of monetary policy. But while the replacement of currency is probably the threat to receive the greatest recent attention, improvements in IT might well erode demand for other components of the monetary base as well.

In the case of the demand for reserves owing to reserve requirements, faster information processing facilitates the transfer of funds between accounts not subject to such requirements and the 'transactions balances' that are, thus allowing payments to be made while maintaining low average balances subject to the reserve requirements. This possibility has made the concept of 'transactions balances' increasingly unsustainable from a conceptual point of view, and is surely one of the reasons for the worldwide trend toward the elimination of reserve requirements. It is likely that countries like the USA will follow suit before long.

However, monetary policy remains effective, even in those countries that have completely eliminated required reserves, even if the methods that they use to implement monetary policy are rather different than those still employed in the USA. Still, this arguably depends on a residual demand for central-bank settlement balances. The demand for these might also be reduced by advances in IT. For, even if all payments are cleared through the central bank, commercial banks' demand for a non-zero level of settlement balances depends on their inability to perfectly forecast their payment flows, and to arrange transactions in the interbank market throughout the day so as to maintain settlement balances constantly at zero. With more efficient communications between banks, it should, in principle, be possible to borrow overnight cash from another bank only in the instant that it is needed for final settlement of a payment, at which time the paying bank's settlement account would return to a zero balance. Since every payment that is made is received by someone, a sufficiently efficient market for the reallocation of funds among banks should allow all banks to operate with settlement balances near zero.

A final possibility, raised by Mervyn King in particular, is the eventual elimination of the demand for settlement balances owing to the development of electronic networks allowing payments to be settled without even the involvement of central-bank settlement accounts. This prospect is highly speculative at present; most current proposals for variants of 'electronic money' still depend on the final settlement of transactions through the central bank, even if payments are made using electronic signals rather than old-fashioned instruments such as paper checks. And some, such as Charles Freedman (2000), doubt that the special role of central banks in providing for final settlement could ever be replaced. Yet the idea seems conceivable at least in principle, since the question of finality of settlement is ultimately a question of the quality of one's information about the accounts of the parties with whom one transacts – and while the development of central banking has undoubtedly been a useful way of economizing on limited information-processing capacities, it is not clear that advances in technology could not make other methods viable.

I shall not here seek to evaluate which of these various attempts to imagine the payments technologies of the future are more likely to be correct. Instead, I shall argue that concerns about the consequences of the IT revolution for the role of central banks are exaggerated, not so much on the ground that advances in computing are unlikely to fundamentally transform the payments mechanism, but on the ground that even such radical changes as might someday develop are unlikely to interfere with the conduct of monetary policy.

There are several reasons why I believe that the articles mentioned above exaggerate the potential problem. These all have to do with the inadequacy of the common assumption that the effects of monetary policy depend on a mechanical connection between the monetary base and the volume of nominal spending, which is then presumably dependent on a need to use base money as a means of payment. This assumption leads easily to a number of misconceptions.

The first misconception is a failure to recognize that a central bank only needs to be able to control the level of short-term nominal interest rates to achieve its stabilization goals. In practice, central banks generally seek to achieve an operating target for an overnight interest rate in the inter-bank market for reserves held at the central bank. Control of this rate then directly affects other short-term interest rates, which, in turn, determine longer-term interest rates and exchange rates, which ultimately determine spending and pricing decisions.

It is important to note that there need not be a stable relation between this overnight interest rate and the size of the monetary base for the central bank to effectively control overnight interest rates. Innovations in means of payment may complicate the use of quantity targets to achieve a given level of overnight interest rates, or even to render it infeasible. As a result, some central banks, like the US Federal Reserve, may have to modify their operating procedures, so as to more directly fix overnight interest rates. But this would require no change in the way in which the Federal Reserve adjusts its operating target for the federal funds rate in response to changing economic conditions and should not, in any way, impair the effectiveness of the Federal Reserve's stabilization policy.

A second misconception is the apparent assumption that the use of *currency* for retail transactions is important for the monetary transmission mechanism. It is true that the demand for currency is the largest part of private-sector demand for the monetary base under current conditions[4] – and so a significant reduction in the use of currency would greatly reduce the size of the monetary base – but a large monetary base is in no way essential for effective central-bank control of short-term interest rates.

Furthermore, the overnight interest rate that a typical central bank actually seeks to control is determined in the interbank market for bank reserves. The public's demand for currency affects this only insofar as it affects the *supply of bank reserves*. If people wish to hold more currency, then banks must reduce their reserves at the central bank in order to acquire the currency. For this not to reduce the supply of bank reserves, an offsetting open-market operation by the central bank is required, but, under typical circumstances, this is a relatively minor complication. Furthermore, the complete elimination of the use of currency in minor transactions would only make monetary control under current operating procedures *easier*, by making it simpler for the central bank to control the supply of bank reserves.

A final misconception is the assumption that in order to 'tighten' policy – raising overnight interest rates – the central bank must ration bank reserves, making reserves scarce enough for banks to be willing to hold the remaining supply, even though the opportunity cost of holding reserves has risen. To have this effect the capacity for rationing of supply would obviously depend on the non-existence of sufficiently good substitutes for the use of bank reserves, so that even a large spread between the interest rate available on other liquid assets and that paid on reserves does not result in complete substitution away from reserves. It thus requires a sort of monopoly power on the part of the central bank, and one might worry that innovations in means of payment could seriously undermine this.

However, conventional analysis on this point implicitly assumes a *zero rate of interest on reserves*, so that raising interest rates in the economy at large (what the central bank needs to do to rein in spending) requires that the central bank be able to increase this *spread*. This standard assumption remains true in the USA, but is not true in many other countries. Furthermore, in several

---

[4]For example, it accounts for more than 84% of central bank liabilities in countries such as the USA, Canada and Japan (Bank for International Settlements, 1996, Table 1).

other countries (below I shall discuss in particular the implementation of policy in Canada, Australia and New Zealand), changes in the *level* of interest rates are currently brought about without any variation in the size of the spread between the overnight rate available in the interbank market and the interest rate paid on funds held overnight with the central bank. Instead, the interest rate in the interbank market and the interest rate on reserves are always raised (or lowered) in tandem.

Because such a system does not require variation in the spread between the return on other assets and that on bank reserves, or even the *existence* of any substantial spread, it does not depend on bank reserves fulfilling a unique function that gives the central bank monopoly power. My conclusion is that while advances in IT may well require changes in the way in which monetary policy is implemented in countries like the USA, the ability of central banks to control inflation will not be undermined; and in the case of countries like Canada, Australia or New Zealand, the method of interest-rate control that is currently used (the 'channel' system to be described below) should continue to be perfectly effective, even in the face of the most radical of the technical changes that are currently envisioned.

I now elaborate on each of these points. I shall first consider the effects of erosion of demand for central-bank liabilities in the case that diminution of monetary frictions does not eliminate the central bank's ability to control the interest-rate spread between its own liabilities and other financial assets, and argue that, in this case, monetary policy could still be effective, even in the absence of interest payments on reserves. I shall then consider the more radical possibility of a loss of the central bank's ability to materially affect this spread. In this case, I shall argue that more significant changes in the implementation of monetary policy would be required in countries like the USA, but that the method currently used in countries like Canada, Australia and New Zealand would continue to be perfectly effective.

As the crucial monetary policy decision would continue to be the adjustment of the central bank's operating target for an overnight interest rate (such as the US federal funds rate), this would still require no fundamental change in the way in which monetary policy is conceived, and would imply no reduction in a central bank's ability to stabilize either economic activity or inflation. Thus there is every reason to expect that, in the coming century, the role of central banks in the control of inflation will be essentially the same as it is now.

III. Interest-Rate Control with Zero Interest on Bank Reserves

In considering whether interest-rate control should still be possible even without the payment of interest on base money, it is useful to begin by discussing

how short-term nominal interest rates are determined under current US institutional arrangements (which involve no interest payments on bank reserves).
We can then take up the question of what changes might be required by the
development of new payments media.

In the United States, Federal Reserve policy is formulated in terms of an
operating target for the federal funds rate, an overnight interest rate in the
interbank market for reserves held at the Federal Reserve. The determination
of the equilibrium federal funds rate is explained in Figure 1. The effective
supply of reserves at any given level of the funds rate can be described by a
relation of the form

$$TR = NBR + b(FF - DR) \qquad (1)$$

where TR denotes total reserves, NBR the quantity of non-borrowed reserves,
and the function $b(s)$ the quantity of reserves that banks are willing to borrow
at the discount window, as a function of the spread s between the federal funds
rate FF and the discount rate DR.

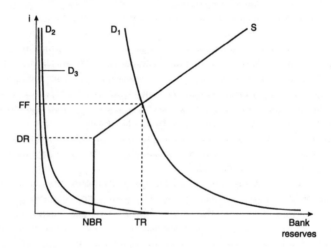

Figure 1: The market for bank reserves (USA)

This last function increases from zero in the case of a zero spread, becoming
a progressively greater positive quantity as the spread increases. Here the idea
is that there will be no willingness to borrow at the discount window if
reserves are obtainable on the interbank market at a funds rate lower than the
discount rate. When the funds rate exceeds the discount rate, banks are willing

Monetary Policy in a World Without Money 237

to borrow, but not an unlimited amount in the case of only a small difference in rates, as there are also implicit costs of borrowing at the discount window. These implicit marginal costs are generally assumed to be increasing in the amount borrowed, resulting in a well-documented increasing relationship between discount-window borrowing and the differential between the funds rate and the discount rate. The total effective supply of reserves implied by equation (1) can then be graphed as the schedule S in Figure 1.

Banks' aggregate demand for reserves, primarily as a result of reserve requirements, plotted as a function of the funds rate, is indicated by the schedule D_1 in the figure. The equilibrium funds rate FF and the associated level of total reserves TR are then determined by the intersection of the two schedules. The Federal Reserve influences the equilibrium funds rate through open-market purchases or sales of government securities that change the quantity of non-borrowed reserves NBR available to the banks in aggregate. Such an open-market operation shifts the entire schedule S horizontally. This, in turn, changes the equilibrium funds rate. (Specifically, an open-market sale of securities decreases non-borrowed reserves, resulting in a higher equilibrium funds rate.) Typically, the demand for reserves schedule D_1 is assumed to be relatively interest-inelastic, especially in the short run. Then the size of open-market operation required to bring about a given increase in the funds rate depends mainly on the amount by which the willingness to borrow at the discount window is expected to be increased by the higher spread between the funds rate and the discount rate. One reduces the supply of non-borrowed reserves, requiring the banks in aggregate to increase their discount-window borrowing by that amount, so that the funds rate is bid up to a level reflecting the implicit cost of discount-window borrowing to the increased extent.

How should this mechanism be affected by the development of electronic means of payment? As noted earlier, the development of 'electronic cash' as a substitute for the use of currency in small transactions should have no material effect on the possibility of monetary control through this mechanism at all. Note that nothing has been said about the demand for currency at all in the above account. In fact, if the demand for currency is interest-sensitive, this complicates the story only slightly; the size of the open-market operation required to raise short-term interest rates a given amount has to be corrected for the increase in the supply of non-borrowed reserves that occurs when households and firms choose to reduce their currency holdings by depositing the currency with banks. If the development of 'electronic cash' were to eliminate the use of currency altogether – or if currency came to be used solely for special types of transactions, such as illegal ones, so that the remaining currency demand became more completely interest-inelastic – then the above method of control of the federal funds rate through open-market operations would work all the more perfectly.

A less trivial question arises in the case of innovations that might sharply reduce the demand for bank reserves, for reasons of the sort discussed earlier. One might envisage a radical shift to the left of the demand schedule D_1, to a schedule such as D_2 or D_3 instead. This would admittedly create problems for the Federal Reserve's method of achieving its funds rate targets, as set out above. That method is based on creating a shortfall of non-borrowed reserves (relative to banks' aggregate desired reserves) of a sufficient size to induce the desired interest-rate spread. However, if desired reserves themselves came to be negligible, it would not be possible in this way ever to induce any very substantial quantity of borrowing at the discount window.

Of course, one could still vary the supply of reserves through open-market operations, but if the demand for reserves were extremely inelastic (as implied by schedule D_2 or D_3), and it were also not possible to bring about significant variations in discount-window borrowing, it would be quite hard to calculate the exact size of (very small) open-market operation required to bring about a given size change in the funds rate. In particular, if the remaining demand for bank reserves were also *unstable* – say, fluctuating arbitrarily between schedules D_2 and D_3 – then control of the quantity of non-borrowed reserves through open-market operations could result in extreme funds-rate volatility.[5]

Still, this is really just a problem with the attempt to achieve one's funds-rate targets through choice of *a target level of non-borrowed reserves*, which is then arranged through a given size of open-market operation; there is no genuine infeasibility of interest-rate control by the central bank in such an environment. The demand schedules D_2 and D_3 still imply that any positive funds rate is a possible equilibrium, in the case of an appropriate supply of bank reserves; it is simply necessary that the Federal Reserve supplies the quantity of reserves that happens to be demanded at its target funds rate. Neither a highly inelastic demand for reserves nor an unstable demand would

---

[5]In practice, countries in which bank reserves are held only for settlement purposes (as required reserves have been eliminated) find that the aggregate quantity of overnight settlement cash held by commercial banks can vary sharply over short periods of time, in the absence of any notable changes in interest rates or the volume of real transactions in the economy. See, for example, the high-frequency variation in settlement cash in New Zealand plotted in Figure 3 on page 244, in a period in which the overnight interest rate (Figure 4 on page 249) is extremely stable from one day to the next. There are, in particular, two surges in settlement cash holdings in the space of a year, in which the level of settlement cash briefly achieves levels as much as 50 times the normal level of overnight settlement cash. This sort of instability of banks' desired settlement cash holdings would clearly make interest-rate control through adjustment of a quantity target for settlement cash unreliable, at least as far as day-to-day variation in overnight rates would be concerned. The reduction in the volatility of overnight interest rates under the 'channel' system described in the next section is considered to be one of its more obvious advantages; see Brookes and Hampton (2000).

create any problem, as long as the Federal Reserve were simply to announce the interest rate at which it intended to supply reserves to the market, rather than trying to calculate in advance the quantity of reserves that should be supplied to achieve a particular funds-rate target.[6]

This would require some modification of the Federal Reserve's current operating procedures. Variations in the supply of non-borrowed reserves would no longer be a useful policy tool, and it would be sensible to maintain a target supply of zero non-borrowed reserves.[7]

Such reserves as banks wished to hold would be supplied at the discount window. There would furthermore be little point in the Federal Reserve continuing to use 'moral suasion' to limit discount-window borrowing, thus making the implicit cost of funds from this source significantly higher than the discount rate; for borrowed reserves would in any event always be quite small. The discount window might as well be operated as a borrowing facility of the kind provided by many other central banks, at which an arbitrary quantity of reserves may be borrowed (with suitable collateral) at an announced rate.[8] Under such circumstances, the equilibrium federal funds rate should simply equal the discount rate. Variations over time in the discount rate would then be the crucial tool by which desired variations in the federal funds rate would be achieved.

This analysis assumes that there still remains *some* small positive demand for bank reserves, no matter how large the interest-rate spread between the federal funds rate and the (zero) rate paid on reserves may be. Woodford (1998) provides a simple model of technical progress in payment media that illustrates how that could easily be the case. In this model, households purchase a large number of differentiated goods; some of these ('cash goods')

---

[6]Even if desired reserves came to be *completely* interest-inelastic, there would be no reason for the Federal Reserve not to be able to determine the equilibrium funds rate. As long as banks are required (in aggregate) to borrow at the discount window to satisfy their inelastic demand for reserves, any bank that borrows will assign a value to marginal funds obtained on the interbank market equal to the cost of funds at the discount window. If funds were furthermore supplied freely at the discount window (contrary to current practice), it would not be possible for the equilibrium funds rate in the interbank market to be either higher or lower than the discount rate.

[7]This would still require open-market operations, to offset the effects on the supply of non-borrowed reserves of changes in currency holdings (if these have not entirely vanished) and of government payments (which surely would not vanish). This is the residual function of open-market operations under 'channel' systems like those discussed in Section III, under which the target level of settlement cash is never adjusted as an instrument of monetary policy. For a discussion of the use of open-market operations for 'liquidity management' under the current regime in New Zealand, see Brookes (1999).

[8]See Borio (1997) for a survey of alternative provisions.

must be purchased using a means of payment that requires households to (directly or indirectly) hold base money in proportion to the volume of expenditure on these goods, while others – 'credit goods', adopting the terminology of Lucas and Stokey (1987) – may be purchased using a payment technology that requires no base money at all. The fact that no interest is paid on the monetary base increases the cost of purchases using 'cash'; so, optimizing households will substitute away from consumption of these goods to some extent, and the extent depends on the level of nominal interest rates. However, the preferences assumed imply that, for any finite level of interest rates, a positive level of consumption of 'cash' goods is still desired, and there thus remains a positive demand for the monetary base. This continues to be true no matter how small the number of goods that are 'cash goods', as long as *some* such goods continue to exist.

This model allows one to show, not only that central-bank control of short-term nominal interest rates need not be problematic even in a world in which cash has been displaced as a means of payment for virtually all purchases, but also that such a development introduces no complications for the way in which such control of nominal interest rates affects the economy and, in particular, the price level. Woodford (1998) shows the existence of a well-defined 'cashless limit', in the sense that the equilibrium price level path (as a function of the sequence of disturbances affecting the economy, including random variation in the central bank's rule for setting short-term nominal interest rates) is virtually the same in *all* cases in which the number of 'cash' goods is *sufficiently small*. This is because the effects of interest rates on spending and pricing decisions depend on the way the marginal utility of additional expenditure (and hence of additional income) varies with the level of real expenditure at that point in time. This relation depends in general on the nature of the monetary frictions, and on the level of real money balances in the economy; but in the case of any economy sufficiently close to the 'cashless limit', this relation is essentially the same, and essentially *independent* of variations in the level of real money balances.

Thus, while shifts over time in the demand for base money from a schedule like D_2 to one like D_3 – due, for example, to time variation in the fraction of purchases that happen to be of 'cash' goods – create problems for the use of *quantity-targeting techniques* to control interest rates, they do not necessarily create any problems for successful control of short-term nominal interest rates. Moreover, they need not create any problems for the central bank's determination of the level of interest rates that is required at each point in time for successful stabilization of the price level. In practice, this will often involve difficult questions of judgement on the part of the central bank – essentially, it will need to track variation over time in the Wicksellian 'natural rate of interest' (Woodford 1999) – but these problems are made no *more* difficult by the substitution of electronic means of payment for payments using central-bank money. Thus, there is no reason to regulate the development of such means of payment in order to facilitate this aspect of monetary control, either.

IV. Interest-Rate Control without Control of a Rate Spread

The analysis in Section II assumed that, even in the 'cashless limit', it continues to be possible for the central bank to vary the spread between the return on base money and on other financial assets to an arbitrary extent. It has been argued that this may well continue to be possible even if total demand for the monetary base comes to be minimal in size and subject to arbitrary (percentage) variations, and under circumstances where the remaining uses for the monetary base impose only trivial costs on the private sector. Nonetheless, one may wonder whether sufficient progress in IT might not lead to an alternative endpoint, in which the central bank ceases to be able to induce private parties to hold base money *at all*, in the event of any substantial return differential between base money and other liquid assets.

In terms of our simple diagram, one might conjecture that instead of the demand for bank reserves shifting from D_1 to something like D_2 or D_3 in Figure 1, technical progress might lead to a shift from D_1 to something like D_2 in Figure 2. Here it is assumed that there is a certain finite cost advantage to using central-bank money, proportional to the size of the transaction, so that it will not be used *at all* in the event of a return spread larger than a critical value determined by the proportional cost.[9]

If advances in IT are imagined to lower this cost, then the interest rate at which the base money demand schedule intersects the vertical axis becomes progressively closer to zero. In such a case, it will not be possible for the central bank to force the interest rate above the level represented by that intercept, no matter how much it restricts the supply of the monetary base.

Given the fact that there is also necessarily a limit (of zero) on how much this interest-rate spread can be reduced by increasing the supply of the monetary base, a situation of the kind represented by the schedule D_2 in Figure 2 would severely limit the extent to which a central bank could move

---

[9]It is important for our argument that we now assume that the demand for *all* components of the monetary base vanishes at some finite interest rate. In Figure 1, it suffices that the demand for *reserves* remain positive at arbitrarily high interest rates; the demand for the monetary base will then remain positive whether there continues to be positive currency demand or not. But our argument here that the central bank should be unable to increase market interest rates more than a finite amount above the zero rate paid on base money would not be valid if there continued to be a positive demand for central-bank-supplied currency.

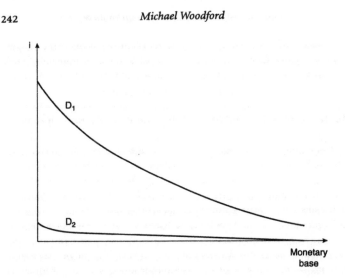

Figure 2: Alternative possibility for reduction in demand

short-term interest rates through variation in the terms on which it supplies reserves. In particular, as Ingemar Bengtsson (2000) and Bennett McCallum (2000) note, in a *fully* frictionless economy – one in which the demand for money has fallen to exactly zero at any positive interest differential, and not simply to a very small positive quantity – the method of price-level control expounded in Section II would be inapplicable.

However, an inability to affect the interest-rate *spread* between base money and other assets does not imply that a central bank is powerless to control short-term nominal interest rates. For it is still possible to change the equilibrium short-term nominal interest rate by changing the *interest paid on reserves*. We have assumed above that the interest on reserves equals zero at all times, but there is no necessity for this interest rate to be zero, or even for it to be constant; a central bank could easily enough vary it daily should it choose. Furthermore, the choice of the nominal rate of interest on central-bank liabilities is an arbitrary choice of the central bank's. There is thus another instrument through which a central bank can seek to affect the level of overnight nominal interest rates, an instrument that happens not to be used when, as in the USA at present, there is no interest on reserves. This additional instrument is, in fact, redundant when the central bank can effectively control the interest-rate differential by varying the supply of base money.[10] But if new

---

[10]Of course, it has often been argued that the payment of interest on bank reserves is desirable in order to reduce the cost to banks of holding such reserves, and so to reduce inefficient attempts to economize on reserves and on reservable deposits; see Friedman (1959) for a classic

Monetary Policy in a World Without Money 243

payments technologies were to eliminate the possibility of substantial variation in the interest-rate spread, it would still be possible to vary equilibrium short rates by varying the interest paid on base money, and this would then become a crucial tool in the implementation of monetary policy.[11]

Would a variable rate of interest payments on the monetary base be feasible? When one thinks of the currency component of the base, there is an obvious technical advantage to a fixed nominal yield of zero: a bill that is stamped 'ten dollars' at the time of issuance is simply worth ten dollars at all later points in time, and there is no need to track it as it changes hands. Charles Goodhart (1986) and Huston McCulloch (1986) have nonetheless proposed that interest payments on currency would be feasible, through a lottery based on the serial numbers of individual notes. However, interest payments on currency would not really be necessary under the system of interest-rate control just proposed; it would suffice to pay a time-varying (non-negative) interest rate on bank reserves. Under the hypothesis represented in Figure 2 – that a small positive interest-rate spread would suffice to induce complete substitution away from all uses of base money – this might mean the complete elimination of currency holdings. However, that would pose no threat to the control of short-term nominal interest rates by varying the interest paid on bank reserves; interest rates would simply be determined in the market for bank reserves.[12] Indeed, this is the crucial nexus under current arrangements already.

Also, there is no doubt that it is easy to pay interest on bank reserves. Indeed, a number of countries do so already.[13] Indeed, there are already central banks that control short-term interest rates by *varying* the interest rate paid on balances held with the central bank, rather than by varying the

---

statement of this position. A similar argument would apply to the payment of interest on currency, were that feasible at low cost, but such *efficiency* considerations are independent of the question of price-level *control* with which we are concerned here.

[11]Hall (1983, 1999) and Woodford (1999) both propose this as a method of price-level control in the complete absence of monetary frictions. Grimes (1992) similarly shows that this method would be effective in an environment in which central-bank reserves are no more useful for carrying out transactions than other liquid government securities, so that open-market purchases or sales of such securities are completely ineffective. Hall also proposes a specific kind of rule for adjusting the interest rate on bank reserves in order to ensure a constant equilibrium price level; but this particular rule is not essential to the general idea. One might equally well simply adjust the interest paid on reserves according to a 'Taylor rule' or a Wicksellian price-level feedback rule (Woodford 1999).

[12]The same would be true if there remained a positive demand for currency, say for illegal transactions, that was almost completely interest-inelastic.

[13]See Borio (1997) for a comparative survey of international arrangements as of a few years ago.

244   *Michael Woodford*

differential between that interest rate and overnight interest rates paid by banks to one another. This is true of the 'channel' system of interest-rate control used by central banks such as the Bank of Canada, the Reserve Bank of Australia, and the Reserve Bank of New Zealand.[14] The successful experience of these central banks indicates that such a system of monetary control is perfectly feasible under current circumstances; but given such a system, there is little reason to expect monetary control to be any more difficult following the development of new electronic media for making payments.

The basic mechanism through which the overnight interest rate in the interbank market is determined under a 'channel' system can be explained using Figure 3.[15] We again focus on the market for bank reserves, which in the countries just referred to are maintained as settlement balances, despite the fact that reserve requirements no longer exist.[16] Under a 'channel' system, the central bank chooses a target overnight interest rate (indicated by TR in Figure 3), which is periodically adjusted in response to changing economic conditions. This is called the 'official cash rate' (OCR) in New Zealand.

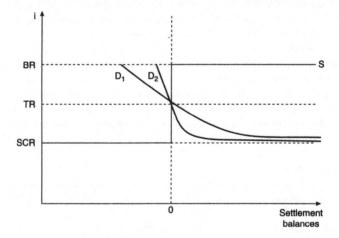

Figure 3: The market for settlement balances (N.Z.)

---

[14]For details of these systems see, e.g. Archer et al. (1999), Bank of Canada (1999), Borio (1997), Brookes and Hampton (2000), Clinton (1997), Reserve Bank of Australia (2000), Reserve Bank of New Zealand (1999) and Sellon and Weiner (1997).

[15]For the sake of concreteness, I shall describe in particular the system used in New Zealand since March 1999, as I am writing this at the Reserve Bank of New Zealand.

[16]Under the hypothesis of this section – innovations in payment mechanisms of a kind that would result in a complete abandonment of methods of payment requiring the use of

In addition to supplying a certain aggregate quantity of settlement cash (which can be adjusted through open-market operations), the central bank offers a lending facility, through which it stands ready to supply an arbitrary amount of additional overnight settlement cash at a fixed interest rate, which is slightly higher than the target overnight interest rate. (The lending rate is indicated by the level BR in Figure 3, which stands for 'Bank Rate', the term for this lending rate in Canada.) In New Zealand, this lending occurs through reverse repo transactions, at the overnight repo facility (ORF), and the ORF rate is generally set exactly 25 basis points higher than the OCR.

Finally, commercial banks that clear transactions through the central bank also have the right to deposit excess settlement cash overnight with the central bank at a deposit rate (indicated by the level SCR in Figure 3), which is positive but slightly lower than the target overnight rate. Typically, the target rate is the exact centre of the band whose upper and lower bounds are set by the lending rate and the deposit rate, and it is actually only the latter two rates that have any significance in terms of central-bank commitment to intervene in the market for settlement balances.[17] In New Zealand, the deposit rate is called the 'settlement cash rate' (hence the label in Figure 3), and is generally set exactly 25 basis points lower than the OCR.[18]

The lending rate on the one hand and the deposit rate on the other define a 'channel' within which overnight interest rates should be contained. Because these are both standing facilities (unlike the Federal Reserve's discount window in the USA), no bank has any reason to pay another bank a higher rate for overnight cash than the rate at which it could borrow from the central bank; similarly, no bank has any reason to lend overnight cash at a rate lower than the rate at which it can deposit with the central bank. Furthermore, the

---

central-bank balances in the event of any cost differential above a small ceiling – it seems particularly plausible to suppose that reserve requirements would be abandoned, in order to maintain the clearing of payments through the central bank. Hence, in this section, we shall assume a system under which reserve requirements no longer exist.

[17]While policy announcements at some central banks, such as the Reserve Bank of New Zealand, emphasize the current setting of a target rate (the OCR in New Zealand) in the centre of the 'channel' established by the lending and deposit rates, the Bank of Canada instead announces the setting of the Bank Rate (that is the lending rate), with the deposit rate being defined as 50 basis points below Bank Rate. However, the centre of the channel is still considered to define the Bank's target overnight rate (Bank of Canada 1999).

[18]A 50 basis-point spread between the lending rate and the deposit rate is also typical under current practice at the Bank of Canada and the Reserve Bank of Australia. However, the Reserve Bank of New Zealand briefly narrowed its channel to a width of only 20 basis points late in 1999, so as to reduce the cost to banks of holding larger-than-usual settlement balances in order to deal with possible unusual liquidity demands as a result of 'Y2K' panic. See Hampton (2000) for details of the latter episode.

spread between the lending rate and the deposit rate give banks an incentive to trade with one another (with banks that find themselves with excess settlement cash lending it to those that find themselves short) rather than depositing excess funds with the central bank when long and borrowing from the lending facility when short. The result is that the central bank can control overnight interest rates without having to engage in large transactions volumes itself through either of the standing facilities; the bank's willingness to transact in large volume largely eliminates any need for it to do so (Brookes and Hampton 2000).

The two standing facilities result in an effective supply curve for settlement cash of the form indicated by schedule S in Figure 3. The vertical segment corresponds to the central bank's settlement cash target (essentially equivalent to the supply of non-borrowed reserves in Figure 1); in Figure 3, this is shown as being zero, since in practice central banks using this sort of system choose a settlement cash target that is very small relative to the size of daily transactions flows in the economy, and that remains largely unchanged from day to day.[19] The horizontal segment to the right at the lending rate (unlike the upward sloping schedule in Figure 1) indicates that overnight borrowing is possible at a standing facility, unlike the Federal Reserve's discount window. The horizontal segment to the left at the deposit rate indicates that the payment of interest on deposits puts a floor on how low the equilibrium overnight rate can fall, no matter how low the demand for settlement balances may be. (One may view such a segment as also existing in Figure 1, but at a federal funds rate of zero.)

The equilibrium overnight rate is then determined by the intersection of this schedule with a demand schedule for settlement balances, represented in the figure by the curve D_1. A simple model of the determinants of this schedule is provided by Graeme Guthrie and Julian Wright (2000).[20] Guthrie

---

[19]Keeping the equilibrium overnight rate near the target rate seems generally to require a small positive target value for settlement balances. In New Zealand, the settlement cash target under the OCR system has generally been about $20 million NZ. At the Bank of Canada, the target level of settlement balances was actually zero during the early months of the LVTS system, but this led to overnight rates above the target rate (that is the centre of the channel) on average, and sometimes even above the Bank Rate at times of particular liquidity demand. Since late in 1999, the Bank has switched to targeting a positive level of settlement balances, typically about $200 million Canadian, and this target is increased on days when especially high transactions volume is expected (Bank of Canada 1999, Addendum II).

[20]Guthrie and Wright introduce their model as a way of explaining how monetary policy was implemented in New Zealand prior to the introduction of the OCR system in 1999; under this system, both the lending rate and the deposit rate were 'market-linked', as discussed further below. However, the Guthrie–Wright analysis of the determinants of the demand for settlement balances given standing facilities of the two types applies equally well in the case that the interest rates associated with the standing facilities are determined in some other way, and we use it here for that purpose. Similar models are discussed in Grimes (1992) and in Henckel et al. (1999).

and Wright model the overnight rate as being determined in competitive trading among commercial banks, prior to complete knowledge of their end-of-day clearing positions. The trades made in the interbank market thus shift the mean of each bank's probability distribution of possible end-of-day positions, without being able to alter the bank's degree of uncertainty about where it will end up relative to that conditional mean. Each of the risk-neutral banks trades to the point where the marginal reduction in the expected cost of borrowing from the lending facility (in the case that the bank ends up short) by borrowing additional cash on the interbank market exactly matches the marginal increase in the expected loss from having to deposit with the central bank (in the case that the bank ends the day with positive settlement cash). The mean end-of-day position that each bank will target will thus depend on where the interest rate in the interbank market lies relative to the two boundaries of the channel; the closer the interbank rate is to the deposit rate, the greater the positive level of settlement balances that each bank will wish to target, as the cost of being short is increased relative to the cost of ending the day with excess cash. (Once the interbank rate falls to the level of the deposit rate, there is no opportunity cost to holding additional settlement cash, and so if there is any risk at all of a large negative payment flow late in the day, a bank's target level of settlement cash should become very large, as assumed in Figure 3.)

The specific relation implied by the model of Guthrie and Wright takes the form

$$F\left(-\frac{C}{V}\right) = \frac{OR - SCR}{BR - SCR} \qquad (2)$$

where C is the quantity of settlement cash targeted the banks (through trades in the interbank market) as a function of the overnight rate OR in that market.[21] Here BR and SCR are the lending and deposit rates (as in Figure 3), V is a parameter that scales the banks' uncertainty about their end-of-day cash positions, and $F(x)$ denotes the probability that end-of-day cash will be no more than Vx greater than its expected value. The fact that the cumulative distribution function F is increasing means that C will be a decreasing function of OR, as indicated by the schedule D_1 in Figure 3.

Symmetry of the probability distribution of possible levels of end-of-day cash then implies that each bank will target a zero end-of-day balance if the

---

[21]Grimes (1992) derives a similar relation in a model with lending and deposit facilities of the kind just described. However, the inter-bank market for overnight cash is not modelled by Grimes; in his model, it is the equilibrium interest rate on bank loans that plays the role of OR in equation (2).

overnight rate is exactly halfway between the deposit rate and the lending rate. Hence the schedule D_1 in Figure 3 implies zero aggregate desired settlement cash when the overnight rate exactly equals the target rate. This implies that a settlement cash target of zero on the part of the central bank should achieve an overnight rate equal to the target rate, regardless of what that target interest rate may be. In practice, it seems that a small positive level of aggregate settlement balances are typically desired when the overnight rate remains in the centre of the channel. The more important prediction of the model, however, is that the demand for settlement balances should be a function of the location of the overnight rate *relative to the lending rate and deposit rate*, but *independent* of the absolute *level* of any of these interest rates. This means that an adjustment of the level of overnight rates by the central bank need not require any change in the supply of settlement cash, as long as the location of the lending and deposit rates relative to the target overnight rate do not change.

Thus under a 'channel' system like New Zealand's, changes in the level of overnight interest rates are brought about simply by announcing a change in the OCR, which has the implication of changing the lending and deposit rates at the central bank's standing facilities; no quantity adjustments in the Reserve Bank's settlement cash target are required.[22]

The degree to which the system succeeds in practice is shown in Figures 4 and 5. Figure 4 plots the New Zealand overnight interest rate since the adoption of the OCR system in March 1999. (Here the vertical lines mark the dates of the five increases in the OCR during this period.) One observes that the overnight interest rate is extremely stable between adjustments of the OCR; in fact, it is exactly equal to the OCR (to the nearest basis point) on all but 11 days within the sample period. Also, on the dates at which the OCR was raised by either 25 or 50 basis points, the overnight interest rate immediately jumped to equal the new target rate. As shown in Figure 5, these dates were not associated with reductions of the aggregate level of settlement cash. Thus the ability of the Reserve Bank to 'tighten' policy is in no way dependent on the creation of a greater 'scarcity' of bank reserves. This is a direct consequence of the fact that interest rates are raised under this system without any attempt to change the *spread* between market rates of return and the interest paid on bank reserves.

This does not mean that the supply of settlement cash has become completely irrelevant for overnight interest-rate determination. The degree to

---

[22]Guthrie and Wright (2000) document the fact that under the system used in New Zealand prior to 1999, interest-rate changes were also achieved without any change in the Reserve Bank's settlement cash target, though, under that regime, the lending and deposit rates adjusted automatically in response to market interest-rate movements, rather than as a direct result of a policy decision of the Reserve Bank.

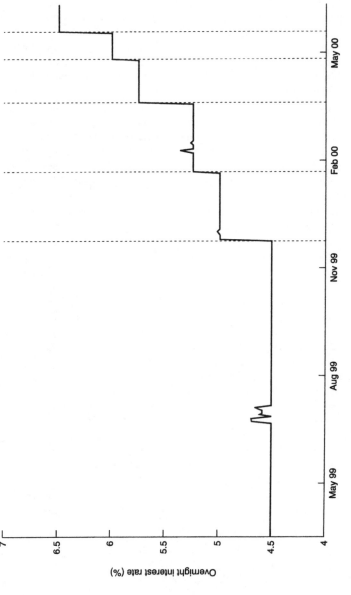

Figure 4: Overnight cash rate under the OCR system (New Zealand)

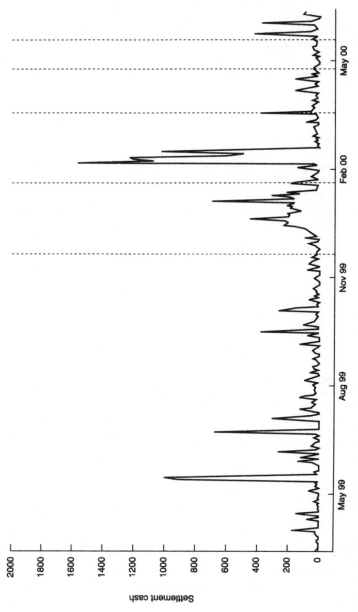

Figure 5: Settlement cash balances under the OCR system (New Zealand)

Monetary Policy in a World Without Money 251

which the overnight interest rate tracks the OCR in New Zealand at present is due to an implicit convention among the commercial banks, according to which overnight cash is lent among them at the OCR rather than any other rate. This convention obviously simplifies negotiations among the banks, and does not represent a great departure from the trade that would result from an idealized competitive auction market, if the equilibrium demand for settlement cash is approximately that predicted by the model described above.[23] On the other hand, the convention comes under pressure when desired liquidity (at an interest rate equal to the OCR) is too great relative to the Reserve Bank's settlement cash target.

In general, the Reserve Bank of New Zealand does still engage in daily open-market operations, to offset changes in the supply of settlement cash (owing to changes in the demand for currency or to government payments, for example) that would otherwise occur. If these 'liquidity management operations' did not occur, the supply of settlement cash would be quite variable relative to its average level, and the convention of trading overnight cash at the OCR would likely be unsustainable on most days.[24] Indeed, on at least two important occasions since the introduction of the OCR system in New Zealand (in May 1999 and February 2000), large government payments have meant that the Reserve Bank has been unable to conduct 'liquidity management operations' of sufficient size to prevent a shortage of settlement cash from developing.[25] On these occasions, those banks with excess settlement cash have not been willing to lend at the OCR, so that the overnight rate has temporarily risen above the OCR.[26] It is quite possible

---

[23]This particular convention is presumably one of a large number of patterns of exchange that could be sustained as a Nash equilibrium of the repeated game played by the relatively small number of banks that clear payments with one another in New Zealand. Note that each bank's reservation level of expected profits would be the one that would result from a refusal of other banks ever to trade with it in the interbank market, in which case it would always have to borrow from the central bank when short and deposit with the central bank when long at the end of the day. Since the variability of each bank's end-of-day position (in the absence of interbank lending of settlement cash) is large relative to the average level of settlement cash per bank, this would imply a significant expected loss from the spread between the lending rate and deposit rate, relative to what can be achieved by trading in the interbank market so as to never hold much more than the average level of settlement cash. The size of the possible losses from failure to cooperate can be judged from the size of the increases in aggregate settlement cash on those occasions when cooperation has actually broken down, namely in May 1999 and February 2000.

[24]See, for example, Figure 6 in Brookes (1999).

[25]I am grateful to Andy Brookes for discussion of these episodes.

[26]On these occasions, the 'short' banks have resisted the attempts of 'long' banks to lend their excess balances at a rate above the OCR, and, instead, in many cases, have borrowed from the ORF despite the higher interest rate, leaving the 'long' banks to deposit their funds with the

that more frequent occurrences of a similar sort would break down the convention altogether.

Furthermore, it is clear that the Reserve Bank would be able to force a change in overnight rates, should it wish to, through a sufficiently drastic change in the settlement cash target. This can be illustrated by the occasional use of this tool by the Reserve Bank prior to the introduction of the OCR system, when the interest rates associated with the standing facilities were given by a fixed spread over 'market' interest rates (Huxford and Reddell 1996; Guthrie and Wright 2000). That system relied on market interest rates to follow a suggested path indicated by Reserve Bank announcements; on occasion, a failure of market rates to follow the Reserve Bank's suggestions required action by the Reserve Bank to demonstrate its capacity to intervene if necessary. For example, a failure of interest rates to rise as suggested by the Reserve Bank in the last two weeks of 1992 resulted in the settlement cash target being cut from $20 million NZ to zero on 7 January 1993. This resulted in an immediate 500 basis point increase in overnight interest rates, and significant increases in longer rates as well (Guthrie and Wright 2000, sec. 3.1). However, under a system with zero reserve requirements like New Zealand's, this sort of quantity adjustment seems a rather blunt instrument, one that could be used to 'discipline' the banks but that would not provide a precise means of directly achieving a desired level of overnight interest rates without the use of other means of guiding the banks to that level.

Given a 'channel' system for the implementation of monetary policy like that currently used in New Zealand and several other countries, there is little reason to fear that either the development of 'electronic cash' for retail transactions or of alternative electronic methods of settlement of payments among banks should threaten a central bank's ability to control the path of overnight nominal interest rates, and, through them, spending and pricing decisions in the economy. Let us first consider the possibility of the replacement of currency by 'electronic cash' of one kind or another. Once again, this would merely *simplify* the task of controlling overnight interest rates using a 'channel' system, by eliminating one source of variations in total settlement cash that have to be offset by 'liquidity management operations' on the part of the central bank. Similarly, the development of systems that payments to be

Reserve Bank. The result was very large temporary surges in aggregate settlement balances, owing to the breakdown of cooperation; these can be seen in Figure 5. The possibility of such events from time to time, of course, despite the efforts of the Reserve Bank to target the aggregate quantity of settlement cash through 'liquidity management operations' and despite the mutual interest of the commercial banks in trading among themselves to avoid use of the standing facilities, is an important reason why variation in the settlement cash target is not a useful tool for achieving the Reserve Bank's desired variations in overnight interest rates.

made without holding any significant wealth in bank deposits subject to reserve requirements poses no threat, as we have seen that a 'channel' system is perfectly effective in the absence of bank reserves held to satisfy reserve requirements.

A more subtle question would be the consequences of improvements in the ability of banks to accurately forecast their end-of-day cash positions, allowing them to maintain their end-of-day positions nearer to exactly zero. This would correspond to a secular decrease in the parameter V in equation (2), so that, according to the Guthrie–Wright model, the demand curve for settlement balances would shift from D_1 to something like D_2 in Figure 3. However, such a development would not change the fact that desired settlement balances are a function of the location of the overnight rate within the channel rather than of the absolute level of overnight rates, so that it should still be possible to move the overnight rate by simply moving the lending and deposit rates, holding fixed the settlement cash target.[27]

The only possible problem would result from the demand for settlement balances becoming less interest-elastic (as shown in Figure 3). This could significantly increase the need for precisely calibrated open-market operations to prevent variations in settlement cash of a size sufficient to shift the location of the equilibrium overnight rate within the channel to an undesirable extent. Now, this problem could be dealt with by shrinking the width of the channel. This would obviously limit the size of possible variations in the overnight rate. But even more, equation (2) implies that the elasticity of the demand for settlement balances is increased by narrowing the spreads between the deposit rate, the target rate and the lending rate, reducing the size of the shift in the equilibrium overnight rate that should result from a given size forecast error in the central bank's 'liquidity management operation'. Thus an appropriate reduction in the width of the channel can fully offset the effect on the elasticity of demand resulting from the reduction in V. Furthermore, the main reason for not choosing too narrow a channel – concern for the degree to which the standing facilities might be resorted to in this case instead of re-allocation of cash among banks through the interbank market (Brookes and Hampton 2000) – becomes less of a concern under our hypothesis of improved forecastability of end-of-day positions, so a narrower channel would seem entirely reasonable.

---

[27]A similar conclusion was reached in the pioneering analysis of Grimes (1992). The conclusion to that paper considers a future in which uncertainty about end-of-day cash positions has been eliminated as a result of 'real-time banking accompanied by a continuously operating, competitive interbank market'. Grimes argues that such a development would undermine the effectiveness of open-market operations as instrument of policy, but that the central bank should still be able to control interest rates, and hence the price level, by varying the interest rate paid at the central bank's deposit facility.

Finally, let us consider the threat that may be posed by the development of payment systems that do not require payments to be cleared using central-bank settlement balances. In the world imagined by Mervyn King (1999), there would be no *necessity* for clearing payments using accounts held with the central bank. What this would mean – assuming that the problems with assuring parties of the finality of payments not guaranteed by the central bank could be solved – is that there would be a limit on the costs that clearing payments through the central bank could impose on the banks, before they would choose to simply abandon the use of that clearing system. But even granting this, it is not obvious that banks should cease to settle payments through the central bank.

For the success of a 'channel' system of interest-rate control does not depend on the imposition of any significant costs on commercial banks (similar to those resulting, for example, from a requirement to hold non-interest-earning reserves). As we have seen, a system without reserve requirements like New Zealand's results in extremely low aggregate settlement balances at most times, and the spread between market overnight rates and the interest paid on these balances is relatively modest (only 25 basis points at present). And the sorts of improvements in IT that we have hypothesized should only make these costs lower: banks should be able to maintain lower average settlement balances by forecasting their end-of-day cash position more precisely, and central banks should be willing to reduce the width of their channels under such circumstances.

There are a variety of reasons why clearing payments through the central bank ought to remain attractive, even in the absence of a legal requirement to do so, as Charles Freedman (2000) stresses. These include the fact that the creditworthiness of the central bank cannot be doubted, and the fact that banks will need to clear at least some payments through the central bank if the government maintains its own account with the central bank.[28] But even if many payments came to be cleared through some independent mechanism, and, indeed, even if a settlement account at the central bank ceased to be of any interest whatsoever as a convenient way of clearing payments arising out of private transactions, there should still be no reason why the central bank could not continue to determine the level of overnight interest rates with a high degree of precision.

For the logic of the method of interest-rate control sketched above does not depend on the continued use of central bank settlement balances as a means of clearing payments between banks. Suppose that balances held with the

---

[28]Both of these arguments depend on the government not severing its traditional links with the central bank. However, a privileged relation between the central bank and the government does not restrict private transactions in the way that regulations suppressing the development of private clearing mechanisms would.

Monetary Policy in a World Without Money 255

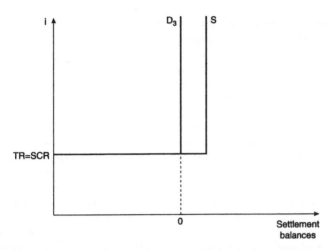

Figure 6: The interbank market when central-bank balances are no longer used for clearing purposes

central bank ceased to be any more useful to commercial banks than any other equally riskless overnight investment. In this case, the demand for settlement balances would collapse to a vertical line at zero for all interest rates higher than the settlement cash rate, as shown in Figure 6, together with a horizontal line to the right at the settlement cash rate. That is, banks should still be willing to hold arbitrary balances at the central bank, as long as (but only if) the overnight cash rate is no higher than the rate paid by the central bank. In this case, it would no longer be possible to induce the overnight cash market to clear at a target rate higher than the rate paid on settlement balances. The central bank could still control the equilibrium overnight rate, though, by choosing a positive settlement cash target, so that the only possible equilibrium would be at an interest rate equal to the settlement cash rate, as shown in Figure 6.

Such a system would differ from current channel systems in that an overnight lending facility would no longer be necessary, so that there would no longer be a 'channel' and the rate paid on central-bank balances would no longer be set at a fixed spread below the target overnight rate; instead, it would be set at exactly the target rate.[29] Perfect control of overnight rates should still be possible though, through adjustments of the rate paid on central-bank balances,

---

[29]This presumes a world in which no payments are cleared using central-bank balances. Of course, there would be no harm in continuing to offer such a facility as long as the central-bank clearing system were still used for at least some payments.

and changes in the target overnight rate would not have to involve any change in the settlement cash target, just as is true under current channel systems.

V. The Source of Central Bank Control over Short-Term Interest Rates

In contemplating this final, most radical possibility, we are led back to the puzzle on which Benjamin Friedman (1999) remarks: how is it that such small trades by central banks can move rates in such large markets? In the complete absence of any monopoly power on the part of central banks – because their liabilities no longer supply any services not also supplied by other equally riskless, equally liquid financial claims – it might be thought that any remaining ability of central banks to affect market rates should depend on a capacity to adjust their balance sheets by amounts that are large relative to the overall size of financial markets. One might still propose that central banks should be able to engage in trades of any size that turned out to be required, owing to the fact that the government stands behind the central bank and can use its power of taxation to make up any trading losses, even huge ones.[30]

I shall argue, instead, that massive adjustments of central-bank balance sheets would not be necessary to move interest rates, even in a world where central-bank liabilities ceased to supply any services in addition to their pecuniary yield. Note that, in the situation depicted in Figure 6, the central bank can raise the equilibrium overnight rate without any change in the quantity of central-bank balances at all. Furthermore, the constant supply of central-bank liabilities – the settlement cash target, in the terminology used under current channel systems – can be quite small relative to the overall volume of financial transactions in the economy, though it needs to be positive.

Why is this possible? Certainly, if a government were to decide to peg the price of some commodity (say, oil), it might be able to do so, but only by holding stocks of the commodity that were sufficiently large relative to the world market for that commodity, and by standing ready to vary its holdings of the commodity by large amounts as necessary. What is different about controlling short-term nominal interest rates?

The key to an answer is to note that there is no inherent 'equilibrium' level of interest rates to which the market would tend in the absence of central-bank intervention, and against which the central bank must exert a significant countervailing force in order to achieve a given operating target. This is because there is no inherent value (in terms of real goods and services) for a fiat unit of account such as the 'dollar', except insofar as a particular exchange value results

---

[30]This seems to be the position of Goodhart (2000).

Monetary Policy in a World Without Money 257

from the monetary policy commitments of the central bank. Alternative price-level paths are thus equally consistent with market equilibrium in the absence of intervention, and associated with these alternative paths for the general level of prices are alternative paths for short-term nominal interest rates.

Even recognizing this, one might suppose – as Fischer Black (1970) once did – that, in a fully deregulated system, the central bank should have no way of using monetary policy to select among these alternative equilibrium; the path of money prices (and similarly nominal interest rates, nominal exchange rates, and so on) would then be determined solely by the self-fulfilling expectations of market participants.[31] Whence does any special role of the central bank in equilibrium determination derive?

The answer is that the unit of account in a purely fiat system is *defined* in terms of the liabilities of the central bank.[32] A financial contract that promises to deliver a certain number of 'dollars' at a specified future date is promising payment in terms of settlement balances at the central bank – the Federal Reserve in the case of the US dollar, the Reserve Bank in the case of the NZ dollar, and so on – or in terms of some kind of payment that the payee is willing to accept as a suitable equivalent. In the technological utopia imagined by Mervyn King, financial market participants are willing to accept as final settlement transfers using electronic networks in which the central bank is not involved; but settlement balances at the central bank still define the thing to which these other claims are accepted as equivalent.[33]

This explains why the nominal interest yield on settlement balances at the central bank can determine overnight rates in the market as a whole. The central bank can clearly define the nominal yield on overnight deposits in its settlement accounts as it chooses; it is simply promising to increase the nominal amount credited to a given account, after all. It can also allow banks to exchange such deposits among themselves on whatever terms they like. But the market value of a dollar deposit in such an account cannot be anything other than a dollar – because this defines the meaning of a 'dollar'!

---

[31]Bengtsson (2000) offers a recent example of a similar view, but allows for the possibility that the central bank can provide a 'focal point' that serves to coordinate the expectations of private parties on a particular future path of prices, making this path self-fulfilling.

[32]See Hall (1999) for a similar view.

[33]White (2000) makes much the same point, stressing the role of legal tender statutes in defining the meaning of a particular currency such as the New Zealand dollar. It is important, however, to stress that such statutes do not represent a restriction on the means of payment that can be used within a given geographical region – or at any rate that there need be no such restrictions on private agreements for White's point to be valid. What matters is simply the definition of what contracts written in terms of a particular unit of account are taken to mean.

258   *Michael Woodford*

This is not possible for a private financial institution, which can offer to the market liabilities that promise to pay a certain number of dollars in the future, but must accept the market's view as to the number of dollars that such liabilities are worth at present. More precisely, even if the liabilities of the private entity are not regarded as perfect substitutes for other financial instruments, it cannot determine *both* the quantity that it issues *and* the nominal yield on the investment – it must either auction a certain quantity and let the market determine the price (and hence the yield), or it can announce a yield and see what quantity the market will buy. However, a central bank can determine both the quantity of settlement balances in existence and the nominal yield on those balances; central banks do so daily. And the power to do so does not depend on the non-existence of close substitutes for these liabilities of the central bank. The central bank's position as monopoly supplier of an asset that serves a special function is necessary in order for variations in the quantity supplied to affect the yield *spread* between this asset and other market yields, but not in order to allow separate determination of the yield on central bank liabilities and the quantity of them in existence.

The special feature of central banks, then, is that they are entities the liabilities of which happen to be used to define the unit of account in a wide range of contracts that other people exchange with one another. There is perhaps no deep, universal reason why this need be so; nor, perhaps, is it essential that there be one such entity per national political unit. One might imagine, as Friedrich Hayek (1986) did, a future in which private entities manage competing monetary standards in terms of which people might choose to contract. But even in such a world, the Federal Reserve would still be able to control the exchange value of the US dollar, the Reserve Bank of New Zealand would be able to control the exchange value of the New Zealand dollar, and so on, by adjusting the nominal interest rates paid on the respective central banks' liabilities.

The only real question about such a future is how much the central banks' monetary policies would *matter*. This would depend on how many people still chose to contract in terms of the currencies the values of which they continued to determine. Under present circumstances, it is quite costly for most people to attempt to transact in a currency other than the one issued by their national government, and under these conditions, the central bank's responsibility for maintaining a stable value for the national currency is a grave responsibility. In a future in which transactions costs of all sorts have been radically reduced, that might no longer be the case, and if so, the harm that bad monetary policy can do would be reduced. Nonetheless, it would surely still be convenient for contracting parties to be able to make use of a unit of account with a stable value, and the provision and management of such a standard of value would still be a vital public service. Thus central banks that demonstrate both the commitment and the skill required to maintain a stable value for their countries' currencies should continue to have an important role to serve in the century to come.

Michael Woodford
Economics Department, Princeton University
111 Fisher Hall, Princeton, NJ 08544, USA
woodford@princeton.edu

References

Archer, David, Andrew Brookes and Michael Reddell (1999), 'A Cash Rate System for Implementing Monetary Policy', *Reserve Bank of New Zealand Bulletin*, 62, 51–61.

Bank for International Settlements (BIS) (1996), *Implications for Central Banks of the Development of Electronic Money*, Basel: BIS, October.

Bank of Canada (1999), 'The Framework for the Implementation of Monetary Policy in the Large Value Transfer System Environment', revised March 31, (see also Addendum II, November 1999). [Available at www.bank-banque-canada.ca/english/lvtsmp.htm.]

Bengtsson, Ingemar (2000), 'Superseding the Quantity Theory of Money – The Contractual Approach to Nominal Prices', unpublished manuscript, Lund University, Sweden, May. [Available at www.nek.lu.se/nekibe/priceco2.pdf.]

Black, Fischer (1970), 'Banking in a World without Money: The Effects of Uncontrolled Banking', *Journal of Bank Research*, 1, 9–20.

Borio, Claudio E. V. (1997), *The Implementation of Monetary Policy in Industrial Countries: A Survey*, Economic Paper no. 47, Bank for International Settlements.

Brookes, Andrew (1999), 'Monetary Policy and the Reserve Bank Balance Sheet', *Reserve Bank of New Zealand Bulletin*, 62(4), 17–33.

——, and Tim Hampton (2000), 'The Official Cash Rate One Year On', unpublished manuscript, Economics Department, Reserve Bank of New Zealand, June.

Clinton, Kevin (1997), 'Implementation of Monetary Policy in a Regime with Zero Reserve Requirements', Bank of Canada working paper no. 97-8, April.

Freedman, Charles (2000), 'Monetary Policy Implementation: Past, Present and Future – Will the Advent of Electronic Money Lead to the Demise of Central Banking?', *International Finance*, 3, 211–27.

Friedman, Benjamin M. (1999), 'The Future of Monetary Policy: The Central Bank as an Army with Only a Signal Corps?', *International Finance*, 2, 321–38.

Friedman, Milton (1959), *A Program for Monetary Stability*. New York: Fordham University Press.

Goodhart, Charles A. E. (1986), 'How Can Non-Interest-Bearing Assets Coexist with Safe Interest-Bearing Assets?', *British Review of Economic Issues*, 8, Autumn, 1–12.

—— (2000) 'Can Central Banking Survive the IT Revolution?', *International Finance*, 3, 189–209.

Grimes, Arthur (1992), 'Discount Policy and Bank Liquidity: Implications for the Modigliani–Miller and Quantity Theories', Reserve Bank of New Zealand discussion paper no. G92/12, October.

Guthrie, Graeme, and Julian Wright (2000), 'Open Mouth Operations', *Journal of Monetary Economics*, 48, 489–516.

Hall, Robert E. (1983), 'Optimal Fiduciary Monetary Systems', *Journal of Monetary Economics*, 12, 33–50.

—— (1999), 'Controlling the Price Level', NBER working paper no. 6914, January.

Hampton, Tim (2000), 'Y2K and Banking System Liquidity', *Reserve Bank of New Zealand Bulletin*, 63, 52–60.

Hayek, Friedrich A. (1986), 'Market Standards for Money', *Economic Affairs*, 6(4), 8–10.

Henckel, Timo, Alain Ize and Arto Kovanen (1999), 'Central Banking without Central Bank Money', IMF working paper, March.

Huxford, Julie and Michael Reddell (1996), 'Implementing Monetary Policy in New Zealand', *Reserve Bank of New Zealand Bulletin*, 59(4), 309–22.

King, Mervyn (1999), 'Challenges for Monetary Policy: New and Old', *Bank of England Quarterly Bulletin*, 39, 397–415.

Lucas, Robert E., Jr, and Nancy L. Stokey (1987), 'Money and Interest in a Cash-in-Advance Economy', *Econometrica*, 55, 491–513.

McCallum, Bennett T. (2000), 'The Present and Future of Monetary Policy Rules', *International Finance*, 3, 273–86.

McCulloch, J. Huston (1986), 'Beyond the Historical Gold Standard', in C. D. Campbell and W. R. Dougan, eds, *Alternative Monetary Regimes*. Baltimore: Johns Hopkins University Press.

Reserve Bank of Australia (2000), 'About the RBA: Monetary Policy', revised May 3. [Available at www.rba.gov.au/about/ab_monpol.html.]

Reserve Bank of New Zealand (1999), 'Monetary Policy Implementation: Changes to Operating Procedures', *Reserve Bank of New Zealand Bulletin*, 62(1), 46–50.

Sellon, Gordon H., Jr, and Stuart E. Weiner (1996), 'Monetary Policy Without Reserve Requirements: Analytical Issues', *Federal Reserve Bank of Kansas City Economic Review*, 81(4), 5–24.

—— (1997), 'Monetary Policy Without Reserve Requirements: Case Studies and Options for the United States', *Federal Reserve Bank of Kansas City Economic Review*, 82(2), 5–30.

White, Bruce (2000), 'What Makes a Central Bank a Central Bank?', unpublished manuscript, Economics Department, Reserve Bank of New Zealand, June.

Woodford, Michael (1998), 'Doing Without Money: Controlling Inflation in a Post-Monetary World', *Review of Economic Dynamics*, 1, 173–219.

—— (1999), 'Price-Level Determination under Interest-Rate Rules', unpublished manuscript, Princeton University, April. [Available at www.princeton.edu/~woodford.]

[8]

MICHAEL WOODFORD

How Important Is Money in the Conduct of Monetary Policy?

I consider some of the leading arguments for assigning an important role to tracking the growth of monetary aggregates when making decisions about monetary policy. First, I consider whether ignoring money means returning to the conceptual framework that allowed the high inflation of the 1970s. Second, I consider whether models of inflation determination with no role for money are incomplete, or inconsistent with elementary economic principles. Third, I consider the implications for monetary policy strategy of the empirical evidence for a long-run relationship between money growth and inflation. And fourth, I consider reasons why a monetary policy strategy based solely on short-run inflation forecasts derived from a Phillips curve may not be a reliable way of controlling inflation. I argue that none of these considerations provides a compelling reason to assign a prominent role to monetary aggregates in the conduct of monetary policy.

JEL codes: E52, E58
Keywords: monetarism, two-pillar strategy, cashless economy.

IT MIGHT BE THOUGHT obvious that a policy aimed at controlling inflation should concern itself with ensuring a modest rate of growth of the money supply. After all, every beginning student of economics is familiar with Milton Friedman's dictum that "inflation is always and everywhere a monetary phenomenon" (e.g., Friedman 1992), and with the quantity theory of money as a standard account of what determines the inflation rate. Yet nowadays monetary aggregates play little role in monetary policy deliberations at most central banks. King (2002, p. 162) quotes then-Fed Governor Larry Meyer as stating that "money plays no explicit role in today's

Prepared for the Conference in Honor of Ernst Baltensperger, University of Bern, June 8, 2007. An earlier version was presented as the 2006 W.A. Mackintosh Lecture, Queen's University, Canada. I would like to thank Jordi Galí, Stefan Gerlach, Charles Goodhart, Tmar Issing, Robert E. Lucas, Jr., Klaus Masuch, Bennett McCallum, Rick Mishkin, Ed Nelson, Christian Noyer, Athanasios Orphanides, Lucrezia Reichlin, Julio Rotemberg, Gregor Smith, Lars Svensson, Harald Uhlig, Volker Wieland, and an anonymous referee for helpful discussions and comments on earlier drafts, while absolving them of any responsibility for the opinions expressed, and the (U.S.) National Science Foundation for research support through a grant to the National Bureau of Economic Research.

MICHAEL WOODFORD *is from Columbia University* (*E-mail:* Mw2230@columbia.edu).

Received November 27, 2006; and accepted in revised form August 10, 2007.

Journal of Money, Credit and Banking, Vol. 40, No. 8 (December 2008)
© 2008 The Ohio State University

1562 : MONEY, CREDIT AND BANKING

consensus macro model, and it plays virtually no role in the conduct of monetary policy."

Not all agree that this de-emphasis of money growth as a criterion for judging the soundness of policy has been a good thing. Notably, the European Central Bank (ECB) continues to assign a prominent role to money in its monetary policy strategy. In what the ECB calls its "two-pillar strategy," one pillar is "economic analysis," which "assesses the short-to-medium-term determinants of price developments." According to the ECB, this analysis "takes account of the fact that price developments over those horizons are influenced largely by the interplay of supply and demand in the goods, services and factor markets." But in addition, a second pillar, "monetary analysis," assesses the medium- to long-term outlook for inflation, "exploiting the long-run link between money and prices." The two alternative frameworks for assessing risks to price stability are intended to provide "cross-checks" for one another (ECB 2004, p. 55).

But what exactly is the nature of the additional information that can be obtained by tracking trends in the growth of monetary aggregates, and why should it be of such crucial importance for the control of inflation as to constitute a separate "pillar" (not infrequently characterized as the "first pillar") of the ECB's policy strategy? And does "monetary analysis" genuinely represent a distinct and complementary perspective on the determinants of inflation, that cannot be subsumed into an "economic analysis" of the inflationary pressures resulting from the balance of supply and demand in product and factor markets, and that can be used to guide policy decisions?

I here review several of the most important arguments that have been made for paying attention to money, considering both the purported omissions made by "economic analysis" alone and the asserted advantages of the information revealed by monetary trends. Of course, it is impossible to review the voluminous literature on this topic in its entirety, so I shall have to stick to a few of the most prominent themes in recent discussions.

First, I consider whether ignoring money means returning to the conceptual framework that allowed the high inflation of the 1970s. The architects of the ECB's monetary policy strategy were undoubtedly concerned not to repeat past mistakes that have often been attributed to a failure to appreciate the role of money in inflation determination. Have those central banks that assign little importance to money, like the current Federal Reserve, forgotten the lessons of the crucial debates of a quarter century ago? Second, I consider the theoretical status of models of inflation determination with no role for money. Are such models incomplete, and hence unable to explain inflation without adding the additional information provided by a specification of the money supply? Or, even if complete, are they inconsistent with elementary economic principles, such as the neutrality of money? Third, I consider the implications for monetary policy strategy of the empirical evidence for a long-run relationship between money growth and inflation. And finally, I consider reasons why a monetary policy strategy based solely on short-run inflation forecasts derived from a Phillips curve may not be a reliable way of controlling inflation, and ask whether "monetary analysis" is an appropriate way to increase the robustness of the conclusions reached regarding the conduct of policy.

MICHAEL WOODFORD : 1563

1. THE HISTORICAL SIGNIFICANCE OF MONETARISM

One of the more obvious reasons for the ECB's continuing emphasis on the prominent role of money in its deliberations is a concern not to ignore the lessons of the monetarist controversies of the 1960s and 1970s. Monetarists faced substantial opposition to their theses at the time, but they largely won the argument with their Keynesian critics, especially in the minds of central bankers. Moreover, those central banks, such as the Bundesbank, that took on board monetarist teachings to the greatest extent had the best performance with regard to inflation control in the 1970s and 1980s. Hence it may be feared that abandoning an emphasis on monetary aggregates in the conduct of monetary policy would mean returning to the intellectual framework of 1960s-vintage Keynesianism, with the consequent risk of allowing a return of the runaway inflation experienced in many countries in the 1970s.[1]

But is this fear well-founded? Monetarism did surely represent an important advance over prior conventional wisdom, and it would indeed be a grave mistake to forget the lessons learned from the monetarist controversy. Yet I would argue that the most important of these lessons, and the ones that are of greatest continuing relevance to the conduct of policy today, are not dependent on the thesis of the importance of monetary aggregates.[2]

First, monetarism established that monetary policy can do something about inflation, and that the central bank can reasonably be *held accountable* for controlling inflation. This was not always accepted—in the 1950s and 1960s, many Keynesian models treated the general price level as given, independent of policy, or only affected by policy under relatively extreme circumstances (when capacity constraints were reached), but not in the most common situation. Even in the 1970s, when inflation could no longer be considered a minor detail in macroeconomic modeling, it was often argued to be due to the market power of monopolists or labor unions rather than to monetary policy.

Monetarists contested these skeptical theses about the possibility of controlling inflation through monetary policy, and the quantity theory of money provided them with an important argument. Given that central banks obviously could affect—and even to a certain extent control—the quantity of money, the quantity-theoretic view of inflation made it clear that central banks *could* affect inflation, and indeed could contain it, at least over the medium to long run, if they had the will to do so.

1. For example, Lucas (2006) admits that "central banks that do not make explicit use of money supply data have recent histories of inflation control that are quite as good as the record of the ECB," but then warns: "I am concerned that this encouraging but brief period of success will foster the opinion, already widely held, that the monetary pillar is superfluous, and lead monetary policy analysis back to the muddled eclecticism that brought us the 1970s inflation" (p. 137).

2. I do not pretend, of course, in the brief discussion that follows, to provide an exhaustive account of the desirable elements in monetarist thought. Many other ideas originated or championed by monetarists, such as the importance of the distinction between real and nominal interest rates and the concept of the natural rate of output, have had a profound effect on contemporary monetary economics and policy analysis—but these are even more obviously independent of any thesis about the importance of monetary aggregates.

1564 : MONEY, CREDIT AND BANKING

But it is not true that monitoring monetary aggregates is the *only* way that a central bank can control inflation. Present-day central banks that pay little attention to money do *not,* as a consequence, deny their responsibility for inflation control. To the contrary, many have public inflation targets and accept that keeping inflation near that target is their primary responsibility. And while the Fed has no explicit target of this kind, Federal Reserve officials speak often and forcefully about their determination to ensure price stability, and the record of the past decade makes such statements highly credible. Nor do the models used for policy analysis within such banks, even when these do not involve money at all, imply that monetary policy cannot affect inflation, as is discussed further in the next section.

Second, monetarism emphasized the importance of a *verifiable commitment* by the central bank to a noninflationary policy. Monetarists were the first to emphasize the importance of containing inflation *expectations* and to stress the role that commitment to a policy rule could play in creating the kind of expectations needed for macro-economic stability. Research over the past several decades has only added further support for these views.[3]

The prescription of a money growth target provided a simple example of a kind of commitment on the part of a central bank that should guarantee low inflation, at least over the long run, and moreover of a type that would be relatively straightforward for the public to monitor.[4] But, once again, this is not the *only* kind of commitment that would serve, and a central bank can fully accept the importance of commitment, and of making its commitments clear to the public, without having a money growth target. Indeed, inflation targeting central banks do clearly bind themselves to a specific, quantitative commitment regarding what their policy will aim at, and they have given great attention to the issue of how to show the public that their policy decisions are justified by their official target, notably through the publication of *Inflation Reports* like those of the Bank of England or the Swedish Riksbank.

Thus, in neither case does preservation of the important insights obtained from the monetarist controversy depend on continuing to emphasize monetary aggregates in policy deliberations. And the fact that inflation targeting central banks dispense with monetary targets and analyze their policy options using models with no role for money does not imply any return to the policy framework that led to (or at any rate allowed) the inflation of the 1970s.[5] Indeed, not even Friedman continued, in his later years, to view monetary targets as a prerequisite for controlling inflation.[6]

---

3. For example, both the importance of expectations in the monetary transmission mechanism and the advantages of suitably designed policy rules are central themes of Woodford (2003).

4. Neumann (2006), in a review of monetary targeting by the Bundesbank, stresses the desire to influence public expectations of inflation as a central motivation for the strategy and a key element in its success.

5. In Section 4, I consider some specific errors in policy analysis that may have contributed to the "Great Inflation" of the 1970s, and discuss whether the avoidance of such errors requires a central bank to monitor the supply of money.

6. London (2003) reports an interview in which Friedman stated that "the use of quantity of money as a target has not been a success," and that "I'm not sure I would as of today push it as hard as I once did." In a more recent interview, Kuttner (2006) quotes Friedman as having said,"I believe [that] economists in general have . . . overestimate[d] how hard it is to maintain a stable price level. We've all worked on getting

Are there nonetheless reasons to assign a greater importance to money than central banks other than the ECB generally do at present? To consider this, it is useful to begin with a discussion of the theoretical framework behind optimization-based dynamic general-equilibrium models such as that of Smets and Wouters (2003, 2007), now widely used for quantitative policy analysis in central banks, and the role of money in such models.

2. CAN ONE UNDERSTAND INFLATION WITHOUT MONEY?

A first question about the role of monetary aggregates in a sound strategy for monetary policy is whether one can reasonably base policy decisions on models of the transmission mechanism for monetary policy that make no reference to monetary aggregates. Many of the quantitative models now used in central banks are of this kind, and this is surely one of the reasons for the minor role now played by monetary statistics in policy deliberations at many central banks, as the quotation above from Meyer indicates. But is there perhaps something inherently problematic about relying upon models with this feature, especially in a central bank that takes the maintenance of price stability as its primary objective? At the ECB, for example, the fact that "economic analysis" of inflation risks is expected to mean analysis in the context of models that include no role for money is one of the primary justifications given for the inclusion of a second "pillar" of the policy strategy, the cross-check provided by monetary analysis.[7]

There are a variety of misgivings that one might have about the soundness of "cashless" models as a basis for policy analysis. One sort of doubt may concern their theoretical coherence, or at least their consistency with a fundamental principle of economic theory, the *neutrality of money*. One might suppose that a model that makes no reference to must either be inconsistent with monetary neutrality, or leave the general level of prices indeterminate—so that such a model could not be used to predict the consequences for inflation of alternative policies. Alternatively, one might suppose that the models are coherent as far as they go, but that they are incomplete. For example, Nelson (2003) argues that standard "new Keynesian" models that make no reference to money only model the (temporary) departures of the inflation rate from an assumed long-run steady-state inflation rate, and that this steady-state inflation rate can only be understood by taking account of the long-run growth rate of money. And finally, even if one grants that cashless models provide a theoretically coherent

rules, my money rule and others, [on the ground that] it's such a hard job to keep prices stable. Then along comes the 1980s, and central banks all over the world target price stability; and lo and behold, all of them basically succeed. . . . So it must be that that [it] is easier to do than we thought it was. . . . Once [central banks] really understood that avoiding inflation, keeping prices stable, was their real objective, their first order objective, and put that above everything else, they all turned out to be able to do it."

7. According to the ECB, an important limitation of "economic analysis" is the fact that "important information, such as that contained in monetary aggregates, is not easily integrated into the framework used to produce the [staff macroeconomic] projections" (ECB 2004, p. 61).

account of inflation determination, it may be argued that they fly in the face of well-established empirical regularities. For example, Alvarez, Lucas and Weber (2001, p. 219) assert that current consensus models involve "a rejection of the quantity theory" and argue as a consequence that some quite different theory of the monetary transmission mechanism needs to be developed.

2.1 A Model without Money

In order to address these questions about the general structure of "cashless" models of inflation determination, it is useful to give an explicit example of a model of this kind. The most basic "new Keynesian" model[8] consists of three equations. The first is an aggregate supply relation,[9]

$$\pi_t - \bar{\pi}_t = \kappa \log \left(Y_t / Y_t^n \right) + \beta E_t [\pi_{t+1} - \bar{\pi}_{t+1}] + u_t, \tag{1}$$

where π_t represents the rate of inflation between periods t and $t + 1$, $\bar{\pi}_t$ is the perceived rate of "trend inflation" at date t, Y_t is aggregate output, Y_t^n is the "natural rate of output" (a function of exogenous real factors, including both technology and household preferences), u_t is a possible additional exogenous "cost-push" disturbance, and the coefficients satisfy $\kappa > 0, 0 < \beta < 1$. This equation represents a log-linear approximation to the dynamics of aggregate inflation in a model of staggered price-setting of the kind first proposed by Calvo (1983) and incorporated into a complete monetary DSGE model by Yun (1996). In the variant of the model presented here, in periods when firms do not reoptimize their prices, they automatically increase their prices at the trend inflation rate $\bar{\pi}_t$; departures of aggregate output from the natural rate and/or cost-push shocks give firms that reoptimize their prices an incentive to choose a price increase different from the trend rate, and so create a gap between π_t and $\bar{\pi}_t$. This assumption of automatic indexation was first used in the empirical model of Smets and Wouters (2003), who assume indexation to the current inflation target of the central bank,[10] as discussed further below.

The second equation is a log-linear approximation to an Euler equation for the timing of aggregate expenditure,

$$\log(Y_t / Y_t^n) = E_t \left[\log(Y_{t+1} / Y_{t+1}^n) \right] - \sigma \left[i_t - E_t \pi_{t+1} - r_t^n \right], \tag{2}$$

---

8. In Woodford (2003) I call models of this kind "neo-Wicksellian," in order to draw attention to the fundamental role in such models of a transmission mechanism in which interest rates affect intertemporal spending decisions, so that monetary policy need not be specified in terms of an implied path for the money supply, but the terminology "New Keynesian" for such models has become commonplace, following Clarida et al. (1999), among others.

9. See Woodford (2003, chaps. 3–5) for discussion of the microeconomic foundations underlying equations (1) and (2), as well as more complicated versions of the model, including some small empirical models that are close cousins of the model presented here.

10. Actually, their empirical model assumes indexation to an average of the current inflation target and a recent past inflation rate. The assumption here of simple indexation to the inflation trend or inflation target simplifies the algebra of the discussion below of equilibrium determination, while still conveying the essential flavor of the Smets–Wouters model of price adjustment.

sometimes called an "intertemporal IS relation," by analogy to the role of the IS curve in Hicks' exposition of the basic Keynesian model. Here i_t is a short-term nominal interest rate (a riskless "one-period rate" in the theoretical model, earned on money market instruments held between periods t and $t + 1$) and r_t^n is the Wicksellian "natural rate of interest" (a function of exogenous real factors, like the natural rate of output). This equation is the one that indicates how monetary policy affects aggregate expenditure: the expected short-term real rate of return determines the incentive for intertemporal substitution between expenditure in periods t and $t + 1$. The equation is here written in terms of the output gap $\log(Y_t/Y_t^n)$ rather than the level of aggregate real expenditure Y_t in order to facilitate solution of the model.

The remaining equation required to close the system is a specification of monetary policy. We might, for example, specify policy by a rule of the kind proposed by Taylor (1993) for the central bank's operating target for the short-term nominal interest rate,

$$i_t = r_t^* + \bar{\pi}_t + \phi_\pi(\pi_t - \bar{\pi}_t) + \phi_y \log(Y_t/Y_t^n). \tag{3}$$

Here $\bar{\pi}_t$ is the central bank's inflation target at any point in time, and r_t^* represents the central bank's view of the economy's equilibrium (or natural) real rate of interest and hence its estimate of where the intercept needs to be in order for this policy rule to be consistent with the inflation target; ϕ_π and ϕ_y are positive coefficients indicating the degree to which the central bank responds to observed departures of inflation from the target rate or of output from the natural rate, respectively. I shall assume that both $\bar{\pi}_t$ and r_t^* are exogenous processes, the evolution of which represent shifts in attitudes within the central taken to be independent of what is happening to the evolution of inflation or real activity. This is a simplified version (because the relation is purely contemporaneous) of the empirical central bank reaction function used to specify monetary policy in the empirical model of Smets and Wouters (2003). Note that while (3) includes two distinct types of "monetary policy shocks," corresponding to innovations in r_t^* and $\bar{\pi}_t$, respectively, there is no economic significance to anything but the sum $r_t^* + (1 - \phi_\pi)\bar{\pi}_t$ the two components are empirically identified only insofar as their fluctuations are assumed to exhibit different degrees of persistence. Like Smets and Wouters, I shall assume that the inflation target follows a random walk,

$$\bar{\pi}_t = \bar{\pi}_{t-1} + v_t^\pi, \tag{4}$$

where v_t^π is an i.i.d. shock with mean zero, while r_t^* is stationary (or, if the natural rate of interest has a unit root, $r_t^* - r_t^n$ is stationary).

It might be thought unrealistic to assume that the output gap to which the central bank responds is identical to the theoretical conception of the output gap that appears in the aggregate-supply relation (1). However, if the central bank responds to a different measure (e.g., to $\log Y_t$ minus a deterministic trend), the discrepancy between the central bank's conception of the output gap and the theoretically relevant one can be taken to be included in the intercept term r_t^*. (As long as the discrepancy is a function of purely exogenous variables, as in the example just proposed, this changes nothing in my analysis.)

It might also be thought extraordinary to suppose that the inflation target of the central bank, denoted $\bar{\pi}_t$ in (3), should coincide with the rate of inflation, denoted $\bar{\pi}_t$ in (1), to which price setters index their prices when not reoptimizing them. One interpretation of this, proposed by Smets and Wouters (2003), is that the private sector observes the central bank's inflation target and indexes prices to it. If one does not wish to postulate a behavioral relation for the private sector that depends on an assumption of a particular type of monetary policy (namely, the existence of a well-defined inflation target at each point in time), one can interpret the indexation rate $\bar{\pi}_t$ in (1) as the Beveridge–Nelson (stochastic) trend of the inflation process,[11]

$$\bar{\pi}_t \equiv \lim_{T \to \infty} E_t \pi_T. \tag{5}$$

As we shall see, in the equilibrium of the present model, the inflation rate π_t fluctuates around a stochastic trend given by the central bank's inflation target, and since (4) implies that $E_t \bar{\pi}_T = \bar{\pi}_t$ for any future date T, under definition (5) the indexation rate will in fact equal the central bank's inflation target at each point in time, assuming that this is part of the information set of price setters.

2.2 Can Such a Model Explain the Rate of Inflation?

A first question about this model is whether such a model—which has thus far made no reference to the economy's supply of money—has any implication for the general level of prices and for the rate of inflation. It is easily shown that it does. Using (3) to substitute for i_t in (2), the pair of equations (1)–(2) can be written in the form

$$z_t = A \, E_t z_{t+1} + a \left(r_t^n - r_t^* \right), \tag{6}$$

where

$$z_t \equiv \begin{bmatrix} \pi_t - \bar{\pi}_t \\ \log \left(Y_t / Y_t^n \right) \end{bmatrix},$$

where A is a 2×2 matrix of coefficients and a is a 2-vector of coefficients. The system (6) has a unique nonexplosive solution (a solution in which both elements of z_t are stationary processes, under the maintained assumption that the exogenous process

---

11. This is well defined as long as monetary policy implies that the inflation rate is difference stationary, and that the first difference of inflation has an unconditional mean of zero; that is, there is no long-run inflation trend. Atheoretical characterizations of inflation dynamics in countries like the United States that lack an official inflation target, often have this property (e.g., Stock and Watson 2006). And the model sketched here implies that equilibrium inflation should have this property as well.

$r_t^n - r_t^*$ is stationary) as long as both eigenvalues of A are inside the unit circle;[12] this condition holds if[13]

$$\phi_\pi + \frac{1 - \beta}{\kappa}\phi_y > 1. \tag{7}$$

If this condition holds (as it does for many empirical Taylor rules), the unique non-explosive solution is given by

$$z_t = \sum_{j=0}^{\infty} A^j a\, E_t\left[r_{t+j}^n - r_{t+j}^*\right]. \tag{8}$$

This implies, in particular, a solution for equilibrium inflation of the form

$$\pi_t = \bar{\pi}_t + \sum_{j=0}^{\infty} \psi_j E_t\left[r_{t+j}^n - r_{t+j}^*\right], \tag{9}$$

where

$$\psi_j \equiv [1\,0]\, A^j\, a$$

for each j.[14] This shows how inflation is determined by the inflation target of the central bank, and by current and expected future discrepancies between the natural rate of interest and the intercept adjustment made to central bank's reaction function. (If the intercept r_t^* is adjusted so as to perfectly track r_t^n, the central bank should perfectly achieve its inflation target.) So the model does imply a determinate inflation rate. Moreover, given an initial price level (a historical fact at the time that one begins to implement the policy represented by equation (3)), the model correspondingly implies a determinate path for the price level.[15]

---

12. The analysis here treats the inflation trend to which price-setters index in (1) as being given by the central bank's inflation target in (3); thus the $\bar{\pi}_t$ appearing in both equations represents the same quantity, and this is exogenously specified by (4). If, instead, one supposes that the $\bar{\pi}_t$ appearing in (1) is defined by (5), one must consider the possibility of an equilibrium in which the inflation trend differs from the central bank's target rate. But one can show that under the condition (7) stated in the text, there cannot exist an equilibrium of that kind.

13. See Woodford (2003, Prop. 3). Note that in equation (7) there, a factor of 4 appears because the Taylor rule coefficients are quoted for the case in which the interest rate and inflation rate are annualized, while the "period" of the discrete-time model is assumed to be a quarter. Here instead (3) is written in terms of "one-period" rates for simplicity.

14. For plots of these coefficients in some numerical examples, see Woodford (2003, Figures 4.5 and 4.6). The coefficients are denoted ψ_j^π in the figures.

15. It is not true, as sometimes supposed, that the initial price level fails to be determined by the model. If t_0 is the first period in which the policy begins to be implemented, a higher price level P_{t_0} will correspond to a higher inflation rate π_{t_0} and so will provoke a higher interest rate target from the central bank. Given the value of P_{t_0-1}, which is at that point a historical fact—and not one that is irrelevant for the central bank's policy rule—there is a uniquely determined equilibrium value for P_{t_0}, and similarly for P_t in any period $t \geq t_0$.

1570 : MONEY, CREDIT AND BANKING

Does the fact that this model determines the equilibrium price level without any reference to the money supply imply a violation of the long-established economic principle of the *neutrality of money*? It does not. The most important aspect of monetary neutrality, and the one that represents a genuinely deep principle of economic theory, is the proposition that decisions about the supply and demand of goods and services should (if decision makers are rational) depend only on the *relative prices* of different goods, and not on the *absolute* price (price in terms of money) of anything. This has an important implication for the theory of inflation, which is that one cannot expect there to be a theory of the general price level (at least, not one founded on rationality and intertemporal general equilibrium) for a world *without government*— in the way that one can, for example, speak of what the relative price of oil would be in a hypothetical world in which there were no government petroleum reserves or other government interventions in the market for oil. The equilibrium price level, or alternatively the real purchasing power of the monetary unit, depends crucially on government policy, and more specifically on monetary policy: it is only the fact that the central bank's actions are *not* independent of the absolute price level that gives a nation's currency unit any specific economic significance.[16]

Thus, one should not expect a well-formulated model to explain the general level of prices *except* as a result of the way in which monetary policy is specified. But this does not mean that the model must involve any reference to the supply of money. For example, the monetary policy rule might specify that the national currency is convertible into some real commodity (gold being the most popular choice, historically). The parity at which the central bank is committed to maintain convertibility is then the crucial determinant of the real purchasing power of the currency unit; the nominal stock of money that ends up being held in such an economy is neither a policy decision by the central bank nor an essential element of an account of equilibrium determination under such a regime. The kind of policy represented by (3) is another example of a way that a central bank policy that does not involve a target for the quantity of money, and that can be implemented without even measuring any monetary aggregates, can determine the general level of prices.

The model is in fact fully consistent with monetary neutrality, as I have defined this principle above. Each of the two private-sector behavioral relations, (1) and (2), relates real variables only to *relative* prices. Indeed, not only is the absolute level of prices irrelevant in these equations, but the absolute rate of inflation is irrelevant as well (a property sometimes referred to as "superneutrality"): in (1) only the inflation rate relative to the inflation trend matters, and in (2) only the inflation rate relative to the nominal interest rate matters. Thus a permanent increase in the inflation rate (shifting the perceived inflation trend by the same amount), if accompanied by a

16. In theory, it is possible to have a regime under which the equilibrium price level is determined by *fiscal* policy, even though the central bank behaves in a way that is independent of the absolute level of prices; this is illustrated by the theory of the functioning of a wartime bond price-support regime proposed in Woodford (2001). I shall leave aside this possibility, however, for purposes of the present discussion. Even if one accepts this type of regime as a theoretical possibility, there is no reason to think of it as a practical alternative to the assignment to the central bank of responsibility for maintaining price stability; the adoption of such schemes during wartime represents a temporary sacrifice of the goal of inflation control to increased flexibility of government finance.

corresponding increase in the level of nominal interest rates (so as to keep the short-run real rate of interest unchanged), would make the same pattern of real economic activity over time consistent with these equations. The equilibrium inflation rate is only determinate because the policy rule (3) does *not* have this property.

It is sometimes asserted that models like the one sketched above do not actually explain the rate of inflation without reference to money growth, but only departures of inflation from its trend rate, with the trend needing to be determined somewhere else—specifically, by the long-run rate of money growth. For example, Nelson (2003, Section 2.2) attributes to McCallum (2001) the argument that in such models "inflation ... can still be regarded as pinned down in the long run by the economy's steady-state nominal money growth rate."[17] In particular, Nelson argues that because equations like (1)–(3) have been log-linearized, analyses using these equations "take as given" the long-run average inflation rate rather than determining it within the model; the economic relation through which money growth determines the long-run inflation rate "is buried in the constant terms" and "suppressed altogether in the dynamic equations that are expressed in terms of deviations from the steady state."[18]

But this is a misunderstanding. While (8) represents a solution for the evolution of the "inflation gap" (i.e., the deviation of the inflation rate from the trend $\bar{\pi}_t$), the trend inflation rate $\bar{\pi}_t$ is *also* determined within the system: it corresponds to the central bank's target rate, incorporated into the policy rule (3). Of course one could determine it in other ways as well; if, for example, one were to close the model by specifying a loss function for the central bank, rather than a Taylor rule, then one could derive the trend rate of inflation from this model of central-bank behavior as well. (Again it would depend on the central bank's inflation target, specified in the loss function.) The fact that the equations are log-linearized does not mean that one simply *assumes* an average inflation rate; the equations allow one to derive the average inflation rate corresponding to a given policy, though one only expects the log-linearized equations to be accurate if the solution obtained in this way is one in which endogenous variables such as the "inflation gap" turn out not to be very different from the steady-state values around which the equations have been log-linearized.[19] So while it is true that a model like this does not determine the inflation rate independently of *monetary policy,* it *does*

17. This is not an obvious reading of what McCallum (2001) actually says. McCallum is concerned with whether *the aggregate-supply relation alone* can be viewed as determining the equilibrium inflation rate, independently of *monetary policy,* and his answer is that, in the New Keynesian model that he discusses, "the long-run average rate of inflation ... is controlled entirely by the central bank—the monetary authority" (p. 146). Similarly, I have shown that in the model sketched here, the inflation trend is determined purely by the central bank's policy rule. But this does not mean that the complete model, *including* equation (3), is incomplete, nor does McCallum suggest otherwise.

18. Reynard (2006) criticizes mainstream monetary policy analysis on similar grounds, arguing that linearized models "focus on relative instead of general price level fluctuations," while the issue of importance for policy is the control of the inflation trend (pp. 2–3). Lucas (2006) echoes this view, stating that a unified treatment of the inflation trend and fluctuations around the trend "remains an unsolved problem on the frontier of macro-economic theory. Until it is resolved, the use of monetary information should continue to be used as a kind of add-on or cross-check, just as it is in ECB policy formulation today" (p. 137).

19. The restriction of attention above to the nonexplosive solution of (6) does not mean assuming that the variables z_t must have zero means, though that is true in the example discussed above if one supposes that r_t^* is equal to r_t^n on average. And if one were *not* to restrict attention to nonexplosive solutions, there would be a multiplicity of solutions to equation system (6), but this problem would *not* be eliminated by

determine the inflation rate without any reference to money growth and without any need to specify additional relations beyond those listed above.

Some may object that an assumption that the central bank can *implement* the policy represented by equation (3) over the long run is unwarranted, unless it does so by paying attention to money growth and not solely to the variables appearing in the equation. Friedman's (1968) celebrated critique of attempts to peg nominal interest rates might be cited as illustration of the proposition that pursuit of an interest rate rule without reference to the resulting growth in the money supply can easily lead to eventual infeasibility of the policy. But the set of interest rate rules that lead to unstable dynamics of the kind described by Friedman can be characterized simply in terms of the degree to which the nominal interest rate operating target responds to variations in inflation (or the price level), output, and inflation expectations; thus, one can identify rules that it *should* be possible to implement indefinitely, and others that one should *not* be able to implement.[20] In the case of a rule like (3), which leads to stable dynamics under plausible assumptions about expectation formation, there is no problem with the assumption that the rule determines monetary policy indefinitely. Following the rule may *imply* a stable long-run rate of growth of the money supply,[21] but there is no need to monitor money growth in order to implement the rule, and the predicted consequences of following the rule for inflation and output are the same whether money demand remains stable or not.

2.3 How Gross Is the Abstraction from Reality in Ignoring Money?

Thus far I have argued that there is nothing conceptually incoherent about a model of inflation determination that involves no role whatsoever for measures of the money supply. But is such a model, while internally consistent, nonetheless patently unrealistic, so that it would be foolish to base practical analyses of monetary policy options on a model of this kind? One answer to this question would be to point out that more complicated versions of the model just sketched, such as the model of Smets and Wouters (2003, 2007), are able to account fairly well for the historically observed dynamics of inflation and other key macroeconomic variables in both the United States and the euro area. For example, Smets and Wouters (2007) show that their model compares favorably with atheoretical VAR or BVAR models in terms of out-of-sample forecasting performance, especially over horizons from 1 to 3 years.

---

adjoining a quantity equation to the system. Indeed, it would not be solved even if the policy rule (3) were to be replaced by an exogenously specified path for the money supply.

20. Bullard and Mitra (2002) and Preston (2005) provide examples of analyses of this kind, in the context of a New Keynesian model similar to the one sketched in the previous section, supplemented by a model of adaptive expectation formation in the spirit of Friedman's (1968) analysis of expectational dynamics. These formal analyses confirm Friedman's assertion that an interest rate peg should lead to explosive dynamics (and hence be eventually unsustainable) but find that a Taylor rule satisfying (7) is instead associated with stable expectational dynamics, and eventual convergence to a determinate rational-expectations equilibrium like that characterized in (9).

21. This will be true if there exists a money–demand relation, such as (10) below, that remains stable over the long run.

Are such models nonetheless obviously unrealistic on dimensions other than those with which Smets and Wouters are concerned, so that one might nonetheless suspect that this apparent empirical success is accidental—and that the estimated "structural" relations might not prove to be structural at all—if one were to choose policies substantially different from those followed over the sample period? Of course these models, like all models, abstract from a vast number of complications of actual economies; the practical question is not whether a model is literally correct, but whether the simplifications that it involves are fatal to a realistic analysis of the types of questions for which it is intended to be used. Here I wish to focus on whether the omission of money is likely to distort key relationships that matter for an analysis of the effects of alternative monetary policy decisions.

It is especially important to address a common misunderstanding about the implications of a moneyless model like the one presented above. Such a model does not require one to believe that efforts by the central bank to control the money supply will have no effect on the economy, owing to the completely elastic character of the velocity of money, as held by some extreme Keynesians in the 1950s (the UK "Radcliffe Report" being the best-known expression of such views (see, e.g., Radcliffe Committee 1959, para. 391). It is true that the model presented above includes no description of a demand for money; derivation of the relations (1) and (2) does not require one to take any particular view of whether money is or is not perfectly substitutable for other financial assets in private portfolio decisions. In fact, the equations as written are *compatible* with a world in which there is no special role for money in facilitating transactions, and hence no reason for money not to be perfectly substitutable with any other similarly riskless nominal asset, and deriving the model in this "frictionless" case is one way to clarify that the key relationships in the model have no intrinsic connection with the evolution of the money supply. But despite the pedagogical value of considering that case, the use of such a model to understand inflation determination in an actual economy does not require one to suppose that open-market operations are in fact irrelevant, or that there is not a uniquely defined path for the money supply associated with the policy described by rule (3).

For the model equations presented above are also *consistent* with the existence of a well-defined money–demand curve of a conventional sort, giving rise to an additional equilibrium relation of the form

$$\log(M_t/P_t) = \eta_y \log Y_t - \eta_i i_t + \epsilon_t^m, \tag{10}$$

in which M_t is the (nominal) money supply in period t, the positive coefficients η_y and η_i are the income elasticity and interest rate semielasticity of money demand, respectively, and ϵ_t^m is an exogenous disturbance to money demand. This standard "quantity equation" does not contradict any of the equations written earlier; in the case of a monetary policy of the kind described by (3), equation (10) simply indicates the way in which the money supply will have to vary as the central bank implements the interest rate target specified by (3). Adjoining the quantity equation to the previous system provides additional detail about what happens in the equilibrium previously described, and about what is involved in policy implementation. The additional equation is not needed, however, in order for the model to predict the evolution of inflation, output and interest rates under a given interest rate rule, and it is accordingly not needed in order to judge whether one interest-rate rule or another would have more desirable features, as long as the objectives of policy relate only to the evolution of these variables. One's conclusions about these matters would be the same regardless of the coefficients of the money–demand specification, or indeed whether a stable money–demand relation even exists.

The model is thus not one that requires the existence of a money–demand relation such as (10), but not one that is incompatible with the existence of such a relation either. It is thus incorrect to claim, as Alvarez, Lucas, and Weber (2001) do, that models like the one set out above "reject" the quantity theory of money, and can accordingly be dismissed in light of the empirical support for that theory. No matter how strong one might believe the evidence to be in favor of a stable money–demand relation, this would not *contradict* any of the equations of the "New Keynesian" model, and would thus provide no ground for supposing that an alternative model is needed in order to reach sound conclusions about monetary policy.[22]

Still less is the model inconsistent with such elementary observations as the fact that non-interest-earning currency continues to be held even in financially developed economies like that of the United States. It is true that a fully "frictionless" model would not allow currency to be held if it pays an interest rate lower than the interest rate on other riskless nominal assets. And it would certainly be a mistake for a central bank to take literally the prediction of such a model that it should be impossible to raise short-term nominal interest rates above zero as long as there are no plans to retire the entire stock of currency from circulation. But one can adjoin to the model a money demand equation that solves the "paradox" of the existence of different interest rates on currency and on T-bills (or in the federal funds market), without requiring any material change in the relations relied upon above to predict equilibrium inflation.

It may be objected that while an equation of the form (10) is not *mathematically* inconsistent with the structural relations derived earlier, it is nonetheless not economically plausible that the transactions frictions that account for the existence of a "liquidity premium" should not also change the correct specification of relations such as (1) and (2). In fact, it is theoretically plausible that transactions frictions do have *some* effect on the correct specification of these structural relations. For example, if one motivates the existence of a liquidity premium by supposing that households obtain a service flow from cash balances, and accordingly write the period flow of utility of the representative household not as $U(C_t)$, where C_t is real consumption expenditure, but as $U(C_t, M_t/P_t)$, then except in the special case of additive separability in the two arguments—a familiar case in textbook expositions, but one that is hard to defend as realistic—the marginal utility of real income each period depends on the level of real money balances in addition to the level of consumption. This in

---

22. See, for example, McCallum (2001) and Svensson (2003) for previous discussions of this point.

MICHAEL WOODFORD : 1575

turn means that the equilibrium real rate of interest should depend not only on current and expected future real activity (which determines equilibrium consumption), as in equation (2) but also on current and expected future real money balances, as discussed in Woodford (2003, chap. 2, section 3). This change in the relation between real activity and the marginal utility of income also implies that real money balances should generally enter the aggregate-supply relation (1) as well (Woodford 2003, chap. 4, section 3).[23]

The question is how large this correction is likely to be in practice. McCallum (2001), Woodford (2003, pp. 117–121, 304–311), and Ireland (2004) all examine this issue in the context of New Keynesian models that include transactions frictions of a kind that give rise to a money demand relation of the form (10). McCallum and Woodford each calibrate their model specifications so that the implied money–demand relation agrees with estimated relations for the United States, while Ireland presents maximum-likelihood estimates of a complete structural model using U.S. data on money growth, inflation, output, and interest rates. All find that under an empirically realistic specification, the real-balance corrections are nonzero, but quite small, and that they make little difference for the quantitative predictions of the model with regard to a variety of monetary policy experiments.

And even granting that one wishes to take corrections of this kind into account, for the sake of greater accuracy, it is not obvious that this implies that money balances should become an important state variable. While in the nonseparable case, the marginal utility of income is no longer a function solely of consumption and exogenous preference parameters, the missing variable can as well be described as the *interest rate differential* between nonmonetary and monetary assets (which represents the opportunity cost of holding wealth in the form that yields transactions services), as some measure of the *quantity* of liquid wealth. At least in some cases, expressing the relationship in terms of the interest rate differential is clearly superior. Suppose, for example, that the utility in period t is given by a (nonseparable) function of the form

$$U(C_t, M_t/(P_t \bar{m}_t)),$$

where $\bar{m}_t$ is an exogenous disturbance representing changes in the transactions technology. In this case, the marginal utility of (real) income λ_t will depend on C_t and $M_t/(P_t \bar{m}_t)$, and the equilibrium interest rate differential Δ_t will *also* be a function of those two quantities, so that there exists a functional relationship

$$\lambda_t = \lambda(C_t, \Delta_t)$$

that is invariant to changes in the transaction technology. (The relationship between λ_t, C_t, and M_t/P_t will instead also involve the disturbance $\bar{m}_t$.) Using this relation, one can express the generalized versions of the structural relations (1) and (2) in terms

---

23. Other, more explicit, models of the way in which cash balances facilitate transactions often have a similar implication; see, for example, Woodford (2003, appendix, section A.16).

of inflation, output, and *two* short-term nominal interest rates (the interest rate on non-monetary assets and the interest rate paid on money, if any), as discussed in Woodford (2003, chap. 4). Since the payment of interest on money is not commonly used as an independent instrument of policy, this does not introduce any additional state variables, though the dynamics of the effects of interest rates on inflation and output are now somewhat more complex than in the baseline model presented above. Writing the model in terms of inflation, output, the nominal interest rate (on nonmonetary assets) and money balances would not only introduce an additional state variable but would introduce dependence of all three structural equations on an additional structural disturbance ($\bar{m}_t$), that could be eliminated by writing the model in terms of the *cost* of liquidity rather than the *quantity* of liquid balances.

More generally, it is often observed that the basic New Keynesian model abstracts from financial frictions of all sorts when it refers to a single interest rate that is taken to be both the central bank's policy rate and the unique measure of the relative cost of current and future expenditure by the private sector. This is obviously an oversimplification, and some feel that a more complete account of the monetary transmission mechanism, distinguishing among the variety of interest rates and asset returns that co-exist in a typical economy, would inevitably restore an important role to monetary aggregates as a key determinant (or crucial indicator) of changes in the structure of asset returns.[24] This is too large a topic to address here in detail, but two brief comments are appropriate.

First, there is nothing essential to the logic of the New Keynesian model that requires that it abstract from financial frictions and extensions of the basic New Keynesian model to incorporate various types of credit-market frictions have been proposed by Bernanke et al. (1999), Christiano et al. (2003, 2007), and Goodfriend and McCallum (2007), among others. To the extent that such frictions are judged to be of quantitative importance for monetary policy analysis, they can be incorporated into a mainstream New Keynesian framework; belief that they are important is neither a reason to reject the empirical relevance of such a framework nor a reason to consider money and credit developments within a wholly distinct and competing analytical framework, as under the ECB's "two pillar" strategy.[25]

Second, it is far from obvious that assigning an important role to *credit* frictions in the monetary transmission mechanism implies that the monetary aggregates stressed in the traditional monetarist literature should be important state variables. For example, in the influential "financial accelerator" model of Bernanke et al. (1999), the key innovation relative to a standard New Keynesian model is the introduction of an endogenous wedge between the required *ex ante* rate of return on investment projects and the rate of return received by savers, the size of which depends on the aggregate

24. Nelson (2003) argues for this view, though without offering a specific theory of how money is related to other asset returns and how these matter to the monetary transmission mechanism. Goodfriend and McCallum (2007) present an explicit model with financial frictions that result in multiple interest rates and use it to argue for the quantitative importance of "money and banking" to the transmission mechanism.

25. The suggestion of ECB Vice President Lucas Papademos (2006) that one can eventually imagine the two separate analyses being combined in a "single ... larger pillar" is surely a sensible one, though it remains to be seen how "prominent" a role there is for money in the eventual synthesis.

net worth of entrepreneurs; the evolution of the net worth of entrepreneurs, in turn, depends mainly on the equilibrium returns to capital. The size and evolution of this friction have no essential connection with any monetary aggregate, and indeed, it would be possible to simplify the model, abstracting from the use of cash to facilitate transactions altogether, without any fundamental change in the model's predictions with regard to the response of output and inflation to either real disturbances or monetary policy (specified in terms of an interest rate rule such as (3)).[26]

In this, as in other models of the "financial accelerator" type, the key impediment to efficient financial intermediation derives from the circumstances of the borrowers (a lack of internal funds or of suitable collateral) rather than some inability of intermediaries to obtain sufficient funds to lend, as in traditional discussions of the "bank lending channel" of monetary policy. Credit frictions of this kind seem more likely to be quantitatively significant for economies like the United States, where there are many substitutes for bank credit and banks have many sources of funds other than the supply of transactions deposits, so it is not obvious that variations in the money supply should have much connection with the relevant credit frictions. Moreover, even if lending by banks is assumed to play a crucial role (on the ground that other sources of finance are imperfect substitutes), it would seem to be variations in the volume of *bank credit* that would be of greatest macroeconomic significance, rather than variations in the volume of those specific bank liabilities that are counted as part of the money supply.[27]

3. IMPLICATIONS OF THE LONG-RUN RELATIONSHIP BETWEEN MONEY AND PRICES

The monetarist argument for the importance of attention to monetary aggregates in a strategy to control inflation is above all an empirical one. The association of money growth with inflation is argued, as an empirical matter, to be highly robust, confirmed by data from different centuries, from different countries, and from economies with different financial institutions and different monetary and fiscal policies. Empirical work in the monetarist tradition often emphasizes simple correlations (and sometimes lead–lag relationships) rather than structural estimation, but it may be argued that the relations thus uncovered represent more certain knowledge because they are independent of any maintained assumption of the correctness of a particular structural model. Monetarists argue that the causal relation between money growth and inflation is as a consequence one that can more safely be relied upon in designing a policy aimed at controlling inflation than the relations (such as the Phillips curve) that make up a structural macroeconometric model.

---

26. This is illustrated by the work of Cúrdia (2007), who develops an open-economy extension of the model of Bernanke et al. (1999) that is purely "cashless."

27. Although Goodhart (2007) argues that central banks ought still to pay attention to "monetary aggregates," his argument is primarily for the significance of variations in the efficiency of intermediation by commercial banks, and indeed he remarks that he "believe[s] that the rate of growth of bank lending to the private sector is as, or a more, important monetary aggregate than broad money by itself" (p. 60).

1578 : MONEY, CREDIT AND BANKING

It is important, then, to consider the nature of the long-run evidence to which the monetarist literature frequently refers. My goal here will not be to criticize the soundness of the statistical evidence itself but rather to ask—even taking the evidence at face value—how much of a case one can build on it for the importance of using monetary aggregates in assessing the stance of monetary policy.

While early advocacy of money-growth targets was often based on analyses of the correlation between money growth and real and/or nominal national income at business-cycle frequencies, these correlations have broken down in the United States since the 1980s,[28] and the more recent monetarist literature has instead emphasized the wide range of evidence that exists for a long-run relationship between money growth and inflation. This relationship is argued to be more robust and to suffice as a justification for controlling money growth given a central bank's proper concern with the character of long-run inflation trends.

Studies of the long-run or low-frequency relationship between money and prices are of several types. First, cross-country correlations between money growth and inflation, averaged over long periods, typically show a strong positive relationship, and even a certain tendency of the data points for different countries to fall near a line with a slope of 45 degrees, as predicted by the quantity theory of money, at least when countries with very high average inflation rates are included in the sample. McCandless and Weber (1995) provide a number of plots of this kind, one of which (comparing 30-year averages of M2 growth and CPI inflation for a sample of 110 countries) was included in Robert Lucas's (1996) Nobel lecture as empirical confirmation of that theory.[29] Further cross-country comparisons are presented by King (2002) and Haug and Dewald (2004).[30]

Second, low-frequency movements in money growth and in inflation can be compared in a single country if sufficiently long time series are available to allow consideration of how low-frequency trends change over time. Bandpass filtering of the respective time series has become a popular method in studies of this kind; essentially, this means taking long moving averages of the data, so as to average out high-frequency fluctuations. For example, Benati (2005) compares the low-frequency variations in money growth and inflation in both the United Kingdom and the United States using various measures of money and prices, and data from the 1870s to the present; his bandpass filters retain only fluctuations with a period of 30 years or longer. Even with this degree of smoothing of the data, several long swings in the

---

28. See, for example, Estrella and Mishkin (1997), Hafer and Wheelock (2001), and Walsh (2003, Figure 1.3). More recently, relations of this kind have been much less stable in the euro area as well. For a recent discussion of the stability of M3 demand in the euro area, and its implications for the usefulness of "excess liquidity" measures based on cumulative M3 growth, see Bordes et al. (2007). Fischer et al. (2008) document the reduced reliance on estimated money–demand relations in recent years in the monetary analysis of the ECB.

29. Lucas argues that "it is clear from these data ... that ... the quantity theory of money ... applies, with remarkable success, to co-movements in money and prices generated in complicated, real-world circumstances. Indeed, how many specific economic theories can claim empirical success at the level exhibited in [the figure of McCandless and Weber]? ... The kind of monetary neutrality shown in this figure needs to be a central feature of any monetary or macro-economic theory that claims empirical seriousness" (Lucas 1996, p. 666). The same figure is repeated, with similar comments, in Lucas (2006).

30. See, however, de Grauwe and Polan (2001) for criticism of evidence of this kind.

rate of money growth have occurred in each country over the sample period, and the timing and magnitude of the shifts in the low-frequency trend are similar for both money growth and inflation. Similar results are obtained (albeit with shorter time series and hence averaging over a somewhat shorter window) for euro-area data on money growth and inflation by Jaeger (2003) and Assenmacher-Wesche and Gerlach (2006).

Another popular approach to studying the long-run relationship between money growth and inflation in a single country is cointegration analysis. Two (or more) non-stationary series are said to be cointegrated if there is nonetheless a linear combination of the series that is stationary. Assenmacher-Wesche and Gerlach (2006), for example, find that in the euro area, broad money growth and inflation are each nonstationary series (stationary only in their first differences), but that the two series are cointegrated. This implies that they have a common (Beveridge–Nelson) "stochastic trend": changes in the predicted long-run path of one series are perfectly correlated with changes in the predicted long-run path of the other series. Moreover, one cannot reject the hypothesis that the linear combination of the two series that is stationary is their difference (i.e., real money growth), so that a 1% upward shift in the predicted long-run growth rate of broad money is associated with precisely a 1% upward shift in the predicted long-run rate of inflation, in accordance with the quantity theory of money. Cointegration analysis is similarly used to establish a long-run relationship between euro-area money growth and inflation by Bruggeman et al. (2003) and Kugler and Kaufmann (2005). Thus, the results obtained from all three approaches to studying the long-run relationship between money growth and inflation are quite consistent with one another, and with the predictions of the quantity theory of money.

But what does the existence of such a long-run relationship imply for the use of monetary aggregates in the conduct of monetary policy? For the sake of argument, I shall take for granted that the empirical case has been established, and ask what would follow from this for policy. Of course, there are always questions that can be raised about the certainty with which econometric results have been established—claims about the "long run" in particular are notoriously difficult to establish using short time series—and about whether correlations observed under historical conditions should be expected to persist under an alternative policy, designed in order to exploit them. But I think that the monetarist interpretation of these data is indeed the most plausible one, and I shall not challenge it.

In particular, I shall suppose that it has been established that—for example, in the euro area—there really is a reliable structural equation of the form

$$\log M_t - \log P_t = f(X_t), \tag{11}$$

representing money demand behavior, and holding independently of the monetary policy that may be followed by the central bank.[31] Here, $f(X_t)$ represents some

---

31. Benati (2005) argues that because (in the case of United Kingdom data since 1870) the low-frequency relation between money growth and inflation has remained similar despite a succession of fairly different monetary policy regimes, one can best interpret the relation as structural. The same argument had earlier been made by Batini and Nelson (2001).

function of both real and nominal variables with the property that, given the exogenous processes for real disturbances, $f(X_t)$ will be a *difference-stationary* process in the case of any monetary policy that makes the inflation rate a difference-stationary process, with an unconditional growth rate

$$g \equiv E[\Delta f(X_t)]$$

that is independent of monetary policy. If this is the case, then if inflation is difference-stationary (or I(1)), money growth will also have to be difference-stationary, and money growth and inflation will have to be cointegrated, with a cointegrating vector $[1 - 1]$, since first-differencing (11) implies that $\mu_t - \pi_t$ must equal the stationary process $\Delta f(X_t)$. Moreover, the unconditional mean of this process is

$$E[\mu_t - \pi_t] = g, \tag{12}$$

so that over the long run, the average rate of inflation will be the average rate of money growth minus g, regardless of what that rate of money growth may be. The hypothesis of a relation of the form (11) is thus a simple interpretation of the empirical relations asserted in the literature just mentioned.

The important question is, even granting the existence of a reliable structural relation of this kind, what are the implications for the conduct of monetary policy? A first proposal might be that the existence of a well-established empirical relation of this kind implies that "cashless" models of inflation determination are incorrect and hence not a sound basis for policy analysis. But this would not follow. As explained in the previous section, the possibility of explaining inflation dynamics without any reference to monetary aggregates does not depend on a denial that a stable money–demand relation exists—it requires only that the system of equilibrium conditions (including the quantity equation) have a certain recursive structure. I have shown that a cashless model can be consistent with a standard form of money–demand relation, and one can also easily show that such a model is consistent with the existence of a cointegrating relation between money growth and inflation of the kind often found empirically.

Let us consider again the same log-linear "New Keynesian" model as above, extended to include a money–demand relation of the form (10), and assume once more a monetary policy of the form (3), with an inflation target that evolves as a random walk (4) just as in the empirical model of Smets and Wouters (2003). Finally, let us suppose either that both r_t^n and r_t^* are stationary processes, or at any rate that the difference $r_t^n - r_t^*$ is stationary, indicating that the central bank succeeds in tracking variations in the natural rate of interest, at least over the long run. Then the solution (9) implies that the inflation rate π_t is an I(1) random variable, with a stochastic trend equal to $\bar{\pi}_t$. First-differencing (10) furthermore implies that

$$\mu_t - \pi_t = \eta_y \gamma_t - \eta_i \Delta i_t + \Delta \epsilon_t^m, \tag{13}$$

where $\gamma_t \equiv \Delta \log Y_t$ is the growth rate of output. Solution (8) similarly implies that the output gap is stationary, so that as long as the (log) natural rate of output is at least difference-stationary, γ_t will be stationary. Moreover, (2) implies that

$$i_t = r_t^n + E_t \pi_{t+1} + \sigma^{-1} E_t \left[\gamma_{t+1} - \gamma_{t+1}^n \right]$$
$$= r_t^* + \pi_t + \left(r_t^n - r_t^* \right) + E_t[\Delta \pi_{t+1}] + \sigma^{-1} E_t \left[\gamma_{t+1} - \gamma_{t+1}^n \right],$$

where γ_t^n is the growth rate of the natural rate of output, so that $i_t - r_t^n - \bar{\pi}_t$ is a sum of stationary variables and hence stationary. Since the last two of these terms have been assumed (or just shown) to be difference-stationary, i_t must also be difference-stationary. Then if we also assume that ϵ_t^m is at least difference-stationary, every term on the right-hand side of (13) is stationary, so that $\mu_t - \pi_t$ is predicted to be stationary.

It would then follow that μ_t must be an I(1) random variable, like π_t, but that the two variables are cointegrated, with a cointegrating vector equal to [1 − 1]. Hence the New Keynesian model is consistent with cointegration evidence of the kind found, for example, by Assenmacher-Wesche and Gerlach (2006). This in turn implies that the average growth rates of money and prices will necessarily be similar if one averages over a sufficiently long period of time, as the stationary difference between μ_t and π_t will have a long-run average value of zero. It follows that the theoretical model of the previous section is equally consistent with the other kinds of "long run" or "low frequency" evidence cited above. Hence, such facts, no matter how thoroughly established, provide no evidence against the validity of nonmonetary models of that type.[32]

A second view might be that the long-run relation between money and prices provides an argument for the desirability of a money–growth target. If a structural relation of the form (11) is believed to exist regardless of the monetary policy chosen, then it follows that as long as the central bank ensures that the money supply grows at some rate $\bar{\mu}$—or at least that the rate of money growth μ_t fluctuates in a stationary way around the average level $\bar{\mu}$—then over the long run the rate of inflation will have to equal $\bar{\mu} - g$, on account of (12). It is true that such a rule is only guaranteed to yield the desired rate of inflation as an average over a sufficiently long period of time. Nonetheless, it can be argued that such an approach is an especially *reliable* way of ensuring the desired long-run rate of inflation, founded as it is on a robust empirical relation; and that this is not only *one* goal of monetary policy, but perhaps the only one that can be reliably achieved.

---

32. In Woodford (2008) I illustrate this through simulation of a calibrated version of the New Keynesian model described above. When the simulated data for money growth and inflation are bandpass filtered, the low-frequency components exhibit strong comovement of the kind found in historical data by authors such as Benati (2005) and Assenmacher-Wesche and Gerlach (2006). (The low-frequency movements in money growth even appear to "lead" the low-frequency movements in the inflation rate, though this does not indicate any *causal* priority of the changes in the rate of money growth.) The simulated data are also consistent with the results obtained by Assenmacher-Wesche and Gerlach when they estimate reduced-form inflation equations using different frequency components of the data: low-frequency inflation is mainly "explained" by low-frequency money growth and output growth, whereas the output gap is instead the most significant of the regressors "explaining" high-frequency inflation. The success of this exercise shows that "two-pillar Phillips curve" estimates do not imply that standard New Keynesian models are incomplete as models of inflation determination.

But nothing in the argument just given implies that a money growth target is the *only* way in which a desired long-run inflation rate can be ensured. If a structural relation of the form (11) exists, it follows that any policy that succeeds in making the inflation rate equal some target rate $\bar{\pi}$ on average over the long run will *also* have to make the rate of money growth equal $\bar{\pi} + g$ on average over the long run. But this does not imply that a successful policy must involve a target for money growth; it need not involve measurement of the money supply at all.

In fact, if all that one cares about is whether an average inflation rate of 2% is maintained over a period of several decades, this is quite easy to ensure. It is only necessary that one be able to measure the inflation rate itself—and not necessarily in real time; it suffices that the lag in data availability be one of weeks rather than years—and that one be able to tell whether policy is being adjusted in a way that should lower inflation as opposed to raising it (for which an interest rate instrument suffices). A suitable policy is then one that monitors the cumulative increase in prices relative to the 2% per year target, and tightens policy if prices have risen too much, loosening it if they have risen too little. One does not need to monitor money growth to tell if an undesirable long-run inflation trend is developing; measurement of *inflation itself* suffices for this! As long as one does in fact know how to measure price increases, and to use policy to accelerate or decelerate the rate of inflation (at least over the next few years), there is little difficulty in ensuring a desired rate of inflation over a sufficiently long period of time. Of course, there are significant practical questions connected with the measurement of current inflation *at high frequencies,* and even greater difficulties in assessing the near-term inflation outlook given the current stance of policy, but the existence of a *long-term* relation between money growth and inflation does not imply any advantage of money-growth statistics in addressing those questions.

Finally, it might be thought that the existence of a long-run relation between money growth and inflation should imply that measures of money growth will be valuable in forecasting inflation, over "the medium to long run" even if not at shorter horizons. But this is not the case. Cointegration of money growth with the inflation rate would imply that *if* one were to know what the average rate of money growth will be over some sufficiently long future horizon, one would need no other information in order to be able to forecast the average inflation rate over that same horizon. But one does not know in advance what the rate of money growth over the long run will be (i.e., unless one knows it because the central bank is determined to adjust policy to ensure a particular rate of money growth). And there is no reason to assume that the *recent* rate of growth of the money supply provides the best predictor of the future long-run rate of money growth. If money were something exogenous with respect to the central bank's actions, like the weather, then it might make sense to try to discern long-run trends from moving averages of recent observations. But the long-run growth rate of the money supply will depend on future monetary policy decisions, and there is no sense in which the existence of a "trend" toward faster money growth in recent years dooms an economy to continue to have fast money growth over some medium to long term.

As a simple example, consider the New Keynesian model presented above, in the special case in which the interest rate gap $r_t^g \equiv r_t^n - r_t^*$ is a white noise process. (This could be true either because both r_t^n and r_t^* are white noise processes or because the central bank adjusts r_t^* to track the changes in the natural rate of interest that are forecastable a period in advance, setting $r_t^* = E_{t-1}r_t^n$.) In this case, the solution (8) is of the form

$$\pi_t = \bar{\pi}_t + ar_t^g,$$
$$\log Y_t = \log Y_t^n + br_t^g,$$

for certain coefficients a, b. If inflation evolves in this way, the optimal forecast of future inflation at any horizon $j \geq 1$ is given by

$$E_t\pi_{t+j} = \bar{\pi}_t = \pi_t + (a/b)\log(Y_t/Y_t^n). \tag{14}$$

Thus, if one uses the current inflation rate and the current output gap to forecast future inflation, one cannot improve upon the forecast using information from any other variables observed at time t.

Forecasting future inflation using the output gap *alone* would not be accurate since inflation has a stochastic trend while the output gap is stationary; one needs to include among the regressors some variable with a similar stochastic trend to that of inflation. But this need not be money growth; *inflation itself* is also a variable with the right stochastic trend, and using current inflation to forecast future inflation means that one need not include any other regressors that track the stochastic trend. What one needs as additional regressors are *stationary* variables that are highly correlated with the current *departure* of inflation from its stochastic trend, that is, the Beveridge–Nelson "cyclical component" of inflation. In the simple example presented above, the output gap is one example of a stationary variable with that property. More generally, the thing that matters is which variables are most useful for tracking relatively high-frequency (or cyclical) variations in inflation and *not* which variables best track long-run inflation. This is true regardless of the horizon over which one wishes to forecast inflation.

Of course, this hardly proves that monetary statistics cannot be of any use as indicator variables. In general, central banks use measures of a wide range of indicators in assessing the state of the economy and the likely effects of alternative policy decisions, and it is right for them to do so. There is no *a priori* reason to exclude monetary variables from the set of indicators that are taken into account. But the mere fact that a long literature has established a fairly robust long-run relationship between money growth and inflation does not, in itself, imply that monetary statistics must be important sources of information when assessing the risks to price stability. Nor does that relationship provide the basis for an analysis of the soundness of policy that can be formulated without reference to any structural model of inflation determination and that can consequently be used as a "cross-check" against more model-dependent analyses. To the extent that money growth is useful as an indicator variable, its interpretation will surely be dependent on a particular modeling framework, that identifies the structural significance of the state variables that the rate of money growth helps to identify (the natural rate of output and the natural rate of interest, in their example).

1584 : MONEY, CREDIT AND BANKING

Thus, a fruitful use of information revealed by monetary statistics is more likely to occur in the context of a model-based "economic analysis" of the inflationary consequences of contemplated policies than in some wholly distinct form of "monetary analysis."

4. PITFALLS OF PHILLIPS-CURVE-BASED MONETARY POLICY ANALYSIS

One of the most important arguments given by the ECB for its "two-pillar" strategy is a desire to ensure a more robust framework for deliberations about monetary policy than would result from complete reliance upon any single model or guideline.[33] "The two-pillar approach is designed to ensure ... that appropriate attention is paid to different perspectives and the cross-checking of information.... It represents, and conveys to the public, the notion of diversified analysis and ensures robust decision making" (ECB, 2004, p. 55).[34]

The issue of robustness is certainly an important concern in choosing a monetary policy strategy, and skepticism is appropriate about the accuracy of any currently existing quantitative models of the monetary transmission mechanism. But is the practice of "cross-checking" the conclusions of "economic analysis" by monitoring money growth (along with other related statistics) the most appropriate way of ensuring robustness? In order to consider the possible advantages of such an approach, it is necessary to consider what some of the more obvious pitfalls might be of making policy on the basis of a Phillips-curve-based model of inflation dynamics alone.[35]

4.1 The Pitfall of Reliance upon Inaccurate Estimates of Potential Output

One obvious potential problem with basing monetary policy on forecasts of the near-term outlook for inflation is that the forecasts may be biased. In such a case, it might be possible for policy to be more inflationary than is intended, perhaps even for many years, because the central bank's biased forecasts persistently predict a lower inflation rate than actually occurs on average. One obviously should not wish to make it too easy for such an outcome to occur, and this is a reason for caution about making policy on the basis of a single, possibly unreliable, forecasting model.

33. This consideration is emphasized by Issing (2006), who stresses that in adopting a monetary policy strategy for the ECB, the Governing Council was equally unwilling to rely upon monetary analysis *alone*.

34. The asserted greater robustness of policies that respond to monetary developments is an important theme of the defense of the monetary pillar by Masuch et al. (2003), one of the background studies for the ECB's re-evaluation of its monetary policy strategy in 2003.

35. Here I consider only the question of whether the use of information from monetary aggregates as a "cross-check" (as part of a two-pillar framework) is a particularly suitable way of curing specific potential defects of a Phillips-curve-based policy analysis. A somewhat different argument, often made by monetarists, asserts that a monetary targeting rule is more robust than an "activist" policy based on a specific economic model, precisely because it requires no model for its implementation. Von zer Muehlen (2001)—originally written in 1982—remains a useful discussion of the reasons why there is no logical connection between a preference for robustness to Knightian uncertainty and choice of a "nonactivist" policy.

A Phillips-curve-based short-run forecasting model might be especially vulnerable to problems of this kind, owing to the crucial role in such a model of the "output gap" as a determinant of inflationary pressures. In fact, real-time measures of the output gap are notoriously controversial because of the difficulty of recognizing changes in the "natural" (or potential) level of output at the time that they occur. Orphanides (2003a) illustrates how large the mistakes are that may easily be made by comparing "real-time" measures of the U.S. output gap available to the Fed during the 1970s to the Fed's subsequent assessment of what the output gap during that period had been. According to the view at the time (based on estimates of potential output by the President's Council of Economic Advisors), the output gap was negative throughout the 1970s, often by 5% or more (including the entire 5-year period between 1974 and 1979), and reached a level as low as -15% in 1975. Based on this statistic, policy might have been viewed as relatively "tight." But from the vantage point of the 1990s,[36] the Fed had substantially revised its view of the output gap during the 1970s: according to the revised data, the output gap was instead *positive* during much of the 1970s, and only negative by a few percent even during the worst quarters of the 1974–75 recession. (The key to the change in perspective was an eventual recognition that productivity growth had been lower during the 1970s than during the previous two decades—something that had not been immediately recognized at the time.)

This type of mistake—persistently overestimating potential output for many years in sequence—could easily result in a persistent inflationary bias to policy, at least if the output gap estimate were used to assess the stance of policy in a naive or mechanical way. This is in fact the explanation of the United States' "Great Inflation" of the 1970s proposed by Orphanides (2003a, 2003b). According to Orphanides, the Fed's target for the federal funds rate throughout the 1970s was set in almost exactly the way that would be implied by a "Taylor rule," with the same inflation target and other coefficients said by Taylor (1993) to characterize Fed policy during the early Greenspan years. In his interpretation, the similar policy rule resulted in much higher inflation during the 1970s because interest rates were kept low in response to the (incorrectly) perceived large negative output gaps.

This is clearly an important practical problem. Avoiding a repetition of the "Great Inflation" of the 1970s should be a key goal in the choice of a monetary policy strategy. It is perhaps too much to expect any strategy to ensure against all possible policy errors, but a wise policymaker will surely strive at the least not to commit exactly the *same* mistake twice.

To what extent would a reliance upon monetary indicators in the conduct of policy solve this problem? It is true that, in a model like the one sketched above (to which we adjoin a standard money–demand relation, such as (10)), an inflationary policy that arises from an overestimate of potential output through the mechanism hypothesized by Orphanides would be associated with a high rate of money growth. Hence, a policy committed to a money growth target, or that would at least respond to persistent

36. At the time of Orphanides' study, the most recent Federal Reserve estimates of historical output gaps that had been made public dated from 1994.

observations of excessive money growth by subsequently tightening policy, would not allow the inflationary policy stance to continue, even if the overestimate of potential output were to persist for many years (as was the case in the United States in the 1970s).

But this is hardly the *only* kind of policy that would preclude the possibility of an entire decade of undesirably high inflation. One did not need the signal provided by money growth to realize that policy was allowing inflation to remain high in the 1970s; the inflation data themselves were evident enough, for many years prior to the eventual dramatic shift in policy under Paul Volcker (beginning in the fall of 1979).[37] According to Orphanides' interpretation of the policy mistake, the Fed was aware of the rate of inflation but nonetheless believed that tighter policy would be inappropriate, because of the severely negative output gap.[38] (Tighter policy, to bring down inflation at the cost of an even more negative output gap, would not have struck a proper balance between the two objectives of stabilization policy.) The additional information provided by statistics on money growth would not have dispelled this misconception. There is not, for example, any reason to suppose that if the output gap really *had* been so negative, money would not have grown at a similar rate, so that the facts about money growth should have disconfirmed the policymakers' analysis of the situation. For money demand depends on the actual level of transactions in an economy, *not* on how that level of activity compares to the "natural rate"—and as a result money is not especially useful as a source of information about the mistake that was made in the 1970s.

One thing that *would* help to avoid this kind of mistake would be the use of information other than direct measures of real activity and estimates of trends for those variables (by filtering the observations of these variables alone) in constructing one's estimate of the current "output gap."[39] An optimal estimate, based on a Kalman filter, would take into account the fact that an observation of higher inflation than had been expected should lead one to question one's view of how much "slack" there currently is in the economy, so that inflation outcomes should themselves be an important factor in the central bank's estimate of the output gap, as discussed by Svensson and Woodford (2003). Of course, money growth could also be one among the indicator variables used in such a filtering exercise, but once again, there is no

37. Here I refer to the period following the removal of price controls in 1974. In the presence of price controls, there is obviously a particular need for indicators of the stance of policy other than the inflation rate itself. But signs of distortions created by the controls, of the sort that eventually required them to be abandoned, should provide an important clue even in the presence of price controls.

38. As noted in Section 1, other intellectual errors may have contributed to the explanation of policy in the 1970s as well, such as skepticism about the ability of monetary policy to restrain inflation. But as discussed there, attention to money would not be necessary in order to avoid those mistakes either.

39. In particular, measures of labor costs should be an important additional source of information. The output gap appearing in (1) as a source of inflationary pressures appears there because, in the basic New Keynesian model, the average real marginal cost of supplying goods covaries with the output gap; it is really real marginal cost that should appear in a more general version of the aggregate–supply relation (Woodford 2003, chap. 3). This suggests that measures of marginal cost relative to prices should be valuable in judging when policy is generating inflationary pressure. In empirical estimates of the New Keynesian Phillips curve (e.g., Gali and Gertler 1999, Sbordone 2002), the level of real unit labor costs has proven to be a useful proxy for this variable.

reason to suppose that it should receive particular weight, given its lack of any direct causal connection with the underlying state variable that one is trying to estimate.

Of course, the construction of an optimal Kalman filter is only a complete solution to the problem of conducting policy under uncertainty when the only uncertainty is about the economy's current state,[40] rather than uncertainty about the correct *model* to use. And one should be equally concerned about the possibility of systematic policy mistakes owing to the use of a model that is incorrect in more fundamental ways. But the most obvious approach to that problem, in my view, is also one under which it is important to closely monitor *inflation outcomes* but under which there is no obvious importance to monitoring money growth as well.

The key to avoiding the possibility of an entire decade of inflation well above the target level, even when the model that one uses to judge the current stance of policy may produce biased forecasts of near-term inflation, is to be committed to *correct past target misses,* rather than conducting policy in a *purely forward-looking* fashion.[41] That is, a year or two of inflation higher than was desired should result in policy that deliberately aims at an inflation rate *lower* than the long-run inflation target for the next few years, so as to correct the overshoot and keep a long-run average of the inflation rate close to the target despite the temporary deviation. In this way, even if the central bank uses a model that produces a downward-biased forecast of inflation for many years in a row (due, for example, to a persistent overestimate of potential output), it will not allow excess inflation to occur for very long before policy is tightened.

One simple way to institutionalize this kind of error–correction would be through commitment to a target path for the *price level,* rather than only to a prospective *inflation rate.* The two targets are equivalent if the target is always hit, but not in what they imply about the consequences of target misses for subsequent policy— thus it is precisely the issue of robustness to model errors (or other failures of policy implementation) that gives one a reason to choose between them.[42] A price-level target path is especially simple to explain, but much the same kind of error correction could alternatively be achieved through a commitment to a target for the *average*

40. Here the "state" is understood to mean the current value of a vector of additive stochastic terms in the structural equations of one's model, rather than (for example) the current values of the coefficients that multiply the state variables in those equations.

41. Orphanides and Williams (2002) propose an alternative way of insulating policy from the consequences of inaccurate estimates of the natural rate of output and/or the natural rate of interest, which is to set interest rates in accordance with a "difference rule" rather than a Taylor rule of the form (3). In the rule that they propose, the *change* in the interest rate operating target is a function of inflation and the *growth rate* of output, so that there is no need for any measure of the *levels* of the interest rate or of output that are consistent with the inflation target. As with the proposal discussed here, the Orphanides–Williams policy is one that makes no use of measures of money. The desirable features of the Orphanides–Williams rule are related to those the desirable consequences of price-level targeting described below. For example, in the case of the basic New Keynesian model presented above, the Orphanides–Williams rule implies a trend stationary price level, so that departures of the price level from its deterministic trend path are subsequently corrected.

42. Even if, as is true for most if not all central banks, one does not aim at complete inflation stabilization but is instead willing to trade off some short-run variation in inflation for the sake of greater stability of real activity, a corresponding contrast remains possible between commitment to an output-gap-adjusted inflation target and commitment to an output-gap-adjusted price-level target path.

inflation rate over a period of years, where the period in question would not be wholly in the future.[43]

Many central bankers seem to be resistant to error correction as an aim in the conduct of policy on the ground that "bygones should be bygones"—however disappointed one may be with past outcomes, one should always aim to do the best thing for the economy from the present time onward, which implies that only purely forward-looking considerations should be relevant. But this is incorrect reasoning, even in the case that the central bank has complete certainty about the correctness of its model of the economy (and about the private sector's understanding the economy in exactly the same way), to the extent that private-sector behavior is *forward looking,* as models derived from intertemporal optimization imply that it should be. For if private-sector behavior depends on anticipations of the subsequent conduct of policy, then the way that the central bank can be counted on to respond subsequently to target misses has an important effect on what is likely to occur on the occasions that generate those target misses.

For example, in the context of the simple New Keynesian model presented above, let us consider the policy that would minimize a loss function of the form

$$E_0 \sum_{t=0}^{\infty} \beta^t \left[\left(\pi_t - \pi^*\right)^2 + \lambda \left(x_t - x^*\right)^2 \right], \tag{15}$$

representing dual inflation and output-gap stabilization objectives (with some relative weight $\lambda > 0$ on the output objective), in response to exogenous cost-push shocks of the kind represented by the term u_t in (1). One can show[44] that the optimal policy is one that will allow inflation to temporarily increase above the long-run target level π^* in response to a positive (temporary) cost-push shock, but that will be committed to subsequently bringing the price level back to the path (a path growing deterministically at the rate π^* per period) that it would have been predicted to follow in the absence of the shock. It is desirable for people to be able to rely upon the central bank's tendency to react in this way, for then a positive cost-push shock will bring with it an *expectation of subsequent policy tightening,* the anticipation of which gives people a reason to moderate their wage and price increases despite the current cost-push shock. The shift in inflation expectations will partially offset the effect of the cost-push shock on the short-run aggregate–supply trade-off, so that the central bank would not face so painful a choice between allowing significant inflation or reducing output substantially below potential.[45]

---

43. This was pointed out by King (1999), who suggested that inflation targets may lead to error-correcting behavior, to the extent that a central bank expects its success at meeting its target on average over a period such as a decade to be a subject of scrutiny.

44. See Clarida et al. (1999) or Woodford (2003, chap. 7) for details of this analysis.

45. The optimality of this kind of response to cost-push shocks depends, of course, on details of the correct dynamic specification of the inflation-output trade-off, as stressed by Batini and Yates (2003). It is sometimes argued that subsequent reversal of price increases due to cost-push shocks is only optimal in the case of a "purely forward-looking" version of the New Keynesian Phillips curve that cannot account for

Eggertsson and Woodford (2003) similarly show that there are important advantages to a commitment to error correction in the case that a central bank is temporarily unable to hit its inflation target owing to the zero lower bound on nominal interest rates. In the case of a purely forward-looking inflation target, a period when the natural rate of interest is temporarily negative—as arguably occurred in Japan in the late 1990s—can lead to a prolonged contraction and deflation, owing to the expectation that prices will not be allowed to rise even when the central bank regains the ability to hit its inflation target at a non-negative level of short-term interest rates. A price level target would instead imply that a period of reflation should be expected following any period of price declines due to the binding lower bound on interest rates; because a greater price level decline would then automatically create expectations of more future inflation (causing the zero nominal interest rate during the constrained period to correspond to a lower real interest rate), such a policy would if credible limit the price declines (and the associated contraction of real activity) during the period of the binding zero lower bound.

Thus a commitment to error correction can be valuable even if the central bank can be certain of the effects of its policy decisions; the argument is only strengthened when one also considers the uncertainty under which monetary policy is actually conducted. In an analysis that is especially apposite to our discussion of the policy errors of the 1970s, Gorodnichenko and Shapiro (2006) note that commitment to a price-level target reduces the harm done by a poor real-time estimate of productivity (and hence of the natural rate of output) by a central bank.[46] If the private sector expects that inflation greater than the central bank intended (owing to a failure to recognize how stimulative policy really was, on account of an overly optimistic estimate of the natural rate of output) will cause the central bank to aim for lower inflation later, this will restrain wage and price increases during the period when policy is overly stimulative. Hence, a commitment to error correction would not only ensure that the central bank does not exceed its long-run inflation target in the same way for many years in a row; in the case of a forward-looking aggregate–supply trade-off of the kind implied by (1), it would *also* result in less excess inflation in the first place, for any given magnitude of misestimate of the natural rate of output.

Similarly, Aoki and Nikolov (2005) show that a price-level rule for monetary policy is more robust to possible errors in the central bank's economic model. They assume that the central seeks to implement a "target criterion," using a quantitative model to

---

observed inflation inertia. However, the specification (1) proposed here is able to account for the observed inertia in inflation dynamics over the past few decades—that is, the failure of inflation to revert rapidly to a "long run" value that is constant over time—as due to variation over time in the inflation target $\bar{\pi}_t$ of the kind found by Smets and Wouters (2003). Other interpretations of observed inflation inertia that would also imply that it is optimal to subsequently undo price increases due to cost-push shocks are discussed in Woodford (2006).

46. Gorodnichenko and Shapiro argue that uncertainty about a possible change in the trend rate of productivity growth in the United States in the late 1990s did not cause the kind of inflation instability observed in the 1970s precisely because the Greenspan Fed followed an error-correction policy, as if it had a price-level target. Their argument assumes that this feature of Fed policy was correctly understood by the public, despite its not being made explicit in the Fed's public discussions of its policy.

determine the level of the short-term nominal interest rate that will result in inflation and output growth satisfying the criterion. Aoki and Nikolov compare two alternative target criteria, one specified as an output-gap-adjusted target for the inflation rate, and the other as a gap-adjusted target for the price level; the two policy rules would be equivalent if the target criterion could be fulfilled at all times, but they have different dynamic implications in the case of target misses owing to errors in calculating the interest rate required to hit the target. They find that the price-level target criterion leads to much better outcomes when the central bank starts with initially incorrect coefficient estimates in the quantitative model that it uses to calculate its policy, again because the commitment to error correction that is implied by the price-level target leads price-setters to behave in a way that ameliorates the consequences of central bank errors in its choice of the interest rate.

Some of the advantages of a price-level target (or alternatively, a commitment to error correction) can also be achieved by a money-growth target, if this is understood as commitment to a target *path* for the money supply that is not reset each time money growth differs from the target rate—that is, if one does not allow "base drift." The ECB's computation of an "excess liquidity" statistic based on the cumulative growth in broad money over several years relative to its "reference value" for money growth would be consistent with a target of this kind. If excess liquidity results in policy being tighter than it would otherwise be, this would tend to correct the consequences of excessively inflationary policy (resulting in excess money growth) due, for example, to an overly optimistic estimate of potential output. This is presumably the reasoning behind Jürgen Stark's statement that "evaluating the money stock and liquidity situation helps to ensure that central banks look at developments in the level of key nominal variables, and not just their rate of change" (Stark 2006).

While this is a valid point, one should note that tracking cumulative excess *inflation*—that is, departures from a "reference path" for the price level—would be even more effective for this purpose than tracking excess money growth. Excess money growth is an equally useful indicator only to the extent that excess money growth (over a period of a year or two) is a reliable measure of excessively inflationary policy. But money growth can diverge widely from inflation over a period of several years, while inflation itself can be measured fairly accurately within a few months. Thus, the superior method for ensuring robustness against the type of policy error discussed above would seem to be a commitment to respond to the measured evolution of the price level itself, without any need to track measures of the money supply.

4.2 The Pitfall of Ignoring the Endogeneity of Expectations

Another well-known potential problem with policy based on an estimated Phillips curve is the trap of failing to recognize the difference between the *short-run* tradeoff between inflation and real activity, which is available for given inflationary expectations, and the *long-run* trade-off that is available when the eventual adjustment of expectations is taken into account. The best-known exposition of this trap is in the analysis of discretionary policy by Kydland and Prescott (1977) and Barro and

Gordon (1983). These classic expositions assumed a particular type of expectations-augmented Phillips curve that was popular in the "New Classical" literature of the 1970s, but discretionary policy has a similar inflationary bias in a New Keynesian model of the kind expounded above, as shown in Clarida et al. (1999) and Woodford (2003, chap. 7).

Suppose that each period, the central bank chooses a nominal interest rate i_t so as to minimize its loss function

$$(\pi_t - \pi^*)^2 + \lambda(x_t - x^*)^2, \tag{16}$$

given the trade-off between inflation and output implied by the Phillips-curve relation (1) and the effects of interest rates on expenditure implied by (2). Suppose furthermore that in its evaluation of these structural relations, the central bank takes as given the inflation trend $\bar{\pi}_t$ to which price setters index their prices, and current private-sector expectations $E_t\pi_{t+1}, E_t x_{t+1}$; it assumes that none of these are affected by its choice of policy in period t, so that it simply faces trade-offs of the form

$$\pi_t = a_t + \kappa x_t,$$
$$x_t = b_t - \sigma i_t,$$

where the intercepts a_t and b_t are independent of the choice of i_t. Note that the static loss function (15) is consistent with the intertemporal objective (14) assumed above, if the central bank acts in a discretionary fashion (never making any advance commitments regarding its future policies) and understands (as is true in the Markov equilibrium of this model) that the choices of π_t, Y_t, and i_t have no consequences for equilibrium outcomes in any periods after t. Similarly, the assumption that the central bank's policy decision will not affect expectations (including expectations regarding the inflation trend[47]) is correct if the private sector has rational expectations and the economy evolves in accordance with the Markov equilibrium. Thus, the assumed behavior of the discretionary central bank does not involve any incorrect understanding of the effects of its policy decision, given that it is only deciding what to do in the current period.

Given the slope of the (correctly) perceived Phillips curve trade-off, the central bank will choose to achieve the point on that trade-off that satisfies the first-order condition

$$(\pi_t - \pi^*) + \frac{\lambda}{\kappa}(x_t - x^*) = 0. \tag{17}$$

Let us suppose furthermore, for simplicity, that there are no cost-push shocks u_t. Then since both the objective and the constraints are the same (in terms of the variables π_t, x_t, and $i_t - r_t^n$) in all periods, a Markov equilibrium involves constant values for

---

47. Here the indexation rate $\bar{\pi}_t$ is understood to be defined by (5), so that it depends only on expectations regarding policy far in the future.

each of those variables, and the constant value of π will also be the constant value of the inflation trend $\bar{\pi}$. Substitution of identical constant values for π and $\bar{\pi}$ into (1) indicates that any Markov equilibrium must involve a constant output gap $x = 0$. Condition (14) then implies that the constant equilibrium inflation rate is equal to

$$\pi = \pi^* + + \frac{\lambda}{\kappa} x^*, \tag{18}$$

which is necessarily greater than the target inflation rate π^* under the assumptions that $\lambda > 0$ and $x^* > 0$ in (15).

This is not, however, an optimal policy, from the standpoint of the bank's own objectives. In the case of any constant inflation rate π, (1) implies a constant output gap $x = 0$. Hence, the loss function (15) is equal to

$$(\pi - \pi^*)^2 + \lambda x^{*2}$$

each period. This expression is minimized at $\pi = \pi^*$, and not at the higher inflation rate (17). The lower value of losses could easily be achieved by committing to a policy that delivers the target inflation rate π^* each period. Thus, discretionary policy results in an inflationary bias, as in the analysis of Kydland and Prescott and of Barro and Gordon, even when the central bank correctly assesses the current values of Y_t^n and r_t^n, and more generally, when it correctly assesses the consequences of alternative possible choices. The bank's mistake is that it only considers the action to take in the current period and so fails to realize how it could shape expectations (and hence the location of the Phillips curve trade-off between inflation and output) by committing to a policy in advance.

An approach to policy choice of this kind clearly leads to an unsatisfactory outcome, despite being based on optimization, and I believe that it is generally what central bankers have in mind when they speak of the importance of maintaining a "medium-run" or "long-run orientation" for monetary policy, rather than allowing policy to be dictated by "short-run" considerations alone. It thus represents one possible interpretation of what the ECB seeks to guard against by insisting that its "economic analysis" of short-term inflation risks be subject to a "cross-check" from a monetary analysis that takes a longer-term perspective.

But would attention to the growth rate of monetary aggregates solve the problem illustrated by the above analysis? If we adjoin a money–demand relation such as (10) to our model, then the Markov equilibrium with overly inflationary policy will also involve a correspondingly high rate of money growth, but once again, one need not monitor money growth in order to see that the policy is inflationary. (In the equilibrium just described, the central bank is under no illusions about the inflation rate resulting from its policy.) Supposing that the central bank monitors the money supply, that it is aware of the structural relation (10), and indeed that it chooses a target for M_t (rather than i_t) each period—but again, in a discretionary fashion, with no commitment regarding future policy—would change nothing about our analysis above of the inflation rate resulting from discretionary policy.

Of course, the famous diagnosis of the problem by Kydland and Prescott (1977) was that monetary policy should be conducted in accordance with a *policy rule,* rather than on the basis of a procedure aimed at minimization of an objective such as (14). And at the time that they wrote, a money-growth rule of the kind advocated by Friedman was clearly what they had in mind. But there is no reason why a policy rule, intended to prevent the central bank from giving in to the temptation to exploit the short-run Phillips curve trade-off, would have to involve a target for money growth. If all one cares about is eliminating the undesirably high average rate of inflation—or if one ignores the existence of random shocks, as in the simple analysis above— then *any* policy rule that implies a suitably low average inflation rate would work as well. In particular, an *inflation target* will suffice to eliminate the problem, if it is taken seriously—if it does not simply mean that the central bank's loss function (15) penalizes deviations from a well-defined target π^* but rather that the central bank is pledged to ensure that the long-run average inflation rate remains within a fairly narrow range.[48] As explained above, it is certainly possible to design a policy framework that will ensure the desired average inflation rate, over a sufficiently long period of time, without any reference to monetary aggregates.

Nor is it correct to say that in the discretionary "trap," the central bank's mistake is reliance upon an inadequate model of the determinants of inflation or of the effects of policy—one that is accurate in the short run but not in the medium to long run—so that the inflationary bias of policy could be avoided by basing policy on an alternative (presumably quantity-theoretic) model that gives a more accurate account of the determinants of long-run inflation trends. As I have just noted, the quantity-theoretic relation (10) can be part of the model used to determine the optimal action each period without this implying any change in the logic of discretionary policy. Nor is there any mistake in the central bank's forecast of the inflation rate resulting from its policy, either in the short run or later.

The central bank's mistake is instead one of failing to recognize that a sequence of optimizing decisions about policy in one period, taking as given the way that policy will be conducted subsequently, does not lead to an optimal overall pattern of action. It fails to see that committing to a *systematically* different policy that is maintained over time would make possible a different inflation-output trade-off than the one that the central bank faces in each of the succession of periods in which it considers an alternative policy in that period only, owing to the endogeneity of inflationary expectations, and the relevance of those expectations to the inflation-output trade-off in (1).

In order to avoid making this kind of error, a central bank that seeks to minimize an objective such as (14) needs to have a correct view of the nature of the

---

48. Proponents of "flexible inflation targeting" sometimes argue that it suffices that a central bank have a well-defined loss function of the form (14), to which it is publicly committed, and that the central bank be able to defend its policy decisions as being aimed at minimizing such an objective. But the discretionary policy, shown above to lead to undesirably high inflation, has all of these features. It is therefore important to recognize that a successful inflation-targeting regime must also involve a commitment to a decision procedure that does not allow discretionary choice of the policy action each period that would minimize the loss function.

aggregate–supply relation (1) and of the nature of private-sector expectations. Belief in a particular view of the relation between money growth and aggregate nominal expenditure is quite beside the point! While it is true that monetarists like Friedman and Lucas played a crucial role in the 1960s and 1970s as advocates of the view that the long-run Phillips curve trade-off should be vertical, this view does not follow from the quantity theory of money itself. The existence of a stable money–demand relation such as (10) implies nothing about the correct specification of the aggregate–supply relation. And one could accept the view that a permanent n percent increase in the rate of growth of the money supply will eventually result in a permanent n percent increase in the inflation rate while still believing in a (nonvertical) long-run Phillips-curve trade-off; the type of long-run relation between money growth and inflation discussed in Section 3 would exist even in this case, as long as permanently higher inflation has a permanent effect on only the *level* of output and not its *growth rate*.

Thus, what is needed to avoid such mistakes is not greater attention to the relation between money growth and inflation or to the estimation of money–demand relations; it is deeper study of the dynamics of wage and price setting, and especially of the role of expectations in such decisions. But this is precisely the topic of what the ECB calls "economic analysis" as opposed to monetary analysis. While the mistake illustrated above may result from an inadequate understanding of the nature of the Phillips curve, the problem cannot be solved by resort to an analytical framework that dispenses with a Phillips curve. And if excessive emphasis on the importance of monetary analysis draws resources within the central bank away from the task of improved modeling of wage and price dynamics, the likelihood of policy mistakes stemming from an inadequate understanding of aggregate supply will only be increased.

5. CONCLUSION

I have examined a number of leading arguments for assigning an important role to tracking the growth of monetary aggregates when making decisions about monetary policy. I find that none of them provides a convincing argument for adopting a money growth target, or even for assigning money the "prominent role" that the ECB does, at least in its official rhetoric. Of course, this is hardly a proof that no such reason will ever be discovered. But when one examines the reasons that have been primarily responsible for the appeal of the idea of money growth as a simple diagnostic for monetary policy, one finds that they will not support the weight that they are asked to bear. Thus, while one must admit that it is always possible that monetary targeting might yet be discovered to have unexpected virtues, there is little ground for presuming that such virtues must exist, simply because of the familiarity of the hypothesis.

Nor do the arguments offered here imply that central banks should make a particular point of *not* seeking to extract any information from monetary aggregates. An inflation-targeting central bank should make use of all of the sources of information available to it, in judging the interest rate policy that should be consistent with a projected evolution of the economy consistent with its target criterion (Svensson and Woodford 2005). While I see no reason for either the policy instrument or the target criterion to involve a measure of the money supply, the model used to calculate the economy's projected evolution under alternative policy paths may involve a large number of state variables, and given that many of the state variables in such a model are not directly observed, or not with perfect precision, a large number of other variables may provide relevant information in judging the economy's state and hence the appropriate instrument setting. There is no reason why a variety of monetary statistics should not be among the large number of indicators that are used by a central bank in preparing its projections. But this appropriate use of the information contained in monetary statistics would not make money a target in its own right, and neither would it make monetary analysis a distinct basis for forming a judgment about the stance of monetary policy, independent of the considerations involved in an explicit economic model of wage and price setting.

LITERATURE CITED

Alvarez, Fernando, Robert E. Lucas Jr., and Warren Weber. (2001) "Interest Rates and Inflation." *American Economic Review,* 91:2, 219–25.

Aoki, Kosuke, and Kalin Nikolov. (May 2005) "Rule-Based Monetary Policy under Central Bank Learning." CEPR Discussion Paper No. 5056.

Assenmacher-Wesche, Katrin, and Stefan Gerlach. (April 2006) "Interpreting Euro Area Inflation at High and Low Frequencies." CEPR Discussion Paper No. 5632.

Barro, Robert J., and David B. Gordon. (1983) "A Positive Theory of Monetary Policy in a Natural Rate Model." *Journal of Political Economy,* 91, 589–610.

Batini, Nicoletta, and Edward Nelson. (2001) "The Lag from Monetary Policy Actions to Inflation: Friedman Revisited." *International Finance,* 4:4, 381–400.

Batini, Nicoletta, and Anthony Yates. (2003) "Hybrid Inflation and Price-Level Targeting." *Journal of Money, Credit and Banking,* 35, 283–300.

Benati, Luca, "Long-Run Evidence on Money Growth and Inflation." *Bank of England Quarterly Bulletin,* Autumn 2005, pp. 349–55.

Bernanke, Ben S., Mark Gertler, and Simon Gilchrist. (1999) "The Financial Accelerator in a Quantitative Business Cycle Framework." In *Handbook of Macroeconomics,* Vol. 1C, edited by John B. Taylor and Michael Woodford. Amsterdam: North Holland.

Bordes, Christian, Laurent Clerc, and Velayoudom Marimoutou. (February 2007) "Is There a Structural Break in Equilibrium Velocity in the Euro Area?" Banque de France Working Paper No. 165.

Bruggeman, Annick, Paola Donati, and Anders Warne. (2003) "Is the Demand for Euro Area M3 Stable?" In *Background Studies for the ECB's Evaluation of its Monetary Policy Strategy,* edited by Otmar Issing et al. Frankfurt: European Central Bank.

Bullard, James, and Kaushik Mitra. (2002) "Learning about Monetary Policy Rules." *Journal of Monetary Economics,* 49, 1105–29.

Calvo, Guillermo A. (1983) "Staggered Prices in a Utility-Maximizing Framework." *Journal of Monetary Economics,* 12, 383–98.

1596 : MONEY, CREDIT AND BANKING

Christiano, Lawrence J., Roberto Motto, and Massimo Rostagno. (2003) "The Great Depression and the Friedman-Schwartz Hypothesis." *Journal of Money, Credit and Banking,* 35, 1119–98.

Christiano, Lawrence J., Roberto Motto, and Massimo Rostagno. (April 2007) "Shocks, Structures or Monetary Policies? The Euro Area and the US after 2001." Unpublished manuscript, Northwestern University.

Clarida, Richard, Jordi Galí, and Mark Gertler. (1999) "The Science of Monetary Policy: A New Keynesian Perspective." *Journal of Economic Literature,* 37, 1661–707.

Cúrdia, Vasco. (June 2007) "Monetary Policy under Sudden Stops." In *Essays in Open Economy Macroeconomics,* Ph.D. Dissertation, Department of Economics, Princeton University.

de Grauwe, Paul, and Magdalena Polan. (June 2001) "Is Inflation Always and Everywhere a Monetary Phenomenon?" CEPR Discussion Paper No. 2841.

Eggertsson, Gauti B., and Michael Woodford. "The Zero Bound on Interest Rates and Optimal Monetary Policy." *Brookings Papers on Economic Activity,* 2003:1, 139–211.

Estrella, Arturo, and Frederic S. Mishkin. (1997) "Is There a Role for Monetary Aggregates in the Conduct of Monetary Policy?" *Journal of Monetary Economics,* 40, 279–304.

European Central Bank. (2004) *The Monetary Policy of the ECB.* Frankfurt: European Central Bank.

Fischer, Bjorn, Michele Lenza, Huw Pill, and Lucrezia Reichlin. (2008) "Money and Monetary Policy: The ECB Experience 1999–2006." In *The Role of Money: Money and Monetary Policy in the 21st Century,* edited by Andreas Beyer and Lucrezia Reichlin. Frankfurt: European Central Bank.

Friedman, Milton. (1968) "The Role of Monetary Policy." *American Economic Review,* 58, 1–17.

Friedman, Milton. (1992) *Money Mischief: Episodes in Monetary History.* New York: Harcourt Brace Jovanovich.

Galí, Jordi, and Mark Gertler. (1999) "Inflation Dynamics: A Structural Econometric Analysis." *Journal of Monetary Economics,* 44, 195–222.

Goodfriend, Marvin, and Bennett T. McCallum. (June 2007) "Banking and Interest Rates in Monetary Policy Analysis: A Quantitative Exploration." NBER Working Paper No. 13207.

Goodhart, Charles A.E. (2007) "Whatever Became of the Monetary Aggregates?" *National Institute Economic Review,* 200, 56–61.

Gorodnichenko, Yuriy, and Matthew D. Shapiro. (May 2006) "Monetary Policy when Potential Output is Uncertain: Understanding the Growth Gamble of the 1990s." NBER Working Paper No. 12268.

Hafer, R.W., and David C. Wheelock. "The Rise and Fall of a Policy Rule: Monetarism at the St. Louis Fed, 1968–86." *Federal Reserve Bank of St. Louis Review,* January/February 2001, pp. 1–24.

Haug, Alfred A., and William G. Dewald. (2004) "Longer-Term Effects of Monetary Growth on Real and Nominal Variables, Major Industrial Countries, 1880–2001." ECB Working Paper No. 382.

Ireland, Peter. (2004) "Money's Role in the Business Cycle." *Journal of Money, Credit and Banking,* 36, 969–83.

Issing, Otmar. "The ECB's Monetary Policy Strategy: Why Did We Choose a Two-Pillar Approach?" Address at the Fourth ECB Central Banking Conference, November 10, 2006.

Jaeger, A. (2003) "The ECB's Money Pillar: An Assessment." IMF Working Paper No. 03/82.

King, Mervyn A. (1999) "Challenges for Monetary Policy: New and Old." In *New Challenges for Monetary Policy*. Kansas City: Federal Reserve Bank of Kansas City.

King, Mervyn A. (2002) "No Money, No Inflation—The Role of Money in the Economy." *Bank of England Quarterly Bulletin*, Summer 2002, pp. 162–77.

Kugler, Peter, and Sylvia Kauffman. (2005) "Does Money Matter for Inflation in the Euro Area?" Oesterreichische Nationalbank, Working Paper No. 103.

Kuttner, Robert. "Agreeing to Disagree: Robert Kuttner Speaks with Milton Friedman." *The American Prospect*, January 5, 2006.

Kydland, Finn E., and Edward C. Prescott. (1977) "Rules Rather than Discretion: The Inconsistency of Optimal Plans." *Journal of Political Economy*, 85, 473–91.

London, Simon. (2003) "Lunch with the *FT:* Milton Friedman." *Financial Times*, June 7.

Lucas, Robert E., Jr. (1996) "Nobel Lecture: Monetary Neutrality." *Journal of Political Economy*, 104, 661–82.

Lucas, Robert E., Jr. (2006) "Panel Discussion: Colloquium in Honor of Otmar Issing." Remarks presented at the ECB colloquium "Monetary Policy: A Journey from Theory to Practice." Frankfurt.

Masuch, Klaus, Sergio Nicoletti-Altimari, Huw Pill, and Massimo Rostagno. (2003) "The Role of Money in Monetary Policy Making." In *Background Studies for the ECB's Evaluation of its Monetary Policy Strategy*, edited by Otmar Issing et al. Frankfurt: European Central Bank.

McCallum, Bennett T. (2001) "Monetary Policy Analysis in Models without Money." *Federal Reserve Bank of St. Louis Review*, 83, 145–60.

McCandless, George T., Jr., and Warren E. Weber. "Some Monetary Facts." *Federal Reserve Bank of Minneapolis Quarterly Review*, Summer 1995, pp. 2–11.

Nelson, Edward. (2003) "The Future of Monetary Aggregates in Monetary Policy Analysis." *Journal of Monetary Economics*, 50, 1029–59.

Neumann, Manfred J.M. (2006) "Pre-commitment and Guidance: Lessons from the Bundesbank's History." A paper presented at the ECB colloquium "Monetary Policy: A Journey from Theory to Practice." Frankfurt.

Orphanides, Athanasios. (2003a) "The Quest for Prosperity without Inflation." *Journal of Monetary Economics*, 50, 633–63.

Orphanides, Athanasios. (2003b) "Historical Monetary Policy Analysis and the Taylor Rule." *Journal of Monetary Economics*, 50, 983–1022.

Orphanides, Athanasios, and John C. Williams. (2002) "Robust Monetary Policy Rules with Unknown Natural Rates." *Brookings Papers on Economic Activity*, 2002: 63–118.

Papademos, Lucas. (2006) "The Role of Money in the Conduct of Monetary Policy." Speech at the Fourth ECB Central Banking Conference, Frankfurt.

Preston, Bruce. (2005) "Learning about Monetary Policy Rules When Long-Horizon Expectations Matter." *International Journal of Central Banking*, 1, 81–126.

Radcliffe Committee. (1959) *Report of the Committee on the Workings of the Monetary System*, London: Her Majesty's Stationery Office.

Reynard, Samuel.. (2006) "Maintaining Low Inflation: Money, Interest Rates, and Policy Stance." Working paper, Swiss National Bank.

Sbordone, Argia M. (2002) "Prices and Unit Labor Costs: A New Test of Price Stickiness." *Journal of Monetary Economics,* 49, 265–92.

Smets, Frank R., and Raf Wouters. (2003) "An Estimated Dynamic Stochastic General Equilibrium Model of the Euro Area." *Journal of the European Economic Association,* 1, 1123–175.

Smets, Frank R., and Raf Wouters. (2007) "Shocks and Frictions in U.S. Business Cycles: A Bayesian DSGE Approach." *American Economic Review,* 97, 586–606.

Stark, Jürgen. (2006) "Introductory Remarks." Remarks at the Fourth ECB Central Banking Conference, Frankfurt.

Stock, James H., and Mark W. Watson. (2006) "Why Has U.S. Inflation Become Harder to Forecast?" NBER Working Paper No. 12324.

Svensson, Lars E.O. (2003) "Comment: The Future of Monetary Aggregates in Monetary Policy Analysis." *Journal of Monetary Economics,* 50, 1061–70.

Svensson, Lars E.O., and Michael Woodford. (2003) "Indicator Variables for Optimal Policy." *Journal of Monetary Economics,* 50, 691–720.

Svensson, Lars E.O., and Michael Woodford. (2005) "Implementing Optimal Monetary Policy through Inflation-Forecast Targeting." In *The Inflation Targeting Debate,* edited by B.S. Bernanke and M. Woodford Chicago: University of Chicago Press.

Taylor, John B. (1993) "Discretion versus Policy Rules in Practice." *Carnegie–Rochester Conference Series on Public Policy,* 39, 195–214.

von zur Muehlen, Peter. "Activist versus Non-Activist Monetary Policy: Optimal Rules under Extreme Uncertainty." FEDS Paper no. 2001-2, Federal Reserve Board, January.

Walsh, Carl E. (2003) *Monetary Theory and Policy,* 2nd ed. Cambridge, MA: MIT Press.

Woodford, Michael. (2001) "Fiscal Requirements for Price Stability." *Journal of Money, Credit and Banking,* 33, 669–728.

Woodford, Michael. (2003) *Interest and Prices: Foundations of a Theory of Monetary Policy.* Princeton: Princeton University Press.

Woodford, Michael. (2007) "Interpreting Inflation Persistence: Comments on the Conference on Quantitative Evidence on Price Determination." *Journal of Money, Credit and Banking,* 39: 203–10.

Woodford, Michael. (2008) "Does a 'Two-Pillar Phillips Curve' Justify a Two-Pillar Monetary Policy Strategy?" In *The Role of Money: Money and Monetary Policy in the 21st Century,* edited by Andreas Beyer and Lucrezia Reichlin. Frankfurt: European Central Bank.

Yun, Tack. (1996) "Nominal Price Rigidity, Money Supply Endogeneity, and Business Cycles." *Journal of Monetary Economics,* 37, 345–70.

[9]

Monetary Policy Analysis in Models Without Money

Bennett T. McCallum

It has recently become common practice—indeed, virtually standard practice—for monetary policy analysis to be conducted in models that include no reference to any monetary aggregate.[1] Although there have been a few protests,[2] this general tendency is true of research conducted by both central bank and academic economists.[3] The purpose of the present paper is to consider whether there is anything fundamentally misguided about this practice.

The paper begins by specifying a small prototype model that reflects today's standard approach and asking whether its adoption implies that monetary policy has little or nothing to do with money. The answer developed here is "no." Next it is argued that the prototype model excludes monetary aggregates only because of an assumption concerning the monetary transactions technology that seems unjustifiable in principle. We go on to consider whether elimination of this assumption, and the implied inclusion of a monetary aggregate, would be of quantitative importance in business cycle analysis. Again the apparent answer is "no."

The paper's third main topic involves *indeterminacy* issues that have been prominent in recent discussions of models and interest-rate policy rules of the type under consideration. Here it is argued that the undesirability of basing policy on forecasts of future inflation rates has been overstated in the theoretical literature, which has emphasized non-fundamental solutions that may be irrelevant empirically. As a related matter, the paper takes up the type of indeterminacy implied by a rule that does not respect the Taylor principle (i.e., that interest rates should be made to increase by more than point-for-point with inflation). It is argued that the nature of the problem in this case is different and

of genuine importance. Finally, it is noted that although these answers suggest that policy analysis in models without money is not fundamentally misguided, they do not imply that conducting policy in this manner is necessarily a desirable strategy.

ARE MODELS WITHOUT MONEY NON-MONETARY MODELS?

Let us begin by writing down a simple schematic prototype model without money of the sort that has been popular recently. Here and in the rest of the paper we use y_t to denote the logarithm of real output during period t with $\bar{y}_t$ being the natural-rate (i.e., flexible price) value of y_t so that $\tilde{y}_t = y_t - \bar{y}_t$ is the output gap. Also p_t is the log of the price level so that Δp_t is the inflation rate, while g_t represents the log of real government purchases and R_t is the short-term nominal interest rate that the central bank uses as its instrument. Then the prototype model is:

(1)
$$y_t = b_0 + b_1 \left(R_t - E_t \Delta p_{t+1} \right) + E_t y_{t+1} + b_2 \left(g_t - E_t g_{t+1} \right) + v_t$$
$$b_1 < 0,\ b_2 > 0$$

(2)
$$\Delta p_t = \beta E_t \Delta p_{t+1} + \alpha \left(y_t - \bar{y}_t \right) + u_t$$
$$0 < \beta < 1,\ \alpha > 1$$

(3)
$$R_t = \mu_0 + E_t \Delta p_{t+1} + \mu_1 \left(E_t \Delta p_{t+j} - \pi^* \right) + \mu_2 \left(y_t - \bar{y}_t \right) + e_t.$$
$$\mu_1, \mu_2 > 0$$

Here, equation (1) represents a forward-looking expectational IS function of the type that can be justified by dynamic optimization analysis, as explained by Kerr and King (1996), McCallum and Nelson (1999b), Woodford (1995, 1999), and many others. The stochastic disturbance v_t represents the effects of taste shocks and is assumed to be exogenous, as are the "cost push" and policy shocks u_t and e_t. Relation (2) is a price adjustment specifica-

---

Bennett T. McCallum is the H.J. Heinz professor of economics at Carnegie Mellon University, a research associate of the National Bureau of Economic Research, and a research advisor at the Federal Reserve Bank of Richmond. The author is indebted to Marvin Goodfriend, Douglas Laxton, John Leahy, Allan Meltzer, Edward Nelson, and Alex Wolman for helpful comments.

[1] For some prominent examples, see Clarida, Gali, and Gertler (1999), Rotemberg and Woodford (1997), and most of the papers in Taylor (1999).

[2] For example, Meltzer (1999) and Nelson (2000).

[3] The similarity of research strategies being used by central bank and academic economists can be seen by perusal of the June 1999 issue of the *Journal of Monetary Economics*, which include papers from two major conferences on the topic of monetary policy rules.

tion of the Calvo-Rotemberg type, which is the most nearly standard of those currently in use.[4] For present purposes it will suffice to treat $\bar{y}_t$ as exogenous, as is usually done in small models, although Casares and McCallum (2000) show that it is not too difficult to endogenize investment and therefore $\bar{y}_t$.[5]

Finally, equation (3) represents a policy rule of the Taylor (1993) type, which has the effect of adjusting upward the real interest rate $R_t - E_t \Delta p_{t+1}$ when current or expected inflation (depending on the value of j) exceeds its *target* value π^* and/or the output gap is positive. For best performance the central bank will choose the parameter μ_0 to equal $\bar{r}$, the long-run average real rate of interest, which in turn will equal $-b_0/b_1$, presuming that $E(g_t - E_t g_{t+1}) = 0$ (i.e., that we are abstracting from growth in $\bar{y}_t$ and g_t). Often an additional term in R_{t-1} is included in the policy rule to represent interest rate smoothing.

Clearly, the system given by equations (1) through (3) includes no monetary aggregates. Yet it is complete, in the sense that the three relations govern time paths for the three endogenous variables, y_t, Δp_t, and R_t. It would be possible to add to the system a (base) money demand relation such as

(4) $\log M_t - p_t = c_0 + c_1 y_t + c_2 R_t + \eta_t, \qquad c_1 > 0, c_2 < 0$

but the latter would be superfluous, in the sense that it would not affect the behavior of y_t, Δp_t, or R_t.[6] Its only function would be to specify the amount of base money that is needed to implement the policy rule (3). Thus policy analysis involving y_t, $\bar{y}_t$, Δp_t, and R_t can be carried out without even specifying a money demand function such as equation (4) or collecting measurements on the stock of money, M_t.

Nevertheless, it would be wrong to view this system without any monetary aggregate, equations (1) through (3), as representing a non-monetary model. For the central bank's control over the one-period nominal interest rate ultimately stems from its ability to control the quantity of base money in existence. If some entity other than the central bank could exogenously manipulate the path of M_t, then (4), (1), and (2) would determine paths for y_t, Δp_t, and R_t with (3) being overruled.

Of course, the preceding statement presumes institutional arrangements much like those in existence today, in which it is appropriate to assume that the central bank has (monopoly) control over the issue of base money. Some writers, such as Friedman (1999), have suggested that technological progress in the payments and information process-

ing industries may critically alter this situation in coming years and leave central banks with no control over the short-term interest rates that matter for macroeconomic purposes. Most of the Summer 2000 special issue of *International Finance* is devoted to a discussion of that possibility. In my opinion, Goodhart (2000) is correct to argue that, because central banks can be supported by governmental powers of regulation and taxation, they are unlikely to lose their control over interest rates in the foreseeable future.

In any event, there is an additional way to express the basic point at issue. This is to ask whether, according to the model (1) through (3), inflation is viewed as a non-monetary phenomenon, governed by the Phillips curve relationship (equation (2)). It is my contention that such a suggestion would be unjustified. Specifically, the primary issue in this regard is what controls the long-run average rate of inflation. And in the prototype model, that rate is controlled entirely by the central bank—the monetary authority. For this argument let us assume that the long run average value of $\bar{y}_t$ is zero, i.e., that $E(y_t - \bar{y}_t) = 0$ as is implied by the strict version of the natural rate hypothesis.[7] Then from equation (1) we have that, in the absence of growth, $E(R_t - \Delta p_{t+1}) = -b_0/b_1$ so equation (3) implies that

(5) $\qquad -b_0/b_1 = \mu_0 + \mu_1 \left(E \Delta p_{t+j} - \pi^* \right) + \alpha E \bar{y}_t$.

Thus it follows that, with $E\bar{y} = 0$,

(6) $\qquad E\Delta p_t = \pi^* - \left((b_0/b_1) + \mu_0 \right) (1/\mu_1)$.

Consequently, if the central bank sets μ_0 equal to the average real interest rate, $-b_0/b_1$, as a sensible central bank would, then the average inflation rate will equal the central bank's chosen target value π^*. And if it errs by, for instance, ε in setting μ_0, the average inflation rate will differ from π^* by ε/μ_1, which becomes smaller as the policy rule's response to

---

[4] There has recently been much controversy over the adequacy of the Calvo-Rotemberg specification since it itself supplies no persistence to the inflation rate; see Estrella and Fuhrer (2000) and Gali and Gertler (1999) for an introduction to the controversy.

[5] This, of course, requires that equation (1) be replaced by a set of equations representing an "expectational IS sector."

[6] Here M_t is the nominal money stock. For present purposes we can think of it both as base money and as the relevant monetary aggregate that facilitates transactions.

[7] This version is due to Lucas (1972). For more discussion, see McCallum and Nelson (1999a).

FEDERAL RESERVE BANK OF ST. LOUIS

discrepancies of inflation from its target becomes stronger. Basically, then, the average inflation rate is determined by central bank behavior. Parameters α and β from the Phillips relationship (equation (2)) play no role.

There is an apparent problem with the foregoing demonstration, namely, that the Calvo-Rotemberg relation (2) becomes $E\pi = \beta E\pi + \alpha E\tilde{y}$ in the steady state, which implies (with $\beta < 1$) that $E\tilde{y} > 0$. The latter condition, however, violates the natural rate hypothesis, in contradiction with the assumption made above. In my opinion this points to a flaw in the usual formulation of the Calvo-Rotemberg model.[8] Instead of a derivation pertaining to the costs or impossibility of changing prices in relation to the previous period's level, a rational version of the model would be concerned with changes relative to the previous period's level plus the average one-period inflation rate, as in the version of the model used by Ireland (2000). In that case, there would be no problem with the foregoing argument. Furthermore, although the inflation rate would depend upon Phillips curve parameters if one were to insist on retaining (2), the same would be true if the central bank were to control the monetary base as its instrument variable, assuming that the policy feedback rule was one that involved both $\pi-\pi^*$ and $\tilde{y}$ as objectives.

IS NEGLECT OF MONEY QUANTITATIVELY IMPORTANT?

The objective of this section is to look into the theoretical foundations for the prototype model (equations (1) through (3)) and follow up with a quantitative analysis.[9] Actually, the focus will be only on equations (1) and (4) because the policy rule (3) is simply being taken as an object of investigation, whereas issues relating to the price adjustment specification (2) are quite distinct and beyond the scope of this paper.[10] Thus we begin by reviewing the optimizing rationale for (1) and (4), which is reasonably familiar from the references mentioned on p. 1.

For simplicity, suppose that capital is treated as a constant, k. Then a typical household, which supplies inelastically one unit of labor per period, seeks at time $t = 1$ to maximize

$$\sum_{t=1}^{\infty} \beta^{t-1} u(c_t, \zeta_t),$$

where c_t represents Dixit-Stiglitz consumption bundles and ζ_t is a stochastic shock to preferences. The household's budget constraints for $t = 1, 2, \ldots$ are

$$(7) \quad \begin{aligned} & Y_t^A \left(P_t / P_t^A \right)^{1-\theta} - tx_t - w_t(n_t-1) = \\ & c_t + m_t - (1+\pi_t)^{-1} m_{t-1} + (1+r_t)^{-1} b_{t+1} - b_t + \psi(c_t, m_t). \end{aligned}$$

Here Y_t^A is aggregate per-household demand while P_t/P_t^A is the price of the household's specialized output relative to the implied Dixit-Stiglitz price index of goods in general. Also, tx_t is lump-sum taxes paid (net of transfers); n_t is labor employed in production so with a real wage of w_t we have $w_t(n_t-1)$ as the household's net payment to hired labor; m_t is real money balances held at the end of period t; $\pi_t = (P_t^A/P_{t-1}^A)-1$ is the inflation rate; and b_{t+1} is the number of real bonds purchased, at a real price of $1/(1+r_t)$, during t. Finally, $\psi(c_t, m_t)$ represents the resources used in conducting transactions (i.e., in shopping for the precise bundle of consumption goods that the household chooses). The household produces output subject to the production function $Y_t = f(A_t n_t, k)$, where A_t is a technology shock, and its amount produced is equal to the quantity demanded:

$$(8) \quad f(A_t n_t, k) = Y_t^A \left(P_t / P_t^A \right)^{-\theta}.$$

As is common, we assume $0 < \beta < 1$, $\theta > 1$, and that f is well behaved. The transaction technology is such that $\psi_1(c_t, m_t) > 0$ and $\psi_2(c_t, m_t) \leq 0$.

In this setup the household's first order conditions are as follows for $t = 1, 2, \ldots$, with λ_t and ξ_t being the Lagrange multipliers on (7) and (8):

$$(9) \quad u_1(c_t, \zeta_t) - \lambda_t \left[1 + \psi_1(c_t, m_t) \right] = 0$$

$$(10) \quad -\lambda_t w_t + \xi_t A_t f_1(A_t n_t, k) = 0$$

$$(11) \quad -\lambda_t \left[1 + \psi_2(c_t, m_t) \right] + \beta E_t \lambda_{t+1} (1+\pi_{t+1})^{-1} = 0$$

$$(12) \quad -\lambda_t (1+r_t)^{-1} + \beta E_t \lambda_{t+1} = 0$$

$$(13)$$

$$\lambda_t Y_t^A (1-\theta) P_t^{-\theta} / \left(P_t^A \right)^{1-\theta} + \xi_t Y_t^A \theta P_t^{-(\theta+1)} / \left(P_t^A \right)^{-\theta} = 0.$$

Thus equations (7) through (13) determine the household's choices of c_t, m_t, n_t, b_{t+1}, P_t, λ_t, and ξ_t

---

[8] My own preferred price adjustment scheme is the "P-bar" model used by McCallum and Nelson (1999a).

[9] The issue at hand has been addressed previously by Ireland (2001), McCallum (2000), and Nelson (2000). Here we take a somewhat different approach.

[10] Details concerning price adjustment are, in other words, basically unrelated to this paper's central concern.

REVIEW

in response to exogenous, market-given, or govern-ment-specified values of w_t, A_t, π_t, r_t, Y_t^A, and P_t^A.

For general equilibrium, the additional relations are

$$(14) \qquad\qquad n_t = 1$$

$$(15) \qquad\qquad m_t = M_t / P_t$$

$$(16) \quad G_t - tx_t = m_t - \left(1 + \pi_t\right)^{-1} m_{t-1} + \left(1 + r_t\right)^{-1} b_{t+1} - b_t$$

$$(17) \qquad\qquad \pi_t = \left(P_t^A / P_{t-1}^A\right) - 1.$$

Then with M_t, G_t, and tx_t given exogenously by policy, and assuming symmetry among households so that $P_t = P_t^A$ and $Y_t^A = f(A_t n_t, k)$, the system also determines endogenously the values of w_t, r_t, P_t, and π_t.

This last statement presumes that the monetary authority—part of the "government"—exogenously controls M_t. But if we introduce the nominal rate of interest R_t defined by the Fisher identity,

$$(18) \qquad 1 + R_t = \left(1 + r_t\right) E_t \left(1 + \pi_{t+1}\right),$$

then we could reverse the roles of R_t and M_t, mak-ing the latter endogenous and the former policy-governed.

Also, we could introduce stickiness of nominal product prices. Suppose we did so by adding another relation such as

$$(19) \qquad \Delta p_t = \beta E_t \Delta p_{t+1} + \alpha \left(y_t - \bar{y}_t\right),$$

which is the same as (2). Here $p_t = \log P_t$ and again $y_t = \log Y_t$ with $\bar{y}_t$ being the flexible-price value of y_t that would be produced if there were no price stickiness, that is, $\bar{y}_t = f(A_t, 1, k)$. The introduction of (19) requires, in order to prevent overdetermination, that one of the previously prevailing conditions be eliminated. The simplest option, and in my opinion the most realistic, is to eliminate the condition for labor market equilibrium—equation (14). Then labor and output will both be demand determined.

The crucial issue, in the present context, is whether a relation such as (1)—with no money term involved—can be justified by our optimizing equi-librium analysis. In that regard we solve (9) for λ_t and substitute into (12):

$$(20) \quad \frac{u_1\left(c_t, \zeta_t\right)}{\left[1 + \psi_1\left(c_t, m_t\right)\right]} = \left(1 + r_t\right) \beta E_t \left\{ \frac{u_1\left(c_{t+1}, \zeta_{t+1}\right)}{\left[1 + \psi_1\left(c_{t+1}, m_{t+1}\right)\right]} \right\}.$$

Now, if $\psi(c_t, m_t)$ were separable, so that ψ_1 did not

involve m, equation (20) would include only c_t, c_{t+1}, and r_t (plus shock terms). It would then be possible to write a log-linearized approximation of the form

$$(21) \qquad \log c_t = b_0' + E_t \log c_{t+1} + b_1' r_t + v_t',$$

where v_t' represents $\zeta_t - E_t \zeta_{t+1}$. The latter is a familiar consumption Euler equation, although it differs from the most common version by incorporating the influences of the transactions term $\psi(c_t, m_t)$. Contin-uing, a log-linearized approximation to the overall resource constraint for the economy at hand, with constant capital, is

$$(22) \qquad \log Y_t = (c/Y) \log c_t + (G/Y) \log G_t,$$

where (c/Y) and (G/Y) are steady-state shares. Substitution of (21) into (22) then yields

$$(23) \log Y_t + E_t \log Y_{t+1} + b_0 + b_1 r_t + b_2 \left(g_t - E_t g_{t+1}\right) + v_t,$$

where $g_t = \log G_t$. This relation is of the form of equation (1), so the latter can be justified. But this justification relies upon the assumption that $\psi(c_t, m_t)$ is separable, and in fact that seems implausible. Much more likely, I would think, would be a $\psi(c_t, m_t)$ function that made the cross partial derivative negative, so that the marginal benefit of holding money—i.e., the reduction in transaction costs—increases with the volume of consumption spending.

In McCallum (2000a), I proposed the following as a first-guess specification for ψ:

$$(24) \quad \psi\left(c_t, m_t\right) = c_t a_1 \left(c_t / m_t\right)^{a_2}. \qquad a_1, a_2 > 0$$

Furthermore, it is shown there that the resulting implication for (23) is that it should then include an additional term, namely,

$$(25) \quad \begin{aligned} &b_3 \left(\log m_t - E_t \log m_{t+1}\right) \equiv \\ &(c/Y) \phi \left(\phi + \sigma\right)^{-1} \left(\log m_t - E_t \log m_{t+1}\right), \end{aligned}$$

with $\phi = a_1(1 + a_2) a_2 (c/m)^{a_2}$, where σ is the inverse of the intertemporal elasticity of substitution in consumption. This equation can then be written

$$(1') \quad \begin{aligned} y_t = &b_0 + b_1 \left(R_t - E_t \Delta p_{t+1}\right) + E_t y_{t+1} \\ &+ b_2 \left(g_t - E_t g_{t+1}\right) + b_3 \left(\log m_t - E_t \log m_{t+1}\right) + v_t. \end{aligned}$$

Numerical values for a_1 and a_2 will be considered shortly.

Another implication of the assumed specifica-tion (24) concerns the implied demand for money function. We see that (11) and (12), together with the Fisher identity, imply

(26) $$1+\psi_1(c_t, m_t)=(1+R_t)^{-1}$$

or, approximately,

(27) $$-\psi_1(c_t, m_t)=R_t.$$

But with (24) this gives

(28) $$a_1 a_2(c_t/m_t)^{1+a_2}=R_t$$

or

(29) $$\log m_t = \left[(\log a_1 a_2)/(1+a_2)\right]+\log c_t -\left(1/(1+a_2)\right)\log R_t.$$

Thus we have a money demand function with a constant elasticity with respect to R_t of $-1/(1 + a_2)$ and an elasticity with respect to spending of 1.0. This relation can now be added to our model, which becomes (2), (3), (29), and (1′); these govern the behavior of y_t, Δp_t, R_t, and m_t.

Furthermore, equation (29) (or (28)) is useful in assigning values to a_1 and a_2, i.e., in calibration. Let us begin by assuming a money demand elasticity of -0.2; that choice implies $a_2 = 4$. Also, for a quarterly model let us assume an average interest rate of 0.0125 (i.e., 5 percent per year) and an average c/m ratio of 1.25. Then (28) becomes $a_1(4)(1.25)^5 =$ 0.0125, implying $a_1 = 0.00102$. Then the crucial parameter ϕ becomes

(30)

$$\phi=0.00102\,(5)\,(4)\left(1.25\right)^4 = 0.0204(2.44) = 0.0498,$$

and the slope coefficient b_3 in (25) is, assuming $\sigma = 2$ and $(c/Y) = 0.7$,

(31) $$(c/Y)\phi(\phi+\sigma)^{-1}=(0.7)(0.0498)/(2.0498)=0.017.$$

The remainder of our calibration is more standard: $\beta = 0.99$, $\alpha = 0.05$, $\theta = 5$, and the policy rule parameters $\mu_1 = 0.5$, $\mu_2 = 0.1$, $\mu_3 = 0.8$. The latter value refers to an extension of the Taylor rule to reflect interest rate smoothing:

(3′)

$$R_t =$$
$$(1-\mu_3)\left[\mu_0 +E_t\Delta p_{t+1}+\mu_1\left(E_t\Delta p_{t+1}-\pi^*\right)+\mu_2 E_{t-1}\,\bar{y}_t\right]$$
$$+\mu_3 R_{t+1}+e_t.$$

Note that in the latter we have used $E_t\Delta p_{t+1}$, setting $j = 1$ in (3). Also, v_t is white noise and we have

generated $\bar{y}_t$ by the process $\bar{y}_t = 0.95\ \bar{y}_{t-1} + a_t$, with a_t white noise. Finally, we have made one more modification to the model at hand, in an attempt to have fairly realistic specifications for parts of the system not under scrutiny. This modification is to replace the price adjustment relation (2) with the following:

(2′) $$\Delta p_t =0.5\beta\left[E_t\Delta p_{t+1}+ \Delta p_{t-1}\right]+\alpha\,\bar{y}_t +e_t.$$

Here we have included the Δp_{t-1} term to reflect inflation inertia that appears to exist in many developed economies.

The model at hand consists, then, of relations (1′), (2′), (3′), and (4), specified to approximate (28).[11] The object is to see if the inclusion of the term (25) in (1′) substantially affects the behavior of Δp_t and y_t—i.e., whether theoretically incorrect exclusion of money from the system is of quantitative importance. For this purpose, impulse response functions are very well suited. As a tool for comparing a model with actual economic behavior, impulse response functions are of dubious value because of the need for shock identification. But they are more sensitive than autocorrelation functions to model specification, so are highly appropriate for the purpose at hand. Consequently, Figure 1 shows impulse response functions for y_t, Δp_t, and R_t for unit shocks to v_t, e_t, and a_t. In the top half of the figure we have included the m_t terms in (1′), whereas in the bottom half they are excluded. It is obvious that there is no appreciable difference.

That there would be an appreciable difference, if the coefficient in (25) were larger, is illustrated in Figure 2. There we take the coefficient to be 0.2, holding everything else (including c_2) unchanged. Now the output and inflation responses are noticeably different, especially in response to a monetary policy shock.

In addition, as a quick robustness check we assume that the money demand elasticity is -0.1, rather than -0.2, implying that $a_2 = 9$ instead of 4. This change yields $b_3 = 0.033$ and $c_2 = -8$. The results, shown in the bottom half of Figure 2, are scarcely different from those in Figure 1. Finally, we note that decreasing rather than increasing a_2 (making money demand more elastic) would make the effect even smaller than in our initial case.

Our investigation suggests, then, that although it is theoretically incorrect to specify a model without money, the magnitude of the error thereby

---

[11] Thus c_2 in (4) equals $-1/(R(1 + a_2))$, which equals -16 when $a_2 = 4$.

REVIEW

Figure 1

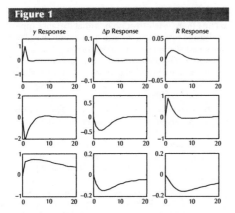

NOTE: Unit shocks to IS (top), policy rule (mid), and tech with money (b_3=0.017).

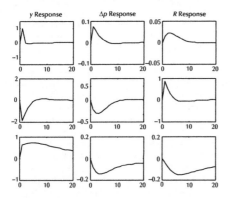

NOTE: Unit shocks to IS (top), policy rule (mid), and tech without money (b_3=0.0).

Figure 2

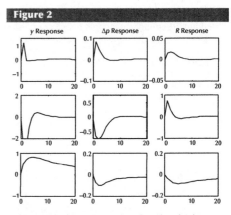

NOTE: Unit shocks to IS (top), policy rule (mid), and tech with money (b_3=0.2).

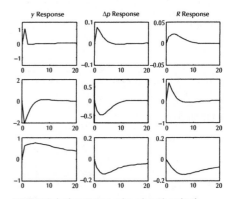

NOTE: Unit shocks to IS (top), policy rule (mid), and tech with money (a_2=9).

introduced is extremely small. This finding is basically consistent with those of Ireland (2001), who finds that econometric estimates of a parameter analogous to b_3 are insignificantly different from zero.[12]

ARE RATIONAL-EXPECTATION INDETERMINACIES IMPORTANT?

Models without money are typically ones in which an interest rate serves as the policy instrument that is adjusted in response to macroeconomic

conditions, prominently including inflation. Central bankers and practical analysts stress the need to move *preemptively*, i.e., to adjust the policy stance when inflation forecasts get out of line without waiting for realized inflation to depart strongly from its target path (see, e.g., Goodfriend, 1997, and Svensson, 1997). There is, however, a line of theoretical analysis that warns of the danger of

[12] Ireland (2001) shows that, for his preferred rationalization of sticky prices, a term involving m_t also appears in the price adjustment relation.

"indeterminacy" if central banks' R_t policy rules respond too strongly to rational forecasts of *future* inflation, even if the same responses to current inflation would not be problematic. This argument was first developed by Woodford (1994) and has subsequently been promoted, or discussed with apparent approval, by Bernanke and Woodford (1997); Kerr and King (1996); Clarida, Gali, and Gertler (1997); Svensson (1997); Christiano and Gust (1999); Carlstrom and Fuerst (2000); Isard, Laxton, and Eliasson (1999); and Bullard and Mitra (2000). Its main message, that variants of inflation-forecast targeting are likely to generate undesirable outcomes, seems rather surprising in light of the descriptions of actual policy procedures used by the Bank of England, Reserve Bank of New Zealand, and Bank of Canada.[13] Note in this regard that for very large values of μ_1, in a policy rule like (3), the implied policy is virtually the same as exact targeting of an expected inflation rate, as promoted by Svensson (1997) and others. Thus the argument seems to deserve scrutiny. The present section extends and elaborates on an alternative argument briefly outlined in McCallum (1999, pp. 634-35), which suggests that the danger identified by the line of analysis in question represents a theoretical curiosity that is probably not of practical relevance.

Let us begin the discussion by noting the way in which the term "indeterminacy" is used in this body of literature. The term first became prominent in monetary economics from a series of writings by Patinkin—beginning with (1949) and culminating with (1961) and (1965)—that grew out of observations made by Lange (1942) about a putative logical inconsistency in classical monetary theory. Some of Patinkin's conclusions were disputed in a notable book by Gurley and Shaw (1960), and the resulting controversy was prominently reviewed in an influential survey article by Johnson (1962). In all of this earlier literature, it must be noted, the form of indeterminacy under discussion was "price level indeterminacy" such that the models in question fail to determine the value of *any* nominal variable, including the money supply. That type of failure occurs basically because of postulated policy behavior that is entirely devoid of any nominal anchor—i.e., there is no concern by the central bank for nominal variables.[14] Since rational private households and firms care only about real variables, according to standard neoclassical analysis, the absence of any "money illusion" by them *and* by the central bank must imply that no agent (in the

model) has any concern for any nominal variable. Thus there is in effect no nominal variable appearing anywhere in the model, so naturally it cannot determine the value of such variables.

Arguably, a dynamized, rational expectations version of this type of price-level indeterminacy, in the context of an interest rate policy rule, was developed by Sargent and Wallace (1975) and exposited in Sargent's influential textbook (1979, pp. 362-63). But of course this type of indeterminacy disappears if the central bank provides a nominal anchor, as was recognized by Parkin (1978) and McCallum (1981), even in the presence of rational expectations and the complete absence of private money illusion.

The type of indeterminacy under discussion in the current literature cited at the beginning of this section is very different. Instead of a failure to determine any nominal variable (without any implied problematic behavior for real variables), the recent Woodford-warning[15] literature is concerned with a multiplicity of stable equilibria in terms of *real* variables.[16] This type of aberrational behavior stems not from the absence of any nominal anchor (a static concept) but from the (essentially dynamic) fact that various paths of real money balances can be consistent with rational expectations under some circumstances. In order to avoid possible semantic confusions, McCallum (1986) proposed that different terms be used for the two types of aberrational behavior—nominal indeterminacy and solution multiplicity, respectively.[17] It is necessary to report, however, that this proposal has not met with widespread acceptance.

Of what importance is the distinction emphasized in the last paragraph? As an example of the sort of confusion that can arise if the distinction is not recognized, let us refer to the analysis of "price level indeterminacy" under an interest rate rule in the famous *JPE* paper by Sargent and Wallace (1975) mentioned above. It has long been my own belief

---

[13] See, for example, descriptions by King (1999), Archer (2000), and Freedman (2000).

[14] See Patinkin (1965, p. 309).

[15] This term is due to Lars Svensson.

[16] It is dynamically stable equilibria that are relevant because explosive paths of real variables are normally ruled out by transversality conditions that show them to be suboptimal for individual private agents.

[17] The adjective "nominal" was omitted from my original proposal, but seems clearly to be desirable.

R E V I E W

that the Sargent-Wallace (1975) paper was concerned with nominal indeterminacy—see McCallum (1981, 1986). Woodford (1999, Chap. 2), by contrast, interprets this Sargent and Wallace discussion as pertaining to solution multiplicity. My position is strengthened by the fact that the only substantive reference cited by Sargent and Wallace is Olivera (1970), which is clearly concerned with nominal indeterminacy. But there is something to be said for Woodford's position: under his interpretation the Sargent-Wallace result is valid, whereas under mine it is invalid (see McCallum, 1986, p. 148). Possibly Sargent and Wallace were undecided in their own thinking about which of the two concepts was being considered. In any event, their paper and the writings that have followed illustrate clearly the importance of making the distinction.

Let us now consider the substance of the Woodford warning of multiple solutions when policy is based on rational forecasts of future inflation.[18] It can be illustrated in a model such as our prototype (1) through (3) presented above. For convenience, let us rewrite the model here, omitting for simplicity the g_t term and treating $\bar{y}_t$ as a constant normalized to zero. Also, let us ignore constant terms that are tedious and for present purposes uninteresting. Finally, let us suppose that $E_t \Delta p_{t+1}$ is the inflation-forecast variable to which the policy rule pertains. Then the system can be written as

$$(32) \qquad y_t = b_1\left(R_t - E_t \Delta p_{t+1}\right) + E_t y_{t+1} + v_t$$

$$(33) \qquad \Delta p_t = \beta E_t \Delta p_{t+1} + \alpha y_t$$

$$(34) \qquad R_t = \left(1 + \mu_1\right)E_t \Delta p_{t+1} + \mu_2 y_t + e_t.$$

Here we suppose that u_t is absent from (2) while e_t in (3) is white noise, but that v_t in (1) is generated by a first-order autoregressive process—denoted AR(1)—as follows:

$$(35) \qquad v_t = \rho_1 v_{t-1} + \varepsilon_{1t}.$$

Here ε_{1t} is white noise and the AR parameter satisfies $\left|\rho_1\right| < 1$.[19]

In this model the unique minimum-state-variable (MSV) rational expectations solution is of the form[20]

$$(36) \qquad y_t = \phi_{11} v_t + \phi_{12} e_t$$

$$(37) \qquad \Delta p_t = \phi_{21} v_t + \phi_{22} e_t.$$

Then we have $E_t y_{t+1} = \phi_{11}\rho_1 v_t$ and $E_t \Delta p_{t+1} = \phi_{21}\rho_1 v_t$;

consequently, standard undetermined coefficient calculations yield

$$(38a) \qquad \phi_{11} = 1/\left[1 - \rho_1 - b_1\mu_2 - \left(\alpha b_1\mu_1\rho_1\right)/\left(1 - \beta\rho_1\right)\right]$$

$$(38b) \qquad \phi_{12} = b_1/\left(1 - b_1\mu_2\right)$$

$$(38c) \qquad \phi_{21} = \alpha/\left[\left(1 - \beta\rho_1\right)\left(1 - \rho_1 - b_1\mu_2\right) - \alpha b_1\mu_1\rho_1\right]$$

$$(38d) \qquad \phi_{22} = \alpha b_1/\left(1 - b_1\mu_2\right).$$

It is easy to verify that $\phi_{11} > 0$, $\phi_{12} < 0$, $\phi_{21} > 0$, and $\phi_{22} < 0$—i.e., that both y_t and Δp_t respond positively to a demand shock and negatively to a random, policy-induced blip in R_t. Thus the MSV solution suggests that there is no problem with the inflation-forecast targeting rule (34).

Suppose, however, that a researcher looks for non-MSV solutions of the form

$$(39) \qquad y_t = \phi_{11} v_t + \phi_{12} e_t + \phi_{13}\Delta p_{t-1}$$

$$(40) \qquad \Delta p_t = \phi_{21} v_t + \phi_{22} e_t + \phi_{23}\Delta p_{t-1},$$

where the extraneous state variable Δp_{t-1} is included. These expressions imply $E_t y_{t+1} = \phi_{11}\rho_1 v_t + \phi_{13}(\phi_{21}v_t + \phi_{22}e_t + \phi_{23}\Delta p_{t-1})$ and $E_t\Delta p_{t+1} = \phi_{21}\rho_1 v_t + \phi_{23}(\phi_{21}v_t + \phi_{22}e_t + \phi_{23}\Delta p_{t-1})$. Then undetermined coefficient reasoning implies that the values for the ϕ_{ij} are given by six relations analogous to (38) among which are

$$(41) \qquad \phi_{13} = b_1\mu_1\phi_{23}^2 + b_1\mu_2\phi_{13} + \phi_{13}\phi_{23}$$

and

$$(42) \qquad \phi_{23} = \beta\phi_{23}^2 + \alpha\phi_{13}.$$

From these ϕ_{13} can be solved out, yielding the cubic equation

$$(43) \qquad \phi_{23} = \beta\phi_{23}^2 + \alpha b_1\mu_1\phi_{23}^2/\left(1 - b_1\mu_2 - \phi_{23}\right).$$

Inspection of the latter indicates that one solution

---

[18] Note that I am not disputing the different point that central banks need to base policy on their own information and structural models, also discussed by Woodford (1994) and Bernanke and Woodford (1997).

[19] It will be observed that the current system is somewhat simpler than the one used in the third section of the paper ("Is the Neglect of Money Quantitatively Important?"). The reason is to have one in the current section that permits some analytical results to be obtained, so that more understanding of the numerical results will be possible. The basic results also pertain to more general models.

[20] The MSV concept is discussed at length in McCallum (1999), where it is interpreted as the unique solution that includes no bubble or sunspot components. A solution procedure is there proposed that generates a unique solution by construction in a very wide class of linear RE models.

is provided by $\phi_{23} = 0$, which implies $\phi_{13} = 0$. This, of course, gives the MSV solution obtained previously. But (43) is also satisfied by roots of the quadratic

(44) $\quad \beta\phi_{23}^2 - [1 + \beta + \alpha b_1\mu_1 - b_1\mu_2\beta]\phi_{23} + (1 - b_1\mu_2) = 0,$

i.e., by

(45) $\quad \phi_{23} = \dfrac{d \pm [d^2 - 4\beta(1 - b_1\mu_2)]^{0.5}}{2\beta},$

where d is the term in square brackets in (44). Therefore, for some values of the parameters α, β, b_1, μ_1, and μ_2 there may be other real solutions in addition to the MSV solution.[21]

To keep matters relatively simple, let $\mu_2 = 0$ so that the policy rule responds only to expected inflation. Then d becomes $1 + \beta + \alpha b_1\mu_1$, and there will be two real roots to (44) if $\mu_1 < 0$ or $\mu_1 > \mu_1^c \equiv [2\beta^{0.5} + 1 + \beta]/(-b_1\alpha)$. Furthermore, while one of the ϕ_{23} values in (44) will exceed 1.0 in absolute value when $\mu_1 > \mu_1^c$, the other will not—it will be a (negative) stable root. Consequently, there will be no transversality condition to rule out that root's implied trajectory as a rational expectations (RE) equilibrium. Thus there is, for $\mu_1 > \mu_1^c$, an infinite multiplicity of stable RE solutions indexed by the initial start-up value of Δp_{t-1}. In such cases, moreover, "sunspot" solutions are also possible in the sense of not being ruled out by the conditions of RE equilibria.[22] This is the danger pointed out by the Woodford warning, and it is made more likely when values of μ_2 exceed zero.[23]

I now wish to argue that the foregoing danger may not be of any practical significance, for it is entirely possible that non-MSV—i.e., bubble and sunspot—solutions are empirically irrelevant.[24] That such is the case is a cogent and plausible hypothesis, which to my knowledge has not been convincingly contradicted by any empirical tests, despite the enormous amount of interest shown by researchers over the past 25 years. In support of this position, I will offer two infrequently-stated lines of argument.

The first line of argument, in favor of the proposition that only MSV solutions are of empirical relevance, concerns the nature and role of the RE hypothesis. No one, I would think, believes that the orthogonality conditions for RE literally obtain precisely in real world economies, any more than do the conditions for exact profit and utility maximization. The hypothesis is extremely fruitful and attractive nevertheless because it points to a pow-

erful force, the desirability (for purposeful agents) of eliminating any systematic component of their expectational errors. And it keeps analysts from constructing models in which it is possible for agents to repeatedly commit the same type of expectational error, over and over again. But to suggest that the "expectation function,"[25] which describes actual expectational behavior, can jump from one specification (e.g., the MSV form $\Delta p^e_{t+1} = \phi_{21}\rho_1 v_t$) to another (e.g., the non-MSV form $\Delta p^e_{t+1} = \phi_{21}\rho_1 v_t + \phi_{23}[\phi_{21}v_t + \phi_{22}e_t + \phi_{23}\Delta p_{t-1}]$) with different ϕ_{ij} values) at any point of time—without any particular stimulus—seems downright whimsical. Much more plausible, I would contend, is the idea that such expectation functions are uniquely given at any point of time for any specified economy and policy regime. This does not imply, of course, that expectations themselves, e.g., Δp^e_{t+j}, cannot jump abruptly from one period to the next.

In this regard, the theoretical work of Evans (1986) and Evans and Honkapohja (1999, 2001) is in my opinion predominantly supportive of the hypothesis that the unique MSV solution is relevant for macroeconomic analysis.[26] With respect to the model at hand, for example, it is shown by Bullard and Mitra (2000, Figure 3) that the MSV solutions are *E-stable*, and therefore learnable by a real-time least-squares learning procedure, for the cases with large μ_1 and/or μ_2 values.[27] Bullard and Mitra do not analyze the E-stability/learnability properties of the non-MSV solutions, but very closely related cases have been analyzed by Evans (1986, pp. 150-53) and

---

[21] An analysis is provided by Bullard and Mitra (2000, p. 26).

[22] By a sunspot solution I mean one that includes random variables (of a martingale difference variety) that have no connection with other elements of the model.

[23] See, e.g., Bullard and Mitra (2000).

[24] At least, in macroeconomic contexts.

[25] An expectations function is a formula relating an expectational variable, such as the period-t expectation of z_{t+j}, denoted $_t z^e_{t+j}$, to observable variables.

[26] Evans and Honkapohja themselves might not agree. In any event, their recent terminology differs from mine in that they use the term MSV to refer to solutions that in some cases obtain in addition to the one that is specified by my concept of the MSV procedure. (See Evans and Honkapohja, 1999, p. 488; 2001, Chaps. 8-10.)

[27] E-stability pertains to the convergence of meta-time iterations that may or may not drive non-RE expectations functions to their RE values. Evans and Honkapohja (1999, 2001) show that in the cases at hand E-stability implies convergence of a real-time least-squares learning process like that of Marcet and Sargent (1989). For a useful introduction, see Bullard and Mitra (2000).

REVIEW

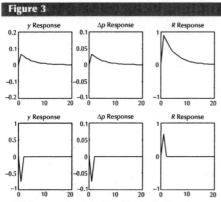

Figure 3

NOTE: Responses to unit shocks to IS (top) and policy rule (bottom) with $\mu_1=53.0$.

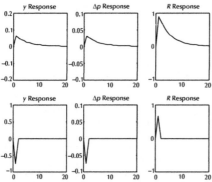

NOTE: Responses to unit shocks to IS (top) and policy rule (bottom) with $\mu_1=53.1$.

Evans and Honkapohja (1999, pp. 487-506; 2001, Chap. 10). These results indicate that their method of determining an expectation function would lead to the MSV solution in the case at hand.

The second line of argument to be developed here is to emphasize (i) that the unique MSV solution is available in the high-μ_1 cases pointed to by the Woodford warning and (ii) that this solution is well behaved in the sense of experiencing no discontinuity when passing through the critical values that delineate the region of multiple stable solutions. Specifically, impulse response functions for the MSV

solution are virtually indistinguishable for μ_1 values just above and just below the μ_1^c critical value at which solution multiplicity sets in. By contrast, the non-MSV solutions are highly different for the same pairs of μ_1 values (i.e., just above and just below μ_1^c).[28]

To illustrate this, let us take a numerical example in which $b_1 = -0.75$, $\beta = 0.99$, $\alpha = 0.1$, and $\rho_1 = 0.8$. In this case the critical value of μ_1 will be

$$(46) \quad \mu_1^c = \left[2\left(0.99^{0.5}\right)+1.99\right]/(0.75)(0.1) = \left[1.99+1.99\right]/0.75 = 53.07.$$

For values of μ_1 less than 53.07, there will be a single stable solution; for values above 53.07 there will be multiple stable solutions.[29] But for values of μ_1 close to 53.07, the behavior of the MSV solution will be virtually identical regardless of whether μ_1 is slightly below, equal to, or slightly above 53.07. This is demonstrated in Figure 3, where impulse response functions for y, Δp, and R are shown for unit shocks to the IS function (i.e., $v_t = 1.0$) and the policy rule (i.e., $e_t = 1.0$). The plots with $\mu_1 = 53.0$ and $\mu_1 = 53.1$ are, it seems fair to say, virtually indistinguishable.

More generally, properties of the MSV impulse response functions change continuously with values of μ_1. This is illustrated in Figures 4 and 5. In the former, we have cases with $\mu_1 = 10$ and $\mu_1 = 20$, both of which imply unique stable solutions. The response peaks in y and Δp are reduced smoothly in size as μ_1 increases from 10 to 20 to 53. Then these reductions continue to obtain, in a smooth manner, as μ_1 is increased further to 80 and 200; see Figure 5.

Behavior of the non-MSV solution contrasts sharply, and is distinctly non-continuous. For $0 < \mu_1 < 53.07$, roots to (44) are complex so (38) gives the only solution. Then with $\mu_1 = 53.1$, we obtain a stable non-MSV solution (in addition to the stable MSV solution) as shown in the top panel of Figure 6.[30] Since the responses to e_t involve coefficients in which the denominator equals the AR(1)

[28] I am indebted to Doug Laxton for suggesting comparisons based on impulse response functions.

[29] This is verified by Matlab calculation of solutions using my modification of Klein's (2000) QZ algorithm.

[30] These non-MSV solutions are obtained by adding to the Matlab file mentioned previously a subroutine written by Christopher Sims, qzswitch.m, to generate the solution implied by a different ordering of the system's generalized eigenvalues, in the manner mentioned on p. 633 of McCallum (1999).

Figure 4

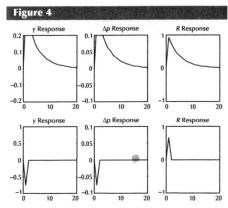

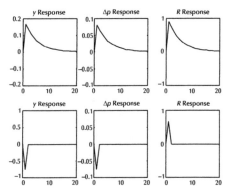

NOTE: Responses to unit shocks to IS (top) and policy rule (bottom) with μ_1=10.0.

NOTE: Responses to unit shocks to IS (top) and policy rule (bottom) with μ_1=20.0.

Figure 5

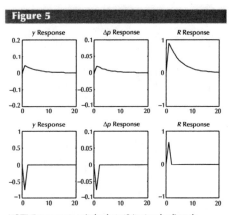

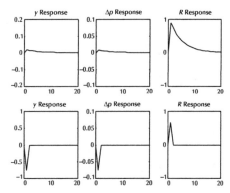

NOTE: Responses to unit shocks to IS (top) and policy rule (bottom) with μ_1=80.0.

NOTE: Responses to unit shocks to IS (top) and policy rule (bottom) with μ_1=200.0.

parameter for the e_t process, these responses are "infinite" when e_t is white noise. Consequently, a value of 0.01 is used for this AR(1) parameter in the model for Figure 6. A comparison with Figure 3 shows, not surprisingly, that this non-MSV solution is not at all similar to the MSV solution with μ_1 = 53.0. Next, consider the bottom panel of Figure 6, where μ_1 = 80. It can be seen that the increase in μ_1 *decreases* the responsiveness of R_t and leaves larger peaks for y_t and Δp_t in response to both shocks. Also note that y_t and Δp_t blip *upward* in response to a surprise increase in R_t and that the responses of

y_t and R_t are huge. Finally, if we let the autoregressive parameter generating e_t be 0.04 instead of 0.01, the direction of the y_t and Δp_t responses to e_t flips over to become negative. (This case is not shown.)

These results illustrate, for one representative set of parameter values, the well-behaved nature of the MSV solution and the erratic nature of the non-MSV (bubble) solutions. Such results also obtain for other parameter values and clearly suggest the desirability of considering the MSV solutions as the sole economically relevant solution. If this strategy is adopted, i.e., if the MSV solution is taken to rep-

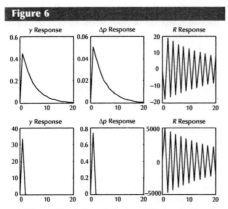

NOTE: Non-MSV solution; unit shocks to IS (top) and policy rule (bottom) with $\mu_1=53.1$.

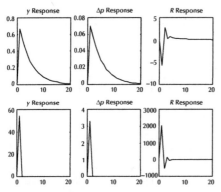

NOTE: Non-MSV solution; unit shocks to IS (top) and policy rule (bottom) with $\mu_1=80.0$.

resent implied behavior for the model at hand, then there is no compelling reason to believe that large μ_1 values will generate undesirable behavior. In that case, preemptive inflation forecast targeting with an R_t instrument will not be subject to the dangers mentioned above.

ON THE VALIDITY OF THE TAYLOR PRINCIPLE

As a related matter, let us now consider the consequences of having a policy rule that fails to

satisfy the Taylor principle, i.e., that an interest rate policy rule should respond by more than point-for-point to inflation or its expectation. Both Taylor (1999) and Clarida, Gali, and Gertler (1999) emphasize that this requirement, which translates into $\mu_1 > 0$ in our model (32) through (34), implies that the *real* rate of interest will be moved upward (tightening policy) when inflation exceeds its target (and vice versa). Our analysis of the previous section was principally concerned with cases in which $\mu_1 > \mu^c$, but it was shown using (44) that solution multiplicity also obtains when $\mu_1 < 0$. Thus it might be thought that our argument for downplaying the importance of solution multiplicity would also apply to cases with $\mu_1 < 0$, thereby contradicting the Taylor principle. Such is not the case, however, and it is the task of this section to explain why. In other words, we will determine what is the true problem posed, from the MSV perspective, by $\mu_1 < 0$.

For our argument to be different for "indeterminacies" with $\mu_1 < 0$, as compared with those with $\mu_1 > \mu^c$, it must not be the existence of solution multiplicities per se that is considered problematic when $\mu_1 < 0$. Instead, there must be some other condition that prevails when $\mu_1 < 0$ and represents a problem that is, according to the present argument, of genuine importance.

Once again this problem is the absence of E-stability. Bullard and Mitra (2000) show that $\mu_1 < 0$ implies the absence of E-stability, and therefore the failure of least-squares learning, for separate cases in which π_t, π_{t-1}, and $E_{t-1}\pi_{t+j}$ enter the policy rule.[31] This can be seen by inspection of their Figures 1 through 3. Since E-stability of an MSV solution enhances the attractiveness of that solution by indicating that it may be of empirical relevance, its absence for $\mu_1 < 0$ suggests that policy rules with $\mu_1 < 0$ should be avoided.

An interesting application of this argument concerns the special case in which $\mu_1 = -1$ with Δp_t in the rule and $\mu_2 = 0$, i.e., the case of a pure interest rate peg: $R_t = $ constant. Then the Bullard-Mitra results imply that E-stability does not prevail. This constitutes a version, with an optimizing model, of the argument of Howitt (1992). Note that it applies to a maintained interest rate peg, not to the use of an interest rate instrument.

An alternative argument for the case with $-1 < \mu_1 < 0$ can be developed as follows. Consider a model in which the endogenous variable x_t is generated by the relationship

---

[31] Here I am discussing cases with $\mu_2 = 0$. Bullard and Mitra's results are more general, since they also consider $\mu_2 > 0$.

(47) $x_t = a_0 + a_1 E_t x_{t+1} + a_2 x_{t-1} + z_t,$

where z_t is a stationary exogenous forcing variable with an unconditional mean of zero. Now apply the unconditional expectation operator to get

(48) $Ex_t = a_0 + a_1 Ex_{t+1} + a_2 Ex_{t-1} + 0.$

Assuming stationarity, we then have

(49) $Ex_t = a_0 / (1 - a_1 - a_2).$

Clearly, as $a_1 + a_2$ approaches 1.0 from below, the unconditional mean of x_t approaches $+\infty$, whereas if $a_1 + a_2$ approaches 1.0 from above, then the mean of x_t approaches $-\infty$. Thus there is an infinite discontinuity at $a_1 + a_2 = 1$. So to be well formulated, the model needs to include a parameter restriction that rules out $a_1 + a_2 = 1$. From a purely mathematical perspective, $a_1 + a_2 > 1$ would do as well, but for economic plausibility the preferred restriction is $a_1 + a_2 < 1$. Note that if $a_2 = 0$, this amounts to $1 - a_1 > 0$.

To see the relevance of the foregoing for the model (32) through (34), with $\mu_2 = 0$, write the system as

(50)

$$\begin{bmatrix} 1 & 0 \\ -\alpha & 1 \end{bmatrix} \begin{bmatrix} y_t \\ \Delta p_t \end{bmatrix} = \begin{bmatrix} 1 & b_1\mu_1 \\ 0 & \beta \end{bmatrix} E_t \begin{bmatrix} y_{t+1} \\ \Delta p_{t+1} \end{bmatrix} + \begin{bmatrix} 1 & 0 \\ 0 & 1 \end{bmatrix} \begin{bmatrix} v_t \\ e_t \end{bmatrix}$$

or

(51) $x_t = AE_t x_{t+1} + Cz_t,$

where $x_t = [y_t \ \Delta p_t]'$, $z_t = [v_t \ e_t]'$, and

(52) $A = \begin{bmatrix} 1 & 0 \\ -\alpha & 1 \end{bmatrix}^{-1} \begin{bmatrix} 1 & b_1\mu_1 \\ 0 & \beta \end{bmatrix} = \begin{bmatrix} 1 & b_1\mu_1 \\ \alpha & \alpha b_1\mu_1 + \beta \end{bmatrix}.$

Now the counterpart of $1 - a_1 > 0$ in the previous example is that $\det(I-A) > 0$. If that condition does not hold, the model is not well formulated and the unconditional mean of x_t passes through an infinite discontinuity. But the value of $\det(I-A)$ in the case at hand is $-\alpha b_1\mu_1$. Thus with $\alpha > 0$ and $b_1 < 0$, the requirement for this model to be well formulated is $\mu_1 > 0$. This follows the original development and promotion of the MSV solution, in which McCallum (1983, p. 160) points out "the desirability of specifying admissible parameter values as an integral part of the model."

The main conclusion of this section is that the Taylor principle is basically correct. If μ_2 is positive,

then μ_1 can be negative to some extent without losing E-stability; according to Bullard and Mitra (2000), the necessary and sufficient condition for E-stability is $\alpha\mu_1 + (1-\beta)\mu_2 > 0$. But that is a modification, not a fundamental contradiction, of the principle. Its basic logic is sound.

CONCLUDING REMARKS

In the foregoing sections the following arguments have been developed: (i) models without monetary aggregates do not imply that inflation is a non-monetary phenomenon and are not necessarily non-monetary models; (ii) theoretical considerations suggest that such models are misspecified, but the quantitative significance of this misspecification seems to be very small; (iii) arguments based on "indeterminacy" findings, e.g., regarding policy rules that respond strongly to expected future inflation rates, are of dubious merit: there are various reasons for believing that findings of solution multiplicity are theoretical curiosities that have little or no real world significance; (iv) monetary policy rules that violate the Taylor principle, by contrast, possess another characteristic—the absence of E-stability and least-squares learnability—that suggests undesirable behavior in practice.

These points are mostly supportive of the notion that policy analysis in models without money, based on interest rate policy rules, is not fundamentally misguided. It is important, consequently, to mention explicitly that they do not imply that policy rules with an interest rate instrument are necessarily preferable to ones based on a controllable monetary aggregate, such as total reserves or the monetary base. My own preference has been, for many years, for base instrument rules. Furthermore, my recent (2000b) study of the counterfactual historical performance of alternative rules for the United States, the United Kingdom, and Japan suggests that—for reasons that are not entirely clear—base instrument rules would have provided better policy guides than interest instrument rules over 1965-98. But the topics considered in the present paper are ones of considerable fundamental interest, and it is important in choosing among different types of rules—i.e., different ways of conducting policy—that central bankers not be misled by dubious economic analysis.[32]

---

[32] In that regard, the analysis in the fourth section of the paper ("Are Rational-Expectation Indeterminacies Important?") also suggests that some results used to argue in favor of an interest rate instrument, rather than the monetary base—see, e.g., Woodford (1999)—are also dubious.

REVIEW

REFERENCES

Archer, David J. "Inflation Targeting in New Zealand." Paper presented at the International Monetary Fund Institute Seminar on Inflation Targeting, 20-21 March 2000.

Bernanke, Ben S. and Woodford, Michael. "Inflation Forecasts and Monetary Policy." *Journal of Money, Credit and Banking*, November 1997, *29*(4), pp. 653-84.

Bullard, James and Mitra, Kaushik. "Learning About Monetary Policy Rules." Working Paper 2000-001B, Federal Reserve Bank of St. Louis, July 2000.

Carlstrom, Charles T. and Fuerst, Timothy S. "Forward-Looking Versus Backward-Looking Taylor Rules." Working Paper, April 2000.

Casares, Miguel and McCallum, Bennett T. "An Optimizing IS-LM Framework with Endogenous Investment." Working Paper, September 2000.

Christiano, Lawrence J. and Gust, Christopher J. "Comment" in Taylor (1999), pp. 299-316.

Clarida, Richard; Gali, Jordi and Gertler, Mark. "The Science of Monetary Policy: A New Keynesian Perspective." *Journal of Economic Literature*, December 1999, *37*(4), pp. 1661-707.

_____, _____ and _____. "Monetary Policy Rules and Macroeconomic Stability: Evidence and Some Theory." Working Paper 6442, National Bureau of Economic Research, March 1998.

Estrella, Arturo and Fuhrer, Jeffrey C. "Dynamic Inconsistencies: Counterfactual Implications of a Class of Rational Expectations Models." Working Paper, July 2000.

Evans, George W. "Selection Criteria for Models with Non-Uniqueness." *Journal of Monetary Economics*, September 1986, *18*(2), pp. 147-57.

_____ and Honkapohja, Seppo. "Learning Dynamics," in John B. Taylor and Michael Woodford, eds., *Handbook of Macroeconomics*, Volume 1A. New York: North-Holland, 1999, pp.449-542.

_____ and _____. Learning and Expectations in Macroeconomics. Princeton, NJ: Princeton University Press, 2001.

Freedman, Charles. "The Canadian Experience with

Targets for Reducing and Controlling Inflation." Paper presented at the International Monetary Fund Institute Seminar on Inflation Targeting, 20-21 March 2000.

Friedman, Benjamin M. "The Future of Monetary Policy: The Central Bank as an Army with Only a Signal Corps?" *International Finance*, November 1999, *2*(3), pp. 321-38.

Gali, Jordi and Gertler, Mark. "Inflation Dynamics: A Structural Econometric Analysis." *Journal of Monetary Economics*, October 1999, *44*(2), pp. 195-222.

Goodfriend, Marvin. "Monetary Policy Comes of Age: A 20th Century Odyssey." Federal Reserve Bank of Richmond *Economic Quarterly*, Winter 1997, *83*(1), pp. 1-22.

Goodhart, Charles. "Can Central Banking Survive the IT Revolution?" *International Finance*, July 2000, *3*(2), pp. 189-209.

Gurley, John G. and Shaw, Edward S. *Money in a Theory of Finance*. Washington, DC: The Brookings Institution, 1960.

Howitt, Peter. "Interest Rate Control and Nonconvergence to Rational Expectations." *Journal of Political Economy*, August 1992, *100*(4), pp. 776-800.

Ireland, Peter N. "Money's Role in the Monetary Business Cycle." Working Paper 8115, National Bureau of Economic Research, February 2001.

Isard, Peter; Laxton, Douglas and Eliasson, Ann-Charlotte. "Simple Monetary Policy Rules Under Model Uncertainty." *International Tax and Public Finance*, November 1999, *6*(4), pp. 537-77. Also in P. Isard, A. Razin, and A.K. Rose, eds., *International Finance and Financial Crises: Essays in Honour of Robert P. Flood, Jr.* New York: Kluwer Academic Publishers, 2000.

Johnson, Harry G. "Monetary Theory and Policy." *American Economic Review*, June 1962, *52*(3), pp. 335-84.

Kerr, William and King, Robert G. "Limits on Interest Rate Rules in the IS Model." Federal Reserve Bank of Richmond *Economic Quarterly*, Spring 1996, *82*(2), pp. 47-77.

King, Mervyn A. "The Monetary Policy Committee Two Years On." *Bank of England Quarterly Bulletin*, August 1999, *39*, pp. 297-303.

Klein, Paul. "Using the Generalized Schur Form to Solve a

Multivariate Linear Rational Expectations Model." *Journal of Economic Dynamics and Control*, September 2000, *24*(10), pp. 1405-23.

Lange, Oscar. "Say's Law: A Restatement and Criticism," in O. Lange, F. McIntyre, and T.O. Yntema, eds., *Studies in Mathematical Economics and Econometrics*. Chicago: 1942.

Lucas, Robert E., Jr. "Econometric Testing of the Natural Rate Hypothesis," in O. Eckstein, ed., *Econometrics of Price Determination*. Washington, DC: Board of Governors of the Federal Reserve System, 1972.

Marcet, Albert and Sargent, Thomas J. "Convergence of Least Squares Learning Mechanisms in Self-Referential Linear Stochastic Models." *Journal of Economic Theory*, April 1989, *4*(2), pp. 337-68.

McCallum, Bennett T. "Price Level Determinacy with an Interest Rate Policy Rule and Rational Expectations." *Journal of Monetary Economics*, November 1981, *8*(3), pp. 319-29.

_____. "On Non-Uniqueness in Rational Expectations Models: An Attempt at Perspective." *Journal of Monetary Economics*, March 1983, *11*(2), pp. 139-68.

_____. "Some Issues Concerning Interest Rate Pegging, Price Level Determinacy and the Real Bills Doctrine." *Journal of Monetary Economics*, January 1986, *17*, pp. 135-50.

_____. "Role of the Minimal State Variable Criterion in Rational Expectations Models." *International Tax and Public Finance*, November 1999, *6*, pp. 621-39. Also in P. Isard, A. Razin, and A.K. Rose, eds., *International Finance and Financial Crises: Essays in Honor of Robert P. Flood, Jr.* New York: Kluwer Academic Publishers, 2000.

_____. "Theoretical Analysis Regarding a Zero Lower Bound on Nominal Interest Rates." *Journal of Money, Credit and Banking*, November 2000a, *32*(4), pp. 870-94.

_____. "Alternative Monetary Policy Rules: A Comparison with Historical Settings for the United States, the United Kingdom, and Japan." Federal Reserve Bank of Richmond *Economic Quarterly*, Winter 2000b, *86*(4), pp. 49-79.

_____ and Nelson, Edward. "Performance of Operational Policy Rules in an Estimated Semiclassical Structural Model," in Taylor (1999), pp. 15-45.

_____ and _____. "An Optimizing IS-LM Specification for Monetary Policy and Business Cycle Analysis," *Journal of Money, Credit and Banking*, August 1999b, *31*(3, Part 1), pp. 296-316.

Meltzer, Allan H. "Commentary: Monetary Policy at Zero Inflation," in *New Challenges for Monetary Policy*. Federal Reserve Bank of Kansas City, 1999, pp. 261-76.

Nelson, Edward. "Direct Effects of Base Money on Aggregate Demand." Working Paper, May 2000.

Olivera, Julio H. "On Passive Money." *Journal of Political Economy*, July/August 1970, *78*(4, Part 2), pp. 805-14.

Parkin, Michael. "A Comparison of Alternative Techniques of Monetary Control Under Rational Expectations." *Manchester School*, September 1978, *46*(3), pp. 252-87.

Patinkin, Don. "The Indeterminacy of Absolute Prices in Classical Economic Theory." *Econometrica*, January 1949, *17*(1), pp. 1-27.

_____. "Financial Intermediaries and the Logical Structure of Monetary Theory: A Review Article." *American Economic Review*, March 1961, *51*(1), pp. 95-116.

_____. *Money, Interest, and Prices*. 2nd Ed. New York: Harper and Row, 1965.

Rotemberg, Julio J. and Woodford, Michael. "An Optimization-Based Econometric Framework for the Evaluation of Monetary Policy," in B.S. Bernanke and J.J. Rotemberg, eds., *NBER Macroeconomics Annual, 1997*. Cambridge, MA: MIT Press, 1997.

Sargent, Thomas J. *Macroeconomic Theory*. New York: Academic Press, 1979.

_____ and Wallace, Neil. "'Rational' Expectations, the Optimal Monetary Instrument, and the Optimal Money Supply Rule." *Journal of Political Economy*, April 1975, *83*(2), pp. 241-54.

Svensson, Lars E.O. "Inflation Forecast Targeting: Implementing and Monitoring Inflation Targets." *European Economic Review*, June 1997, *41*(6), pp. 1111-46.

Taylor, John B. "Discretion Versus Policy Rules in Practice." *Carnegie-Rochester Conference Series on Public Policy*, December 1993, *39*, pp. 195-214.

REVIEW

_____, ed. *Monetary Policy Rules*. Chicago: University of Chicago Press for NBER, 1999.

Woodford, Michael. "Nonstandard Indicators for Monetary Policy: Can Their Usefulness Be Judged From Forecasting Regressions?" in G.N. Mankiw, ed., *Monetary Policy*. Chicago: University of Chicago Press for NBER, 1994, pp. 99-115.

_____. "Price-Level Determinacy Without Control of a Monetary Aggregate." *Carnegie-Rochester Conference Series on Public Policy*, December 1995, 43, pp. 1-46.

_____. "Price Level Determination Under Interest Rate Rules" in *Interest and Prices*. Unpublished manuscript, 1999, Chap. 2.

Part IV
Uncertainty and Policy

[10]

Central bankers and uncertainty

In this speech,[1] Professor Charles Goodhart, member of the Bank's Monetary Policy Committee, discusses how central banks do, and how they should, change short-term interest rates in response to economic developments.

For the majority of my professional life, I have had the good fortune to be simultaneously involved both as a participant in, and as an academic observer of, central banks. Today, and as is suitable for this occasion and audience, I shall be primarily emphasising my academic observations. Nevertheless, my study of central bank behaviour is inevitably informed and coloured by my previous years as a Bank official, and current position as an external member of the Monetary Policy Committee (MPC), but my comments today are unauthorised, not necessarily representative of any of my colleagues or of other central bankers, independent and, I trust, reasonably objective — and where they are mistaken I have no one to blame but myself, except of course for the econometrics, where I have had help from the Bank staff.

Let me plunge into the central policy issue. The key decision that the monetary authorities take each month is whether, and by how much, to change the short-term interest rate. There was a time when a vocal segment of the academic community advocated a notably different operating mechanism, of monetary base control, but that debate has faded.

The question has, instead, become how central banks actually do, and how they should, vary interest rates in response to economic developments. The suggestion has now been made by a number of academics, notably by John Taylor, that most central bank reaction functions (except for those pegging their exchange rates and hence their interest rates to some other country) can in practice be reasonably well described by a relatively simple function, often now termed the Taylor rule; and that this rule approximates quite closely to the social welfare optimum, when examined in the context of a variety of models established for a variety of countries (Taylor, 1998a, b and c, and papers at the June 1998 Stockholm Conference). Under such a Taylor reaction function, the nominal level of the interest rate is determined by the current level of two variables, the rate of inflation and an (inherently somewhat uncertain) measure of the output gap, the deviation of actual output from potential, so:

$$i_t = a + b_1 \pi_t + b_2 (y_t - y^*) .$$

where a is the equilibrium real interest rate (usually about 2% or 3%).[2]

My first point is that virtually all attempts to estimate the Taylor rule empirically require the addition of a lagged dependent variable, ie the interest rate in the previous period, in order to fit well. Moreover, with monthly, or quarterly data, the coefficient on the lagged dependent variable is usually close to, and in some estimated cases greater than, unity. This means that central banks have historically changed rates by only a small fraction of their ultimate cumulative reaction in response to an inflationary shock or to a deviation of output from potential. Thus, the equation actually fitted becomes:

$$i_t = a + (1 - \rho) b_1 \pi_t + (1 - \rho) b_2 (y_t - y^*) + \rho i_{t-1}$$

My main theme today is to enquire further into this phenomenon whereby virtually all central banks change interest rates, in response to shocks, by a series of small steps in the same direction, rather than attempting more aggressively to offset that shock quickly in order to return the economy to equilibrium.

Some academics studying this subject deal with this issue by positing that changes in interest rates enter the authorities' loss function. But why should that be so? One can easily understand the social loss arising from inflation and deviations of output from potential, but what exactly is the social loss arising from changes in interest rates themselves? We shall attempt to pursue this question further soon, but in the interim I want to raise a few points about the use of such a reaction function and its application to the United Kingdom.

First, the generally quite good fit of an estimated Taylor rule is not to say that in some countries, over some time periods, one cannot improve the fit by adding other variables. In small open economies, especially those pegging their exchange rate, the interest rate in the home country will also respond significantly to interest rates in its larger neighbour (Peersman and Smets, 1998). Nor, of course, are the coefficients closely similar for all countries (and over all time periods) in such estimated reaction functions.

(1) The annual Keynes lecture, given at the British Academy on 29 October 1998. The author would like to thank the British Academy, which holds the copyright of this speech and discussion and will be publishing them in its *Proceedings*, for permission to publish them here.
(2) Indeed, in some cases, notably Germany, evidence has been presented that such a reaction function fits the observed data better than the explanations given by the central bank of its own behaviour. Thus, Clarida and Gertler (1997) show that the addition of monetary variables to a Taylor-rule reaction function for Germany adds nothing to the explanatory power of that equation.

One of the curious lacunae in this literature has been the failure so far to integrate the Taylor reaction function literature with the literature on central bank independence.[1] I would expect the measure of independence to be positively associated with the size, and perhaps the speed, of the authorities' reaction to inflation shocks.[2] There is some partial and preliminary evidence that this conjecture is correct. For example, Stephen Wright at Cambridge (1997) tested such reaction functions for Germany, the United States and the United Kingdom over the time period 1961 Q1–94 Q4, and found that over this time period the estimated cumulative response of the monetary authorities in the United Kingdom to an inflationary shock, ie the size of the coefficient b_1, at 0.8, was both considerably less than that of the Federal Reserve and of the Bundesbank, and also below the value of unity required to guarantee price stability. But when I asked Stephen to re-run his equation over the last decade, he obtained the much higher value of 1.6 for the b_1 coefficient in the United Kingdom, as large as that in Germany, and slightly larger than the standard value of 1.5 incorporated in the normative versions of the Taylor rule.

Similarly, a preliminary study of a number of separate, and quite short, monetary regimes in the United Kingdom, undertaken in the Bank by Ed Nelson (1998), has found the coefficients in the Taylor reaction function, especially the b_1 (inflation response) coefficient, to be strongly time-varying, as shown below:

Table A
Taylor reaction function coefficients; United Kingdom, 1972–97

	b_1	b_2	ρ	
1972/76	0.00	0.69 (a)	0.70 (a)	Quarterly
1976/79	0.44 (b)	0.58	0.70 (a)	Monthly
1979/87	0.46 (a)(b)	0.08	0.75 (a)	Monthly
1987/90	-ve	0.25 (a)	0.66 (a)	Monthly
1992/97	1.32 (a)(b)	0.24	0.40 (a)	Quarterly

(a) Significant, t > 2.
(b) Forward-looking; using instrumental variables.

One of the most visible and widely remarked aspects of current central banking mores is that they, especially when independent, are supposed to give absolute primacy to the achievement of price stability. The level of output is not supposed to enter, for example, the objective function of the ECB or of the Bank of England. Yet, as described, the revealed preference of all monetary authorities appears to be to respond both to current inflation and to the current output gap. Actually, this seeming conundrum is very simply resolved. There are two ways to answer this question. The first is that these two variables, ie current inflation and the current output gap, are the critical variables needed to forecast future inflation. A regression of current inflation for the United Kingdom on the levels of inflation and a measure of the output gap one year previously, a measure that is as always somewhat arbitrary and uncertain, gives the following result:

$$\pi_t = 0.010 + 0.840\ \pi_{t-1} + 0.527\ (y - y^*)_{t-1}$$
$$\quad\ \ (0.011)\quad (0.113)\qquad (0.199)$$

$R^2 = 0.739$, SEE $= 0.029$ (1974–97 annual data).

This is not to say that the vast efforts put in by the Bank staff and others to construct the inflation forecast do not add value to our estimates of future inflation, but it does suggest that knowledge of current inflation and where the country stands on the output gap, or equivalently using Okun's Law with respect to the natural rate of unemployment, can take one most of the way there. Given that lags in the transmission mechanism mean that the authorities can only reasonably target an inflation forecast (Svensson, 1997, a and b, and Svensson and Rudebusch, 1998), appearing to respond to current inflation and to the current output gap may well appear superficially much the same as targeting a pure inflation forecast.

The second leg of the answer, which was discussed in greater depth by Mervyn King in his 1997 Financial Markets Group lecture, is that even if we knew exactly how our economies worked, subject only to additive, stochastic shocks with mean zero, such shocks would still, from time to time, drive us away from our longer-term objectives of holding output close to productive potential with low, or zero, inflation. As is well known, the problem is particularly acute with supply shocks. That gives rise to the well understood complication that if one tries to restore inflation back very rapidly to its equilibrium, the lagged effects of monetary policy can lead both to large-scale, 'excessive' variations in output (around productive potential), and in many cases also to instrument instability (when the changes in interest rates needed to offset last time's disequilibrium become explosively greater over time). On the other hand, enormous concern to prevent any large deviation of output from its equilibrium can lead to continuing and excessive deviations of inflation from target. This leads to a trade-off between output-variability and inflation-variability of the general form shown in Chart 1.

Chart 1
Output/inflation variability trade-off

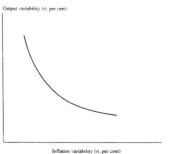

Output variability (σ, per cent)

Inflation variability (σ, per cent)

(1) This void is being rapidly filled now; see, for example, Murchison and Siklos (1998).
(2) Though there is evidence that the Bundesbank, and perhaps other more independent central banks, react as or more slowly than those that have been more subservient (see Goodhart (1997) and Fischer, A M (1996)).

Bank of England Quarterly Bulletin: February 1999

Fortunately for the MPC, the empirical evidence for the United Kingdom currently indicates that this is not a serious problem. The work of Haldane, Batini and Whitley at the Bank of England (1997) suggests that if one chooses an appropriate horizon for returning inflation to its target, one will achieve about as good an outcome for both inflation and output variability together as is practicably possible. Thus, in Chart 2, the choice of lag length (*j* in the chart) for returning inflation to its target simultaneously more or less minimises both inflation deviations and output variability following a shock.

Chart 2
j-loci: full and no pass-through cases[a]

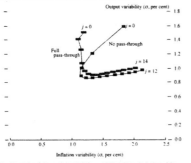

(a) Chart 2 plots the locus of output/inflation variability points as the horizon of the inflation forecast (*j*) is varied, one assuming full and immediate import-price pass-through (a shorter transmission lag), and the other, no immediate pass-through (a longer transmission lag).

In another independent exercise, my discussant, Charlie Bean (1998), estimated such a policy frontier between the standard deviations of inflation and output (see Chart 3).

Chart 3
Policy frontiers

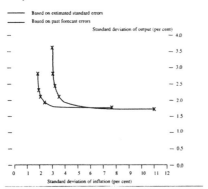

He then wrote: 'The most striking thing about these frontiers are how sharply curved they are—indeed they are almost rectangular—and how close together are the optimal points for relative weights in the range 1:3 to 3:1. This

rectangular quality is also found in the work of Haldane and Batini (1998),...., suggesting that it is not simply an artefact of the rather simple model structure employed here. This rectangularity has an important implication: a wide range of possible weights on output *vis-à-vis* inflation lead to the selection of rather similar points on the policy frontier. Hence little is lost by the government being able to write only an incomplete contract with the central bank, which does not explicitly prescribe the relative weight the central bank is supposed to place on output volatility versus inflation volatility; the central bank only needs to know that preferences are not extreme. Furthermore such an incomplete contract is likely to lead to a better outcome than a more completely specified contract that encourages the central bank to select a policy that is at the upper end of the policy frontier. One interpretation of the UK inflation remit is that it is precisely such an incomplete contract'.

So the evidence suggests that the short-term trade-off between the variance of inflation and output, over which so much blood has been spilt, is, in the United Kingdom at least, in practice not such a difficult and troublesome issue. The key point is that the MPC should choose an appropriate future horizon at which to aim to return to the inflation target set by the Chancellor. By doing so, they should be able to minimise the variance of both output and inflation. Given that horizon, how then should the monetary authorities operate, according to the principles that flow from our models of the economy, always remembering, and I really want to emphasise this, that in most of these models the only uncertainty in the system is additive and stochastic?

The answer to that conditional question is fairly clear. We should each month alter interest rates so that the expected value of our target, the forecast rate of inflation at the appropriate horizon about 18 months to two years hence, should exactly equal the desired rate of 2^{1}/$_{2}$%. Lars Svensson has written several papers on the optimality of such a procedure. If we start from an initial position in which the predicted forecast value of inflation is already close to the objective, then as a first approximation we should expect interest rates to respond to the unanticipated element in the incoming news. Since this is by definition a martingale series, often somewhat loosely termed a 'random walk', then, on these assumptions, an optimally conducted interest rate path also ought to be nearly random walk, as should also, of course, be the voting pattern of individual members of the MPC. This is, broadly, what the generality of our economic models imply.

I shall shortly demonstrate how, and why, no central bank actually does behave in such a random walk fashion. But before I do so, I want to contrast the normative theory inherent in our basic models with the public perception that such random walk behaviour is not optimal in practice. Thus, in *The Times* on Thursday, 11 June, under the headline 'Anger grows at Bank's U-turn' (page 29), Janet Bush and Anne Ashworth state that,

'Critics of the increase described the Bank's apparent shift in policy as 'almost laughable'. One said: 'It is like a drunk staggering from side to side down the street''.

You will appreciate that this latter is an almost perfect description of a random walk path. Similarly, the *Sunday Business* main leader of 7 June was entitled 'The fickleness of hawks today and doves tomorrow'; the unnamed writer commented,

'Where the committee lost credibility last week is in its inconsistency.... What is the outside world meant to make of members who can change their view so readily? It suggests a fickle committee, influenced by the latest anecdotal or statistical evidence, swaying its opinions one way or the other and back again'.

One of the arguments used by Wim Duisenberg, the President of the ECB, in rejecting the publication not only of individual voting records but also of minutes for some long duration is apparently, and this passage is in direct quotes in Robert Chote's *Financial Times* article on 1 June (page 10), that:

'Publication of the minutes soon after decisions have been taken or meetings have taken place will—and this is only human—make it more difficult for individual participants in the discussion to change their minds and be convinced of the arguments of others'.

Now this struck a particular chord with me; for example, yet another commentator, Jonathan Loynes, writing in *Greenwell Gilt Weekly* on 18 May, wrote,

'Of course, this does not mean that Professor Goodhart cannot switch *back* to the Hawks. If his change of heart was driven by recent softer earnings numbers then the latest pick-up could cause him to think again. But an immediate about-turn is most unlikely, if only for reasons of credibility'.

Wim Duisenberg presumably now doubts my humanity, Jonathan Loynes my credibility. Yet let me reprise once again. If policy is roughly on course to deliver the desired objective, then policy should be finely balanced, and should react to incoming unanticipated news in an approximately random walk fashion. A committee, or an individual within that, who consistently votes the same way for month after month either has got the balance of policy seriously wrong, or individually must think that that balance is seriously wrong.

I previously qualified the term 'random walk behaviour' with the adverb 'approximately'. The first point to make is that the dynamic structure of the economy involves strong serial correlation and long lags in monetary policy effects. If we seek to optimise monetary policy in a model with such inherent lags, even if we still use a certainty-equivalent model only involving additive stochastic uncertainty, then

we could expect to find some degree of serial correlation in the path of interest rates. The dynamic structure of the economy itself can account for part of the observed persistence in the directional movement of interest rates. To repeat, interest rates should not be random walk even under certainty-equivalence. But the degree, the extent, of gradualism exhibited in interest rate policy is far higher than the dynamic structure of serial correlation in the economy alone can justify.

An excellent paper by Brian Sack (1998a; see also 1998b) of the staff in the Fed's Board examined, by using a VAR model, initially with additive uncertainty, what the expected policy in adjusting the fed funds rate would have been if policy was to be optimised. He found (page 4) that:

'The optimal policy displays a tendency to move in a particular direction over sustained periods of time, as found in the data. Still, the optimal policy responds more aggressively to changes in the state of the economy than the observed policy. As a result, the funds rate path under the expected policy is more volatile than the actual funds rate. Moreover, the observed policy tends to lag behind the expected policy, limiting any changes in the funds rate and gradually moving towards the optimal policy over a period of six months. The actual policy is therefore described by an excessive amount of interest rate smoothing that cannot be explained strictly by the dynamic behaviour of the variables to which the Fed is responding. The interest rate smoothing that is observed indicates that the analysis under additive uncertainty ignores an important element of policy making'.

One way of expressing this difference visually is to compare the path of the calculated 'optimal' and actual fed funds rate, as Sack does in his Figure 2, here Chart 4. You can see that the green optimal expected line is more jagged, with more reversals of direction than the actual fed funds path. As you can see from the time path of the actual planned target rate

Chart 4

Actual and optimal funds rate under additive uncertainty

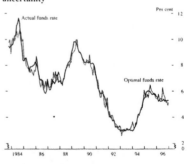

Note: The optimal funds rate is based on the policy rule that solves the dynamic programming problem. It is the rate predicted by the policy rule given the actual history of the economy at each point in time.

Bank of England Quarterly Bulletin: February 1999

(see Chart 5), most of the changes amount to small steps in the same direction. The cumulative distribution for the expected optimal policy with additive uncertainty is very different from that of the actual policy followed.

Chart 5
Actual federal funds rate

There are, however, some technical problems relating to the estimation and assessment of the calculated optimal interest rate change at any time. For example, should this be done on a one step ahead basis, starting from the actual level of interest rates in the preceding period, or on a dynamic basis starting from what would have been the optimal level of interest rates in the preceding period? In practice, when the actual level of interest rates is not too far from the estimated optimal level, the results are qualitatively pretty similar.

Anyhow, both sets of results are shown in Table B. This compares the actual changes in interest rates in each month in the United States with those that would have been made under the optimal policy rule(s), assuming stochastic additive uncertainty. The interest changes, which in the model can take any size, are here grouped into 'bins', whereby any optimal change between plus and minus 12½ basis points is counted as a 'no change' decision, any optimal change between 12½ and 37½ basis points is grouped into the 25 basis point (¼%) change 'bin', and so on. You should also note that, for reasons that will become increasingly obvious, I have grouped all changes that were continuations of an existing direction of change on the left

of the table, and all changes that reversed the direction of movement on the right hand side. Let me draw three features to your attention. First, under the optimal policy, there would have been 55 (47) changes[1] over this time period of ½% or more; in reality, there were 23. So policy is less aggressive than the model would suggest was optimal. Second, no change was made in practice more than twice as often as this model indicated would be optimal. Third, whereas the number of continuations in the model, 76 (58), was very close to the number actually made, the number of reversals in the model, 36 (55), was about four times those made historically (10). Compared with the model predictions, the Fed has a bias to make no change, appeared extraordinarily reluctant to reverse the direction of change, and tended to eschew large, aggressive movements.

Because of the importance I attach to this kind of analysis, I have been encouraging the Bank staff to complete a companion study for the United Kingdom to that done by Sack for the United States—not that they needed much encouragement from me; it was already on their agenda. Unfortunately, the estimation of satisfactory VAR models for the United Kingdom is a much more complex exercise. The United Kingdom a more open economy, which requires a model with a larger dimension; policy regime changes have been more frequent and more drastic; and the price puzzle[2] has been even more stubbornly pervasive in the UK than in US models. Be that as it may, despite all the difficulties, Chris Salmon and Ben Martin of the Bank of England staff are now constructing a VAR model (on a broadly similar basis to that estimated for the United States) for the United Kingdom. I hope that their work will soon appear as a Bank of England *Working Paper*. This VAR is quarterly, from 1981 Q2 to 1998 Q2. A serious problem with this is that there were several major monetary policy regime changes during this period, which have, perforce, to be averaged out in this exercise.

Moreover, in the United Kingdom, for a variety of reasons relating to shifting policy regimes (eg Medium Term Financial Strategy, shadowing the DM, exchange rate mechanism, etc), and/or possibly to policy errors, actual interest rates were often markedly out of line for persistent periods from the optimal policies estimated from VARs. So the only comparison that made sense in the United Kingdom was that between actual policy and that estimated

Table B
Optimal interest rate changes from the United States

Certainty	Number of continuations							Number of reversals						
	Up >0.5	Down >0.5	Up 0.5	Down 0.5	Up 0.25	Down 0.25	No change	Up 0.25	Down 0.25	Up 0.5	Down 0.5	Up >0.5	Down >0.5	
(a) One step ahead change on actual	9	6	11	10	21	19	40	8	9	7	6	3	3	152
(b) Dynamic change on own lag	7	3	4	11	12	21	39	20	13	5	8	3	6	152
(c) Actual policy	1	6	9	5	9	20	92	4	4	1	1	0	0	152

(1) The number refers to row (a) and the number in brackets refers to row (b) of Tables B and F throughout this article.
(2) In such VAR models, the initial response of inflation to an interest rate increase is often, perversely, to increase.

Table C
Actual number of interest rate changes

	Number of continuations									Number of reversals							
	Up >1	Down >1	Up 0.75	Down 0.75	Up 0.5	Down 0.5	Up 0.25	Down 0.25	No change	Up 0.25	Down 0.25	Up 0.5	Down 0.5	Up 0.75	Down 0.75	Up >1	Down >1
UK additive uncertainty (a)	4	6	2	3	3	5	3	1	1	2	4	7	5	2	2	8	8
UK actual policy (a)	2	8	2	3	2	9	2	8	14	1	0	1	2	2	1	5	4
US actual policy (b)	2	1	2	5	3	5	2	7	15	1	2	1	0	1	1	0	1

(a) 1981.3–1998:2 (66 observations).
(b) 1984.3–1996:4 (49 observations).

Table D
Percentage of total interest rate decisions

	Number of continuations									Number of reversals							
	Up >1	Down >1	Up 0.75	Down 0.75	Up 0.5	Down 0.5	Up 0.25	Down 0.25	No change	Up 0.25	Down 0.25	Up 0.5	Down 0.5	Up 0.75	Down 0.75	Up >1	Down >1
UK additive uncertainty (a)	6	9	3	5	5	8	5	2	2	3	6	11	8	3	3	12	12
UK actual policy (a)	3	12	3	5	3	14	3	12	21	2	0	2	3	3	2	8	6
US actual policy (b)	4	2	4	10	6	10	4	14	31	2	4	2	0	2	2	0	2

(a) 1981.3–1998:2 (66 observations).
(b) 1984.3–1996:4 (49 observations).

as the optimal dynamic change on the previous optimal value.

Anyhow, we have now used this quarterly model for the United Kingdom to try to replicate Sack's results. This is shown for quarterly data in Table C, on the assumption of stochastic additive uncertainty only (ie certainty-equivalence). Recall, however, that Sack's model was monthly, which accords more closely with the periodicity of monetary decision-making. So if there were three consecutive monthly 25 basis point changes in the quarter in the United Kingdom, this would come out in our quarterly figures as a single 75 basis point change. To facilitate comparison, we have also recalculated Sack's results for US actual policy at a quarterly frequency, and this is also shown in Table C for the actual numbers, and in Table D for exactly comparable proportions.

What this shows is that, as in the United States, 'optimal' policy, subject only to additive uncertainty, would be far more activist (only one 'no change' in 17 years, compared with 14 in reality), and much more prone to reversals (38 under the optimal policy, compared with 16 in reality); the number of continuations in practice (36) was again quite close to that under the optimal policy. What is, however, strikingly different between the two countries is the apparently much greater willingness in the United Kingdom to change interest rates by considerably larger steps. We believe that this is because UK policy had to respond to larger shocks, more regime changes and perhaps worse policy errors.

So the gist of my assessment is that, both in the United Kingdom and the United States, there are about the same number of steps in the same continuing direction, many more 'no change' decisions, and many fewer reversals of

direction than might appear optimal under a certainty-equivalent model. In the United States, but not in the United Kingdom, there were also fewer large changes in interest rates than would have appeared optimal. Moreover, this is not just an Anglo-Saxon phenomenon. A general dislike of making large aggressive changes in interest rates, and the bias towards 'no change' decisions, is well documented for all developed countries. What I would like to emphasise here is that a concern to avoid reversals of direction is also well-nigh universal, as documented in the latest 1998 BIS *Annual Report*. This *Report* comments (page 68), and I quote,

'There is some evidence that a dislike of reversals of this sort is not uncommon in the industrial countries. Central banks generally move interest rates several times in the same direction before reversing policy. Moreover, the interval between policy adjustments is typically considerably longer when the direction is changed. As the size of the steps at turning-points is not systematically larger than at other times, this pattern of adjustments risks being interpreted as a tendency to move 'too little, too late'. One possible rationalisation for such behaviour is uncertainty about the policy impulses. Such uncertainty is likely to be greatest at the turning-points of the interest rate cycle. A further reason for wishing to avoid frequent interest rate reversals is the desire to provide clear guidance to markets, both to strengthen the pass-through along the yield curve and to avoid destabilising markets'.

If you rank countries in terms of the ratio of continuations to reversals, with the top being Austria with 63 continuations to 2 reversals, the United Kingdom comes 9th out of 12, well below the median, so the evidence suggests that we have actually been comparatively more willing than most to change direction.

Bank of England Quarterly Bulletin: February 1999

Table E
Policy rate adjustments

Sequence of adjustment

	Number of changes				Average duration (a)				Average change (b)			
	++	+-	-+	--	++	+-	-+	--	++	+-	-+	--
United States	6	1	2	22	41	108	321	39	0.46	0.25	0.25	0.28
Germany	65	31	31	107	22	24	34	14	0.25	0.19	0.12	0.15
France	8	5	6	86	47	72	77	31	0.51	0.40	0.83	0.21
Italy	9	6	6	24	122	182	121	83	1.31	0.88	0.96	0.73
United Kingdom	28	17	18	84	36	69	49	23	0.94	0.50	0.77	0.37
Canada	10	1	2	21	22	57	103	21	0.43	0.25	0.25	0.25
Spain	4	5	4	33	56	72	67	35	0.42	0.24	0.35	0.38
Australia	2	1	1	17	43	413	264	67	1.00	0.50	0.75	0.79
Netherlands	55	27	28	108	16	15	32	15	0.42	0.53	0.40	0.21
Belgium	9	7	8	82	17	10	82	10	0.45	0.24	0.34	0.14
Sweden	14	1	2	24	16	132	146	10	0.12	0.25	0.27	0.18
Austria	15	1	1	48	70	42	150	34	0.38	0.50	0.25	0.16

Notes: + + = two successive increases (tightenings), + - = increase followed by decrease;
- + = decrease followed by increase; - - = two successive decreases (easings)

Policy rates and starting dates of the sample periods. Australia, official target rate, 23 January 1990; Austria, GOMEX, 6 May 1985; Belgium, central rate,
29 January 1991; Canada, operating bands 15 April 1994. France, tender rate, 4 January 1982; Germany, repurchase rate, 19 June 1979; Italy, discount rate,
1 January 1978; Netherlands, special advances rate, 1 January 1978; Spain, repurchase rate, 14 May 1990; Sweden, repurchase rate, 1 June 1994; United Kingdom,
Band 1 bank bills, 1 January 1978; United States, federal funds target rate, 10 August 1989. End of sample periods: 31 March 1998.

(a) In days.
(b) In percentage points.

So the common practice among central banks is to make long series of small steps in the same direction. This behavioural pattern is partly, but only partly, picked up in the econometrics for the Taylor rule, in the guise of the near-unitary value of the lagged dependent variable.

John Taylor, of the eponymous rule, has studied the comparative virtues of rules of this kind, both with and without smoothing of the form empirically observed, in simulations carried out in some ten models of various economies. His conclusions (1998d, page 11) are that, 'Comparing such rules [with smoothing] with the two rules that do not respond to the lagged interest rate shows that neither type of rule dominates across all models. However, for a number of models the rules with lagged interest rates have very poor performance with extraordinarily large variances. These could be Great Depression or Great Inflation scenarios in some models. It turns out, however, that the models that predict very poor performance for the lagged interest rate rules are models without rational expectations, or in which forward looking effects are not strong in the model. Why? Interest rate rules which respond with a lag exploit people's forward-looking behaviour; these rules assume that people will expect later increases in interest rates if such increases are needed to reduce inflation'.

Put another way, it is alright for the authorities to act slowly in a series of cautious small steps, just as long as a forward-looking public can effectively undo such cautious lags by immediate anticipation. In a similar vein, Marvin Goodfriend (1991) has argued that an anticipated series of small steps in short rates will trigger off a large change in longer-term bond yields when the sequence starts, and that it may be the latter that has more effect in some economies in influencing demand. This may be particularly the case in countries where the objectives, and forecasts of the likelihood of reaching those objectives, are not regularly and publicly quantified.

It surely must be the case that the eventual determination to vary interest rates enough to defeat inflation is more important than the speed, or path, by which this is done: the Bundesbank, for example, is even more prone to smoothing than has been the case in the United Kingdom. When the reputation for determination is in place, then the ultimate measures will probably be broadly anticipated by the public. But even if it can thus be claimed that smoothing is, in general, a fairly harmless exercise, it still leaves the question of why the monetary authorities in virtually all major countries have adhered to this behaviour pattern so determinedly. What have we failed to understand?

The failings, of course, lie far more in the standard economic models than in the practical behaviour of central bankers. One of the central problems is that uncertainty is far more complex, insidious and pervasive than represented by the additive error terms in standard models. The more essential uncertainty is multiplicative, ie attached to the coefficients in the models—or, in simpler terms, we do not know the true workings of the economic system. In some cases, we do not even know which coefficients are non-zero, ie which variables are relevant. But even when we do know which variables to include in our equations, we certainly do not know what the true value of their coefficients may be.

Let me give you just two topical examples of such general uncertainties. First, in an open economy, one of the main ways in which interest rate changes have an impact on the economy is via their effect on exchange rates. But can anyone, you, me, the MPC, predict the market's response at all accurately in advance? Second, to revert to the Taylor rule, discussed earlier, life would be so much easier if we knew exactly, when we come to take decisions, what was the sign of the output gap, or of its kissing cousin, the natural rate of unemployment, let alone their true arithmetic values. The regressions on the Taylor rule that I showed you earlier were predicated on the assumption that the way we estimate the underlying rate of productive potential is absolutely correct, and known with certainty.[1] Whereas, in practice, most governments' supply-side measures are intended to give a beneficial shift to the growth of productive potential and to the natural rate of unemployment. Moreover, it is patently obvious that such supply-side factors have varied over time, though, as in continental Europe, not always for the better.

As the Governor recently said in his speech to the TUC,

'The truth is that neither we, nor they, nor anyone else, can know with any great certainty *precisely* where demand is in relation to capacity in the economy as a whole. Still less do we know where it is likely to be over the next couple of years—and that is the more relevant consideration, given the time it takes before changes in interest rates have their full effects'.

What even is the current sign of the output gap? As is evidenced by our differing votes, we in the MPC can and do individually see the same underlying data having different implications for that gap. Even in the United States, where the natural rate has been historically most stable, there are always arguments that new developments, a new paradigm, may have caused significant shifts in underlying productivity and the natural rate.

Such uncertainty would matter less if it was not for the associated stylised fact that policy actions, notably monetary policy, only take effect with long lags. In the presence of multiplicative uncertainty, it would seem optimal to proceed cautiously, as Bill Brainard (1967) first demonstrated. Indeed, but if there were not such long lags, then the sensibly cautious tendency to underdo the dosage would become rapidly apparent, and just as rapidly rectified. But the problem is that it can take so long for cautious moves to become recognised as such, that the inherent dynamic of the economy can lead to inflationary, or deflationary, momentum building up in the meantime. Or in simpler terms, excessive caution, even though entirely understandable in an uncertain world, can lead to the syndrome of 'too little, too late', or, as the Americans put it, 'falling behind the curve'.

It is, perhaps, in this latter context that the publication of a central bank's inflation forecast becomes so crucial. Despite being properly hedged around with probability distributions, where our uncertainties decently peep out from under our fan charts, and with, of course, the repeated mantra that we never take the forecast either literally or slavishly, the publication of the forecast nevertheless acts as a discipline on us. Against the natural tendency to defer action in an uncertain context, the publication of the forecast holds the MPC's feet to the fire. If the projected outcome for prospective inflation is significantly different from the target (and please allow me just for today to duck the question of how one might assess exactly what is a 'significant' difference), then the MPC comes under strong pressure to rectify the situation. We all know that forecasts are fallible, but without a published forecast, in a world of long lags, the tendency towards 'too little, too late' would become much worse.

'Too little, too late' could, in principle, be perfectly symmetric, in the sense that the response to deflationary pressures could be just as delayed and hesitant as the response to inflationary pressures. And we can all think of episodes, though mostly in other countries, where we might have preferred a more aggressively expansionary response to deflationary pressures. Yet it is my personal opinion that this syndrome is likely to be somewhat asymmetric. Interest rate increases are rarely popular, while expansionary measures are so. In a world of uncertainty, where what you surely know is that you do not know either the future, or even really the present state of the economy, there is in my view an absolutely natural, and perfectly human, tendency towards delaying restrictive action for longer than expansionary measures. I must, however, add that an equally common public perception is that central bankers so hunger for 'credibility' that they have an asymmetric bias towards tightening. Perhaps the two biases roughly balance out?

Again, my discussant, Charlie Bean, got the analysis absolutely right. Having, correctly in my view, largely dismissed the idea that politicians underhandedly try to aim for output levels intentionally in excess of the equilibrium, he goes on to say,

---

(1) There is some (slight) distinction between parameter uncertainty, whereby $Y_t = a + (b + \varepsilon_t)X_t + u_t$,

$\mu\varepsilon = 0$, $\sigma^2\varepsilon = K_1$, $\mu u = 0$, $\sigma^2 u = K_2$

and measurement error of Y_t, (or less likely in most cases of X_t), whereby the ultimate best estimate of Y is inaccurately measured, especially at first, by $\hat{Y}_t$, with

$Y_t = \hat{Y}_t + \eta_t$, so that

$(\hat{Y}_t + \eta_t) = a + b(X_t) + u_t$

$\mu\eta = 0$, $\sigma^2\eta = K_3$, $\mu u = 0$, $\sigma^2 u = K_2$ (K's are constants),

as my discussant, Charlie Bean, has pointed out. As the above formulation indicates, however, their implications are very closely similar.

Orphanides (1998b, also see 1998a) commented as follows:

'In summary, the presence of noise in the data acts as a counterweight to the highly responsive policy that policy-makers might have otherwise adopted to stabilise the economy. This result can be understood intuitively. When a policy-maker suspects that the information he is being provided with regarding the state of the economy is subject to significant noise, he should be reluctant to adjust his policy instrument as much as he would if he could trust the picture of the economy being painted with the data. This suggests that policy will be less activist than would be efficient with better information. More generally, in an environment where the observed behaviour of the economy does not conform well with the policy-maker's beliefs about the underlying state of the economy, the policy-maker ought to properly take into account that much of the information he is provided with describes the economy with substantial error. This, then will call for a cautious response to apparent imbalances in the economy.

It is worth noting that the motivation for this caution differs from the one associated with uncertainty regarding the model's parameters. Following Brainard (1967), it has been recognised that parameter uncertainty may lead a Bayesian policy-maker to reduce the policy instrument responsiveness to economic imbalances'.

Bank of England Quarterly Bulletin: February 1999

'A far more plausible explanation as to why governments might be inclined to push output above the natural rate is that they are expected to deliver a high level of output through the *whole range* of their policies, and are rewarded by the electorate if they achieve this, and punished if they do not. The level of economic activity thus becomes a signal of government competence. Furthermore the natural rate is not known with any certainty, and the beneficial output effects of monetary policy expansion typically show through a year or so ahead of their effects on inflation. Thus governments, particularly near election time, may be more prepared to risk an expansionary monetary policy than is really prudent, arguing that such a policy is not likely to be inflationary, but rather is consistent with their successful effects to raise the output potential of the economy'.

The point that I would like to make here is that such pressures affect central bankers, and even independent members of MPCs, in exactly the same kind of way, even if not to the same extent, that they affect politicians. Nevertheless, there are reasons to hope, and indeed to expect, that an operationally independent monetary authority should be much more resistant to an asymmetric, and excessive, caution in response to uncertainty. First, we do not have colleagues who look to us for re-election. Second, we have a publicly stated, quantified, and symmetric, inflation target to meet, and we can and should be held accountable for achieving that. Third, we have imposed on ourselves the discipline of a regularly published forecast of inflation, which provides a continuing public score-card of how we feel that we are doing in meeting that objective, and we are more likely to respect that discipline than politicians have, perhaps, been in the past.

Let me revert to my central concern about the nature of uncertainty. Unless there is a good reason, and there usually is not, to believe that there is negative inverse correlation between the additive and multiplicative sources of uncertainty, then the existence of multiplicative uncertainty and measurement noise will generally cause the authorities to move in smaller steps. On average, they should underdo the dosage, since a larger change in the instrument, given multiplicative uncertainty, will add to the variance of outcomes. Given the loss function, there is a trade-off between getting as near as possible to the desired value of the target variable and increasing the prospective variance of the target variable(s).

From my personal viewpoint, the essential features of the economy that both set the agenda for, and complicate the life of, the monetary authorities are the interaction between the effects, and implications, of multiplicative uncertainty on the one hand and long lags in the effects of monetary policy on the other. I need hardly remind you that virtually all analysis of monetary policy games, going well beyond textbooks to what are presumed to be state-of-the-art articles, has been based on models in which neither feature appears at all.

We all know that, in principle, such multiplicative Brainard uncertainty should lead to greater caution in varying policy instruments, here interest rates, because a large change in rates will have an uncertain effect on outcomes, and hence raise the possibility of potentially large social losses. But a problem for practitioners is that no one until recently has made much empirical study of how quantitatively important such Brainard uncertainty should be regarded as in practice. Let me put it another way: the manner in which monetary authorities around the world appear to vary interest rates in a series of consecutive small steps of the same sign might be optimal if, and very likely only if, multiplicative uncertainty was indeed a problem of the first order of importance.

Is it such? Even if practical central bankers may not have known that they were talking prose all their lives, have they in practice been acting almost optimally? Until recently, there was no serious attempt to measure this empirically. But now, Brian Sack of the staff of the Fed's Board of Governors has made an excellent first stab of doing just that, in the article that I have already quoted. He uses a five-variable VAR model with production, unemployment, inflation and commodity prices as the non-policy variable, and the federal funds rate as the policy variable. This exercise can both incorporate the long lags involved, and allow one to estimate the variance/co-variance matrix for the coefficients, and hence the extent of multiplicative uncertainty.

Not surprisingly, he found that such an exercise brought the actual historical conduct of US monetary policy much closer into line with what the model indicated would be optimal — see, for example, his Figure 5, here Chart 6. Thus he concluded (page 28),

Chart 6
Actual and optimal funds rate under parameter uncertainty

Note: The optimal funds rate is based on the policy rule that solves the dynamic programming problem. The optimal funds rate value is the rate predicted by the policy rule given the actual history of the economy at each point in time.

'Gradual movements in the federal funds rate do not necessarily indicate that the Federal Reserve has an interest rate smoothing incentive. Dynamic structure and parameter uncertainty can account for a considerable portion of the gradual funds rate movements that are observed. The intertemporal behaviour of the targeted variables causes the funds rate to move in a particular direction over substantial periods of time. However, under additive uncertainty, the expected path of the funds rate is much more volatile and reacts to changes in the economy more aggressively than the observed funds rate. This smoothing of the interest rate can be explained by the fact that the Fed does not know perfectly the structure of the economy. Uncertainty arising from imprecise estimation of the VAR coefficients is minimised at the level of the funds rate predicted by the policy rule that has been historically implemented. An aggressive policy would result in high expected variance for the targeted variables because the Fed has traditionally smoothed the funds rate. The policy rule that accounts for parameter uncertainty therefore reacts to changes in the state of the economy with gradual movements in the funds rate, which reduces the excess volatility of the expected policy and limits the deviation of this policy from the observed level of the funds rate.

Although the uncertain dynamic structure results in gradual funds rate movements, there remains an element of interest rate smoothing that cannot be explained in this exercise'.

Nonetheless, there are still several remaining differences between such central bank behaviour in practice and those actions that would appear optimal, even after taking account of multiplicative Brainard uncertainty. Let me revert to Table B, showing the implied distribution of interest rate changes, but this time also including the result with multiplicative Brainard uncertainty.

What this table, Table F, shows is that once one takes Brainard uncertainty into account, the paucity of large

aggressive jumps in interest rates becomes largely explained. With Brainard uncertainty, there would only have been 23 (24) changes[1] of 50 basis points, or more in the US case, compared with the 23 found historically.

What, however, the empirical application of Brainard uncertainty still largely fails to explain is the small number of reversals. Under our VAR models, with or without Brainard uncertainty, the number of reversals of direction of policy should have been some three to five times as common as found in practice, depending on whether one uses as the basis for judgment the one step ahead or the dynamic prediction from the model.

Once again, I have been encouraging the Bank staff to replicate this same study for the United Kingdom, and for the VAR model, already briefly described, the results of the dynamic optimal policy under multiplicative uncertainty are shown in Table G (alongside the optimal policy with additive uncertainty only, and actual policy). As with the United States, recognition of multiplicative uncertainty should make policy-makers far more cautious, with many fewer large step changes. Indeed, what is remarkable from Table G is that the actual number of large step changes (more than 1% in a quarter), at 19, was more than four times the number (4) that should have been made in this period had policy-makers been consistently following an average optimal policy adjusted for multiplicative uncertainty.

What is also remarkable is that such reversals as occurred in practice in the United Kingdom were predominantly very large (9 of 1% or more, as compared with 7 under 1%), in contrast with actual continuations (10 of 1% or more, 26 under 1%). Under multiplicative uncertainty, the numbers

Table F
Optimal interest rate changes for the United States

Certainty	Number of continuations							Number of reversals						
	Up >0.5	Down >0.5	Up 0.5	Down 0.5	Up 0.25	Down 0.25	No change	Up 0.25	Down 0.25	Up 0.5	Down 0.5	Up >0.5	Down >0.5	
(a) One step ahead change on actual	9	6	11	10	21	19	40	8	9	7	6	3	3	152
(b) Dynamic change on own lag	7	3	4	11	12	21	39	20	13	5	8	3	6	152
(c) Actual policy	1	6	9	5	9	20	92	4	4	1	1	0	0	152
Uncertainty	Number of continuations							Number of reversals						
	Up >0.5	Down >0.5	Up 0.5	Down 0.5	Up 0.25	Down 0.25	No change	Up 0.25	Down 0.25	Up 0.5	Down 0.5	Up >0.5	Down >0.5	
(a) One step ahead change on actual	1	0	7	9	31	18	50	12	18	5	0	1	0	152
(b) Dynamic change on own lag	1	0	5	8	19	35	57	8	9	3	3	2	2	152
(c) Actual policy	1	6	9	5	9	20	92	4	4	1	1	0	0	152

		Total continuations			Total reversals	
		Up	Down	No change	Up	Down
(a) One step ahead change on actual	Certainty	41	35	40	18	18
	Uncertainty	39	27	50	18	18
(b) Dynamic change on own lag	Certainty	23	35	39	28	27
	Uncertainty	25	43	57	13	14
(c) Actual policy		19	31	92	5	5

1984:5-1996:12 (152 observations).

(1) See footnote (1) on page 106.

Bank of England Quarterly Bulletin: February 1999

Table G
Optimal interest rate changes for the United Kingdom

	Number of continuations								No change	Number of reversals							
	Up >1	Down >1	Up 0.75	Down 0.75	Up 0.5	Down 0.5	Up 0.25	Down 0.25		Up 0.25	Down 0.25	Up 0.5	Down 0.5	Up 0.75	Down 0.75	Up >1	Down >1
Additive uncertainty	4	6	2	3	3	5	3	1	1	2	4	7	5	2	2	8	8
Multiplicative uncertainty	0	3	3	2	1	7	6	10	14	4	4	3	3	3	2	0	1
Actual policy	2	8	2	3	2	9	2	8	14	1	0	1	2	2	1	5	4

1981 3–1998 2 (66 observations).

for reversals were 1 of 1% or more, 19 under, and for continuations, 3 of 1% or more, 29 under. If we should make the (admittedly extreme) assumption that these really large reversals were mainly due to regime changes and recognition of prior policy errors, then the UK figures show roughly the same ratio of smaller reversals between optimal policy under multiplicative uncertainty to those in practice, ie 19 to 7, as in the United States.

Thus, in the United Kingdom, one problem is to explain why there were so many really large changes in interest rates in practice, given that under Brainard uncertainty, the optimal changes should have ideally been smaller. If these, especially the reversals, can be accounted for by regime changes/policy errors, then we are left, as in the US case, with a problem of accounting for a general, apparent reluctance to reverse the direction of change. And let me emphasise and repeat that I do not think that this latter is just an Anglo-Saxon propensity. It is, I believe, common to all major central banks.

The distributions from such a VAR model probably provide an upper bound on the degree of caution, and interest rate smoothing, that should theoretically be undertaken, because the construction of this model completely leaves out the advantage that can be obtained from more aggressive action, whereby one then learns more about the working of the economy—which should, in principle, reduce *future* uncertainty (see, for example, Sack (1998b)). Thus, Volker Wieland (1998, page 2) wrote,

'There are a number of reasons to believe that such a Brainard-type analysis overstates the case for gradualism. For example, Caplin and Leahy (1996) show that in a game between a policy-maker who attempts to stimulate the economy and potential investors, a cautious policy move may be ineffectual, because investors anticipate lower interest rates in the future. Another reason, investigated in this paper, is that a more aggressive policy move may generate more information, which would improve the precision of future estimates and thereby future policy performance'.

Indeed, two eminent American economists, Tom Sargent (1998) and James Stock (1998), have recently argued that a central bank seeking to insure against the worst risks coming about (a 'minimax' strategy) in the context of multiplicative uncertainty should actually be more aggressive, not less. The implied corollary, of course, is that if such aggression should prove to have been unnecessary,

the measures can be reversed in a subsequent period. But such a reversal of policy is just what central banks appear, on this evidence, loth to do.

Not only the evidence that I have presented here, but also other anecdotal reports, suggest that central bankers are, as a class, notably reluctant to make a move on interest rates that might subsequently need to be reversed (except under crisis conditions, eg relating to a pegged exchange rate target, or after a major policy regime change), and much more so than our currently best models suggest would be optimal.

There are two reasons, not mutually exclusive, why this might be so. The first I owe mainly to Michael Woodford (1998). Assume that for some reason the central bank wants to reduce the variance of the level of short-term interest rates. Nevertheless, the central bank wants to maintain the ability to have a quick and strong effect on the economy at a time of a major shock hitting the economy. If the central bank can commit to behaving in such a way that any small reversal in direction of change will be followed by several similar steps in the same direction, then forward-looking rational agents will make large changes to their behaviour whenever reversals occur. But the downside for the central bank, the corollary, is that it must be cautious about reversing direction in the face of minor shocks, since too many short-lived reversals would limit its power to combat major shocks, given of course the initial reluctance to increase the variance of short-term rates.

The second reason is tied up with the credibility issue. As I explained earlier, when policy is already just about on course, so that the decision is finely balanced, it might indeed be technically optimal to change one's views and one's decisions, and the direction of movement of interest rates, as news comes in, even from month to month, certainly from quarter to quarter. It seems difficult to explain this to outside commentators, who often perceive such reversals as evidence of inconsistency, patent error, and irresolution. We all react to criticism. As long as commentators castigate the monetary authorities for moves that turn out after the event to have been inappropriate and unnecessary, then that will tend to reinforce the tendency towards 'too little, too late'. The lessons from such outside criticism on changing one's mind is that no change in interest rates should be made unless and until the probability is quite strong that a subsequent change in the same direction will also subsequently be needed. That is, I would argue, not the optimal way to conduct policy, but it is, I believe, what happens around the world.

To conclude, there is an absolute yawning gap between the general perception of non-economist outsiders that reversals of policy, changes of mind, are to be deplored and castigated as evidence of error, irresolution and general incompetence, and the apparent findings from our economic models that such reversals should optimally occur some four, or so, times more frequently than they do in practice. Maybe our models are missing something important. If not, we have then singularly failed to explain to the world at large how policy should be carried out. Either way, there is still an enormous amount of work to be done.

References

Bank for International Settlements (1998), (BIS), *Annual Report*, Basle, Switzerland.

Bean, C (1998), 'The New UK Monetary Arrangements: A View from the Literature', paper presented to the Academic Panel of HM Treasury, Centre for Economic Performance, LSE, March.

Brainard, W C (1967), 'Uncertainty and the Effectiveness of Policy', *American Economic Review*, 57(2), pages 411–25.

Caplin, A and Leahy, J (1996), 'Monetary Policy as a Process of Search', *American Economic Review*, 86(4), pages 689–702.

Clarida, R and Gertler, M (1997), 'How the Bundesbank Conducts Monetary Policy', C Romer and D Romer (ed), *Reducing Inflation*, (Chicago: University of Chicago Press).

Fischer, A M (1996), 'Central Bank Independence and Sacrifice Ratios', *Open Economies Review*, 7, pages 5–18.

George, E A J (1998), 'The objectives and current state of monetary policy', *Bank of England Quarterly Bulletin*, 38(4), pages 376–78, November.

Goodfriend, M (1991), 'Interest Rates and the Conduct of Monetary Policy', Carnegie-Rochester Conference Series on Public Policy, 34, pages 7–30.

Goodhart, C A E (1997), 'Why do the Monetary Authorities Smooth Interest Rates', Chapter 8 in *European Monetary Policy*, S Collignon (ed), (Pinter: London).

Haldane, A G, Batini, N and Whitley, J (1997), 'A Forward-Looking and Probabilistic Approach to Monetary Policy', paper prepared for the NBER Conference on 'Monetary Policy Rules' in January 1998, Bank of England, December.

King, M A (1997), 'The inflation target five years on', *Bank of England Quarterly Bulletin*, 37(4), pages 434–42, November.

Murchison, S and Siklos, P (1998), 'Central Bank Reaction Functions in Inflation and Non-Inflation Targeting Economies: Are They Informative About the Conduct of Monetary Policy', *Working Paper*, Department of Economics, Wilfrid Laurier University, Waterloo, Ontario, August.

Nelson, E (1998), 'Taylor Rule Estimates for the UK, 1972–1997', *Bank of England Draft Working Paper*, October.

Bank of England Quarterly Bulletin: February 1999

Orphanides, A (1998a), 'Monetary Policy Rules Based on Real-Time Data', *Finance and Economics Discussion Series*, 1998–03, Board of Governors of the Federal Reserve System.

Orphanides, A (1998b), 'Monetary Policy Evaluation with Noisy Information', *Working Paper*, Board of Governors of the Federal Reserve System, October.

Peersman, G and Smets, F (1998), 'The Taylor Rule: A Useful Monetary Policy Guide for the ECB?', paper presented at the Conference on Monetary Policy of the ESCB: Strategic and Implementation Issues, Bocconi University, Milan, 6–7 July.

Sack, B (1998a), 'Does the Fed Act Gradually? A VAR Analysis', *Finance and Economics Discussion Series* # 1998–17, Board of Governors of the Federal Reserve System, April.

Sack, B (1998b), 'Uncertainty, Learning and Gradual Monetary Policy', *Finance and Economics Discussion Series*, Board of Governors of the Federal Reserve System, July.

Sargent, T J (1998), Discussion of 'Policy Rules for Open Economies' by Laurence Ball, papers presented at the NBER Conference on 'Monetary Policy Rules', Islamorada, Florida, January.

Stock, J H (1998), 'Monetary Policy in a Changing Economy: Indicators, Rules, and the Shift towards Intangible Output', paper presented at the Eighth International IMES, Bank of Japan Conference, Tokyo, June.

Svensson, Lars E O (1997a), 'Inflation Forecast Targeting: Implementation and Monitoring Inflation Targets', *European Economic Review* 41, pages 1,111–46.

Svensson, Lars E O (1997b), 'Inflation Targeting: Some Extensions', *NBER Working Paper No 5962*.

Svensson, Lars E O (1998), 'Inflation Targeting as a Monetary Policy Rule', in preparation.

Svensson, Lars E O and Rudebusch, G R (1998), 'Policy Rules for Inflation Targeting', paper presented at the Conference on 'Central Bank Inflation Targeting', FRB San Francisco, March.

Taylor, J B (1998a), 'An Historical Analysis of Monetary Policy Rules', in Taylor (1998b), forthcoming.

Taylor, J B (1998b), 'Monetary Policy Rules', *Chicago University Press*, forthcoming.

Taylor, J B (1998c) (ed), 'The Robustness and Efficiency of Monetary Policy Rules as Guidelines for Interest Rate Setting by the European Central Bank', prepared for Sveriges Riksbank-IIES Conference on Monetary Policy Rules, Stockholm, June 12–13.

Taylor, J B (1998d), 'Information Technology and Monetary Policy', paper prepared for the Eighth International IMES/Bank of Japan Conference, Tokyo, June.

Wieland, V (1998), 'Monetary Policy and Uncertainty about the Natural Unemployment Rate', *Finance and Economics Discussion Series*, pages 1,998–2,022, Board of Governors of the Federal Reserve System.

Woodford, M (1998), 'Optimal Monetary Policy Inertia', paper presented at the Money Macro Conference in London, and at the Monetary Policy Conference in Frankfurt; Department of Economics, Princeton University, September.

Wright, S (1997), 'Monetary Policy, Nominal Interest Rates, and Long-Horizon Inflation Uncertainty', *Working Paper*, Cambridge University, November.

[11]

Available online at www.sciencedirect.com

SCIENCE DIRECT®

ELSEVIER   Journal of Monetary Economics 50 (2003) 605–631

www.elsevier.com/locate/econbase

Monetary policy evaluation with noisy information ☆

Athanasios Orphanides*

Division of Monetary Affairs, Board of Governors of the Federal Reserve System, Washington, DC 20551, USA

Received 15 November 2000; received in revised form 12 July 2002; accepted 9 September 2002

Abstract

This study investigates the implications of noisy information regarding the measurement of economic activity for the evaluation of monetary policy. Using a simple model of the U.S. economy, I show that failing to account for the actual level of information noise in the historical data provides a seriously distorted picture of feasible macroeconomic outcomes and produces inefficient policy rules. Naive adoption of policies identified as efficient when this difficulty is ignored results in macroeconomic performance worse than actual experience. When the noise content of the data is properly taken into account, policy reactions are cautious and less sensitive to the apparent imbalances in the unfiltered data. The resulting policy prescriptions reflect the recognition that excessively activist policy can increase rather than decrease economic instability.
Published by Elsevier Science B.V.

JEL classification: E52; E58

Keywords: Policy evaluation; Taylor rule; Optimal control; Observation noise; Inflation targeting; Natural growth targeting

---

☆ I would like to thank Richard Anderson, Charles Calomiris, Carl Christ, Bill English, Milton Friedman, Greg Hess, David Lindsey, Brian Madigan, Allan Meltzer, Dick Porter, Simon van Norden, Kendrew Witt, participants at presentations at Johns Hopkins, Berkeley, Columbia, the Federal Reserve Bank of St. Louis, the International Monetary Fund, and at meetings of the Econometric Society and the Federal Reserve System Committee on Macroeconomics, for valuable discussions and comments. The opinions expressed are those of the author and do not necessarily reflect views of the Board of Governors of the Federal Reserve System.

*Tel.: +1-202-452-2654.

E-mail address: athanasios.orphanides@frb.gov (A. Orphanides).

0304-3932/03/$ - see front matter Published by Elsevier Science B.V.
doi:10.1016/S0304-3932(03)00027-8

606   *A. Orphanides / Journal of Monetary Economics 50 (2003) 605–631*

1. Introduction

Monetary policy decisions are made in real time and are based, by necessity, on preliminary data and estimates that contain considerable noise and are often substantially revised months or years after the event. While part of everyday life for policymakers, this aspect of the monetary policy process is often neglected in theoretical formulations of monetary policy, introducing a wedge between the promise of macroeconomic theory and the reality of macroeconomic practice.

Recognition of the complications resulting from the presence of noise is important for the study of monetary policy for two reasons: First, the evaluation of past policy is incorrect when it is based on the wrong data. That is, our understanding of the past becomes distorted. Second, the evaluation of alternative policy strategies is unrealistic and likely to mislead if it is based on the assumption that policy can react to either data that are not really available to policymakers when policy must be set or that are only available with substantial noise. That is, recommendations for better policy in the future become flawed.

Failing to recognize the extent of our ignorance leads to the false promise that an activist stabilization policy can have considerable success in fine-tuning the economy. Policy reactions that are unduly influenced by apparent imbalances in the data that may be mere artifacts of faulty measurement, however, risk increasing rather than reducing economic instability. This problem is by no means new to macroeconomic policy. For at least the past fifty years, it has been articulated many times by Milton Friedman, for instance in several of the essays he collected in 1953 and 1969 (Friedman, 1969). As early as 1947, Friedman (1947) questioned the value of control theory for taming business cycle fluctuations by observing:

> Contemporary interpreters of the course of business have notoriously failed not only to predict the course of business but even to identify the current state of affairs. It is not abnormal for some to assert that we are in the early stages of deflation and others that we are entering into an inflation (1947, p. 414).

Rather surprisingly, half a century later and despite considerable advances in the evaluation of monetary policy performance, the quantitative relevance of this issue for monetary policy design has yet to receive proper attention. On one hand, those who believe that our knowledge of the economy is seriously lacking suggest adopting passive rules that generally forego short-run stabilization. On the other, proponents of activist policy implicitly suggest that the information problem does not present a serious handicap.[1] This paper attempts to bridge this gap. My analysis draws on

---

[1] Earlier work that bears on this is issue includes Meltzer (1987), who presents evidence confirming substantial errors in assessing the economic outlook to argue against activist policy and McCallum (1994) who recognizing the difficulty of policy formulated with contemporaneous information, suggests that activist policy should be based on lagged information. Several authors, including Taylor (1999a), McCallum (1999), and Orphanides (2001), argue that measurement problems should be of concern for activist stabilization, and many others, including Estrella and Mishkin (1999), Kuttner (1992), Orphanides and van Norden (2002), and Wieland (1998) discuss the difficulties associated with the measurement of the concept of full employment in the context of stabilization policy. Since the working paper version of this study was completed, several

recent work that evaluates the performance of monetary policy formulated in terms of reactive interest-rate-based policy rules. Using a simple estimated model of the U.S. economy, I follow recent studies and evaluate alternative policy rules to assess the proper degree of monetary policy responsiveness to fluctuations in inflation and economic activity. However, instead of only performing these evaluations based on the assumption that the policymaker can observe the data promptly and accurately, I perform parallel experiments that recognize that in real time the policymaker observes the data with noise. Using the actual historical data that were available to policymakers in real time I am able to calibrate the degree of data imperfections to exactly match the level of noise faced by policymakers in practice. Comparison of the resulting alternative counterfactual experiments then presents a straightforward quantification of the impact of data noise on monetary policy.

The results confirm the common finding obtained in many recent stochastic simulation studies that, in the absence of noise, activist control could substantially improve upon the actual macroeconomic performance of the U.S. economy. However, I show that this improvement is illusory: It provides a seriously distorted picture of feasible outcomes that would occur once the noise in the data is taken into account. The resulting outcomes that would obtain had the supposedly optimal policies been adopted are in fact worse than the actual performance of the U.S. economy over the 1980s and early 1990s. The presence of noise acts as a counterweight to the highly responsive policy that would otherwise be appropriate to adopt. Recognition of the false promise of activist policies when the state of the economy cannot be confidently ascertained by the data leads to policy that tends to downplay the apparent short run fluctuations in the economy.

Even considering the limitations of the information available to policymakers in real time, however, my results suggest that there may be some room for short-run stabilization policy. In this sense, the suggested strategy for monetary policy is neither at the extreme of total passivity nor at the alternative of reckless activism. Paradoxically, by demonstrating that actual monetary policy since 1980 has not been activist enough to live up to the "promise" of stabilization policies that appear optimal when the information limitations are ignored, my analysis suggests that policy over the past two decades may have actually exhibited a balance which may also explain its success. Indeed, recognition of the limitations facing policymakers in practice significantly enhances our understanding of forces that may have shaped policy over this period. The results provide an explanation both for the aversion of policy to commit to any specific reactive policy rule, as well as for the apparent caution characterizing monetary policy in practice. As Blinder (1998) noted explaining the policy process during his tenure as Vice-Chairman at the Federal Reserve, "a little stodginess at the central bank is entirely appropriate". I show that data noise induces such stodginess. Further, since the degree of uncertainty regarding the reliability of incoming information continuously changes with the

---

(footnote continued)

authors have examined the quantitative significance of this problem for monetary policy. See, for example, Orphanides et al. (2000), Ehrmann and Smets (2001) and references therein.

evolution of the economic environment, the apparent degree of caution in policy decisions changes in tandem. The result, as Chairman Greenspan (1997) pointed out, is that "some element of discretion appears to be an unavoidable aspect of policymaking," and policy will appear eclectic, even though the Federal Reserve "has sought to exploit past patterns and regularities in a systematic way." In the end, "policymakers shy away from rule-based decisions because the rules assume that they know too much", as Kohn (1999, p. 197) observed.

2. The nature of the information problem

I restrict my attention to a family of simple reactive rules that specify that the Federal Reserve set the federal funds rate (the short nominal interest rate) as a linear function of the output gap y (that is deviations of output from its potential, $q - q^*$), and the difference between actual inflation, π, and its desired level, π^*. Defining the short-term real interest rate, r, as the nominal interest rate, f, minus inflation, the stance of monetary policy can be described by comparing the real rate to its long-run equilibrium level, r^*:

$$r - r^* = \gamma(\pi_t - \pi^*) + \delta y_t. \tag{1}$$

An appealing feature of this specification is that it encompasses the interest-rate rule suggested as descriptive of recent U.S. monetary policy by Taylor (1993). Taylor's rule can be obtained by re-writing Eq. (1) in terms of the federal funds rate: $f_t = r^* + \pi_t + \gamma(\pi_t - \pi^*) + \delta y_t$, and substituting the parameters $r^* = \pi^* = 2$, and $\gamma = \delta = \frac{1}{2}$. Starting with the large-scale model comparison studies reported in Bryant et al. (1993), rules of this type have been investigated in depth in simulation studies. (See, e.g. Henderson and McKibbin, 1993; and the collection of studies in Taylor, 1999b). As Taylor (1999a) observes in surveying this work, the simulation analysis has already produced a number of positive conclusions. Taylor's rule appears to perform rather well in a variety of models and as such appears to be quite robust to model specification. However, these studies also suggest that Taylor's rule is not efficient in terms of stabilizing output and inflation, and specifically find that rules with considerably higher response coefficients than Taylor's suggested parameters, $\gamma = \delta = \frac{1}{2}$, would result in better performance.

The information problem associated with these policy rules is that the performance of the rules is examined under the maintained assumption that the policymaker has accurate information regarding the current values of inflation and the output gap at his disposal when setting the interest rate. In fact, however, both inflation and the output gap are measured with considerable noise. Thus, as Orphanides (2001) points out, a more accurate representation of reality should take into account that the policymaker's observation regarding inflation, $\tilde{\pi}$, and the output gap, $\tilde{y}$, at the time policy decisions are being made, may in fact differ from the true underlying levels of inflation, π, and the output gap, y. Letting x denote the noise in the observation of inflation and z the noise in the observation of the output gap, we have:

$$\pi_t = \tilde{\pi}_t + x_t,$$

$$y_t = \tilde{y}_t + z_t.$$

Further, the true real interest rate corresponding to a chosen nominal interest rate is not the observed difference between the nominal interest rate and observed inflation, $\tilde{\pi}$, but the unobserved difference between the nominal interest rate and actual inflation, π.[2] It is important to note that in this formulation, $\tilde{\pi}_t$ and $\tilde{y}_t$ do not represent *filtered* estimates/forecasts of the true values of π_t and y_t but noisy observations. The errors, x_t and z_t are correlated with π_t and y_t and uncorrelated with $\tilde{\pi}_t$ and $\tilde{y}_t$, respectively.[3] I return to the filtering problem later on.

Once the presence of noise is recognized, it is evident that the proper specification of a simple rule specified to set the interest rate in terms of observed inflation and output is not Eq. (1) but rather:

$$\tilde{r}_t - r^* = \gamma(\tilde{\pi}_t - \pi^*) + \delta\tilde{y}_t, \tag{2}$$

where $\tilde{r} \equiv f - \tilde{\pi}$. Of course, in the absence of noise, $\pi_t = \tilde{\pi}_t$ and $y_t = \tilde{y}_t$ in which case Eqs. (1) and (2) are identical. Written in terms of the true measures of inflation and the gap, the interest rate policy corresponding to rule (2) is:

$$r_t - r^* = \gamma(\pi_t - \pi^*) + \delta y_t - \underbrace{((1+\gamma)x_t + \delta z_t)}_{\text{noise}}. \tag{3}$$

This reveals the nature of the information problem. By choosing positive response coefficients to the inflation and output gaps—as is appropriate for the stabilization of output and inflation—the policymaker inadvertently also reacts to the noise processes. This introduces undesirable movements in the interest rate, which feed back to the economy and generate unnecessary fluctuations in output and inflation. As a result, an efficient policy that properly accounts for the noise in the data might seek a balance and call for less activism than would be appropriate in the absence of noise.

---

[2] By concentrating attention on an ex-post concept of the real interest rate, instead of an ex-ante concept, I sidestep the issue of separating the noise in the policymaker's observation of inflation from the noise in the policymaker's observation of the public's inflation expectations. I discuss the obvious omitted complications later on. As written, the policy rule also reflects the assumption that the policymaker knows the level of the equilibrium real interest rate, r^*. In practice, this introduces additional complications for monetary control.

[3] Conceptually, as emphasized by Sargent (1989), one could envision two alternative models of measurement: the classical model in which observed data are reported with noise, and the filtering model in which the policymaker is presented with optimally filtered estimates/forecasts. Thus, the choice of model depends on the particular application. With regard to real-time assessments of inflation and the output gap available historically at the Federal Reserve, which is relevant for this analysis, Orphanides (2001) documents that the noise formulation is the most appropriate.

610   *A. Orphanides / Journal of Monetary Economics 50 (2003) 605–631*

3. A minimalist model

Most of the models employed in policy rule evaluations are sufficiently complicated that the reaction function in Eq. (1) is at best only approximately efficient. To assess the degree to which observation noise influences the performance of otherwise efficient policy rules, however, it is more convenient to start with a baseline case under which optimal policy can be exactly characterized by the simple reaction function in Eq. (1). To that end, I rely on the following minimalist model of the economy:

$$\pi_t = \pi_{t-1} + \alpha y_t + e_t, \tag{4}$$

$$y_t = \rho y_{t-1} - \xi(r_{t-1} - r^*) + u_t, \tag{5}$$

where α and ξ are positive, ρ is between zero and one, and e_t and u_t are disturbances drawn from independent normal distributions with zero means and variances σ_e^2 and σ_u^2.

The major advantage of this simple model is that the underlying state of the economy at the end of a period is completely described by just two things, inflation and the output gap during the period. Of course, this is too simplistic to characterize the short-run dynamic behavior of the economy at a high frequency, such as at monthly or quarterly intervals. Rather, a coarser division of time is required. As a result, I interpret the length of the period to be half a year.

The objective of monetary policy is to minimize a weighted sum of the unconditional variances of inflation and the output gap.

$$\mathscr{L} = \omega Var(\pi_t - \pi^*) + (1 - \omega)Var(y_t).$$

The weight, ω, which is assumed to be a fixed fraction between zero and one, reflects the tenacity with which the policymaker is willing to pursue inflation stabilization in the short run, at the expense of continuously aiming for full employment.[4]

3.1. Perfect information

Under the assumption that the observations of inflation and the output gap are timely and not subject to noise, derivation of the optimal policy in this model is a straightforward exercise in linear-quadratic control. (See Appendix A for details.) The solution takes exactly the form of Eq. (1) and optimal policy is described by:

$$r_t - r^* = \gamma^N(\pi_t - \pi^*) + \delta^N y_t. \tag{6}$$

---

[4] Thus, a weight approaching one would reflect King's (1997) "inflation nutter," a policymaker who places no weight on output stabilization.

A. Orphanides / Journal of Monetary Economics 50 (2003) 605–631   611

The optimal response coefficients, γ^N and δ^N, can be computed analytically in terms of the model parameters, α, ξ and ρ, and the policymaker's preferences, ω:

$$\gamma^N = \frac{-\alpha\omega + \sqrt{4(1-\omega)\omega + (\alpha\omega)^2}}{2(1-\omega)\xi},$$

$$\delta^N = \frac{\rho}{\xi}.$$

As can be seen, the optimal response to the output gap, δ^N, is simply a function of the persistence of output, ρ, and the interest responsiveness of aggregate demand, ξ. The optimal response to inflation, γ^N, depends on all parameters of the model, including ω. In fact, γ^N is increasing in the inflation stabilization weight, with a lower limit of zero as $\omega \to 0$ and an upper limit of $1/\alpha\xi$ as $\omega \to 1$. This latter response generates an output gap exactly equal to what is necessary to bring inflation to its target in just one period (in expectation), as an "inflation nutter" would be expected to attempt to do.

3.2. Naive policy

The policy reaction function derived under the assumption of perfect state information also serves as a useful baseline case to consider when noise actually *is* present in the data. To be sure, the resulting policy:

$$\tilde{r}_t - r^* = \gamma^N(\tilde{\pi}_t - \pi^*) + \delta^N \tilde{y}_t \tag{7}$$

is not necessarily efficient since it does not reflect the proper informational assumptions. It is, however, exactly the policy that would be adopted if one were tempted to take the results of the perfect information analysis at face value and blindly apply the suggested recommendations using the data available. In this sense, this rule reflects naive policy.

3.3. Efficient simple rules

Naive monetary control is efficient in the absence of noise but is clearly inefficient when noise is present in the data. To characterize the set of comparable efficient policies when the policymaker correctly takes the presence of noise into consideration for policy design requires solution of a constrained minimization problem. The solution is the set of response coefficients γ^S and δ^S which minimize the policymaker's objective for different possible values of the preference weight ω, when policy follows the simple rule:

$$\tilde{r}_t - r^* = \gamma^S(\tilde{\pi}_t - \pi^*) + \delta^S \tilde{y}_t \tag{8}$$

and the policymaker properly accounts for the noise in the data.

Obviously, in the absence of noise, the efficient policy will coincide with the naive policy reaction function. When noise is present in the data, determination of the efficient rules requires a complete characterization of the stochastic processes

612   A. Orphanides / Journal of Monetary Economics 50 (2003) 605–631

governing the observation noise. Anticipating the empirical description of the data in
Section 4, I assume that the inflation noise, x, can be adequately modeled as a serially
uncorrelated process. The noise process for the output gap, on the other hand,
exhibits considerable persistence arising from both persistent errors in the
measurement of actual output (e.g. benchmark revisions) as well as persistent errors
in the measurement of potential output. To capture this persistence, I assume that
the output gap noise, z, is described by the autoregressive process:

$$z_t = \beta z_{t-1} + v_t. \tag{9}$$

I assume that x and v are drawn from independent zero mean normal distributions
with variances σ_x^2 and σ_v^2, respectively. With these additional assumptions, we can
describe the economy for an arbitrary choice of response parameters in the
simple rule (8) in terms of a first order autoregressive system of the vector
$(\pi_t - \pi^*, y_t, z_t, r_t - r^*)'$. The asymptotic covariance of this vector can be computed
analytically from the resulting autoregressive system in terms of the parameters of
the system, α, ρ, ξ and β, the preference weight, ω, the rule responses γ and δ and the
covariance of e_t, u_t, x_t and v_t. Using this covariance matrix, I resort to numerical
optimization to determine the efficient rule responses γ^S and δ^S that minimize the
associated policymaker loss function.

3.4. Optimal control and certainty equivalence

Although the focus of my analysis is efficient simple rules, it is instructive to also
examine the performance of the economy with optimal control in the presence of the
noisy data. When the underlying data describing the economy are noisy, the most
recent observations do not provide the best assessment of the underlying inflation
and output gap measures by themselves. Recognizing that he receives noisy data, the
policymaker may employ his assumed model to remove the noise component from
the data as best as possible, before formulating his policy. This filtering of the data
entails forming the conditional expectation of the true underlying states, π_t and y_t,
consistent with the most recent data, $\tilde{\pi}_t$ and $\tilde{y}_t$, and the policymaker's model and
prior assessment of the economy. (The appendix provides details on the
implementation of this filter for the model.) The outcome of this filtering, $\hat{\pi}_t$, and
$\hat{y}_t$, represents the policymaker's best assessment of the state of inflation and output in
the economy. With substantial noise, this assessment could be tenuous and the
policymaker may recognize that he cannot ascertain the state of the economy with
much confidence. However, once this first step is completed, application of the
certainty equivalence principle yields the optimal policy:

$$\hat{r}_t - r^* = \gamma^N(\hat{\pi}_t - \pi^*) + \delta^N \hat{y}_t, \tag{10}$$

where $\hat{r}_t \equiv f_t - \hat{\pi}_t$ and the response coefficients, γ^N and δ^N are the same as the ones
corresponding to the naive policy which is optimal in the absence of noise. The
policy described by Eq. (10), coupled with the appropriate filtering constitutes the
optimal policy design in this economy under the assumption that the model is
properly specified and known with certainty. However, the rule cannot be written in

A. Orphanides / Journal of Monetary Economics 50 (2003) 605–631   613

terms of just the current values of the observed data, $\tilde{\pi}_t$ and $\tilde{y}_t$, and is not equivalent to the simple efficient rule (8). In essence, a simple efficient rule setting the interest rate in terms of observed noisy data collapses the filtering and control steps of the optimal stochastic control solution to the policymaker's problem into a single step. This allows policy to be formulated in terms of just current data but entails some loss of performance relative to the theoretical ideal optimal control policy.[5]

4. Data and model parameters

Assessing the extent of noise in the data requires a comparison of the real-time data available to the policymakers when interest rate decisions are made as well as measures of the true underlying state of the economy. Information is needed for three concepts, nominal output, the output deflator and potential output. The only additional variable needed in the model, the federal funds rate, is not subject to similar measurement problems. For the information available to policymakers in real time, I rely on data associated with the production of the Federal Reserve Board staff's analysis for the macroeconomic outlook. This is presented in a document that is prepared for the FOMC before each FOMC meeting—the Greenbook. A detailed description of this data is provided in Orphanides (2001). My sample starts in 1980 and ends in 1992 (the last year for which data where available to the public when the analysis was completed). From each year, I use data from the May Greenbook for the first semi-annual observation and the November Greenbook for the second semi-annual observation, reflecting the model assumption that the choice of the average federal funds rate for a period incorporates information available towards the end of the period.

Historical information on nominal output, the output deflator, and potential output, the three central series for my analysis, is continuously refined and updated. Given the difficulties associated with their measurement, including problems with the underlying disaggregated data and a continuing debate regarding methodological issues, it is impossible to know what the true value of either inflation or the output gap has been in the past with much confidence.[6] If, however, measurement regarding

---

[5] This discussion can also help clarify a potential source of confusion relating to the application of certainty equivalence in this setting. Although noise appears to represent uncertainty that is "additive", the certainty equivalence principle does not imply that the optimal rule is impervious to it. The sense in which additive uncertainty does not matter in this setting is not with regard to the variance of the noise in the data but with regard to the variance of the conditional expectation which characterizes the policymaker's best assessment of the state of inflation and output after the noise is filtered from the data.

[6] A voluminous literature has examined the problems associated with and suggested improvements for the measurement of both output and inflation. Zellner (1958), Cole (1969a), and Mankiw and Shapiro (1986) have studied the revisions in output measures. The annual revisions of the national income and product accounts published in the *Survey of Current Business* detail the continuing effort for improvement in the data. Orphanides and van Norden (2002) document the impact of these revisions on the measurement of the output gap in real time. The measurement of inflation has been the subject of heightened attention in recent years including the studies by Boskin et al. (1996), Shapiro and Wilcox (1996), and Bryan et al. (1997).

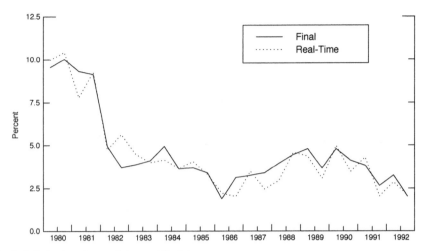

Fig. 1. Inflation based on real-time and final data.

Notes: Semiannual data. Inflation is constructed as the rate of change in the implicit output deflator during the period at an annual rate using seasonally adjusted data. Real-time data reflect information as of May and November for the first and second halves of each year, respectively. Final data reflect historical information with data available at the end of 1994.

the past improves as time progresses, using the most recent available data might offer a sufficient approximation of the "truth" to provide a useful measure of the noise in the real-time data. Here, I rely on data available at the end of 1994 as providing proxies of the true measures of inflation and the output gap for the sample.[7]

Figs. 1 and 2 plot the real-time and final data for inflation and the output gap, respectively. Table 1 presents summary statistics for these series and the inflation and output gap noise. As would be expected for noisy data, the standard deviations of the real-time series, $\tilde{y}$ and $\tilde{\pi}$, are larger than those of the final data, y and π. The noise in the inflation data, x, defined as the difference between the final and real-time series, is considerable at times, ranging from -1.91 to $+1.53$ percentage points. However no significant bias or serial correlation patterns can be detected. (The mean is 0.12 and the first order serial correlation is -0.07.) Thus, modeling x as a white noise process appears reasonable. The estimated standard deviation of the process, an estimate for σ_x, is 0.69 percent.

The data reveal a different pattern for the output gap noise. The difference between the final and real-time output gap, z, is noticeably different from zero on average, and exhibits substantial serial correlation in this sample. An AR(1) process, however, provides a satisfactory model. Estimation with least squares yields the

---

[7] The choice is driven by data availability. Although more recent vintages of output and the output deflator data are available from the Commerce Department, 1994 marked the latest corresponding series for historical potential output data available from the Federal Reserve when the analysis was completed.

A. Orphanides / Journal of Monetary Economics 50 (2003) 605–631   615

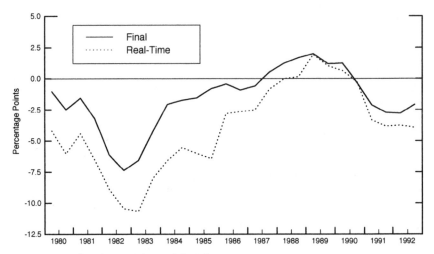

Fig. 2. Output gap based on real-time and final data.

Notes: Semiannual data. The output gap is the average difference between real output and potential output, measured as a fraction of potential output using seasonally adjusted data. Real-time data reflect information as of May and November for the first and second halves of each year respectively. Final data reflect historical information with data available at the end of 1994.

following estimates (standard errors in parentheses):

$$z_t = \underset{(0.063)}{0.911}\, z_{t-1} + v_t, \quad \hat{\sigma}_v = 0.93.$$

The 0.911 point estimate for the output gap noise persistence parameter, β, confirms the substantial serial correlation in the output gap noise.[8]

To obtain parameters for the output and inflation equations of the model, I estimate Eqs. (4) and (5) with least squares using semiannual data for the sample from 1980 to 1992, the same period over which I am able to construct the data for the noise. The estimation is based on the final data series since the objective of the model is to capture the evolution of the actual inflation and output processes.

$$\pi_t = \pi_{t-1} + \underset{(0.070)}{0.180}\, y_t + e_t, \quad \hat{\sigma}_e = 1.04,$$

$$y_t = + \underset{(0.611)}{0.835} + \underset{(0.101)}{0.764}\, y_{t-1} - \underset{(0.135)}{0.293}\, r_{t-1} + u_t, \quad \hat{\sigma}_u = 1.16.$$

---

[8] In fact, the data would not reject the hypothesis that z is integrated of order 1. However, given that in such short samples (13 years), tests of the null hypothesis of a unit root often lack power, and given the strong theoretical prior that the noise should be stationary, this should not be a major concern. Although the output gap noise deviated noticeably from zero in this sample—the average between the final and real-time data is 2.34 percentage points—allowing for an intercept term in the regression yields an estimate not statistically different from zero. The appearance of a bias is due to the serial correlation of the process. A simple way to see this is by noting that $z_t - 0.9z_{t-1}$ has a mean very close to zero. As a result, I impose the restriction that the noise is a mean zero process on the data to recover the estimates for β and σ_v.

Table 1
Summary statistics: 1980H1–1992H2

	Mean	SD	Min	Max	AR
y_t	−1.64	2.44	−7.36	1.99	0.87
$\tilde{y}_t$	−3.99	3.46	−10.67	1.93	0.90
z_t	2.35	1.53	−0.07	5.62	0.81
π_t	4.60	2.27	1.89	10.02	0.75
$\tilde{\pi}_t$	4.48	2.37	2.02	10.44	0.67
x_t	0.12	0.69	−1.90	1.53	−0.07

Notes: y_t is the output gap, defined as actual real output minus potential, as a fraction of potential, in percent, based on data available at the end of 1994. $\tilde{y}_t$ is the corresponding real-time measure. π_t is inflation of the implicit deflator from the last quarter of the previous period to the last quarter of the current period, in percent annual rate, based on data available at the end of 1994. $\tilde{\pi}_t$ is the corresponding real-time measure. x_t is the difference between the final and real-time inflation series. z_t is the difference between the final and real-time output gaps. SD is the standard deviation and AR is the first order serial correlation coefficient.

Despite its simplicity, the model characterizes semiannual U.S. data over this period rather well. The data are compatible with the accelerationist restriction in the Phillips curve and a check for structural stability based on the maximum likelihood-ratio test statistic proposed by Andrews (1993) does not suggest evidence for instability.[9]

5. Policy evaluation

Armed with a parameterized model of the U.S. economy, estimates of the variances of the underlying supply and demand shocks and, importantly, estimates of the stochastic processes of the noise in the inflation and output gap data, I next provide comparisons of the performance from naive policies, efficient simple rules, and optimal control in the presence of noise.[10]

5.1. Naive policy

My benchmark for comparison is the performance of the economy if rules deemed optimal in the absence of noise were naively followed. The solid line in Fig. 3 shows the counterfactual variability frontier that would result if policy were set according to (7) and noise were absent from the data. The different points on the line trace the

---

[9] For additional details regarding the estimated model see the working paper version of this study.

[10] My objective is to highlight the implications of erroneously ignoring the presence of noise in the data. As a result, in all experiments, I maintain a litany of other assumptions embedded in policy rule evaluations of this nature, such as that the model is assumed to be properly specified, that the estimated parameters are constant over time, invariant to the choice of policy, and known with certainty by the policymakers, and that the stochastic processes of the shocks, including the noise processes, are constant over time and known with certainty. Since the spirit of my analysis is to illustrate the limitations of one specific aspect of policy evaluation, it is only proper to acknowledge the presence of other significant limitations at the outset.

A. Orphanides / Journal of Monetary Economics 50 (2003) 605–631   617

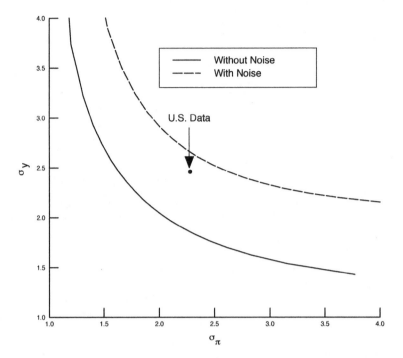

Fig. 3. Output-inflation variability frontier with naive control.

Notes: The solid line shows the (infeasible) frontier constructed assuming no noise in the data. The dashed line shows the variability that would actually result if the naive control policies were followed.

performance of the economy in terms of the unconditional standard deviations of inflation and the output gap for different values of ω. The dot marks the actual variability of inflation and the output gap over the same sample from which the stochastic shocks are drawn, that is 1980–1992. Since actual experience over this period has been away from the efficient variability frontier, this model confirms the usual finding that, however commendable monetary policy may have been over this period, substantial room for improvement would appear to remain.

Of course, by ignoring the noise in the data, the frontier shown in the solid line presents outcomes that are infeasible in practice, even if all the other assumptions in the model held. Computation of the outcomes that would have resulted if the naive policies were followed ought to properly account for the noise in the data. Doing so results in the variability pseudo-frontier shown in the dashed line in Fig. 3. With the appropriate inclusion of the forgotten noise, it becomes evident that the policies recommended as optimal result in performance that is not only substantially worse than advertised, but is also worse than the actual historical outcome of the variability of output and inflation in the data.

Table 2 examines the quantitative magnitude of this deterioration in performance more closely for three alternative preference weights, ω. Each row shows the

Table 2
Naive policy performance deterioration

Noise	$\omega = 0.25$		$\omega = 0.50$		$\omega = 0.75$	
	σ_π	σ_y	σ_π	σ_y	σ_π	σ_y
$s = 0$	2.45	1.77	1.93	2.11	1.56	2.58
$s = 1$	3.35	2.24	2.48	2.53	1.89	3.06
$s = 2$	5.20	3.30	3.66	3.51	2.65	4.17

Notes: Each pair, σ_π, σ_y, shows the standard deviation of inflation and the output gap when policy follows $\tilde{r}_t - r^* = \gamma^N(\tilde{\pi}_t - \pi^*) + \delta^N \tilde{y}_t$, with the response parameters γ^N and δ^N which are optimal in the absence of noise ($s = 0$) for the preference weight, ω.

standard deviation of inflation and the output gap corresponding to a different level of noise in the data. The noise scale parameter, s, measures the presence of noise in units of standard deviations relative to the actual noise in this sample. That is, $s = 0$ shows the (infeasible) performance of the naive rules in the absence of noise (as the solid line in Fig. 3), $s = 1$ the performance with noise of the magnitude estimated in the data (as the dashed line in Fig. 3) and $s = 2$ reflects noise with twice the standard deviation of both the inflation and output gap noise in the data.

Two interesting results are evident in the table. First, the deterioration of performance in the presence of noise, especially the variability of inflation, is relatively bigger the smaller the weight put on inflation stability. Second, the deterioration of performance is not proportional to the degree of noise as measured by s. When $\omega = 0.5$, for instance, the standard deviation of inflation rises from 1.93 to 2.48 as s moves from 0 to 1, roughly a 30 percent increase, but rises to 3.66, an increase of almost 90 percent, as s moves to 2. Thus, naive policies are disproportionately more deleterious the less weight is placed on inflation stability and the more noise is present in the data the policymaker is reacting to.

5.2. Efficient simple rules and optimal control

Policymakers who properly take into account the noise in the data, of course, can improve upon the naive policy rules. Fig. 4 compares the naive frontier in the presence of noise derived in Fig. 3 to the variability frontier corresponding to the family of efficient simple rules (Eq. (8), the dotted line), and the variability frontier corresponding to optimal control policies in this model (Eq. (10), the dash-dot line). As noted before, computation of these frontiers explicitly incorporates the presence of noise in the data. For the optimal control rules, the solution also reflects filtering the noise from the observed inflation and output gap. (This step is detailed in Appendix A.)

As is evident, policies that properly account for the noise in the data can yield substantial improvements over the naive policies. The optimal control frontier presents the best feasible set of outcomes under the assumptions of the model. In practice, however, the presence of model uncertainty and, especially, concern for misspecification (as recently illustrated by Levin et al., 1999, for instance) imply that

A. Orphanides / Journal of Monetary Economics 50 (2003) 605–631   619

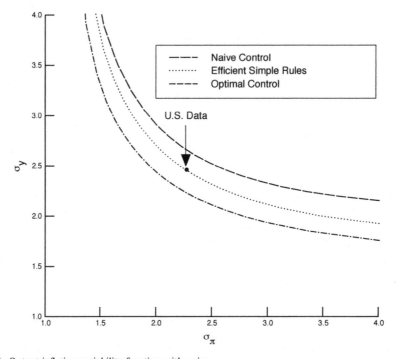

Fig. 4. Output-inflation variability frontiers with noise.

Notes: The efficient simple rule frontier reflects outcomes when policy follows the rule: $\tilde{r}_t - r^* = \gamma(\tilde{\pi}_t - \pi^*) + \delta \tilde{y}_t$, with efficient choice of the response parameters γ, δ.

optimal control outcomes are not truly feasible so it is more instructive to concentrate on the frontier corresponding to the efficient simple rules (8). The historical performance of the U.S. economy over this period is right on the efficient simple rule frontier, raising doubts about the claim suggested by naive policy evaluations that much improvement in performance would have been possible with better macroeconomic control.

Two key lessons emerge from the policy frontier comparisons in Figs. 3 and 4. First, naive policy evaluation that ignores the presence of noise in the data can be extremely misleading and can lead to seriously flawed policy recommendations. Second, policy design that properly accounts for the informational limitations facing policymakers can mitigate, though not eliminate entirely, the deleterious effects of noise.

5.3. The efficiency of policy stodginess

Examination of the simple efficient rules in the presence of noise relative to the naive control rules that are efficient in the absence of noise also permits comparison of the suggested responsiveness of the federal funds rate instrument to the observed

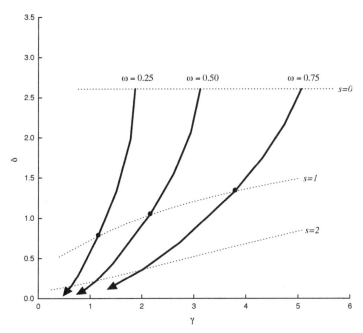

Fig. 5. Efficient simple rule response to inflation and output.

Notes: Points on the figure reflect efficient choices of the response parameters γ and δ when policy follows the rule: $\tilde{r}_t - r^* = \gamma(\tilde{\pi}_t - \pi^*) + \delta\tilde{y}_t$. The solid lines show variation in efficient choices corresponding to alternative preference weights, ω, for different levels of noise, s. The arrows, indicate the direction of movement of the efficient choices with increasing levels of noise. The dotted lines reflect iso-noise loci of efficient choices with $s = 0$ indicating efficient choices in the absence of noise, $s = 1$ reflecting the estimated level of noise in the data, and $s = 2$ reflecting noise with standard deviation twice the estimated level.

inflation and output gap. To that end, it is useful to parameterize the response parameters, γ and δ, of the simple efficient rule (8) to indicate their variation with the scale parameter measuring the noise in the data, s, and the inflation-stabilization-preference weight, ω.

Fig. 5 provides a graphical summary of these results. Points on the figure show the optimal response pairs γ (horizontal axis) and δ (vertical axis) corresponding to different levels of noise, s, and preference weight, ω. The three dotted lines correspond to the loci of efficient responses for three different levels of noise, $s = 0, 1$, and 2. Each locus shows the efficient responses for different values of ω, with points to the right corresponding to greater weights. The three solid lines in the figure correspond to loci of efficient responses for three different levels of the inflation stabilization weight, $\omega = 0.25, 0.5$ and 0.75. Each locus shows the efficient responses for different values of s. The points with the highest values for γ and δ correspond to the baseline of no noise $s = 0$, with the direction of the arrows indicating the direction in which the efficient choices for γ and δ move as noise increases. As can be

Table 3
Efficient simple rule response parameters

Noise	$\omega = 0.25$		$\omega = 0.50$		$\omega = 0.75$	
	γ	δ	γ	δ	γ	δ
$s = 0$	1.87	2.61	3.12	2.61	5.05	2.61
$s = 1$	1.15	0.77	2.16	1.04	3.78	1.33
$s = 2$	0.64	0.15	1.12	0.22	2.02	0.36

Notes: The entries reflect efficient choices of the response parameters γ and δ when policy follows the rule: $\tilde{r}_t - r^* = \gamma(\tilde{\pi}_t - \pi^*) + \delta\tilde{y}_t$, corresponding to alternative preference weights, ω, and levels of noise, s.

Table 4
Estimated policy reaction functions with optimal control

Noise	$\omega = 0.25$		$\omega = 0.50$		$\omega = 0.75$	
	γ	δ	γ	δ	γ	δ
$s = 0$	1.87	2.61	3.12	2.61	5.05	2.61
$s = 1$	1.02	0.99	1.87	1.21	3.31	1.48
$s = 2$	0.64	0.43	1.19	0.62	2.12	0.90

Notes: The entries reflect least squares estimates of the slope parameters of the reaction function, $f_t - \pi_t = c_0 + \gamma\pi_t + \delta y_t + \eta_t$, using final data when the policymaker follows the optimal control policy, $f_t - \hat{\pi}_t = c_0 + \gamma^N\hat{\pi}_t + \delta^N\hat{y}_t$. Results are shown for alternative preference weights, ω, and levels of noise, s.

seen, regardless of the preference weight, the response to the output gap in particular drops sharply as the magnitude of noise increases. For convenience, Table 3 shows the efficient response parameters associated with the simple policy rule (8) for selected values of s and ω.

Examination of the optimal control policies in the presence of noise is also illuminating for understanding the appearance of attenuation in estimated reaction functions. Consider, for instance, least squares estimation of the policy reaction function:

$$f_t - \pi_t = c_0 + \gamma\pi_t + \delta y_t + \eta_t \tag{11}$$

using the final ("true") values of the data, π and y, when policy is set based on Eq. (10).[11] Table 4 shows the estimated slope parameters from the regression (11) for different values of the noise scale parameter, s and preference weight, ω.[12] As can be seen, in the presence of noise the estimated slope parameters become considerably smaller providing an appearance of attenuated responses to inflation and output.

---

[11] Obviously, this regression does not characterize the true policy reaction function in the presence of noise and the error term, η_t, is neither orthogonal to the regressors nor does it represent a policy disturbance. See Sargent (1989) and Christiano et al. (1998) for discussions of the estimation issues arising from the presence of noise.

[12] These are based on regressions with data generated by drawing from the stochastic distributions of the model disturbances and tracking the filtering and control process for each pair of s and ω shown.

Policy reaction functions estimated over long samples invariably produce shifting parameter estimates exhibiting instability. This is sometimes interpreted as reflecting shifts in policy preferences or strategies, suggesting that policy may be formulated in unsystematic fashion. The results above suggest that this need not be the case. Even if policy were based on a simple reactive rule, mere variations in a policymaker's confidence in his knowledge of the economy in real time would lead to substantial changes in the efficient response of policy to developments in both inflation and the output gap. This is the case even with a stable model of the economy, stable and fixed distributions of supply and demand shocks, and constant preferences. As a result, interpreting estimated policy reaction functions and mapping the estimated response coefficients into the underlying policy objectives may be misleading. Until a better understanding of the determinants and evolution of confidence regarding our understanding of the economic outlook evolves, it will remain difficult to uncover the underpinnings of the apparent variation in estimated policy reaction functions. Integration of the process of learning from past experience (as recently investigated by Sargent, 1999, and Wieland, 2000) may be essential for a better understanding and evaluation of monetary policy.

5.4. Are less ambitious policies more robust?

In light of the unfavorable performance associated with the pursuit of apparently "optimal" policies when the information problem is not properly accounted for, it is also of interest to examine whether less ambitious policies may be more robust to such errors in policy design. In particular, given the potential errors associated with real-time measures of the output gap, consider the following two families of policy rules that are based on the Taylor rule but forego the activism associated with responding to the level of the output gap altogether.

Inflation targeting rule:

$$r_t - r^* = \theta^\pi(\pi_t - \pi^*).$$

Natural growth targeting rule:

$$r_t - r^* = \theta^n(n_t - n_t^*),$$

where $n \equiv \Delta q + \pi$ reflects nominal output growth, and $n^* \equiv \Delta q^* + \pi^*$ the natural growth of nominal output consistent with the policymaker's inflation target.[13] By foregoing any attempt at activist response to the business cycle, as measured by the level of the output gap, these rules are closer in spirit to the non-activist policies advocated by Friedman (1953), Meltzer (1987,1998) and others. Surely such policies are suboptimal when the assumption of perfect information can be maintained. Since in the absence of noise the *optimal* rule requires a response to the level of the output gap, the performance of these rules will be clearly inferior. The top lines in

---

[13] Note that $(n_t - n_t^*) = (\pi_t - \pi^*) + \Delta y_t$ since, by definition, $\Delta y = \Delta q - \Delta q^*$. Thus, the natural growth targeting rule can be thought of as a version of the Taylor rule that replaces the output gap with its change. As with the Taylor rule, one could also examine a generalized version of the natural growth targeting rule that allows for different responses to the two components of the rule $(\pi - \pi^*)$ and Δy.

Table 5
Performance deterioration with inflation targeting rule

Noise	$\omega = 0.25$		$\omega = 0.50$		$\omega = 0.75$	
	σ_π	σ_y	σ_π	σ_y	σ_π	σ_y
$s = 0$	3.00	2.33	2.47	2.67	2.11	3.15
$s = 1$	3.04	2.39	2.52	2.74	2.17	3.27
$s = 2$	3.15	2.55	2.64	2.96	2.33	3.61

Notes: Each pair, σ_π, σ_y, denotes the standard deviation of inflation and the output gap when policy follows the rule, $r_t - r^* = \theta^\pi(\pi_t - \pi^*)$. The response parameters, θ^π, corresponding to the preference weights 0.25, 0.50 and 0.75 are 0.60, 1.02, and 1.75, respectively. These reflect the efficient choices in the absence of noise ($s = 0$).

Table 6
Performance deterioration with natural growth targeting rule

Noise	$\omega = 0.25$		$\omega = 0.50$		$\omega = 0.75$	
	σ_π	σ_y	σ_π	σ_y	σ_π	σ_y
$s = 0$	2.96	2.29	2.50	2.58	2.24	2.96
$s = 1$	3.00	2.35	2.55	2.69	2.31	3.14
$s = 2$	3.12	2.53	2.71	2.97	2.53	3.62

Notes: Each pair, σ_π, σ_y, denotes the standard deviation of inflation and the output gap when policy follows the rule, $r_t - r^* = \theta^n(n_t - n_t^*)$. The response parameters, θ^n, corresponding to the preference weights 0.25, 0.50 and 0.75 are 0.66, 1.16, and 1.91, respectively. These reflect the efficient choices in the absence of noise ($s = 0$).

Tables 5 and 6 ($s = 0$), show the performance of the economy that can be achieved when the policymaker is restricted to follow the simple inflation targeting or natural growth targeting rules, respectively, with complete information. Comparison with the top line of Table 2, which shows the performance of the optimal rule confirms a substantial deterioration in both cases. For example, from Table 5, when $\omega = 0.25$, the standard deviations of inflation and output deteriorate by 22 and 32 percent, respectively, when the policymaker is restricted to respond only to inflation when accurate information regarding both inflation and the output gap is available.

But a more relevant comparison is to assess the potential for deterioration in performance when the policymaker incorrectly formulates policy under the assumption of perfect information when, in reality, information is noisy. (In essence, this serves as a robustness check against the possibility that the policymaker may incorrectly downplay the magnitude of the information problem.) The second and third rows in Tables 5 and 6 ($s = 1, 2$) show the deterioration due to noise and are directly comparable to the corresponding rows of Table 2 which show the deterioration with the "optimal" rule. Comparison across the three tables indicates that the deterioration of performance with either the inflation targeting or natural growth targeting rule is comparatively much smaller than with the "optimal" rule. Indeed, with substantial noise ($s = 2$), both the inflation targeting and natural

624 *A. Orphanides / Journal of Monetary Economics 50 (2003) 605–631*

growth targeting rules yield uniformly better performance than the performance suggested by naive formulation of optimal policies that ignore the information problem. Foregoing the activism inherent in responding to the output gap appears to be a robust policy prescription when it is difficult to interpret apparent deviations of aggregate demand from the economy's potential in real time and the extent of mismeasurement is hard to gauge.

6. Noise and expectations

The baseline model examined thus far did not directly examine economic agent expectations. Explicit modeling of expectations when complete information about the state of the economy is not available presents a number of additional interesting complications.[14] Clearly, the policymaker's difficulty in interpreting the incoming data remains. But additional problems arise which, if anything, may magnify the consequences of noise. Fundamentally, the issue is that with rational expectations, the beliefs of economic agents become an important determinant of current economic activity and, as Lucas (1973) demonstrated, private agent misperceptions become central in the analysis.

As is well documented, data noise leads to substantial deterioration in the reliability of forecasts (e.g. Cole, 1969b). Since forecasts influence current outcomes, their reliability is an implicit but important factor in determining the performance of the economy in rational expectations models. But by introducing additional noise in the economy, activist policies may increase the unreliability of these forecasts. Therefore, the evaluation of alternative policies in such models would need to factor the indirect influence of noise on forecasts in addition to the direct effect of noise on policy.

A thornier issue is that with noisy information the policymaker's perception of reality may differ from that of other agents in the economy. For instance, individuals may have better information regarding their own income than the policymaker does. As a result, even if all agents in the economy share common beliefs regarding the true nature of the economy (an unlikely premise), heterogeneity in either the available information or merely the confidence with which that information is being read will result in a divergence between the policymaker's and other agents' expectations about the future. In the presence of noise, explicit modeling of the resulting parallel realities perceived by the policymaker and other agents may become necessary to describe the economic equilibrium.[15]

---

[14] Examples of models employed for policy evaluation that incorporate expectations explicitly include both structural rational expectations models such as Taylor (1979), Fuhrer (1994), Orphanides and Wieland (1998) and Williams (1999), as well as models based more explicitly on optimizing behavior such as King and Wolman (1999), McCallum and Nelson (1999) and Rotemberg and Woodford (1999).

[15] In practice, policymakers may attempt to draw some inference as to the state of private expectations. For inflation sources include household survey data, professional forecasts, information in the prices of nominal and indexed bonds and so forth. Consumer sentiment surveys and surveys of manufacturing managers sometimes provide independent information on consumption and production plans. But as with other data sources, the noise content of this information could be considerable.

A. Orphanides / Journal of Monetary Economics 50 (2003) 605–631   625

These issues suggest that a full exploration of the implications of noise for policy evaluation in a forward looking model, might require adding considerable complexity to the baseline model. Nonetheless, it is useful to demonstrate that the key lessons from the baseline model continue to hold in a forward looking context. To that end, I employ a simple forward-looking variation of the model and examine the implications of two alternative assumptions regarding information availability and the formation of expectations. Specifically, I modify the inflation equation from the accelerationist Phillips curve in the baseline model to a simplified version of the forward-looking specification in the Fuhrer and Moore (1995) model:

$$\pi_t = \phi E_t \pi_{t+1} + (1 - \phi)\pi_{t-1} + \alpha y_t + e_t \tag{12}$$

with $\phi = \frac{1}{2}$.[16] As with the Fuhrer–Moore model, the output gap equation retains its autoregressive nature. To keep results comparable to the baseline model, I retain the same parameters as before with the exception of ϕ and concentrate my attention on the formation of expectations.

To evaluate policy in the forward looking model I examine policies that take the form of the optimal policies in the baseline model under commitment—that is I assume that once a policy rule is chosen by the policymaker, that rule is fully credible and remains in effect without change in subsequent periods. In the absence of noise, expectations are formed rationally, properly taking into account the policy rule adopted by the policymaker. Thus, the optimal policy within the class of rules of the form of Eq. (6), is simply the policy rule that minimizes the policymaker's loss function taking into account the influence of the policy rule on the formation of expectations. This policy with response parameters γ^N and δ^N that are optimal for the forward looking specification of the model. In the absence of any informational problems, inflation expectations when private agents expect the policymaker to follow the optimal policy rule can be simply written as a linear function of the two state variables, $E_t \pi_{t+1} = f(\pi_t, y_t)$.

Table 7 shows the deterioration in economic performance from the presence of noise with this specification under alternative assumptions. The table parallels Table 2 which showed a similar comparison for the baseline model. The top row, ($s = 0$), shows the standard deviations of inflation and output with optimal policy in this forward looking specification for alternative weights placed on inflation stabilization in the absence of noise. Comparing it to the top row of Table 2 shows that moving to the forward-looking specification while leaving all other elements in the model unchanged, yields a lower variability of inflation and output. This reflects the well-known expectational benefit from following well-designed rules that anchor inflation expectations around the policymaker's target, π^*.

The remaining rows in the table reflect outcomes when the policymaker naively follows the policy rules that are optimal in the absence of noise when in fact noise is present. In this case, we also need to explicitly specify what information is available to private agents in the model and how expectations are formed. To highlight the

---

[16] See Fuhrer and Moore (1995) and Fuhrer (1997) for comparisons of this specification with alternative forward looking price-setting specifications and the accelerationist Phillips curve.

Table 7
Noise and naive policy performance deterioration with forward-looking specification

Noise	$\omega = 0.25$		$\omega = 0.50$		$\omega = 0.75$	
	σ_π	σ_y	σ_π	σ_y	σ_π	σ_y
$s = 0$	1.92	1.40	1.59	1.62	1.33	1.99
Uninformed						
$s = 1$	2.21	1.91	1.76	2.03	1.44	2.38
$s = 2$	2.89	2.96	2.19	2.94	1.73	3.30
Informed						
$s = 1$	3.53	1.58	2.29	1.79	1.65	2.19
$s = 2$	6.22	2.03	3.67	2.20	2.36	2.70

Notes: Each pair, σ_π, σ_y, denotes the simulated standard deviation of inflation and the output gap with naive policy based on the model specification indicated and with the preference weights, ω, as shown. For each specification and preference weight the table shows both the simulated performance in the absence of noise ($s = 0$) as well as the outcome if the same policy were followed in the presence of noise ($s = 1, 2$). Informed and Uninformed reflect alternative assumptions regarding the formation of expectations in the presence of noise.

range of possibilities I examine two alternatives that could be viewed as opposite extremes. The first case assumes that private agents observe the same data as the policymaker, $\tilde{\pi}_t$ and $\tilde{y}_t$ and are equally *uninformed* or naive in the same sense the policymaker is assumed to be naive. That is, private agents behave, as if the data are free of noise. Expectations are formed using the reduced form corresponding to rational expectations in the absence of noise, $E_t\pi_{t+1} = f(\tilde{\pi}_t, \tilde{y}_t)$. These expectations are consistent with the model and are "rational" from the perspective of private agents who believe that the observed inflation and output gap data are free of noise. In fact, in this case both the policymaker and private agents believe that policy is optimal and expectations rational. But these beliefs are based on a false premise.

The second case assumes that unlike the policymaker, private agents have full knowledge of the true state of the economy in addition to the noisy data employed by the policymaker to set policy. Expectations are formed rationally taking into account this information as well as the policy process. I refer to this as the case of *informed* agents. This case reflects expectations based on correct beliefs and full information on the part of private agents and is therefore closer to the traditional usage of the rational expectations concept.

Examining the results in Table 7 suggests two key findings. The first is that as with the baseline model in Table 2, the presence of noise leads to a noticeable deterioration of the variability of inflation and output. This is evident for all three preference weights, ω, shown and for both alternatives regarding expectations formation. The second is that the extent of this deterioration depends significantly on the information governing the formation of expectations. The deterioration in inflation variability is considerably worse with informed agents but the deterioration of the output variability is less pronounced.

Table 8
Efficient simple rule response parameters with forward-looking specification

Noise	$\omega = 0.25$		$\omega = 0.50$		$\omega = 0.75$	
	γ	δ	γ	δ	γ	δ
$s = 0$	1.30	2.11	2.22	1.85	3.80	1.68
$s = 1$	1.33	0.53	2.09	0.52	3.45	0.60
$s = 2$	1.07	0.16	1.68	0.17	2.67	0.22

Notes: The entries reflect efficient choices of the response parameters γ and δ when policy follows the rule: $\tilde{r}_t - r^* = \gamma(\tilde{\pi}_t - \pi^*) + \delta\tilde{y}_t$, corresponding to alternative preference weights, ω, and levels of noise, s.

As with the baseline model, it is also of interest to examine the impact of noise on efficient simple rule responses when the policymaker recognizes the presence of noise in the data. Table 8 shows the results for the forward looking specification. I consider the case of informed agents here so expectations are rationally formed and based on correct beliefs. This table parallels Table 3 in the baseline model. As with that table, the top row ($s = 0$), indicates the optimal control responses since in the absence of noise the simple rule and optimal control responses coincide. As can be seen by comparing the top rows in Tables 3 and 8, in the forward looking specification the optimal response coefficients, especially to the inflation gap are smaller in the forward looking model. Again, this reflects the automatic stabilization influence of rational expectations with a fully credible policy rule. Finally, comparing the top row in Table 8 with the subsequent rows that show the efficient responses with noise confirms that the caution exhibited is the baseline model is present in the forward looking specification as well.

In summary, the two key lessons drawn from the baseline model continue to hold in this forward looking model. The presence of noise can lead to a significant deterioration of policy outcomes and the proper policy response in the face of this noise is for the policymaker to exhibit caution in responding to apparent imbalances in economic developments.

7. Conclusion

Unless the practical limitations facing monetary policy are properly acknowledged, policy evaluations will always suggest that activist monetary policy can improve macroeconomic performance. Such gains may be illusory. As I show within the context of interest-rate-based monetary policy rules, while short-run economic stabilization gains from pursuing activist policies may appear substantial, these gains all but disappear once the informational limitations facing policymakers are taken into consideration. Indeed, a cautious response to apparent imbalances in the data is appropriate. A prudent policymaker should recognize that much of the information at his disposal is fraught with noise, and avoid overreaction. This caution is especially relevant when considering apparent deviations of aggregate demand from

628   A. Orphanides / Journal of Monetary Economics 50 (2003) 605–631

the economy's potential. Though well intentioned, naive policy that downplays such informational problems may become a source of instability.

The main objective of this analysis is to serve as a reminder and provide some concrete evidence for some old wisdoms regarding monetary policy. As Modigliani (1977) pointed out, the recognition that inappropriately activist monetary policy can be destabilizing "has had a salutary effect on reassessing what stabilization policies can and should do, and on trimming down fine-tuning ambitions" (p. 17). For as Friedman (1968) observed: "The first and most important lesson that history teaches about what monetary policy can do—and it is a lesson of the most profound importance—is that monetary policy can prevent money itself from being a major source of economic disturbance." (p. 12).

Appendix A

A.1. Control with perfect information

Let

$$
\mathbf{X}_t = \begin{bmatrix} \pi_t - \pi^* \\ y_t \end{bmatrix}, \quad \mathbf{V}_t = \begin{bmatrix} e_t + \alpha u_t \\ u_t \end{bmatrix}, \quad \mathbf{A} = \begin{bmatrix} 1 & \alpha\rho \\ 0 & \rho \end{bmatrix}, \quad \text{and} \quad \mathbf{B} = \begin{bmatrix} -\alpha\xi \\ -\xi \end{bmatrix}.
$$

Then, the economy can be compactly written as

$$
\mathbf{X}_{t+1} = \mathbf{A}\mathbf{X}_t + \mathbf{B}(r_t - r^*) + \mathbf{V}_{t+1}.
$$

The policy-maker objective can be written in terms of the quadratic form $\mathbf{X'QX}$ where $\mathbf{Q}$ reflects the weights in the policymaker's preferences:

$$
\mathbf{Q} = \begin{bmatrix} \omega & 0 \\ 0 & 1 - \omega \end{bmatrix}.
$$

Following standard results from linear-quadratic control theory, for instance as described in Bertsekas (1995), the optimal policy is given by

$$
r_t - r^* = -(\mathbf{B'KB})^{-1}\mathbf{B'KAX}_t,
$$

where $\mathbf{K}$ solves the algebraic Riccati equation:

$$
\mathbf{K} = \mathbf{A'}(\mathbf{K} - \mathbf{KB}(\mathbf{B'KB})^{-1}\mathbf{B'K})\mathbf{A} + \mathbf{Q}.
$$

This yields the solution shown in the text for γ^N and δ^N.

A.2. Kalman filtering with noisy information

With imperfect state observation, the optimal policy entails application of the Kalman filtering algorithm to filter the noise from the observed data before determining the optimal setting of the policy instrument. Because the noise process for the output gap is serially correlated, it is convenient to redefine the state vector by adding one lag of the output gap in order to formulate the filtering algorithm in its canonical form. Thus let

$$
\underline{\mathbf{X}}_t = \begin{bmatrix} \pi_t - \pi^* \\ y_t \\ y_{t-1} \end{bmatrix}, \quad \mathbf{Z}_t = \begin{bmatrix} \tilde{\pi}_t - \pi^* \\ \tilde{y}_t - \beta \tilde{y}_{t-1} \end{bmatrix}, \quad \mathbf{U}_t = \begin{bmatrix} -x_t \\ -v_t \end{bmatrix},
$$

$$
\text{and} \quad \mathbf{C} = \begin{bmatrix} 1 & 0 & 0 \\ 0 & 1 & -\beta \end{bmatrix}.
$$

With this redefinition, the observation equations can be simply written as

$$
\mathbf{Z}_t = \mathbf{C}\underline{\mathbf{X}}_t + \mathbf{U}_t.
$$

The model can be written as before by redefining $\mathbf{V}$, $\mathbf{A}$, $\mathbf{B}$ and $\mathbf{Q}$ to accommodate the expanded state as follows:

$$
\underline{\mathbf{V}}_t = \begin{bmatrix} e_t + \alpha u_t \\ u_t \\ 0 \end{bmatrix}, \quad \mathbf{A} = \begin{bmatrix} 1 & \alpha\rho & 0 \\ 0 & \rho & 0 \\ 0 & 1 & 0 \end{bmatrix}, \quad \mathbf{B} = \begin{bmatrix} -\alpha\xi \\ -\xi \\ 0 \end{bmatrix},
$$

$$
\text{and} \quad \underline{\mathbf{Q}} = \begin{bmatrix} \omega & 0 & 0 \\ 0 & 1-\omega & 0 \\ 0 & 0 & 0 \end{bmatrix}.
$$

With these redefinitions the steady state Kalman filtering algorithm can be applied directly (e.g. Bertsekas, 1995, Chapter 5). The updated states $\hat{\pi}_{t+1}$ and $\hat{y}_{t+1}$ are then obtained from the first two entries of the updated state vector, $\underline{\hat{\mathbf{X}}}_{t+1}$. Let $\mathbf{M}$ denote the covariance matrix of $\underline{\mathbf{V}}$ and $\mathbf{N}$ the covariance matrix of $\mathbf{U}$. Then, the filter is given by

$$
\underline{\hat{\mathbf{X}}}_{t+1} = (\underline{\mathbf{A}} + \underline{\mathbf{B}}\,\underline{\mathbf{L}})\underline{\hat{\mathbf{X}}}_t + \bar{\Sigma}\mathbf{C}'\mathbf{N}^{-1}(\mathbf{Z}_{t+1} - \mathbf{C}(\underline{\mathbf{A}} + \underline{\mathbf{B}}\,\underline{\mathbf{L}})\underline{\hat{\mathbf{X}}}_t),
$$

where

$$
\bar{\Sigma} = \Sigma - \Sigma\mathbf{C}'(\mathbf{C}\Sigma\mathbf{C}' + \mathbf{N})^{-1}\mathbf{C}\Sigma,
$$

$$
\underline{\mathbf{L}} = -(\underline{\mathbf{B}}'\underline{\mathbf{K}}\,\underline{\mathbf{B}})^{-1}\underline{\mathbf{B}}'\underline{\mathbf{K}}\,\underline{\mathbf{A}}
$$

and $\underline{\mathbf{K}}$ and Σ are the unique positive semidefinite symmetric solutions of the Riccati equations:

$$
\underline{\mathbf{K}} = \underline{\mathbf{A}}'(\underline{\mathbf{K}} - \underline{\mathbf{K}}\,\underline{\mathbf{B}}(\underline{\mathbf{B}}'\underline{\mathbf{K}}\,\underline{\mathbf{B}})^{-1}\underline{\mathbf{B}}'\underline{\mathbf{K}})\underline{\mathbf{A}} + \underline{\mathbf{Q}},
$$

$$
\Sigma = \underline{\mathbf{A}}(\Sigma - \Sigma\mathbf{C}'(\mathbf{C}\Sigma\mathbf{C}' + \mathbf{N})^{-1}\mathbf{C}\Sigma)\underline{\mathbf{A}}' + \mathbf{M}.
$$

References

Andrews, D., 1993. Tests for parameter instability and structural change with unknown change point. Econometrica 61 (4), 821–856.

Bertsekas, D., 1995. Dynamic Programming and Optimal Control, Vol. I. Athena Scientific, Belmont, MA.

Blinder, A., 1998. Central Banking in Theory and Practice. MIT Press, Cambridge, MA.

Boskin, M.J., Dulbergen, E.R., Gordon, R.J., Griliches, Z., Jorgenson, D.W., 1996. Toward a more accurate measure of the cost of living, Final Report to the Senate Finance Committee, December 4.

Bryan, M.F., Cecchetti, S.G., Wiggin II, R.L., 1997. Efficient Inflation Estimation, Federal Reserve Bank of Cleveland, Working Paper 9707.

Bryant, R.C., Hooper, P., Mann, C. (Eds.), 1993. Evaluating Policy Regimes: New Research in Empirical Macroeconomics, Brookings, Washington DC.

Christiano, L.J., Eichenbaum, M., Evans, C.L., 1998. Monetary Policy Shocks: What Have We Learned and to What End? NBER Working Paper, No. 6400, February.

Cole, R., 1969a. Errors in Provisional Estimates of Gross National Product. National Bureau of Economic Research, New York.

Cole, R., 1969b. Data errors and forecasting accuracy. In: Jacob, M. (Ed.), Economic Forecasts and Expectations. National Bureau of Economic Research, New York.

Ehrmann, M., Smets, F., 2001. Uncertain Potential Output: Implications for Monetary Policy. European Central Bank WP No. 59, April.

Estrella, A., Mishkin, F.S., 1999. Rethinking the Role of the NAIRU in Monetary Policy: Implications of Model Formulation and Uncertainty. In: Taylor, B. (Ed.), Monetary Policy Rules. University of Chicago, Chicago.

Friedman, M., 1947. Lerner on the economics of control. Journal of Political Economy 55 (5), 405–416.

Friedman, M., 1953. Essays in Positive Economics. University of Chicago, Chicago.

Friedman, M., 1968. The role of monetary policy. American Economic Review 58 (1), 1–17.

Friedman, M., 1969. The Optimum Quantity of Money and Other Essays. University of Chicago, Chicago.

Fuhrer, J.C., 1994. Optimal Monetary Policy and the Sacrifice Ratio. In: Fuhrer, J. (Ed.), Goals, Guidelines, and Constraints Facing Monetary Policymakers. Federal Reserve Bank of Boston, Boston.

Fuhrer, J.C., 1997. The (Un)Importance of forward-looking behavior in price specifications. Journal of Money, Credit, and Banking 29 (3), 338–350.

Fuhrer, J.C., Moore, G.R., 1995. Inflation Persistence. Quarterly Journal of Economics 110 (1), 127–159.

Greenspan, A., 1997. Remarks at the 15th Anniversary Conference of the Center for Economic Policy Research at Stanford University, September 5.

Henderson, D., McKibbin, W. J., 1993. A Comparison of Some Basic Monetary Policy Regimes for Open Economies: Implications of Different Degrees of Instrument Adjustment and Wage Persistence. Carnegie-Rochester Conference Series on Public Policy, Vol. 39, pp. 221–318.

King, M., 1997. Changes in UK monetary policy: rules and discretion in practice. Journal of Monetary Economics 39 (1), 81–97.

King, R.G., Wolman, A.L., 1999. What Should the Monetary Authority Do When Prices are Sticky? In: Taylor, B. (Ed.), Monetary Policy Rules. University of Chicago, Chicago.

Kohn, D., 1999. Comment. In: Taylor, B. (Ed.), Monetary Policy Rules, University of Chicago, Chicago.

Kuttner, K., 1992. Monetary Policy with Uncertain Estimates of Potential Output. Economic Perspectives: Federal Reserve Bank of Chicago, January/February, pp. 2–15.

Levin, A., Wieland, V., Williams, J., 1999. Robustness of simple policy rules under model uncertainty. In: Taylor, B. (Ed.), Monetary Policy Rules. University of Chicago, Chicago.

Lucas, R.E., 1973. Some international evidence on output-inflation tradeoffs. American Economic Review 63, 326–334.

Mankiw, G.N., Shapiro, M.D., 1986. News or noise: an analysis of GNP revisions. Survey of Current Business, May, pp. 20–25.

McCallum, B.T., 1994. Specification of policy rules and performance measures in multicountry stimulation studies. Journal of International Money and Finance 13 (3), 259–275.

McCallum, B.T., 1999. Issues in the design of monetary policy rules. In: Taylor, B., Woodford, M. (Eds.), Handbook of Microeconomies. Elsevier, Amsterdam.

McCallum, B.T., Nelson, E., 1999. Performance of operational policy rules in an estimated semi-classical structural model. In: Taylor, B. (Ed.), Monetary Policy Rules. University of Chicago, Chicago.

Meltzer, A.H., 1987. Limits of short—run stabilization policy. Economic Inquiry 25, 1–14.

Meltzer, A.H., 1998. Monetarism: the issues and the outcome. Atlantic Economic Journal 26 (1), 8–31.

Modigliani, F., 1977. The monetarist controversy or, should we forsake Stabilization policies? American Economic Review 67 (2), 1–19.

Orphanides, A., 2001. Monetary policy rules based on real-time data. American Economic Review 91 (4), 964–985.

Orphanides, A., van Norden, S., 2002. The unreliability of output gap estimates in real time. Review of Economics and Statistics 84 (4), 569–583.

Orphanides, A., Wieland, V., 1998. Price stability and monetary policy effectiveness when nominal interest rates are bounded at zero. Finance and Economics Discussion Series, 98-35, Board of Governors of the Federal Reserve System, June.

Orphanides, A., Porter, R., Reifschneider, D., Tetlow, R., Finan, F., 2000. Errors in the measurement of the output gap and the design of monetary policy. Journal of Economics and Business 52 (1/2), 117–141.

Rotemberg, J., Woodford, M., 1999. Interest-rate rules in an estimated sticky price model. In: Taylor, B. (Ed.), Monetary Policy Rules. University of Chicago, Chicago.

Sargent, T.J., 1989. Two models of measurements and the investment accelerator. Journal of Political Economy 97 (2), 251–287.

Sargent, T.J., 1999. The Conquest of American Inflation. Princeton University Press, Princeton.

Shapiro, M.D., Wilcox, D.W., 1996. Mismeasurement in the consumer price index: an evaluation. NBER Macroeconomic Annual.

Taylor, J.B., 1979. Estimation and control of a macroeconomic model with rational expectation. Econometrica 47 (5), 1267–1286.

Taylor, J.B., 1993. Discretion versus policy rules in practice. Carnegie-Rochester Conference Series on Public Policy, Vol. 39, December, pp. 195–214.

Taylor, J.B., 1999a. The robustness and efficiency of monetary policy rules as guidelines for interest rate setting by the European central bank. Journal of Monetary Economics 43 (3), 655–679.

Taylor, J.B. (Ed.), 1999b. Monetary Policy Rules. University of Chicago, Chicago.

Wieland, V., 1998. Monetary policy under uncertainty about the natural unemployment rate. Finance and Economics Discussion Series, 98-22, Board of Governors of the Federal Reserve System.

Wieland, V., 2000. Monetary policy, parameter uncertainty and optimal learning. Journal of Monetary Economics 46 (1), 199–228.

Williams, J.C., 1999. Simple Rules for Monetary Policy, Finance and Economics Discussion Series, 99-12, Board of Governors of the Federal Reserve System, February.

Zellner, A., 1958. A Statistical analysis of provisional estimates of gross national product and its components, and of personal saving. Journal of the American Statistical Association 53 (281), 54–65.

Further reading

Orphanides, A., 1998. Monetary policy evaluation with noisy information. Finance and Economics Discussion Series, 1998-50, Federal Reserve Board, October.

Part V
Lessons from
Recent Monetary Policy Experience

[12]

The Monetary Policy Debate Since October 1979: Lessons for Theory and Practice

Marvin Goodfriend

Monetary theory and policy have been revolutionized in the two decades since October 1979, when the Federal Reserve under the leadership of Paul Volcker moved to stabilize inflation and bring it down. On the side of practice, the decisive factor was the demonstration that monetary policy could acquire and maintain credibility for low inflation, and improve the stability of both inflation and output relative to potential. On the theory side, the introduction of rational expectations was decisive because it enabled models of monetary policy to incorporate forward-looking elements of aggregate demand and price-setting, long known to be critically important for policy analysis, so as to understand how monetary policy achieved the favorable results found in practice.

Federal Reserve Bank of St. Louis *Review*, March/April 2005, *87*(2, Part 2), pp. 243-62.

1 INTRODUCTION

In retrospect, the Federal Reserve tightening of monetary policy begun under the leadership of Paul Volcker in October 1979 stands as a decisive turning point in the postwar monetary history of the United States. With some ups and downs, inflation rose from around 1 percent to over 10 percent in the preceding two decades. The Volcker Fed brought inflation down to around 4 percent by 1984 after a difficult period of sustained disinflationary monetary policy. In the two decades since, inflation has been reduced to a range in 2003 that Chairman Greenspan characterized as "effective price stability," thanks to the consistent inflation-fighting actions of the Greenspan Fed.

The Volcker disinflation and the stabilization of inflation has had an enormous influence on the theory and practice of monetary policy.[1] This paper reviews how monetary policy has been shaped by that experience. A large part of the story is that central bankers and academic economists learned from each other and both learned

from evidence accumulated in the conquest of inflation. Monetarist theory and evidence on money supply and demand, and on the relationship between money and inflation, encouraged the Volcker Fed to act against inflation. The successful stabilization and eventual elimination of inflation at reasonable cost in light of subsequent benefits, without wage and price controls, and without supportive fiscal policy actions, vindicated the main monetarist message. However, the Fed's reliance on interest rate policy since then appears to contradict monetarist teaching that money must play a central role in the execution of monetary policy. Modern models of interest rate policy owe more to post-monetarist rational expectations reasoning and notions of credibility and commitment to policy rules born of the rational expectations revolution.

Much macroeconomic theory developed before October 1979 remains at the core of models of monetary policy in use today. The notion of a permanent trade-off between inflation and unemployment has been discredited. However, the forward-looking theory of consumption and

---

[1] See, for instance, Blinder (2004) and Fischer (1994).

Marvin Goodfriend is senior vice president and policy advisor at the Federal Reserve Bank of Richmond. The paper benefited from conversations with Bennett McCallum, Athanasios Orphanides, and the discussant Larry Ball.

investment developed decades ago remains at the
core of the modern theory of aggregate demand.
And Keynesian dynamic rational expectations
sticky-price models of monetary policy pioneered
in the late 1970s and early 1980s by Guillermo
Calvo, Stanley Fischer, and John Taylor remain
at the core of models of aggregate supply today.
Keynesian models predict an inverse relationship
between the change in inflation and the output
gap. That view was confirmed by the severe recession accompanying the Volcker disinflation. Since
then, the success in stabilizing inflation has given
credence in practice to the rational expectations
idea that a central bank committed to making low
inflation a priority can anchor inflation expectations and improve the stability of both inflation
and output relative to potential.

Section 2 sets the stage for the discussion to
follow by reviewing the practice and theory of
monetary policy as of October 1979. Section 3
describes the key empirical features of the Volcker
disinflation and the lessons that they teach.
Section 4 summarizes current consensus views
on the theory and practice of monetary policy that
emerged from the disinflation experience and
related theoretical developments. Topics covered
are as follows: the consensus theoretical model
of monetary policy, implicit inflation targeting
in practice, explicit interest rate policy, and
communication policy. In Section 5 we consider
current controversies related to each aspect of
monetary theory and practice discussed in
Section 4.

2 EXPERIENCE AND THEORY AS OF OCTOBER 1979

The Volcker Fed was encouraged to embark
on a disinflationary course by a practical appreciation of the problems in failing to make low
inflation a priority, and by a theoretical understanding that inflation should and could be stabilized and brought down with monetary policy.
This section describes the destabilizing go-stop
policy cycles that characterized inflationary monetary policy prior to 1979 and summarizes briefly
Keynesian and monetarist thinking as it related

to the promise and prospects for the stabilization
of inflation as of 1979.

2.1 Inflationary Go-Stop Monetary Policy Prior to 1979

A combination of factors explains the unprecedented peacetime inflation that tripled the general
price level in the two decades prior to the Volcker
disinflation.[2] Most important was the willingness
to tolerate each burst of inflation in the expectation that it would soon die down. In retrospect,
the public's willingness to accept the upward drift
of the price level after World War II was probably
the origin of the loss of credibility for low inflation that eventually helped to unhinge inflation
expectations in the 1960s and thereafter. There
was little understanding at first of the role played
by inflation expectations in propagating wage
and price inflation and the scope for monetary
policy to anchor inflation expectations. Finally,
the idea that inflation could permanently reduce
unemployment, which gained currency in the
1960s, appeared to provide a benefit to some
inflation.

When one adds to the above inclinations and
beliefs that the Fed was charged with conducting
monetary policy on a discretionary basis, one
can understand the go-stop monetary policy that
characterized the decades prior to October 1979.
During that period the Fed tended to justify periodic actions to contain inflation against an implicit
objective for low unemployment. Inflation would
rise slowly as monetary policy stimulated employment in the go phase of the policy cycle. By the
time the public and Fed became sufficiently concerned about rising inflation for monetary policy
to act against it, pricing decisions had already
begun to embody higher inflation expectations.
At that point, a given degree of restraint on inflation required a more aggressive increase in short-
term interest rates, with greater risk of recession.
There was a relatively narrow window of broad
public support for the Fed to tighten monetary
policy in the stop phase of the policy cycle. The
window opened after rising inflation was recog-

---

[2] See, for instance, Hetzel (1998) and Orphanides (2002).

nized as the major concern and closed when tighter monetary policy caused the unemployment rate to begin to rise. Often the Fed did not take full advantage of the window of opportunity to raise rates because it wanted more confirmation that higher rates were called for and it was concerned about the recessionary consequences. Once the unemployment rate peaked and began to fall, however, the public's anxiety about it diminished. And the Fed could fight inflation less visibly by lowering interest rates gradually and prolonging the stop phase of the policy cycle.[3]

The tolerance for rising inflation and the sensitivity to recession meant that go-stop cycles became more inflationary over time. The average unemployment rate rose, too, perhaps because increasingly restrictive monetary policy was needed on average to prevent inflation from rising still faster. Aggressive price- and wage-setting behavior tended to neutralize the favorable employment effects of monetary stimulus in the go phase of the policy cycles. As the Fed attempted to offset these unfavorable developments, inflation and expected inflation moved higher. Lenders demanded unprecedented inflation premia in long-term bond rates, and the absence of an anchor for inflation caused inflation expectations and long bond rates to fluctuate widely.

2.2 The Theory of Monetary Policy as of October 1979

James Tobin's (1980) comprehensive review of stabilization policy written for the 10th anniversary of the *Brookings Papers on Economic Activity* contains a good summary of macroeconomic theory as it related to monetary policy, unemployment, and inflation at the time. The five main points of what he calls the consensus macroeconomic framework, *vintage 1970*, are as follows[4]:

---

[3] Friedman (1964) discusses go-stop monetary policy. Also, see Goodfriend (1997) and Shapiro (1994). Taylor (1979) provides quantitative evidence that can be interpreted as inefficient go-stop policy. See, especially, his Figure 1. Romer and Romer (1989) document that since World War II the Fed tightened monetary policy decisively to contain inflation on six occasions: October 1947, September 1955, December 1968, April 1974, August 1978, and October 1979. The unemployment rate rose sharply each time.

[4] The five points are taken from Tobin (1980, pp. 23-25).

(1) Prices are marked up labor costs, usually adjusted to normal operating rates and productivity trends...and rates of price and wage increase depend partly on their recent trends, partly on expectations of their future movements, and partly on the tightness of markets for products and labor.

(2) Variations in aggregate demand, whether a consequence of policies or of other events, affect the course of prices and output, and wages and employment, by altering the tightness of labor and product markets, and in no other way.

(3) The tightness of markets can be related to the utilization of productive resources, reported or adjusted unemployment rates, and capacity operating rates. At any given utilization rate, real output grows at a steady pace...reflecting trends in supplies of labor and capital and in productivity. According to Okun's law, in cyclical fluctuations each percentage point of unemployment corresponds to 3 percent of GDP [gross domestic product].

(4) Inflation accelerates at high employment rates because tight markets systematically and repeatedly generate wage and price increases in addition to those already incorporated in expectations and historical patterns. At low utilization rates, inflation decelerates, but probably at an asymmetrically slow pace. At the Phelps-Friedman "natural rate of unemployment," the degrees of resource utilization generate no net wage and price pressures up or down and are consistent with accustomed and expected paths, whether stable prices or any other inflation rate. The consensus view accepted the notion of a nonaccelerating inflation rate of unemployment (NAIRU) as a practical constraint on policy, even though some of its adherents would not identify NAIRU as full, equilibrium, or optimum employment.

(5) On the instruments of demand management themselves, there was less consensus. The monetarist counterrevolution had provided

debate over the efficacy of monetary and fiscal measures, the process of the transmission of monetary policies to total spending, and the proper indicators and targets of monetary policy.

Remarkably, much of this consensus remains at the core of modern mainstream models of monetary policy today, as discussed in Section 4.

Tobin was more pessimistic than other Keynesian economists, such as Arthur Okun (1978), that disinflationary monetary policy alone could bring down inflation at an acceptable unemployment cost. Tobin's views are worth recalling because they capture the more pessimistic Keynesian thinking about the power of monetary policy to control inflation, and they provide some contrast with more optimistic monetarist views discussed below that gained currency in the inflationary decades prior to October 1979. For instance, in the same paper, we learn that Tobin thought that the path of real variables would have been disastrously worse had the path of nominal GDP growth been held to 4 percent per year since 1960. He regarded "the inertia of inflation in the face of nonaccommodative policies [as] the big issue." Tobin's view was that "the price- and wage-setting institutions of the economy have an inflation bias. Consequently, demand management cannot stabilize the price trend without chronic sacrifice of output and employment unless it is assisted, occasionally or permanently, by direct incomes policies of some kind."[5] A few pages later Tobin says that he thinks it would be "recklessly imprudent to lock the economy into a monetary disinflation without auxiliary incomes policies."[6]

Monetarists led by Milton Friedman, Karl Brunner, and Allan Meltzer were optimistic that the Fed could and should use monetary policy alone to bring inflation down. Monetarist theory and its prescriptions for monetary policy were based on the quantity theory of money, evidence from many countries showing that sustained inflation was associated with excessive money growth,

and evidence that inflation could be stopped by slowing the growth of the money supply.[7]

In particular, monetarists demonstrated convincingly that the demand for money was sufficiently stable in the United States to enable the central bank to bring the inflation rate down by reducing the trend rate of growth of the monetary aggregates. And monetarists argued successfully that, although the introduction of money substitutes could adversely impact the stability of money demand in the short run, money demand was sufficiently stable and money supply sufficiently controllable by a central bank over time that financial innovations did not fundamentally alter the central bank's power over inflation. By assembling a convincing body of theory and evidence that controlling money was necessary and sufficient for controlling inflation, and that a central bank could control money, monetarists laid the groundwork for the Volcker Fed to take responsibility for inflation after October 1979 and bring it down.

Monetarists, however, like Keynesians, believed that a disinflation would be costly. Previous experience with go-stop policy made it clear that there was a short-run unemployment cost of fighting inflation. The temporary unemployment cost of a large permanent disinflation would likely exceed the cost of previous temporary attempts to contain inflation in the stop phase of the policy cycle. Both Keynesians and monetarists then understood that the unemployment cost of permanent disinflation could be reduced greatly if the Fed could acquire credibility for low inflation.[8] In a credible disinflation, money growth and inflation would slow together, with little increase in unemployment.[9]

On the other hand, if the disinflation were not credible, then wage and price inflation would

---

[5] Tobin (1980, p. 64).

[6] Tobin (1980, p. 69).

[7] See, for example, Friedman (1968, 1989), Meltzer (1963), Poole (1978), Sargent (1986), and the regular reports of the Shadow Open Market Committee led by Karl Brunner and Allan Meltzer.

[8] Fellner (1979), Sargent (1986), and Taylor (1982) contain early discussions of the role of credibility in minimizing the cost of disinflation.

[9] In fact, Ball (1994) pointed out that a fully credible disinflation could produce a temporary increase in employment for some sticky price specifications.

continue as before, and the public would drive interest rates up and asset prices down as it competed for increasingly scarce real money balances. In that case, unemployment would rise and come down only as the disinflation gained credibility, wage and price inflation slowed, interest rates fell, asset prices rose, and aggregate demand rebounded.

Monetarists tended to be more optimistic than Keynesians about the potential role for credibility because monetarists saw a greater role for expectations in wage and price setting and a smaller role for inertia. And monetarists thought that monetary policy could exert a greater influence over expected inflation than did Keynesians. At any rate, in October 1979 it was not at all clear how quickly the Volcker Fed could acquire credibility for low inflation, how costly a disinflation might be, or even whether it could succeed at all, given the pressure that would be brought to bear on the Fed as a result of the accompanying recession.

3 LESSONS FROM THE VOLCKER DISINFLATION

By October 1979 the level and volatility of inflation and inflation expectations resulting from two decades of inflationary go-stop monetary policy greatly complicated the pursuit of stabilization policy. Large real interest rate policy actions were necessary to stabilize the economy. Moreover, it became increasingly difficult to track the public's inflation expectations to tell how nominal federal funds rate policy actions translated into real rate actions. The public found it increasingly difficult to discern the Fed's policy intentions, and the Fed found it increasingly difficult to gauge the state of the economy and how the economy would respond to its policy actions. The opportunity for policy mistakes was enlarged. In short, there was a breakdown in mutual understanding between the public and the Fed.

The Fed rarely sought publicity for its monetary policy actions. However, confidence had deteriorated to such an extent by October 1979 that the Fed broke sharply with tradition and grabbed the headlines with a dramatic high-profile

announcement that it had changed operating procedures to place greater emphasis on controlling money.[10] That dramatic announcement served three main purposes: (i) it associated the Fed with monetarists and thereby bought some credibility against inflation, (ii) it enabled the Fed to blame high interest rates on tighter monetary control, and (iii) it signaled that the Fed would take responsibility for inflation and staked the Volcker Fed's reputation on containing inflation in order to build the Fed's credibility as an inflation fighter. Importantly, the Volcker Fed did not talk much about *disinflation* in October 1979. Its public statements and Federal Open Market Committee (FOMC) transcripts from the fall of 1979 make clear that its objective was more modest: *to stabilize and contain* an increase in inflation and inflation expectations. A reading of the FOMC transcripts also makes clear that the Fed came to regard disinflation as a feasible and preferable course of action only gradually as events unfolded in 1980 and 1981. What follows is a brief summary of the key aspects of the Volcker disinflaton and their lessons for monetary policy. In reviewing these events we will see why and how the Volcker Fed produced the sustained disinflation.

3.1 Loss of Room to Maneuver

The big surprise for the Volcker Fed in the months after October 1979 was that its room to maneuver between fighting inflation and fighting recession disappeared.[11] In effect, the Fed lost the leeway to choose between stimulating employment in the go phase of the policy cycle and fighting inflation in the stop phase. The Volcker Fed raised the nominal federal funds rate by about 3 percentage points in the fall of 1979 in its opening fight against inflation. But evidence that the economy was moving into recession caused the Fed to pause in its aggressive tightening. January 1980 later turned out to be a National Bureau of Economic Research business cycle peak, validating

---

[10] See Lindsey, Orphanides, and Rasche (2005).

[11] See, for instance. FOMC (1980; Report on Open Market Operations, February 4-5, pp. 3-4; and Joseph F. Ziesel. Chart Show, February 5).

the Fed's concern about a recession. But with the federal funds rate held steady, the 30-year (long) bond rate jumped by around 2 percentage points between December and February, despite a weakening economy. A number of factors contributed to the unprecedented collapse of bond prices and increase in inflation expectations evident in the sharp rise in the bond rate. Among the most important were the spike in inflation in early 1980, the ongoing increase in oil prices, the incredible rise in the price of gold to around $850 per ounce in January, and the Soviet invasion of Afghanistan. That said, the Fed's hesitation to tighten policy at the first sign of recession probably contributed to the inflation scare by creating doubts in the public's mind of the Fed's willingness to incur the unemployment cost to contain inflation.

The unprecedented challenge to its credibility as an inflation fighter made clear that the Fed had lost the *flexibility* to use interest rate policy to stabilize employment and output. The Fed reacted aggressively to the inflation scare by raising the federal funds rate 3 percentage points to 17 percent in March! The short recession that occurred in the first half of 1980 resulted from the tightening of monetary policy in conjunction with the imposition of credit controls.[12] When the magnitude of the downturn became clear, however, the Fed cut the federal funds rate by around 8 percentage points between April and July to act against it. Real GDP fell anyway, at around a 10 percent annual rate in the second quarter. But the recession ended quickly with the aggressive easing of monetary policy and the lifting of credit controls in June, and real GDP bounced back with 8 percent annual growth in the fourth quarter of 1980. Unfortunately, inflation remained high throughout 1980.

3.2 Tactics, Credibility, and Cost

Observing the resurgence of economic activity, the Fed quickly moved the federal funds rate back up by early 1981 to 19 percent. As measured by personal consumption expenditures (PCE) inflation, which was around 10 percent at the time, real short-term interest rates were then a very high

9 percent. A recession began in July 1981 that would take the unemployment rate from around 7 percent to nearly 10 percent at the recession trough in November 1982. PCE inflation fell by around 5 percentage points to the 5 percent range by the first quarter of 1982, and the Fed brought the funds rate down by 5 percentage points as well. Thus, the Fed maintained real short-term interest rates of 9 percent, even as the unemployment rate continued to rise. One reason that policy remained extraordinarily tight even after the break in inflation is that the behavior of long bond rates suggested that the Fed's credibility as an inflation fighter continued to deteriorate.[13] The long rate actually rose by 3 percentage points from January 1981 to more than 14 percent in October, even as the economy weakened. And the bond rate remained in the 13 to 14 percent range until it began to come down in the summer of 1982. Only then, in the third quarter of 1982, did the Fed begin to reduce real short-term interest rates and pave the way for a recovery. Thereafter, inflation stabilized at around 4 percent and real GDP grew by around 6.5 percent and 4.5 percent in 1983 and 1984, respectively.

A number of factors help to explain why the Fed went ahead with the disinflation in 1981 and why the disinflation succeeded. First, the disastrous developments in 1980 taught the Fed that attempting to stabilize inflation *at a high level* was costly for the following reasons[14]: (i) High inflation invited inflation scares that the Fed was compelled to counteract by raising short-term real interest rates, with great risk of recession; (ii) high inflation invited interventions, such as credit controls, that could be equally damaging to the economy; and (iii) containing inflation at a high level would likely require the Fed to maintain a larger average output gap than otherwise to prevent inflation from rising further.

Second, the events of 1980 heightened the public's unhappiness with high inflation. Public

---

[12] See Schreft (1990).

[13] A reading of the 1981 transcripts reveals the FOMC's concern with high long-term interest rates and the high inflation expectations that they reflect. For instance, see Chairman Volcker's remarks on page 39 of the August 18, 1981, transcript.

[14] For instance, see Chairman Volcker's remarks in the FOMC transcript from July 7, 1981, p. 36.

support, together with the support of the new Reagan administration, encouraged the Volcker Fed to pursue disinflationary monetary policy in 1981.

Third, the Fed did the hard work of raising the federal funds rate to 17 percent in the spring of 1980. The Fed then took advantage of the window of opportunity that presented itself during the rebound in economic activity in the second half of 1980 to return the federal funds rate to that range. Moving the federal funds rate back up aggressively signaled the Fed's commitment and determination to renew the fight against inflation in 1981. By positioning itself with a 19 percent nominal, and 9 percent real, federal funds rate, the Fed could then let the economy disinflate without having to *raise* the nominal funds rate further and could *lower* the nominal federal funds rate as the disinflation took hold.

3.3 The Inflation Scare Problem and Preemptive Interest Rate Policy

Severe credibility problems flared up during the Volcker era as "inflation scares" in the bond market—falling bond prices due to sharply rising inflation premia in long-term interest rates.[15] Inflation scares presented the Fed with a costly dilemma: Ignoring them could encourage more skepticism about the Fed's fight against inflation, but raising real short rates in response risked precipitating a recession or worsening a recession already in progress. There were four prominent inflation scares in the Volcker era. As discussed above, the first scare in early 1980 shocked the Fed into a 3-percentage-point tightening of the federal funds rate in March and was pivotal in persuading the Fed to pursue a more explicitly disinflationary course. The second scare in 1981, with bond rates remaining high through mid-1982, contributed to the Fed's prolonging the 1981-82 recession.

The third inflation scare took the long-term rate from the 10 percent range in mid-1983 to over 13 percent in the summer of 1984. Remarkably, the bond rate was then only about 1 percentage point below its peak in 1981 even though inflation

was about 6 percentage points lower in 1984 and inflation remained in the 4 percent range throughout the inflation scare of 1983-84! In this case, the Fed followed the long rate up with the federal funds rate, taking the funds rate up by around 3 percentage points to the 11 percent range in mid-1984 before the bond rate began to come down. The bond rate then fell by 6 percentage points to the 7 percent range by early 1986, about 3 percentage points below where it had been at the start of the inflation scare. The Fed's aggressive containment of the scare apparently made the public confident of another 3-percentage-point reduction in the trend rate of inflation.

The successful containment of the 1983-84 inflation scare was the most remarkable feature of the Volcker disinflation. The Fed had succeeded in reducing inflation temporarily in many preceding go-stop policy cycles.[16] Preemptive interest rate policy actions in 1983-84 finally put an end to inflationary go-stop policy. This success was particularly important for the future because it showed that well-timed, aggressive interest rate policy actions could defuse an inflation scare and preempt rising inflation without creating a recession.

The Volcker Fed was confronted with a fourth inflation scare in 1987, the last year of Chairman Volcker's leadership of the Fed. The 1987 scare was marked by a 2-percentage-point rise in the bond rate between March and October. This time the Volcker Fed reacted little to the scare, perhaps because GDP growth was weaker than in 1983-84 and there was less risk of an increase in the actual inflation rate. In light of the Volcker Fed's demonstrated determination to act against inflation earlier in the decade, however, the 1987 scare was striking evidence of the fragility of the credibility of the Fed's commitment to low inflation.

4 CONSENSUS THEORY AND PRACTICE OF MONETARY POLICY

The period since October 1979 has seen a considerable convergence in the theory and prac-

---

[15] See Goodfriend (1993), Gurkaynak, Sack, and Swanson (2003), Ireland (1996), and Orphanides and Williams (2005).

[16] This point is emphasized by Shapiro (1994).

tice of monetary policy. On the theory side, New Neoclassical Synthesis models (alternatively called New Keynesian models) of monetary policy embody key components from Keynesian, monetarist, rational expectations, and real business cycle macroeconomics. On the policy side, it is widely agreed that central banks can and should use monetary policy to maintain low inflation over time and that the commitment to price stability enhances the power of monetary policy to stabilize employment over the business cycle. The agreed-upon desirability and feasibility of a priority for price stability was born of the practical experience reviewed above in conjunction with theory developed since October 1979.

In what follows, we review the nature and origin of key elements of the current consensus. First, we review the components of the consensus theory of monetary policy. Second, we review the reasons for the rise of implicit inflation targeting as the strategy of monetary policy in practice. Third, we explain the emergence of explicit interest rate policy as the means of implementing, discussing, and analyzing monetary policy. Fourth, we discuss the transition from the practice of secrecy to transparency in communicating monetary policy actions, concerns, and intentions to the public.

4.1 The Consensus Model

The modern New Neoclassical Synthesis (or New Keynesian) consensus macroeconomic model of monetary policy is a dynamic general equilibrium model with a real business cycle core and costly nominal price adjustment. The consensus model and its implications for monetary policy have been exposited from somewhat different perspectives in Goodfriend and King (1997), Clarida, Galí, and Gertler (1999), Woodford (2003), and Goodfriend (2004).[17] A convergence in thinking is clear from a reading of these diverse expositions. The heart of the baseline model is compactly represented by the following two equations.

There is a "forward-looking IS function" in which current aggregate demand relative to poten-

tial output depends positively on expected future income and negatively on the short-term real interest rate. It resembles the original Keynesian IS function except for its reliance on expected future income. The dependence of current aggregate demand on expected future income dates back to the theory of consumption developed by Fisher (1930) and Friedman (1957).

There is an "aggregate supply function," also called a price-setting function, that relates current inflation inversely to the current markup (or output gap) and expected future inflation. This aggregate supply function can be derived directly from Calvo's (1983) model of staggered price setting and is closely related to the pioneering work of Stanley Fischer and John Taylor (see Taylor, 1999b).

The modeling of expected future income in the IS function and expected future inflation in the aggregate supply function reflects the introduction of rational expectations into macroeconomics by Robert Lucas in the 1970s.[18] Rational expectations theory and solution methods provided a convincing and manageable way to model expectations. Moreover, rational expectations theory taught that it is critically important in analyzing monetary policy to let expectations rationally reflect changes in the way that monetary policy is imagined to be conducted.

By solving the IS function forward, it is possible to express current aggregate demand relative to potential in terms of the expected path of future short-term real interest rates and future potential output. To the extent that price-level stickiness enables monetary policy to exert leverage over the path of real interest rates, both current and expected interest rate policy actions determine current aggregate demand.

By solving the inflation-generating function forward, one can see that the current inflation rate depends inversely on the path of expected future markups. The model implies that inflation will remain low and stable if monetary policy manages aggregate demand to stabilize the output gap to keep the average markup at the profit-maximizing markup. In other words, monetary

---

[17] See also the papers in Mankiw and Romer (1991).

[18] See Lucas (1976, 1981).

policy maintains price stability by anchoring expected future markups at the profit-maximizing markup so firms do not wish to change prices. Monetary policy that stabilizes the markup at its profit-maximizing value makes the macroeconomy behave like the underlying core real business cycle model with flexible prices. From this perspective, "flexible price real business cycle models of aggregate fluctuations are of practical interest, not as descriptions of what aggregate fluctuations should be like *regardless* of the monetary policy regime, but as descriptions of what they would be like under an *optimal* monetary policy regime."[19]

Looking back at Tobin's summary of consensus thinking about monetary policy in 1980, much remains from that time. There is the idea that prices are marked up over costs; that price trends depend on expectations and on tightness of labor and product markets; that variations in aggregate demand alter inflation by influencing the tightness of markets; that there is a natural rate of unemployment (where output equals potential) at which wage and price setters perpetuate the going rate of inflation (presumably at the profit-maximizing markup); that inflation accelerates when output is expected to exceed potential (the markup is expected to be compressed); and that inflation decelerates when output is expected to fall short of potential (the markup is expected to be elevated). The main advances since then are due to (i) the proven power of monetary policy to reduce and stabilize inflation and inflation expectations at a low rate and (ii) the progress in modeling expectations rationally to understand how monetary policy consistently committed to stabilizing inflation can achieve favorable results.

The model of monetary policy is closed with a description of how policy is imagined to be conducted. Rational expectations teaches that it is not possible to tell how a monetary policy action influences behavior unless it is modeled as part of systematic *policy*. Hence, the model cannot be employed to analyze policy actions without specifying how policy is conducted. There are two ways to do this. One can assume that the central bank

employs a rule for its policy instrument, such as a Taylor interest rate rule or a McCallum monetary base rule. Or one can assume that the central bank chooses its instrument each period to maximize a welfare function, which could be derived to reflect household utility in the model. Each way of closing the model has advantages and disadvantages. An ad hoc policy rule can be chosen to approximate a central bank's reaction function in practice. The problem is that an ad hoc rule is unlikely to be optimal in the model in question. On the other hand, optimal policy in the model may not give rise to a policy rule that a central bank would follow in practice, and it may not be optimal at all if the model is incorrect.[20] Kydland and Prescott (1977) first pointed out that optimal monetary policy is likely to be time inconsistent and that monetary policy may be suboptimal if a central bank cannot commit to a policy rule.[21]

4.2 Implicit Inflation Targeting

With respect to the practice of monetary policy, the most important development since October 1979 has been the rise of *implicit* inflation targeting as the core of the Fed's strategy of monetary policy.[22] This is remarkable in retrospect because no one would have predicted it in October 1979. For instance, although monetarists insisted that price stability ought to be the primary goal of monetary policy, their reading of monetary history suggested that the inflation rate itself could not serve as a practical guide for monetary policy and an operational criterion for performance because of the long and variable lags of nearly two years in the effect of monetary policy on inflation.[23] Hence, monetarists recommended monetary targeting as the means by which a central bank should control the inflation rate.

---

[19] Woodford (2003, p. 410). Goodfriend and King (1997) and Goodfriend (2004) emphasize this point.

[20] See McCallum (1999) and Svensson (1999).

[21] See, also, Barro and Gordon (1983).

[22] The Fed does not have a formal inflation target. But Goodfriend (2003b) argues that monetary policy conducted by the Greenspan Fed may be characterized as a form of implicit inflation targeting. See Bernanke and Mishkin (1997) for a formal definition of inflation targeting.

[23] See Friedman (1960, pp. 87-88).

The rise of implicit inflation targeting is the result of a number of factors.[24] Most important, the Fed has shown that a consistent commitment to price stability *can* stabilize inflation within a relatively narrow range at a low rate over the business cycle. Second, the unemployment cost (associated with go-stop policy and inflation scares) of *failing* to make low and stable inflation a priority is now well understood. Third, anchoring inflation expectations is understood to produce three critical benefits: (i) It helps the Fed to know how its nominal federal funds rate target changes translate into real interest rate movements, which helps the Fed gauge the likely impact of its policy actions on the economy; (ii) it enables the Fed to buy time to recognize and counteract threats to price stability before they develop into inflation or deflation scares; and (iii) it enhances the flexibility of interest rate policy to react aggressively (without an inflation scare in bond markets) to shocks that threaten to destabilize financial markets and/or create unemployment. Fourth, macroeconomic performance since the Volcker disinflation has produced two of the longest expansions in U.S. economic history, with two of the shortest contractions in 1990-91 and 2001.

4.3 Explicit Interest Rate Policy

A second practical development of considerable importance since October 1979 has been the Fed's decision since February 1994 to announce publicly its federal funds rate target immediately after each FOMC meeting. This development marked the return to an explicit interest rate policy, last fully acknowledged in the early 1920s. When the Fed embarked on its first campaign to tighten monetary policy in the aftermath of World War I, it did so with widely publicized increases in its discount rate, which the public then understood to anchor money market rates in much the same way the Bank of England's "bank rate" had anchored rates since the 19th century.[25] High interest rates were suspected to have caused the

deflation and recession of 1920-21. According to Meltzer's (2003) account, it is no exaggeration to say that the Fed was traumatized by its first use of open interest rate policy.[26] Shortly after that experience, the Fed moved to adopt operating procedures to pursue interest rate policy less visibly. It did so by targeting borrowed reserves.

Borrowed-reserve targeting enabled the Fed to talk about monetary policy in terms of the "degree of pressure on reserves," rather than in terms of interest rates, and to create the illusion that money market rates were determined largely if not completely by market forces. There were three reasons for this.[27] Money market rates floated relative to the discount rate, with a spread that fluctuated with credit risk and the volume of bank reserves that the Fed forced the banking system to borrow from Reserve Banks. Money market rates could be manipulated quietly, without changing the high-profile discount rate, by forcing the banking system to borrow more or less of its reserves at the discount window. The Fed could create the impression that visible (discount rate) interest rate policy *followed* market rates. For instance, if the Fed wanted to raise rates it could first force banks into the window by selling securities. That would raise market rates without raising the discount rate. Later, the Fed could raise and realign the discount rate while buying securities to bring the volume of forced borrowings back down. Of course, the Fed retained the option of *leading* with discount rate changes when it wanted to grab the headlines.

Thus, borrowed-reserve targeting was noisy interest rate policy in which the Fed continued to manage short-term interest rates closely but in a relatively invisible way. It afforded the Fed a means of implementing interest rate policy actions quietly or loudly, depending on what was called for.[28] With some notable exceptions, such as the 1974-79 period, until 1994 the Fed often managed

---

[24] Feldstein (1997) and Schmitt-Grohé and Uribe (2002), for instance, provide quantitative support for making low inflation a priority.

[25] See Hawtrey (1938).

[26] See Meltzer (2003, pp. 13, 112-16, and 127).

[27] See Goodfriend (2003a).

[28] Goodfriend (1991, p. 21) quotes Governor Strong from 1927 and Chairman Greenspan from 1989, explaining why it is useful for the Fed to have the option to take policy actions quietly or loudly.

short-term interest rates by targeting borrowed reserves.[29]

A number of factors account for the Fed's decision to return to explicit interest rate policy in 1994. The period of high interest rates in the 1970s and 1980s, especially during the Volcker disinflation, gave the Fed a high profile, which it never lost. Greater public scrutiny of monetary policy created pressure for increased transparency of interest rate policy actions. Second, increased instability in the demand for M1 and M2 in the 1980s and early 1990s undermined the case for operating procedures that involved bank reserves and monetary targeting. Third, academic papers (e.g., Goodfriend, 1991, 1993, and Taylor, 1993) began to talk about monetary policy explicitly in terms of interest rates. Fourth, academics learned how to analyze monetary policy in models without money (e.g., Kerr and King, 1996, McCallum, 2001, and Woodford, 2003) and economists at the Board developed models of monetary policy without money (e.g., Brayton et al., 1997). Fifth, with inflation low and stable, the federal funds rate could be expected to move in a relatively low and narrow range. In short, the consensus to implement, discuss, and analyze monetary policy as explicit interest rate policy became overwhelming.

4.4 Communicating Policy Concerns and Intentions

A third practical development of importance since October 1979 has been the remarkable increase in transparency in communicating the concerns and intentions of monetary policy in addition to announcing the federal funds rate target. One can understand this transition as a *change in the means* by which a central bank achieves its primary monetary policy mission: to contribute to macroeconomic stability in a way that leaves maximum freedom of action to private markets. The idea is that monetary policy should be conducted as unobtrusively as possible to mini-

mize interference in markets. Hence, central banks developed a reputation for secrecy.[30] Recent theory and practice reviewed above, however, teaches that a central bank enhances the performance of markets by creating an environment of dependable low inflation. Since transparency creates understanding of the tactics and strategy of monetary policy, transparency rather than secrecy is more apt to strengthen credibility for low inflation. Broadly speaking, that is what accounts for the striking increase in communication with the public that has characterized monetary policy in recent years.[31]

The return to fully explicit interest rate policy in 1994 initiated greater use of communications in support of monetary policy actions. The enhanced visibility of interest rate policy actions increased the public's appetite for transparency and encouraged even more Fed communication with markets. The train of events worked like this: Announcing the federal funds rate targets enabled the federal funds rate futures market to mature. That, in turn, made the path of expected future interest rate policy actions more visible to the public. Market participants and the public began to debate Fed concerns and intentions for future interest rates more openly. By measuring the distance between market expectations and its internal intentions for the future funds rate, the Fed could judge the effectiveness of its communications about monetary policy and how they might be adjusted to achieve a desired effect. The "conversation" between markets and the Fed became particularly important in 2003, when the federal funds rate was 1 percent and the Fed wished to lower the yield curve to fight the deflation risk by steering expected future interest rates lower with language that signaled its intention to be patient in raising interest rates.

Interestingly enough, these developments appear to have re-created the option for the Fed to make interest rate policy actions quietly or loudly. To move interest rates quietly, the Fed moves federal funds rate futures in the desired direction by gradually signaling its intentions

---

[29] Cook and Hahn (1989) point out that the Fed chose to control the federal funds rate so firmly from September 1974 until September 1979 that the public was able to perceive most changes in the target on the day they occurred. The extent to which the Fed employed borrowed reserve targeting from 1979 to 1994 is controversial. See Cook (1989) and Poole (1982) on the 1979-82 period, and Thornton (2004) on the period after 1982-84.

[30] Goodfriend (1986).

[31] See Blinder (2004) and Ferguson (2002).

through its communications. Later, the Fed simply confirms expectations that it created previously by adjusting its federal funds rate target as expected. On the other hand, if circumstances are such that the Fed wishes to get more attention for its actions, it can surprise markets with federal funds rate policy actions not prepared for in advance. In this way, the Fed can appear either to follow or to lead the market, as it could do with the borrowed-reserve targeting procedures used earlier in its history.

5 CURRENT CONTROVERSIES

There are many controversies within the broad consensus described above—on the theory of monetary policy, inflation targeting, interest rate policy, and communications—that matter for the conduct of monetary policy. Some of these are discussed below.

5.1 Specification and Interpretation of the Monetary Policy Model

The most important controversies in the theory of monetary policy involve the aggregate supply function (price-setting function), because it determines the nature of the short-run trade-off between inflation and unemployment.[32] Clearly, shocks to aggregate demand present no conflict between stabilizing inflation around its objective and stabilizing output around potential. What about shocks to aggregate supply? To appreciate the issues, consider first the baseline price-setting function discussed above derived from Calvo (1983), in which current inflation depends positively on expected future inflation or the current output gap or the current markup. Goodfriend and King (1997, 2001), King and Wolman (1999), and Goodfriend (2002) emphasize that in this baseline case, fully credible price stability keeps output at its potential and employment at its natural rate. In other words, there is no short-run trade-off between inflation and unem-

ployment, even for shocks to aggregate supply.[33] From this perspective, even those who care mainly about output and employment can support strict price stability.

Yet, many would say that the baseline case is not realistic and, indeed, taking other potential features of the macroeconomy into account can overturn the strong implication that price stability is always welfare-maximizing monetary policy. For instance, John Taylor has emphasized a trade-off in the *long-run variance* of inflation and output relative to potential in models of monetary policy that results from a short-run trade-off in the levels of inflation and unemployment. See, for instance, the papers in Taylor (1999a). Any of the following modifications of the Calvo price-setting function produce a short-run trade-off in inflation and unemployment, adding (i) a "cost" shock that feeds directly into inflation irrespective of expectations or the current markup, (ii) lagged inflation that reflects structural inflation inertia in the price-setting process, and (iii) nominal wage stickiness to the baseline model, which otherwise presumes that wages are perfectly flexible.

With any of these modifications, it is no longer always possible to stabilize both inflation and output at potential. Monetary policy must create a shortfall of aggregate demand relative to potential output to offset the effect of a cost shock or inertial inflation on current inflation. Nominal wage stickiness creates a trade-off with respect to productivity shocks even without modifications (i) and (ii). To see this, first consider a temporary negative shock to productivity in the baseline model. In that case, markup and inflation stabilization both call for a contraction in aggregate demand to conform to the contraction in potential output. And nominal and real wages both fall with productivity, offsetting the effect of the negative shock to productivity on marginal cost and the markup. Thus, when wages are flexible, monetary policy can simultaneously stabilize the output

---

[32] The aggregate supply function derived from Calvo (1983) has a small long-run trade-off between unemployment and inflation that is ignored in practical applications.

[33] Fully credible price stability means that current inflation and expected future inflation are identical (and consistent with a low-inflation target). In this case, the Calvo price-setting function implies that actual output equals potential output or, equivalently, in the baseline model, that the actual markup equals the profit-maximizing markup.

gap and inflation. Things don't work out as neatly if nominal wages are sticky.[34] Then, monetary policy must steer aggregate demand below potential (to raise the marginal physical product of labor) to offset the effect of negative productivity growth on marginal cost in order to stabilize the markup and the inflation rate.

Although these modifications seem realistic, there are reasons to question their importance in practice. First, because marginal cost is already taken into account in the underlying theory, strictly speaking there is no role for a "cost" shock in the price-setting function. The statistical residual found in practice might just reflect measurement error or noise in the modeling of expectations. If one argues that some costs flow directly to prices in a perfectly competitive sector, then theory suggests that the central bank should consider stabilizing only a "core" index of monopolistically competitive sticky prices. Second, theory that justifies structural inertia in the inflation-generating process is controversial.[35] Lags of inflation in an estimated inflation-generating function could reflect persistence introduced into the inflation rate by central bank behavior, especially in the presence of measurement or other specification errors. There is evidence that apparent inflation persistence is reduced when inflation is low and stable.[36] Third, an inflation target of 1 to 2 percent coupled with productivity growth of around 2 percent produces nominal wage growth in the 3 to 4 percent range. Such high average nominal wage growth should keep the economy away from situations in which significant downward nominal wage stickiness, as opposed to slower nominal wage growth, is required to keep price inflation stable and output at potential.

5.2 Should the Fed Adopt an Inflation Target?

Given the Fed's established commitment to low inflation, and the widely agreed-upon benefits

derived from putting a priority on price stability, the question is this: Should the Fed adopt an explicit, numerical target range for inflation and strive to keep inflation in or near that range? This debate is well illustrated by an exchange between Goodfriend (2003b) and Kohn (2005). Goodfriend argues that the Greenspan Fed has been targeting inflation *implicitly* in the following senses. First, Chairman Greenspan testified in 1989 in favor of a qualitative low-inflation objective for the Fed, defined as a situation in which "the expected rate of change of the general level of prices ceases to be a factor in individual and business decision-making."[37] Thus, it is reasonable to think that the Greenspan Fed sought to make that definition of price stability a reality over time. Second, the Greenspan Fed targeted inflation *flexibly*. It achieved price stability gradually by leaning against rising inflation in the late 1980s, bringing it down gradually in the early 1990s, holding the line on inflation in 1994, and keeping a measure of inflation favored by the Fed, core PCE inflation, in the 1 to 2 percent range thereafter. Third, it is difficult to imagine that, henceforth, the Greenspan Fed deliberately would target core PCE inflation above 2 percent or below 1 percent. Fourth, the Greenspan Fed has implicitly practiced inflation targeting as *constrained countercyclical stabilization policy*. The Greenspan Fed exploited its credibility for low inflation to lower short-term interest rates aggressively to fight the recession in 2001 and to keep short-term interest rates at historic lows since then to stimulate employment and guard against deflation. Thus, Goodfriend argues that to help perpetuate its current practice of flexible inflation targeting as constrained stabilization policy, the Fed should acknowledge an explicit 1 to 2 percent *long-run* target range for core PCE inflation.

Contrary to Goodfriend, Kohn (2005) argues that the Fed would not have been able to adapt as flexibly to the changing conditions described above if an explicit inflation target had already been in place. So Kohn would not characterize policy pursued by the Greenspan Fed as implicit inflation targeting. Moreover, Kohn argues that

---

[34] See Erceg, Henderson, and Levin (2000).

[35] See Fuhrer and Moore (1995).

[36] See Cecchetti (1995) and Cogley and Sargent (2001).

[37] Greenspan (1990, p. 6).

even without explicit inflation targeting the economy has enjoyed most of the benefits of low and stable inflation and inflation expectations. He sees little need to adopt a formal inflation target to help perpetuate the focus on price stability in the future. In effect, Kohn thinks that a formal inflation target would exert a needless constraint on countercyclical stabilization policy, in part because he worries that it might be imposed with more unproductive conditions than Goodfriend thinks would be the case.

In return, Goodfriend emphasizes three points. In the long run there are *no* circumstances in which sustained inflation should or need be much higher or lower than today. Monetary policy best encourages employment and economic growth in the long run by stabilizing inflation and inflation expectations. A central bank has an *obligation* to inform Congress formally of these lessons learned from theory and experience of monetary policy since October 1979 and to ask to be held accountable for keeping inflation in or near a 1 to 2 percent target range over time in order to improve congressional oversight of monetary policy.

5.3 Interest Rate Policy with No Role for Money

It is ironic that monetarists deserve much of the credit for laying the groundwork for the Fed's defeat of inflation, yet the Fed currently ignores money in both the implementation and analysis of monetary policy.[38] Moreover, monetarists have long emphasized the dangers inherent in implementing monetary policy using the federal funds rate instead of using bank reserves or the monetary base as the policy instrument.[39] Yet, the Fed has pursued an explicit interest rate policy since 1994. It is worth recalling, then, the nature of the monetarist concerns and to consider more generally the robustness of interest rate policy without any role for money.

Poole (1978) presents the classic monetarist criticism of monetary policy: The Fed has tended to smooth short-term interest rates excessively

over the business cycle in the following sense.[40] The Fed has been reluctant to raise short-term interest rates promptly and aggressively enough when the economy strengthens after a recession trough; and the Fed has not lowered rates promptly and aggressively enough when the economy weakens at the start of a recession. Hence, interest rate policy has imparted an excessively procyclical bias to money growth that has exacerbated the business cycle. Poole points out that, in the past, the smoothing of short-term interest rates has actually caused both short- and long-term rates to become more volatile over time. Although Poole doesn't mention it, interest rate smoothing probably played a large part in creating the increasingly inflationary and excessively volatile go-stop cycles before October 1979.

The Fed has learned to adjust interest rates more preemptively since October 1979. It moved interest rates aggressively during the Volcker disinflation, and inflationary go-stop policy cycles are no more. A closer look, however, indicates that some residual problems associated with interest rate smoothing in Poole's sense may remain. For instance, the Fed did not respond with higher short-term interest rates during the 1987 inflation scare—and may have held rates too low for too long after the October 1987 stock market crash, given the increase in inflation that followed. On the other hand, the Fed did move aggressively and preemptively to head off rising inflation in 1994, without creating a recession. Later in the decade, though, the Fed may have exacerbated cyclical instability by holding the federal funds rate target too low for too long.[41]

Only time will tell whether the monetarist argument that interest rate policy is inherently destabilizing will reassert itself. Before leaving this point, however, it must be mentioned that Woodford (2003) has shown that "inertial" interest rate policy may be advantageous. Specifically, if interest rate smoothing is measured by the coefficient on $R(t-1)$ in a rule for $R(t)$, the federal funds rate, then Woodford argues that coefficients above 1 (superinertial interest rate rules) may be optimal.

---

[38] See Brayton et al. (1997).

[39] McCallum (2000b) presents evidence that monetary base rules performed better over 1970-98 than Taylor-style interest rate rules.

[40] Poole (1978, p. 105-10).

[41] See Goodfriend (2002).

Of course, this requires that the rule also respond vigorously to inflation or expected future inflation and possibly to the output gap.

Whatever one thinks about interest rate policy, there are good reasons why money ought to be integrated into the Fed's operating procedures to some extent. First, the Fed should have a contingency plan to implement "quantitative" policy by expanding its balance sheet in case the zero bound becomes a constraint on interest rate policy. Second, the Fed should have a contingency plan for returning to monetary targeting in the event that high and volatile inflation and inflation expectations cause trouble again. Third, the Fed needs to understand better how interest rate policy should be modified to counteract shocks to the production and use of broad money in the presence of extreme asset price movements or crises of confidence in credit markets.[42]

A final, crucial concern about interest rate policy is this: Explicit interest rate policy as conducted by the Fed today relies heavily for its effectiveness on the *credibility* of the Fed's commitment to price stability.[43] There has been no *explicit* nominal anchor for U.S. monetary policy at least since the United States left the gold standard when the Bretton Woods fixed exchange rate system collapsed in 1973.[44] Six years of monetary chaos after that persuaded the Volcker Fed in October 1979 to work toward establishing an *implicit* nominal anchor by restoring and maintaining credibility for low inflation. Monetary economists have taught, and central bankers have commonly believed, that monetary policy ought to have an explicit nominal anchor such as a link to gold, a fixed foreign exchange rate, an announced path for a monetary aggregate, or an inflation target.[45] Yet Congress has not designated one and the Fed has not adopted an explicit nominal anchor to replace the link to gold. Practical and theoretical developments since October 1979 suggest that monetary policy may not need an

explicit nominal anchor after all, at least in some circumstances. It is debatable, however, whether Fed credibility for low inflation alone will prove to be a robust substitute for an explicit nominal anchor in the face of the monetary policy challenges to come, especially since the Fed's commitment to low inflation needs the support of conforming fiscal policy to be fully credible.

5.4 Clarifying Short-Run Communications

Because the Fed does not publicly and explicitly specify a target range for inflation, it must signal its short-run concerns and intentions about inflation and deflation entirely in post-FOMC meeting statements and minutes and in the Chairman's speeches and reports to Congress. Problems that the Fed experienced in 2003 in signaling its concern about deflation raise questions as to whether statements and speeches substitute adequately for an explicit inflation target. For instance, the statement following the May 2003 FOMC meeting, that further disinflation was unwelcome, came as a surprise, and media commentary amplified the nervousness about deflation well beyond what was justified. Expected future funds rates fell sharply and pulled longer-term interest rates down sharply as well. The Fed reduced the federal funds rate less than the widely expected 50 basis points at the June meeting, and longer-term interest rates promptly reversed field.

Broaddus and Goodfriend (2004) point out that if an inflation target range had been in place in 2003, the public could have inferred the Fed's growing concern about disinflation gradually as the inflation rate drifted down earlier in the year. Expected future interest rates likely would have come down smoothly with less chance of overshooting the Fed's intended policy stance. The authors went on to assert that this experience illustrates a more general point. Rational expectations reasoning teaches that the public has difficulty gauging the intent of a Fed policy action taken out of context and, therefore, the Fed will find it particularly difficult to predict the effect of an ad hoc unsystematic policy action. Since the announcement that any more disinflation would be unwelcome was ad hoc by definition, it is not

---

[42] See Goodfriend (forthcoming).

[43] See Blinder (2000).

[44] The gold standard ceased to provide an effective nominal anchor for monetary policy long before that. See Goodfriend (1988).

[45] See McCallum (2000a).

Goodfriend

surprising that it caused confusion. In this case, the reaction was excessive, but in another situation there might have been an insufficient reaction. The point is that the scope for misunderstanding in discretionary communications is great.[46] On this basis, a case can be made that an inflation target would be a valuable addition to the Fed's short-run communications procedures. From this perspective, Broaddus and Goodfriend argue, the Fed has authority from Congress to set an inflation target as part of its operational independence.

In the second half of 2003, the Fed had difficulty convincing financial markets of its inclination to maintain a low federal funds rate for a "considerable period." One possible reason, also argued by Broaddus and Goodfriend, is that policy statements emphasized strong real economic growth during the period but paid insufficient attention to the sizable *gap* in employment and to the cumulative deflation in unit labor costs that had almost certainly widened the gap between actual and profit-maximizing markups. The apparent size of these gaps likely helped to produce the disinflation that occurred in 2003 and contributed to the deflation risk that inclined the Fed to keep the federal funds rate low. Broaddus and Goodfriend argue that the Fed ought to clarify its short-run concerns and intentions by referring to gaps in markups, employment, and output more prominently in its communications in order to make expected future federal funds rates conform more closely to the Fed's preemptive policy intentions. Talking in terms of gap indicators is controversial because of the unfortunate experience in the 1960s and 1970s, when calling attention to employment and output gaps created pressure that led to inflationary monetary policy and poor macroeconomic performance. Nevertheless, Broaddus and Goodfriend argue that times have changed and the Fed could deal with such pressures by announcing an explicit inflation target.

6 CONCLUSION

Monetary theory and policy have been revolutionized in the two decades since the Federal

[46] See McCallum (2004).

Reserve moved in October 1979 to stabilize inflation and bring it down. It is true that much of today's core theory and practice was already in place by October 1979. For instance, the stickiness of prices was understood to be important, current inflation was understood to depend on expected inflation, and inflation was understood to respond inversely to the output gap. But the advances were revolutionary nevertheless. On the side of practice, the decisive and revolutionary factor was the demonstration that monetary policy has the power to acquire and maintain credibility for low inflation so as to improve the stability of both inflation and output relative to potential. On the theory side, the introduction of rational expectations was decisive because it enabled models of monetary policy to incorporate forward-looking elements of aggregate demand and price setting, long known to be critically important for policy analysis, so as to understand how monetary policy consistently committed to stabilizing inflation could achieve the favorable results found in practice. In short, the period since October 1979 was a remarkable one in which major parallel developments in both theory and experience reinforced each other, making monetary economists and central bankers both more confident of their respective advances.

REFERENCES

Ball, Laurence. "Credible Disinflaton with Staggered Price-Setting." *American Economic Review*, March 1994, *84*, pp. 282-89.

Barro, Robert J. and Gordon, David B. "A Positive Theory of Monetary Policy in a Natural Rate Model." *Journal of Political Economy*, 1983, *91*, pp. 589-610.

Bernanke, Ben S. and Mishkin, Frederic S. "Inflation Targeting: A New Framework for Monetary Policy?" *Journal of Economic Perspectives*, 1997, *11*, pp. 97-116.

Blinder, Alan S. "Central-Bank Credibility: Why Do We Care? How Do We Build It?" *American Economic Review*, December 2000, *90*, pp. 1421-31.

Blinder, Alan S. *The Quite Revolution: Central Banking Goes Modern.* New Haven, CT: Yale University Press, 2004.

Brayton, Flint; Levin, Andy; Tryon, Ralph and Williams, John. "The Evolution of Macro Models at the Federal Reserve Board." *Carnegie-Rochester Conference Series on Public Policy*, December 1997, *47*, pp. 43-81.

Broaddus, J. Alfred Jr. and Goodfriend, Marvin. "Sustaining Price Stability." Federal Reserve Bank of Richmond *Economic Quarterly*, Summer 2004, *90*, pp. 3-20.

Calvo, Guillermo A. "Staggered Prices in a Utility Maximizing Framework." *Journal of Monetary Economics*, September 1983, *12*, pp. 383-98.

Cecchetti, Stephen G. "Inflation Indicators and Inflation Policy," in Ben S. Bernanke and Julio J. Rotemberg, eds., *NBER Macroeconomics Annual.* Cambridge, MA: MIT Press, 1995, pp. 189-219.

Clarida, Richard; Galí, Jordi and Gertler, Mark. "The Science of Monetary Policy: A New Keynesian Perspective." *Journal of Economic Literature*, December 1999, *37*, pp. 1661-707.

Cogley, Timothy and Sargent, Thomas J. "The Evolution of Postwar U.S. Inflation Dynamics," in Ben S. Bernanke and Kenneth S. Rogoff, eds., *NBER Macroeconomics Annual.* Cambridge: MIT Press, 2001, pp. 331-73.

Cook, Timothy. "Determinants of the Federal Funds Rate: 1979-1982." Federal Reserve Bank of Richmond *Economic Review*, January/February 1989, pp. 3-19.

Cook, Timothy and Hahn, Thomas. "The Effect of Changes in the Federal Funds Rate Target on Market Interest Rates in the 1970s." *Journal of Monetary Economics*, November 1989, *24*, pp. 331-51.

Erceg, Christopher J.; Henderson, Dale W. and Levin, Andrew T. "Optimal Monetary Policy with Staggered Wage and Price Contracts." *Journal of Monetary Economics*, October 2000, *46*(2), pp. 281-313.

Federal Open Market Committee. Transcripts. Washington, DC: Board of Governors of the Federal Reserve System, 1979-81.

Feldstein, Martin. "The Costs and Benefits of Going from Low Inflation to Price Stability," in Christina D. Romer and David H. Romer, eds., *Reducing Inflation: Motivation and Strategy.* Chicago: University of Chicago Press, 1997, pp. 123-66.

Fellner, William. "The Credibility Effect and Rational Expectations: Implications of the Gramlich Study." *Brookings Papers on Economic Activity*, 1979, *1*, pp. 167-89.

Ferguson, R. "Why Central Banks Should Talk." Remarks at the Graduate Institute of International Studies, Geneva, Switzerland, January 2002.

Fischer, Stanley. "Modern Central Banking," in Forrest Capie et al., eds., *The Future of Central Banking: The Tercentenary Symposium of the Bank of England.* Cambridge: Cambridge University Press, 1994, pp. 262-308.

Fisher, Irving. *The Theory of Interest.* Fairfield, NJ: Augustus M. Kelly, [1930] 1986.

Friedman, Milton. *A Theory of the Consumption Function.* Princeton: Princeton University Press, 1957.

Friedman, Milton. *A Program for Monetary Stability.* New York: Fordham University Press, 1960.

Friedman, Milton. Statement before the U.S. Congress, House of Representatives, Committee on Banking and Currency in *The Federal Reserve System After Fifty Years.* Subcommittee on Domestic Finance. Hearings. 88 Cong. 2 Sess. Washington, DC: U.S. Government Printing Office, 1964.

Friedman, Milton. "The Role of Monetary Policy." *American Economic Review*, March 1968, *58*(1), pp. 1-17.

Friedman, Milton. "Quantity Theory of Money," in John Eatwell, Murray Milgate, and Peter Newman, eds., *The New Palgrave: Money.* New York: W.W. Norton & Company, 1989, pp. 1-40.

Goodfriend

Fuhrer, Jeffrey and Moore, George. "Inflation
Persistence." *Quarterly Journal of Economics*,
February 1995, *110*(1), pp. 127-59.

Goodfriend, Marvin. "Monetary Mystique: Secrecy
and Central Banking." *Journal of Monetary
Economics*, 1986, *17*, pp. 63-92.

Goodfriend, Marvin. "Central Banking Under the
Gold Standard." *Carnegie-Rochester Conference
Series on Public Policy*, Autumn 1988, *29*, pp. 85-124.

Goodfriend, Marvin. "Interest Rates and the Conduct
of Monetary Policy." *Carnegie-Rochester Conference
Series on Public Policy*, Spring 1991, *34*, pp. 7-30.

Goodfriend, Marvin. "Interest Rate Policy and the
Inflation Scare Problem: 1979-1992." Federal
Reserve Bank of Richmond *Economic Quarterly*,
Winter 1993, *79*, pp. 1-24.

Goodfriend, Marvin. "Monetary Policy Comes of
Age: A 20th Century Odyssey." Federal Reserve
Bank of Richmond *Economic Quarterly*, Winter
1997, *83*, pp. 1-22.

Goodfriend, Marvin. "The Phases of U.S. Monetary
Policy: 1987 to 2001." Federal Reserve Bank of
Richmond *Economic Quarterly*, Fall 2002, *88*, pp.
1-17.

Goodfriend, Marvin. Book Review: Allan H. Meltzer,
*A History of the Federal Reserve, Volume I: 1913-
1951*. Federal Reserve Bank of Minneapolis *The
Region*, December 2003a, *1*, pp. 82-89.

Goodfriend, Marvin. "Inflation Targeting in the United
States?" NBER Working Paper No. 9981, National
Bureau of Economic Research, September 2003b
(also in Ben S. Bernanke and Michael Woodford,
eds., *The Inflation Targeting Debate*. Cambridge,
MA: National Bureau of Economic Research, 2005,
pp. 311-37).

Goodfriend, Marvin. "Monetary Policy in the New
Neoclassical Synthesis: A Primer." Federal Reserve
Bank of Richmond *Economic Quarterly*, Summer
2004, *90*(3), pp. 21-45 (reprinted from *International
Finance*, 2002, *5*, pp. 165-92).

Goodfriend, Marvin. "Narrow Money, Broad Money,
and the Transmission of Monetary Policy," in
Faust, Jon, Athanasios Orphanides, and David
Reifschneider, eds., *Models of Monetary Policy:
Research in the Tradition of Dale Henderson,
Richard Porter, and Peter Tinsley*. Proceedings of a
Federal Reserve Board conference (March 26-27,
2004). Washington, DC: Board of Governors of the
Federal Reserve System (forthcoming).

Goodfriend, Marvin and King, Robert G. "The New
Neoclassical Synthesis and the Role of Monetary
Policy," in Ben S. Bernanke and Julio J. Rotemberg,
eds., *NBER Macroeconomics Annual*. Cambridge:
MIT Press, 1997, pp. 231-82.

Goodfriend, Marvin and King, Robert G. "The Case
for Price Stability," in A.G. Herrero et al., eds.,
*First ECB Central Banking Conference, Why Price
Stability?* Frankfurt: European Central Bank, 2001,
pp. 53-94; NBER Working Paper No. 8423, National
Bureau of Economic Resarch, August 2001.

Greenspan, Alan. Statement before the U.S. Congress,
House of Representatives, Subcommittee on
Domestic Monetary Policy of the Committee on
Banking, Finance and Urban Affairs, *Zero Inflation*.
Hearing, 101 Cong. 1 Sess. Washington, DC: U.S.
Government Printing Office, 1990.

Gurkaynak, Refet S.; Sack, Brian and Swanson, Eric.
"The Excess Sensitivity of Long-term Interest Rates:
Evidence and Implications for Macroeconomic
Models." Finance and Economics Discussion
Series 2003-50, Board of Governors of the Federal
Reserve System, February 2003.

Hawtrey, R.G. *A Century of Bank Rate*. London:
Longran, 1938.

Hetzel, Robert L. "Arthur Burns and Inflation."
Federal Reserve Bank of Richmond *Economic
Quarterly*, Winter 1998, *84*, pp. 21-44.

Ireland, Peter. "Long-Term Interest Rates and Inflation:
A Fisherian Approach." Federal Reserve Bank of
Richmond *Economic Quarterly*, Winter 1996, *82*(1),
pp. 21-35.

Kerr, William and King, Robert G. "Limits on Interest
Rate Rules in the IS Model." Federal Reserve Bank

of Richmond *Quarterly Review*, Spring 1996, *82*, pp. 47-75.

King, Robert G. and Wolman, Alexander L. "What Should the Monetary Authority Do When Prices Are Sticky?" in John B. Taylor, ed., *Monetary Policy Rules*. Chicago: University of Chicago Press, 1999, pp. 349-404.

Kohn, Donald. "Comments on Marvin Goodfriend's 'Inflation Targeting in the United States?'" in Ben S. Bernanke and Michael Woodford, eds., *The Inflation Targeting Debate*. Cambridge, MA: National Bureau of Economic Research, 2005, pp. 337-50.

Kydland, Finn and Prescott, Edward C. "Rules Rather than Discretion: The Inconsistency of Optimal Plans." *Journal of Political Economy*, June 1977, *85*(3), pp. 473-91.

Lindsey, David; Orphanides, Athanasios and Rasche, Robert H. "The Reform of October 1979: How It Happened and Why." Federal Reserve Bank of St. Louis *Review*, March/April 2005, *87*(2. Part 2), pp. 187-235.

Lucas, Robert E. Jr. "Econometric Policy Evaluation: A Critique." *Carnegie-Rochester Conference Series on Public Policy*, 1976, *1*, pp. 19-46.

Lucas, Robert E. Jr. *Studies in Business-Cycle Theory*. Cambridge, MA: MIT Press, 1981.

McCallum, Bennett T. "Issues in the Design of Monetary Policy Rules," in John B. Taylor and Michael Woodford, eds., *Handbook of Macro-economics*. Amsterdam: Elsevier Science B.V., 1999, pp. 1483-530.

McCallum, Bennett T. "The United States Deserves a Monetary Standard." Unpublished manuscript, Shadow Open Market Committee, 2000a.

McCallum, Bennett T. "Alternative Monetary Policy Rules: A Comparison with Historical Settings of the United States, the United Kingdom, and Japan." Federal Reserve Bank of Richmond *Economic Quarterly*, Winter 2000b, pp. 49-79.

McCallum, Bennett T. "Monetary Policy Analysis in

Models without Money." NBER Working Paper No. 8174, National Bureau of Economic Research, 2001.

McCallum, Bennett T. "Misconceptions Regarding Rules vs. Discretion for Monetary Policy." *Cato Journal*, Winter 2004, *23*(3), pp. 365-72.

Mankiw, N. Gregory and Romer, David H., eds. *New Keynesian Macroeconomics*. Volumes 1 and 2. Cambridge, MA: MIT Press, 1991.

Meltzer, Allan H. "The Demand for Money: The Evidence from the Time Series." *Journal of Political Economy*, June 1963, *71*, pp. 219-46.

Meltzer, Allan H. *A History of the Federal Reserve*. Volume 1: 1913-1951. Chicago: University of Chicago Press, 2003.

Okun, Arthur M. "Efficient Disinflation Policies." *American Economic Review*, May 1978, *68*, pp. 348-52.

Orphanides, Athanasios and Williams, John C. "Inflation Scares and Forecast-Based Monetary Policy." *Review of Economic Dynamics*, 2005 (forthcoming).

Poole, William. *Money and the Economy: A Monetarist View*. Reading: Addison-Wesley Publishing Co., 1978.

Poole, William. "Federal Reserve Operating Procedures: A Survey and Evaluation of the Historical Record Since October 1979." *Journal of Money, Credit, and Banking*, 1982, *14*(4). pp. 575-96.

Romer, Christina D. and Romer, David H. "Does Monetary Policy Matter? A New Test in the Spirit of Friedman and Schwartz," in Oliver J. Blanchard and Stanley Fisher, eds., *NBER Macroeconomics Annual*. Cambridge, MA: MIT Press, 1989, pp. 121-69.

Sargent, Thomas J. *Rational Expectations and Inflation*. New York: Harper & Row, 1986.

Schmitt-Grohé, Stephanie and Uribe, Martin. "Optimal Fiscal and Monetary Policy under Sticky Prices." NBER Working Paper No. 9220, National Bureau of Economic Research, 2002.

Goodfriend

Schreft, Stacey L. "Credit Controls: 1980." Federal Reserve Bank of Richmond *Economic Review*, November/December 1990, pp. 25-55.

Shapiro, Matthew D. "Federal Reserve Policy: Cause and Effect," in N. Gregory Mankiw, ed., *Monetary Policy*. Chicago: University of Chicago Press, 1994, pp. 307-34.

Svensson, Lars E.O. "Inflation Targeting as a Monetary Policy Rule." *Journal of Monetary Economics*, June 1999, *43*, pp. 607-54.

Taylor, John B. "Estimation and Control of a Macroeconomic Model with Rational Expectations." *Econometrica*, September 1979, *47*(5), pp. 1267-86.

Taylor, John B. "Establishing Credibility: A Rational Expectations Viewpoint." *American Economic Review Papers and Proceedings*, May 1982, *72*(2), pp. 81-85.

Taylor, John B. "Discretion Versus Policy Rules in Practice." *Carnegie-Rochester Conference Series on Public Policy*, December 1993, *29*, pp. 195-214.

Taylor, John B., ed. *Monetary Policy Rules*. Chicago: University of Chicago Press, 1999a.

Taylor, John B. "Staggered Price and Wage Setting in Macroeconomics," in John B. Taylor and Michael Woodford, eds., *Handbook of Macroeconomics*. Amsterdam: Elsevier Science B.V., 1999b, pp. 1009-50.

Thornton, Daniel L. "When Did the FOMC Begin Targeting the Federal Funds Rate? What the Verbatim Transcripts Tell Us." Working paper, Federal Reserve Bank of St. Louis, August 2004.

Tobin, James. "Stabilization Policy Ten Years After." *Brookings Papers on Economic Activity*, 1980, *1*, pp. 19-71.

Woodford, Michael. *Interest and Prices: Foundations of a Theory of Monetary Policy*. Princeton: Princeton University Press, 2003.

[13]

Panel Discussion I

What Have We Learned Since October 1979?

Ben S. Bernanke

The question asked of this panel is, "What have we learned since October 1979?" The evidence suggests that we have learned quite a bit. Most notably, monetary policymakers, political leaders, and the public have been persuaded by two decades of experience that low and stable inflation has very substantial economic benefits.

This consensus marks a considerable change from the views held by many economists at the time that Paul Volcker became Fed Chairman. In 1979, most economists would have agreed that, in principle, low inflation promotes economic growth and efficiency in the long run. However, many also believed that, in the range of inflation rates typically experienced by industrial countries, the benefits of low inflation are probably small—particularly when set against the short-run costs of a major disinflation, as the United States faced at that time. Indeed, some economists would have held that low-inflation policies would likely prove counterproductive, even in the long run, if an increased focus on inflation inhibited monetary policymakers from responding adequately to fluctuations in economic activity and employment.

As it turned out, the low-inflation era of the past two decades has seen not only significant improvements in economic growth and productivity but also a marked *reduction* in economic volatility, both in the United States and abroad, a phenomenon that has been dubbed "the Great Moderation." Recessions have become less frequent and milder, and quarter-to-quarter volatility in output and employment has declined significantly as well. The sources of the Great Moderation remain somewhat controversial, but, as I have argued elsewhere, there is evidence for the view that improved control of inflation has contributed in important measure to this welcome change in the economy (Bernanke, 2004). Paul Volcker and his colleagues on the Federal Open Market Committee deserve enormous credit both for recognizing the crucial importance of achieving low and stable inflation and for the courage and perseverance with which they tackled America's critical inflation problem.

I could say much more about Volcker's achievement and its lasting benefits, but I am sure that many other speakers will cover that ground. Instead, in my remaining time, I will focus on some lessons that economists have drawn from the Volcker regime regarding the importance of credibility in central banking and how that credibility can be obtained. As usual, the views I will express are my own and are not necessarily shared by my colleagues in the Federal Reserve System.

Volcker could not have accomplished what he did, of course, had he not been appointed to the chairmanship by President Jimmy Carter. In retrospect, however, Carter's appointment decision seems at least a bit incongruous. Why would the President appoint as head of the central bank an individual whose economic views and policy goals (not to mention personal style) seemed, at least on the surface, quite different from his own? However, not long into Volcker's term, a staff economist at the Board of Governors produced a paper that explained why Carter's decision may in

Ben S. Bernanke is a member of the Board of Governors of the Federal Reserve System.

Federal Reserve Bank of St. Louis *Review*, March/April 2005, *87*(2, Part 2), pp. 277-82.
© 2005, The Federal Reserve Bank of St. Louis.

fact have been quite sensible from the President's, and indeed the society's, point of view. Although the question seems a narrow one, the insights of the paper had far broader application; indeed, this research has substantially advanced our understanding of the links among central bank credibility, central bank structure, and the effectiveness of monetary policy.

Insiders will have already guessed that the Board economist to whom I refer is Kenneth Rogoff, currently a professor of economics at Harvard, and that the paper in question is Ken's 1985 article, "The Optimal Degree of Commitment to an Intermediate Monetary Target" (Rogoff, 1985).[1] The insights of the Rogoff paper are well worth recalling today. Rather than considering the paper in isolation, however, I will place it in the context of two other classic papers on credibility and central bank design, an earlier work by Finn Kydland and Edward Prescott and a later piece by Carl Walsh. As I proceed, I will note what I see to be the important lessons and the practical implications of this line of research.[2]

Central bankers have long recognized at some level that the credibility of their pronouncements matters. I think it is fair to say, however, that in the late 1960s and 1970s, as the U.S. inflation crisis was building, economists and policymakers did not fully understand or appreciate the determinants of credibility and its link to policy outcomes. In 1977, however, Finn Kydland and Edward Prescott published a classic paper, entitled "Rules Rather than Discretion: The Inconsistency of Optimal Plans" (Kydland and Prescott, 1977), that provided the first modern analysis of these issues.[3] Specifically, Kydland and Prescott demonstrated why, in many situations, economic outcomes will be better if policymakers are able to make credible

commitments, or promises, about certain aspects of the policies they will follow in the future. "Credible" in this context means that the public believes that the policymakers will keep their promises, even if they face incentives to renege.

In particular, as one of Kydland and Prescott's examples illustrates, monetary policymakers will generally find it advantageous to commit publicly to following policies that will produce low inflation. If the policymakers' statements are believed (that is, if they are credible), then the public will expect inflation to be low and demands for wage and price increases should accordingly be moderate. In a virtuous circle, this cooperative behavior by the public makes the central bank's commitment to low inflation easier to fulfill. In contrast, if the public is skeptical of the central bank's commitment to low inflation (for example, if it believes that the central bank may give in to the temptation to overstimulate the economy for the sake of short-term employment gains), then the public's inflation expectations will be higher than they otherwise would be. Expectations of high inflation lead to more aggressive wage and price demands, which make achieving and maintaining low inflation more difficult and costly (in terms of lost output and employment) for the central bank.

Providing a clear explanation of why credibility is important for effective policymaking, as Kydland and Prescott did, was an important step. However, these authors largely left open the critical issue of how a central bank is supposed to obtain credibility in the first place. Here is where Rogoff's seminal article took up the thread.[4] Motivated by

---

[1] Rogoff's paper was widely circulated in 1982, a sad commentary on publication lags in economics.

[2] In focusing on three landmark papers, I necessarily ignore what has become an enormous literature on credibility and monetary policy. Walsh (2003, Chap. 8) provides an excellent overview. Rogoff (1987) was an important early survey of the "first generation" of models of credibility in the context of central banking.

[3] In another noteworthy paper, Calvo (1978) made a number of points similar to those developed by Kydland and Prescott (1977). The extension of the Kydland-Prescott "inflation bias" by Barro and Gordon (1983a) has proved highly influential.

[4] Rogoff was my graduate school classmate at M.I.T., and I recently asked him for his recollections about the origins of the "conservative" central banker. Here (from a personal e-mail) is part of his response:

[T]he paper was mainly written at the Board in 1982...It came out as an IMF working paper in February 1983 (I was visiting there), and then the same version came out as an International Finance Discussion paper [at the Board of Governors] in September 1983...The original version of the paper...featured inflation targeting. Much like the published paper, I suggested that having an independent central bank can be a solution to the time consistency [that is, credibility] problem if we give the bank an intermediate target and some (unspecified) incentive to hit the target...I had the conservative central banker idea in there as well, as one practical way to ensure the central bank placed a high weight on inflation. Larry Summers, my editor at the [*Quarterly Journal of Economics*], urged me to move that idea up to the front

the example of Carter and Volcker, Rogoff's paper showed analytically why even a President who is not particularly averse to inflation, or at least no more so than the average member of the general public, might find it in his interest to appoint a well-known "inflation hawk" to head the central bank. The benefit of appointing a hawkish central banker is the increased inflation-fighting credibility that such an appointment brings. The public is certainly more likely to believe an inflation hawk when he promises to contain inflation because they understand that, as someone who is intrinsically averse to inflation, he is unlikely to renege on his commitment. As increased credibility allows the central bank to achieve low inflation at a smaller cost than a noncredible central bank can, the President may well find, somewhat paradoxically, that he prefers the economic outcomes achieved under the hawkish central banker to those that could have been obtained under a central banker with views closer to his own and those of the public.

Appointing an inflation hawk to head the central bank may not be enough to ensure credibility for monetary policy, however. As Rogoff noted in his article, for this strategy to confer significant credibility benefits, the central bank must be perceived by the public as being sufficiently independent from the rest of the government to be immune to short-term political pressures. Thus Rogoff's proposed strategy was really two-pronged: The appointment of inflation-averse central bankers must be combined with measures to ensure central bank independence. These ideas, supported by a great deal of empirical work, have proven highly influential.[5] Indeed, the credibility

benefits of central bank autonomy have been widely recognized in the past 20 years, not only in the academic literature but, far more consequentially, in the real-world design of central banking institutions. For example, in the United Kingdom, the euro area, Japan, and numerous other places, recent legislation or other government action has palpably strengthened the independence of the central banks.[6]

Rogoff's proposed solution to the credibility problems of central banks does have some limitations, however, as Ken recognized both in his paper and in subsequent work. First, although an inflation-averse central banker enhances credibility and delivers lower inflation on average, he may not respond to shocks to the economy in the socially desirable way. For example, faced with an aggregate supply shock (such as a sharp rise in oil prices), an inflation-averse central banker will tend to react too aggressively (from society's point of view) to contain the inflationary impact of the shock, with insufficient attention to the consequences of his policy for output and employment.[7] Second, contrary to an assumption of Rogoff's paper, in practice, the policy preferences of a newly appointed central banker will not be precisely known by the public but must be inferred from policy actions. (Certainly the public's perceptions of Chairman Volcker's views and objectives evolved over time.) Knowing that the public must make such inferences might tempt a central banker to misrepresent the state of the economy (Canzoneri, 1985) or even to take suboptimal policy decisions; for example, the central banker may feel compelled to tighten policy more aggres-

---

section and place inflation targeting second. This, of course, is how the paper ended up.

[Regarding the Fed], Dale Henderson and Matt Canzoneri liked the paper very much...[M]any other researchers gave me feedback on my paper (including Peter Tinsley, Ed Offenbacher, Bob Flood, Jo Anna Gray, and many others)... Last but perhaps most important, there is absolutely no doubt that the paper was inspired by my experience watching the Volcker Fed at close range. I never would have written it had I not...ended up as an economist at the Board.

[5] Walsh (2003, Section 8.5) reviews empirical research on the correlations of central bank independence and economic outcomes. A consistent finding is that more-independent central banks produce lower inflation without any increase in output volatility.

[6] The benefits of central bank independence should not lead us to ignore its downside, which is that the very distance from the political process that increases the central bank's policy credibility by necessity also risks isolating the central bank and making it less democratically accountable. For this reason, central bankers should make communication with the public and their elected representatives a high priority. Moreover, central bank independence does not imply that central banks should never coordinate with other parts of the government, under the appropriate circumstances.

[7] Lohmann (1992) shows that this problem can be ameliorated if the government limits the central bank's independence, stepping in to override the central bank's decisions when the supply shock becomes too large. However, to preserve the central bank's independence in normal situations, this approach would involve stating clearly in advance the conditions under which the government would intercede, which may not be practicable.

sively than is warranted in order to convince the public of his determination to fight inflation. The public's need to infer the central banker's policy preferences may even generate increased economic instability, as has been shown in a lively recent literature on the macroeconomic consequences of learning.[8]

The third pathbreaking paper I will mention today, a 1995 article by Carl Walsh entitled "Optimal Contracts for Central Bankers," was an attempt to address both of these issues.[9] To do so, Walsh conducted a thought experiment. He asked his readers to imagine that the government or society could offer the head of the central bank a performance contract, one that includes explicit monetary rewards or penalties that depend on the economic outcomes that occur under his watch. Remarkably, Walsh showed that, in principle, a relatively simple contract between the government and the central bank would lead to the implementation of monetary policies that would be both credible and fully optimal. Under this contract, the government provides the central banker with a base level of compensation but then applies a penalty that depends on the realized rate of inflation—the higher the observed inflation rate, the greater the penalty.

If the public understands the nature of the contract and if the penalty assessed for permitting inflation is large enough to affect central bank behavior, the existence of the contract would give credence to central bank promises to keep the inflation rate low (that is, the contract would provide credibility).[10] Walsh's contract has in common with Rogoff's approach the idea that, in

a world of imperfect credibility, giving the central banker an objective function that differs from the true objectives of society may be useful. However, Walsh also shows that the contracting approach ameliorates the two problems associated with Rogoff's approach. First, under the Walsh contract, the central banker has incentives not only to achieve the target rate of inflation but also to respond in the socially optimal manner to supply shocks.[11] Second, as the inflation objective and the central banker's incentive scheme are made explicit by the contract, the public's problem of inferring the central banker's policy preferences is significantly reduced.

There have been a few attempts in the real world to implement an incentive contract for central bankers—most famously a plan proposed to the New Zealand legislature, though never adopted, which provided for firing the governor of the central bank if the inflation rate deviated too far from the government's inflation objective.[12] But Walsh's contracts are best treated as a metaphor rather than as a literal proposal for central bank reform. Although the pay of central bankers is unlikely ever to depend directly on the realized rate of inflation, central bankers, like most people, care about many other aspects of their jobs, including their professional reputations, the prestige of the institutions in which they serve, and the probability that they will be reappointed.

Walsh's analysis and many subsequent refinements by other authors suggest that central bank performance might be improved if the government set explicit performance standards for the central bank (perhaps as part of the institution's charter or enabling legislation) and regularly compared objectives and outcomes. Alternatively, because central banks may possess the greater expertise in determining what economic outcomes are both feasible and most desirable, macroeconomic goals might be set through a joint exercise of the govern-

---

[8] Evans and Honkopohja (2001) is the standard reference on learning in macroeconomics. Recent papers that apply models of learning to the analysis of U.S. monetary policy include Erceg and Levin (2001) and Orphanides and Williams (forthcoming).

[9] Persson and Tabellini (1993) provided an influential analysis of the contracting approach that extended and developed many of the points made by Walsh (1995).

[10] An objection to this conclusion is that, although the central bank's incentives are made clear by the contract, the public might worry that the government might renege on its commitment to low inflation by changing the contract. Those who discount this concern argue that changing the contract in midstream would be costly for the government, because laws once enacted are difficult to modify and because changing an established framework for policy in an opportunistic way would be politically embarrassing.

[11] A key assumption underlying this result is that the central banker cares about the state of the economy as well as about the income provided by his incentive contract.

[12] In personal communications, Walsh reports to me that he was visiting a research institute in New Zealand at the time of these discussions. Walsh's reflection on the New Zealand proposals helped to inspire his paper.

ment and the central bank. Many countries have established targets for inflation, for example, and central bankers in those countries evidently make strong efforts to attain those targets. The Federal Reserve Act does not set quantitative goals for the U.S. central bank, but it does specify the objectives of price stability and maximum sustainable employment and requires the central bank to present semiannual reports to the Congress on monetary policy and the state of the economy. Accountability to the public as well as to the legislature is also important; for this reason, the central bank should explain regularly what it is trying to achieve and why. In sum, Walsh's paper can be read as providing theoretical support for an explicit, well-designed, and transparent framework for monetary policy, one which sets forth the objectives of policy and holds central bankers accountable for reaching those objectives (or at least for providing a detailed and plausible explanation of why the objectives were missed).

In the simple model that Walsh analyzes, the optimal contract provides all the incentives needed to induce the best possible monetary policy, so that appointing a hawkish central banker is no longer beneficial. However, in practice—because Walsh's optimal contracts can be roughly approximated at best, because both the incentives and the policy decisions faced by central bankers are far more complex than can be captured by simple models, and because the appointment of an inflation-averse central banker may provide additional assurance to the public that the government and the central bank will keep their promises—the Walsh approach and the Rogoff approach are almost certainly complementary.[13] That is, a clear, well-articulated monetary policy framework, inflation-averse central bankers, and autonomy for central banks in the execution of policy are all likely to contribute to increased central bank credibility and hence better policy outcomes. Of course, other factors that I could not cover in this short review, such as the central bank's reputation for veracity as established

over time, may also strengthen its credibility (Barro and Gordon, 1983b; Backus and Driffill, 1985).[14]

Let me end where I began, with reference to Paul Volcker and his contributions. I have discussed today how Volcker's personality and performance inspired one seminal piece of research about the determinants of central bank credibility. In focusing on a few pieces of academic research, however, I have greatly understated the impact of the Volcker era on views about central banking. The Volcker disinflation (and analogous episodes in the United Kingdom, Canada, and elsewhere) was undoubtedly a major catalyst for an explosion of fresh thinking by economists and policymakers about central bank credibility, how it is obtained, and its benefits for monetary policymaking. Over the past two decades, this new thinking has contributed to a wave of changes in central banking, particularly with respect to the institutional design of central banks and the establishment of new frameworks for the making of monetary policy.

Ironically, the applicability of the ideas stimulated by the Volcker chairmanship to the experience of the U.S. economy under his stewardship remains unclear. Though the appointment of Volcker undoubtedly increased the credibility of the Federal Reserve, the Volcker disinflation was far from a costless affair, being associated with a minor recession in 1980 and a deep recession in 1981-82.[15] Evidently, Volcker's personal credibility notwithstanding, Americans' memories of the inflationary 1970s were too fresh for their inflation expectations to change quickly. It is difficult to know whether alternative tactics would have helped; for example, the announcement of explicit inflation objectives (which would certainly have been a radical idea at the time) might have helped guide inflation expectations downward more quickly, but they might also have created a political backlash that would have doomed the entire effort. Perhaps no policy approach or set of institutional

---

[13] Several authors have shown this point in models in which the inflation bias arising from noncredible policies differs across states of nature; see, for example, Herrendorf and Lockwood (1997) and Svensson (1997).

[14] But see Rogoff (1987) for a critique of models of central bank reputation.

[15] Evidence on the behavior of inflation expectations after 1979 supports the view that the public came to appreciate only very gradually that Volcker's policies represented a break from the immediate past (Erceg and Levin, 2001).

arrangements could have eliminated the 1970s inflation at a lower cost than was actually incurred. If so, then the significance of Paul Volcker's appointment was not its immediate effect on expectations or credibility but rather that he was one of the rare individuals tough enough and with sufficient foresight to do what had to be done. By doing what was necessary to achieve price stability, the Volcker Fed laid the groundwork for two decades, so far, of strong economic performance.

REFERENCES

Backus, David and Driffill, John. "Inflation and Reputation." *American Economic Review*, June 1985, *75*(3), pp. 530-38.

Barro, Robert J. and Gordon, David B. "A Positive Theory of Monetary Policy in a Natural Rate Model." *Journal of Political Economy*, August 1983a, *91*(4), pp. 589-610.

Barro, Robert J. and Gordon, David B. "Rules, Discretion, and Reputation in a Model of Monetary Policy." *Journal of Monetary Economics*, July 1983b, *12*(1), pp. 101-21.

Bernanke, Ben S. "The Great Moderation." Remarks before the Eastern Economic Association, Washington, DC, February 20, 2004.

Calvo, Guillermo A. "On the Time Consistency of the Optimal Policy in a Monetary Economy." *Econometrica*, November 1978, *46*(6), pp. 1411-28.

Canzoneri, Matthew B. "Monetary Policy Games and the Role of Private Information." *American Economic Review*, September 1985, *75*(5), pp. 547-64.

Erceg, Christopher J. and Levin, Andrew T. "Imperfect Credibility and Inflation Persistence." Finance and Economics Discussion Series 2001-45, Board of Governors of the Federal Reserve System, October 2001.

Evans, George W. and Honkopohja, Seppo. *Learning and Expectations in Macroeconomics.* Princeton, NJ: Princeton University Press, 2001.

Herrendorf, Berthold and Lockwood, Ben. "Rogoff's 'Conservative' Central Banker Restored." *Journal of Money, Credit, and Banking*, November 1997, *29*(4, Part 1), pp. 476-95.

Kydland, Finn E. and Prescott, Edward C. "Rules Rather than Discretion: The Inconsistency of Optimal Plans." *Journal of Political Economy, 85*(3), June 1977, pp. 473-92.

Lohmann, Suzanne. "Optimal Commitment in Monetary Policy: Credibility versus Flexibility." *American Economic Review,* March 1992, *82*(1), pp. 273-86.

Orphanides, Athanasios and Williams, John C. "Imperfect Knowledge, Inflation Expectations, and Monetary Policy," in Ben S. Bernanke and Michael D. Woodford, eds., *The Inflation Targeting Debate.* Chicago, IL: University of Chicago Press for NBER (forthcoming).

Persson, Torsten and Tabellini, Guido. "Designing Institutions for Monetary Stability." *Carnegie-Rochester Conference Series on Public Policy,* December 1993, *39*, pp. 53-84.

Rogoff, Kenneth. "The Optimal Degree of Commitment to an Intermediate Monetary Target." *Quarterly Journal of Economics*, November 1985, *100*(4), pp. 1169-89.

Rogoff, Kenneth. "Reputational Constraints on Monetary Policy." *Carnegie-Rochester Conference Series on Public Policy,* Spring 1987, *26*, pp. 141-82.

Svensson, Lars E.O. "Optimal Inflation Contracts, 'Conservative' Central Banks, and Linear Inflation Contracts." *American Economic Review*, March 1997, *87*(1), pp. 98-114.

Walsh, Carl E. "Optimal Contracts for Central Bankers." *American Economic Review*, March 1995, *85*(1), pp. 150-67.

Walsh, Carl E. *Monetary Theory and Policy.* Second Ed. Cambridge, MA: MIT Press, 2003.

What Have We Learned Since October 1979?

Alan S. Blinder

My good friend Ben Bernanke is always a hard act to follow. When I drafted these remarks, I was concerned that Ben would take all the best points and cover them extremely well, leaving only some crumbs for Ben McCallum and me to pick up. But his decision to concentrate on one issue—central bank credibility—leaves me plenty to talk about.

Because Ben was so young in 1979, I'd like to begin by emphasizing that Paul Volcker retaught the world something it seemed to have forgotten at the time: that *tight monetary policy can bring inflation down at substantial, but not devastating, cost.* It seems strange to harbor contrary thoughts today, but back then many people believed that 10 percent inflation was so deeply ingrained in the U.S. economy that we might be doomed to, say, 6 to 10 percent inflation for a very long time. For example, Otto Eckstein (1981, pp. 3-4) wrote in a well-known 1981 book that "To bring the core inflation rate down significantly through fiscal and monetary policies alone would require a prolonged deep recession bordering on depression, with the average unemployment rate held above 10%." More concretely, he estimated that it would require 10 point-years of unemployment to bring the core inflation rate down a single percentage point,[1] which is about five times more than called for by the "Brookings rule of thumb."[2] As it turned out, the Volcker disinflation followed the Brookings rule of thumb rather well. About 14 cumulative percentage point–years of unemploy-

ment above the nonaccelerating inflation rate of unemployment (NAIRU) drove core inflation down by 6.2 percentage points over the six years spanning 1980 to 1985.[3] Yes, disinflation hurt, but much less than what the pessimists envisioned. Volcker may have enhanced the Fed's credibility; I certainly think so. But that did not improve the inflation-unemployment trade-off.

The forced march of core inflation down from 10 percent to 4 percent in the early 1980s taught us a second lesson that, I believe, is the essence of Paul Volcker's legacy: that *sometimes the central bank has to be single-minded about fighting inflation*, and that the strong will of a determined leader like Volcker is one key ingredient. When Volcker took the helm, the nation's problem was clear—too much inflation—and so was the solution—sustained tight money. It only required someone with iron will to apply the solution to the problem. Lindsey, Orphanides, and Rasche (2005) ask at this conference whether Volcker was a monetarist, a Keynesian, an inflation targeter, and so on. They seem to answer no in each case. To me, the right short characterization of Paul Volcker as Chairman of the Fed is simple: He was a highly principled and determined inflation hawk.

I would like to contrast these two Volcker lessons, which are the foci of this conference, with two quite different lessons that we can take away from the Greenspan era. The first is that, in apparent contradiction to what I just said, *flexibility in monetary policy is very important*. The contradiction is only apparent, not actual, because the worlds faced by Paul Volcker and Alan Greenspan were starkly different. During the Greenspan years, inflation has flared up only once, in 1990-91, and then only briefly. Instead, Greenspan has faced, among other things, two severe stock market crashes, a period of fragile bank balance sheets in the early 1990s, the rolling international financial

[1] Eckstein (1981, p. 46).

[2] This rule of thumb was due to a number of members of the Brookings Panel on Economic Activity in the 1970s, including Arthur Okun, George Perry, and William Nordhaus, but especially arose from a series of papers by Robert Gordon.

[3] The calculation assumes a NAIRU of 5.8 percent, which was the actual unemployment rate of 1979.

Alan S. Blinder is a professor and a co-director of the Center for Economic Policy Studies at Princeton University.

Federal Reserve Bank of St. Louis *Review*, March/April 2005, *87*(2, Part 2), pp. 283-86.

crises of 1997 and 1998,[4] the surprising productivity acceleration after 1995, a brief flirtation with
deflation, and the need to pull off several "soft
landings." Excruciatingly tight money was not
the right solution to any of these problems. I dare-
say that history will not remember Alan Greenspan
as the man who took 17 years to bring inflation
down from 4 percent to 2 percent. Rather, it will
remember him as the Fed Chairman who dealt
so well with a remarkable variety of difficult
challenges over a prolonged period of time.

Here's a test. Try a little mental free-association
with the phrase "accomplishments of Paul Volcker
as Chairman of the Fed."[5] I think all of you will
immediately think of "conquering inflation," or
something synonymous with that. Now try
"accomplishments of Alan Greenspan as Chairman
of the Fed." Here there are so many choices that
I doubt that even this well-informed group could
ever agree on a single answer. My own choice
would be how spectacularly well he recognized
and dealt with the productivity acceleration after
1995. But others will have their own favorite on
the long and impressive Greenspan hit parade.

That hit parade brings me naturally to the
fourth lesson, which is that *fine tuning is actually
possible* if you combine enough skill with a mo-
dicum of good luck. I began my economic education in the halcyon days of Walter Heller, when
a number of economists really believed in fine-
tuning. By the time I started teaching at Princeton
in 1971, however, this belief had been shattered.
But Alan Greenspan's remarkable performance
should bring it roaring back. Greenspan probably
shuns the label "fine-tuner." But his record is
replete with delicate decisions over moves of 0
versus 25 basis points or 25 versus 50 basis points,
with careful management of the exact monthly
timing of this rate increase or that rate decrease,
with several actual and attempted soft landings,
with influencing markets with minor variations
in wording, and so on. If that is not fine-tuning,
I don't know what is. And you know what? It

worked. We've had only two mild recessions
during Greenspan's long watch. As a result, the
bar for the next Chairman of the Fed has been set
extraordinarily high.

My fifth lesson goes back to the Volcker years.
Curiously, it seems not to have been mentioned
at this conference yet. So let me say it: *Money-
supply targeting can be hazardous to a nation's
health.* Lindsey, Orphanides, and Rasche (2005)
have discussed whether or not we should view
the money-growth rule as a "political heat shield"
that Volcker selected opportunistically to fend off
criticisms of excruciatingly tight money. Frankly,
after reading their paper I'm not sure whether
their answer is yes or no. (My own view is yes.)
But regardless, two things seem clear—and I
state them here, at the Federal Reserve Bank of
St. Louis, of all places. First, the Fed overdid
monetary stringency in 1980-81 partly because
of the misbehavior of velocity.[6] And second, res-
cuing the economy in 1982 required abandoning
the experiment with monetarism. I shudder to
think what might have happened to the U.S.
economy in 1982 and thereafter if the Federal
Open Market Committee (FOMC) had stubbornly
stuck to its money growth targets. But Volcker and
his colleagues were too smart—and insufficiently
doctrinaire—to do that. (By the way, that's a good
combination of attributes for a central banker.)

If a central bank abandons monetary aggregates, what should it put in their place? Many
experts now answer: inflation targets. But that
just pushes the question back one stage to this:
What instrument should the central bank use to
pursue its inflation target? After all, no matter how
much theoretical models try to pretend that it is,
the inflation rate is *not* a control variable. Milton
Friedman taught us years ago that the nominal
interest rate is a bad choice; fixing it can even lead
to dynamic instability. The *real* interest rate, we
have learned in the Volcker and Greenspan years,
is a far better choice. And that is my sixth lesson.

Greenspan, in particular, has focused attention on an update of Wicksell's "natural interest
rate" concept that we now call the *neutral real
federal funds rate.* And, more by his actions than

---

[4] Analogously to these last two, Volcker had to devote a great deal
of time and energy to debt crisis in the developing countries that
erupted in 1982 and the consequent concentration of risks on the
balance sheets of many money center banks.

[5] The last five words are important. I am in awe of Volcker's many
accomplishments since leaving the Federal Reserve System.

[6] Specifically, I do not believe the Fed ever intended to cause a
recession as deep as the one we had.

by his rhetoric, he has called attention to the Taylor rule as a useful benchmark. For current purposes, I write the Taylor rule as a guide for setting the *nominal* funds rate in a way that stabilizes both inflation and output:

$$i = r^* + \pi + \alpha(\pi - \pi^*) + \beta(y - y^*),$$

where i is the nominal funds rate, r^* is the neutral level of the real funds rate, π is the inflation rate, y is the (log) of output, and π^* and y^* are the targets for inflation and output, respectively. We think of monetary policy as "easy" when $i < r^* + \pi$ and as "tight" when $i > r^* + \pi$.

I view the Taylor rule as a useful way of thinking about monetary policy, although it is not, and John Taylor did not intend it to be, a literal rule in the Friedmanite sense. Several aspects of the Taylor rule are worth mentioning. The first is that *both* α and β are positive. This means, for example, that there may be times when it is appropriate for the central bank to hold its interest rate *below* neutral even though the inflation rate is *above* target.[7]

The second aspect constitutes my seventh lesson. The requirement that α be positive means that *the central bank should react more than point for point to changes in the inflation rate.* For example, under Taylor's choice of $\alpha = \frac{1}{2}$, each 1-point move in the inflation rate would induce the central bank to adjust its policy rate by 150 basis points in the same direction, meaning that the real funds rate moves by 50 basis points in that direction. If α is not positive, the central bank would be allowing rising inflation to *reduce* the real federal funds rate—a potentially destabilizing policy.

My last few lessons were learned in the Greenspan era. The eighth lesson is hardly ever mentioned, but I think it should be. Three times during the Greenspan era, the Fed demonstrated that *doing nothing can constitute a remarkably effective, even bold, monetary policy.*

The first such episode started in July or September 1992 and lasted until February 1994.[8] To stimulate an economy that seemed to be fight-

ing substantial financial "headwinds," the Fed held the nominal funds rate at 3 percent, which at the time meant that the *real* funds rate was kept at around zero, for about 18 months. This sizable and long-lasting monetary stimulus helped get the economy rolling in 1994 and thereafter. The third such episode was a similar effort to stimulate a sluggish economy. The Fed lowered the nominal funds rate to 1.25 percent in November 2002 and then to 1 percent in June 2003—and then held it there until June 30, 2004, a period of 12 to 19 months, depending on when you want to start counting. In both of these cases, the degree of monetary stimulus was quite large and the length of time for which it was applied was very long, by the standards of central banking. In that sense, each of these periods of "doing nothing" constituted a boldly expansionary policy.[9]

The middle episode of "doing nothing" was a bit different from the other two but, if anything, was an even bolder departure from standard central banking practice. From January 1996 until June 1999, the Fed did not raise interest rates to restrain the booming economy even though the unemployment rate kept falling through any reasonable estimate of the NAIRU.[10] Janet Yellen and I (2001) have called this episode the years of "forbearance," and it constituted a real gamble that Greenspan took over the objections of a number of FOMC members.[11] Other than his oft-expressed skepticism about the NAIRU concept, the stated basis for Greenspan's refusal to raise rates was his belief—which was subsequently ratified by the data—that productivity had accelerated and would continue on a high trajectory, thereby justifying a faster trend growth rate.[12] The gamble paid off handsomely.

---

[7] Conversely, if y is high enough, the central bank will want "tight money," even if inflation is already below target.

[8] The Fed cut the funds rate to 3.25 percent in July 1992 and to 3 percent in September 1992.

[9] During much of the more recent episode, the inflation rate was drifting down, so the real funds rate was actually rising slightly. In the 1992-94 episode, inflation was quite constant.

[10] There was actually one 25-basis-point rate hike in March 1997. But the FOMC also reduced the funds rate by 75 basis points following the financial crisis in the fall of 1998.

[11] For more details on this episode from an insider's perspective, see Meyer (2004).

[12] Higher productivity growth, by itself, does not lead to an ever-decreasing NAIRU. But favorable supply shocks and the related hypothesis that *actual* productivity was running ahead faster than productivity as *perceived* by workers will lead to a transitory decline in NAIRU. On the latter, see Blinder and Yellen (2001, Chap. 6).

All three of these episodes, but especially the last, lead naturally to my ninth lesson. Another significant part of the Greenspan legacy is the demonstration that *a central bank can be strongly pro-growth without being irresponsible.* This, I think, is a genuine benefit of the Federal Reserve's much-maligned dual mandate to support *both* low inflation *and* high employment, coupled with a Chairman willing to make use of it. It would, I believe, have been much more difficult for an inflation-targeting central bank, or for a bank like the European Central Bank with a mono-goal, to forbear in 1996-99 the way the Fed did.

During these three periods of FOMC "inaction," intermediate and long rates were not marking time. Similarly, during the most recent Federal Reserve tightening (June 1999–May 2000) and easing (January 2001–June 2004) cycles, bond rates moved around quite a bit—generally in the direction the Fed wanted. This leads to the tenth lesson learned since 1979: If the central bank lets the markets in on its thinking, *the markets can do part of the work of monetary policy.* Specifically, if the markets believe the central bank will soon be raising (lowering) rates, intermediate and long rates will rise (fall) in anticipation, thereby tightening (easing) "monetary policy" before the policymakers lift a finger.

Outsourcing part of the work to the bond market in this way has two interesting, and probably salutary, implications for monetary policy. First, and less important, the central bank should not have to move its policy rate around as much, in either direction, as would be necessary without the anticipatory behavior of the bond market. Second, and more important, the lags in monetary policy should be reduced by the bond market's reactions. Not so many years ago, central bankers and economists viewed long rates as *following* short rates with a substantial lag—which slowed down the transmission of monetary policy impulses into the real economy. Nowadays, many central bankers and economists see long rates as *leading* short rates.

This anticipatory process can work, however, only if the central bank communicates its intentions to the markets effectively. Thus, and this is my final lesson from post-1979 experience, *greater transparency can enhance the effective-*

ness of monetary policy. The old tradition at central banks was, of course, to say little and to say it cryptically. That's how the temple kept secrets. There is still far too much secrecy for my taste. But the unmistakable trend, both at the Fed and around the world, is toward greater transparency.

I could go on and on about why I think this is a salutary trend, both for democracy and for monetary policy—and I have.[13] But I think it is now time to relinquish the platform to Ben McCallum. Suffice it to say that while the Federal Reserve has often hesitated over specific incremental increases in disclosure, and while it has sometimes warned of adverse consequences from greater transparency, virtually none of these adverse consequences have ever come to pass, and the Fed has never regretted its step-by-step movements toward greater openness.[14] At least that's my reading of the history since 1994. If they disagree, there are plenty of current and former Federal Reserve officials present here today to dispute what I have just said.

REFERENCES

Blinder, Alan S. *The Quiet Revolution: Central Banking Goes Modern.* New Haven, CT: Yale University Press, 2004.

Blinder, Alan S. and Yellen, Janet L. *The Fabulous Decade: Macroeconomic Lessons from the 1990s.* New York: Century Foundation Press, 2001.

Eckstein, Otto. *Core Inflation.* Englewood Cliffs, NJ: Prentice-Hall, 1981.

Lindsey, David E; Orphanides, Athanasios and Rasche, Robert H. "The Reform of October 1979: How It Happened and Why." Federal Reserve Bank of St. Louis *Review*, March/April 2005, *87*(2, Part 2), pp. 187-235.

Meyer, Laurence H. *A Term at the Fed: An Insider's View.* New York: Harper Business, 2004.

---

[13] On this trend, see Blinder (2004, Chapter 1).

[14] After this October 2004 St. Louis conference, the FOMC took yet another step in the direction of greater transparency by deciding to release its minutes earlier.

Panel Discussion I

What Have We Learned Since October 1979?

Bennett T. McCallum

MODEL COMPARISON

The question posed for this panel cannot be answered entirely straightforwardly, for different analysts knew (i.e., believed) different things about monetary policy in October 1979, and the same is true now. But I will try to speak to the spirit of the question in an operational way by briefly contrasting mainstream models that are being used now, for policy analysis, with ones that were being used then. For the "now" portion of this comparison it is easy to write down a prototypical model, which is basically the one labeled as the "consensus" model by Goodfriend (2005) in his contribution to this conference. One might quibble with the term consensus, since some economists do not approve of this model, but it is in fact a very standard starting point, among policy analysts, for elaboration or in some cases disagreement. So, the agenda now is to compare it to its counterpart of 1979. How might one select a 1979-vintage model for that purpose? Well, in October of 1979, I was in the midst of writing a paper (McCallum, 1980) that was designed to demonstrate the effects of incorporating rational expectations (RE) into an otherwise mainstream macro model. Using that paper's model to represent those typical in 1979 might not be a perfect solution, but it is probably as good as anyone could reasonably expect.

Consider, then, the following basic model, circa 1979:

$$(1)\ y_t = b_0 + b_1(R_t - E_t\Delta p_{t+1}) + v_t \qquad b_1 < 0$$

$$(2)\ \Delta p_t = E_{t-1}\Delta p_t + \alpha_1(y_t - \bar{y}_t)$$
$$+ \alpha_2(y_{t-1} - \bar{y}_{t-1}) + u_t \qquad \alpha_1 > 0, \alpha_2 < 0$$

$$(3)\ m_t + \mu_0 + \mu_1 m_{t-1}$$
$$+ \mu_2(y_t - \bar{y}_{t-1}) = e_t \qquad \mu_1 > 0, \mu_2 < 0$$

$$(4)\ m_t - p_t = c_0 + c_1 y_t + c_2 R_t + \eta_t \qquad c_1 > 0, c_2 < 0$$

$$(5)\ \bar{y}_t = \gamma_0 + \gamma_1 \bar{y}_{t-1} + a_t \qquad \gamma_1 > 0$$

Here the symbols are as follows: y_t = log of output, $\bar{y}_t$ = log of natural-rate output, p_t = log of price level, m_t = log of money stock, R_t = one-period interest rate, and $v_t, u_t, e_t, \eta_t, a_t$ = stochastic shocks. Equation (1) represents an IS function in which the rate of spending on goods and services is taken to depend (negatively) on the real rate of interest. Equation (2) is a "natural rate" type of Phillips curve or price adjustment relationship, with the unit coefficient on $E_{t-1}\Delta p_t$ implying the absence of any long-run trade-off, as in Fischer (1977) or Lucas (1973). In addition, (4) is a money demand (or "LM") function of a standard type, while (3) represents monetary policy behavior with the central bank adjusting the money supply[1] each period in a way that responds to the current (or possibly a recent past) output gap. The latter concept refers to the fractional difference between output and its natural rate value, with the latter being generated (exogenously, for simplicity) in equation (5).

Using models of basically the foregoing specification, researchers such as Lucas (1973), Fischer (1977), Sargent (1973), Taylor (1979), and McCallum (1980) conducted RE analysis to determine the dynamic properties of various systems and alternative policy rules. One of the main objects of analysis was to determine whether the systematic components of monetary policy rules, or only the purely random components, have effects on the cyclical properties of real variables—including employment and especially the output gap—when expectations are formed rationally.

---

[1] Researchers who were concerned with operationality, such as Andersen and Jordan (1968) and Brunner and Meltzer (1976), tended to use the monetary base as the instrument variable in policy specifications that would be represented by (3) in the model.

Bennett T. McCallum is a professor at Carnegie Mellon University and a research associate at the National Bureau of Economic Research. The author thanks Marvin Goodfriend and Edward Nelson for helpful comments on an earlier draft.

Federal Reserve Bank of St. Louis *Review*, March/April 2005, *87*(2, Part 2), pp. 287-91.

Panel Discussion I

Lucas (1972, 1973), Sargent (1973), and most notably Sargent and Wallace (1975) argued that the behavior of the gap would be unaffected by alternative monetary policy rules, while Fischer (1977) and Taylor (1979) took the opposing position. My review (McCallum, 1980) concluded that there were plausible specifications that would support each position. It should be emphasized, however, that most policy analysis being conducted at the time was not of this type, focusing on properties of dynamic systems, but instead featured point-in-time exercises of the type that RE analysis showed to be (in many cases) fundamentally misleading.

For comparison, today's prototype model can be written, in its simplest form, as follows:

$$(6)\ y_t = b_0 + b_1(R_t - E_t\Delta p_{t+1}) + E_t y_{t+1} + v_t \qquad b_1 < 0$$

$$(7)\ \Delta p_t = \beta E_t \Delta p_{t+1} + \alpha_1(y_t - \bar{y}_t) + u_t \qquad \alpha_1 > 0$$

$$(8)\ R_t = \mu_0 + \Delta p_t + \mu_1(\Delta p_t - \pi^*) \\ + \mu_2(y_t - \bar{y}_{t-1}) + e_t \qquad \mu_1 > 0,\ \mu_2 > 0$$

$$(9)\ m_t - p_t = c_0 + c_1 y_t + c_2 R_t + \eta_t \qquad c_1 > 0,\ c_2 < 0$$

$$(10)\ \bar{y}_t = \gamma_0 + \gamma_1 \bar{y}_{t-1} + a_t \qquad \gamma_1 > 0$$

Here, there are three major changes from the model of 1979. First, the term $E_t y_{t+1}$ enters the counterpart of the IS function (1), reflecting that equation's origin as a consumption Euler equation, with consumption substituted out in favor of output, to represent optimizing behavior by rational optimizing households.[2] Second, the usual Phillips or price adjustment relation (7) differs from (2) by having $\beta E_t \Delta p_{t+1}$ instead of $E_{t-1}\Delta p_t$ as the reference expected inflation rate. Again, this specification is more readily justified by optimizing analysis, due in this version to Calvo (1983) and a host of follow-up papers, including King and Wolman (1996). Finally, the most striking change is in the monetary policy rule (8), which is here expressed in terms of the one-period nomi-

nal interest rate, used as an instrument variable, instead of the growth rate of the (base) money supply. This change in the usual modeling practice, which was given an important impetus by Taylor (1993), undoubtedly represents a move in the direction of realism since actual central banks of industrial countries almost invariably use some short-term nominal interest rate as their "operating target." Whether that mode of policy behavior is socially desirable is not an entirely settled matter, although the preponderance of opinion has certainly moved in that direction, partly under the forceful influence of Woodford (1999, 2003).

Of course, today's models often do not include any money demand relation such as (9). Given the absence of monetary aggregate variables from (6) and (7), this omission becomes formally innocuous when policy is conducted as in (8), as has been explained numerous times (e.g., McCallum, 1999). Today's models do not imply that no such money demand relation obtains, of course, but merely that their specification does not influence the dynamic behavior of the main macro variables given the remainder of the (recursive) system.

There are two other ways, besides this change in the monetary policy instrument, in which today's policy analysis usually differs from that of 1979. The first has already been mentioned; it is that today the standard mode of policy analysis involves a comparison of the behavior of target variables (e.g., inflation and the output gap) under different maintained policy rules, rather than point-in-time exercises.[3] The other is that today's models are constructed in a manner that attempts to respect both theory and evidence, by using optimization-based general equilibrium analysis in an attempt to develop systems that are potentially structural—and thus immune to the Lucas critique (Lucas, 1976)—and by specifying the models quantitatively, either as a result of econometric estimation or by selection of their parameter values on the basis of a careful calibration (of the type emphasized in the real business cycle literature).

---

[2] This simplest version of the model does not include endogenous investment spending, as distinct from consumption. Endogenous investment can be included fairly readily, but some users instead calibrate the sensitivity of spending to the real interest rate so as to match the consumption-plus-investment value, rather than the one appropriate to consumption alone.

[3] I would definitely include the design of optimal policy rules under the former heading, despite various reservations mentioned in McCallum and Nelson (2004).

PROMINENT TOPICS

A second way to approach the question "What have we learned?" would be to consider specific topics that have been prominent—of major professional interest—among monetary economists since October 1979. A list of such topics that I have put together fairly quickly includes those given below. The ordering is roughly, but not strictly, chronological.

    i. Operating procedures
    ii. Sacrifice ratios
    iii. Credibility
    iv. Commitment versus discretionary policy optimization
    v. Central bank independence
    vi. Vector autoregression (VAR) models
    vii. Real business cycle models
    viii. New Keynesian models
    ix. Structural VAR models
    x. New neoclassical synthesis models
    xi. Transparency and communication
    xii. Interest rate smoothing
    xiii. Taylor rules
    xiv. Inflation targeting
    xv. Analysis with real-time data
    xvi. The zero lower bound on nominal interest rates
    xvii. Optimality from a "timeless perspective"
    xviii. Targeting versus instrument rules
    xix. Indeterminacy, learnability, and E-stability

Most of these topics are of considerable intellectual content and interest; indeed, I have been interested in a majority of them myself. But, in trying to answer "What have we learned?" it would seem best to strive for a shorter and more practically oriented list, in part because merely to specify the meaning of each of the terms and provide a citation of the key references would require several pages. In the next and final section, accordingly, I will try to produce one.

WHAT HAVE WE LEARNED?
A SHORT LIST

First, we have learned to conduct monetary policy analysis in a manner that seems reasonable to both academic and central bank economists. This is important because it facilitates communication between these two groups of analysts. I have argued (McCallum, 1999) that this convergence of viewpoints has proceeded to the point where one usually cannot tell from examination of a particular research paper whether it was written by an academic or a central bank economist. For this healthy development I would give much credit to the simple but insightful exposition of Taylor (1993). It is, of course, possible to worry about how much of today's highly technical research actually influences policymakers, such as members of the FOMC. But there are positive indications, both at the Board of Governors and at regional Federal Reserve Banks. Not only in the Fed, but also in the central banks of other countries (e.g., the Bank of England, the European Central Bank, the Bank of Japan), it has become fairly common for the top monetary policymaking committee to include research economists among its voting members. (Indeed, several are present at this conference!)

Second, we have learned that the crucial requirement for a central bank is to give top priority to the task of keeping inflation low. At least this is the message that I perceive from all the attention that has been paid to "inflation targeting." Terminologically, there is a bit of a problem with respect to the formal literature on that subject, for it is unclear why an optimizing central bank with an objective function of the form

(11) maximize

$$E_0 \sum_{t=0}^{\infty} \beta^t \left[(\pi_t - \pi^*)^2 + \lambda(y_t - \bar{y}_t)^2 \right] \qquad \lambda \geq 0$$

should be called an inflation targeter rather than an "output gap targeter," especially if λ is relatively large. But in practice, each recognized inflation-targeting central bank has emphasized achievement of a low inflation rate as its top priority. So I think that it can be said that there is much agreement on what I regard as the crucial requirement.

With respect to the objective function (11), several researchers (e.g., Orphanides, 2001, 2003; McCallum, 2001) have argued that it would be dangerous for the central bank to respond strongly to an operational measure of the output gap, in part because of the great difficulty that prevails in practice in obtaining satisfactory estimates of the natural-rate value, $\bar{y}_t$, or even in agreeing on the proper concept to utilize for the latter. A strong response to the level of the gap is not necessarily the same as adopting a large value of λ in (11), it should be noted. It is the same under discretionary optimization, but with the "timeless perspective" approach the implied optimality condition involves the *change* in the output gap, in which case the undesirable effects of natural-rate mismeasurement tend to cancel out to a substantial extent (Orphanides, 2003).[4]

Finally, I think that we have seen that it is possible for central banks to avoid the inflation bias that results from period-by-period discretionary re-optimization when the target level of output exceeds the natural-rate value. I hope that this is because central banks are now avoiding discretionary period-by-period re-optimization, choosing instead to make policy in a committed, rule-like fashion. Some form of timeless perspective behavior, that does not try to exploit conditions that happen to prevail currently, is necessary to avoid several types of suboptimality, including the one mentioned above. But it remains somewhat unclear what the actual current situation is, in terms of central bank behavior.

REFERENCES

Andersen, Leonall C. and Jordan, Jerry L. "The Monetary Base—Explanation and Analytical Use." Federal Reserve Bank of St. Louis *Review*, August 1968, *50*(8), pp. 7-11.

Brunner, Karl, and Meltzer, Allan H. "An Aggregative Theory for a Closed Economy," in Jerome Stein, ed., *Monetarism*. Amsterdam: North-Holland, 1976.

---

[4] For a discussion of the timeless-perspective approach, see Woodford (2003, Chap. 7).

Calvo, Guillermo A. "Staggered Prices in a Utility-Maximizing Framework." *Journal of Monetary Economics*, September 1983, *12*(3), pp. 383-98.

Fischer, Stanley. "Long-Term Contracts, Rational Expectations, and the Optimal Money Supply Rule." *Journal of Political Economy*, February 1977, *85*(1), pp. 191-205.

Goodfriend, Marvin. "The Monetary Policy Debate Since October 1979: Lessons for Theory and Practice." Federal Reserve Bank of St. Louis *Review*, March/April 2005, *87*(2, Part 2), pp. 243-62.

King, Robert G. and Wolman, Alexander L. "Inflation Targeting in a St. Louis Model of the 21st Century." Federal Reserve Bank of St. Louis *Review*, May/June 1996, *78*(3), pp. 83-107.

Lucas, Robert E. "Expectations and the Neutrality of Money." *Journal of Economic Theory*, April 1972, *4*(2), pp. 103-24.

Lucas, Robert E. "Some International Evidence on Output-Inflation Tradeoffs." *American Economic Review*, June 1973, *63*(3), pp. 326-34.

Lucas, Robert E. "Econometric Policy Evaluation: A Critique." *Carnegie-Rochester Conference Series on Public Policy*, 1976, *1*, pp. 19-46.

McCallum, Bennett T. "Rational Expectations and Macroeconomic Stabilization Policy: An Overview." *Journal of Money, Credit, and Banking*, November 1980, *12*(4, Part 2), pp. 716-46.

McCallum, Bennett T. "Recent Developments in the Analysis of Monetary Policy Rules." Federal Reserve Bank of St. Louis *Review*, November/December 1999, *81*(6), pp. 3-12.

McCallum, Bennett T. "Should Monetary Policy Respond Strongly to Output Gaps?" *American Economic Review*, May 2001, *91*(2), pp. 258-62.

McCallum, Bennett T. and Nelson, Edward. "Targeting vs. Instrument Rules for Monetary Policy." NBER Working Paper 10612, National Bureau of Economic Research, June 2004.

Orphanides, Athanasios. "Monetary Policy Rules
  Based on Real-Time Data." *American Economic
  Review*, September 2001, *91*(4), pp. 964-85.

Orphanides, Athanasios. "The Quest for Prosperity
  Without Inflation." *Journal of Monetary Economics*,
  April 2003, *50*(3), pp. 633-63.

Sargent, Thomas J. "Rational Expectations, the Real
  Rate of Interest, and the Natural Rate of
  Unemployment." *Brookings Papers on Economic
  Activity*, 1973, *2*, pp. 429-72.

Sargent, Thomas J. and Wallace, Neil. "Rational
  Expectations, the Optimal Monetary Instrument,
  and the Optimal Money Supply Rule." *Journal of
  Political Economy*, April 1975, *83*(2), pp. 241-54.

Taylor, John B. "Estimation and Control of a
  Macroeconomic Model with Rational Expectations."
  Econometrica, September 1979, *47*(5), pp. 1267-86.

Taylor, John B. "Discretion versus Policy Rules in
  Practice." *Carnegie-Rochester Conference Series on
  Public Policy*, November 1993, *39*, pp. 195-214.

Woodford, Michael. "Optimal Monetary Policy
  Inertia." NBER Working Paper 7261, National
  Bureau of Economic Research, July 1999.

Woodford, Michael. *Interest and Prices: Foundations
  of a Theory of Monetary Policy.* Princeton: Princeton
  University Press, 2003.

Part VI
Policymaking:
Challenges for the Future

[14]

Challenges for monetary policy: new and old

Deputy Governor, Mervyn King[1] *argues that central banks have reached a record high in terms of their power and reputation. But to retain that position, they have to face two major challenges in a low inflation environment. The first is to decide on the objective for monetary policy. He considers the appropriate definition of price stability and the degree to which central banks should aim to stabilise output. The second challenge is to improve central banks' understanding of the transmission mechanism. Mervyn King concludes by speculating about the future of central banks.*

1   Introduction

The turn of the Millennium seems an appropriate moment to assess the role of central banks in the modern world. On second thoughts, perhaps a Millennium is not the correct unit, for it is the past century which has seen the rise and rise of central banks. One hundred years ago there was no Federal Reserve System. Indeed, in 1900 there were only 18 countries with central banks. Today that number is 172. How many will there be one hundred years from now? Will central banks exist at all?

At the beginning of this century, outside continental Europe only Japan and Indonesia had central banks. The number— and status—of central banks rose throughout the century, and has risen to the point where well over 90% of the countries represented at the United Nations have central banks (see Chart 1). Part of this rise resulted from the conversion of colonial currency boards into central banks of independent countries. But a further impetus was given by the creation of new central banks in eastern and central Europe in the 1990s. And only this year the latest, and arguably the most important, of the new central banks was created with the establishment of the European Central Bank.

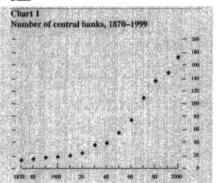

Chart 1
Number of central banks, 1870–1999

It is not just the number of central banks that has increased steadily throughout the century. Their power and independence has also increased substantially, especially over the past decade. Although the definition of 'independence' is as much a matter of practice as of legal status, ten years ago it was possible to argue that the only large countries with independent central banks were the United States, Germany and Switzerland. Since then, in all three principal time zones there have been significant moves towards independence of central banks. In the Americas, independence was granted in varying degrees to central banks in Argentina, Brazil, Chile and Mexico. In Asia, the Bank of Japan was made independent. And in Europe, not only was the European Central Bank set up, but the Old Lady of Threadneedle Street herself acquired independence in 1997. The result is that after a century of expansion, central banks now find themselves in a position of power and responsibility unrivalled in their history.

Today, central banks are rarely out of the headlines. Monetary policy is news. It is news in the G7, where newspapers continually speculate about future policy moves, and it is news in emerging markets, where the very stability of a country sometimes seems to depend on a resolution of its currency and financial problems.

But this is no time for hubris. For much of the century discretionary monetary policy, freed from the constraints of, first, the gold standard and subsequently the Bretton Woods system of pegged exchange rates, produced inflation (see Chart 2). Unfettered discretion has not been a success. It is no accident that the inflation target approach to monetary policy, so popular in the 1990s, has been described as 'constrained discretion' (Bernanke and Mishkin (1997), King (1997a)). Mechanical policy rules are not credible— in the literal sense that no one will believe that a central bank will adhere rigidly to such a rule irrespective of circumstances. No rule could be written down that describes how policy would be set in all possible outcomes. Some discretion is inevitable. But that discretion must be constrained by a clear objective to which policy is directed

(1) Paper prepared for the Symposium on 'New challenges for monetary policy' sponsored by the Federal Reserve Bank of Kansas City at Jackson Hole, Wyoming, on 27 August 1999. This paper may also be found on the Bank's web site at www.bankofengland.co.uk/speeches/speech51.pdf. I am very grateful to Ravi Balakrishnan, Nicoletta Batini, Mark Cornelius, Spencer Dale, Ben Martin, Ed Nelson, John Vickers and Anthony Yates of the Bank of England, who not only made helpful comments and suggestions but also contributed most of the ideas to this paper.

Bank of England Quarterly Bulletin: November 1999

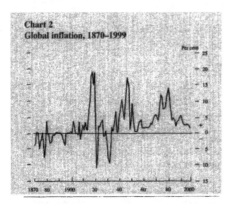

Chart 2
Global inflation, 1870–1999

and by which performance against the objective can be assessed.

Giving a central bank a clear remit of maintaining price stability, and holding it accountable for achieving that, is seen as a *sine qua non* of a credible monetary policy regime. The language in which that remit is embodied varies from country to country. But the view that price stability is the overriding objective of monetary policy is now common to both industrialised countries and emerging markets. In part that reflects the intellectual revolution which 'rediscovered' the absence of a trade-off in the long run between inflation and output. But it also reflects the experience of the past 30 years in which high and unstable inflation led to greater fluctuations in output and employment than accompanied periods of low and stable inflation. A commitment to price stability is now seen as the key to achieving broader economic stability. Indeed, John Taylor has described the past 15 years, which contained the two longest post-war expansions, in the United States as the 'Long Boom'. In Europe, the past 15 years might be more accurately described as the 'Long March' to stability.

There is now a widespread intellectual consensus—almost a conventional wisdom—about the objectives which central banks should pursue, and the means by which they should pursue them. This is a very dangerous position. Could it be that 1999 is the apogee of the power of central banks? I believe that if central banks are to retain their central position in economic policy making, they must face up to the intellectual and technological challenges that lie ahead. Unless they do so, popularity will turn to disillusion.

Those challenges are in two main areas of monetary policy. They are: (a) the objectives of monetary policy, and (b) the transmission mechanism through which monetary policy affects those objectives. I discuss these issues in Sections 2 and 3, respectively. Section 4 discusses, more briefly, the international arena in which central banks operate. I return to the future of central banks in Section 5.

2   Monetary policy in a low inflation world: objectives

It may seem strange to identify the objectives of monetary policy as a challenge to central banks. Surely, there is a consensus that price stability is the overriding objective of monetary policy. A decade ago, when Alan Greenspan (1989) defined price stability as—'price levels sufficiently stable so that expectations of change do not become major factors in key economic decisions'—many industrial countries were some way from price stability. A more precise definition was unnecessary. It was clear along which path policy should proceed. But now that inflation has fallen in the main OECD countries, from 12.4% in 1980, to 5.2% in 1990 and 1.6% in 1998, the fact of price stability raises a number of challenges for both the formulation and explanation of the objectives of monetary policy.[1]

Irrespective of the words used to describe it, any monetary policy can be thought of as a combination of an *ex ante* inflation target and a strategy for responding *ex post* to unanticipated shocks (King (1996), (1997b)). The relevant shocks are those to which the central bank can respond before the private sector is able to adjust nominal wages and prices. In a world of low inflation, the private sector will want to know three things about the corresponding monetary policy reaction function. First, how 'low' is the inflation rate at which the central bank is aiming? Second, what precisely does the central bank mean by the exercise of its 'constrained discretion' to respond to shocks in order to stabilise inflation and output? Third, does the central bank intend to bring the price level back towards some desired longer-term path? The efficiency of monetary policy increases when central banks are open about all three aspects of their policy. Consider them in turn.

2(i)   The optimal inflation rate

What is the optimal rate of inflation? As inflation has fallen from earlier high levels towards something approaching price stability, the question of what is the optimal inflation rate has become more important. Indeed a growing number of central banks have adopted an explicit and numerical target for inflation. Milton Friedman (1969) argued that anticipated inflation should, on average, be negative. Steady deflation—at a rate equal to the real rate of interest—is optimal because only at a zero nominal interest rate is the marginal opportunity cost of holding cash equal to its marginal production cost (close to zero in practice).

Other considerations suggest that a changing price level—whether inflation or deflation—creates costs. These include the distortionary effects of an unindexed tax system, especially on capital income, and increased menu costs as prices have to be adjusted more frequently. As a result, many have argued for the objective of pure price stability, that is zero measured inflation (for example, Feldstein (1996)). One problem with the objective of zero inflation is that the official indices used to measure inflation are subject

---
[1] The countries excluded from these comparisons are Greece, Hungary, Mexico, Poland and Turkey.

to biases of several kinds. Most studies suggest that these measures overstate the 'true' rate of inflation by an amount that could lie in a range from 0.5% to 2% a year. The Boskin Commission (1996) produced a central estimate of the overstatement of inflation in the US consumer price index of 1.1% a year.[1]

Such estimates are not uncontroversial and there is no reason to presume that the bias remains constant from year to year. Moreover, there is no unique price index to measure general inflation in a world in which relative prices move around. When average inflation is high, the differences in inflation recorded by different indices are small. But when overall inflation is low, differences between indices are more apparent. For example, Johnson, Small and Tryon (1999) found sizable discrepancies between alternative inflation measures in the United States since 1975. The Bank of England discusses a number of measures of inflation in its quarterly *Inflation Report*. No one measure fully captures all of the information that is relevant to the setting of monetary policy. A single measure, and a single target, for inflation are useful in terms of the transparency of the objectives of policy and the accountability of those responsible for decisions. But the need to examine different measures of inflation highlights the difficulty of identifying precisely an 'optimal' rate of inflation. Nevertheless, concern about the measurement bias problem has led to suggestions that the optimal measured rate of inflation is positive.

Yet other economists have argued that an inflation rate well above zero is desirable because it leads to higher output and employment. Krugman (1996), for example, proposed a long-run inflation target of 3%–4%. Two reasons, in particular, have been advanced for aiming at a positive inflation rate. The first concerns the significance of downward nominal rigidities in wages and prices. If nominal wages and prices are inflexible downwards, then a higher rate of inflation might enable a faster adjustment of real relative wages and prices which would improve efficiency. Second, the fact that nominal interest rates cannot fall below zero may constrain monetary policy in a time of recession. Both arguments have attracted some support recently, and I consider them in turn.

2(i) a Downward nominal rigidities

In a provocative and much-cited paper, Akerlof, Dickens and Perry (1996) claimed that 'targeting zero inflation will lead to a large inefficiency in the allocation of resources, as reflected in a sustainable rate of unemployment that is unnecessarily high'. They studied how downward nominal wage rigidity affects the optimal inflation rate. Their contribution was twofold. First, they reported the empirical evidence on the frequency of nominal wage cuts in the United States. Second, they argued that the existence of downward nominal wage rigidity implied that, at low rates of inflation, there is a permanent trade-off between inflation

and unemployment—a trade-off whose existence many of us expend a great deal of energy denying.

It is not surprising that downward nominal rigidity in wages and prices means that zero inflation will be costly for unemployment. But is such rigidity theoretically plausible? And does theory imply that inflation would be a cure? The assumptions required to generate downward nominal rigidities, for which inflation would be a cure, are complex. For example, it is commonly thought that if wage earners were subject to 'money illusion' then positive inflation would provide room for periodic real wage cuts without necessitating cuts in nominal wages or undesirable increases in unemployment. There is indeed some evidence that supports the existence of money illusion. For example, Shiller (1996) found that 59% of his respondents stated that they would be happier with higher money wages though unchanged real wages. Even 10% of economists displayed this kind of money illusion! However, money illusion is not by itself sufficient to generate downward nominal rigidities whose effects could be mitigated by inflation (see Yates (1998)). Money illusion means that people care about nominal wages in addition to real wages. But it does not explain why people care more about a fall in nominal wage growth from 0% to -3% than a change from 3% to 0%.

Akerlof, Dickens and Perry argued that the proportion of salary earners accepting nominal pay cuts could be as low as 2%–3%. The evidence on the frequency of nominal wage cuts is not so clear-cut if we look at other studies.[2] Product markets also exhibit a prevalence of nominal price cuts. For example, towards the end of 1998, more than 25% of the components of the US CPI were falling. Broadly the same was true for the RPI index in the United Kingdom.

Moreover, it is difficult to believe that any downward inflexibility of nominal wages would be unaffected by changes in inflation. As low inflation becomes the norm, resistance to nominal wage cuts could well disappear. In Japan, money wages have been falling since the beginning of 1998. And trend increases in productivity leave scope for changes in relative real wages, without reductions in the level of nominal wages. For example, an inflation target of 2% a year and productivity growth also of 2% a year, mean that nominal wages would rise at an average rate of 4% a year, leaving scope for reductions in relative real wages without cuts in nominal wages.

It is important to focus not only on the frequency of price or wage cuts at any one time, but also on how the distribution of prices and wages evolves over time. If the world were characterised by downward nominal rigidities we would expect to find that the skewness of price changes increases, with more zero changes, as the inflation rate falls. Charts 3 and 4 suggest that this does not happen: as inflation falls, so the proportion of the index that is falling goes up. The evidence from more formal regression studies is also

---

[1] Broadly similar estimates were produced for the United Kingdom by Cunningham (1996).
[2] Crawford and Harrison (1998) found that between 9%–20% of employees experienced nominal wage cuts in Canada between 1995 and 1996.

Bank of England Quarterly Bulletin: November 1999

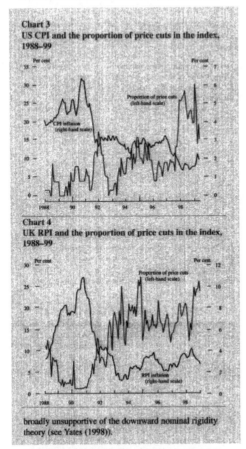

Chart 3
US CPI and the proportion of price cuts in the index, 1988–99

Chart 4
UK RPI and the proportion of price cuts in the index, 1988–99

broadly unsupportive of the downward nominal rigidity theory (see Yates (1998)).

Finally, the most casual, but at the same time the most striking, piece of evidence relates to recent experience. Akerlof *et al* argued that, at inflation rates below 3%, the existence of a permanent trade-off meant that unemployment would rise. In fact, since their paper was presented to a Brookings Panel in March 1996 there have been only four months when the recorded annual inflation rate in the United States was above 3%, yet during that period unemployment has continued to fall. No doubt there are many reasons why this might have happened, but at least one of them is that any downward nominal rigidity is too small for the Fed to worry about. A new Akerlof *et al* study is in the pipeline, to be presented in the autumn. Until that is available, I remain unconvinced that nominal rigidities mean we should abandon the pursuit of price stability.

2(i) b   Zero bound on nominal interest rates

A second argument for targeting moderate inflation rather than price stability is that nominal interest rates cannot fall

below zero. Given the existence of this lower bound, the ability to reduce interest rates in response to large and persistent negative demand shocks is likely to be constrained if the average level of interest rates, and hence inflation, is low. This is no theoretical curiosum. In Japan, official interest rates have now been below 1% since September 1995 and have been virtually zero since February 1999. And in Europe, where the average inflation rate is at present close to 1% a year, interest rates have been reduced to 2.5%, a level not seen even in Germany for over 20 years. The experience of Japan, in particular, poses a serious challenge to central bankers and economists alike in how to think about monetary policy in a world of low inflation.

The proposition that the inability to reduce interest rates below zero might create problems for monetary policy was emphasised by Keynes (1936) in the 1930s, later by Vickrey (1955), and, more recently, by Phelps (1972), Summers (1991) and Fischer (1996). For most of the post-war period, those problems seemed to belong to the past. But the return to price stability raises the question of whether such concerns may be more pressing in future. The significance of the zero lower limit on nominal short-term interest rates hinges on whether monetary policy becomes impotent at the point when the constraint begins to bind. In other words, can a 'liquidity trap' render monetary policy ineffective? I return to this question in Section 3.

The welfare analysis of the optimal inflation target depends on both (i) the probability that nominal interest rates will be constrained at zero, and (ii) the cost of that constraint should it bind. In the rest of this section I focus on (i), because if the constraint is unlikely to bind then (ii) is redundant. The cost of the constraint depends critically upon whether monetary policy is impotent at that point and is discussed in Section 3.

There are few historical episodes that throw light on the question. In the 1930s, nominal short-term interest rates were close to zero in a number of countries, including the United States, for a decade or more; and the same was true of Switzerland in the 1970s. History can, however, shed light on the frequency of negative real interest rates in past cycles. Is it common for real rates to be negative? That is of interest because the lower limit on nominal interest rates implies a bound on real interest rates equal to minus the expected rate of inflation. The lower the expected rate of inflation, the higher the lower bound on real interest rates. In the limit, if prices are expected to be stable, then real interest rates too cannot become negative.

So how likely is it that negative real interest rates will be needed? Summers (1991) suggested that 'the real interest rate [in the United States] has been negative in about a third of the years since World War II'. He did not specify the details of exactly which real interest rate had been negative. Defining the real rate as the one-year Treasury constant maturity rate less the actual CPI inflation rate, the *ex post* rate was negative for about 20% of the period since 1950. But the relevant concept is the *ex ante* expected short-term

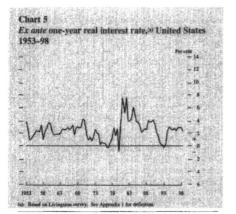

Chart 5
Ex ante one-year real interest rate,(a) United States 1953–98

real interest rate. That rate cannot be observed directly. Estimates using survey-based measures of inflation expectations produce much lower frequencies of negative real rates than for *ex post* rates. Chart 5 shows the *ex ante* real rate of interest in the United States from 1953 to 1998 H2 defined as the one-year Treasury constant maturity rate less the expected inflation rate from the Livingston survey. There are only three brief episodes of negative real rates. These are 1976 H2–1977 H1, 1980 H1 and 1993 H1. So *ex ante* real interest rates have been negative only rarely in the post-war period. A similar finding holds for the United Kingdom (see Chart 6).[1]

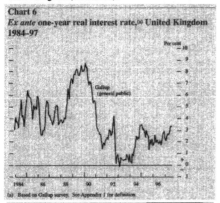

Chart 6
Ex ante one-year real interest rate,(a) United Kingdom 1984–97

Data on the past behaviour of real interest rates, even *ex ante* rates, are not conclusive. Low inflation, and the associated change of monetary policy regime, is likely to have altered the cyclical profile of interest rates. So theoretical models of monetary policy may throw further light on the potential importance of the lower limit on

nominal interest rates. There has in the past two or three years been an explosion of interesting and imaginative technical research on exactly this question.[2]

It is helpful to start, however, by considering a back of the envelope calculation, based on the assumption that the central bank follows a 'Taylor rule' under which interest rates are raised or lowered according to whether output is above or below trend and inflation is above or below its target level. That rule may be represented by the following equation for nominal short-term interest rates:

$$i_t = i^* + \lambda_1 (y_t - y^*) + \lambda_2 (\pi_t - \pi^*) \tag{1}$$

where i is the short-term nominal interest rate, i^* is the 'neutral' nominal interest rate, y and y^* are the logarithms of the levels of actual and trend output respectively, π is the inflation rate and π^* the target inflation rate. The two parameters λ_1 and λ_2 represent how active monetary policy is in responding to deviations of output from trend and inflation from its target level.

Negative demand shocks mean that output can temporarily be below trend and inflation fall below its target. Suppose that the inflation target was 2% a year, and the 'neutral' real interest rate was 3% a year. Then the 'neutral' nominal interest rate would be 5% a year. Imagine a large negative demand shock which led output to fall some 4% below its trend level, and inflation to fall from its target level of 2% a year to zero. Suppose that before the shock output and inflation were at their desired levels and interest rates were at their neutral level. The impact of the shock would require a reduction in interest rates. But by how much? That would depend on the coefficients in the Taylor rule. Typical estimated values for the coefficients λ_1 and λ_2 on output and inflation, respectively, are 0.5 and 1.5. The latter coefficient must exceed unity in order that the policy response to an inflationary shock is a rise in real interest rates. In our example, interest rates would fall by 2 percentage points because of the shortfall of output from trend, and by 3 percentage points because of the shortfall of inflation below its target. Hence interest rates would fall from 5% to zero if policy followed the simple rule.

What does this tell us about the likelihood that interest rates would hit zero? Only shocks which had a large impact on either output or inflation would create a problem. Such shocks are not inconceivable, but are unusual. The example suggests that policy would most likely be constrained when demand shocks were persistent, and a negative shock to output and inflation occurred when output and inflation were already below their normal levels. Suppose that output was 2% below trend and inflation 1% below target when a negative demand shock occurred. Then interest rates would already be 2.5 percentage points below their normal level, and a shock of only 2% to output and another 1% to

(1) Details of the construction of the *ex ante* real interest rate are given in Appendix 1. Chart 6 uses data from Gallup. *Ex ante* real interest rates for the United Kingdom were also calculated using the Basix survey. According to measures of inflation expectations from this survey, UK *ex ante* real rates have not been negative since 1986, when the survey began.
(2) Among this work are papers by Fuhrer and Madigan (1997), Krugman (1998), Orphanides and Wieland (1998), Rotemberg and Woodford (1997), Wolman (1998), and a recent conference volume edited by Taylor (1999). The literature is surveyed by Johnson *et al* (1999).

Bank of England Quarterly Bulletin: November 1999

inflation would be sufficient to reduce interest rates to zero. That suggests that in practice the constraint is likely to bind primarily when either shocks are persistent or policy-makers have failed to react quickly to demand shocks in the first place, and find themselves with slow growth and inflation below target when another negative shock occurs. A pre-emptive policy that is symmetric around the inflation target will help to make less likely the need for extremely low interest rates.

The idea that monetary policy does or should follow a Taylor rule has been extremely influential. Like most good ideas, its virtue is simplicity. It is not a mechanical rule to guide policy, but a vehicle to clarify issues. The calculation above is extremely simple. To analyse the frequency of interest rates being close to zero requires a more careful analysis of the shocks hitting the economy. The more recent technical literature (see footnote 2 on page 401) has tried to do exactly that.

More sophisticated policy rules have been developed. These imply that it may be better to act more 'aggressively' in response to shocks to inflation or output than in the above example of the Taylor rule. Changing interest rates quickly and sharply in response to news reduces the volatility of inflation and output. This is the case for pre-emptive monetary policy action in which interest rates should move in anticipation of likely prospects for inflation.

At first sight, one might think that interest rates would hit the zero bound more often with a pre-emptive strategy than with less aggressive policies. There is, indeed, some truth in this proposition. But matters are more complicated. And it is instructive to see why. Look at the simple Taylor rule described by equation (1). It is tempting to think that the larger are the coefficients, λ_1 and λ_2, which describe the response of interest rates to output and inflation respectively, the greater will be the movement in interest rates over the cycle. But equation (1) alone does not determine the path of interest rates over time. That depends on how inflation and output themselves respond to earlier movements in interest rates. In technical jargon, inflation and output are endogenous variables, and equation (1) is a policy reaction function, not a reduced form describing the time path followed by interest rates. If a more aggressive policy response reduced the volatility of output and inflation, then interest rates might actually be less volatile over the cycle as a whole than under a less aggressive strategy. Hence pre-emptive monetary policy does not necessarily mean that interest rates are volatile over the cycle.

The benefits of a pre-emptive policy depend upon the transmission mechanism. That lesson comes from exploring modifications of the simple Taylor rule. One such, which I shall call the extended Taylor rule, takes the form:

$$i_t = i^* + \lambda_1 (y_t - y^*) + \lambda_2 (\pi_t - \pi^*) + \lambda_3 i_{t-1} \qquad (2)$$

where not only are the coefficients λ_1 and λ_2 typically larger than in the simple Taylor rule, reflecting a bigger response

to current deviations of output from trend and inflation from its target, but interest rates also depend on their previous level.

The table shows the probability that interest rates might hit the zero bound implied by four different models of the transmission mechanism published recently in the conference volume entitled 'Monetary Policy Rules' edited by John Taylor (1999). Each model simulated the behaviour of interest rates for two different policy reaction functions. The first was a simple Taylor rule with coefficients $\lambda_1 = 0.5$ and $\lambda_2 = 1.5$, as in equation (1). The second was the extended Taylor rule, as in equation (2), with coefficients $\lambda_1 = 0.8$, $\lambda_2 = 3.0$ and $\lambda_3 = 1.0$. For two of the models, the simple rule is sufficient to reduce to negligible proportions the risk of zero interest rates. But the extended rule significantly increases the risk that interest rates might hit the zero bound. Indeed, for those two models the risk of zero interest rates is between one quarter and one third under the extended rule. These models are traditional macroeconomic models where private sector behaviour is more backward-looking than forward-looking.

Probability of zero interest rates in different economic models

Per cent

Model	Simple Taylor Rule	Aggressive Taylor Rule
Batini-Haldane	1	31
Levin-Wieland-Williams	2	24
McCallum-Nelson	11	16
Rotemberg-Woodford	12	2

Note: The probabilities are calculated on the assumption that the exogenous shocks are normally distributed using the reported standard deviation of interest rates under the two policy rules, and that the average nominal interest rate is 5.0%.

In the other two models, private sector expectations play a key role. This forward-looking element to behaviour changes the conclusions quite dramatically. The simple rule generates a higher, though not large, probability that interest rates might need to fall to zero. But the extended rule does not, in one case, lead to a significant rise in that probability, and, in the other, actually leads to a very substantial fall in the risk of zero interest rates. The reason is that in those models aggregate demand is sensitive to long-term interest rates. With the extended Taylor rule, a rise in interest rates is expected to persist. This will increase the leverage of monetary policy. Hence a small rise in interest rates today may induce quite large changes in private sector demand, followed by equally rapid responses of output and inflation. In turn that makes it less likely that nominal interest rates will have to fall towards zero.

So the relationship between the simple and the extended forms of the Taylor rule is sensitive to assumptions about the nature of the transmission mechanism of monetary policy. These models are not yet sufficiently robust for strong conclusions about policy to be drawn. But they do have one interesting implication for the interpretation of central bank behaviour. Much of the academic literature tends to describe extended Taylor rules which contain a lagged interest rate as interest rate smoothing: interest rates have a tendency to stay at their current level. Such smoothing is often described as evidence of an inherent central bank degree of caution, or 'gradualism'. This is often contrasted with more 'activist' policies. Yet, as we have seen, the presence of lagged interest rates in a policy reaction function could, depending on the transmission mechanism, be evidence of an aggressive or pre-emptive policy stance. Moreover, the lagged interest rate in (2) could also be an appropriate response to the fact that future inflation depends on lagged values of output and inflation. A central bank that followed the extended Taylor rule, could be described as either 'activist' or 'gradualist'. Hence such words should be used with enormous care. Their meaning is not at all obvious outside a well-defined economic model.

The insight that a prompt response to shocks may prevent the need for larger subsequent movements ('a stitch in time saves nine'), and hence a less volatile path for interest rates is general. The lessons of recent research provide many insights into the way monetary policy should be set. But they do not provide an accurate quantitative guide to the risk that interest rates may need to fall to zero. In part, this reflects our incomplete understanding of the way the economy behaves. But it also reflects the fact that the probability of zero interest rates depends on the likelihood of extreme shocks. That is very hard to assess from historical experience when the frequency of such shocks is small. Econometricians require a large number of observations before their conclusions can be firm. So, as ever, central banks will need to keep an open mind. They must be prepared not only to act quickly but to think quickly.

All in all, the observations that there may be downward nominal rigidities in wages and prices and that there is a zero lower limit on nominal interest rates, do not appear to justify a policy of deliberately targeting a higher rate of inflation than is currently pursued by most central banks. Summers (1991) concluded that 'the optimal inflation rate is surely positive, perhaps as high as 2 or 3%'. In his latest book, Krugman (1999) argued that the United States and Europe should 'make sure that inflation does not get too low when times are good: to set a target rate of at least 2%, so that real interest rates can be reduced to minus 2 rather than merely to zero if the situation demands' (*op cit* pages 161–62). Although the evidence for such propositions does not seem to me conclusive, the practical difference between the inflation targets recommended by Summers and Krugman and the inflation targets pursued by central banks is in practice small. The inflation target agreed by the Reserve Bank of New Zealand and its government is a range of 0% to 3%; the Bank of England has been given an inflation target of 2.5% a year; and the European Central Bank has a quantitative target for inflation of 'a year-on-year increase in the Harmonised Index of Consumer Prices (HICP) for the euro area of below 2%'. Academic economists and central bankers—and an increasing number are both—are perhaps closer to each other than their rhetoric sometimes suggests.

2(ii)   Stabilising output and employment

What can and should central banks do to stabilise output and employment? There are two overriding constraints on the ability of central banks to target real variables. First, in the long run, when the lags in the monetary policy transmission mechanism have worked themselves out, monetary policy affects the price level, not output or employment. Second, in the short run, before policy has fully worked through, the effect of monetary policy on real variables is extremely uncertain because the transmission mechanism is neither sufficiently well understood nor sufficiently stable over time for policy easily to target real variables. Nevertheless, monetary policy does have real effects in the short run. As Benjamin Friedman (1998 page viii) has pointed out, 'the tension created by the joint effect of central bank actions on inflation and on aggregate output, or employment, is usually of the essence whenever public policy discussion turns to monetary policy'.

Faced with shocks that tend to shift output and inflation in opposite directions, central banks have a choice. They can try either to bring inflation back to its target level as soon as possible, which might exacerbate the initial impact of the shock on output, or they can accommodate the change in inflation, bringing inflation back to the target more slowly and so reducing the impact on output. Although there is no stable trade-off between inflation and output, there is a trade-off between the variability of inflation and the variability of output. Such a trade-off is known as a—yes, you've guessed it—Taylor curve (Taylor (1979)). Chart 7 shows the Taylor curve. The position of the curve is determined by the structure of the economy (in particular by the variances of the shocks hitting the economy) and the behaviour of monetary policy. The Taylor curve plots the locus of combinations of inflation and output variability that can be attained by appropriate monetary policies. It is traced out by changing the relative weights on inflation and output variability in the central bank's 'loss function', or, in other words, by changing the implicit horizon for the inflation target. Moving down the curve from left to right is equivalent to choosing a shorter horizon over which to bring

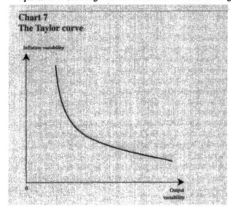

Chart 7
The Taylor curve

Inflation variability

Output variability

Bank of England Quarterly Bulletin: November 1999

inflation back to target, thus lowering the variability of inflation and increasing the variability of output.

So a central bank has 'constrained discretion' about the horizon over which to bring inflation back to target; that is, a choice about how to trade off variability of output against variability of inflation. This choice has no implications for the average level of either output or inflation, but reflects a choice about whether inflation or output should bear the strain of the initial impact of any shock. And it is at the heart of public debate over monetary policy.

Is it possible in practice to exploit the trade-off described by the Taylor curve? The curve is a useful expositional device to explain the choices facing central banks. But its empirical value is limited for two reasons.

First, the curve is a 'volatility possibility frontier' which can be identified from actual data only if the central bank is pursuing the best of all possible monetary policies. That cannot be independently verified. Second, the curve is likely to shift over time as the variances of the shocks hitting the economy themselves move around. Empirical estimates of Taylor curves are highly model specific, and can be estimated in practice only by the use of model simulation. Research by Bean (1998) and Batini (1999) suggests that the Taylor curve appears to bend sharply around the point where the standard deviation of fluctuations in GDP relative to trend is equal to the standard of deviation of inflation. Hence policy-makers with different preferences might well generate very similar outcomes for inflation and output variability. This, however, is conjecture. The Taylor curve is a useful conceptual tool, but is difficult to use empirically.

There are further reasons for supposing that monetary policy should focus on keeping inflation close to its target and not on fine-tuning output. The particular difficulty with implementing policy rules of the Taylor kind is that, as formulated, they presume a knowledge of output relative to its trend level. Estimates of the output gap, or the difference between unemployment and the current NAIRU, not only vary greatly from one method to another, but are often of opposite signs. Ignorance not only of the transmission mechanism of monetary policy but also of underlying productive potential, means that basing monetary policy on short-term movements in output can be hazardous. In a recent study of US monetary policy in the post-war period, Orphanides (1999) found that simple policy rules behaved extremely well when interest rates were set with the benefit of hindsight—using retrospective knowledge about movements in output that identified the trend path for productivity. But when they were based on information available to policy-makers at the time, they performed much less well. Orphanides concluded that there were risks in responding too aggressively to estimates of deviations of output from trend, and that 'the stabilisation promise suggested by these activist policy rules is indeed illusory'.

Changing interest rates in response to movements in inflation appears to be a relatively robust policy rule. Moving interest rates in response to changes in output, however, is much more sensitive to a knowledge of both the structure of the economy and, in particular, the forces determining the long-run growth of productive potential. To illustrate this, Christiano and Gust (1999) found that in a rather different model of the transmission mechanism than the conventional sticky price model used by many, the only robust policy rule was one which targeted inflation.

So although there are, in principle, reasons for using constrained discretion to respond to shocks, central banks would do well to have modest ambitions about the scope for output stabilisation. A keen appreciation of how limited is our present knowledge of the economy should be central to the policy-making process. It is precisely that lack of knowledge which makes mechanical policy rules incredible. The use of constrained discretion is sensible. But, as Orphanides pointed out, such a strategy 'requires continued vigilance against mechanical attempts to exploit historical relationships to fine-tune the performance of the economy'. Beware of (non-Greek) econometricians bearing false relationships. Perhaps one of the strongest arguments for delegating decisions on interest rates to an independent central bank is that, whereas democratically elected politicians do not often receive praise when they say 'I don't know', those words should be ever present on the tongues of central bankers. And, in a state of ignorance, it is important for the central bank to be transparent about both what it thinks it understands and what it knows it does not understand. In so doing, it may reduce the scale of wasted resources devoted to discovering the secrets of central bank thinking, and reduce the numbers of players in financial markets who fear that others have inside information.

2(iii)   Targeting prices or inflation

The third challenge to the objectives of central banks is whether monetary policy should be directed to meeting a target inflation rate or a target price level. The case for price stability suggests that it is the stability of the long-run price level which creates confidence in the monetary standard and enables nominal contracts to play an important role in the economy. The long-term lender knows what her return will be in real terms, and equally the long-term borrower knows what he will pay. Yet the arguments presented in section 2(i) imply that a positive average measured inflation rate, might be desirable. Can price stability be reconciled with low inflation? The choice between price-level targeting and inflation targeting has attracted some interest recently.[1] The proponents of price-level targeting point out that under inflation targeting the variance of the price level increases without limit as deviations of inflation from the target level are treated as bygones. This is analogous to base level drift with monetary targeting. Proponents of inflation targeting point out that to return prices to their previous level might imply significant volatility of output.

---

(1) See Hall (1984), Bank of Canada (1994), Svensson (1999), McCallum (1990), McCulloch (1991), and Dittmar, Gavin and Kydland (1999).

I find this contrast somewhat artificial. The reason is that the dichotomy between the two approaches is analysed in models in which the target variable, whether inflation or the price level, is returned to its desired level in the following period. Earlier, I suggested that it was useful to think in terms of the horizon over which inflation was brought back to its target level in the context of an inflation target strategy. Equally, one can think in terms of the horizon over which policy-makers wish to bring the price level back to some desired pre-determined path.

To make this clearer, consider the current framework for UK monetary policy. The Bank of England's Monetary Policy Committee (MPC) has been given an inflation target of 2.5% a year by the Government. Members of the Committee will be held accountable for their actions in achieving that target. Imagine that the parliamentary committee to which the MPC is accountable holds hearings in 2007 to discover whether the new arrangements had been successful in meeting the inflation target. They might well ask what the average inflation rate was over the first ten years of the Committee's existence. Most commentators would regard that as a framework for inflation targeting. But asking whether the Committee had achieved an average inflation rate over that period would in fact be equivalent to price level targeting, in the sense that the Committee would be asking whether the price level after ten years was close to its desired pre-determined path implied by the objective that prices should rise by 2.5% a year. Hence an average inflation rate target is equivalent in many ways to price-level targeting. Although that is not the objective of the MPC—which is to aim continuously to meet the 2.5% target irrespective of past inflation outturns—it is worth exploring the implications of an average inflation rate target.

Just as the pursuit of an inflation target requires a judgment about the horizon over which inflation should be brought back to its target level following a shock, there is a second question that arises in the context of price-level or average inflation rate targeting. That concerns the horizon over which the price level should be brought back to its desired pre-determined path. Suppose that the average inflation target is π^*. That defines the desired price level path over time, P^*_t, which rises at the rate π^*. Policy might respond not only to deviations of output from trend and inflation from the target level, but also to deviations of the price level from its desired path. A key policy choice is the horizon over which the price level is brought back to that path. To avoid sharp changes in the current operational inflation target this horizon (denoted by H) could be a decade or more. The operational inflation target each period would be equal to the constant π^*, adjusted for the fact that prices had deviated from their desired path. The current operational inflation target is then given by:

$$\pi^{**}_t = \pi^* - \frac{1}{H}\left(\frac{P_t - P^*_t}{P^*_t}\right) \qquad (3)$$

Substituting this expression into equation (1) for the Taylor rule gives the average inflation rate targeting rule as:

$$i_t = i^* + \lambda_1\left(y_t - y^*\right) + \lambda_2\left(\pi_t - \pi^*\right) + \lambda_3\left(\frac{P_t - P^*_t}{P^*_t}\right) \qquad (4)$$

where $\lambda_3 = \lambda_2/H$.

Equation (4) shows that the difference between inflation and price-level targeting is a matter of degree and not a qualitatively different choice. At one extreme, where the horizon H increases without limit, then 'pure' inflation targeting means that policy follows a simple Taylor rule and the variance of the future price level increases without limit. At the other extreme, where the horizon $H = 0$, policy brings the price level back to its pre-determined path as quickly as possible. That implies greater volatility of output. Both in theory and in practice, policy-makers are likely to choose an intermediate horizon. To reduce short-run volatility in output and employment, central banks will bring inflation back to target gradually. But if central banks target an average inflation rate, then policy will aim also to return the price level to its pre-determined path. In this way, a policy rule such as (4) combines the advantages of the nineteenth century achievement of maintaining stability and predictability of the price level in the long run, with the twentieth century achievement of reducing short-run fluctuations in inflation and output. That would be an appropriate policy rule to take into the twenty-first century.

In practice, the operational inflation target could be adjusted either at discrete intervals, such as five years, or when the deviation of the price level from its desired deterministic path exceeded some critical level, rather than continuously, so that the target could be expressed as a round(ish) number.

A concern with the predictability of the long-run price level does not necessarily imply greater volatility of output and inflation in the short run. Dittmar, Gavin and Kydland (1999) and Svensson (1999) have shown that if there is persistence in shocks to output (that is, persistence in the short-run Phillips curve), then price-level targeting may actually imply lower volatility of output and inflation. Again, the optimal policy rule is sensitive to the behaviour of the economy, about which there is great uncertainty (see also Batini and Yates (1999)).

Simulations of macroeconomic models which incorporate policy rules such as (4) show that significant reductions in the variance of the future price level can be achieved at small cost in terms of increases in the volatility of output. This should not be surprising. The commitment to predictability of the long-run price level does not mean sharp changes in the inflation target from year to year. Small changes, even at discrete intervals, are sufficient to maintain predictability of the long-run price level without much change in either the average inflation rate targeted over a decade or so, or the response of output to changes in interest rates. Simulations suggest that there may be a rather small sacrifice in terms of output volatility for significant reductions in future price level volatility. Chart 8 shows simulation results from a three-equation macroeconomic

Bank of England Quarterly Bulletin: November 1999

model calibrated to quarterly data for the United Kingdom. They illustrate the qualitative properties of mixed inflation-price level targeting. The three equations describe aggregate demand as a function of the real interest rate, aggregate supply as a function of price 'surprises' and a stochastic supply shock, and interest rates by the policy reaction function (4). The first two panels of Chart 8 show

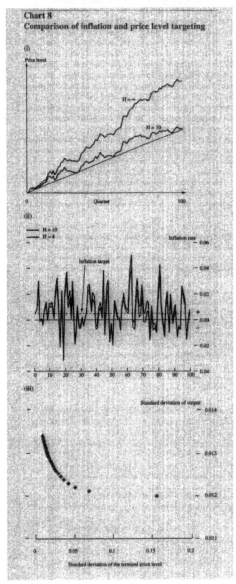

Chart 8
Comparison of inflation and price level targeting

(i)

Price level

H = ∞

H = 10

0   Quarter   100

(ii)

H = 10
H = ∞

Inflation rate
— 0.06

Inflation target
— 0.04

— 0.02

+
— 0.00

— 0.02

0   10   20   30   40   50   60   70   80   90   100   0.04

(iii)

Standard deviation of output
— 0.014

— 0.013

— 0.012

— 0.011

0   0.05   0.1   0.15   0.2

Standard deviation of the terminal price level

the paths for the price level and inflation, respectively, for a particular sequence of shocks over 100 quarters. Two lines are plotted, in addition to a line corresponding to the long-run inflation target of 2% a year, one corresponding to pure inflation targeting (H = ∞) and the other to mixed inflation-price level targeting (H = 10). The long-run price level is much more predictable with the mixed strategy than with pure inflation targeting and there is rather little difference in terms of the inflation profile. The trade-off between variability of the price level and the variability of output around its trend is shown in the third panel. In terms of standard deviations, this shows that significant reductions in price level uncertainty can be achieved at relatively low cost in terms of output variability, but that beyond a certain point further reductions are costly or difficult to attain.

3   Monetary policy in a low inflation world: transmission mechanism

In Section 2, several questions arose to which the answers depended crucially on the transmission mechanism of monetary policy. Do central banks have the power to stabilise output in the short run, and is this objective jeopardised by the pursuit of long-run price stability? Differences of view certainly exist, but there is broad agreement on the conceptual framework within which these questions should be answered. Before joining the FOMC, William Poole (1998) wrote that,

> 'macroeconomists share a common core model, and most are well aware of the uncertainty over estimates of key parameters in the model. Some lean a bit one way, some another way. This fact makes a debate less exciting than in earlier days but is a sign of real progress in macroeconomics.'

That is, I think, a fair description of the way economists see themselves. But is the current state of economic knowledge similar to that of nineteenth century physics, when many theories appeared to be settled but were soon shown to be inadequate in important cases? Certainly, there is much that we do not understand. The recent experience of Japan has reopened the question of whether a 'liquidity trap' can exist and how best to respond to it. In the United States, and elsewhere, asset prices have risen to levels that make it difficult for even the most sober central banker to avoid speaking of 'asset price bubbles'. Although there are many aspects of the transmission mechanism about which central banks would like to know more, I focus in this section on the following question. Is monetary policy impotent when nominal interest rates are close to zero?

The issue of how monetary policy works when interest rates are at or close to zero has been contentious since the possibility of a 'liquidity trap' was suggested by Keynes (1936) formalised by Hicks (1937) and revived by Krugman (1998). But it is only the recent experience of Japan, where interest rates have been virtually zero since February 1999, that the subject has again acquired immediate policy relevance. There are two views:

(i) When interest rates are zero, households and firms have an infinitely elastic demand for money balances. An increase in the money supply is absorbed passively in higher balances, and there are no implications for broader measures of money or demand and output. Monetary policy is impotent; there is a liquidity trap.[1]

(ii) When interest rates are zero, households and firms become satiated with money balances, and any increase in the money supply leads to changes in household portfolios with consequent changes in relative yields on different financial and real assets, and direct and indirect effects on spending.

The policy implications of the two views are clearly very different, but which one is the more attractive theoretically and empirically? In part, this depends on the demand for money. The response of the short-term nominal interest rate (a price variable) and of the monetary base (a quantity variable) to central bank operations are opposite sides of the same coin (or is it note?). The preferences of households and firms for money balances can be described in terms of either their demand for quantities of money or their response to interest rates. What happens when the nominal interest rate goes to zero—effectively making money and short-term securities perfect substitutes? If the demand for money balances tended to infinity, as the interest rate tended to zero, then monetary policy would have no effect on real demand and output because any additional money created would simply be absorbed passively in money holdings. But if preferences for money balances exhibit satiation such that the demand is finite at a zero price, then the creation of money beyond that amount would be translated into demand for other assets and ultimately—via effects on relative yields—into nominal spending. So, in principle, empirical estimates of the demand for money should help us to resolve the issue. These two possible views of the money demand curve are shown in Chart 9. Of course, there is rather little evidence on the demand for money at zero interest rates.[2]

In principle, all relevant relative prices should enter the demand for money. With a myriad of financial assets, and unobservable shadow interest rates on different consumer durables, there are many candidates for the prices or interest rates to include in a model of money demand. Both in theory and in practice, it is sensible to try to limit these. But that choice leaves room for disagreement about whether the relevant rates have been included, and it is precisely that scope for disagreement which continues to divide Keynesians and monetarists. (These differences are explored in detail in the symposium on the Monetary Transmission Mechanism published in the *Journal of Economic Perspectives* in 1995.)

Keynes himself realised that other assets had to be included in the model for a satisfactory account of the demand for

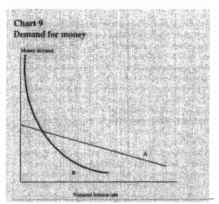

Chart 9
Demand for money

money. He focused on long-term government bonds. When short-term interest rates were extremely low, long-term bond yields would also be low, albeit above zero. But at such low rates the prices of long-term bonds would become extremely volatile with respect to small changes in the interest rate. For example, a consol with a yield of 5% would fall in price by almost 5% if the long-term interest rate were to rise by 25 basis points, whereas it would fall by 20% for the same absolute rise in interest rates if the yield were only 1%. Hence, as has been seen in Japan over the past two years, bond prices become extremely volatile at low interest rates. That might lead to a significant risk premium on long-term bonds which, in turn, would place a floor under the long-term interest rate. As Keynes argued,

> 'Circumstances can develop in which even a large increase in the quantity of money may exert a comparatively small influence on the rate of interest. For a large increase in the quantity of money may cause so much uncertainty about the future that liquidity-preferences due to the precautionary-motive may be strengthened; whilst opinion about the future of the rate of interest may be so unanimous that a small change in present rates may cause a mass movement into cash'. (Keynes (1936), page 172.)

At low interest rates, holding bonds was unattractive because they presented almost a one-way option—the interest rate could only go up. Stability in such circumstances required differences of opinion about the future direction of interest rates. Only then would control of the money supply be a potent weapon in the hands of central banks.

The alternative view is that monetary policy retains its potency even when short-term interest rates are zero. The demand for money depends upon the yields of a wide variety of assets. It is not infinitely elastic at extremely low

---

(1) The Keynesian response to a liquidity trap is either to expand fiscal policy or to find ways to tax cash balances. The former became the staple diet of policy-makers in the immediate post-war period, before the difficulties of stabilisation policy became apparent, and the latter is rarely suggested as a serious option (although it is discussed by Buiter and Panigirtzoglou (1999)).
(2) It is interesting that the Lucas (1994) logarithmic money demand function is equivalent to the Keynesian infinitely elastic demand for money at a zero interest rate.

Bank of England Quarterly Bulletin: November 1999

interest rates, and so an increase in the money supply will lead to changes in portfolio behaviour, changes in relative asset prices across a spectrum of assets, and, in turn, an increase in nominal demand and output. Expansionary monetary policy can take the form of open market operations in which the central bank purchases a wide variety of assets, not just short-term government securities. In this way, changes in base money feed through to changes in broader measures of money. For there to be a liquidity trap, base money must be a perfect substitute for all other assets. In open economies, the exchange rate is one of the important relative prices that may respond to an increase in the monetary base. The essence of this 'monetarist' model of the transmission mechanism is the impact of a change in money supply on the quantities and yields of a wide range of financial and real assets (Meltzer (1995)). In that model, an increase in the monetary base would not lower the interest rate below the zero bound, but would affect the yields on other assets. Asset prices in general would rise, and would have an impact on spending. There would be no liquidity trap.

To support this view, Meltzer (1999) has argued that there are three episodes in US monetary history between 1914 and 1950 in which the monetary base was a better empirical indicator of the policy stance than measures of short-term interest rates. In two of those three episodes (1937–38 and 1948–49) short-term interest rates were close to zero. Meltzer finds a significant impact of money base growth on consumption, even after taking into account the effect of interest rates and lagged consumption growth. Nelson (1999b) has replicated these results for the United Kingdom, and finds sizable effects of real base money growth on growth in output, over and above effects via real interest rates. The orders of magnitude of the US and UK responses appear similar, although, if anything, the impact is larger in the United Kingdom than in the United States.

What is the mechanism by which increases in base money affect demand and output when short-term interest rates are zero? It is hard to believe that an increase in real money balances induces a sizable wealth effect—they are too small relative to other forms of wealth. Their impact must come, at least in part, from a change in the yields on other assets. In turn that is likely to reflect changes in risk premia. With short rates stuck at zero, the pure expectations theory of the term structure of interest rates and the uncovered interest parity arbitrage theory of exchange rates provide no way for monetary policy to affect other yields. Those theories ignore risk premia. A full explanation of the transmission mechanism of monetary policy at zero interest rates will require a general equilibrium theory of risk premia and how those risk premia are affected by monetary policy. Neither the Keynesian idea of a liquidity trap nor the monetarist rejection of such a concept are based on a rigorous and fully articulated theory of risk premia. How risk premia are determined is the key question for future research on the impact of monetary policy on asset prices. Perhaps such a theory will be the equivalent in economics of the special and general theories of relativity in physics.

So the question of whether monetary policy is impotent when short-term interest rates are zero remains, for the present, largely open. A rapid expansion of the monetary base in Japan might be an experiment from which we would learn much. But central banks are not in the business of engaging in experiments. In qualitative terms, it seems implausible that a sustained increase in money supply would simply lead to an addition to holdings of cash. But the quantitative impact on spending remains unclear.

The Japanese economy has been in recession for some time; interest rates have been low for several years, and virtually zero for much of 1999 (see Chart 10). Many commentators have urged the Bank of Japan to expand the monetary base. Since short-term government instruments have now become almost perfect substitutes for cash, open market operations should, so it is argued, concentrate on purchases of long-term government bonds, private sector financial assets and foreign currency. Such purchases would change relative

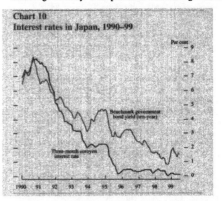

Chart 10
Interest rates in Japan, 1990–99

asset yields, including the exchange rate, and produce a rise in private sector demand. In contrast, the Bank of Japan has argued against such a strategy on three grounds (Okina (1999)). First, an increase in base money would be unlikely to produce corresponding increases in broader measures of money because banks do not wish to expand their assets by lending to the private sector. Second, it is unlikely that long-term interest rates could fall further because of a risk premium reflecting the price volatility of bonds when interest rates are low. Third, there may be political obstacles to a significant depreciation of the yen—namely, opposition from the United States and in Asia itself. Although there has, indeed, been substantial foreign exchange intervention by Japan over the past year, that has been directed to stabilising the yen-dollar exchange rate, and the intervention has been sterilised.

Support for the rejection of money base expansion as a way out comes from McKinnon and Ohno (1999). They pointed out that, in an open economy with no capital controls, long-term interest rates in Japan should reflect expectations of future currency appreciation. Bond yields could have fallen to their present levels only if the market believed that the yen would continue to appreciate in future as it has over the past 20 years. They regard the expectation of further yen appreciation as given, which leads to an externally generated liquidity trap. Attempts to weaken the yen would, they argue, fail because investors believe that any depreciation would be only temporary. Quite why expectations of future yen appreciation cannot be influenced by monetary policy is unclear. The announcement of a medium-term commitment to an inflation target comparable with those elsewhere should eliminate expectations of perpetual yen appreciation.

In future, economists will surely learn much about monetary policy at low interest rates from the current experience of Japan. There is no doubt that monetary policy becomes more complicated when nominal interest rates are very low. There may be institutional or political objections to the consequences of a policy of base money expansion. Nevertheless, it is hard to believe that monetary policy is completely impotent.

4 The international monetary system

No central bank can be an island of stability. Interdependence among countries is a feature of modern economic life. For most countries their exchange rate is one of the most important relative prices in the economy, and some countries have gone further and either delegated monetary policy to another country—as with a currency board—or have determined to decide monetary policy collectively—as in a monetary union.

Over the past ten to fifteen years, since freely floating exchange rates and unrestricted capital movements characterised the world financial system, two 'stylised facts' have emerged. First, with floating exchange rates the volatility of real exchange rates has risen significantly compared with earlier regimes of various types of fixed exchange rate. Second, the size and volatility of international capital flows has often made fixed but adjustable exchange rate pegs hard to sustain.

This experience poses three questions for the design of the international monetary system. First, should currency arrangements take one of two extreme forms, either (a) a floating regime with a domestic nominal anchor (such as a money growth or inflation target), or (b) abandonment of a national currency through unilateral 'dollarisation' or multilateral monetary unions? Several countries, ranging from Britain to Brazil, have abandoned fixed exchange rate pegs and adopted floating regimes with domestic nominal targets. Other countries, such as Argentina and members of the euro area, have moved towards either rigid currency boards or a fully-fledged monetary union.

Second, if this is indeed the choice, how should a country decide between retaining its own currency with a domestic nominal target or allowing its monetary policy to be determined elsewhere?

Third, what should be the arrangements for the 'governance' of the international monetary system? Changes in the number of currencies, and the associated number of central banks, have already led to active discussion about the appropriate fora in which decisions on the international monetary system are discussed and made.

The proposition that the world is becoming polarised into countries with freely floating exchange rates and countries with rigidly fixed rate regimes is, on the face of it, plausible. It describes the failed experience of many countries who tried to pursue a middle path of fixed but adjustable rates. But recent experience may tell us more about the need for clarity in a country's monetary policy framework, and the resulting credibility which that generates, than an iron law of exchange rate regimes. For countries that have acquired credibility in their willingness to take whatever measures are necessary to maintain a fixed exchange rate, a fixed but adjustable peg may be a feasible regime. And there may be cases in which countries in transition from a state of hyperinflation to more conventional rates of inflation can benefit, at least for a time, from the clarity and simplicity of a commitment to an exchange rate objective. Nevertheless, it is likely that the number of countries choosing the two extremes will continue to increase.

As far as the choice between the two extremes is concerned, the issue hinges on the costs and benefits of an exchange rate agreement with other countries. This is not the place to rehearse the costs and benefits of a monetary union. In Europe, the greatest potential economic benefit is, in my view, the impact on growth of trade resulting from the greater exploitation of the larger market made possible by a single currency. Against that benefit must be set the economic cost of more pronounced business cycles which may result from interest rates which are inappropriate for the country concerned, even if they are in the interests of the monetary union as a whole. It will be interesting to see whether the example of the Economic and Monetary Union in Europe leads to an expansion of the number of regional monetary unions in other parts of the world.

The immediate implication of a monetary union is that a wide range of decisions which were previously taken within a country are now made collectively. That requires mechanisms for those joint decisions on matters such as exchange rates and fiscal policy. For example, the Euro 11 Group of finance ministers has an important role to play in the operation of monetary union. Its role is not to provide a political input into monetary policy. It is to provide a forum for member countries to reach agreement on those issues which are not the responsibility of the ECB. These include fiscal policy and any formal exchange rate arrangements between the euro and other currencies. They also need to develop a common view on a range of issues which will then be represented to other countries on the international stage.

Changes in currency arrangements will have implications for the international monetary system. Will fixed exchange

Bank of England Quarterly Bulletin: November 1999

rates spring up within the three regions in which the dollar, the euro and the yen are the most important currencies? Or will currency boards emerge which link emerging market currencies to the dollar, irrespective of their regional affiliation? How will the three major currencies relate to each other? The answers will depend on politics at least as much as on economics.

There has been much talk, and even some action, about the architecture of the international financial system. Some of this relates to international monetary co-operation. The proliferation of meetings means that there are now many groups of a Gx form, where x is almost any integer between two and 182. Indeed, there is even a group called GX which has not yet determined the composition of its membership. The international monetary system is now very different from when the Bretton Woods institutions were set up. Free capital mobility has changed the playing field. The role of those institutions, and the way in which the member countries interact, is certain to continue to evolve. The G7 might become smaller (perhaps a G3); or it might become larger (including the leading emerging market countries); or it might even stay the same.

5   The future of central banks

Despite some ups and downs, central banks are ending this century well ahead of where they started it. There are more of them, and they have greater power and influence. But is this the peak? Will future historians look back on central banks as a phenomenon largely of the twentieth century?

Although central banks have matured, they have not yet reached old age. There remains much to be done. The case for price stability, and the role of central bank independence in achieving it, needs to be made to a wide audience. We must build a constituency for low inflation, without having to resort to episodes of high inflation to prove that instability is costly. To that end, communication has become more important—central banks have moved from mystery and mystique to transparency and openness. The language of central banking must evolve to reflect the need to maintain broader support for the objective of stability and the legitimacy of independent central banks in pursuing it.

Looking further ahead, the future of central banks is not entirely secure. Their numbers may decline over the next century. The enthusiasm of governments for national currencies has waned as capital flows have become liberalised and exchange rates more volatile. Following the example of the European Central Bank, more regional monetary unions could emerge. Short of this, the creation of currency boards, or even complete currency substitution, might also reduce the number of independent national monetary authorities.

But much more important is the potential impact of technological innovation. At present, central banks are the monopoly supplier of base money—cash and bank reserves.

Because base money is the ultimate medium of exchange and of final settlement, central banks have enormous leverage over the value of transactions in the economy, even though the size of their balance sheet is very small in relation to those of the private sector. For years, economists have had difficulty in incorporating money into rigorous general equilibrium models. To the elegance of the Walrasian model of an exchange economy has been bolted on an assumption about the technology of making payments such as a 'cash in advance' constraint. These untidy ways of introducing money into economic models are not robust to changes in institutions and technology. Is it possible that advances in technology will mean that the arbitrary assumptions necessary to introduce money into rigorous theoretical models will become redundant, and that the world may come to resemble a pure exchange economy?

Electronic transactions in real time hold out that possibility. There is no reason, in principle, why final settlements could not be carried out by the private sector without the need for clearing through the central bank. The practical implementation of such a system would require much greater computing power than is at present available. But there is no conceptual obstacle to the idea that two individuals engaged in a transaction could settle by a transfer of wealth from one electronic account to another in real time. Pre-agreed algorithms would determine which financial assets were sold by the purchaser of the good or service according to the value of the transaction. And the supplier of that good or service would know that incoming funds would be allocated to the appropriate combination of assets as prescribed by another pre-agreed algorithm. Eligible assets would be any financial assets for which there were market-clearing prices in real time. The same system could match demands and supplies of financial assets, determine prices and make settlements.

Financial assets and real goods and services would be priced in terms of a unit of account. The choice of a unit of account (perhaps a commodity standard, which would produce broad stability in the price level) would be a matter for public choice and regulation, along the lines of existing weights and measures inspectors. Final settlement could be made without any recourse to the central bank. Only if the unit of account was managed would there be a role for a body such as a central bank. Whether the unit of account should be determined by a mechanical rule, as other weights and measures, or managed in a discretionary way depends on some deep issues about the nature of 'nominal rigidities' in such an economy. As Henckel et al (1999) have noted, the key to a central bank's ability to implement monetary policy is that it 'remains, by law or regulation, the only entity which is allowed to 'corner' the market for settlement balances'.

Without such a role in settlements, central banks, in their present form, would no longer exist; nor would money. Economies of this kind have been discussed by Black (1970), Fama (1980), Friedman (1999), Hall (1983) and Issing (1999). The need to limit excessive money creation would be replaced by a concern to ensure the integrity of the computer systems used for settlement purposes. A regulatory body to monitor such systems would be required. Existing regulators, including central banks, would no doubt compete for that responsibility. Moreover, in just the same way as the Internet is unaware of national boundaries, settlement facilities would become international.

The key to any such developments is the ability of computers to communicate in real time to permit instantaneous verification of the creditworthiness of counterparties, thereby enabling private sector real time gross settlement to occur with finality. Any securities for which electronic markets exist could be used as part of the settlement process. There would be no unique role for base money, and hence the central bank monopoly of base money issue would have no value. Central banks would lose their ability to implement monetary policy. The successors to Bill Gates would have put the successors to Alan Greenspan out of business.

As a central banker interested in information technology, should I regard this prospect as a dream or a nightmare? Perhaps the answer is that central bankers should enjoy life today. I shall place my faith in the words of Walter Bagehot who, in *Lombard Street* (1873), wrote that:

> 'Nothing would persuade the English people to abolish the Bank of England; and if some calamity swept it away, generations must elapse before at all the same trust would be placed in any other equivalent.'

Central banks may be at the peak of their power. There may well be fewer central banks in the future, and their extinction cannot be ruled out. Societies have managed without central banks in the past. They may well do so again in the future. The web site of my favourite football team has the banner 'heroes and villains'. For some, central bankers are heroes—more powerful and responsible than political leaders—and for others they are villains—too fanatical to be entrusted with the world economy. For all our sakes, it is important that central bankers are seen neither as heroes nor villains. They should be modest technicians, striving to improve the way they use the tools of their trade, and always eager to learn. Openness of mind and fleetness of foot will be the best way to avoid extinction.

Bank of England Quarterly Bulletin: November 1999

Appendix 1

The construction of survey based *ex ante* and *ex post* real interest rates for the United States and United Kingdom

1   Background to the surveys

1.1   Gallup (United Kingdom)

The survey started in January 1984 but was discontinued in September 1997. It was conducted on a monthly basis, in the first two weeks of the month. The survey covered 1,000 employees, drawn from a stratified sample of the population of Great Britain. Respondents were asked to forecast inflation in the following ranges: 0–1, 1–2, 3–4, 5–6, 7–8, 9–10, 11–12, 13–14, 15–20, and 20 plus. Gallup calculated an average by taking the mid-point of each range and weighting by the number of respondents within it. The mid-point of the 20 plus range was assumed to be 24%.

1.2   Basix (United Kingdom)

The survey is conducted by Barclays Bank on a quarterly basis in early March, early June, early September and early December. It began in December 1986. It looks at the inflation expectations of six separate groups of people: general public, business economists, academic economists, finance directors, trade unions and investment analysts. The question relates to twelve month ahead RPI inflation expectations, except for the general public group for which the inflation measure is not specified.

1.3   Livingston (United States)

The survey asks a range of 'professional' forecasters and academics to forecast US CPI inflation. The number of participants has been fairly steady over time averaging about 50 respondents in each survey. One set of questionnaires is sent out in May and must be returned in early June, and the other set of questionnaires is sent out in November and must be returned in early December.

The timing conventions of the Livingston Survey have been consistent throughout the period that the Federal Reserve Bank of Philadelphia has managed the survey (it took responsibility for the survey in 1990), and seem to be generally consistent with the above pattern before that time.

2   Nominal interest rates

2.1   UK nominal interest rate

The UK nominal rate is the twelve-month London interbank offer rate (Libor).

2.2   US nominal interest rate

The nominal interest rate is the one-year Treasury constant maturity rate. Yields on Treasury securities at 'constant maturity' are interpolated by the US Treasury from the daily yield curve. This curve, which relates the yield on a security to its time to maturity, is based on the closing market bid yields on actively traded Treasury securities in the over-the-counter market.

3   Constructing a survey based *ex ante* measure of the real rate

3.1   UK real rates

To calculate the survey based *ex ante* real rate, the average of the twelve-month Libor rate over the dates of the survey is calculated. The survey based inflation expectation corresponding to these dates is subtracted from this average nominal interest rate. The Gallup inflation expectations series tended to overpredict inflation outturns. If this were allowed for by subtracting the average error of 1.61 percentage points from the Gallup series, then there would be no examples of negative real rates in Chart 6.

3.2   US real rates

The majority of the Livingston sampling period lies in May and November, the real interest rate is calculated as the monthly average for the nominal interest rate in either May or November less the appropriate inflation expectation. The Livingston expectations series has tended to under predict inflation outturns. If this were allowed for by adding the average error of 0.65 percentage points to the Livingston series, then real interest rates would be negative in 10 half years out of 92, compared with four half years when no adjustment was made.

4   The *ex post* real rate

4.1   The UK *ex post real rates*

The nominal interest rate is again twelve-month Libor rate. The actual RPIX inflation outturn is subtracted from the appropriate month-average nominal interest rate.

4.2   The UK *ex post real rates*

As with the *ex ante* real rate, the nominal interest rate is the one-year Treasury constant maturity rate. The actual CPI inflation outturn is subtracted from the appropriate month-average nominal interest rate.

References

Akerlof, G A, Dickens, W T and Perry, G L (1996), 'The macroeconomics of low inflation', *Brookings Papers on Economic Activity*, No 1, pages 1–76.

Bagehot, W (1873), *Lombard Street: a description of the money market*, William Clowes and Sons, London.

Bank of Canada (1994), *Economic Behaviour and Policy Choice Under Price Stability*, Ottawa.

Batini, N (1999), 'The shape of stochastic-simulation generated Taylor curves', Bank of England, *mimeo*.

Batini, N and Haldane, A (1999), 'Forward-looking rules for monetary policy', *Bank of England Working Paper*, No 91.

Batini, N and Yates, A (1999), 'Inflation or price level targeting?', Bank of England, *mimeo*.

Bean, C (1998), 'The new UK monetary arrangements: a view from the literature', *Economic Journal*, Vol 108, pages 1,795–809.

Bernanke, B S and Mishkin, F S (1997), 'Inflation targeting: a new framework for monetary policy?', *NBER Working Paper*, No 5893.

Black, F (1970), 'Banking and interest rates in a world without money', *Journal of Bank Research*, Autumn, pages 9–20.

Boskin, M (1996), 'Toward a more accurate measure of the cost of living', *Final Report of the Advisory Commission To Study the Consumer Price Index*, Washington DC.

Buiter, W H and Panigirtzoglou, N (1999), 'Liquidity traps: how to avoid them and how to escape them', Bank of England, *mimeo*.

Christiano, L J and Gust, C J (1999), 'Taylor Rules in a limited participation model', *NBER Working Paper*, No 7017.

Crawford, A and Harrison, A (1998), 'Testing for downward nominal rigidity in wages', in *Price Stability, Inflation Targets and Monetary Policy*, proceedings of a conference held by the Bank of Canada, May 1997.

Cunningham, A W F (1996), 'Measurement bias in price indices: an application to the UK's RPI', *Bank of England Working Paper*, No 47.

Dittmar, R, Gavin, W T and Kydland, F E (1999), 'The inflation-output variability trade-off and price-level targets', *Federal Reserve Bank of St Louis Review*, January/February.

Fama, E F (1980), 'Banking in the theory of finance', *Journal of monetary economics*, Vol 6, pages 39–57.

Feldstein, M (1996), 'The costs and benefits of going from low inflation to price stability', *NBER Working Paper*, No 5469.

Feldstein, M (ed) (1999), *The costs and benefits of price stability*, University of Chicago Press for NBER.

Fischer, S (1996), 'Why are central banks pursuing long-run price stability?', in *Achieving price stability*, Federal Reserve Bank of Kansas City, pages 7–34.

Friedman, B M (1998), 'Introduction', in Solow, R M and Taylor, J B, *Inflation, unemployment, and monetary policy*, The MIT Press, Cambridge, Massachusetts.

Friedman, B M (1999), 'The future of monetary policy: the central bank as an army with only a signal corps?', *International Finance*, forthcoming.

Bank of England Quarterly Bulletin: November 1999

Friedman, M (1969), 'The optimum quantity of money', in *The optimum quantity of money and other essays*, Chicago: Aldine Publishing Company.

Fuhrer, J C and Madigan, B F (1997), 'Monetary policy when interest rates are bounded at zero', *Review of economics and statistics*, Vol 79, pages 573–85.

Greenspan, A (1989), 'Statement by Chairman, Board of Governors of the Federal Reserve System before the Committee on Banking, Finance and Urban Affairs, US House of Representatives, 24 January 1989', *Federal Reserve Bulletin*, March 1989, pages 139–42.

Hall, R E (1983), 'Optimal fiduciary monetary systems', *Journal of Monetary Economics*, Vol 12, pages 33–50.

Hall, R E (1984), 'Monetary strategy with an elastic price standard', in *Price stability and public policy*, Federal Reserve Bank of Kansas City.

Henckel, T, Ize, A and Kovanen, A (1999), 'Central banking without central bank money', IMF, *mimeo*.

Hicks, J R (1937), 'Mr Keynes and the 'Classics': a suggested interpretation', *Econometrica*, Vol 5, pages 147–59.

Issing, O (1999), 'Hayek—currency competition and European Monetary Union', Annual Hayek Memorial Lecture, hosted by the Institute of Economic Affairs, London, 27 May.

Johnson, K, Small, D and Tryon, R (1999), 'Monetary policy and price stability', *Board of Governors of the Federal Reserve System International Finance Discussion papers*, No 641, *mimeo*, Washington DC.

Keynes, J M (1936), 'The general theory of employment, interest and money', Volume VII of *The Collected Writings of John Maynard Keynes (1973)*, Macmillan, London.

King, M A (1996), 'How should central banks reduce inflation?—Conceptual issues', in *Achieving price stability*, Federal Reserve Bank of Kansas City.

King, M A (1997a), 'The inflation target five years on', *Bank of England Quarterly Bulletin*, Vol 37(4), pages 434–42.

King, M A (1997b), 'Changes in UK monetary policy: rules and discretion in practice', *Journal of Monetary Economics*, Vol 39, pages 81–97.

Krugman, P (1996), 'Stable prices and fast growth: just say no', *The Economist*, 31 August, pages 19–21.

Krugman, P (1998), 'It's baaack! Japan's slump and the return of the liquidity trap', *Brookings Papers on Economic Activity*, No 2, pages 137–205.

Krugman, P (1999), *The return of depression economics*, W W Norton and Co, New York.

Levin, A, Wieland, V and Williams, J C (1998), 'Robustness of simple monetary policy rules under model uncertainty', *Federal Reserve Board Finance and Economics Discussion Series*, No 45.

Lucas, R E (1994), 'The welfare costs of inflation', *CEPR Working Paper*, No 394.

McCallum, B T (1990), 'Could a monetary base rule have prevented the Great Depression?', *Journal of Monetary Economics*, Vol 26, pages 3–26.

McCallum, B T and Nelson, E (1999), 'Performance of operational policy rules in an estimated semi-classical structural model', in J B Taylor (ed), *Monetary policy rules*, Chicago: University of Chicago Press for NBER, pages 15–45.

McCulloch, J H (1991), 'An error-correction mechanism for long-run price stability', *Journal of Money, Credit and Banking*, Vol 23, pages 619–24.

McKinnon, R and Ohno, K (1999), 'The foreign exchange origins of Japan's economic slump in the 1990s: the interest rate trap', Stanford University, *mimeo*.

Meltzer, A H (1995), 'Monetary, credit and (other) transmission processes: a monetarist perspective', *Journal of Economic Perspectives*, Vol 9, pages 49–72.

Meltzer, A H (1999), 'The transmission process', paper prepared for conference on the *Monetary transmission process: recent developments and lessons for Europe*, Bundesbank, Frankfurt, 25–27 March.

Nelson, E (1999a), 'UK monetary policy 1972–97: a guide using Taylor Rules', Bank of England, *mimeo*.

Nelson, E (1999b), 'Direct effects of base money on aggregate demand: theory and evidence', Bank of England, *mimeo*.

Okina, K (1999), 'Monetary policy under zero inflation: a response to criticisms and questions regarding monetary policy', *Bank of Japan Institute for Monetary and Economic Studies Discussion Paper Series*, No 99-E-20.

Orphanides, A and Wieland, V (1998), 'Price stability and monetary policy effectiveness when nominal interest rates are bounded at zero', *Federal Reserve Board Finance and Economics Discussion Series*, No 35, August.

Orphanides, A (1999), 'The quest for prosperity without inflation', Federal Reserve Board, May, *mimeo*.

Phelps, E (1972), *Inflation policy and unemployment theory*, MacMillan, London.

Poole, W (1998), 'Comments', in Solow, R M and Taylor, J B, *Inflation, unemployment, and monetary policy*, The MIT Press, Cambridge, Massachusetts.

Rotemberg, J J and Woodford, M (1997), 'An optimization-based econometric framework for the evaluation of monetary policy', in Bernanke, B S and Rotemberg (eds), *NBER Macroeconomics Annual 1997*, MIT Press, pages 297–346.

Shiller, R (1996), 'Why do people dislike inflation?', *NBER Working Paper*, No 5539, April.

Summers, L (1991), 'How should long term monetary policy be determined?', *Journal of Money Credit and Banking*, Vol 123, pages 625–31.

Svensson, L E O (1999), 'Price level targeting vs inflation targeting', *Journal of Money Credit and Banking*, forthcoming.

Taylor, J B (1979), 'Estimation and control of a macroeconomic model with rational expectations', *Econometrica*, Vol 47, pages 1,267–86.

Taylor, J B (1998), 'Monetary policy and the long boom', *Federal Reserve Bank of St Louis Review*, November/December.

Taylor, J B (ed) (1999), *Monetary policy rules*, University of Chicago Press for NBER.

Vickrey, W (1955), 'Stability through inflation', in Kurihara, K (ed), *Post-Keynesian Economics*, George Allen and Unwin Ltd, London.

Wolman, A L (1998), 'Real implications of the zero bound on nominal interest rates', Federal Research Bank of Richmond, *mimeo*.

Yates, A (1998), 'Downward nominal rigidity and monetary policy', *Bank of England Working Paper*, No 82.

[15]

Monetary Policy Today:
Sixteen Questions and about Twelve Answers

Alan S. Blinder

There have been three great inventions since the beginning of time: fire, the wheel, and central banking,
   -- Will Rogers

Victorians heard with grave attention that the Bank Rate had been raised. They did not know what it meant. But they knew that it was an act of extreme wisdom.
   -- John Kenneth Galbraith

My assignment is to survey the *main* questions swirling around monetary *policy today*. I emphasize three words in this sentence, each for a different reason. "Main" is because one person's side issue is another's main issue. So I had to be both selective and judgmental in compiling my list, else this paper would have been even longer than it is. "Policy" indicates that I have restricted myself to issues that are truly relevant to real-world policymakers, thus omitting many interesting but purely academic issues. "Today" means that I focus on current issues, thus passing over some illustrious past issues. All these omissions still leave a rather long list; so I will treat some issues quite briefly.

I have compiled a list like this once before. In December 1999, at what I believe was the first conference ever organized by the brand-new European Central Bank (ECB) in Frankfurt, I offered (over dinner, no less!) a list of 15 questions that would have to be answered by anyone starting a central bank from scratch at the time (Blinder, 2000). In this paper, I will declare two of my 15 Frankfurt issues largely resolved, and note that two others have dropped off the radar screen without being resolved. However, I will add five new issues. Thus the list of issues has grown longer, not shorter, since 1999. But do not mistake that for lack of progress. Both the art and science of monetary policy have advanced considerably since then.

Before proceeding further, let me mention some issues that I will *not* take up, for their omission is, in some sense, a measure of that progress. My Frankfurt list included the old debate over the choice between interest-rate targets and monetary-aggregate targets, which seems to have been resolved everywhere except in the ECB's rhetoric. It also included the issue of whether electronic money poses a threat to central banks, which was a hot issue then but seems to have faded from view.[1] Earlier discussions of central banking issues devoted a great deal of attention to the need for central bank independence.[2] But that debate is all but over, and I will simply *assume* that the central bank is independent.[3] Similarly, some earlier authors thought it necessary to defend the proposition that low inflation is a central goal of monetary policy, a proposition that no longer needs defense.[4] In addition, a huge amount of ink has been spilled on the time consistency debate and the so-called inflation bias[5]—another debate that I consider to be over, although others may disagree.

What, then, will I discuss? Part I, the longest part of the paper, takes up five critical questions regarding the *institutional design* of the monetary policy authority:

1. What is the proper objective function for monetary policy?

2. How transparent should the central bank be?

---

[1] See, for example, the papers by Charles Goodhart, Charles Friedman, and Michael Woodford in the July 2000 special issue of the journal *International Finance*.
[2] See, for example, Fischer (1994).
[3] However, there are those who worry about fiscal dominance and/or budgetary independence of the central bank.
[4] Again, see Fischer (1994). However, the issue of whether monetary policy should target the *inflation rate* or the *price level* remains a live one. See Issue 15 below.
[5] The original sources were Kydland and Prescott (1977) and Barro and Gordon (1983).

2

3. Should the central bank be an inflation targeter, as that term is commonly used nowadays?

4. Should monetary policy decisions be made by a single individual or by a committee--and, if the latter, what type of committee?

5. Should the central bank also regulate and/or supervise banks?

After that, I turn in Part II to *operating principles* for monetary policy, discussing six issues:

6. Is the observed proclivity of central bankers to avoid policy reversals justifiable?

7. Does the revealed preference of central bankers for gradualism make sense?

8. Is "fine tuning" possible after all? And if so, should central bankers attempt to fine-tune their economies?

9. Should central banks lead or follow the financial markets?

10. Should central banks in floating exchange rate regimes intervene in the foreign-exchange market?

11. Should central banks use derivatives in the conduct of monetary policy?

Finally, I briefly discuss five issues pertaining to the *transmission mechanism* for monetary policy in Part III:

12. Transmission through the term structure of interest rates

13. Transmission through the exchange rate

14. How should the central bank deal with asset-market bubbles?

3

15. How should the central bank deal with the zero lower bound on nominal interest rates?

16. Do the world's giant central banks have global responsibilities?

I. The Design and Structure of the Central Bank

The first set of five issues pertains to how central banks should be designed and organized—to their "constitutions," so to speak.

Issue 1: What is the proper objective function for monetary policy?

My jumping-off point for this discussion is the loss function that has become ubiquitous in academic writings on monetary policy:

$$(1a) \quad L = (\pi - \pi^*)^2 + \lambda(y - y^*)^2 \quad \text{or}$$

$$(1b) \quad L = (\pi - \pi^*)^2 + \lambda(u - u^*)^2,$$

where L is the period loss, π is the inflation rate and π^* its target value, y is real output and y^* its "natural" or "equilibrium" or "potential" value, and u is the unemployment rate and u^* is the NAIRU. Two variants are given because some authors prefer to represent the central bank's real economic activity objective by the output gap while others prefer the unemployment gap. I will return to this choice briefly below; but, for the most part, it is immaterial.

Nowadays, the live argument is over the size of λ, with some authors fretting that it not be set too large. It thus seems almost quaint to recall that Fischer (1994) went to great lengths to argue that $(\pi - \pi^*)^2$ should figure prominently in the loss functions of central banks—that is, that $\lambda < \infty$. No one needs to make that argument today.

4

Making (1) operational, even in a metaphorical sense, requires that the central bank choose three parameters: λ, π^*, and either y^* or u^*. Each raises important practical issues.

Let us start with π^*, where two main issues arise. The first is obvious and has been so extensively discussed that I will treat it briefly: What's the number? A consensus of sorts seems to have developed around an inflation target of 2% or so for advanced, industrial countries. Berg (2005) surveyed practices at 20 inflation-targeting central banks, eight of which are from rich countries, and every one of the eight uses either 2% or 2.5% as the midpoint of its target range. The ECB, of course, targets inflation "below, but close to, 2%," and the Federal Reserve's all-but-announced target is similar.[6] At 2% inflation, the price level doubles every 35 years. Why not set the target lower? The two main arguments are (a) that price indexes are biased upward and (b) that π^* should be set high enough to provide a reasonable cushion against deflation (see Issue 15 below). Neither seems controversial nowadays, so I move on to a question that is: What measure of inflation should be used?

One important choice is whether inflation should be measured by a "headline" or "core" concept,[7] that is, should it include or exclude energy prices?[8] I am firmly

---

[6] The Fed's preferred index of consumer prices is not the CPI, but rather the deflator for core personal consumption expenditures in the national income and product accounts, which normally runs below the core CPI measure. In its February 2006 monetary policy report, the FOMC implicitly set its target for core PCE inflation at 1.75-2%.

[7] This is not the only issue. For example, Mankiw and Reis (2003) argue for using wage increases rather than price increases. Strum (2006) argues for a PPI measure rather than a CPI measure. Reis (2005) explores the role of asset prices in the price index. Yet another issue is whether monetary policy should target inflation (the usual choice) or the price level. This last question is dealt with briefly under Issue 15 below.

5

in the "core" camp for three related reasons. First, monetary policy is unlikely to have much leverage over energy (or food) prices; so it makes sense to focus the central bank's attention on the inflation it can actually do something about. Second, even if the bank's true concern is headline inflation—which is, after all, the inflation that consumers actually experience—it can probably forecast future headline inflation better by using current and lagged values of core inflation. Ricardo Reis and I (2005) demonstrate this conclusion statistically for the United States, and I suspect it holds in many countries. Third, I believe that concentrating on core inflation is likely to produce more sensible monetary policy in the face of oil shocks (see below).

Despite these powerful arguments, virtually all central banks and governments have opted for headline over core. The ECB, of course, is the most prominent example in this part of the world. But Berg's (2005) list shows that 18 of the 20 inflation-targeting central banks use a headline concept of inflation.

If the choice is controversial, it must be because of the third reason given earlier: the response to supply shocks. So let me briefly defend my position.[9] Consider, first, the case that is dominant in the data: a supply shock that raises the relative price of oil *temporarily*. In that case, oil prices are a source of *inflation* as they rise, but subsequently become a source of *deflation* as they fall—which happens automatically, with no need for central bank action. Given the long lags

---

[8] In most countries, "core" inflation also excludes food prices. (In Japan, the core consumer price index excludes fresh food but includes energy products.) However, food prices have not been an issue for more than 30 years, so I concentrate on energy.
[9] I have dealt with this topic in more detail in Blinder and Reis (2005), especially pages 41-45.

from monetary policy to inflation, there is essentially nothing the central bank can do to remove this bit of inflation volatility.

The other empirically relevant case is when oil prices rise to *permanently* higher levels. Then oil prices are an engine of inflation, but one that naturally peters out unless "second-round effects" on *core* inflation are large. The recent evidence suggests only minor second-round effects, perhaps due to central banks' greater determination to stop inflation in the 1990s and in this decade as compared to the 1970s (Hooker, 2002). Why? The presumed answer is better anchoring of inflationary expectations (Bernanke, 2006). In any case, returning to the main question, there is little that monetary policy can or should do to limit the "first-round effects" of an oil shock. For example, targeting *headline* inflation during a period of rising (falling) oil prices might make monetary policy excessively tight (loose). Hence my conclusion: Stick to core inflation.

The choice of a full-employment target (y* or u*) also merits some discussion. Let me first assume that the target is y*, and then consider whether u* might be the better choice.

The empirical literature contains at least three distinct ways to estimate y*. The oldest is *potential GDP*, which can be defined as:

(2) $y^* = AF(L^*(1-u^*), K)$,

where F(.) is the aggregate production function, A is the Solow residual (in levels), L* is the full-employment labor force (so L*(1-u*) is the "natural" level of employment), and K is the capital stock. A second concept--which is closely related in principle, but is estimated very differently in practice—is the *natural* *rate* of output, defined as the level of production (= aggregate demand) at which

the price level is neither accelerating nor decelerating. It is often "backed out" of

an estimated Phillips curve using Okun's law, thereby making no direct use of

time series data on either K or L (not to mention A). A third approach is to define

y* as the "trend," which is then estimated in some mechanical way (e.g., by a

Hodrick-Prescott filter).

In the context of an objective function like (1), which trades off output volatility

against inflation volatility, the natural rate of output derived from a Phillips-curve

framework (the second of the three concepts above) seems to be a sensible

working definition of y*. Often, the empirical procedure begins with an estimate of

u* from a statistical Phillips curve. Needless to say, that number cannot be

known with precision. Most European countries, in fact, never had a widely-

accepted estimate of the NAIRU; and the days when a 6% NAIRU was a

consensus choice in the United States are long gone. So, at a minimum,

estimates of u* must be treated as time-varying and having large standard errors

(Staiger, Stock, and Watson, 2001).

Notice that, while academics seem to have a revealed preference for output

gaps over unemployment gaps, a second empirical step is needed to move from

the latter to the former—which adds an additional element of statistical

uncertainty. That element is productivity, which translates labor input into output.

At times when projecting (or even estimating) productivity is difficult, estimating

the path of y* becomes extremely hazardous.[10] For this very practical reason, I

have a mild preference for using an unemployment-gap concept rather than an

---

[10] Orphanides (2003) emphasizes this point.

8

output-gap concept. But I do not want to exaggerate the strength of this preference. As Blinder and Yellen (2001) and others have noted, an *unrecognized* acceleration (deceleration) of productivity growth can temporarily depress (raise) the NAIRU.

The next issue is the choice of the weight λ in (1). A higher value of λ connotes more concern with output or unemployment gaps, relative to inflation gaps, and vice-versa. It is tempting to identify λ with the coefficients α and β in a Taylor rule:

$$(3) \quad i = r^* + \pi + \alpha(\pi - \pi^*) + \beta(u^* - u),$$

where i is the nominal interest rate and r^* is the equilibrium real interest. But Svensson (1997) has shown that the mapping from λ to α and β is by no means straightforward. A higher λ need not even lead to a higher ratio β/α, for example. Nonetheless, Blinder and Reis (2005) estimate that Alan Greenspan had a much higher β/α than either Paul Volcker or the Bundesbank prior to the advent of the euro—a reflection, I believe, of his much higher λ. Furthermore, Rudebusch's (2001) calculations of optimal α and β for a simple linear model of the U.S. economy under different choices of λ show substantial sensitivity of the ratio β/α to λ, and in the intuitive direction.[11]

Theoretical discussions of the loss function generally end about here. But central bankers should ponder two more issues. The first is the functional form. The quadratic, of course, is motivated solely by mathematical convenience and gives rise, among other things, to certainty equivalence. Never mind the specific

---

[11] Specifically, when $\lambda=1$ (his base case), $\beta/\alpha=.58$; if $\lambda=4$, β/α rises to .95; and if $\lambda=0.25$, β/α falls to .41. See Rudebusch (2001, Table 1, p. 206).

9

quadratic shape; that's a quibble I do not want to raise. The more fundamental question is why low unemployment should be penalized as much as high unemployment—or, indeed, should be penalized *at all* (Cukierman, 2004). The main reason why central bankers worry about low unemployment is that tight markets produce rising inflation. But that should be taken care of by the first term in (1). If, speaking hypothetically, monetary policy could push u down further without pushing π up, why shouldn't it? The late 1990s in the United States is an historical case in point. Did America suffer some loss because the unemployment rate dropped as low at 3.9%?

One obvious answer is the standard micro-inefficiency argument: Deviations from the real competitive equilibrium *in either direction* impose welfare losses. But this argument is not terribly compelling if the real world is not perfectly competitive. For example, monopolistic competition models suggest that output is systematically too low, in which case raising it should yield efficiency *gains*, not losses. Furthermore, some of us believe that low unemployment yields notable social benefits that are at least partially non-economic in nature. Another possible answer, suggested by Cuckierman (2004), is that the inflation bias discussed by Kydland and Prescott (1977) returns if low unemployment is not penalized symmetrically. This may be the best rationale for doing so.

The other oft-forgotten issue in specifying the loss function is that every central bank has either statutory or tacit responsibility for maintaining financial stability. At certain critical times, this objective takes precedence over everything else. So financial stability seems far too important to be left out of the loss

10

function. Researchers commonly model this third objective by adding a term like

$\gamma(r_t - r_{t-1})^2$ to (1), on the theory that interest-rate volatility and financial-market

instability are highly correlated. Such a crude proxy surely misses many

important aspects of financial instability, however, especially during a banking or

financial crisis, when financial stability may dominate the central bank's other

concerns. So some other approach seems warranted. One possibility is a quasi-

lexicographic ordering under which the central bank minimizes (1) unless serious

financial instability arises, in which case it turns its attention to the latter.

Issue 2: How transparent should the central bank be?

Much has been written on why central banks should be transparent, some of it

by me.[12] In fact, there is by now a sizable scholarly literature on this topic, which I

will not summarize here.[13] Instead, let me just remind readers that there are *two*

main reasons to favor transparency. The one on which economists always focus

is that greater openness should make monetary policy more effective by

tightening the gears between central bank actions and market expectations. But

there is another reason, one which real-world central bankers should never

forget: democratic accountability.

One or both of these arguments appear to have persuaded most of the

world's central bankers (and/or their governments), because there is an

unmistakable trend in the direction of greater openness virtually all over the

world. In a quotation from the 1980s of which I have long been fond, Karl Brunner

(1981) wrote that:

---

[12] See, for example, Blinder *et al.* (2001) and Blinder (2004).
[13] For two recent overviews, see Geraats (2002) and Woodford (2005).

> Central Banking [has been] traditionally surrounded by a peculiar
> mystique... The possession of wisdom, perception and relevant
> knowledge is naturally attributed to the management of Central
> Banks... The relevant knowledge seems automatically obtained
> with the appointment and could only be manifested to holders of the
> appropriate position. The mystique thrives on a pervasive
> impression that Central Banking is an esoteric art. Access to this art
> and its proper execution is confined to the initiated elite. The
> esoteric nature of the art is moreover revealed by an inherent
> impossibility to articulate its insights in explicit and intelligible words
> and sentences.

This was a caricature, of course, but it captured the underlying reality of the time.

The received wisdom in central banking circles then was: Say as little as

possible, and say it cryptically. But attitudes toward transparency have changed

dramatically since then, and central banks around the world have opened up.

Although it is still more of a laggard than a leader in terms of transparency,

the Federal Reserve is a case in point. Prior to February 1994, the FOMC did not

even announce its interest rate decisions as it made them, preferring to let

money market professionals figure them out by observing the Fed's open market

operations. Highly stylized minutes of FOMC meetings were published at the

time, but only after the *following* meeting. Contemporaneous statements after

FOMC meetings, however, were rare (and extremely terse) until May 1999.

That is when the Fed made several major changes in its disclosure policies,

changes that amounted to a quantum leap in the volume of useful information it

provided. First, the FOMC started announcing its "bias" (later changed to

"balance of risks") immediately. Second, it began issuing statements after every

meeting (whether or not there was a change in interest rates). And third, its

12

statements became longer and more substantive. Here is one simple quantitative measure. In the three years 1996-1998 inclusive, the FOMC issued a total of *five* post-meeting statements, with an average of 58 substantive words per statement—thus *under 100 words per year*![14] And the Fed said nothing at all after its first two meetings in 1999 (in February and March). But then it issued a statement after *each* of the remaining six FOMC meetings in 1999, averaging 135 words per statement—thus raising the annual rate to over 1,000 words. This pattern has prevailed (approximately) ever since.

The FOMC took another step toward greater transparency early in 2002, when it began announcing its vote immediately after each meeting, naming names. And finally, starting at the beginning of 2005, the Fed began releasing the minutes of each meeting with approximately a three-week delay—thus *before* the next meeting. None of these changes can be said to constitute a great leap forward. But together they add up to a huge increase in the amount of information released by the formerly-mum Fed—as I once called it, a quiet revolution (Blinder, 2004). And in my view and, much more important, in Chairman Ben Bernanke's view (Bernanke, 2004b), there is more to come.

People often ask if there are limits to (optimal) transparency.[15] My answer is to paraphrase Einstein: Every central bank should be as transparent as possible, but not more so.[16] By this I mean that the default option should be disclosure; a

---

[14] I include in this count only words pertaining either to the economic situation or to the policy decision, excluding standard boilerplate such as the opening sentence, which simply states what the FOMC did ("The Federal Open Market Committee decided today to..."), and the closing paragraphs that announce the vote and the discount rate recommendations of the district banks.
[15] See, for example, Mishkin (2004) and Cukierman (2006).
[16] Einstein said: "Everything should be made as simple as possible, but not simpler."

central bank should keep things secrets only when there are good reasons for doing so.[17] And good reasons do exist. For example, the central bank must preserve the confidentiality of proprietary information given to it by private banks—for example, in its role as bank supervisor. (See Issue 5 below.) Similarly, the central bank must maintain the confidentiality of certain information provided to it by governments, both domestic and foreign. I would also not want to open monetary policy meetings to the press, because that would likely destroy the deliberative process. Finally, the central bank cannot disclose information it doesn't have. This last "limit" to transparency may sound silly, but I will offer some concrete examples below. But apart from such minor exceptions, all of which are non-controversial, I see few effective limits to transparency. More important, I know of no central banks that have bumped up against the constraint of maximal transparency, with the possible exceptions of the Bank of Norway and the Reserve Bank of New Zealand (RBNZ).

If central banks are not yet near their transparency constraints, what remains to be done? The answer, of course, varies by country. For example, the Federal Reserve will, I believe, soon begin announcing its inflation target, π^*, for the first time—something that many central banks have been doing for years. But I think it is a fair generalization to say that, with some notable exceptions, most central banks around the world still reveal rather little about their forecasts. This may be the next transparency frontier.

---

[17] In contrast, Mishkin (2004, p. 50) suggests that transparency is a good thing only to the extent that it "help(s) the central bank do its job." But, in private conversation, Mishkin has told me that he basically agrees with my position.

Of course, nothing in life is simple. Whenever a central bank forecasts more than, say, six months ahead, *future monetary policy* is among the crucial assumptions that must be built into the forecast. So what future monetary policy should be assumed? The debate to date seems to revolve around three main options:

1. unchanged monetary policy throughout the forecast period

2. the monetary policy path expected by the markets (and therefore embedded in, e.g., futures prices)

3. the central bank's (conditional) forecast of its own future behavior.

The current controversy is focused on option 3, which requires the central bank to reveal sensitive information. Until recently, the RBNZ was the only one brave enough to do this; but lately it has been joined by the Bank of Norway. In neither New Zealand nor Norway did revelation of this sensitive information provoke turmoil in the markets.[18] Some would argue that things might be different if the Fed or the ECB were to start projecting their own policy decisions, given the huge volumes of trading in dollar- and euro-denominated securities. But it is by no means obvious how *better* information on the central bank's intentions can do the markets any harm. My guess is that, after a short period of adjustment, releasing conditional forecasts of future monetary policy would reduce, not increase, market volatility. But many central bankers may disagree with my guess, for they are loath to take this step.

There is, however, another intensely practical issue that should not be ignored: Most central banks, certainly including the Fed, do not even *agree* upon

---

[18] For the case of New Zealand, see Archer (2005).

15

long-term (conditional) forecasts of the path of their policy rate. In such cases,

the failure to *announce* such a path cannot be viewed as a violation of

transparency. Rather, it falls under the seemingly-obvious rubric mentioned

earlier: You cannot reveal information you do not have. The broader question,

then, is whether central banks should (a) *formulate* (conditional) monetary policy

plans running one or two years into the future and then (b) *announce* those plans

as part of their forecasts. My own answers are yes and yes. But doing so clearly

represents a major change in the way most central banks do business. Indeed,

formulating such plans may be a much bigger change in the current *modus*

operandi than *announcing* them once formulated. So option 3 above will probably

remain on the "to do" list, and therefore on the list of current issues for central

bankers, for quite a while.

What can be done in the interim? Many academics have been intensely

critical of option 1—making forecasts based on constant (policy) interest rates.[19]

They point to three main problems: (a) it is logically inconsistent (because, e.g.,

actual market rates are not based on this assumption); (b) it is non-transparent

(because, e.g., the central bank probably does not believe this assumption); and

(c) it leads to dynamic instability for the reason first pointed out by Friedman

(1968): Holding the nominal rate fixed in the face of changes in inflation moves

the real rate in the wrong direction.[20]

I am less critical of the constant interest rate assumption than some of my

colleagues--for two main reasons. First, dynamic instability is unlikely to be

---

[19] For recent comprehensive treatments, see Svensson (2006) and Woodford (2006).
[20] Purely forward-looking models with rational expectations telescope this dynamic instability back into the present, leading to the failure of such models to converge to *any* equilibrium.

16

quantitatively important in forecasts that extend only a year or two into the future. Second, showing that constant interest rates lead to unsatisfactory outcomes serves a useful purpose by providing the predicate for changing monetary policy. Still, the critics' points are valid.

Option 2 above (using market expectations of future central bank policy) eliminates the inconsistency problem and reduces the non-transparency problem. But the instability problem remains because, in dynamic simulations, forecasts taken from *current* market prices will be exogenous rather than endogenous. Using such market-based forecasts also raises the "dog chasing its tail" danger that I mentioned in Blinder (1998) and that Bernanke and Woodford (1997) modeled theoretically.[21]

There is, however, a workable approach that can eliminate all three problems and yet does *not* require that MPC members agree *now* on an entire *path* of future policy decisions. The central bank *staff* can simply use an empirically-estimated reaction function to project the MPC's future behavior mechanically— *without* attributing those forecasts to the MPC itself. This approach should be roughly consistent with market prices because market participants would probably use something similar to forecast the central bank's behavior. It is also totally transparent, as long as the bank reveals the forecasting equation. And finally, it does not lead to dynamic instability as long as the inflation coefficient in the reaction function exceeds one.[22] I would therefore recommend this option to central banks for use right now.

---

[21] Woodford (1994) was an important precursor.
[22] For this reason, the Bank of England staff formerly used a Taylor rule in long-run simulations.

Issue 3: Should a central bank adopt formal inflation targeting?

Recent years have witnessed a notable trend toward a style of monetary policymaking that originated in New Zealand in 1990: inflation targeting. As noted earlier, Berg (2005) counted 20 inflation targeters, and other observers would add a few more central banks to his list. In addition, the ECB can be considered a closet inflation targeter, and both the Fed and the BOJ are actively considering whether to join the ranks.

While much has been written about inflation targeting, I can be brief given what I have already written about transparency (Issue 2) and the central bank's objective function (Issue 1)--because the essence of inflation targeting is announcing a numerical value for π^* and being transparent about it.

Svensson (2005) has argued that transparency should extend to the announcement of the numerical value of λ, the relative weight on the output (or unemployment) gap. But that is another one of those pieces of information that central banks cannot reveal because they do not have it. Most of us, I believe, would have trouble pinning down our own individual λ's.[23] For a monetary policy *committee*, the problem is compounded by having to reach a *group* decision on λ—especially when membership in the committee changes over time.[24]

This discussion does, however, raise an interesting transparency point. All inflation targeting central banks are "flexible" inflation targeters—meaning that they have $\lambda > 0$. Why, then, should their policy be called as "inflation targeting" as opposed to, say, "unemployment targeting"? Equation (1) looks pretty symmetric

---

[23] In fairness to Svensson, this would probably be done by examining alternative optimal paths generated by the bank staff for different choices of λ. It is not impossible.
[24] Svensson has suggested voting, with the median voter's preferences prevailing.

to me. One possible answer is deliberate obfuscation, which Mishkin (2004) argues is iquite prevalent. A second possible answer is that π* is a *choice variable* whereas u* (or y*) is a datum that is *given* to the central bank (Svensson (1999), page 626). To me, that answer is unsatisfactory, however, because proper division of labor dictates that the government should select π* (perhaps in consultation with the bank) and then hand it to the MPC as a datum.[25] The fact that π* is given by law whereas u* is given by "nature" should be irrelevant to the central bank, which should simply take both targets as given and set about minimizing (1), like a bunch of good Keynesian dentists.

Thus, when we translate equations (which only the experts understand) into words, objective functions like (1) seem more consistent with the Federal Reserve's dual mandate than with, say, the ECB's hierarchical goal or the rhetoric of many inflation targeting banks, as Meyer (2006) points out. Calling the minimization of (1) "inflation targeting" therefore seems to be a step away from transparency.

Transparent or not, central banks (or their governments) still need to decide whether to join the ranks of the inflation targeters.[26] Historically, most (but not all) nations that have adopted inflation targeting did so under duress. Either their monetary policy had failed, leaving inflation too high (e.g., New Zealand), or they were forced to change their monetary policy regime owing to, say, the collapse of a fixed exchange rate (e.g., the UK, Brazil).

---

[25] One important caveat: π* should not be chosen so frequently that it becomes a political variable. I like to think of it as being chosen at the "constitutional" stage.
[26] As my colleague Lars Svensson likes to point out, no central bank that has made this choice has subsequently abandoned inflation targeting. That is certainly suggestive.

19

But the past need not be prologue. Recent converts to inflation targeting, such as Norway (and, one might say, the United States), have moved in that direction voluntarily—presumably because they were persuaded that the benefits outweigh the costs. What are the benefits? The most obvious answer is lower inflation, though here the reverse causation problem is severe. (Countries that want to reduce inflation are more likely to adopt IT.[27]) Successful inflation targeting should also make inflation less volatile, as Vega and Winkelried (2005) find, and should anchor expectations at or very close to π*. That nominal anchor, in turn, can give the central bank greater flexibility to respond to short-run exigencies such as high unemployment or oil shocks.

Issue 4: Should monetary policy be made by an individual or a committee?

In yet another "quiet revolution," more and more central banks have begun making monetary policy decisions by committee. Fry *et al.*'s (2000) survey of practices at 88 central banks (about half the total) found that 79 made monetary policy decisions by committee while only nine left those decisions to a single individual. Thus governments around the world have revealed a clear preference for decisionmaking by committee. This phenomenon raises two questions: Why have nations switched from individuals to committees? And is this trend desirable?

The "why" question can be approached in two ways. First, as an *empirical* or *historical* matter, I believe that the main factor underlying the worldwide trend toward monetary policy committees (MPCs) was the perceived success of the Federal Reserve and the Bundesbank, both of which had long made decisions

---

[27] See Ball and Sheridan (2005) and Willard (2006).

20

(at least putatively) by committee. Imitation is, after all, the sincerest form of flattery. In addition, there is no reason to have a monetary policy committee when the central bank is simply taking orders from its government. So the trend toward central bank independence opened the door to committee decisionmaking.

Second, what are some of the *conceptual* or *theoretical* reasons why a central bank might prefer a committee to an individual? Since I have treated this subject at length elsewhere, and because it was recently the topic of an excellent symposium at another European central bank,[28] I can again be brief. In Blinder (2004, Chapter 2), I summarized the main arguments for preferring committee to individual decisionmaking under the following four rubrics:

1. *Pooling:* A committee pools the disparate knowledge of its individual members.

2. *Diversity:* Members of a committee bring different decisionmaking heuristics to a complex problem.

3. *Checks and balances:* Committees are less likely to adopt extreme or idiosyncratic positions.

4. *Reduced volatility:* Owing to "averaging" (which need not be interpreted literally), the decisions of a group are likely to be less volatile.

Perusing these four virtues, only the last might conceivably be turned around and viewed as a vice instead--because one person's low volatility is another's excessive inertia. But Sibert (2005) has pointed to another possible downside of

---

[28] De Nederlandsche Bank held a workshop entitled "Central Banking by Committee" in Amsterdam on November 28, 2005.

21

group decisionmaking: that it might devolve into "groupthink," which is really a polite word for not thinking at all, but merely following the crowd.[29]

Empirical evidence—much of it from psychology—points modestly toward the superiority of group over individual decisionmaking, though the evidence is certainly not dispositive and, of course, does not come from studies of monetary policy.[30] This last point is one of the considerations that led John Morgan and me (2005) to design and carry out a laboratory experiment in which students made synthetic monetary policy decisions both as individuals and as part of five-person groups.[31] It was not surprising, given the literature, that we found that groups outperformed individuals by a modest margin. It was, however, surprising that we found that groups were *not* more inertial—in sharp contrast to 4 above.

Morgan and I are currently working on a sequel to our original experiment, designed to shed light on two further issues. First, do large groups (for us, n=8) outperform small groups (n=4), or vice-versa? This issue is germane to the design of monetary policy committees which, in the real world, range in size from three to 19 members. Second, do groups with designated leaders outperform groups without leaders? This issue is particularly important because all real-world MPCs—indeed, I am tempted to say all real committees—have leaders.

---

[29] Sibert (2005) also devotes a great deal of attention to evidence for free riding and/or social loafing in committees. But I cannot believe this is important on MPCs, where (unlike faculty committees, say) the group decision is the most important task each committee member has.
[30] Kerr *et al.* (1996) is a metastudy of the experimental literature in psychology; they concluded that there is no general answer to the question. See Blinder (2004) for a summary of the economic literature, much of it theoretical. Sibert (2005) offers evidence that questions the superiority of group decisionmaking.
[31] This work was subsequently replicated by researchers at the Bank of England. See Lombardelli *et al.* (2005). Our choice of five-person groups was made long before we heard Sibert's (2005) claim that five is the optimal group size!

In designing an MPC, size is not the only consideration. Blinder *et al.* (2001) first introduced the following typology, which was further developed in Blinder (2004). Committees can either be *individualistic*, meaning that they make decisions by true majority rule with each member voting for his or her own preferred policy—as at the Bank of England, for example; or they can be *collegial*, meaning that they agree in advance to submerge individual differences in order to reach a group consensus—as at the Fed or the ECB. Collegial committees can be further divided into those that are *genuinely collegial*, meaning that the chairman seeks the committee's consensus and then persuades recalcitrant members to go along (e.g., the ECB Governing Council), or *autocratically collegial*, meaning that the chairman more or less dictates the "consensus" to the other members (e.g., the FOMC under Alan Greenspan).

I argued in Blinder (2004) that autocratically-collegial committees are liable to behave too much like individual decisionmakers, thereby leaving most of the benefits of group decisionmaking on the table. This logic seems to point toward either genuinely collegial or individualistic monetary policy committees. I argued in Blinder (2005), incidentally, that the most appropriate communication strategy for a central bank hinges sensitively on the type of MPC that it selects, which links Issues 2 and 4. But, I have neither the time nor the space to go into that linkage here.

Issue 5: Should central banks also be bank supervisors?

One noteworthy recent departure from traditional central banking practice is the trend toward taking central banks out of the business of bank supervision and regulation. This new division of labor has occurred in varying degrees (in some places completely) in the UK, Germany, and Japan, to name just a few major countries.[32] And it is highly controversial, with reasonable arguments on both sides.[33] While there are other aspects, the essence of the debate, it seems to me, boils down to whether *economies of scope* or *conflicts of interest* are the dominant effects when monetary policy (sometimes called "macro prudential" policy) and bank supervision ("micro prudential" policy) are consolidated in the same authority.[34]

The (tacit) traditional view emphasizes economies of scope, which imply that the two functions are best performed by the same institution. Why might that be so? Unlike the case with private businesses, the economies-of-scope issue does *not* turn on cost savings; central banks do not save money by using the same staff for bank supervision and monetary policy. Rather, the main issue is whether there are quantitatively meaningful *complementarities* between the central bank's macro-prudential and micro-prudential responsibilities. The Federal Reserve's former Vice Chairman, Roger Ferguson (2000, p. 301), believes there are: "I think the Fed's monetary policy is better because of its supervisory responsibilities, and its supervision and regulation are better because of its stabilization responsibilities."

For example, having supervisory authority over commercial banks gives the central bank unique access to timely information on the health and operation of

---

[32] See Freytag and and Masciandaro (2005, p. 2) for a more complete list.

[33] For a comprehensive look at the arguments *pro* and *con*, see Goodhart (2000).

[34] Among the other aspects is the question of whether assigning supervisory power to the central bank concentrates too much power in one agency.

the banking system—information that might be relevant, for example, to making judgments about the credit channel of monetary transmission.[35] Such information becomes obviously important at certain critical junctures; the global financial crisis in the summer and fall of 1998 was one dramatic case in point. More generally, there is at least some evidence that supervisory information enhances the Fed's ability to forecast the economy (Peek *et al.*, 1999).

Looking for complementarities in the other direction, having responsibility for monetary policy might force the bank supervisor to internalize the potential macroeconomic consequences of its actions. To cite a prominent U.S. example, bank supervisors were heavily criticized in the early 1990s for exacerbating the "credit crunch," which in turn hampered recovery from the 1990-1991 recession.[36] More generally, it has been suggested that micro-prudential policies can exacerbate business cycles by, for example, forcing banks to rebuild capital during a cyclical downturn.[37] Recently, bank supervisors have been taking this long-neglected issue seriously (White, 2006).

But there are also arguments on the other side. The very things I just cited as potential economies of scope can be viewed as potential sources of conflict of interest instead. For example, should a supervisor allow sick banks to continue to operate just because macroeconomic conditions are weak? I have just suggested why the answer might be yes. But there is a legitimate worry that a

---

[35] The Federal Reserve has made this argument many times. See, for example, see Meyer (1999) or Ferguson (2000).
[36] Among many sources that could be cited, see Bernanke and Lown (1991).
[37] See Kashyap and Stein (2004) and several of the references cited there.

central bank's concern with macroeconomic management might cloud its supervisory judgment, thereby imperiling safety and soundness.

Another set of issues arises from the increasing complexity of financial institutions. A modern universal bank is also an investment bank, a stock brokerage, a funds manager, and an insurance company, to name just a few. The lines that separate one type of financial activity from another are getting blurrier and blurrier all the time, and the activities themselves are growing more complex. For a central bank to monitor all these disparate activities, it needs staff with expertise in securities and insurance (and other things) as well as in banking. It may also find itself bumping heads with the nation's securities and insurance regulators, thereby creating either overlapping jurisdictions or, what is worse, gaps in supervision. Bringing some order to this potential jumble makes it difficult to apply the otherwise-appealing principle of "functional regulation," whereby the banking supervisor watches over banking activities (even if done at Wal-Mart or Merrill Lynch), the securities supervisor polices securities activities (even if done at the Bank of America), and so on. A potentially cleaner approach is to create one financial "super regulator" that can watch over all financial activities at a given institution at once.

Where do I come out on this debate? A bit wishy-washy, I'm afraid, and about where I was when I compiled my 1999 Frankfurt list. There I wrote (Blinder, 2000, p. 69):

> Proprietary information that the central bank receives in bank
> examinations is of some, limited use in formulating monetary policy—and
> is on rare occasions very important. So, on balance, it is probably better to
> have it than not. On the other hand, a bank supervisor may sometimes

26

have to be a protector of banks and sometimes a stern disciplinarian—and either stance may conflict with monetary policy.

I am persuaded that nations should leave at least *some* supervisory responsibility with the central bank. It alone has the broad macroeconomic and even international perspective that is crucial from time to time. It alone has the ultimate responsibility for both macroeconomic and financial stability. And it alone has the resources to serve as lender of last resort should the need arise. Given all that, it seems unwise to deprive the central bank of supervisory information that might be relevant to performing its job. And I do not believe that getting that information secondhand is quite as good as getting it firsthand.

But that does not imply that the central bank must be the sole or even the dominant bank supervisor, especially in countries with hundreds or thousands of non-universal banks. Central bank involvement in bank supervision needs to be thought of as lying along a continuum, not as a "zero-one" variable. The U.S., with four different federal bank regulatory agencies (and 50 more in the states), is a clear example.[38] The Fed should be able to access all the information it needs for monetary policy purposes by serving as the "umbrella supervisor" of all large bank holding companies. And it should be in a good position to monitor systemic risk as long as it has a window into every large financial institution. Neither role requires the Fed to be the primary supervisor of hundreds of small banks--as it is today. In this regard, it is striking that, for example, the Bank of England, which has been entirely excluded from the supervisory arena, has not protested that this exclusion has damaged its ability to conduct monetary policy.

---

[38] Not that I would recommend this crazy-quilt structure to any other country!

27

In any case, regardless of my own views, this is surely a live issue that must be addressed by central banks and governments all over the world.

II. Operating Principles for Monetary Policy

I turn next to a set of six questions related to how central banks should conduct monetary policy.

Issue 6: Should central banks be so averse to policy reversals?

As a broad generalization, the practice of monetary policy seems to be growing closer and closer to the way macroeconomists conceptualize it. Increasingly, central bankers utilize staff analyses, even quite complicated analyses, and think about policy options in the way that technical economists do (e.g., via expectational effects, output gaps, Phillips curves, and the like). In fact, and in contrast to past practice, many central bankers these days even *are* economists. The current heads of the Federal Reserve System, the Bank of England, and the Bank of Israel, for example, are all former academic stars. Yet economic analysis and central banking practice appear to diverge sharply in at least one prominent respect. The matter is what I call *reversal aversion*—the unwillingness of central bankers to reverse direction.

Consider the problem of minimizing the expected discounted present value of a loss function like (1) subject to a dynamic, stochastic model of the economy. Various aspects of the model, including both the shocks and the coefficients, are liable to be changing all the time, which means that the optimal path of the policy instrument is also changing all the time. Suppose the central bank's policy rate

28

has been rising for several meetings, in an attempt to restrain aggregate demand. Now suppose an external shock *reduces* aggregate demand sharply. There is then a reasonable chance that the central bank's *optimal* policy rate would decline even though it has recently been rising.

Although the basic logic of optimization suggests that such *policy reversals* should not be uncommon, central bankers seem to avoid them like the plague. For example, suppose we use the arbitrary but reasonable definition that a policy reversal is a change in direction within three months. Then the allegedly activist British MPC has had only one policy reversal out of 32 interest rate changes in its brief history (which began only in mid 1997).[39] The Swedish Riskbank began using the repo rate as its central policy tool in mid 1994, and since then it has changed the rate 66 times.[40] Only two of these were policy reversals, one coming just after the September 2001 terrorist attacks in the United States. The history of the Greenspan Fed was longer (18½ years) but similar: It shows just three reversals out of 98 policy moves, two of which were associated with the 1987 stock market crash. So reversals are rare. The question is why. And the further question is: Are central banks right to avoid them so assiduously?

As just noted, simple versions of optimization theory say no. There is nothing particularly strange about a sequence of optimal choices that, say, first rises and then falls. Remember Keynes's classic retort to being chided for changing his mind: "When I learn new facts, sir, I change my opinion. What do you do?" So, if

---

[39] Widening the window to four months would add two more reversals. The counts in this paragraph were all current through the end of March 2006.
[40] This count is a bit skewed by 25 changes in 1996, mostly of them small.

29

it is rational to avoid reversals, what factors might standard optimization theory be missing?

One is the dual problem of simultaneous optimization and (re)estimation in a world of pervasive uncertainty. Statistical devices such as Kalman filters (which are just an example) will give rise, e.g., to forecasts and parameter estimates that evolve slowly as new information is received. Policy based on such forecasts and estimates would also evolve slowly.

Another factor is surely central bankers' concern with their *credibility*. If citizens, and perhaps even markets, do not understand the underlying model, do not observe the shocks very well, or do not understand the logic of optimization in the face of "news," they might misinterpret a sequence in which interest rates first rise and then fall as *prima facie* evidence that the bank had erred.[41] That belief, in turn, might undermine the bank's credibility or, in an extreme case, even threaten its independence. At minimum, a quick policy reversal poses a major communication problem. Central banks worry about the loss of credibility a great deal. To cite just one example, Alan Greenspan told the FOMC in July 1996 that, "If we are perceived to have tightened and then have been compelled by market forces to quickly reverse, our reputation for professionalism will suffer a severe blow."[42] Hundreds of similar statements must have been made by central bankers all over the world.

A second factor leading to reversal aversion may be concern with *financial market stability*. Frequent policy reversals by the central bank might induce

---

[41] This point is emphasized by Goodhart (2004).
[42] Quoted by Meyer (2004), p. 56.

unwanted volatility in financial markets as traders felt they were being whipsawed. And a third factor, of course, is the natural unwillingness to be seen as admitting error. So, on balance, the observed aversion to policy reversals is understandable—whether or not it is optimal.

There is, however, a downside to refusing to reverse course. Remember that a central bank that will not change its policy stance even though it is optimal to do so will from time to time find itself falling "behind the curve"—and will subsequently have to play catch-up. That in itself can cause turbulence in financial markets. More important, falling "behind the curve" presumably means either that the inflationary cat gets out of the bag or that the economy suffers a longer slump than is necessary.

Thus reversal aversion is of a different character from the other issues on my list. In the main, I have chosen matters that are currently controversial. This one apparently is not; virtually all central banks seem to exhibit strong aversion to policy reversals. The operational question here is: *Should* the advisability of reversal aversion be a subject of active debate? And my answer is yes.

Issue 7: Is the preference for gradualism rational?

To a greater or lesser degree, central banks around the world also seem to exhibit a strong revealed preference for *gradualism*, that is, for tightening or easing in a series of small steps rather than making fewer, larger rate changes. Econometrically, this means, for example, that when Taylor rules like (3) are estimated on real data they always need to include the lagged dependent variable, viz.:

31

(4) $i = r^* + \pi + a(\pi - \pi^*) + b(u^* - u) + \theta i_{-1} + \varepsilon$.

This equation is typically derived by appending a partial adjustment mechanism,

(5) $i = \theta i_{-1} + (1-\theta)i^*$,

to the specification of the *desired* funds rate, i^*, given by (3). Since a typical

estimate of θ is 0.8 or more in quarterly data (Rudebusch, 2005), the implied

adjustment is very slow.

Table 1 displays the observed distributions of the interest rate changes

actually promulgated by the three central banks mentioned in the previous

section: the Federal Reserve, the Bank of England, and the Swedish Riksbank.

The strong preference for small changes is evident at all three banks: The

fraction of all rates changes that is 25 basis points or less is 79% for the Fed,

88% for the BoE, and 89% for the Riksbank. To put some perspective on this,

remember that Willem Buiter, a member of the Bank of England's original MPC,

once famously derided a 25 basis point rate change as "chicken feed,"

presumably because it is unlikely that 25 basis points would ever be enough to

push "actual" to "desired" anything.

Table 1
Frequency Distributions of Policy Rate Changes

Rate change	Federal Reserve[1]	Bank of England[2]	Sveriges Riksbank[3]
Below 25 bps	17	0	32
Exactly 25 bps	61	28	27
26-49 bps	3	0	2
Exactly 50 bps	17	4	5
Above 50 bps	1	0	0
Total	99	32	66

1. August 1987 through March 2006
2. May 1997 through March 2006
3. June 1994 through March 2006

What the table does *not* show is the huge amount of serial correlation in the data. The Fed is a nice example. It cut rates 24 times between June 1989 and September 1992, and then raised rates seven times between February 1994 and February 1995. Later, it raised rates six times between June 1999 and May 2000, and subsequently cut rates 13 times between January 2001 and June 2003. From June 2004 through June 2006, it raised rates by 25 basis points at 17 consecutive FOMC meetings. None of these episodes was interrupted by even a single move in the opposite direction. If Newton had observed such data, he might have concluded that a central bank in motion tends to stay in motion in the same direction. Why is that?

One reason is *option value*. In a world of constant change, pervasive uncertainty, *and* a strong aversion to policy reversals, a central bank may assign a high value to "keeping its options open"--literally. One way to accomplish that is to move interest rates more gradually than suggested by simple optimization theory (without learning or adjustment costs)—so that you can always stop without having to reverse direction. Notice the crucial role of reversal aversion in this argument. Changing policy *now*, rather than waiting for later, forecloses options *only* if you have reversal aversion—for otherwise, you can quickly undo whatever you have just done. (Analogously, a stock option, once exercised, is gone.) So central bankers' intense aversion to policy reversals is probably one significant factor contributing to monetary policy gradualism.

Whether the gradualism induced by reversal aversion should be decried or applauded is, of course, a matter of debate. Standard optimization theory is often

33

interpreted as saying that the policy instrument should follow something close to a random walk because the central bank should move its policy rate only in response to new information. For example, William Poole (2003, pp. 5-6), a current member of the FOMC who was formerly an academic economist, wrote:[43]

> In my view of the world, future policy actions are almost entirely contingent on the arrival of new information… Given information available at the time of a meeting, I believe that the standing assumption should be that the policy action at the meeting is expected to position the stance of policy appropriately.

But the Greenspan Fed often did not behave this way, and one major reason, I believe, was Greenspan's devotion to keeping his options open. He always wanted to maintain the flexibility to stop at any moment without having to reverse course (Blinder and Reis, 2005). One way to accomplish that is to move cautiously when you move.

A second plausible reason for gradualism is serially-correlated shocks and/or gradual updating of forecasts and parameter estimates, which would keep the central bank moving in the same direction over a series of meetings. Rudebusch (2005) points out that econometricians cannot readily distinguish between partial adjustment and serially-correlated errors. So, rather than observing what appears to be central bank inertia, we might just be observing non-inertial responses to serially-correlated shocks and changing information. Indeed, Goodhart (2004) suggests that serially-correlated forecast errors explain what appears to be gradualism at the British MPC, and Sack (2000) found that serially-correlated

---

[43] I have a hard time squaring this quotation with moving the Federal funds rate by 25 basis points at 16 consecutive meetings. I suspect Poole does, too

shocks help explain the FOMC's observed (and seemingly inertial) reaction function.

A third possible explanation of gradualism derives from what I have labeled "Brainard conservatism" (Blinder, 1998). In a seminal paper, William Brainard (1967) suggested that, unlike additive uncertainty, multiplicative uncertainty should induce a policymaker to move his instrument *less* than he would under certainty equivalence. Even in Brainard's original paper, this was not a tight deduction, but rather a result that held for certain (plausible?) parameter values—basically that covariances were not too large. Subsequent research has verified the fragility of Brainard's result in a variety of more complex settings. There is no Brainard conservatism *theorem.*[44] Yet I still believe what I wrote in Blinder (1998, p.12): "My intuition tells me that this finding is more general—or at least more wise—in the real world than the mathematics will support."[45] Notice that if a wise central banker is conservative in the Brainard sense, he will normally move the policy rate *too little* to put it where he thinks it should be. He will therefore have to move rates again and again--presumably in the same direction.

A fourth motive for gradualism is the desire to smooth interest rates. As I noted earlier, central bankers often associate interest-rate volatility with financial-market instability, perhaps because rate changes lead to asset revaluations. Hence a concern with financial stability can rationalize adding a term like $\gamma(i_t - i_{t-1})^2$ to the central bank's loss function. If that is done, the lagged interest

---

[44] This was clear already in Chow (1975), Chapter 10. See also Rudebusch (2001) and many other sources.
[45] Simulations by Onatski and Williams (2003) suggest this as well.

rate is carried naturally into the monetary policy reaction function, without any need to posit the existence of adjustment costs. In fact, Rudebusch (2001) finds that positing a substantial value of γ helps explain the Fed's observed—and quite inertial--reaction function.

Woodford (2003) has constructed a rather different explanation for gradualism based on the importance of pre-commitment. He uses a specific forward-looking model based on Calvo (1983) pricing, in which only some prices are free to adjust each period. In that setting, he argues that, *if* the central bank can *pre-commit* to a future path of interest rates, then firms that are free to set prices now will expect rates to keep moving in the same direction. They will therefore adjust their prices by more, thereby compensating for those who cannot adjust their prices at all. This is beneficial in Woodford's model because faster price adjustment keeps the economy closer to its full-information equilibrium. While Woodford's paper is frequently cited by academics, I am skeptical that this specific mechanism influences real-world central bank thinking very much. Nonetheless, the basic idea that expected gradual adjustment of *short* rates can lead to strong reactions of *long* rates is probably quite general (Bernanke, 2004a).

In short, we have a plethora of explanations for why gradualism might be rational. I have mentioned five: option value, serially-correlated shocks, Brainard conservatism, the desire to smooth (market) interest rates, and expectational effects on long-term rates. Any one of them will do. The question is: Which are the operative reasons?

36

Issue 8: Is monetary fine tuning possible? Desirable?

Were it not for the success of Alan Greenspan as Chairman of the Federal Reserve, the next issue would not be on my list at all. "Fine tuning" sounds like an archaic phrase left over from the 1960s. Ever since the 1970s, it has been used more often in a pejorative sense than in a prescriptive one, as when my colleague Lars Svensson (2001, p.1) warned that "the complex transmission mechanism of monetary policy, the varying lags and strength of the effects through different channels, unpredictable shocks and inherent uncertainty combine to prevent the use of monetary policy for fine-tuning." In other words: *Do not attempt this at home.*

But Alan Greenspan did, and he succeeded. It is worth asking how. More germane to this paper, it is worth asking whether other central bankers should try to fine tune their own economies. But what, precisely, does that mean? Blinder and Reis (2005), who focus on this question, suggest two aspects:

(a) pursuing an activist stabilization policy that strives to keep inflation and unemployment close to their targets. With a reaction function like a Taylor rule, that would mean utilizing relatively high values of α and β.

(b) adjusting the central bank's policy instrument(s) frequently in pursuit of that goal. Note that, as just argued, frequent adjustment presumably means that the typical interest rate change will be small.

But fine tuning certainly does *not* mean:

(c) achieving or expecting to achieve perfection.

37

We have already noted that most central banks practice (b). What about (a)? I am tempted to answer with Bobby Kennedy's famous rhetorical question: *Why not?* Consistent with (c), no basketball player expects to hit 100% of his shots—and none does. Nonetheless, the objective is always the same: to toss the ball in the center of the basket, in line with (a). Archers behave similarly when they aim their arrows. Indeed, what else should they do? The real fine-tuning issue, it seems to me, is how hard to try.

If there is an argument against trying too hard, that is, against reacting strongly to output and inflation gaps, it must revolve around the dangers of oversteering and, therefore, of accidentally *destabilizing* the economy. How realistic is that danger? Rudebusch's (2001) analysis of optimal versus actual policy in a simple linear model of the U.S. economy points strongly toward the opposite conclusion: that the Fed's α and β are *too small*. On the other hand, some of the simulation findings in Rotemberg and Woodford (1997), Levin, Wieland, and Williams (1999), and Orphanides and Williams (2005) suggest that the Greenspan Fed reacted too strongly to unemployment or output gaps (but not to inflation gaps). The issue seems open. It also strikes me as an important practical issue for central bankers to resolve.

Issue 9: Central banks and financial markets: Who leads and who follows?

In Blinder (1998, pp. 59-62), I argued that central banks should guard their independence from financial markets as zealously as they guard their independence from politics,[46] an argument I picked up in much greater detail in

---

[46] A version of these lectures was first given in 1995, while I was Vice Chairman of the Federal Reserve Board.

Blinder (2004, Chapter 3). But other than the theoretical paper by Bernanke and Woodford (1997), I have seen almost no scholarly attention to this matter. To frame the issue, consider two stereotypes:

- *Old-Fashioned Central Bank* sees itself as a sometimes-stern disciplinarian that lords it over the unruly, and sometimes downright foolish, financial markets. It sees itself both as the adult at the party and as the boss. It therefore expects the markets to follow its lead, even though it knows they will not always oblige.

- *New-Fangled Central Bank*, by contrast, is deeply respectful of markets. It sees itself as more of a student of the financial markets than as a teacher, and it respects the markets for their power and wisdom. It routinely uses asset prices to "read" what the markets expect it to do, and it is loath to deviate much from that expectation.

As a broad generalization, my claim is that Old-Fashioned Central Bank is giving way to New-Fangled Central Bank in the real world. In part, such a movement is inevitable and appropriate—after all, Old-Fashioned Central Bank is a bit of a throwback. But I worry a bit that the shift may be going too far.

Why might this be of concern? One reason is the dog-chasing-its-tail problem mentioned by Blinder (1998) and modeled formally by Bernanke and Woodford (1997). When central banks follow market forecasts, which are in turn based on forecasts of the central bank's own behavior, the result can be either dynamic instability or a failure of equilibrium to exist, depending on whether the model is backward or forward looking. In the real world, this problem would likely manifest

39

itself in a monetary policy that tends to overshoot in both directions, just as speculative markets do.

Finally, there is the related matter of time horizons. Economic models normally pretend that financial markets are populated by coolly-rational, farsighted investors with long (if not infinite) time horizons. But this benign view of markets contrasts sharply with what people in the trenches see every day on trading floors. As Fischer Black slyly put it, financial markets look much more efficient from the banks of the Charles than from the banks of the Hudson. On the banks of the Hudson and in other financial centers where prices are actually made, you find hordes of young traders who are susceptible to fads, herding, and occasional hysteria. These people tend to have incredibly short time horizons, extending at most to the end of the current pay period and maybe only to the end of the trading day.

Notice the great irony here. One of the main reasons why central banks should be independent of politics is that politicians have notoriously short time horizons, extending at most to the next election. Well, the next election is usually much further away than the close of the trading day. Wouldn't it be a shame if central bankers, in an effort to be "modern," escaped from the control of shortsighted politicians only to put themselves under the thumb of even more shortsighted traders?

To be sure, central banks cannot cut themselves off from the markets--and should not try. Markets are not only the main transmission mechanism for monetary policy but also invaluable sources of information. They need to be

40

respected, though perhaps more for their power than for their wisdom.[47] One way to conceptualize my basic point is to contrast the two different meanings of the English verb *to listen*. Should central bankers listen to the markets? Yes, in the sense that we should all listen to news broadcasts; but *not* in the sense that children should listen to their mothers.

Issue 10: Should central banks intervene in foreign exchange markets?

One arena in which the preeminence of market judgments over central bank judgments clearly holds sway is the prevailing attitude toward foreign exchange intervention. Let me break this issue into two closely-linked questions:

1. Do central banks have the power to move exchange rates with *sterilized* intervention?[48]

2. If so, should they use that power?

Question 2, of course, comes straight from the previous issue. If markets always get the exchange rate right, there is certainly no reason for central banks to intervene. So let's at least entertain the possibility that markets sometimes get exchange rates badly wrong. If you reject this possibility, you can skip straight to the next section. But you must also explain the value of the dollar in early 1985— and perhaps today as well.

Current thinking in academic and, even more so, in central banking circles runs strongly against foreign exchange intervention—mostly answering "no" to both questions. Regarding Question 1, the empirical evidence has long been read to say that central banks have little ability to move exchange rates, except

---

[47] On this, see Issues 12 and 13 below.
[48] The power of unsterilized intervention is not at issue. This section pertains only to sterilized intervention.

perhaps fleetingly, without changing their monetary policies. But more recent academic studies, using better data, suggest a bit more scope for unsterilized intervention (Sarno and Taylor, 2001).

The negative consensus always struck me as a bit peculiar, anyway. Why are central banks unable to move currency rates when shifts in private-sector supply and demand move them all the time, and by large amounts? No one thinks that private currency traders are powerless to move exchange rates. Why do they lose this power if they go to work for the public sector? I believe the answer must be quantitative rather than qualitative: Private sector traders regularly buy and sell currencies in far greater volume than central banks do. So, to me, the real question is more normative than positive: *Should* a central bank buy or sell the (possibly large) amount of foreign currency required to move its exchange rate?

A negative answer is certainly tenable. Especially in the case of a major, actively-traded currency like the dollar, euro, or yen, the requisite volume of transactions might be gigantic—which would put the central bank at risk of large capital losses if it is wrong. In such cases, the central bank had better be very sure (a) that it is right and (b) that the exchange rate goal is important enough to justify taking the risk. (And if the exchange rate goal is that important, maybe it should use unsterilized intervention anyway.) Such massive foreign exchange interventions may also have to be asymmetric. While a central bank can always supply as much domestic currency as needed to hold its exchange rate down,[49] it may not have enough foreign exchange reserves to prop its exchange rate up.

---

[49] Assuming it can sterilize the foreign currency inflows.

For the most part, I accept this consensus: Outguessing markets is a hazardous business. But, in my view, we must allow for some exceptions.[50] For example, there are times when currency misalignments are glaringly obvious, even if the "right" exchange rate is not. The dollar in early 1985 (far too high), the dollar again in the spring of 1995 (too low), and the euro in the spring of 2001 (too low) are cases that quickly spring to mind. While neither the timing nor the amount of the market's eventual correction could have been known in advance, it was not hard to recognize that exchange rates were misaligned; and the eventual direction of change was obvious. In cases like that, chances are good that many market participants are aware of the same facts as the central banks, and so are holding their positions nervously. That should make it possible for a large (and hopefully concerted) intervention by central banks to push the forex market in the direction in which it was destined to go anyway.

But Question 2 remains. Is the exchange rate a sufficiently important relative price that the central bank should (a) temporarily take its eye off its true targets (inflation and unemployment) and (b) accept the risk inherent in large-scale currency speculation? My own answer is: normally no, but sometimes yes. For example, there are rare times when exchange rates are so misaligned that they distort trade patterns so much, or interfere so much with demand management, that it becomes rational for the central bank to intervene in large volume. Another possibility, which is exemplified by China today and perhaps by Japan in 2003-2004, is that a nation might believe that its vital interests are best served by a

---

[50] Below, under Issue 14, I outline the conditions necessary to make it sensible for a central bank to try to "burst" an asset-market bubble. Here I am, in essence, claiming that these conditions are occasionally met in the case of exchange rates.

43

lower exchange rate than the free market would deliver—and be willing to pay the price to achieve it.

I realize that I am delivering this paper in a euro-zone country with no exchange rate to worry about. But the ECB may have to deal with the exchange rate issue once again when the markets not only correct the current overvaluation of the dollar but probably overshoot. And, of course, the belief that recent months have constituted one of those rare moments when concerted intervention makes sense is what underlies recent suggestions for a "new Plaza accord" (Cline, 2005). So I would like to resurrect the intervention issue, which has been dead and buried for too long, and commend it to the attention of central bankers.

Issue 11: Should monetary policy use the derivatives markets?

I noted earlier that financial markets are big, powerful, and innovative. Nothing illustrates these traits more dramatically than the explosive growth of the markets for derivatives. Derivatives pose many interesting and difficult issues for supervisors and regulators but, in keeping with my assignment, I confine myself to their potential role in monetary policymaking,[51] which comes in three parts:

1. as a source of market information
2. as part of the monetary transmission mechanism
3. as possible assets for open-market operation.

The first two are uncontroversial. Given the liquidity and volume of trading in, say, interest rate swaps, central banks would be foolish to ignore the signals emanating from those markets—and they don't. Similarly, the most dramatic

---

[51] For this reason, I restrict myself to fixed-income derivatives, such as swaps.

44

early influences of a central bank's policy moves, or even of expectations of policy moves, may well be registered in the markets for derivatives such as interest rae futures. Since these markets, in turn, are linked to the interest rates that matter for real economic decisions, such as those on home mortgages and business loans, they are a key component of the monetary transmission mechanism I don't think anyone doubts either of these propositions.

But the third potential role for derivatives is highly speculative at this point; I do not know of a single central bank that conducts open-market operations in derivatives.[5] I raise the possibility as an issue for the future. Why?

One reason is the sheer size and growing importance of some of these markets, which means they are terrifically deep and liquid. It has often been said that the Federal Reserve conducts open market operations in the U.S. Treasury bill market because that is the deepest, most liquid market in the world; and similar statements are made about other central banks. Well, that may no longer be true. And even if it is true today, it may not be true tomorrow, given the rapid expansion of the derivatives markets. Central banks of the future may discover that they can get faster, more reliable execution in the swaps market, for example.

Another reason stems from the juxtaposition of rapid growth of the derivatives markets against slow growth of central bank balance sheets. Some observers

---

[52] I ignore the Bank of Thailand's use of foreign exchange derivatives in 1997 because that seems to have been motivated by a desire to conceal its true reserve position, not as a way to conduct monetary policy. The Bank of Mexico deals in options on the peso to influence (not peg) its exchange rate—hough transparently. Finally, as part of its efforts to guard against financial disruption at the end of the millennium, the Federal Reserve sold call options on repos in October-December 1999. (See Drossos and Hilton (2000).) I am grateful to Steve Cecchetti for calling these last two cases to my attention.

feel that the markets are already so large and innovative that central banks have

a hard time moving even short-term interest rates via conventional open-market

operations.[53] One obvious answer, of course, is to conduct ever-larger open

market operations--which is where the size of central bank balance sheets

comes in. If, for example, currency shrinks relative to GDP while fixed-income

markets grow, central banks may find their portfolios of T-bills shrinking relative

to the size of the open-market operations needed to move markets.[54] If and when

this happens, *leverage* may be the answer; and that, of course, is where

derivatives come in. Market participants routinely use derivatives to create huge

amounts of leverage, and thus effectively to control large volumes of securities

with relatively little capital. Why can't central banks, who are certainly higher-

rated counterparties, do the same? It's something to think about.

Of course, central banks will want to move into this domain cautiously, if at all.

They are stodgy to begin with, appropriately so in my view; and derivatives have

a vaguely disreputable public image. But most of the "accidents" in the

derivatives markets, not to mention the frauds, have taken place in "exotics," not

in plain-vanilla interest rate swaps, which are simple, transparent, and either are

or can be traded on organized exchanges. And it is, of course, in plain vanillas

that any sensible central bank would operate. For this reason, I believe that

conducting open-market operations in swaps would confer a side benefit by

steering markets away from exotics toward more plain vanilla swaps. Indeed,

were I of a mind to predict the *future* of central banking, as opposed to just

---

[53] I am, personally, rather skeptical of this argument. But one hears it all the time.
[54] Note the parallelism to the previous issue about exchange rate intervention.

analyzing the *present*, I'd be tempted to forecast appearances by central banks in the swaps markets. But for now, it is just something to think about.

III. The Transmission Mechanism for Monetary Policy

I turn, finally and more briefly, to five controversial and/or poorly understood aspects of the transmission mechanism for monetary policy.

Issue 12: Transmission via the term structure of interest rates

The simplest version of the monetary transmission mechanism traces the central bank's influence from overnight rates (which it controls) to longer-term interest rates and thereby on to aggregate demand. The link from short rates to long rates is normally based on the *expectations theory of the term structure* of interest rates, which states that intermediate- and long-term rates are the appropriate weighted averages of expected future short rates.

There is a catch, however. It has been known for years that the expectations theory fails virtually every empirical test miserably, at least when expectations are rational.[55] A one–sentence synopsis of this literature is that long rates are terrible (and biased) predictors of future short rates. To show just one example, I reproduce below a graph from Blinder (2004, p. 78). It shows, on the horizontal axis, the one-year U.S. Treasury bond rate expected to hold nine years ahead *according to the yield curve* and, on the vertical axis, the *actual* one-year rate nine years later. There is hardly any correlation between the two.[56]

---

[55] Among the many references that could be cited, see Campbell (1995). Chow (1989) suggests that the theory fares better under the assumption of adaptive expectations.
[56] The straight line drawn in the graph is *not* the best-fitting regression line. It is a line with a freely-estimated intercept (to allow for a constant risk premium) and a slope of 1.0, which is the

Figure 1
Actual Interest Rates and Predictions from the Term Structure

Actual One-Year Rate (Nine Years Later)

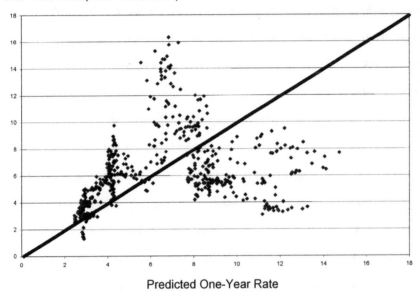

Predicted One-Year Rate

Just why this is so remains a major intellectual puzzle. To blame the puzzle on time-varying term premia is just to give it a name—like blaming machine malfunctions on "gremlins." In Blinder (2004, Chapter 3), I suggested (but certainly did not prove) that the expectations theory fails because long rates are far more sensitive to short rates than "rational" pricing models predict. This hypothesis may or may not be correct. My main purpose in calling attention to the term structure puzzle here is not to resolve it, but rather to urge central bank

---

slope implied by theory. The slope of the actual regression line (not shown) is only 0.27. The underlying data are for U.S. zero-coupon bonds, monthly from December 1949 through February 1991.

research departments to give it high priority. It may be the piece of the monetary transmission mechanism about which we are most in the dark.

This issue relates, by the way, to Issue 9. If markets are so bad at forecasting future short-term interest rates, why should we give so much deference to their forecasts of anything else—including future central bank policy?

Issue 13: Transmission via exchange rates: uncovered interest-rate parity

The mention of unresolved puzzles and terrible forecasts leads naturally to the next issue: the equally-embarrassing failure of *uncovered interest-rate parity*. If one-year interest rates are 5% in the United States and 3% in Germany, the market is implicitly forecasting a 2% depreciation of the dollar against the euro over the coming year. And a similar forecast is implied by every other pair of international interest rates over any horizon. Thought of in terms of monetary policy, when divergent central bank policies engineer international interest rate differentials, those differentials are supposed to first *forecast* and then *become* exchange rate movements. Unfortunately, on average they do not. Not only are uncovered interest-rate parity relationships *terrible* forecasters of future exchange rate movements, they often get the sign wrong.[57]

This is a serious matter. In the usual story of the role of exchange rates in monetary transmission, a country that *raises* its interest rates experiences a currency *appreciation*. The theory of uncovered interest parity explains that this happens in order to induce (rational) expectations that the currency will subsequently *depreciate* back to its original (real) exchange rate. Thus a

---

[57] Among the many sources that could be cited, see Wadhwani (1999) and Meredith and Chinn (2004).

tightening of monetary policy is supposed to lead to a quick appreciation followed

by a depreciation. Nice and logical. But, empirically, it does not happen. How,

then, does monetary policy influence exchange rates? A good question. And until

it gets a good answer, central bankers are operating in a dense fog. So this issue

also ranks high on the research agenda—and high on the list of reasons not to

place excessive trust in market forecasts.

Issue 14: How should central banks react to asset-price bubbles?

Asset prices are an important part of the monetary policy transmission

mechanism. Other things equal, when stock or home prices rise, a central bank

that is targeting, say, a weighted average of the inflation and output gaps will

raise interest rates because wealth effects might otherwise drive aggregate

demand up too fast. This is old hat, uncontroversial, and a standard part of

monetary policy practice.

But should central banks react to asset-market bubbles *per se*, meaning *over*

and above the amount implied by the link from asset prices to wealth to

aggregate demand? In the loss function context, that would mean adding some

asset prices (e.g., stock prices) as a third argument of the loss function. In the

Taylor rule context, it would mean adding those prices as another term in the

equation, as Cecchetti *et al.* (2000) explicitly recommend, so that the central

bank would then raise interest rates as stock prices go up *even if y and π were*

both on target.[58] Both the current and previous chairmen of the Federal Reserve

are on record as opposing this idea (Bernanke and Gertler (1999), Greenspan

---

[58] Cecchetti *et al.* (2000) explicitly state that the central bank should *not* have a target price for the
stock market, but should just "lean against the wind." Thus stock prices enter the Taylor rule with
a positive coefficient, but there is no target level for stock prices.

(2002)), as am I (Blinder and Reis, 2005, pages 64-70). Since so much ink has been spilled on this issue, I can be very terse in outlining the *pros* and *cons*.

Proponents of bubble bursting argue that:

- the central bank has a clear responsibility to preserve financial stability, which is threatened by asset bubbles.

- *sizable* bubbles can, in fact, be detected by applying U.S. Supreme Court Justice Potter Stewart's famous test for pornography: "You know it when you see it." Furthermore, they can be recognized *early enough* to do something about them.

- bubbles lead to misallocations of resources (e.g., the Internet craze) and also damage conventional macroeconomic stability (e.g., when a slump follows a stock market crash).

- the central bank has instruments at its disposal that can deflate bubbles without doing undue harm to its primary goals, inflation and unemployment.

This last argument is usually tacit, not explicit, but it is essential. Without it, bubble-bursting may do more harm than good, even if all the rest is right.

Opponents of bubble-bursting concede that bubbles do happen, do cause resource misallocations, and are sometimes recognizable. But they argue that:

- financial stability can be maintained by what Reis and I (2005) called the "mop up after" strategy.

- bubbles generally become "obvious" only after they have inflated quite far, and attempts to identify them earlier would likely produce many false positives.

- the central bank is not responsible bad private investment decisions, and the macroeconomy is best managed by focusing monetary policy on inflation and unemployment.

- the central bank has no instruments suitable for targeting specifically at bubbles. Raising interest rates enough to burst a bubble would likely burst the economy as well.

I find the second set of arguments far more compelling and, in support, I offer the following quick reflections on the greatest bubble in history: the U.S. stock market bubble of 1998-2000.[59] The idea is that, if the case for bursting bubbles didn't apply then, it may never apply.

First, the stock market bubble was recognizable, but only rather late in the game; and acting too early could have been disastrous. For example, even during its worst months after the crash, the market never returned to where it was on the day in December 1996 that Alan Greenspan declared it to be "irrationally exuberant." Should the Fed have tightened in 1996 and squelched the ensuing boom? My answer is no. Second, the "mop up after" strategy worked extraordinarily well even in this extreme stress test; not a single sizable bank or brokerage firm went bankrupt. Third, despite the fact that a staggering $8 trillion in wealth was vaporized, the post-bubble recession was so small that it

---

[59] Similar facts apply to Europe and Japan. The tech-stock bubble was a worldwide phenomenon.

disappears in annual data. Finally, if the specific concern was tech stocks, what instrument could (or should) the Fed have used to target this idiosyncratic sector?

While my personal opinion is clear, the main point is that real-world central bankers need to make a decision on this issue.

Issue 15: Dealing with the zero lower bound on nominal interest rates

While central banks control the (very) short-term *nominal* interest rate, most economists believe that it is *real* interest rates that influence economic activity.[60] In a deep slump, the central bank would like to make real short rates negative. But this is impossible if the inflation rate is zero or negative, because nominal interest rates cannot fall below zero. For decades, most economists viewed this issue as a theoretical curiosum of no practical importance. But Japan has taught us otherwise.[61]

What to do? First, prevention is clearly better than cure. Bernanke, Reinhart and Sack (2004) creatively examined various unconventional monetary policies-- things that a central bank confronted by the zero lower bound might try--and I would add exchange-rate intervention to their list. I think it is fair to say that such a central bank would not be powerless. That's the good news. However, the unconventional policies are likely to be far weaker than conventional interest-rate policy. That's the bad news. So it is certainly better not to flirt with zero.

---

[60] The truth is not as one-sided as economists often pretend. For example, the front-loading of *real* mortgage payments in a conventional (nominal) fixed rate mortgage makes the *nominal* rate matter quite a lot to capital-constrained home buyers.
[61] When the core CPI inflation rate in the United States dipped to 1.3% in August 2001, the Fed voiced concerns about deflation and the zero lower bound. See Bernanke (2003). At the time of this conference, with *core* HICP inflation at 1.4%, the ECB should have been just as concerned.

Inflation targeting, or rather *successful* inflation targeting, should help. By posting a target, π^*, that is safely above zero, and then achieving it, a central bank can avoid confronting the zero lower bound. At worst, it can always push the short-term real interest rate down to $-\pi^*$, which is why π^* should be bounded away from zero. Of course, with shocks and control errors, even an inflation targeting central bank might find itself below π^*, or even below zero. However, should this happen, a credible commitment to the positive inflation target should keep the current *expected* inflation rate above the current *actual* inflation rate, leaving $r^e = i - \pi^e$ well below $r = i - \pi$.

Targeting the *price level*, rather than the *inflation rate*, provides even greater protection against getting trapped by the zero lower bound. Credible inflation targeting should engender expectations that π, which could go negative for a time, will converge upward to π^*. But credible price *level* targeting should engender expectations that π will actually overshoot π^* for a while in order to get the price level, p_t, back to its target path--thereby pushing π^e higher sooner. For this reason, the earlier verdict that inflation targeting is superior to price level targeting (Fischer, 1994) may need to be revisited for a world of very low inflation. Note, by the way, that adopting a price level target does not imply that the average inflation rate must be zero. The desired price level path can be defined to rise over time at some pre-determined inflation rate: $p_t^* = p_0(1+\pi^*)^t$.

Issue 16: Do the giant central banks have global responsibilities?

There is one last question that most central banks can answer quickly (and in the negative) but that giants like the Federal Reserve and the ECB (and perhaps the Bank of Japan and, one day, the People's Bank of China) must wrestle with: Should a central bank consider the welfare of other countries in making its *domestic* monetary policy decisions? Or, put slightly differently, do the Fed and ECB bear some responsibility for the health of the *world* economy?

Before addressing this question, let me make an important conceptual distinction analogous to the one made under Issue 14 (bubbles). In an interrelated world, what happens in Country B will reverberate somewhat on Country A. For that reason, the central bank of Country A must and will take events in Country B into account in formulating its own domestic monetary policy. To cite just one obvious example, forecasts of foreign economies are needed to generate a forecast of your own net exports. The question for this section is a different one: Should the central bank's objective function have some foreign (or world) variables in it? Or, put more concretely, might there be times when the Fed or the ECB should tighten or ease even though their own domestic economies are not calling for such action?

The case of the "25 basis points that saved the world"—the Fed's rate cut in September 1998, at a time when the U.S. economy was booming—brought this issue into bold relief. While Alan Greenspan was careful to justify the cut by fretting about possible infection from abroad, many observers at the time thought the Fed was doing its part to "save the world."

The question is a vexing one, and one major reason is legal. The Fed was created and derives its mandate from acts of the U.S. Congress; the ECB derives its authority and mandate from the Maastricht Treaty. In both of these cases, and in all others of which I know, the central bank's legal mandate pertains

exclusively to the domestic economy. Other than worrying about possible

reverberations from various Country B's, what right, then, does either the Fed or

the ECB have to take actions designed to help other countries? And if such

actions run counter to domestic needs, has the central bank actually violated the

law? These are serious issues.

But, on the other hand, an elephant walking through the jungle must take care

where it steps. The European and American (and perhaps also the Japanese)

economies are so large, and so important to both real and financial activity

throughout the world, that it can be argued that good international citizenship

gives them special responsibilities. That is why I raise the question, but do not

answer it.

IV. Monetary Policy in the 21st Century

With 16 different issues, it would be foolish to try to summarize all the

arguments. Instead, let me use this concluding section to provoke discussion by

offering overly-crisp and excessively definitive answers to the 16 questions

posed in this paper—leaving out the nuances and counter-arguments.

Organizational structure

1. Monetary policy should target a *core*, not headline, measure of inflation and

set the inflation target well above zero—say, at 2%.

2. Most central banks need to become more transparent in several

dimensions. One is their forecasts, including conditional forecasts of their own behavior. However, a mechanical reaction function might do as an interim solution.

3. Inflation targeters should be more transparent about having an output or unemployment stabilization objective.

4. Monetary policy is best made by committees, but autocratically-collegial committees may not exploit the advantages of group decisionmaking sufficiently.

5. Nations should not exclude their central banks from bank supervision.

Operating principles

6. Central banks need to question their reasons for such extreme aversion to policy reversals.

7. On the other hand, we have, if anything, too many good explanations for the preference for gradualism.

8. Instead of scoffing at "fine tuning," perhaps some central banks should raise their aspiration levels.

9. Central banks should lead the markets rather than follow them.

10. There may be more scope for unsterilized foreign exchange intervention than current central bank rhetoric and practice admit.

11. Some central banks should begin thinking about conducting at least some of their open-market operations in derivatives.

Monetary transmission

12. Figuring out why the expectations theory of the term structure fails so badly is an urgent research priority for central banks.

13. So is the abject failure of uncovered interest parity.

14. Central banks should not use monetary policy to burst asset market bubbles.

15. Central banks should have contingency plans for dealing with the zero lower bound on nominal interest rates.

16. As the world continues to integrate economically, the ECB and the Fed (and eventually also the PBoC) may implicitly have to assume more global responsibilities.

Finally, I confidently predict that, five or ten years from now, some other scholar will have no trouble at all in formulating a list of 16 or more unresolved monetary policy issues. I just hope some of them are different from mine.

LIST OF REFERENCES

1. David Archer (2005). "Central-Bank Communications and the Publication of Interest Rate Projections," paper presented at Sveriges Riksbank conference, "Inflation Targeting: Implementation, Communication, and Effectiveness," Stockholm, June.

2. Laurence Ball and Niamh Sheridan (2005). "Does Inflation Targeting Matter?" in Ben Bernanke and Michael Woodford, eds., *The Inflation-Targeting Debate*. University of Chicago Press, 249-276.

3. Robert Barro and David Gordon (1983). "A Positive Theory of Monetary Policy in a Natural Rate Model," *Journal of Political Economy* 91(4, August): 589-610.

4. Claes Berg (2005)."Experience of Inflation-targeting in 20 Countries," Bank of Sweden *Economic Review* 1: 20-47.

5. Ben Bernanke (2003). "An Unwelcome Fall in Inflation?" speech delivered at University of California, San Diego, July 23.

6. Ben Bernanke (2004a), "Gradualism," Remarks delivered at Federal Reserve Bank of San Francisco (Seattle Branch), May 20, 2004.

7. Ben Bernanke (2004b). "Central Bank Talk and Monetary Policy," speech before the Japan Society, New York, October 7.

8. Ben Bernanke (2006). "The Benefits of Price Stability," speech delivered at Princeton University, February 24.

9. Ben Bernanke and Mark Gertler (1999). "Monetary Policy and Asset Price Volatility," in *New Challenges for Monetary Policy*, Federal Reserve Bank of Kansas City symposium, Jackson Hole, Wyoming, August 26-28.

10. Ben Bernanke and Carla Lown (1991). "The Credit Crunch," *Brookings Papers on Economic Activity* 2: 204-239.

11. Ben Bernanke, Vincent Reinhart, and Brian Sack (2004). "An Empirical Assessment of Monetary Policy Alternatives at the Zero Bound," *Brookings Papers on Economic Activity* 2: 1-78.

12. Ben Bernanke and Michael Woodford (1997). "Inflation Forecasts and Monetary Policy," *Journal of Money, Credit, and Banking* 29(4, November): 653-684.

13. Alan Blinder (1998). *Central Banking in Theory and Practice.* Cambridge: MIT Press.

14. Alan Blinder (2000). "Critical Issues for Modern Central Bankers," in European Central Bank, *Monetary Policymaking under Uncertainty,* 64-74.

15. Alan Blinder (2004). *The Quiet Revolution: Central Banking Goes Modern.* New Haven: Yale University Press.

16. Alan Blinder (2005). "Monetary Policy by Committee: Why and How?" prepared for workshop at De Nederlandsche Bank, November 28.

17. Alan Blinder, Charles Goodhart, Philippe Hildebrand, David Lipton, and Charles Wyplosz (2001). *How Do Central Banks Talk?* Geneva Reports on the World Economy, vol. 3. Geneva: International Center for Monetary and Banking Studies; London: Centre for Economic Policy Research.

18. Alan Blinder and John Morgan (2005). "Are Two Heads Better than One? Monetary Policy by Committee," *Journal of Money, Credit, and Banking* 37(5, October):789-812.

19. Alan Blinder and Ricardo Reis (2005). "Understanding the Greenspan Standard," in *The Greenspan Era: Lessons for the Future,* Federal Reserve Bank of Kansas City symposium, Jackson Hole, Wyoming, August 25-27.

20. Alan Blinder and Janet Yellen (2001). *The Fabulous Decade: Macroeconomic Lessons from the 1990s.* New York: Century Foundation Press.

21. William Brainard (1967). "Uncertainty and the Effectiveness of Policy," *American Economic Review* 57(2, May): 411-425.

22. Karl Brunner (1981). "The Art of Central Banking," Center for Research in Government Policy and Business working paper GPB 81-6, Graduate School of Management, University of Rochester.

23. Guillermo Calvo (1983). "Staggered Prices in a Utility-Maximizing Framework," *Journal of Monetary Economics* 12(3, September): 383-398.

24. John Campbell (1995). "Some Lessons from the Yield Curve," *Journal of Economic Perspectives* 9(3, Summer): 129-152.

25. Stephen Cecchetti, Hans Genberg, John Lipsky, and Sushil Wadhwani (2000). *Asset Prices and Central Bank Policy,* Geneva Reports on the

World Economy, vol. 2. Geneva: International Center for Monetary and Banking Studies; London: Centre for Economic Policy Research.

26. Gregory Chow (1975). *Analysis and Control of Dynamic Economic Systems*. New York: Wiley.

27. Gregory Chow (1989). "Rational versus Adaptive Expectations in Present Value Models," *Review of Economics and Statistics* 71(3, August): 376-384.

28. William Cline (2005). "The Case for a New Plaza Agreement," Policy Brief 05-4, Institute for International Economics, December.

29. Alex Cukierman (2004). "Nonlinearities in Taylor Rules—Causes, Consequences and Evidence," keynote lecture at Central Bank of Uruguay, August.

30. Alex Cukierman (2006). "Central Bank Independence and Monetary Policymaking Institutions—Past, Present, and Future," February 2006, forthcoming in *Economia Chileana*.

31. Alex Cukierman (2005). "The Limits of Transparency," paper presented to the meetings of the American Economic Association, January 2006.

32. Evangeline Drossos and Spence Hilton (2000). "The Federal Reserve's Contingency Financing Plan for the Century Date Change," Federal Reserve Bank of New York *Current Issues in Economics and Finance* 6(15, December): 1-6.

33. Roger Ferguson (2000). "Alternative Approaches to Financial Supervision and Regulation," *Journal of Financial Services Research* 17: 297-303.

34. Stanley Fischer (1994). "Modern Central Banking," in F. Capie, C. Goodhart, S. Fischer, and N. Schnadt, *The Future of Central Banking*. Cambridge University Press.

35. Andreas Freytag and Donato Masciandaro (2005). "Financial Supervision Fragmentation and Central Bank Independence: The Two Sides of the Same Coin?" working paper 14/2005, Friedrich-Schiller-University, Jena.

36. Milton Friedman (1968), "The Role of Monetary Policy," *American Economic Review* 58(1, March): 1-17.

37. Maxwell Fry, DeAnne Julius, Lavan Mahadeva, Sandra Roger, and Gabriel Sterne (2000). "Key Issues in the Choice of a Monetary Policy

61

Framework," in Lavan Mahadeva and Gabriel Sterne, eds., *Monetary Policy Frameworks in a Global Context*. New York: Routledge Publishers.

38.   Petra Geraats (2002). "Central Bank Transparency," *Economic Journal* 112 (483, November): 532-565.

39.   Charles Goodhart (2000). "The Organizational Structure of Bank Supervision," Financial Stability Institute occasional paper 1, Basle, November.

40.   Charles Goodhart (2004). "Gradualism in the Adjustment of Official Interest Rates: Some Partial Explanations," Financial Markets Group special paper 157, London School of Economics, May.

41.   Alan Greenspan (2002). "Opening Remarks," in *Rethinking Stabilization Policy*, Federal Reserve Bank of Kansas City symposium, Jackson Hole, Wyoming, August 29-31.

42.   Mark Hooker (2002). "Are Oil Shocks Inflationary? Asymmetric and Nonlinear Specifications versus Changes in Regime," *Journal of Money, Credit, and Banking* 34(2, May): 540-561.

43.   Anil Kashyap and Jeremy Stein (2004). "Cyclical Implications of the Basle II Capital Standards," Federal Reserve Bank of Chicago *Economic Perspectives* 28(1, January):18-31

44.   Norbert Kerr, Robert MacCoun, and Geoffrey Kramer (1996). "Bias in Judgment: Comparing Individuals and Groups," *Psychological Review* 103(4, March): 687-719.

45.   Finn Kydland and Edward Prescott (1977). "Rules Rather than Discretion: The Inconsistency of Optimal Plans," *Journal of Political Economy* 85(3, June): 473-492.

46.   Andrew Levin, Volker Wieland, and John Williams (1999). "Robustness of Simple Monetary Policy Rules under Model Uncertainty," in John B. Taylor, ed., *Monetary Policy Rules*. National Bureau of Economic Research Conference report, University of Chicago Press.

47.   Clare Lombardelli, James Proudman, and James Talbot (2005). "Committees versus Individuals: An Experimental Analysis of Monetary Policy Decision-Making," *International Journal of Central Banking* 1(1, May):181-205.

48. N. Gregory Mankiw and Ricardo Reis (2003). "What Measure of Inflation Should a Central Bank Target?" *Journal of the European Economic Association* 1(5, September):1058-1086.

49. Guy Meredith and Menzie Chinn (2004). "Monetary Policy and Long-Horizon Uncovered Interest Rate Parity," *IMF Staff Papers* 51(3): 409-430.

50. Laurence Meyer (1999). "Financial Modernization: The Issues," speech delivered at Washington University, March 12.

51. Laurence Meyer (2004). *A Term at the Fed: an Insider's View*. New York: Harper Business.

52. Laurence Meyer (2006). "Coming Soon: An Inflation Target for the FOMC," in Bank of Canada, *Inflation Targeting: Problems and Opportunities*.

53. Frederic Mishkin (2004). "Can Central Bank Transparency Go too Far?" in Reserve Bank of Australia, *The Future of Inflation Targeting*, 48-65.

54. Alexei Onatski and Noah Williams (2003). "Modeling Model Uncertainty," *Journal of the European Economic Association* 1(5, September): 1087-1122.

55. Athanasios Orphanides (2003). "The Quest for Prosperity without Inflation," *Journal of Monetary Economics* 50(3, April): 633-663.

56. Athanasios Orphanides and John Williams (2005). "Robust Monetary Policy with Imperfect Knowledge," Board of Governors of the Federal Reserve System; Federal Reserve Bank of San Francisco. Mimeo.

57. Joe Peek, Eric Rosengren, and Geoffrey Toootell (1999). "Is Bank Supervision Central to Central Banking?" *Quarterly Journal of Economics* 114(2, May): 629-653.

58. William Poole (2003). "Fed Transparency: How, Not Whether," Federal Reserve Bank of St. Louis *Review* 85(6, November/December): 1-8.

59. Ricardo Reis (2005). "Toward a Dynamic Price Index," working paper, Princeton University, April.

60. Julio Rotemberg and Michael Woodford (1997). "An Optimization-Based Econometric Framework for the Evaluation of Monetary Policy," *NBER Macroeconomics Annual* 12: 297-346.

61.   Glenn Rudebusch (2001). "Is the Fed Too Timid?: Monetary Policy in an Uncertain World," *Review of Economics and Statistics* 83(2, May): 203-217.

62.   Glenn Rudebusch (2005). "Monetary Policy Inertia: Fact or Fiction?" paper presented at Sveriges Riksbank conference, "Inflation Targeting: Implementation, Communication, and Effectiveness," Stockholm, June.

63.   Brain Sack (2000). "Does the Fed Act Gradually? A VAR Analysis," *Journal of Monetary Economics* 46(1, August): 229-256.

64.   Lucio Sarno and Mark P. Taylor (2001). "Official Intervention in the Foreign Exchange Market: Is It Effective and, If So, How Does It Work?" *Journal of Economic Literature* 39(3, September): 839-868.

65.   Anne Sibert (2005). "Central Banking by Committee," paper presented at De Nederlandsche Bank, Amsterdam, November 2005.

66.   Douglas Staiger, James Stock, and Mark Watson (2001). "Prices, Wages, and the U.S. NAIRU in the 1990s," in Alan Krueger and Robert Solow, eds., *The Roaring Nineties: Can Full Employment Be Sustained*. New York: Russell Sage Foundation; Century Foundation Press, 3-60.

67.   Brad Strum (2005). "Discretionary Monetary Policy in a Sticky-Price Input/Output Economy," working paper, Princeton University.

68.   Lars Svensson (1997). "Inflation Forecast Targeting: Implementing and Monitoring Inflation Targets," *European Economic Review* 41(6, June): 1111-1146.

69.   Lars Svensson (1999). "Inflation Targeting as a Monetary Policy Rule," *Journal of Monetary Economics* 43(3, June): 607-654.

70.   Lars Svensson (2001). "Independent Review of Monetary Policy in New Zealand: Report to the Minister of Finance," Institute for International Economic Studies working paper, Stockholm University.

71.   Lars Svensson (2005). "Optimal Inflation Targeting: Further Developments of Inflation Targeting," paper presented at Sveriges Riksbank conference, "Inflation Targeting: Implementation, Communication, and Effectiveness," Stockholm, June.

72.   Lars Svensson (2006). "The Instrument-Rate Projection under Inflation Targeting: The Norwegian Example," in Bank of Canada, *Inflation Targeting: Problems and Opportunities*, February.

73. Marco Vega and Diego Winkelried (2005). "Inflation Targeting and Inflation Behavior: A Successful Story?" *International Journal of Central Banking* 1(3, December): 153-175.

74. Sushil Wadhwani (1999). "Currency Puzzles," speech delivered to the London School of Economics, September 16. London: Bank of England.

75. William White (2006). "Procyclicality in the Financial System: Do We Need a New Macrofinancial Stabilization Framework?" BIS working paper 193, Basle, January.

76. Luke Willard (2006). "Does Inflation Targeting Matter?: A Reassessment," CEPS working paper 120, Princeton University, February.

77. Michael Woodford (1994), "Nonstandard Indicators for Monetary Policy," in N. Gregory Mankiw (ed.), *Monetary Policy* (University of Chicago Press for NBER), pp. 95-115.

78. Michael Woodford (2003). "Optimal Monetary Policy Inertia," *Review of Economic Studies* 70, pp. 861-886.

79. Michael Woodford (2005). "Central Bank Communication and Policy Effectiveness," in *The Greenspan Era: Lessons for the Future,* Federal Reserve Bank of Kansas City symposium, Jackson Hole, Wyoming, August 25-27.

80. Michael Woodford (2006). "Comment," in Bank of Canada, *Inflation Targeting: Problems and Opportunities*, February.

[16]

JOHN B. TAYLOR

Thirty-Five Years of Model Building for Monetary Policy Evaluation: Breakthroughs, Dark Ages, and a Renaissance

ONE OF THE most important advances in monetary policy analysis in the past three decades has been the development and use of economy-wide econometric models that combine forward-looking rational expectations and sticky prices or wages. Such models are so commonplace now that the idea hardly deserves comment and indeed the structural models presented at this conference are no exception. But no such models existed at the time that the *Econometrics of Price Determination Conference* was held 35 years ago. The paper by Robert Lucas (1972a) at that conference presented a rational expectations model, but it had perfectly flexible prices—neither time-dependent price setting, as in the future staggered contract models, nor state-dependent price setting, as in the future menu cost models. Other papers at the 1970 conference—still reflecting what was common in econometric macro models at the time—focused on backward-looking models of the wage–price dynamics featuring inflexible markups from wages to prices and adaptive expectations. Expectations of inflation, important for price determination following the Friedman–Phelps hypothesis, were therefore very slow to change unlike in the rational expectations models.

This is a written version of a luncheon address given during the conference marking the 35th anniversary of the 1970 *Econometrics of Price Determination Conference*. It is not meant to be a detailed survey of the literature, but rather a brief overview of research trends during the past 35 years, touching on a few illustrative examples from a huge and rapidly growing literature. I would like to thank David Wilcox for inviting me to speak at the conference and for suggesting this topic, and Pete Klenow, Ben McCallum, John Lipsky, and Ken West for helpful discussions and comments.

JOHN B. TAYLOR *is associated with the Department of Economics and Hoover Institution, Stanford University (E-mail: john.taylor@stanford.edu).*

Received October 7, 2005; and accepted in revised form September 1, 2006.

Journal of Money, Credit and Banking, Supplement to Vol. 39, No. 1 (February 2007)

These two separate strands continued to develop in parallel for years following the conference. One strand was formed by the follow-ups to the Lucas conference paper, including his "Expectations and the Neutrality of Money" paper (1972b), his Lucas critique paper (1976), and the policy ineffectiveness paper of Thomas Sargent and Neil Wallace (1975). The other strand was formed by the research work on price adjustment models for policy at the Federal Reserve Board—including the work estimating the wage–price block of the Fed's model.

Like the gap between desired and actual decision variables in an (S, s) model, the gap between actual and desired models for monetary policy evaluation was growing. As the gap grew, the need to close it in some way in order to do monetary policy analysis became clearer. What exactly was this need? First, the Lucas critique presented a convincing case to many researchers that conventional policy analysis was flawed; the critique offered an alternative method of analysis using rational expectations to evaluate monetary policy rules, though most researchers seemed to ignore or misunderstand that alternative, or to think that the alternative was unattractive or too difficult to follow in practice.

Second, monetary policy evaluation required a realistic model of how monetary policy impacted inflation and the real economy, and that required introducing some form of inflexibility in price formation into the rational expectations models, which was not captured either by the rational expectations models with perfectly flexible prices or by the traditional econometric models with backward-looking adaptive expectations. That the form of monetary policy rules did not even matter in the existing rational expectations models, as shown by Sargent and Wallace (1975), made it virtually impossible to evaluate alternative monetary policy rules in those models as the Lucas critique had suggested one should do.[1] That the traditional models did not have forward-looking expectations made them highly susceptible to the Lucas critique.

1. BREAKTHROUGHS

With this pent-up demand for economy-wide models combining sticky prices and rational expectations it is perhaps understandable that several breakthroughs occurred simultaneously. The paper by Fischer (1977) and the paper coauthored by Phelps (1977) and myself were some of the first responses. Gray's (1976) paper was another. That the editors of the *Journal of Political Economy* (including editor Robert Lucas) decided to publish the Fischer and the Phelps–Taylor papers (1977) back to back in the same issue in 1977 was an indication that many people saw the need to bring the strands together and were adjusting their research accordingly, trying to be one of the first to do so in healthy academic competition. These papers did combine some aspect of sticky prices with rational expectations. By assuming that prices or wages were set

---

1. Another task was to introduce learning into the rational expectations models, which was a path that I first went down before finding how difficult monetary policy evaluation was with learning compared to the simple rational expectations assumption.

one period in advance they thwarted the monetary policy ineffectiveness proposition. More importantly, they opened the possibility that the econometric policy evaluation techniques suggested by Lucas might be used in practice for monetary policy analysis.

But those first-generation models were pretty crude, especially when you look back after three decades, as they could not come close to explaining the aggregate dynamics of inflation and output that the researchers in the other strand of work in traditional econometric models were pursuing. Because the models jumped back fully to the flexible wage–price equilibrium in one period, they could not generate much momentum. In fact, I remember trying to bring versions of the Phelps–Taylor model to the data and soon realized that something more realistic about price setting or wage setting was needed in order to increase the degree of persistence that was virtually nil in those early models.

That was what led me to the staggered wage-setting model (Taylor 1979b) and my 1979 *Econometrica* paper (Taylor 1979a), which, as Ben McCallum stated in his 1999 Homer Jones lecture, "demonstrated that these [econometric policy evaluation] techniques are entirely feasible." In other words you could do practical monetary policy analysis with forward-looking rational expectations. I was able to take the model in that 1979 paper to the data, calculate the optimal rule for the money supply using the methodology that Lucas had suggested—it was effectively a "Taylor rule," though for the money supply—and derive a trade-off between the variability of inflation and output as an alternative to the old Phillips curve trade-off.

A slew of papers in this area were written at this time trying to make things more realistic or more securely founded on economic principles. Julio Rotemberg (1982) showed how a firm's price adjustment decisions could be derived with monopolistic competition assumptions. Guillermo Calvo (1982) introduced his ingenious geometric random version of staggered price setting. Ray Fair and I (1983) worked on an algorithm that was needed to solve nonlinear rational expectations models. Simulations with the models were performed and those simulations showed that the cost of disinflation was less than in the conventional models though more than in the Sargent–Wallace models. Other researchers began using microeconomic data on union wage contracts to calibrate staggered wage setting models.

2. A DARK AGE

But after this flurry of work in the late 1970s and early 1980s, a sort of "dark age" for this type of modeling began to set in. Ben McCallum (1999) discussed this phenomenon in his review lecture, and from the perspective of the history of economic thought, it is an interesting phenomenon. As he put it, there was "a long period during which there was a great falling off in the volume of sophisticated yet practical monetary policy analysis."

McCallum (1999) attributes this period in part to a misunderstanding of the Lucas critique by many researchers, namely that it was taken as a *negative* statement that policy analysis could not be done rather than a *positive* statement of how to do it. Hence, researchers in central banks did not immediately take to these new models and the traditional models of the *Econometrics of Price Determination Conference* continued in use with little in the way of alternatives. I think McCallum is probably right, but if you actually read the Lucas critique paper, it is not hard to see that the clear methodology illustrated in his examples could be applied to other examples, including monetary policy evaluation with sticky prices and rational expectations. Another explanation given by McCallum for the dark ages for this kind of research was the take-off of research on real business cycle models, which absorbed a lot of time and effort by macroeconomists who might otherwise have been applying the Lucas policy methodology to monetary policy. Of course, the real business cycle development was very important in its own right, but it did take emphasis away from new models for monetary policy evaluation.

There were, of course, "keepers of the flame of the rational expectations models with sticky prices" during these dark ages, and for them it was probably not so dark. After all, inflation was plummeting in the United States and the cost, while high, was closer to the estimates of the rational expectations models with sticky prices than to the traditional backward-looking models. Economists at central banks continued to develop models of wage and price dynamics as it was their job to do, and they gradually began to incorporate rational expectations into the models. Svensson (1986) and Blanchard and Kiyotaki (1987) began to build *economy-wide* models with money and with slow price adjustment based on monopolistic competition. West (1988) showed that the unit root implied by many real business cycle models also was implied by the staggered contract models with rational expectations. At Stanford I worked, along with a number of outstanding graduate students (including many who are still very active in this area such as Joe Gagnon, Pete Klenow, Andrew Levin, Ellen McGrattan), on a large-scale multi-country model with rational expectations and sticky wages and prices (see Taylor 1993); this work was motivated by the increased globalization of the world's financial markets and the need to address international monetary policy questions. And McCallum (1988) stressed the importance of robustness in econometric policy evaluation by doing such evaluations with several models.

3. A RENAISSANCE

This all began to change in the late 1980s and the early 1990s. The renewed interest in policy evaluation models with sticky prices and rational expectations can be traced, I believe, to open economy macroeconomic issues and, in particular, to the spread of work on developing larger-scale international monetary policy models, such as the IMF Multimod model developed by Paul Masson, the Federal Reserve Board's MX3 model developed by Joseph Gagnon and Ralph Tryon, and the multi-country econometric model at Stanford that I previously mentioned. The reason that the renewed interest was originally focused on international models was that one could simply not econometrically analyze key international monetary policy issues such as exchange rate policy without combining rational expectations and sticky prices or wages. Questions of fixed exchange rates versus flexible exchange rates are at their heart "regime issues," highly suitable for the new econometric evaluation approach. The Dornbusch (1976) paper on exchange rate overshooting illustrated how to modernize the small open economy model of Mundell–Fleming by incorporating both sticky prices and forward-looking expectations. The international econometric model builders were following that same approach in a large-economy multi-country setting.

Since evaluating exchange rate policy was naturally a question of evaluating regimes, one had no choice but to specify a policy rule for monetary policy; all the international models assumed something close to perfect capital mobility, which meant that the exchange rate regime implied a monetary policy regime. Hence, many policy people began looking at alternative monetary policy rules and they used these new international models with sticky prices and rational expectations to do so. The collection of papers in the book by Bryant, Hooper, and Mann (1993) is the best example of this research; it was from this econometric policy evaluation work that I gleaned a "model consensus" monetary policy rule, which later came to be called the Taylor rule.

Now I believe that this new focus on monetary policy rules in practical policy making in the 1990s—as evidenced, for example, by references in speeches to monetary policy rules by members of the Federal Reserve Board and in articles in central bank publications—in turn brought an even greater increased interest in monetary policy evaluation models with rational expectations and newer forms of sticky prices. In any case many papers were written about such models in the 1990s. The staggered price or wage-setting assumption came under further scrutiny, with Ball (1994) and Fuhrer and Moore (1995) pointing out that these models—originally designed to give more persistence than the first-generation models—themselves did not seem to provide enough persistence. Fuhrer and Moore proposed modifications of the staggered price-setting models that were incorporated into modeling at the Federal Reserve, thereby paving the way for the use of rational expectations and more forward-looking models in policy making.

With the research on policy rules in full force in the 1990s, many researchers began to try to build better models to evaluate monetary policy. A major advance occurred when the techniques of the real business cycle school began to show their influence in these policy evaluation models. King and Wolman (1999) and Chari, Kehoe, and McGrattan (2000) are excellent examples that demonstrate this influence; in these models staggered contracts and rational expectations are embedded in an otherwise real business cycle framework. The real business cycle techniques have the promise of improving identification of structural policy parameters (down to utility and production functions), though their empirical forms are very similar to those derived by West (1988); they still have many of the characteristics of the earlier models used for policy evaluation and tend to yield similar results in policy simulations. The smaller versions of these models have boiled down to three equations, and it is these three equation models that people now frequently refer to as the New Keynesian models, though that term has also been used to describe the entire class of models I am reviewing here.

In sum, I think that this short review makes it clear that tremendous progress has been made in developing econometric models for policy evaluation during the past three decades. One can get a simple measure of this progress by comparing the 1970 *Econometrics of Price Determination Conference* with "post-renaissance" conferences. For example, McCallum (1999) refers to the 1998 NBER conference and the 1998 Riksbank conference on monetary policy rules. Another measure of progress can be seen by comparing Woodford's (2003) book *Interest and Prices* with Don Patinkin's (1965) book *Money, Interest, and Prices*. Like the 1970 *Econometrics of Price Determination*, Patikin's book had no economy-wide models with both rational expectations and sticky prices and wages. In Woodford's book this type of model is the main model used for policy evaluation.

4. FURTHER PROGRESS IN MODEL DEVELOPMENT

While there has been plenty of progress to celebrate, there is much more to do. The most attractive thing about the most recent models is that they can be estimated with microeconomic data, which helps to resolve identification issues inherent in aggregate data. The way in which Golosov and Lucas (2005) use the data put together by Klenow and Kryvtsov (2005) is a wonderful example. One of the interesting findings from Klenow and Kryvtsov is that variations in the number of prices changed in each period is not a major source of variance in inflation fluctuations compared to the size of the price changes. We already knew that the staggered price-setting models of Calvo (1982) have this property since there is no variation in the average number of prices changed each period. Surprisingly, this is also true in the (S, s) models, because, after a large shock, say to the money supply, the increased number of large changes in prices is roughly offset by the smaller number of small changes in prices. Resolution of this "observational equivalence" will require a more detailed look at the Klenow and Kryvtsov micro data.

If I had to give a list of criticisms of the recent work, it would start with the frequent abstraction from wage rigidities. There are important exceptions including work at the Federal Reserve Board by Erceg, Henderson, and Levin (2000), but the approach of the more recent Golosov–Lucas paper with perfectly flexible wages is more common. In my view, wage determination is still a source of inflation dynamics, though not in the same rigid ways as the models in the *Econometrics of Price Determination Conference*. While the (S, s) model makes sense for prices it does not seem accurate for the timing of most wage changes. I think that the study of wage determination needs to be put on the front research burner again. A very important task for future research is an exploration of microeconomic wage data in the BLS's Employment Cost Index, comparable to what Klenow and Kryvtsov (2005) are doing with the CPI. My guess is that the characteristics of the micro wage data will look much different from the price data. Moreover, the micro wage data will permit one to discriminate between different staggered wage-setting models. As Levin et al. (2005) show, the shape of the distribution of wage contracts in staggered wage-setting models matters significantly for monetary policy.

Econometric policy evaluation models are still too rarely used for forecasting. In my view one of the best tests of a model is its ability to forecast, but most forecasting models are still of the reduced form variety, and only loosely connected with structural models, as the Stock and Watson paper at this conference illustrates. Efforts to use the models for forecasting—this will probably require more details for the simple three equation models—would be very worthwhile.

5. IMPACT ON ACTUAL POLICY

What has been the impact on policy of the development of policy evaluation models described here? One might ask if it was influential in building the consensus that led to the end of the Great Inflation. Perhaps, the finding that inflation could be reduced with less disruption than traditional models suggested helped reduce some policymakers' reluctance to take the steps to end inflation, but it seems to me that people supported Paul Volcker's disinflation efforts mainly because they were fed up with inflation.

Perhaps more relevant have been the simulations of alternative monetary policy rules. Clearly, it would not have been possible to even consider such rules systematically if it were not for these models, but the impact of the policy rule research itself is more difficult to prove. Policy rule research has, of course, been useful in comparing policy in different countries and in different time periods, or to characterize good policy versus bad policy. It has enabled central bank staff to work with interest rates as an instrument and to do so with an analytical framework. It has shown that certain monetary policy principles are important, such as reacting in a preemptive fashion to forecasted increases in inflation. It has shown that targeting asset prices can lead to poor results. And it has been helpful anytime forward-looking expectations are important, as in formulating a communication policy during the recent "considerable period" or "measured pace" phases. It is hard to imagine these types of policy issues being analyzed rigorously without the models with rational expectations and sticky prices and wages.

6. FUTURE POLICY ISSUES

There are many important policy issues that these types of models or their successors can be called on to analyze in the future. Understanding the reason for the recent reduction in pass–through coefficients for exchange rates and energy prices is important for monetary policy; the models that incorporate sticky prices, market power, and rational expectations, such as Golosov and Lucas (2005), can be helpful here. Determining when appropriate "deviations" from policy rules should start and when they should end is another important practical topic. Finding better ways to incorporate asset prices into policy formulation is yet another. Nailing down the key reasons among the many conjectures for the recent improvements in output volatility is also important for future policy; in my Homer Jones Lecture (Taylor 1998) I argued that it was improvements in monetary policy, but many other explanations have been raised.

But whether the future policy issues are on this list of policy examples or not, it is important to keep future monetary research focused on policy issues. I think this brief history of econometric policy model development clearly illustrates that economic research is most exciting and productive when it is policy driven.

LITERATURE CITED

Ball, Lawrence. (1994) "Credible Disinflation with Staggered Price Setting." *American Economic Review,* 84, 282–89.

Blanchard, Olivier, and N. Kiyotaki. (1987) "Monopolisitc Competition and the Effects of Aggregate Demand." *American Economic Review,* 77, 647–66.

Bryant, Ralph, Peter Hooper, and Catherine Mann. (1993) *Evaluating Policy Regimes: New Research in Empirical Macroeconomics.* Washington, DC: The Brookings Institution.

Calvo, Guillermo. (1982) "Staggered Contracts and Exchange Rate Policy." In *Exchange Rates and International Macroeconomics,* edited by J.A. Frankel. Chicago: University of Chicago Press.

Chari, V.V., Patrick Kehoe, and Ellen McGrattan. (2000) "Sticky Price Models of the Business Cycle: Can the Contract Multiplier Solve the Persistence Problem." *Econometrica,* 68, 1151–79.

Dornbusch, Rudiger. (1976) "Expectations and Exchange Rate Dynamics." *Journal of Political Economy,* 84, 1161–71.

Erceg, Christopher, Dale Henderson, and Andrew Levin. (2000) "Optimal Monetary Policy with Staggered Wage and Price Setting." *Journal of Monetary Economics,* 46, 281–313.

Fair, Ray C., and John B. Taylor. (1983) "Solution and Maximum Likelihood Estimation of Dynamic Nonlinear Rational Expectations Models." *Econometrica,* 51, 1169–85.

Fischer, Stanley. (1977) "Long Term Contracts, Rational Expectations, and the Optimal Money Supply Rule." *Journal of Political Economy,* 85, 191–206.

Fuhrer, Jeff C., and George R. Moore. (1995) "Inflation Persistence." *Quarterly Journal of Economics,* 110, 127–59.

Golosov, Mikhail, and Robert E. Lucas, Jr. (2005) "Menu Costs and the Phillips Curve." Unpublished paper, University of Chicago.

Gray, Jo Anna. (1976) "Wage Indexation: A Macroeconomic Approach." *Journal of Monetary Economics,* 2, 221–35.

King, Robert G., and Alexander L. Wolman. (1999) "What Should the Monetary Authority Do When Prices Are Sticky?" In *Monetary Policy Rules,* edited by J.B. Taylor, pp. 349–98. Chicago: University of Chicago Press.

Klenow, Peter J., and Oleksiy Kryvtsov. (2005) "State Dependent or Time Dependent Pricing: Does It Matter for Recent U.S. Inflation." Unpublished paper, Stanford University.

Levin, Andrew, Alexei Onatski, John C. Williams, and Noah Williams. (2005) "Monetary Policy Under Uncertainty in Micro-Founded Macroeconomic Models." NBER Working Paper 11523.

Lucas, Robert E., Jr. (1972a) "Econometric Testing of the Natural Rate Hypothesis." In *Econometrics of Price Determination*, edited by Otto Eckstein, pp. 50–59. Washington, DC: Board of Governors of the Federal Reserve Board.

Lucas, Robert E., Jr. (1972b) "Expectations and the Neutrality of Money." *Journal of Economic Theory*, 4, 103–24.

Lucas, Robert E., Jr. (1976) "Econometric Policy Evaluation: A Critique." In *Carnegie Rochester Conference Series on Public Policy 1*. Amsterdam: North-Holland.

McCallum, Bennett. (1988) "Robustness Properties of a Rule for Monetary Policy." In *Carnegie Rochester Conference Series on Public Policy 29*, pp. 173–204. Amsterdam: North-Holland.

McCallum, Bennett. (1999) "Recent Developments in the Analysis of Monetary Policy Rules." In *Review*. Federal Reserve Bank of St. Louis, November/December 1999.

Patinkin, Don. (1965) *Money, Interest and Prices*. New York: Harper and Row.

Phelps, Edmund S., and John B. Taylor. (1977) "Stabilizing Powers of Monetary Policy under Rational Expectations." *Journal of Political Economy*, 85, 163–90.

Rotemberg, Julio. (1982) "Sticky Prices in the United States." *Journal of Political Economy*, 90, 1187–1211.

Sargent, Thomas, and Neil Wallace. (1975) "'Rational' Expectations, the Optimal Monetary Instrument, and the Optimal Money Supply Rule." *Journal of Political Economy*, 83, 241–54.

Svensson, Lars. (1986) "Sticky Goods Prices, Flexible Asset Prices, Monopolistic Competition, and Monetary Policy." *Review of Economic Studies*, 52, 385–405.

Taylor, John B. (1979a) "Estimation and Control of a Macroeconomic Model with Rational Expectations." *Econometrica*, 47, 1267–86.

Taylor, John B. (1979b) "Staggered Wage Setting in a Macro Model." *American Economic Review, Papers and Proceedings*, 69, 108–13.

Taylor, John B. (1993) *Macroeconomic Policy in a World Economy: From Econometric Design to Practical Operation*. New York: W.W. Norton.

Taylor, John B. (1998) "Monetary Policy and the Long Boom." *Review*. Federal Reserve Bank of St. Louis, November/December, 1998.

West, Kenneth. (1988) "On the Interpretation of Near Random Walk Behavior in GNP." *American Economic Review*, 78, 202–09.

Woodford, Michael. (2003) *Interest and Prices*. Princeton, NJ: Princeton University Press.

Name Index

The International Library of Critical Writings in Economics